The Voice of War

The Voice of War

*The Second World War Told by
Those Who Fought It*

EDITED BY JAMES OWEN
AND GUY WALTERS

VIKING
an imprint of
PENGUIN BOOKS

VIKING

Published by the Penguin Group
Penguin Books Ltd, 80 Strand, London WC2R ORL, England
Penguin Group (USA) Inc., 375 Hudson Street, New York, New York 10014, USA
Penguin Books Australia Ltd, 250 Camberwell Road, Camberwell, Victoria 3124, Australia
Penguin Books Canada Ltd, 10 Alcorn Avenue, Toronto, Ontario, Canada M4V 3B2
Penguin Books India (P) Ltd, 11 Community Centre, Panchsheel Park, New Delhi – 110 017, India
Penguin Group (NZ), cnr Airborne and Rosedale Roads, Albany, Auckland 1310, New Zealand
Penguin Books (South Africa) (Pty) Ltd, 24 Sturdee Avenue, Rosebank 2196, South Africa

Penguin Books Ltd, Registered Offices: 80 Strand, London WC2R ORL, England

www.penguin.com

First published 2004
3

The acknowledgements on pp. 621–628 constitute an extension of this copyright page

Set in 11.25/13.75 pt Monotype Bembo
Typeset by Rowland Phototypesetting Ltd, Bury St Edmunds, Suffolk
Printed in Great Britain by Clays Ltd, St Ives plc

A CIP catalogue record for this book is available from the British Library

ISBN 0-670-91423-1

Contents

Maps

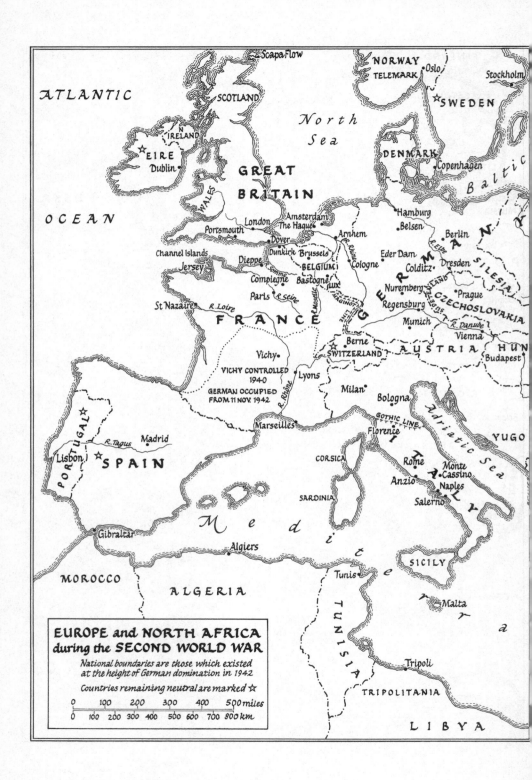

ATLANTIC

OCEAN

Scapa Flow

SCOTLAND

N
IRELAND

★ EIRE
Dublin

WALES

GREAT
BRITAIN

London
Portsmouth
Dover
Channel Islands
Jersey
Dieppe
Compiègne
Paris *R.Seine*
St Nazaire
R.Loire

FRANCE

Vichy

VICHY CONTROLLED
1940
GERMAN OCCUPIED
FROM 11 NOV 1942

Lyons
R.Rhône

Marseilles

PORTUGAL ★
R.Tagus
Lisbon ★
Madrid

SPAIN

Gibraltar

MOROCCO

ALGERIA

*North
Sea*

NORWAY
TELEMARK
Oslo
Stockholm

★ SWEDEN

DENMARK
Copenhagen

Baltic

Hamburg
Belsen
Amsterdam
The Hague
Arnhem
R.Rhine
Brussels
BELGIUM
Cologne
Dunkirk
Somme
Bastogne
Lux.
R.Moselle
MAGINOT
LINE

Berlin
R.Elbe
Eder Dam
Colditz
Dresden
Nuremberg
SILESIA
Regensburg
Prague
CZECHOSLOVAKIA
Munich
R.Danube
Vienna

GERMANY

Berne ★
SWITZERLAND

AUSTRIA HUN
Budapest

Milan
Bologna

Florence
GOTHIC LINE
CORSICA
Rome
Anzio
Monte
Cassino
Naples
Salerno

ITALY

Adriatic Sea

YUGO

SARDINIA

Mediterranea

Algiers

Tunis

SICILY

Malta

TUNISIA

Tripoli

TRIPOLITANIA

LIBYA

EUROPE and NORTH AFRICA
during the SECOND WORLD WAR

*National boundaries are those which existed
at the height of German domination in 1942*

Countries remaining neutral are marked ★

0   100   200   300   400   500 miles
0 100 200 300 400 500 600 700 800 km

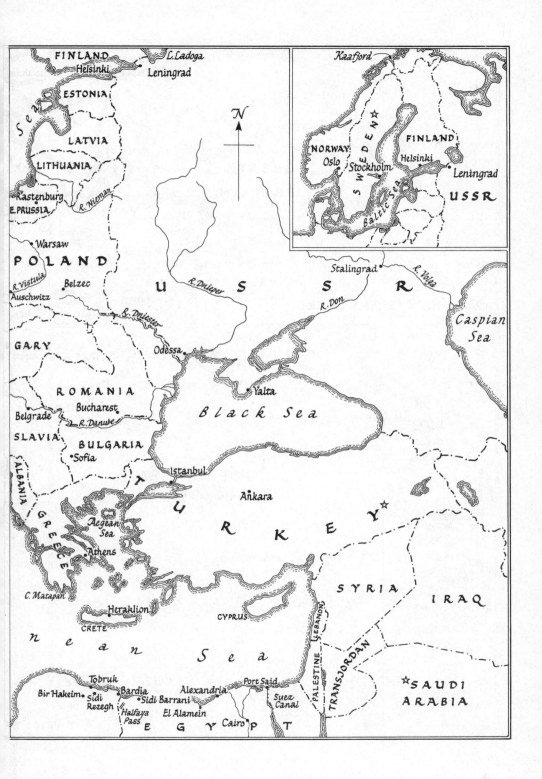

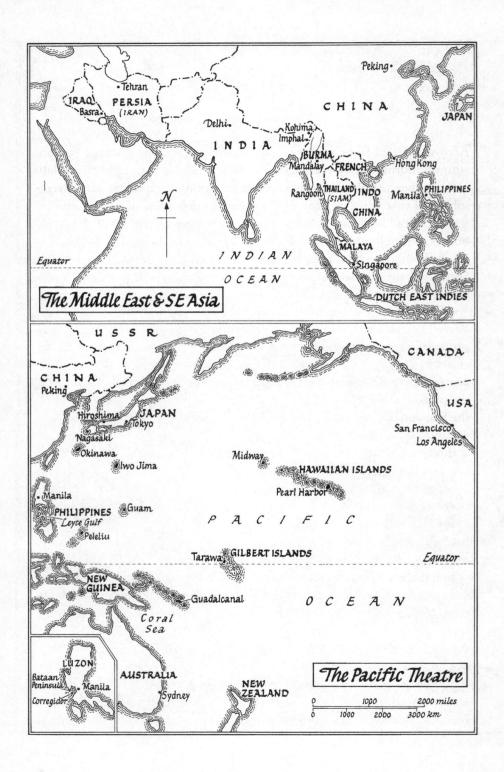

The Middle East & SE Asia

The Pacific Theatre

Preface

Across the field from where we are sitting in this Italian village, on an autumn morning sixty years ago, the soldiers of two nations began to kill one another. As British troops advanced through vineyards, they were subjected to a withering fire by the German defenders of Croce, one of the strongholds on the 'Gothic Line'. Possession of this small group of houses, through which one can drive in less than a minute, changed hands six times in a week in 1944 and cost hundreds of young men their lives. Some lie beneath the rank upon rank of white crosses in the cemetery at Coriano, just down the road from where they died.

Almost everyone lives in a place that was touched by the Second World War. There is a tendency, particularly among the young, to think of it as something remote in history, as irrelevant to our modern lives as the horse and cart, a subject of interest only to film-makers. Yet whether you inhabit one of the world's great cities – London, Berlin, New York, Warsaw – or the most peaceful of rural hamlets, you are somewhere that formed part of the first and only global battlefield, be it as a target of propaganda, training ground, operations centre, manufacturing base or simply a source of manpower. Moreover, you are also somewhere where daily life, borders, taxes, politics and language were and still are fundamentally shaped by the consequences of that conflict. The war remains the central and defining event of the recent past.

Recent indeed, for somehow it tends to be forgotten that this epic struggle in which 40 million people died took place well within living memory, far closer to our time than the battles of the First World War of which there are even now veterans alive. We are both in our early thirties, yet between us we can talk any day with a father and a grandmother who were torpedoed by a German submarine and another grandmother who spent many nights fire-watching on a London rooftop. To share their vivid memories is to understand how near at hand the war remains.

Our aim in this book is to capture that immediacy of experience, to let those who were there tell us what it was really like to invade Okinawa, to endure the Blitz or to suffer at Auschwitz. Their voices are many and of numerous nationalities, ranging from the supreme leaders and the military commanders who planned the war's progress to those who did the fighting, as well as those who played their part on the Home Front.

This is not intended to be a history of the war as such, although we have added short introductions to give extracts context where needed. The available literature is vast, and we looked at several thousand volumes of letters, memoirs and autobiography in making our selection. We firmly believe that we have picked the best, both in the quality of the writing and in its ability to transport one to a street in Hiroshima, a quayside in Tobruk or a beach at Dieppe.

If only for reasons of portability, *The Voice of War* is necessarily representative in nature rather than comprehensive, for we have not had space for every one of the myriad experiences that took place in all the multiple theatres of action. Equally, we have restricted ourselves to accounts available in English (including many not originally written in it) so as to be sure that readers can follow up any they are especially interested in. Indeed, our hope is that all who read this book will long remember the lessons it contains for us, and for the generations to come.

JAMES OWEN   GUY WALTERS
Croce di Montecolombo   Heytesbury
Italy   Wiltshire

Summer 1939

The Coming of War

Having occupied Czechoslovakia with impunity in 1938, Hitler believed that the British and the French would still not fight were he now to further his territorial ambitions by invading Poland. One first-hand witness to these views was the journalist Leonard Mosley.

Then at Bayreuth, one afternoon, Doctor Otto Dietrich, the leader of the Reich Press, took me along to his suite for a drink and a discussion of a coming visit that was being paid to Germany by a British nobleman. I was giving him background information he wanted when – just like that – Hitler walked in. Dietrich when he saw him tried to bundle me from the room, but Hitler stopped him and demanded that I should come forward and be introduced. He was in a good mood; he made a couple of jokes about the English Press when he knew who I was, and then banteringly asked why British journalists in Germany wrote so much about the threat of war. 'There will be no war,' he said. 'Don't you agree?'

This, mark you, was the summer of 1939.

I said that there would be no war if the rights of Poland and the Free City of Danzig were not infringed.

Hitler slapped his thigh, and laughed. 'Even if they are, there will be no war,' he said. 'There was no war over the Sudetenland, nor over Czechoslovakia. There will be no war over Danzig.' When I demurred he repeated: 'There was no war over Sudetenland! There will be none over Poland! The conditions are exactly the same and your actions will be the same.'

It was no job of mine to do Sir Nevile Henderson's job for him, badly though Sir Nevile [the British Ambassador] was doing it himself, and yet I remember trying. I remember quoting my friends in London and saying: 'The conditions are different, Herr Hitler. Almost a year has passed since Munich was signed. Then Britain and France were unprepared. We had no troops, nor arms, nor planes. Now we have had almost a year to get ready. We have had a year of preparation, and this time we shall keep our pledges if Poland's rights are infringed.'

He turned on me sarcastically then. I remember his pale face growing ruddy with passion, and his stubby forefinger with its bitten fingernail jabbing towards me, as he said: 'A year to prepare! What foolishness is that! The position of Britain and France today is worse – far worse – than in September 1938. There will be no war, because you are less in a position to go to war now than you were a year ago. In that year you have achieved less than nothing. You have made things worse, in fact. You have built up your Army? Your Air Force? Your Navy? For every ship you have put on the stocks I have laid one down as well. For every plane you have built I have built twenty. For every tank you have made I have constructed a hundred, and a hundred guns to your single cannon. And for every man you have put in your Army I have conscripted a thousand, and every one of them is trained and has a gun. A year to prepare! You are worse off than you ever were! You will not go to war!'

He strode from the room then. Dietrich looked across at me with a triumphant smile on his greasy face. I remember wondering who was supplying Hitler's information about our arms programme, and how near he was to the truth.

Leonard Mosley

'The inevitability of the struggle'

Few Frenchmen thought war would come, and fewer still doubted that the Maginot Line of defences would hold firm if it did. A rare sceptic was Captain Barlone of the French North African Division.

23 AUGUST 1939

France has been quite bewildered for the last few days; Germany and Soviet Russia have just concluded a pact of non-aggression whilst our Military Mission together with the British is at Moscow, at Stalin's request, to seek agreement with the Red Staff as to possible operations in the event of war. This *volte-face* is being very severely criticised by all the Press except naturally the Communists, who nevertheless are very much embarrassed and unable to give a satisfactory explanation.

Daladier proclaims that exceptional military measures will have to be taken in the near future; one senses a complete reversal of the situation in favour of Germany, without however believing that the position is desperate. Munich in September 1938 and the startling news of March and May have blunted the edge of public opinion. People refuse to envisage the situation except through the tiny peep-hole of Danzig, and a war for 'this provincial town' as Hitler called it, in an attempt to conceal his intentions, would be unthinkable.

Meanwhile, the German press gives vent to more and more exorbitant claims on the Princes of Posen and Silesia and invents 'persecution' of the Germans living in Poland.

My sister and I, on the contrary, have long since believed in the inevitability of the struggle. So I was not surprised when at four o'clock, she telephoned me at my office in Paris that two soldiers had just brought my calling-up notice.

I say good-bye to Benjamin and to the employees, who fully believe that I shall be back at the office by next week. Hastily I make a few purchases: some stout boots, an electric torch, etc. . . . I met de Chaunac, then Samson, a very intelligent German Jew, both of whom arrange to meet me in a fortnight's time.

'So you don't believe that there is going to be a war?' I said to the latter. 'How could anyone believe in any such thing?' he replied; 'France is not ready; she has nothing to go to war with; she would be crushed in a couple of weeks; France will not commit that piece of folly, believe me.'

I shook hands with him without saying a word, amazed to hear such an opinion, for all the German Jews that I have known in recent times urge war like veritable madmen.

24 AUGUST 1939

I take leave of my sister, who is very brave and, as usual, full of energy. Once more I advise her to leave Paris, since no other ties exist to keep her there. She prefers to remain, she isn't afraid. We feel sad, however, believing war to be inevitable. We do not doubt our victory, but wonder what price we shall have to pay.

The train for Toul is full of officers and men; the men as usual joke and laugh. The officers talk to each other about their particular branch of the service. I lunch in the dining-car next to a young lieutenant in the infantry on his way to the Maginot Line. He tells me that he has travelled considerably in Germany for his Insurance Company; only a few weeks ago he did a round there. We agree in thinking that the shortage of food, supposed to exist there, is all eye-wash. He also believes in a long and hard war, and in the swift crushing of Poland. His company is detailed to occupy a gap between two works of the Maginot Line.

We arrived at Toul about four o'clock in the afternoon. The barracks, named after Joan of Arc, stand at the other end of the town. There, I am told to take command of the 92/20 Horse Transport Company of the Headquarters of the 2nd North African Division whose Staff is stationed at Dommartin-les-Toul, a suburb quite near to the barracks. I take possession of the *Journal de Mobilisation* of my company, a bulky volume, which tells me what I have to do and what stores I have to draw day by day. Much work and all perfectly planned. I plunge into this mass of work, endeavouring to get my bearings.

At the local town hall, where I set up my office, I meet Lieutenant Bloch (from Sarreguemines). He is very short, freckled and quite bald, always smiling, and has a pronounced Lorraine accent; always surrounded by friends who remember his cheerfulness on field-days. Good, I'll make him my assistant, I think that we shall get on well together.

Then Second Lieutenant Viry, very correct, very young and serious. He introduces himself to me at the regulation four paces. He has just completed his training in the regular army and was recalled a week ago, as a nucleus for the formation of the company. He has the 'hippo' (horse transport) service at his finger ends, and seems to have a certain contempt for me when I tell him that I know nothing about it, having always served in the infantry and in mechanised units. As he contemplates my temples touched with grey, my old uniform now out of fashion, I feel that he is thinking, 'We're doing fine with an old guy like that.' We shall see . . .

I am lodging with mother Maquin – 82 years old – a nice old woman whose son is a ranker Major of Tirailleurs Algériens (Algerian Rifle Regiment). Mother Maquin is terribly gossipy and very lively, and she tells me all her troubles. Everybody calls her 'Aunty', a nickname I suppose, but she tells me that she has thirty-two nephews and nieces in this tiny village.

She must have reserved my bed for a flea-breeding ground, for in the morning, after a sleepless night, I notice that hundreds of swellings adorn my body. Well, I suppose it can't be helped!

The old dame is delighted, as I have lent Martin, my batman, to her. He is a fine hard-working farmer of the district. I've also lent her a few other *poilus* [French infantrymen] to shake her plum trees, loaded with mirabelles. For four years there have been no mirabelle plums and now that is the only thing that matters in the countryside. Mother Maquin stuffs my pockets full of them, and I eat enough to make me ill.

The men of the reserve come in without undue haste, without the enthusiasm of 1914, or even that of last year, being fully persuaded that they will be sent home in two weeks' time, and annoyed at not being able to complete the harvest. But if one has to go – of course, one will go, and return home to peace and quietness after having given Hitler a good drubbing. The men's great hope is that Hitler will be assassinated because, for the time being, they separate Hitler in their minds from Germany.

Once he is beaten, so they reason, all will be over. They do not realise that Hitler is the manifestation of Germany's predatory instinct, the incarnation of the chosen people whose mission is to dominate the world. Nor do they realise that he is the Leader elected by plebiscite with eighty million votes behind him, of which nine-tenths are probably genuine; that he is also probably the leader of a conspiracy by three great bandits, three devouring monsters: Hitler himself, Mussolini and Japan, and that these are leagued together like gangsters in an attempt to plunder two rich and prosperous nations, the only two who can pay with their immense colonial empires: England and ourselves.

The calmness and the lack of pervasive enthusiasm of our soldiers is moreover due – and this is serious – to the fact that, apart from a desire not to be uprooted every six months, they have no war aims of territorial conquests; but they have one very definite aim, that of finishing off Hitler once and for all. In 1914 – when enthusiasm was unbounded – there was in our hearts after, but only after, war had been declared, the will to reconquer Alsace and Lorraine and a desire for revenge. From the start, France was invaded; we had to retake the lost provinces and free our native soil.

But to-day we desire nothing; we have more than enough colonies, we know that our land is safe from invasion, thanks to the Maginot Line; no one has the least desire to fight for Czecho-Slovakia or for Poland, of which ninety-five Frenchmen out of every hundred are completely ignorant and unable to find on a map; we have no belief that Hitler will hurl himself on us after having swallowed up the little nations, one by one. We tell ourselves that having obtained what he wants, he will leave us in peace.

But the Germans have stupendous war aims: the recovery of what they lost through the treaty of Versailles; to own colonies; to wipe out defeat; to regain their pride; to dominate the world. They scorn the democracies; they have unlimited confidence in their military power and the successes of Hitler have swollen them with pride and self-assurance. Truly these are the war aims of jackals, but offensive aims, whilst ours are merely defensive.

Here the Germans have a considerable advantage over us from the point of view of morale.

25 AUGUST 1939

We begin to collect harness, arms, stores and rations, etc. The requisitioning parties send us fine horses quite unused to sleeping tethered in the open.

An officers' mess is established in a little restaurant half-way between the Jeanne D'Arc barracks and Dommartin; the tables are laid for eighteen to twenty men. We are still cold and reserved in the mess.

Bets are made on the chances of the war. Here, as elsewhere, no one believes that it will come to anything, and the stakes are low and few. I refrain for fear of revealing my pessimism.

D. Barlone

Autumn 1939

The Invasion of Poland

'It is a wonderful feeling now, to be a German'

Wilhelm Prüller was a 23-year-old lieutenant in the German Army. Like Hitler, Prüller was Austrian by birth, one of thousands of his countrymen attracted to the nationalistic Nazi creed in the wake of the collapse of the Habsburg empire after the First World War. Prüller's mood was that of many of the soldiers who advanced into Poland at the beginning of September.

30 AUGUST 1939

In this diary I shall attempt to describe to you, my dearly beloved Henny, all the things that happen to me and my unit. I will also tell you those things about me that you ought to know.

Personally, I think the 'Affaire Poland' will be settled peacefully: perhaps Daladier will at the last minute assume the function of a mediator. But if it really does come to war, I am sure it won't last long. For the Poles won't be able to withstand our attack.

And how could England and France fulfil their promise to help Poland? The West Wall is impregnable. France would sacrifice her sons there to no avail. And England could only rush to help Poland by sea. The Baltic has certainly been closed by us. Gibraltar will be held at bay by Italy and Spain. The only people who could help the Poles are the Soviet Union. And a brilliant stroke of strategy has destroyed this Polish hope, too.

Perhaps the Soviet Union will send an ultimatum to Poland and demand their centuries-old rights.

No matter. The situation is highly satisfactory for us, and it's unthinkable for us, too, as the greatest European power, to sit back and watch the persecution of the *Volksdeutsche* [so-called ethnic Germans] without doing something. It is our duty to rectify this wrong, which cries to Heaven. If we fight, then we know that we are serving a rightful cause. We know, however, that the Führer will do all he can to avoid war.

I SEPTEMBER 1939

It's 4 a.m. We are 2 miles from the border and ready to go.

The Poles haven't accepted our rightful demands.

At 5.45 a.m. the border is supposed to be crossed.

We're a reserve unit. One hundred metres to our side there is a large oil, petroleum or armaments factory. One grenade . . . and we've had it.

We're sitting on our lorries and telling dirty jokes. Everything is camouflaged.

Only a quarter of an hour more. If only this waiting were over. If only something would happen. One way or the other.

For a week they put us up on the bare floor of a school. Waiting, waiting. We haven't slept for nights. And the worst of it is, you're not allowed to write home. Terrible. We're not to write until 4th September.

We've just got paid. One hundred Czech crowns. A joke. In two hours we may not even be in this world. And with 100 crowns in our pockets. And not able to send a last message home, while our dear ones are waiting for news.

One's thoughts go in a circle – as if they wanted to turn a huge mill-stone. Everything on edge. And the feeling that we're in this place: painful when you think of home. The most wonderful feeling as well, though, of manly and loyal devotion to duty!

My darling Henny! I don't know how long it'll last. I want to tell you something lovely: you were the only woman I've ever loved. And if God pleases that I return home, then I know one thing: as long as I live, you'll be the only woman I'll ever love. Before I saw you – yes, there were others, but it wasn't love. You taught that to me. I could start at the Bürgerball, I could talk of your first holiday, of my departure to Berlin and my return. I could recall our marriage, my call-up . . . it wouldn't be complete, though, if I didn't think of our Lore. Guard her well, this little creature. Make her strong, so that one day she can skirt the cliffs of life. And tell her, sometimes, of me, if it should happen that . . .

You both are my hope in this and the coming hours.

And send my best greetings to your mother. She was an idol to me, this wonderful woman. And to my parents, especially my father. And to anyone else who would like to have them. Of course your father, too.

Something else for you: keep on being the wife you always were, be assured that I love only you, and that I live only for you. I don't ask anything from you. Only that you should think of me often, and know that in my life I've only done my duty, nothing but my duty. And stay happy, even in the misfortune of my death.

6.20: the first news: our troops have pushed 3 miles into Poland. The first village has been taken. No shot from the Polish side.

6.45: we move forward.

7.30: the Poles tried a tank attack. They were destroyed and forced to run. While retreating they set fire to six villages.

Our own unit is on our side of the border, although some of our troops are 6 km into Poland. It's begun to rain now. I've wrapped my MG [machine-gun] in a woollen blanket; this might save our lives. To the right are the Tatra Mountains and in front of us a burning village.

We've reached the border.

It is a wonderful feeling now, to be a German.

Flak pushes past us – artillery, tanks and armoured scouting cars, hundreds of them.

We're still on the border. The row of tanks has no end. A quarter of an hour, tanks, tanks, tanks . . . Rain's stopped. The crew of our lorry is all tense. Seven men and a noncom, we all wish we were in Poland . . .

9 o'clock: moving forward at a walking pace. Forward a few feet, then waiting, waiting . . . Just learned that we've occupied Danzig.

9.45: We've crossed the border. We're in Poland. *Deutschland, Deutschland über alles!*

We're 103 km from Krakow. Everywhere we see torn-up roads, trenches, tank traps hastily thrown up. Destroyed bridges make us take long detours across fields. We drive through the first village. They hand flowers into our lorry. In delight they stretch their hands towards us. The blown-up bridges and the torn-up streets continue to slow up our advance. But all the Poles' efforts are shown to be of no avail. The German Wehrmacht is marching! If we look back, or in front of us, or left or right: everywhere the motorised Wehrmacht!

Suddenly, halt! Enemy in front of us. I've got to take my machine-gun section and act as a scouting patrol. About a mile up the hill. Ha! . . . we're shot at from the right. The first time! Machine-gun volley, it doesn't reach us. Then silence. Our lorry climbs the hill. We go back to the Squadron, and leave the lorries.

We march to the attack. Terrific heat now. Battledress. The machine-gun 13.5 kg on our backs. One mile, two, three, on, on . . . We can't go on. But mile after mile is captured. No one can go on. No water, no coffee, no tea. Marching, running, running. Halt! We've reached a PAK (anti-tank gun) and rest in front of a few houses. The family sits in front of the door. All of them crying. But we aren't harming anyone! Why didn't the Polish Government give in? We haven't got anything against the people themselves. But where are our rights? They offer us water and milk. We refuse, because we have to. But this thirst is terrible!

Our artillery begins to fire again. At every shot the Poles wince. Under the shell-fire we march on. It's 16.45. We've marched only 3 hours and have 10 km behind us. I hope we stay here. A hamlet. But there's supposed to be a pub: then we'd have something to drink. Blank goes past and has already got a bottle of beer. It's the last. He chucks it at me. Undrinkable. As if it were warmed up.

It's now 17.30. I am so tired I could drop. My feet ache. I've been on my feet since 1 in the morning. One thing kept me going today, the thought of our seeing each other again. I'm still alive, and so are you and Lore. All of us!

Wilhelm Prüller

Prüller survived the war. In 1959, he could be found running a knick-knack shop in a suburb of Vienna, still wearing a ring engraved with the SS runes.

Not all Germans supported the invasion.

20 SEPTEMBER 1939

So the Nazis (I do not want to speak of the Germans in this connection) . . . the Nazis are conquering, and what else is one to expect? A hopelessly rainy summer has been followed by a clear, sunny autumn, full of the smoky perfumes of that season, with the ground solid and hard-packed and as though made to order for those tanks to roll over and flatten to earth whatever stands in their way . . . the Polish Cavalry, the whole Polish Army . . . and if Poland is ours today, tomorrow it must be the whole world.

Yes, the Nazis are conquering and perhaps internally even more than on the battlefield. The editors exult in bloodthirsty fashion on the news-print into which our forests are to be converted. They have invented a brand-new language to match the great times in which we live, and now proclaim the Realisation of 1899, and the Commitment of the Woman at War, and the Reinforcement by the German Woman, and talk about the ancient piece of German ground, Posen. And when they are reminded that Posen was Polish territory as far back as the time of Frederick the

Great, and that even earlier soldiers from Danzig fought on the Polish side in the First Battle of Tannenberg, they turn nasty and threaten to tell the Gestapo . . .

The Nazis are, indeed, conquering, and their 'war commentators' bring new glory to the German language, as they 'shower the enemy with sparks enough to make him burn for peace' and 'give him something to chew on that lays him flat on the ground'. And when they are told that their German is the German of the latrine wall and the pimp, they turn very nasty indeed, and roar that they are soldiers, and that this happens to be how soldiers talk, and if you don't believe it, you can find out in a concentration camp.

Oh, yes, the Nazis do nothing but conquer, they conquer just as uninterruptedly as Wilhelm's armies did in 1914, and the beer-hall regulars again have the entire world annexed. And in the local café, recently, the old one-time Medical Corps general employed the current jargon in lumping Poles and Englishmen together as 'pigs' – despite the fact that the old man never in his life saw an example of the latter in his 'natural habitat', so to speak.

When I rose and objected to such entirely uncalled-for language, he looked at me with the eyes of a wounded stag, felt that the world had collapsed at his feet, and mumbled something about how he had always thought I was a *patriotic* man.

Friedrich Reck-Malleczewen

The author, a Prussian aristocrat and intellectual, was later executed in Dachau concentration camp.

The view from Westminster

Henry 'Chips' Channon, Parliamentary Private Secretary to 'Rab' Butler at the Foreign Office, had an insider's view of developments in London in early September. Channon was a noted appeaser, and regarded those of his colleagues in the House of Commons who wished to oppose Hitler over Poland as half-crazed warmongers.

2 SEPTEMBER 1939

. . . I had no lunch, walked with Rab to the House of Commons, and tried on the way, forgetting it was Saturday, to buy him a hat. By 2.30 I was back in my room at the House of Commons, and I rang the Private Secretaries asking where the box was with the Statement which the

Chancellor was to make. It had been delayed. At last it arrived, but only two minutes before the Speaker took the chair. Rab and I walked along, and I caught sight of John Simon's bald white head and as we caught him up, he whispered that he had just received an urgent message not to make the statement as important news had come from Italy.

The moment Prayers were over he made a brief announcement to the House that the Prime Minister [Neville Chamberlain] would make a statement later. I rushed out, found Rab in a deep conference, although a peripatetic one, with Halifax. They walked to the Lords together, and I followed, trying to listen. When we reached the Princes Chamber, which was full of eager Peers, my father-in-law seized me and delayed me. When I had broken away Rab told me that the Italians had offered to negotiate and to call together a Five Power Conference, etc. . . .

Then we went, followed by Rab to No. 10. The PM apparently considered Ciano's message of sufficient importance to call together an immediate Cabinet at 4.30 at No. 10, and there was a sauve qui peut from the Front Bench, and the House at once sensed that there was something afoot. I remained in our room so as not to be trapped into saying anything indiscreet . . . Rab rang me about six, the Cabinet had just risen; it has been, he said, stormy, and Ciano was only going to get a very stiff reply though it would be as reasonable as Chamberlain could make it under the circumstances.

Then there was a long, and most unfortunate, wait, which very likely affected the final course of tomorrow's War — for it must be tomorrow now, since we have had our miracle today and did not profit by it; for during the long time which ensued, the nervous House, chafing under delay, and genuinely distressed, some of them, by our guarantee to Poland not having been immediately operative, quenched their thirst in the Smoking Room, and when they returned to hear the PM's statement, many of them were full of 'Dutch Courage'; one noticed their flushed faces . . . Meanwhile the Cabinet had risen and retired. The PM was left behind with Halifax to draft his statement, and a clumsy, or rather inartistic, document it was, too. At the same time they had to ring up Paris and convey to them Ciano's offer (at the time I understood this to be so, though now I believe that the French knew of it this morning). In any case the French Cabinet met immediately and began to discuss it. They demanded more time, and it was first suggested that the Germans should be told that unless they evacuated Poland within a week we should declare War jointly with the French (this proposal is supposed to have originated with Bonnet, who is anti-War). There were long telephonic conversations and the time limit was whittled down to 48 hours. The PM arrived at last, and I instantly woke Rab, who had had ten minutes' sleep, handed him an icy Martini which exhilarated him, and together we walked into the PM's room where we found Alec Dunglass, Rucker and David Margesson. Arthur Greenwood and Archie Sinclair had just been summoned into the inner room and the PM told them of the French evasive delays (they are not so prepared as we are, nor is their evacuation so well advanced). We waited outside, and someone said something funny about Horace Wilson which threw us all into fits of laughter. I suppose it was nerves – the first laugh for weeks, and when Rab gave us his famous cackle, David Margesson and I doubled up, roared until the tears came . . . Suddenly the PM's bell rang, and David was summoned into the presence. By now our spirits were soaring, peace might again be saved, as by a miracle, by Italian intervention . . . We followed the PM into the House, which was crowded and grim. The long wait had irritated everyone, and it would have been longer still had I not reminded the Secretaries that Halifax had probably already made his identical statement in the Lords.

The PM rose, was cheered, but not over-much, and then he read out his statement which I thought ill-conceived. It began by saying that, as yet, no answer had come to our warning to Berlin, and the House, thoroughly prepared to unsheathe the sword, was aghast when it was hinted that peace might yet be saved. Decidedly the PM did not have a very good reception, though Greenwood, who followed him, attempted to soothe the House, whilst maintaining his own dignity. Maxton made an impassioned appeal to the PM to continue his good work, not to be rushed, but he was almost shouted down. All the old Munich rage all over again; all the resentment against Chamberlain: All those who want to die abused Caesar. John McGovern leant over to strike Kirby (Labour member for Euston) but the Speaker pretended not to see . . . there were a few other short speeches, after which Chamberlain rose for the second time, and promised a definite answer by noon tomorrow when the House will meet again – for the first time on a Sunday in all its history.

The Cabinet and the Appeasers were discouraged by the reception the insane House of Commons gave to this glimmer of peace, and began to say that the PM was not accurate in reporting to the House the findings of the Cabinet.

All evening at the FO, Butler and I struggled hard. There were countless telephone calls to Paris and we were told that the French, led by Bonnet, would not shorten their ultimatum to Germany which they insisted should be for a whole week! We know we could not hold the House of Commons for so long, but we offered, as a compromise, 48 hours from tomorrow morning – the Frogs, at first, would not agree. And here the War Party, suddenly strengthened by John Simon, who, I suppose, saw his chance of becoming PM, began to argue for a shorter ultimatum still – the Cabinet sat long. Terrific excitement; wild talk of the French ratting altogether, of our fighting them and the whole world . . . Peter Loxley and I crossed over to No. 10 Downing Street after the Private Secretaries had rung for us to come and join the fun, and it came on to rain – a storm, terrific, ominous – 'When the Rains Came'. I saw Alec Dunglass, 'Are we all mad?', I asked him.

The PM came out of a side room followed by Horace Wilson and Rab. He looked well, almost relieved that the dread decision was taken and the appalling battle on – we were going to give Germany only two hours' ultimatum (this was an answer to the French, to make them ashamed). The Cabinet had insisted; the War Party was led by Simon, Oliver Stanley, Walter Elliot and, I believe Shakespeare Morrison; the overruled Peace Party consisted of the PM and Kingsley Wood. I sat on Rucker's (the most amiable, able Chief Private Secretary) desk, when the door opened into the Cabinet room, and I saw Sam Hoare, alone, in a dinner jacket. The various Chiefs of Staff were wandering about in uniform: Corbin, the steely, grey, Frog Ambassador, was soon in conference with the PM. He was told our decision: we had already instructed Nevile Henderson to ask for an interview tomorrow morning at 9 a.m. and to inform the German Government that unless news came by 11 a.m. that the German Government had ordered the withdrawal of their forces from Poland we should be at War . . . This message was sent, I think, about midnight or after. The French immediately climbed down, and we understood from Corbin that the French Ambassador in Berlin was to ask for an interview tomorrow at noon, and give the German Government 17 hours, that is until 5 a.m. on Monday morning, to withdraw. The French Government have not sufficiently completed their mobilisation and evacuation and all day they had been pressing us to hold back a few more hours. Broken-hearted, I begged David Margesson to do something; but he was already determined. 'It must be War, Chips, old boy,' he said. 'There's no other way out.'

I decided to go home; there were no cars; the rain was blinding – Cabinet Ministers, Chiefs of Staff, all wandered hopelessly about. We left Rab with the PM, who was about to go to bed, for his last night of peace. Wet typists trotted off into the downpour; only people emerging from No. 10 knew the facts . . . Peter and I left: I wanted to walk, as it had cleared a little; he would not. It was dark, a precaution against air-raids. We found a taxi. Peter dropped me. I am home. I shall not sleep; in a few hours we shall be at War, and the PM will have lost his great battle for peace.

Henry Channon

The first air-raid alarm, as witnessed by Winston Churchill.

The Prime Minister's broadcast informed us that we were already at war, and he had scarcely ceased speaking when a strange, prolonged, wailing noise, afterwards to become familiar, broke upon the ear. My wife came into the room braced by the crisis and commented favourably upon the German promptitude and precision, and we went up to the flat top of the house to see what was going on. Around us on every side, in the clear, cool September light, rose the roofs and spires of London. Above them were already slowly rising thirty or forty cylindrical balloons. We gave the Government a good mark for this evident sign of preparation, and as the quarter of an hour's notice which we had been led to expect we should receive was now running out we made our way to the shelter assigned to us, armed with a bottle of brandy and other appropriate medical comforts.

Our shelter was a hundred yards down the street, and consisted merely of an open basement, not even sand-bagged, in which the tenants of half a dozen flats were already assembled. Everyone was cheerful and jocular, as is the English manner when about to encounter the unknown. As I gazed from the doorway along the empty street and at the crowded room below my imagination drew pictures of ruin and carnage and vast explosions shaking the ground; of buildings clattering down in dust and rubble, of fire-brigades and ambulances scurrying through the smoke, beneath the drone of hostile aeroplanes. For had we not all been taught how terrible air raids would be? The Air Ministry had, in natural self-importance, greatly exaggerated their power. The pacifists had sought to play on public fears, and those of us who had so long pressed for preparation and a superior Air Force, while not accepting the most lurid forecasts, had been content that they should act as a spur. I knew that the Government were prepared, in the first few days of the war, with over 250,000 beds for air-raid casualties. Here at least there had been no under-estimation. Now we should see what were the facts.

After about ten minutes had passed the wailing broke out again. I was myself not sure that this was not a reiteration of the previous warning, but a man came running along the street shouting 'All clear', and we dispersed to our dwellings and went about our business.

Winston Churchill

Human wreckage

On 24 September, the Luftwaffe began bombing Warsaw. So ferocious was the attack that the city surrendered just three days later. Here, a Polish nurse describes the conditions in the main hospital.

The procession of wounded from the city was an unending march of death. The lights went out, and all of us, doctors and nurses, had to move about with candles in our hands. As both the operating-theatres and the dressing-stations were destroyed the work was done in the lecture-rooms on ordinary deal tables, and owing to the lack of water the instruments could not be sterilised, but had to be cleansed with alcohol.

I shall remember forever the dreadful night of September 25th–26th, when with one hand I helped to give anaesthetics, holding a candle in the other, while the surgeon was amputating arms or legs. As human wreckage was laid on the table the surgeon vainly endeavoured to save the lives that were slipping through his hands. On the table at which I was assisting tragedy followed tragedy. At one time the victim was a girl of sixteen. She had a glorious mop of golden hair, her face was delicate as a flower, and her lovely sapphire-blue eyes were full of tears. Both her legs, up to the knees, were a mass of bleeding pulp, in which it was impossible to distinguish bone from flesh; both had to be amputated above the knee. Before the surgeon began I bent over this innocent child to kiss her pallid brow, to lay my helpless hand on her golden head. She died quietly in the course of the morning, like a flower plucked by a merciless hand.

That same night, on the same deal table, there died under the knife of the surgeon a young expectant mother, nineteen years of age, whose intestines were torn by the blast of a bomb. She was only a few days before childbirth. We never knew who her husband and her family were, and she was buried, a woman unknown, in the common grave with the fallen soldiers.

That night I tended also two gentle old people, Mr and Mrs N., both of them wounded in the eyes; each had lost one eye, and we did not know if the other eye could be saved. After their wounds were dressed they sat quietly on a bench in the corridor, holding hands and whispering words of encouragement to each other.

The stream of the wounded never ceased. We had to leave the dying in the corridors, as there was no room in any of the wards. Those whom we were able to attend in the improvised operating-theatre we were obliged to place on the floor with a bundle of clothing under their heads. There were so many of them that it became difficult to move about.

Thus the night passed, and the day came, but still the terrible attack was continued without interruption. Warsaw was burning, our hospital was in flames, the windows were smashed, the doors blown in, and there was neither light nor water nor food. The second night of terror passed, and the bombardment of the city never ceased for a moment. We lost all sense of time, and neither minutes nor hours had any significance for this crumbling and collapsing hospital, in which there was no room for the living or the wounded or the dying. Everything became unreal, except the urge to go on tending the human wreckage with which the hospital was choked.

At last, on the third day at 11 a.m., the bombing and the bombardment ceased quite suddenly. Everyone was seized with amazement and terror. I was at the moment in the corridor in which all the dying were placed in rows – long rows of more than a hundred yards of mutilated bodies of soldiers, women and children.

I walked or rather jerked my way among the bodies, to close the eyes of one who had just died, or to hold the head of another who was about to die. Some time after the bombardment ceased it became lighter, and it was then that I saw the most terrible sight – a river of blood literally flowing down the corridor, washing the bodies of the dead, dying, and still living martyrs. The pale light of day entered through the ragged gaps of the broken windows and illuminated the corridor with its rows of shattered bodies. Here lay a little girl beside an aged, white-haired woman – there a soldier beside an old workman in his dungarees. Old and young, children and adults, men and women, all mercilessly murdered.

Jadwiga Sosnkowska

In mid-September, Russia – which had signed a non-aggression treaty with Germany the previous month – also invaded Poland, which she was defeated in less than four weeks and partitioned by Hitler and Stalin.

Harold Nicolson, the author and husband of Vita Sackville-West, was the MP for West Leicester. Like many of his constituents, he was increasingly despondent at the turn of events.

17 SEPTEMBER 1939

Write my *Spectator* article. At 11 a.m. (a bad hour) Vita comes to tell me that Russia has invaded Poland and is striking towards Vilna. We are so dumbfounded by this news that there is a wave of despair over Sissinghurst. I do not think that the Russians will go beyond her old frontier or will wish to declare war on us. But of course it is a terrific blow and makes our victory even more uncertain.

Let me review the situation. It may be that within a few days we shall have Germany, Russia and Japan against us. It may be that Rumania will be subjugated and that the Greeks and Yugoslavs will succumb to Germany. The Baltic and the Scandinavian states will be too frightened to do anything. Holland, Belgium and Switzerland will have to capitulate. Thus the Axis will rule Europe, the Mediterranean and the Far East. Faced by such a combine, France may make her terms. Hitler is then in the position of Napoleon after Austerlitz, with the important difference that whereas we were then in command of the seas, our command of the seas is not now absolute. It is not so much a question of us encircling and blockading Germany; it is a question of them encircling and blockading us. Japan might threaten our position in Australia and the Far East. Russia might threaten us in India. Italy might raise the Arab world. In a few days our whole position might collapse. Nothing could be more black.

And yet and yet, I still believe that if we have the will-power, we might win through. The Germans, who are diffident by nature, can scarcely believe in this fairy-tale. A single reverse and they will be overcome with nervous trepidation. Our position is one of grave danger. A generous offer of an immediate truce with the prospect of an eventual conference might tempt us sorely. But we shall not have a generous offer. What will happen? I suppose that there will be a German ultimatum and a Coalition Cabinet. Chamberlain must go. Churchill may be our Clemenceau or our Gambetta. To bed very miserable and alarmed.

Harold Nicolson

‡

Sinking the Royal Oak

On 13 October the German submarine U-47 slipped into the Royal Navy's base at Scapa Flow, in the Orkneys. Its captain, Gunther Prien, describes how he managed to sink the battleship Royal Oak.

. . . We are in Scapa Flow.

14.10.39. It is disgustingly light. The whole bay is lit up. To the south of Cava there is nothing. I go farther in. To port, I recognise the Hoxa Sound coastguard, to which in the next few minutes the boat must present itself as a target. In that event all would be lost; at present south of Cava no ships are to be seen, although visibility is extremely good. Hence decisions.

South of Cava there is no shipping, so before staking everything on success, all possible precautions must be taken. Therefore, turn to port is made. We proceed north by the coast. Two battleships are lying there at anchor, and further inshore, destroyers. Cruisers not visible, therefore attack on the big fellows.

Distance apart, 3,000 metres. Estimated depth, seven and a half metres. Impact firing. One torpedo fired on northern ship, two on southern. After a good three and a half minutes, a torpedo detonates on the northern ship; of the other two nothing is to be seen.

About! Torpedo fired from stern; in the bow two tubes are loaded; three torpedoes from the bow. After three tense minutes comes the detonation of the nearer ship. There is a loud explosion, roar, and rumbling. Then come columns of water, followed by columns of fire, and splinters fly through the air. The harbour springs to life. Destroyers are lit up, signalling starts on every side, and on land, 200 metres away from me, cars roar along the roads. A battleship had been sunk, a second damaged, and the other three torpedoes have gone to blazes. All the tubes are empty. I decide to withdraw, because: (1) With my periscopes I cannot conduct night attacks while submerged . . . (2) On a bright night I cannot manoeuvre unobserved in a calm sea. (3) I must assume that I was observed by the driver of a car which stopped opposite us, turned around, and drove off towards Scapa at top speed. (4) Nor can I go farther north, for there, well hidden from my sight, lie the destroyers which were previously dimly distinguishable.

At full speed both engines we withdraw. Everything is simple until we reach Skildaenoy Point. Then we have more trouble. It is now low tide. The current is against us. Engines at slow and dead slow; I attempt to get away. I must leave by the south through the narrows, because of the depth of the water. Things are again difficult. Course, 058°, slow – ten knots. I make no progress. At full speed I pass the southern blockship with nothing to spare. The helmsman does magnificently. Full speed ahead both, finally three-quarter speed and full ahead all out. Free of the blockships – ahead a mole! Hard over and again about, and at 02.15 we are once more outside. A pity that only one was destroyed. The torpedo misses I explain as due to faults of course, speed and drift. In tube 4, a misfire. The crew behaved splendidly throughout the operation.

Gunther Prien

Eight hundred and thirty-three members of the Royal Oak*'s company were lost. The Royal Navy would get its revenge on Prien in March 1941, when* U-47 *was depth-charged and destroyed by* Wolverine.

In which we serve

In the early days of the war, the playwright Noël Coward was sent to Paris by what he called 'Hush-Hush Headquarters' to use his contacts for the benefit of Britain's fledgling propaganda effort.

During those two hectic and exasperating weeks I decided to avail myself of Hookie Holland's kind offer, and telephone to Dallas Brooks from the Ministère de la Marine to report progress. Feeling suitably mysterious, but without any noticeable disguise, I arrived at the Ministère after seven o'clock in the evening as Hookie had told me to do. No suspicious sentries challenged me and the whole operation was a good deal simpler than going into the Galeries Lafayette. There was a French PO in the outer office, to whom I said '*Bon soir*' graciously; he replied with a grunt and made no attempt to prevent me from going into the inner office. I gave the special number to the telephone operator, upon which I heard a shrill scream of laughter and, to my intense surprise, was put through to the British Admiralty immediately. Whether or not the operator was laughing at my accent or at a book she was reading I shall never know. I was put through in a few seconds to Electra House, where Dallas Brooks answered the telephone himself. I at once embarked laboriously on the code he had given me. 'This is Diplomat speaking,' I said. (Diplomat was my code name.) To this he replied rather irascibly, 'Who?' 'Diplomat,' I said again slowly and clearly, and then went on with a rush to explain that I had interviewed 'Lion' (Sir Eric) and established successful contact with 'Glory'

(Giraudoux), but had not yet been able to get into touch with 'Triumph' (Daladier), although I had had a charming interview with his Chef-du-Cabinet, whose name I was unable to divulge as we hadn't got a code word for it – He interrupted me at this point by saying: 'What the bloody hell are you talking about?' Repressing my rising irritation I started from the beginning again, articulating very, very slowly as though I were talking to an idiot child. There was a pause and he said wearily: 'It's no good, old boy, I can't understand a word.' At this I really lost patience and explained to him the code, word for word. This foolhardy betrayal of an important secret must have shocked him immeasurably, because there was a moment of silence and then he hung up. I returned fuming to the hotel, where I typed out the whole thing in a letter which I marked 'Secret, Confidential and Dull'.

Noël Coward

‡

The aniseed ball bomb

In the years of struggle ahead for the British, much would depend on the ingenuity of men such as Colonel Stuart Macrae, who was developing weaponry for irregular warfare. His first creation was the limpet mine.

Next day we started in on making our first ship-sinking device. Nobby created an experimental department by sweeping a load of rubbish and more children off a bench. We went shopping in Bedford and bought some large tin bowls from Woolworth's. Some local tinsmith was cajoled into dropping all his other work and fashioning for us rims with annular grooves to fit these bowls and plates which could be screwed on to close these rims. The rims were sweated to the bowls and as many of the little horseshoe magnets as possible were packed into the annular grooves so that the pole pieces were exposed, these pole pieces then being lined up by simply placing a keeper ring over the whole lot. To secure the magnets in place we at first poured bitumen into the groove, but later found that plaster of Paris was a better answer.

The idea was to stuff this bowl full of blasting gelatine or some similar high explosive and then screw the lid in place so that the device was sealed. It had to be carried by a swimmer, so we contrived a belt consisting of a 4" wide steel plate, just long enough to span the magnet ring, to which were attached strips of webbing which could be tied round the swimmer's waist. Obviously the swimmer must not be unduly handicapped by having to travel under water with this contrivance so we wanted it to weigh next to nothing when submerged. Eventually after using up all the porridge in the house in place of high explosive for filling, juggling about with weights and dimensions, and flooding Nobby's bathroom on several occasions, we got this right.

Field trials were the next stage, and we carried them out in Bedford Public Baths which were closed to the public for these occasions. At the deep end we propped a large steel plate reasonably upright to represent the side of a ship and Nobby, who was an excellent swimmer, started his dummy runs. Nobby was exceedingly noble over this. Looking as if he were suffering from advanced pregnancy he would swim to and fro removing the device from his belt, turning it over, and plonking it on the target plate with great skill. We learnt a lot more than we had done in the bathroom. Our magnets were so powerful that when in the water it at first proved difficult to remove the mine from the keeper plate belt without the risk of rupturing oneself. So we had to experiment with various sizes of plate until we had one which gave the required hold and no more. The buoyancy too came in for adjustment as we found it advantageous to have slight positive buoyancy.

It took us only a few days to bring the development to this stage. We then had the basis of Jefferis' magnetic mine which could be plated on the side of a ship by a clever fellow without much difficulty and would stay there provided the ship were not a wooden one and that it was not unduly encrusted with barnacles. We could only hope that the enemy kept his craft in decent condition. At a solemn ceremony back at the works, I christened this thing 'The Limpet' – a name which stuck. It is just as well it did, because quite a different device produced by the Germans later on was called a magnetic mine and this could have caused much confusion.

So far so good. The next thing to do was to devise a delayed action initiator which would cause this gadget to go bang in anything between half an hour and two hours after its installation. There was nothing on the market that would serve the purpose but it was simple enough to think up something. All we needed was a spring-loaded striker, maintained in the cocked position by a pellet soluble in water. When the pellet dissolved, the striker would be released to hit a cap to initiate a detonator which would explode a primer to explode the main charge.

All this was easy enough, but finding a suitable pellet was difficult. There were too many variables. The powder itself was the first one, and the degree to which it was compressed the second one. The temperature of the water made all the difference, and of course so did whether it were fresh water or sea water. Expert chemists were called in to find us the answer, but they failed. One day a pellet would dissolve at a rate which alarmed us and would no doubt have alarmed a Limpeteer. The next day, a similar one might take several hours over the job and we did not want that. There was some hope of a Limpet staying put on a stationary target and every chance of its getting washed off if the target moved off at 20 knots or so as it might well do in time.

One of Nobby's children solved the problem for us. It was only a small one and, in sweeping it off the bench which it much preferred to its play pen, we upset it by knocking its bag of aniseed balls on to the floor. Whilst Nobby was doing a consoling act, I tried one of these sweets. It seemed to stay with me a long time, getting smaller and smaller with great regularity. After trying a couple himself Nobby agreed that this might well be the answer so we commandeered the remainder of the supply and started to experiment. I think I can safely claim to be the first man to drill holes in aniseed balls and devise a fitting to enable this to be done accurately and efficiently. We rigged up some of our igniters with these aniseed balls in place of soluble pellets and tried them out under various conditions. They behaved perfectly, and the next day the children of Bedford had to go without their aniseed balls. For not wishing to be held up for supplies we toured the town and bought the lot.

Stuart Macrae

‡

Struggling writer George Beardmore had recently been let go from his job at the BBC. He and his young family lived in Harrow, north London.

22 OCTOBER 1939

Yesterday was my first day of unemployment this year. Handed in my cards at the Milton Road Exchange, waiting two hours because of the crush, and got signed up. Tuesdays and Thursdays at 11.30 a.m., Box 8. Room crowded and more outside, but only about three other 'jacket-men', the rest artisans and labourers. Yesterday was also the signing-up day for all the 20/21 class but I didn't see any of them and suppose they had been told to report elsewhere.

Sovereigns, if any, are now worth 39/6d. Hamley's of Regent Street have their latest toy in the main window – 'Build Your Own Maginot Line'. On show is a cross-section of the tiered dug-outs and little men in them doing a variety of duties, a blimp hung up from a lorry outside, and an advance patrol crawling through the heavily camouflaged country, meeting with heavy fire. All right, it's only a toy, but a sudden realisation was brought home to me that, historically, purely defence-positions have never held out for long. Or hasn't the French General Staff read Plutarch?

George Beardmore

Winter 1939-40

The Winter War

Helsinki bombed

Russia, seeking territory on the Baltic, invaded Finland on 29 November 1939. The Finns had an army of only 30,000, and a mere handful of tanks and aircraft. Nevertheless, despite their desperate situation, a Swedish journalist found that the Finns maintained an air of unflappability.

The Finns are a calm and immovable people, so calm and immovable that they often irritate even the Swedes, who after all are not among the impulsive races of Europe. Both Finns and Swedes are capable of developing a tremendous temperament when they have drunk a little too much; but in general the Finns are methodical, patient, and have a calf-like calmness. Under the present conditions these characteristics were extremely valuable. At the beginning of the war, at any rate, they used to go down into the trench shelters in the street, and into other ice-cold shelters, in a calm and orderly fashion when the sirens wailed and the bombers thundered above their heads. They walked with natural dignity and without hurry. During one of these bombing attacks I was sitting with a good friend of mine at lunch in a little restaurant in a Helsinki suburb. We had reached about half-way through a very tough beefsteak when the sirens began to wail. Without any particular hurry the middle-aged waitress moved forward to our table, seized our plates, and told us to follow her. In the kitchen she stuck a match-stick into my beefsteak. 'We always do that, so as keep everybody's portion separate,' she said, as she put the plates in the oven. When this was done we continued at the same calm pace, with bombs exploding to the right and left of us, down into the potato-cellar just across the yard which functioned as an air-raid shelter. Our leader lit a candle and took down some knitting which was hanging on the wall in readiness. I had noticed that she had caught up a coarse comb before we left the kitchen and I asked her the reason for this. 'Oh, that is just my "glass comb".' 'What is a "glass comb"?' 'Well, during the first bombardments we noticed that the windows always broke into tiny, tiny splinters, which seemed to have a particular capacity for settling in the hair before we got down to the shelter. It is necessary to try to get the glass out of the hair as quickly as possible, otherwise it is dangerous. So now we always take a "glass comb" with us.'

On another occasion I saw an older man behind the counter of a gentlemen's outfitting shop, where the windows had just been totally broken and the wall had crashed, carrying on the business half an hour after the 'all clear' had sounded. This 'business-as-usual' principle was applied throughout Helsinki without any exception. In the Technical High School, where the drifting snow came in through the roof of the laboratories and the retorts and other chemical apparatus were covered with snow, the students continued their work in the cellars. The rector wrote out his engineering diplomas for examinations passed from a little room in the porter's lodge. He issued about twenty diplomas between the 30th of November, when the institute was bombed, and the end of the year. This unshakable calm permeated everything. It was to be met with in the primitive shelters, where the children sat in rows with pens or combs between their teeth for the sake of their ear-drums, as they had been told to do. No one showed any alarm even among the children. Once or twice during a particularly heavy attack I noticed older people telling them to sing, and then I heard the hymn *Safe in the Arms of Jesus* sung by shrill trebles to the accompaniment of exploding bombs and the hellish music of planes in the sky. The spiritual greatness of Helsinki during those days made the Swedish journalist feel very humble. He asked himself: 'How would the inhabitants of Stockholm react in a similar situation? Those town-dwellers with their elegant, pleasant standards of living, their entire lack of personal experience of warlike conditions? Yes, how would they react if the catastrophe of war stared them in the face?' I think myself that they would stand up to it.

Another phenomenon in Helsinki, from the spiritual point of view, was that all moroseness had entirely disappeared. The Finns are not a laughing nation. They are by nature taciturn and reserved. Let no one accuse me of belonging to those who think that a people cannot keep up its spiritual standard without now and again going through a war, but it was almost a miracle to see how the Finnish people had thawed. In the streets and in the market-places the cold was intense, but the hearts of the Finns seemed to grow warmer and warmer. It was delightful to see the spirit of happy comradeship which was met with in trams and buses, the impulsive helpfulness one to the other which was shown whenever people met. The war seemed to bring forth many fine traits which had not formerly been apparent in the Finnish people. Swedish Finns and pure Finns lived together as cordially as if there were no minority problem in the country. Social barriers fell and were destroyed. In its hour of testing Helsinki was the most friendly and helpful capital in Europe.

Sven Auren

‡

The Battle of the River Plate

Attacking the Graf Spee

By mid-December, the German pocket battleship Graf Spee *had been on the loose in the Atlantic for four months and had sunk nine ships. She was eventually discovered by a force of three Royal Navy cruisers near the mouth of the River Plate, between Argentina and Uruguay. On 13 December, the* Graf Spee's *captain, Hans Langsdorff, deciding that attack was the best form of defence, started the engagement which was to give the British their first significant naval victory of the war. Lt-Cdr Richard Washbourn, a New Zealander, was a gunnery officer on board* Achilles. *His letter gives a vivid account of the 'scrap'.*

The captain was on the bridge, and we turned to each other and said simultaneously, 'My God, it's a pocket battleship!' I legged it as hard as I could go for my box of tricks, and just had time to wonder if there was anything in this gunnery business after all, and where I should be in half an hour's time, before all my lamps lit up and I was able to say 'SHOOT' for the first time in anger. Four minutes only, though most of the sailors were enjoying their very necessary beauty sleep at the time and we were only at cruising stations. We were rather proud of that, even though *Exeter* did beat us to it.

After that my impressions are rather confused. There were a lot of splashes growing up around that target and it wasn't a bit easy picking out my own. I can remember feeling a quite illogical resentment every time he put his great eleven-inch cannon on us, when I saw those damn great pieces belching their unpleasantness at myself and I can remember feeling unspeakably grateful to poor old *Exeter* every time I saw them blazing in her direction.

He came at us for about a quarter of an hour, very obligingly thinking that we were a couple of destroyers in company with *Exeter*. That covered the rather unpleasant stretch of water in which he could outrange us.

He scored a pretty little straddle after twenty minutes and his HE [high explosive] burst on the surface of the water and the pieces peppered us. There weren't as many casualties as one would expect. Our captain acquired a sizish hole in both legs and the chief yeoman on the bridge had a leg smashed up. In my DCT we had rather more than our share. Six pieces came inside. With my usual fantastic luck three pieces impinged on my ample anatomy . . . but caused me little inconvenience, apart from a certain mental vagueness of the ensuing minute or two. Three died quite quickly and definitely, two of whom were actually in physical contact with me, and three were wounded. I don't expect that names mean anything to you at this distance of time, but one of the casualties was an old '*Diomede*', Archibald Cooper Hirst Shaw. E. V. Shirley, another old '*Diomede*', was one of the very severely wounded. The others had the common misfortune of being imperial ratings (NZ).

The survivors behaved just as one expected and hoped. They took no notice of the shambles (and it looked more like a slaughter-house on a busy day than a Director Control Tower) and took over the jobs of those who had been put out as if nothing had happened. One youngster had to seat himself on the unpleasantness that very shortly before had been a very efficient junior gunnery officer and carry out his job. He was a little wide-eyed after we had disengaged but otherwise unmoved. A splinter had jammed the door and prevented the medical parties from reaching us. The wounded never murmured. Shirley quietly applied a tourniquet to himself and saved his life thereby. A sergeant of Marines who was sitting right alongside me never let on that he was wounded. I didn't discover it until the first lull, an hour later, when he nearly fainted from loss of blood.

I learnt this lesson – though it's a difficult one to put into words – that one can wish for nothing better than these troops of ours. They may be a bit of a nuisance in the easy times of peace, but one can't improve on them when things get a bit hot. A spot of trouble of this sort completely changes one's attitude to the troops. I felt very proud of my fellow countrymen [New Zealanders].

Exeter, as you know, bore the brunt. We had the attentions of the 5.8s all the time, but they weren't very effective. I think that we shot up their control fairly early on, and put at least two of the starboard battery out of action.

Tactically my only criticism is that we should have gone in earlier, but that certainly would have meant more damage and casualties than we actually received, and we did achieve the object of the exercise without it.

It was a plain straightforward scrap, with none of the 'hit-and-run' tactics which the Yellow Press credited us with. We hammered away for an hour and a half, and then hauled off under smoke. I must admit to a certain feeling of being baulked of my prey when we were ordered to turn away, because the last twenty minutes at really effective range had been most enjoyable. It turned out to be the psychologically correct moment. We had damn little ammunition left and, as it proved, the job was done. It didn't seem like it at the time. I was very depressed. We had expended most of our bricks and our enemy looked disappointingly undamaged. The after turret was temporarily out of action, and we had seen one fire on board, and he was running like a frightened rabbit, but his fire was distressingly accurate, and his speed was the same as ever, and there was no sign of structural damage.

We shadowed all day. Once or twice we ventured a bit too close and he swung round and let us have it, but he was out of our range and we didn't reply.

In the evening we gave the Uruguayans the thrill of their lives by another little brush just at sunset when we were closing the range to keep him in sight as the visibility lessened. Four times later, during the advancing twilight, he took exception to our presence, but these last Parthian shots were merely gestures.

The morale was magnificent while we were waiting for him to emerge from his hole. The fantastic fleets that Winston [then Minister for the Navy], ably aided and abetted by the BBC, built up outside Montevideo gave us great pleasure. We were pleased to see *Cumberland*, not for any great confidence in her fighting abilities, but from the point of view that she would again provide the first target for *Graf Spee*'s attentions.

We stayed at action stations all night, with the usual 'Hula' parties keeping us amused and awake with their Maori songs. Do you remember Gould, with his guitar and his indiarubber hips?

On the Sunday evening we three went in to finish the job off.

Graf Spee was just visible at sunset when *Ajax*'s aircraft reported that she had blown herself up. Another big moment. We steamed up close past *Ajax*, who was leading us in. Both ships had ordered 'All hands on deck', and were black with bodies who had emerged to see the last of the old enemy. Another big moment. We shouted ourselves hoarse, both ships. The 'Diggers' did their 'Hakas', and sang their songs, and the *Ajax* cheered in reply.

And that was that.

Richard Washbourn

Langsdorff, believing from false reports on the BBC that he was trapped by a large British force, scuttled the Graf Spee *outside Montevideo on 17 December.*

Spring 1940

The Winter War

'Every pilot wondered how much longer his luck could last out'

The 'plucky' Finns fought back against the Russians. Eino Luukkanen was a major in the Finnish air force.

That evening the sauna in the post office building was heated, and after a fine steam bath we rolled, in true Finnish style, naked in the snow, but our enjoyment was marred by the background of rumbling explosions coming from the direction of Luumäki–Viipuri [Vyborg].

The 'Winter War' had now reached its most critical phase, with the Russians at the gates of Viipuri. The enemy had crossed the Viipuri Bay and were forcing their way on to the Vila Peninsula to threaten the key city of Viipuri from the west. The success of our initial ground-strafing foray had evidently not passed unnoticed at headquarters, for this was to remain our principal task until the end of the fighting.

The next morning I received orders to lead two flights on ground-strafing runs between Vilaniemi and Tuppura. I knew that this mission would not be the picnic of our initial strafing essay over the Gulf, for we would now have to fight our way through heavy flak and a strong fighter screen. The cloud base was a little above three thousand feet, so I decided to make our approach in the cloud and then let down for our attack in the south, behind the enemy, thus utilising the element of surprise. It seemed unlikely that the Russians would anticipate an attack from that direction. I carefully briefed the fifteen pilots that were to accompany me, and we took off, formed up in a loose, stepped formation, and set course for Johannes, directly south of Viipuri. We cruised steadily just above the cloud base, catching only occasional glimpses of the terrain below. A Russian formation passed beneath us, flying in the opposite direction. It formed a very tempting target, but we were not on an interception mission and had to allow them to pass unmolested.

The factory chimneys of Johannes showed briefly through a break in the cloud and, for the first time, I broke radio silence to order the formation out of the cloud. Approaching from behind them, the Russian anti-aircraft gunners assumed that we were friendly as I had hoped, and we flew steadily until I banked to port and entered a dive to begin my strafing run. There was certainly no shortage of targets, for the Tuppura–Vilaniemi area was teeming with columns of men, trucks, guns and armoured vehicles. Over Uuraa I could see a formation of I-16 fighters spiralling lazily, and a similar formation was to be seen over Ristiniemi, on our other side, but neither seemed to have spotted us. We had to hit hard and quickly, and then climb back into the cloud to avoid interception.

The distance to our first target was less than a half-mile when the air around us became alive with flak bursts, our aircraft bouncing around in the turbulence of their blast. These puff-balls of black, grey and white were obviously going to reveal our position to the patrolling Russian fighters, but we were quickly through the barrage of bursting shells, and streams of bullets from my quartet of guns were scything through a column of marching men which immediately broke up, the troops running helter-skelter in all directions. I then lined up with a pair of tanks, but my light machine-guns did no apparent damage, the bullets ricocheting from their armoured skins. Banking around at the end of my run, I glanced over my shoulder and noted that the other fifteen Fokkers were following in similar fashion.

Hugging the contours of the ground, we flew westward, then turned sharply north, just in case enemy fighters were chasing us. We did not want to reveal the whereabouts of our base. On landing, I discovered that we had lost one of our number, and later learned that a Russian fighter had managed to get on to the tail of the Fokker, the pilot, Sergeant Fräntilä, receiving a bullet in the chest. However, despite the severity of his wound and loss of blood, Fräntilä had succeeded in landing his fighter in 'No Man's Land' on the ice near Vilaniemi, had crawled from his cockpit into the nearby woods, and been found by a Finnish patrol which quickly carried him to the nearest casualty station. Unfortunately, it was impossible to retrieve his Fokker which had to be destroyed.

For a week we undertook similar strafing sorties, averaging two missions per day, but these became increasingly hazardous as the weather improved. Frequently there was little cloud to cover our approach or protect our retreat, and ever stronger fighter forces were covering the Russian hordes advancing over the ice. After each mission, shrapnel and bullet holes could be found in our planes, and every pilot wondered even more how much longer his luck could last out. These strafing sorties were undoubtedly the toughest missions we had been assigned, and we feared them. It would be naïve to deny this, but we were not frightened. Fear and fright are very different emotions. Fear breeds slowly and grows particularly during periods of helpless inactivity. It is contagious but it can be controlled. Fright is a sudden emotion; unpredictable and rendering clear thinking impossible. There are several types of fear, and their effects differ from pilot to pilot. One type of fear blossoms gradually and paralyses, the pilot becoming panicky. Another type of fear is suppressed, although always present, stimulating courage, eliminating excitement and resulting in a calmness vital in a combat pilot if he is to survive. Fear is a natural emotion and not one to be ashamed of, and although none of us would have spoken of it, we were all experiencing fear. For some, the conquering of fear once airborne was easy; for others it was more difficult. But the combat pilot who was not afraid was already shaking hands with the Grim Reaper. In the heat of action fear seemed to evaporate; it rarely occurred to one that those tracers snaking past the windscreen betrayed a stream of bullets with lethal capabilities. Once tension was relaxed and the flight was over, then fear returned to stand like a shadow at one's shoulder.

Eino Luukkanen

The Winter War was ended by treaty on 12 March. Finland ceded territory to Russia, but it had cost the Soviets 50,000 lives and another 150,000 wounded. The Finns lost 65,000 men. In the air, the Russians had had more than 680 aircraft destroyed to the Finns' tally of just 67. Luukkanen finished the war with 54 kills, ranking him Finland's third highest scoring ace. The lessons learned by the Russians would later be put to use by them against Germany.

Churchill Becomes Prime Minister

On 7 April 1940, the Germans invaded Denmark and Norway. The British attempted to strike back by seizing the Norwegian port of Trondheim but their expeditionary force was able to achieve little and had to be evacuated. The reverse in Norway fatally undermined parliamentary and popular support for Neville Chamberlain, with the choice of his successor seeming to lie between Winston Churchill, First Lord of the Admiralty, who had for so long warned of the Nazis' intentions, and Lord Halifax, the Foreign Secretary, who was identified with the government's appeasement policies. Chamberlain had decided to resign when, on the morning of 10 May, news came of the German invasion of Belgium, Holland and Luxembourg. It was to be a momentous day for many, as Churchill later recalled.

At about ten o'clock Sir Kingsley Wood came to see me, having just been with the Prime Minister. He told me that Mr Chamberlain was inclined to feel that the great battle which had broken upon us made it necessary for him to remain at his post. Kingsley Wood had told him that, on the contrary, the new crisis made it all the more necessary to have a National Government, which alone could confront it, and he added that Mr Chamberlain had accepted this view. At eleven o'clock I was again summoned to Downing Street by the Prime Minister. There once more I found Lord Halifax. We took our seats at the table opposite Mr Chamberlain. He told us that he was satisfied that it was beyond his power to form a National Government. The response he had received from the Labour leaders left him in no doubt of this. The question therefore was whom he should advise the King to send for after his own resignation had been accepted. His demeanour was cool, unruffled, and seemingly quite detached from the personal aspect of the affair. He looked at us both across the table.

I have had many important interviews in my public life, and this was certainly the most important. Usually I talk a great deal, but on this occasion I was silent. Mr Chamberlain evidently had in his mind the stormy scene in the House of Commons two nights before, when I had seemed to be in such heated controversy with the Labour Party. Although this had been in his support and defence, he nevertheless felt that it might be an obstacle to my obtaining their adherence at this juncture. I do not recall the actual words he used, but this was the implication. His biographer, Mr Feiling, states definitely that he preferred Lord Halifax. As I remained silent a very long pause ensued. It certainly seemed longer than the two minutes which one observes in the commemorations of Armistice Day. Then at length Halifax spoke. He said that he felt that his position as a Peer, out of the House of Commons, would make it very difficult for him to discharge the duties of Prime Minister in a war like this. He would be held responsible for everything, but would not have the power to guide the assembly upon whose confidence the life of every Government depended. He spoke for some minutes in this sense, and by the time he had finished it was clear that the duty would fall upon me – had in fact fallen upon me. Then for the first time I spoke. I said I would have no communication with either of the Opposition parties until I had the King's Commission to form a Government. On this the momentous conversation came to an end, and we reverted to our ordinary easy and familiar manners of men who had worked for years together and whose lives in and out of office had been spent in all the friendliness of British politics. I then went back to the Admiralty, where, as may well be imagined, much awaited me.

Winston Churchill

That evening, Churchill was summoned to Buckingham Palace and formally asked by the King, George VI, to form a government.

12 MAY 1940

Such a day as Friday last, the 10th, which began with an invasion and ended with a change of Premier, will not be seen again this lifetime. In a way people are relieved that at last the lies and pretences are done with. Belgium, Holland, and Luxembourg have, almost overnight, suffered the onslaught of the German 'blitzkrieg', after the Polish pattern, i.e. bombing and strafing by planes followed by tanks followed by infantry in over-whelming weight. (Liddell Hart was quoting a Frenchman, Charles de Gaulle, who long ago foretold that for the foreseeable future this is how wars would be fought, rather than by the 1914–18 method of taking up fixed positions and making charges and countercharges. Well, perhaps we shall be spared the slaughter of another generation – and Stoke Station full of wounded.) Everyone is asking where the Maginot Line ends and all are utterly stupefied to discover that it doesn't extend as far as the coast. Another three days and those armies will be staring at us across the Channel. Of course, this invasion of harmless countries has been denied as a possibility *thirteen* times by one Nazi high-up or another.

All day long we have a feeling that while one goes to the office or listens to the blackbirds – this is after all springtime, the only pretty ringtime – somewhere all hell is let loose. But news of it doesn't reach us for at least a week. Meanwhile we hear conflicting reports that German parachute troops, sent forward to capture or destroy key bridges and strong-points, are or are not successful. One hears of how the Allied troops – 'not a man on foot' which presumably means that they ride troop-carriers – poured hour after hour over the Belgian frontier. Germany is said to have lost 200 planes in two days. Reports appear of Rotterdam aerodrome captured and recaptured, of Amsterdam streets in flames, of 200 French civilians dead in widespread raids. But not a raid over England! Too busy elsewhere, one supposes. The hard fact is that we know only that the Low Countries have been invaded by the Germans. All else is conjecture.

Chamberlain has been replaced by soldier-statesman-historian Winston

Churchill. I have always been a Churchillian because he writes well, which in the circumstances doesn't seem an adequate reason. A man of 45, Anthony Eden, has been appointed Minister for War, and a Coalition Government formed that includes Attlee, Arthur Greenwood and Sinclair. Everyone rejoices. The impression was gathering that Chamberlain's government was an assembly of austere, upright, strict maiden aunts.

Tomorrow, Whit Monday, has been cancelled as a holiday, presumably to allow the railways to function normally and to allow the nation as a whole uninterrupted labour.

George Beardmore

'Blood, toil, tears, and sweat'

On Monday, May 13, 1940, I asked the House of Commons, which had been specially summoned, for a vote of confidence in the new Administration. After reporting the progress which had been made in filling the various offices, I said: 'I have nothing to offer but blood, toil, tears, and sweat.' In all our long history no Prime Minister had ever been able to present to Parliament and the nation a programme at once so short and so popular. I ended:

You ask, What is our policy? I will say: It is to wage war, by sea, land, and air, with all our might and with all the strength that God can give us: to wage war against a monstrous tyranny, never surpassed in the dark, lamentable catalogue of human crime. That is our policy. You ask, What is our aim? I can answer in one word: Victory – victory at all costs, victory in spite of all terror; victory, however long and hard the road may be; for without victory there is no survival. Let that be realised: no survival for the British Empire; no survival for all that the British Empire has stood for, no survival for the urge and impulse of the ages, that mankind will move forward towards its goal. But I take up my task with buoyancy and hope. I feel sure that our cause will not be suffered to fail among men. At this time I feel entitled to claim the aid of all, and I say, 'Come, then, let us go forward together with our united strength.'

Winston Churchill

☦

Blitzkrieg

The German invasion of Western Europe, which began on 10 May, was spectacularly rapid. Six days later, having crossed into France, all that stood in the way of Erwin Rommel, commander of the 7th Panzer Division, was the chain of fortified positions known as the Maginot Line.

The way to the west was now open. The moon was up and for the time being we could expect no real darkness. I had already given orders, in the plan for the break-through, for the leading tanks to scatter the road and verges with machine and anti-tank gunfire at intervals during the drive to Avesnes, which I hoped would prevent the enemy from laying mines. The rest of the Panzer Regiment was to follow close behind the leading tanks and be ready at any time to fire salvoes to either flank. The mass of the division had instructions to follow up the Panzer Regiment lorry-borne.

The tanks now rolled in a long column through the line of fortifications and on towards the first houses, which had been set alight by our fire. In the moonlight we could see the men of 7th Motor-cycle Battalion moving forward on foot beside us. Occasionally an enemy machine-gun or anti-tank gun fired, but none of their shots came anywhere near us. Our artillery was dropping heavy harassing fire on villages and the road far ahead of the regiment. Gradually the speed increased. Before long we were 500–1,000–2,000–3,000 yards into the fortified zone. Engines roared, tank tracks clanked and clattered. Whether or not the enemy was firing was impossible to tell in the ear-splitting noise. We crossed the railway line a mile or so south-west of Solre le Château, and then swung north to the main road which was soon reached. Then off along the road and past the first houses.

The people in the houses were rudely awoken by the din of our tanks, the clatter and roar of tracks and engines. Troops lay bivouacked beside the road, military vehicles stood parked in farmyards and in some places on the road itself. Civilians and French troops, their faces distorted with terror, lay huddled in the ditches, alongside hedges and in every hollow beside the road. We passed refugee columns, the carts abandoned by their owners, who had fled in panic into the fields. On we went, at a steady speed, towards our objective. Every so often a quick glance at the map by a shaded light and a short wireless message to Divisional HQ to report the position and thus the success of 29th Panzer Regiment. Every so often a look out of the hatch to assure myself that there was still no resistance and that contact was being maintained to the rear. The flat countryside lay spread out around us under the cold light of the moon. We were through the Maginot Line! It was hardly conceivable. Twenty-two years before we had stood for four and a half long years before this self-same enemy and had won victory after victory and yet finally lost the war. And now we had broken through the renowned Maginot Line and were driving deep into enemy territory. It was not just a beautiful dream. It was reality.

Suddenly there was a flash from a mound about 300 yards away to the right of the road. There could be no doubt what it was, an enemy gun well concealed in a concrete pill-box, firing on 25th Panzer Regiment from the flank. More flashes came from other points. Shell bursts could not be seen. Quickly informing Rothenburg of the danger – he was standing close beside me – I gave orders through him for the regiment to increase speed and burst through this second fortified line with broadsides to right and left.

Fire was opened quickly, the tank crews having been instructed in the method of fire before the attack. Much of our ammunition was tracer and the regiment drove on through the new defence line spraying an immense rain of fire far into the country on either side. Soon we were through the danger area, without serious casualties, but it was not now easy to get the fire stopped and we drove through the villages of Sars Poteries and Beugnies with guns blazing. Enemy confusion was complete. Military vehicles, tanks, artillery and refugee carts packed high with belongings blocked part of the road and had to be pushed unceremoniously to the side. All around were French troops lying flat on the ground, and farms everywhere were jammed tight with guns, tanks and other military vehicles. Progress towards Avesnes now became slow. At last we succeeded in getting the firing stopped. We drove through Semousies. Always the same picture, troops and civilians in wild flight down both sides of the road. Soon the road forked, one going right to Maubeuge, which was now only about 10 miles away, and the other left down into the valley towards Avesnes. The road was now thick with carts and people, who moved off to the side of the tanks or had to be directed into the side by us. The nearer we came to Avesnes the greater was the crush of vehicles through which we had to fight our way. In Avesnes itself, which had been shelled by our artillery shortly before, the whole population was on the move, jammed between vehicles and guns on both sides of the road in front of our moving tank column.

Erwin Rommel

Between the early morning of 16 May and that of 17 May, Rommel's tanks advanced 50 miles. Attempts to block his progress proved futile, as each time the

French chose a new position to hold they discovered that it had already been overrun by the Germans.

Fleeing from Holland

L. de Jong, a Dutch newspaper editor, decided to become a refugee rather than endure life in Amsterdam under the Nazis.

As soon as we woke on Tuesday, the 14th May, we turned on the radio. There was but little news. A German armoured column was reported to have passed the centre of Brabant, which it actually had done thirty-six hours earlier. Moreover the Government was reported 'to have left for a safer place'. Which safer place was not announced.

What to do? I felt pretty unsafe. Perhaps tomorrow or the day after tomorrow the German army would enter Amsterdam and with its usual crowd of Gestapo agents round up the political opponents of the Nazis. But where to go? To Belgium? No, that was almost certainly impossible. Or, perhaps, I could travel by night, and try to reach Belgium by swimming over the rivers when the Germans had occupied the bridges. No, that would be suicidal. To England? That was, perhaps, a possibility. I might place myself under the protection of the British consul. That was a good idea. I could try, anyhow.

By half-past nine my wife and I were standing in front of the British Consulate on the *Rokin* in Amsterdam. There were several hundreds of other people all seeking the protection of the British consul. The consul, however, was inaccessible to anyone who hadn't a British passport, which we had not. Still, our visit to the Consulate was not quite useless, for a policeman told us that boats were leaving the port of Ymuiden and that England would receive all refugees whether they had passes or not.

Two hours later we were driving to Ymuiden at a dangerous speed. There were hundreds of cars all driving in the same direction. At that moment the big oil-tanks near the Noordzee-canal, which connected Amsterdam with the North Sea, were ablaze. Huge columns of black smoke covered part of the sky. It was a nightmare. The shining sun, the beautiful flowers in the grass, the marvellous weather – it all enhanced the cruel character of the events of that day. Fleeing from your country because you think that it is the only way to save your life is in itself cruel enough. But when a thunderstorm is raging you feel that nature is sympathising with you. The lovely character of that spring day made us feel that nature was quite indifferent to our sorrows.

Ymuiden was jammed with cars. It was impossible to reach the boats, even if there were any. So we decided to try our luck on the other side of the North Sea canal. The ferry-boat was tantalisingly slow. There were boats at the side of the canal, but only for those who had a British or French passport. We hadn't. At that moment somebody told us that the burgomaster of Beverwijk, a small town some three miles to the north, could give us exit permits. Perhaps this was meant as a joke. At any rate, if I had thought it over for a minute, I would have come to the conclusion that the burgomaster of a small provincial town hasn't anything to do with the issuing of exit permits. But we were so troubled and so desperate that I would have stripped off all my clothes if somebody had told me that that was a sure way of getting an exit permit.

The town hall of Beverwijk was besieged by hundreds of refugees. After one hour of waiting we were informed that we had better go back to Ymuiden. The burgomaster of Beverwijk couldn't help us, anyhow. So we went back to Ymuiden, weary, hungry, and ashamed. When we arrived there we found that it was impossible to enter the town at all. The military commander had forbidden entry, except to the inhabitants who all carried special passes. So we waited for hours, aimlessly. Several times we tried to find the British Consul, but we couldn't find him. In the meantime there were two raids. More and more people arrived. At about four o'clock we lost our families and friends. All seemed lost. Then, to make things worse, the police ordered everybody to go back home. It was no use to staying in Ymuiden any more. Thousands of people climbed in their cars again, and drove slowly back. Many of them whom I knew quite well – politicians, professors – are now in concentration camps.

We decided to stay. But, of course, we had to hide, for if the police found us, we would be sent back or put into prison. A dear old lady received us in her cottage and gave us a cup of coffee and some bread. We were quite exhausted. After a little while I went out to see if I could find a place where we could spend the night. Next morning, perhaps, we would be allowed to enter the port. I went to a small inn, and got a dirty sofa somewhere in the attics. There we could sleep. Just as I was leaving this place I heard the wireless announcing a special message. It was the Dutch Commander-in-Chief telling us that an armistice had been concluded and that the war in Holland was over. It was one of the greatest shocks I ever got, but I was so weary that I could hardly fully realise it.

The armistice meant, at any rate, that next day the Germans would be in Ymuiden. What was one to do?

I went back to my wife, and we decided to make one last attempt to pass the sentry who guarded the entrance to Ymuiden. And he had disappeared! Just at that moment a car passed us and somebody called my name. It was a friend of mine, a journalist, sitting in the car of one of his friends. The car was crammed with people. We tumbled on top of them. An Ymuiden lad jumped on the running board. 'May I have your car if I bring you to the boat?' 'Of course!' The car jolted forward.

Ten minutes later we were at the boat. We were the last people to arrive.

L. de Jong

The author and his wife arrived in Poole, on the south coast of England, the day after the Dutch surrender on 15 May. Brussels fell on the 17th.

The French in retreat

Roads choked by refugees and abandoned vehicles, a lack of cooperation between the Allies, Germany's complete military superiority – all combined to make the fall of France almost a formality. Here Captain Barlone of the French North African Division describes the ignominious retreat to Dunkirk.

29 MAY 1940

I billet at Erquinghem on the north bank of the Lys, but no divisional orders come to me. I decide in the evening to go to Steenwerek, where the 1st Army Staff, that is to say ours, is quartered. All contact with our North African Division is lost and no orders come through. The exhausted staff officers are rolled up in blankets and sleep on the floor. Those on duty seem depressed. I hear orders given by 'phone to send a few scattered units still holding out to act as stop-gaps and to try to delay, for an hour or two, the closing-in of the infernal circle and so give time to the others to reach Dunkirk. These unlucky troops attack and counter-attack like maniacs and give their lives like heroes. The regiments melt away visibly; our division has received orders to hold out at all costs. The 13th Rifles attacked again yesterday near Houplines – their sixth attack in eight days. They have only 500 men left, nearly all the officers have been killed, but the NCOs carry on and their spirits never falter. The 22nd Rifles tell the same story. With only 700 men left, they are ordered to attack again to-night. While I am there, a staff-officer telephones instructions to the General in command at Lille to fire all petrol dumps and blow up the electric power station as the Germans are expected to enter the town to-night.

The roads are congested by convoys. Thanks to indescribable efforts, the Vet. and I, worn out, manage to rejoin the column at midnight. Without awaiting orders, I decide to make for Poperinghe and Dunkirk. Half a mile from Nieppe, there is a frightful traffic jam. All the village streets are blocked. There are eight or ten lines of traffic: horse-drawn vehicles, guns, motor machine-guns, lorries, ambulances, cars full of refugees; so much so that it took just four hours to cover half a mile. German tanks passed at the head of the great jam, firing a few machine gun belts, then they disappeared. That increased the confusion. At last, towards six o'clock in the morning, we begin to move at a faster pace. I decide to branch off at Neuve Eglise to avoid Poperinghe, which is stated to be under enemy fire.

Large British and French convoys are making for Neuve Eglise, where a counter-attack is being prepared in an attempt to check the advance. British infantry and fifty to sixty British tanks are there in perfect order, so too are French artillery, 155s. Two infantry battalions are mere skeletons. The men look tired, but laugh and joke. They are by no means demoralised. The German planes have quickly located them, and spray all troop concentrations abundantly. On our side, still no aeroplanes in the sky, not even a reconnaissance machine. We fight blindly against an adversary with a hundred eyes, and ten times superior. We climb a slope, and I see the counter-attack developing. The British tanks, very cleverly creeping forward under cover; make a rapid advance. We increase our pace, St Jans Cappel is impracticable, the road having been cut by bombs. Our only way is through a gap of a dozen miles, along which we dodge from side to side over dirt tracks. On arriving at the foot of Mont Noir there is a fresh traffic-block, a mile long, leading to the entrance of Westoutre, where the British have barricaded all exits so that their columns can pass through with greater ease. The French are wild. Some gunners talk of training their guns on them and shooting. As the senior officer present I take command and order two artillery officers to take a hundred men and drag away the heavy British tractors which bar the road. Then I go and find an English major, and in five minutes everything is arranged; they will march off along the Poperinghe road, and the French along the Berguen and Westoutre road. We place a cordon of British and French troops at intervals to mark the route and avoid confusion. The Mont Noir road is cleared of troops in four hours and the columns flow smoothly. We must make up for lost time. We march until nine o'clock in the evening, then we halt for two hours so that men and horses may eat and drink. On once more. We have been pressing forward for twenty-one hours without unharnessing.

At break of day, we find ourselves a dozen miles from Dunkirk. The traffic congestion and disorder on the road are indescribable, because the High Command has omitted to organise traffic control through either staff officers, military police or mobile guards. All kinds of arms are there in unparalleled confusion, but our men do not show the slightest sign of panic. They are calm and do their best to clear the way for their vehicles, in spite of the intermittent firing of the German artillery, which destroys quite a bit of their material. A lot of damaged guns, ambulance vans and motor-cars are thrown into the ditches, in order to relieve the congestion on the road. There they are left together with broken equipment and rifles. After unspeakable efforts, we manage to bring our vehicles more or less in order through this retreating maze, the like of which has never been seen before.

D. Barlone

The evacuation from Dunkirk

On 24 May, Hitler ordered his forces not to advance into the French port of Dunkirk, having been assured by Hermann Goering that his Luftwaffe *would destroy the Allied troops encircled there. Hitler's decision gave the British a chance to rescue the 400,000 servicemen and civilians trapped on the beaches. Among them was a bewildered member of British Field Security.*

I reached the pier. There was no ship there.

I do not know now what I did do. I wandered about. I went down to the sea and looked as far as I could see and I climbed an embankment of stones and looked and I climbed up other places and I looked and there was nothing to see no ship on the sea.

There was a raid, I think there were raids. I remember thinking they would be aiming at the pier and of course they were, there were big bomb craters in the sand all round it and I do remember one was a new one came quite near, it was new I knew because no water had collected in the bottom of it. Yes there were raids there must have been because I remember pressing up against a rock and wondering about rock splinters. Yes there were raids. I was so dreadfully tired. There were raids and raids it was just one long continuous bombardment from the air. I was so dreadfully tired.

Do you know how it is when you have a temperature a very high temperature about one hundred and five or six you lie there and everything is going on. Everything is going on and then you are everything and you are going on it all is awful you are a part of everything and it just goes on. It comes and goes in surges and recedes at a great speed to a great distance and you are with it very far away. You are lying there and you are receding at a great speed to a very great distance and there is a yellow noise like heat and suns in summer. You are a shell on the sea, on the surface of it, and there are troughs and you are at the bottom of it and they enclose you in their heaving folds. There are surges of it and receding and enclosing, you are everything and of it and you do not lose consciousness. You are lying there and everything is awful and you are everything and receding and advancing at a very great speed to a very great distance, like waves on a shell there are surges of it. You do not lose consciousness but you have not consciousness. It advances it recedes it encloses.

I lay on the wet sand and everything was surges of it. I was so tired. My head was on a stone. I was everything happening to me and I could not lose consciousness but I had not consciousness. There was a yellow noise kept coming at a very great speed to a very great distance. I could not think I could only repeat what I tried to think if I could only if only a ship. If I could only if only a ship if I could and if only a ship. If I could only if only a ship if I could only one foot on a ship. If only one foot on a ship if I could only if only a ship. I was so tired. If I could get one foot only one foot on a ship it would be all right because they would pull the other foot after it. I knew they would if only they only if I could. If only if I could. If only a ship if I could.

Like waves folding over there were surges of it.

I felt them kicking me. I had not lost consciousness but I had not got consciousness. They were kicking me. They thought you were dead they said. Two men stood kicking me. It was the tide had come in I was lying in the water.

I got up and sat down on some higher rocks. There was the noise kept coming at a speed from a distance. I groped for it. I concentrated my consciousness on it and dragged it up and held it and asked it what it was. I knew what it was they were shelling the pier. They were shelling the pier. The meaning slipped back to the bottom again. It was too much to mean what it said.

Somewhere inside me was the noise when the gasometer exploded. It was like a large tunnel of roaring sound. It was somewhere inside me and going round.

I walked up over the rocks. It was dawn now. There was a long line of soldiers silhouetted on the embankment. I went to them. Beyond them stretched the pier. At the far end was a black shadow. It was a ship.

I had no capacity left for feeling but I knew it was a ship and the clockwork of my mind went click inside me. I knew if I got on that ship I was in England.

We waited on the embankment. They were shelling it and shelling the pier. I remember nothing about the shells. There were two big gaps in the pier but the structure still held.

They were carrying stretcher cases along it to the ship. At last we filed on. We went a few feet at a time, then we waited. We sat against a low stone parapet. Then we moved on slowly, by inches. We were nearly an hour along that pier.

It was daylight now and time was getting short. I do not know why but we knew it was. I expect it was the tide. We could see now two destroyers. We were half way down the pier. Gradually we began to quicken our pace, and then we were running. There was a part where we ran on single planks over the sea below. It was this getting the stretchers over this had made us move so slowly.

I ran on, the ship was there her bows to the pier. I climbed a small ladder someone hauled me on board and down another ladder and someone said go down, go on down below. I ducked under a rope and ran on. Now down below, no not below.

There was a lifeboat with someone in it and by it a clear space and a post to lean against it. I sat down. I did not mind anything now. I sat down. There was drowning and sinking I did not mind that I did not mind anything now. I sat down.

The captain said through a megaphone to a man on the pier how many more. He said four hundred. The captain said I have only ten minutes. He said four hundred. The captain said all right then if they are there they must come. But hurry, hurry. We manoeuvred alongside the pier and they all came on.

We moved off. It was six or not it was five in the morning. The second destroyer moved too. The sea breezes the sea breezes I swallowed them in wide draughts they were so clean and fresh. We were given life jackets. A sailor came round with tea and a slice of white bread and a piece of cheese. It was wonderful. It did not matter how many of us we were to feed they had enough and enough to feed everyone. The sailors moved about calm and kind and comforting. It was wonderful.

I did not mind anything that had happened. I kept very still. If I moved it might not be. I kept quite still. If I kept still long enough I knew it would be real. It was so wonderful. I was on a ship and any ship yes any ship is England. Any ship yes any ship I was on a ship and on my way to England. It was wonderful. I kept quite still and the sea breezes I swallowed them, no smoke and burning and fire and thick grey oil smoke hazes but sea breezes, I swallowed them they were so clean and fresh and I was alive it was so wonderful.

A. Gwynn-Browne

The 'Little Ships'

On 14 May, the BBC gave out the following announcement: 'The Admiralty have made an Order requesting all owners of self-propelled pleasure craft between 30 foot and 100 foot in length to send all particulars to the Admiralty within 14 days from today if they have not already been offered or requisitioned.' One of those who complied and found himself sailing to Dunkirk to pick up the waiting soldiers was Charles Lightoller.

For some time now we had been subject to sporadic bombing and machine-gun fire, but as the *Sundowner* is exceptionally and extremely quick on the helm, by waiting till the last moment and putting the helm hard over – my son at the wheel – we easily avoided every attack, though sometimes near lifted out of the water.

The difficulty of taking troops on board from the quay high above us was obvious, so I went alongside a destroyer where they were already embarking. I got hold of her captain and told him I could take over a hundred (though the most I had ever had on board was twenty-one). He, after consultation with the military CO, told me to carry on and get the troops aboard. I must say that before leaving England, we had worked all night stripping her down of everything movable, masts included, that would tend to lighten her and make for more room.

I now started to pack them on deck, having passed word below for every man to lie down and keep down; the same applied on deck. I could feel her getting distinctly tender, so took no more. Actually we had exactly a hundred and thirty on board. They were literally packed like the proverbial sardines, even one in the bath and another on the WC, so that all the poor devils could do was sit and be sick. So that after discharging our cargo in Ramsgate at ten p.m., there lay before the three of us a nice clearing-up job.

Charles Lightoller

The author had been involved in another maritime drama 28 years before – he had been the Second Officer of the Titanic. *Some 338,225 British and French troops were taken off from Dunkirk, almost a third of whom crossed the Channel on a 'little ship'; 68,111 more were killed, wounded or taken prisoner.*

‡

Count Galeazzo Ciano was the son-in-law of the Italian dictator, Benito Musso-lini, and his Foreign Minister from 1936. Italy had previously made a strategic alliance with Germany, but he was pessimistic about the consequences of any involvement in the war.

13 MAY 1940

Mussolini began to talk as follows: 'Some months ago I said that the Allies had lost the victory. Today I tell you that they have lost the war. We Italians are already sufficiently dishonoured. Any delay is inconceivable. We have no time to lose. Within a month I shall declare war. I shall attack France and England in the air and on the sea. I am no longer thinking of taking up arms against Yugoslavia because it would be a humiliating replacement.' Today, for the first time, I did not answer. Unfortunately, I can do nothing now to hold the Duce back. He has decided to act, and act he will. He believes in German success and in the swiftness of that success. Only a new turn in military events can induce him to alter his decision, but for the time being things are going so badly for the Allies that there is no hope.

Galeazzo Ciano

‡

Paul Richey, 23, was a fighter pilot with an RAF Hurricane squadron stationed in beleaguered France.

I concentrated on my Heinkel. I had him beautifully steady in the sights and poured short savage bursts into him as I closed. I was wondering why he showed no sign of being hit, because I knew I was hitting him. He had nearly caught his formation up when grey smoke streamed from both his engines, then from his wing-roots and fuselage, and in a second he was completely enveloped. I felt that savage thrill again and said: 'And that for luck, you sod!' as I fired a final burst into the burning mass. It was only half a burst, because I ran out of ammunition with a hiss of compressed air. As I broke lazily away to the left, feeling pretty pleased with myself, I glanced at the still-firing sub-formation and mentally put two fingers up in derision. It was then I learnt a lesson I should have known and will never forget.

Just as I rolled – too slowly – over to the left to dive away, I saw a sudden flash of tracer very close, and in the same second heard several pops, then a deafening 'Bang!' in my right ear. (I think it came from the boys above right, but it's just possible that the rear gunner of the blazing Heinkel was still firing, and if so I raise my hat yet again!) In that instant I knew they'd hit my aeroplane. A shower of blood spurted down my right side. My Hurricane was diving almost vertically, and I was surprised to see my right arm, drenched in blood, raised up in front of me against the hood. There was no feeling in it – the hand was hooked like a dead bird's claw. All this happened in a flash; but so quickly does the mind work that in the same moment I guessed at and assessed the damage and decided how to act. That 'Bang!' still echoed in my right ear, and I said aloud 'Cannon shell in right shoulder – arm may be almost severed – write that off – pull out of dive with left hand, and if necessary bale out, pulling ripcord with left hand.'

But to my horror I found my left arm wouldn't move either! It hung limp and straight down my side. I looked up to find the aircraft plunging earthwards out of control; it was repeatedly diving, gaining speed, flattening out, losing speed and diving again. I had the extraordinary sensation of my head being isolated from the rest of my body inside the cockpit. I was perfectly conscious and could hear the hiss of the airflow rise and fall over the cockpit roof. I looked at my inert body and tried with all my strength to move my arms. My right hand, or claw, was within four inches of the hood handle, but strain as I might I couldn't get it any nearer. The ground was coming up; I could hear myself grunting and straining to move. Then suddenly I heard myself scream. Muffled but clearly audible, I heard myself mutter it, then say it, then shout it: 'God! God! I'm going to be killed! God!'

I stopped shouting abruptly and looked into the bottom of the cockpit, thinking 'I won't feel it!' I looked up again and saw the ground rushing up now – and suddenly my left arm moved. So obsessed had I become with the idea of escape that my hand flew to the hood handle to pull it back. It was jammed! I heaved frantically with the manic strength of desperation, but it didn't budge an inch. I looked again into the cockpit, frightened of fire. Then my right hand suddenly flopped on to the stick, pulled it back, and out of that hellish dive I came. None too soon either, though not desperately low – at about 2,000 feet, to be exact.

I chattered away to myself: 'My God! That's the narrowest squeak *I* ever want! Now get down smartly – you may be on fire – and your engine's stopped.' I glanced over the instruments and noticed the air-speed indicator wasn't registering at all – a bullet or shell must have got the pitot head or some part of the airspeed-indicator system. I had lots of holes in my wings, and a bullet-hole in the windscreen to the right of the bullet-proof section. I wondered where the bullet had gone . . .

I was beginning to feel severe pain in the right side of my neck and face, and thought a cannon shell had struck the side of the cockpit and blown a chunk out of me. I still couldn't get the hood open. I circled as I glided down, picked a field near a village so that I could get help quickly, pumped my flaps down and went into land with my wheels up. As I held off over a harrowed field I braced myself with my left hand against the sight bar. We touched, bounced and bucketed across the field, grinding along in a cloud of dust. Blood splashed over the dashboard and windscreen. Then, just as I thought we were going over, the tail came down with a thump and we came to rest.

I whipped the pin out of my Sutton harness, unclipped my parachute and tried to open the hood. It was still stuck firm, so I jammed both feet against the instrument panel and tugged. No: it wouldn't move. My neck and shoulder throbbed and I was feeling weak, so I rested a moment. From the bottom of the cockpit little wisps of smoke or dust – I wasn't sure which – were rising. I seized the hood-handles once more, heaving and straining with all my remaining strength, but the thing held stubbornly firm and I had to rest again. This was bloody! It looked as though I had escaped a comparatively pleasant death by diving into the ground only to be burnt alive. I wondered if the first lick of flame would give me the strength to bust out of this damned cockpit, or, if not, whether death would come quickly in the heat and smoke. Once again I redoubled my efforts: no good. The emergency panel would not come out with the hood closed, but I bashed out the small break-out panel in the left side of the hood with my fist and put my arm through it, for no reason other than to have access to the outside world.

Why the hell didn't those bloody Frenchmen get a move on? I could hear something dripping and smelt petrol. This galvanised me into one final effort – and suddenly, with a jerk, the hood came half open. I hauled myself out on to the starboard wing and ran away from the aeroplane, expecting an explosion. Panting and exhausted, I stumbled towards a wooded stream.

Paul Richey

The author's wounds were so severe that he was operated on immediately in Paris. He returned to active duty and survived the war.

‡

Undesirable alien

The Hungarian-born writer Arthur Koestler was living in Paris, working on what would become his masterpiece, Darkness at Noon. *A former Communist and an outspoken critic of the Fascist dictators, he had already been interned briefly by the French authorities earlier in the year. Now, as the Germans neared the capital, he was caught up in another sweep of 'undesirable aliens'. If he could not talk himself out of prison, he knew he would find himself in mortal danger when the Nazis arrived.*

I have already said that all the others in the car were Germans and Austrians; I was the only one in the category of Non-Enemy Suspects. So far, the 'enemy aliens' had been concentrated in the Buffalo Stadium, a sports stadium in the south of Paris, and the 'suspects' in the Roland Garros Stadium. On that morning, probably because of the shortage of transport, the *Préfecture* had ordered the local police stations to direct *all* arrested men to the Buffalo camp. But, as appeared on our arrival at that place, they had forgotten to inform the camp authorities at Buffalo of their changed dispositions. It was the usual French muddle. I was the first non-enemy alien to pass through the control bureau of the camp; when I put my passport on the desk and saw the official's surprised face, it all came to me in a flash.

'When and where were you arrested?' asked the official.

'In the Café Dupont, Place de la Convention, an hour ago.'

I did not consciously have to reflect for a second for my answers. The brandy did it for me – or that sly, hairy super-ape, the subconscious. The point is that normally I am a bad actor, and if I try to bluff at poker I am always caught. It was a very odd experience.

'Where is your *carte d'identité*?'

'At home – 10, rue Dombasle, seventh floor. That is why I have been arrested. I just went down to have coffee after lunch and left my *carte d'identité* in the flat; there was a round-up and they took me to the police station. I asked them to let me go home and fetch the *carte d'identité*, but they wouldn't listen – they just shoved me into the car and here I am.'

I *felt* that I was absolutely convincing – the right mixture of polite indignation and honest-to-God stupidity. And all the time I watched my own performance and wondered. Normally I am the rather uninspired type of person; when writing, for instance, I have to sweat out every line with a conscious effort. It was indeed very odd. In the same dream-like exaltation in another age, a person would perhaps have heard voices and produced a mystic vision; now miracles had to happen at police officials' desks; but it was fundamentally the same process.

The man behind the desk turned my passport over and looked at my other papers: Press card, the famous letters from Influential Persons, etc. Over his head, there was a clock on the wall, and it marked 4.30.

'All this is a quite amusing experience for a journalist, but the bother is that I have an appointment at five o'clock,' I said – that is, the brandy said, or the hairy ape.

'What sort of appointment?'

'Why – the daily Press Conference at the Ministry of Information.'

(I had never been at the Press Conference and I had not written an article since the war – but I had kept the Press card.)

'That idiot Lamèche is always making a mess of things,' said the man behind the desk to his assistant; he fumbled irresolutely with my papers. Lamèche, I gathered, was the *commissaire de police* of the XVth Arrondissement. Our escort had left immediately after delivering us.

'Look,' I said. 'I have got to be there at five. If you still have doubts, send a man to accompany me home in a taxi while I fetch my *carte d'identité*. You can give me an armed escort and even a machine-gun if you think it necessary.'

Opposite the desk was the door that led into the camp – and once through that door there was no returning. I had it before my eyes and I knew it was a death-trap; and I knew that the slightest shadow of a false ring in my voice would finish me. But it was not my own voice, and I trusted it entirely.

'No, I don't think that's necessary,' said the man behind the desk and handed my papers back with a smile. 'You are free, monsieur. Sentry, take monsieur to the entrance gate.' And to his secretary: 'Remind me to ring that idiot Lamèche when we are through with the others.' And to me: '*Au revoir, monsieur.* Next time you had better carry your *carte d'identité* on you.'

On the way to the gate I picked up my suitcase which I had left outside the entrance to the office. The sentry did not notice that there was anything wrong about that. At the gate I gave him five francs and asked him to get me a taxi. The taxi arrived. Exit Hyde, enter Jekyll.

But only for a few minutes, while the taxi approached the Porte d'Orléans and the drumming in my chest calmed down. Then the blessings of the brandy began to evaporate and I began to realise the situation in which I was. The camp official would ring Lamèche, or whatever his name was; in half an hour or so the game would be up and the police at my flat – this time perhaps really with a tommy gun. I knocked at the window pane and gave the driver another address, I knew that I would never see my flat again. Exit Jekyll, enter Hyde. But this time for good.

Arthur Koestler

Koestler reached Britain at the end of 1940. He wrote of his French experiences in Pentonville Prison, where he was being held as a political suspect.

Summer 1940

'We shall fight them on the beaches'

With Britain facing the prospect of invasion after the evacuation at Dunkirk, Churchill addressed the Commons on 4 June in bellicose fashion.

Even though large tracts of Europe and many old and famous States have fallen or may fall into the grip of the Gestapo and all the odious apparatus of Nazi rule, we shall not flag or fail. We shall go on to the end. We shall fight in France, we shall fight in the seas and oceans, we shall fight with growing confidence and growing strength in the air; we shall defend our Island, whatever the cost may be. We shall fight on the beaches, we shall fight on the landing-grounds, we shall fight in the fields and in the streets, we shall fight in the hills; we shall never surrender; and even if, which I do not for a moment believe, this Island or a large part of it were subjugated and starving, then our Empire beyond the seas, armed and guarded by the British Fleet, would carry on the struggle, until, in God's good time, the New World, with all its power and might, steps forth to the rescue and the liberation of the Old.

Winston Churchill

‡

Italy enters the war

On 10 June, with France on the point of surrender, Mussolini finally declared war. The French and British ambassadors, André François-Poncet and Sir Percy Loraine, were summoned to Italy's Foreign Ministry by Ciano.

Declaration of war. First I received Poncet, who tried not to show his emotion. I told him, 'You probably understood the reason for your being called.' He answered, with a fleeting smile, 'Although I am not very intelligent, I have understood this time.' After having listened to the declaration of war, he replied. 'It is a blow with a dagger to a man who has already fallen. I thank you nonetheless for using a velvet glove,' he continued, saying that he had foreseen all this for two years, and that he no longer hoped that he could avoid it after the signing of the Pact of Steel. He was unable to consider me an enemy, nor could he consider any Italian an enemy. However, as for the future it was necessary to find some formula for European life, he hoped that an unbridgeable chasm would not be created between Italy and France. 'The Germans are hard masters. You, too, will learn this.' I did not answer. This did not seem to me the time for discussion. 'Don't get yourself killed,' he concluded, pointing to my aviator's uniform, and he clasped my hand.

Sir Percy Loraine was more laconic and inscrutable. He received my communication without batting an eye or changing colour. He limited himself to writing down the exact formula I used and asked me if he was to consider it as advance information or as a general declaration of war. Learning that it was the latter, he withdrew with dignity and courtesy. At the door we exchanged a long and cordial handshake.

Mussolini speaks from the balcony of the Palazzo Venezia. The news of the war does not surprise anyone and does not arouse very much enthusiasm. I am sad, very sad. The adventure begins. May God help Italy.

Galeazzo Ciano

As he left the room, Loraine is supposed to have told Ciano: 'I have the honour to remind Your Excellency that Britain is not in the habit of losing her wars.'

‡

The Fall of France

The occupation of Paris

The French government left Paris on 11 June, followed three days later by the French 7th Army under General Frère. This allowed von Studnitz to lead his 87th Infantry Division into the capital without a shot being fired.

No one remotely guessed what actually did happen. No one foresaw that German troops would come into Paris as peacefully and quietly as they came into Copenhagen or Oslo. No one predicted that Parisians would watch the German entry with the same appearance of bewildered incomprehension the Danes and Norwegians had shown.

We first became aware that Germans were in occupation of the city when Paris fire trucks, manned by Frenchmen, stopped below our hotel on Friday morning and we watched them haul down the four big French flags which encircled the Rond-Point des Champs Elysées. Then they began to tear down posters which urged Frenchmen to buy armament bonds.

We went out then to meet the incoming troops, advancing along the Rue Lafayette, past the Madeleine into the Place de la Concorde. The German high command knew, of course, the conditions which awaited the arrival of their army in Paris. They knew they were coming into an almost empty city. They knew that French gendarmes had been left behind to guard against disorderly incidents.

Nevertheless, it was startling to observe the nonchalance with which those Germans marched through the heart of Paris. They were still at war with France, but they did not even bother to assign guards along the boulevards through which they advanced.

Those first German troops were young and alert and freshly shaved. They had rested during the night in the suburbs and they did not seem tired. To the amazement of Parisians, who had read so much of Germany's mechanised army, those first units were all drawn by horses. We stood at the Madeleine on that sunny morning amid small clusters of Frenchmen and watched the Germans pass. They looked about them with a lively curiosity at the beautiful city which most of them were viewing for the first time. They might have been tourists, out to see the sights, for anything their manner showed. If they felt a sense of exultation, they carefully suppressed demonstrations of triumph. The French people around us watched the procession in silence, bearing themselves with that dignity and sang-froid which their authorities had recommended.

For several days after the occupation the German army authorities simply ignored the population of Paris. The disorganised French civil administration very slowly pulled itself together again. We had curfew at nine o'clock and the blackout continued. And Paris, for the first time since the war began, took on the appearance of a military city. There were continuous troop parades up and down the boulevards, there were military band concerts, there was the incessant roar of planes flying low over the city. We had seen none of these things in Paris during the previous nine months of the war.

On the afternoon of the second day of occupation, as we stood near the American Embassy, the first French prisoners went by in trucks through the Place de la Concorde. The crowds had become larger then, and they surged toward their defeated men. Girls and women ran after them, a few weeping, but most of them shouting encouragement and questions. The Germans did not attempt to hold them back.

Sunday the sixteenth, the third day of the occupation, was a cool sunny day. By this time Paris had become accustomed to the steady roll of army vehicles, carrying German troops and guns and supplies along the boulevards toward the battle lines in the south. We were incapable of astonishment now, even when we saw sight-seeing buses commandeered in Holland and Belgium and Northern France conveying infantrymen to the swiftly shifting front. They looked like some gigantic excursion party, and the eagerness with which the German soldiers snatched their brief view of Paris enhanced the illusion.

Demaree Bess

16 JUNE 1940

I think it was on Tuesday that, while I was wheeling the Enfield down the entry, Jean put her head round the kitchen door and said Italy had joined in. At midnight we were listening to Roosevelt describing this as 'a dagger in the back'. It's all very well making remarks like this from across the Atlantic – what are they going to do? Come in towards the end like last time and say they won the war?

The outstanding personal event of last week was that I was given a 5% cost-of-living rise and a further flat five bob a week for working a 48-hour week. Also the Bank Manager said that he could let me have a further £30 should I need it. The outstanding public event was the German invasion of Paris.

George Beardmore

De Gaulle leaves France

At the start of the war, Brigadier-General Charles de Gaulle was a little-known soldier whose main claim on his fellow Frenchmen's attention was to have warned persistently of the danger of a German invasion. Major-General Edward Spears – an MP and a close friend of Churchill's – was the latter's personal representative to the French government during the weeks of crisis.

Whilst he was cogitating and reconnoitring, De Gaulle and I discussed a little act. He would behave as if he had come to see me off, and at the last moment I was to haul him on board. It was quite possible that amongst the many officers standing about there might be someone watching him, ready to prevent his leaving.

Then suddenly a new difficulty arose. The pilot declared it was essential that De Gaulle's luggage, some of which was heavy, should be lashed. He had, I think, sent ahead a particularly heavy trunk. There was neither cord nor string on the 'plane, so the crew began to work with a will to release from the wooden wheel-blocks the stiff ropes used to pull them away before the machine starts, but do what they would, tearing their nails in a way painful to behold, they could not manage it. There was nothing for it, a ball of string must be found. Courcel set off at the double and soon disappeared in the shoal of 'planes. He was probably not gone for more than ten minutes, but I remember them as holding quite a high priority among the unpleasant periods of waiting I have experienced. De Gaulle showed little and said less, but I noted later in the 'plane that he must have found the tension excruciating. I chatted with the chauffeur, I chatted with De Gaulle, with the crew, then climbed on board to see if, like Sister Ann, I could see anyone coming. It was very trying. There could evidently be no question of leaving the boxes behind to be investigated by Weygand's men. I gathered they contained important papers. On the other hand time was passing, and the possibility of De Gaulle's departure from Bordeaux being detected was increasing. Somebody was sure to think of him in the course of the morning, then steps would be taken to locate him. If it occurred to anyone that he had gone, the aerodrome would be the natural place to look for him. Someone would remember having seen me in the car with him, that would be the clue. Then there would be a telephone call. Thank God the telephone service at Bordeaux was working incredibly badly. At last Courcel appeared, his stilt-like legs carrying him fast, though he appeared to be moving in slow motion. In his hand he carried a ball of string. I hope that never again will this commonplace article be so important to me. Our troubles were over. In a very short time the pilot announced that all was ready. The propellers started making their little private hurricanes. I bade my chauffeur a very sincere and affectionate farewell. He was only an ordinary French chap, but the salt of the earth like a few million others.

We had begun to move when with hooked hands, I hoisted De Gaulle on board. Courcel, more nimble, was in in a trice. The door slammed. I just had time to see the gaping face of the chauffeur and one or two more beside him.

Edward Spears

With France lost, Churchill once more encouraged his own countrymen with stirring words.

What General Weygand called the Battle of France is over. I expect that the Battle of Britain is about to begin. Upon this battle depends the survival of Christian civilisation. Upon it depends our own British life, and the long continuity of our institutions and our Empire. The whole fury and might of the enemy must very soon be turned on us. Hitler knows that he will have to break us in this island or lose the war. If we can stand up to him, all Europe may be free and the life of the world may move forward into broad, sunlit uplands. But if we fail, then the whole world, including the United States, including all that we have known and cared for, will sink into the abyss of a new Dark Age made more sinister, and perhaps more protracted, by the lights of perverted science. Let us therefore brace ourselves to our duties and so bear ourselves that, if the British Empire and its Commonwealth last for a thousand years, men will still say, 'This was their finest hour.'

Winston Churchill

A railway carriage in the woods

The armistice negotiations began at three fifteen p.m. A warm June sun beat down on the great elm and pine trees, and cast pleasant shadows on the wooded avenues as Hitler, with the German plenipotentiaries at his side, appeared. He alighted from his car in front of the French monument to Alsace-Lorraine which stands at the end of the avenue about 200 yards from the clearing where the armistice car waited on exactly the same spot it occupied twenty-two years ago.

The Alsace-Lorraine statue, I noted, was covered with German war flags so that you could not see its sculptured work nor read its inscription. But I had seen it some years before – the large sword representing the sword of the Allies, and its point sticking into a large, limp eagle, representing the old Empire of the Kaiser. And the inscription underneath in French saying: 'TO THE HEROIC SOLDIERS OF FRANCE . . . DEFENDERS OF THE COUNTRY AND OF RIGHT . . . GLORIOUS LIBERATORS OF ALSACE-LORRAINE.'

Through my glasses I saw the Führer stop, glance at the monument, observe the Reich flags with their big swastikas in the centre. Then he strode slowly towards us, towards the little clearing in the woods. I observed his face. It was grave, solemn, yet brimming with revenge. There was also in it, as in his springy step, a note of the triumphant conqueror, the defier of the world. There was something else, difficult to describe, in his expression, a sort of scornful, inner joy at being present at this great reversal of fate – a reversal he himself had wrought.

Now he reaches the little opening in the woods. He pauses and looks slowly around. The clearing is in the form of a circle some 200 yards in diameter and laid out like a park. Cypress trees line it all round – and behind them, the great elms and oaks of the forest. This has been one of France's national shrines for twenty-two years. From a discreet position on the perimeter of the circle we watch.

Hitler pauses, and gazes slowly around. In a group just behind him are the other German plenipotentiaries: Goering, grasping his field-marshal's baton in one hand. He wears the sky-blue uniform of the air force. All the Germans are in uniform, Hitler in a double-breasted grey uniform, with the Iron Cross hanging from his left breast pocket. Next to Goering are the two German army chiefs – General Keitel, chief of the Supreme Command, and General von Brauchitsch, commander-in-chief of the German army. Both are just approaching sixty, but look younger, especially Keitel, who has a dapper appearance with his cap slightly cocked on one side.

Then there is Erich Raeder, Grand Admiral of the German Fleet, in his blue naval uniform and the invariable upturned collar which German naval officers usually wear. There are two non-military men in Hitler's suite – his Foreign Minister, Joachim von Ribbentrop, in the field-grey uniform of the Foreign Office; and Rudolf Hess, Hitler's deputy, in a grey party uniform.

The time is now three eighteen p.m. Hitler's personal flag is run up on a small standard in the centre of the opening.

Also in the centre is a great granite block which stands some three feet above the ground. Hitler, followed by the others, walks slowly over to it, steps up, and reads the inscription engraved in great high letters on that block. It says: 'HERE ON THE ELEVENTH OF NOVEMBER 1918 SUCCUMBED THE CRIMINAL PRIDE OF THE GERMAN EMPIRE . . . VANQUISHED BY THE FREE PEOPLES WHICH IT TRIED TO ENSLAVE.'

Hitler reads it and Goering reads it. They all read it, standing there in the June sun and the silence. I look for the expression on Hitler's face. I am but fifty yards from him and see him through my glasses as though he were directly in front of me. I have seen that face many times at the great moments of his life. But today! It is afire with scorn, anger, hate, revenge, triumph. He steps off the monument and contrives to make even this gesture a masterpiece of contempt. He glances back at it, contemptuous, angry – angry, you almost feel, because he cannot wipe out the awful, provoking lettering with one sweep of his high Prussian boot. He glances slowly around the clearing, and now, as his eyes meet ours, you grasp the depth of his hatred. But there is triumph there too – revengeful, triumphant hate. Suddenly, as though his face were not giving quite complete expression to his feelings, he throws his whole body into harmony with his mood. He swiftly snaps his hands on his hips, arches his shoulders, plants his feet wide apart. It is a magnificent gesture of defiance, of burning contempt for this place now and all that it has stood for in the twenty-two years since it witnessed the humbling of the German Empire.

It is now three twenty-three p.m. and the Germans stride over to the armistice car. For a moment or two they stand in the sunlight outside the car, chatting. Then Hitler steps up into the car, followed by the others. We can see nicely through the car windows. Hitler takes the place occupied by Marshal Foch when the 1918 armistice terms were signed. The others spread themselves around him. Four chairs on the opposite side of the table from Hitler remain empty. The French have not yet appeared. But we do not wait long. Exactly at three thirty p.m. they alight from a car. They have flown up from Bordeaux to a nearby landing field. They too glance at the Alsace-Lorraine memorial but it's a swift glance. Then they walk down the avenue flanked by three German officers. We see them now as they come into the sunlight of the clearing.

General Huntziger, wearing a bleached khaki uniform, Air General Bergeret and Vice-Admiral Le Luc, both in dark blue uniforms, and then, almost buried in the uniforms, M. Noël, French Ambassador to Poland. The German guard of honour, drawn up at the entrance to the clearing, snaps to attention for the French as they pass, but it does not present arms.

It is a grave hour in the life of France. The Frenchmen keep their eyes straight ahead. Their faces are solemn, drawn. They are the picture of tragic dignity.

They walk stiffly to the car, where they are met by two German officers, Lieutenant-General Tippelskirch, Quartermaster General, and Colonel Thomas, chief of the Führer's headquarters. The Germans salute. The French salute. The atmosphere is what Europeans call 'correct'. There are salutes, but no handshakes.

Now we get our picture through the dusty windows of that old wagon-lit car. Hitler and the other German leaders rise as the French enter the drawing-room. Hitler gives the Nazi salute, the arm raised. Ribbentrop and Hess do the same. I cannot see M. Noël to notice whether he salutes or not.

Hitler, as far as we can see through the windows, does not say a word to the French or to anybody else. He nods to General Keitel at his side. We see General Keitel adjusting his papers. Then he starts to read. He is reading the preamble to the German armistice terms. The French sit there with marble-like faces and listen intently. Hitler and Goering glance at the green table-top.

The reading of the preamble lasts but a few minutes. Hitler, we soon observe, has no intention of remaining very long, of listening to the reading of the armistice terms themselves. At three forty-two p.m., twelve minutes after the French arrive, we see Hitler stand up, salute stiffly, and then stride out of the drawing-room, followed by Goering, Brauchitsch, Raeder, Hess, and Ribbentrop. The French, like figures of stone, remain at the green-topped table. General Keitel remains with them. He starts to read them the detailed conditions of the armistice.

Hitler and his aides stride down the avenue towards the Alsace-Lorraine monument, where their cars are waiting. As they pass the guard of honour, the German band strikes up the two national anthems, *Deutschland, Deutschland über Alles* and the *Horst Wessel* song. The whole ceremony in which Hitler has reached a new pinnacle in his meteoric career and Germany avenged the 1918 defeat is over in a quarter of an hour.

William Shirer

Under the terms of the armistice, the Germans were to occupy France to the north and west of a line drawn from Geneva to the Pyrenees that gave the Nazis access to the Atlantic harbours. The remainder of the country was to be governed by a collaborating administration based in Vichy and led by Marshal Pétain and Pierre Laval. Since the start of the blitzkrieg six weeks earlier, the French had lost 92,000 men, the Germans 27,000.

Despite the surrender, the writer and airman Antoine de Saint-Exupéry kept faith with his country.

Since I am one with the people of France, I shall never reject my people, whatever they may do. I shall never preach against them in the hearing of others. Whenever it is possible to take their defence, I shall defend them. If they cover me with shame I shall lock up that shame in my heart and be silent. Whatever at such a time I shall think of them, I shall never bear witness against them. Does a husband go from house to house crying out to his neighbours that his wife is a strumpet? Is it thus that he can preserve his honour? No, for his wife is one with his home. No, for he cannot establish his dignity against her. Let him go home to her, and there unburden himself of his anger.

Thus, I shall not divorce myself from a defeat which surely will often humiliate me. I am part of France, and France is part of me.

Antoine de Saint-Exupéry

The author of The Little Prince *went missing while making a night flight in 1944.*

‡

The British Home Front

The Permanent Under Secretary of the Foreign Office surveys the state of the war.

SATURDAY 29 JUNE 1940

Cabinet at 10. W.S.C. [Churchill] at Chequers, so we got through by about 11.15 . . . T. [his wife, Theodosia] and I drove to the Park and sat and read. Quite peaceful. Then walked a bit in the middle of the Park, but it is parched and seared with guns and trenches – beastly . . . Meinertzhagen [Home Guard] came round to talk to H. [Halifax] and me about blocking the Park Door. He is very gloomy on easy possibility of German descent upon London. I am not terribly impressed: I think it must be more difficult than he makes out. Report from A.E. [Anthony Eden] of a tour in Sussex and Kent, which certainly makes it seem that the Germans can take a penny steamer to the coast and stroll up to London!

. . . Certainly everything is as gloomy as can be. Probability is that Hitler will attempt invasion in next fortnight. As far as I can see, we are, after years of leisurely preparation, completely unprepared. We have simply got to die at our posts – a far better fate than capitulating to Hitler as these damned Frogs have done. But uncomfortable.

Alexander Cadogan

The occupation of the Channel Islands

The Channel Islands were the only British territory to be conquered by the Germans during the war. On 28 June, Jersey was bombed and nine people were killed. On the morning of 1 July, three copies of an ultimatum were dropped on the island threatening further raids unless white flags were displayed. The island's Bailiff, Alexander Coutanche, had little option but to await the arrival of the enemy.

I thought that I would try to relieve my feelings by doing some work in the garden. It was something which I was very fond of doing. I, therefore, changed into an old pair of grey flannels and a sports coat, and went out into the garden in order to do some much needed weeding. I remained engaged in this until my houseman, Coleman, came out to remind me that it was almost dinner time. I came in and told Babs that, if she didn't mind, I would dine as I was without changing.

Towards the very end of dinner, Coleman, who was looking out of the window at the drive, suddenly turned round and said, 'Sir, the drive is full of Jerries. What do we do?'

I said, 'There is only one thing to do and that is to open the door and let them in.'

I remained seated at the table with Babs and into the dining-room walked Aubin. He said, 'I'm awfully sorry but the head man has arrived since you left the airport and he has insisted on coming here with some other officers because the Occupation formalities are apparently not yet complete.'

All this must have happened right at the end of dinner because I remember very well that the decanter of port was already on the table.

I said, 'Very well. Where are they?'

'They're in your drawing room.'

'All right, let's go and meet them.'

I should at this point explain that the ultimatum which had been dropped was addressed to the Governor of the Island. I think that when I arrived at the airport there could have been no doubt in the minds of the German officers there that I was he. However, the present situation was a little different. I was now in gardening clothes and, as I started to walk across the hall, I noticed to my horror that there was a large rent in the knee of my trousers. Aubin was quick to take in the situation. He was a tall, distinguished and impressive figure and he forestalled any questions which my general appearance must have raised by announcing in a commanding tone of voice, as he preceded me through the door, 'His Excellency, the Governor.'

The Germans were all standing in front of the fire-place, which of course was not lit in the middle of summer. Two sentries had been posted, one on either side of the door. There were half a dozen officers and again a civilian to act as interpreter. It was made clear to me who was the commander in charge of the whole operation, when he introduced himself to me as Captain Gussek.

His method of expressing some surprise at my appearance was to put a monocle into his right eye, the better to take me in. In those days I used on occasion to wear a monocle myself and it so happened that it was in the pocket of my jacket now. I was, therefore, able to repay the compliment and I did so. We took good stock of each other.

This momentary confrontation was brought to an end when he turned to one of his subordinates, who handed him a document. It was a proclamation, which he gave to the interpreter to read out. It was exactly the same proclamation as that which had already been read to me at the airport. While this was taking place I could see through the window that Aubin had retired to the dining-room and was fortifying himself with a glass of my port.

Alexander Coutanche

The Channel Islands were not liberated until 9 May 1945. For five years, the islanders suffered increasing hardship, and by December 1944 the Red Cross estimated that the population was surviving on a daily diet of 1,137 calories per head, less than half the recommended amount.

Rationing

Theodora FitzGibbon, a young model, was living in Chelsea with her lover, the photographer Peter Rose Pulham.

At this time we were told to expect an invasion and to stock up our larders accordingly. This was difficult for people with limited incomes like us, for tinned food was expensive, often at black-market prices, when unrationed. We were always hungry for the rations were meagre. One person's weekly rations consisted of one ounce of butter, four ounces of margarine, one ounce of cheese, and between one shilling and one and threepence worth of meat, with a few rashers of bacon. One egg weekly in summer; the winter was unpredictable. Egg powder, that is dried powdered egg, was expected to make up the deficit. The small amounts of sugar (½ lb) and tea (½ lb) we often swapped, illegally, for cheese which was of the uninteresting 'mousetrap' variety, and best made into Welsh rarebit with a little beer.

Tinned fish and meats were on a points system, so many points being allocated each month. A tin of stewed steak or corned beef took two thirds of the allowance. Unless you were pregnant, or a child, milk was only two and a half pints per person a week. Vegetables and fruit were ration-free, but limited and seasonal (in 1941 I queued for an hour to get onions from the greengrocer). Fish was also unrationed, but with mines and U-boats at large it wasn't plentiful, and sometimes didn't seem all that fresh. Chicken was expensive and kept 'under the counter' (a current phrase) for good customers. Technically all offal was free, but as the war progressed it was difficult to find. When I remarked to the butcher that all the animals seemed to be born without tongues, tails, hearts, kidneys, livers or balls, he winked at me, a great arm went under the counter, and he flung up a half-frozen oxtail. I had never cooked one before, but even today I can taste the thick gravy and see our grease-spattered lips as we chewed on the bones.

Unrationed rabbit was the salvation for many people in a low-income group. I made big jellied pies with a scrap of bacon and onion; braised rabbit in dark beer with prunes, which made it taste vaguely like pheasant; or with cider and tomatoes; or with curry spices or paprika; or stuffed and baked rabbit, when we would pretend it was chicken; and if it was very young, Peter would joint it, and we would fry it in a crisp batter. Frying was quite difficult, as lard was rationed and olive oil only obtainable at a chemist on a doctor's prescription, so sometimes we were reduced to liquid paraffin. At least we didn't suffer from constipation! Another 'filler' was pasta, which could be bought freshly made in Soho; rice disappeared as the war went on, and even in Chinese restaurants spaghetti cut to look like rice or pearl barley was served. Housekeeping was made more difficult by the hours spent in queues. Local shopping was done by Peter, who became very good at it – except for the butcher, who gave me bigger cuts, so I bought the meat on Saturday afternoons. I also spread the ration books over different shops, for each one would give a mite over, which added up on three books. Indiscriminate shopping where you saw the best food was not allowed, for you registered at a certain shop, and it involved great bureaucratic difficulties to get the book changed.

Theodora FitzGibbon

After the war, the author made her name as a cookery writer.

‡

John Colville, 25, was seconded from the Foreign Office shortly after the outbreak of war to be one of the Prime Minister's Assistant Private Secretaries. His diaries provide an intimate portrait of Churchill, here seen in pugnacious mood.

After tea I accompanied the PM to a rifle range nearby, where he fired with his Mannlicher rifle at targets 100, 200 and 300 yards away. He also fired his revolver, still smoking a cigar, with commendable accuracy. Despite his age, size and lack of practice, he acquitted himself well. The whole time he talked of the best method of killing Huns. Soft-nose bullets were the thing to use and he must get some. But, said Randolph, they are illegal in war; to which the PM replied that the Germans would make very short work of him if they caught him, and so he didn't see why he should have any mercy on them.

John Colville

✝

The Battle of Britain

Richard Hillary, an Australian, was at Oxford University when, as a member of the RAF Volunteer Reserve, he was called up. He was 21.

I knew that that morning I was to kill for the first time. That I might be killed or in any way injured did not occur to me. Later, when we were losing pilots regularly, I did consider it in an abstract way when on the ground; but once in the air, never. I knew it could not happen to me. I suppose every pilot knows that, knows it cannot happen to him; even when he is taking off for the last time, when he will not return, he knows that he cannot be killed. I wondered idly what he was like, this man I would kill. Was he young, was he fat, would he die with the Führer's name on his lips, or would he die alone, in that last moment conscious of himself as a man? I would never know. Then I was being strapped in, my mind automatically checking the controls, and we were off.

We ran into them at 18,000 feet, twenty yellow-nosed Messerschmitt 109s, about 500 feet above us. Our Squadron strength was eight, and as they came down on us we went into line astern and turned head on to them. Brian Carbury, who was leading the Section, dropped the nose of his machine, and I could almost feel the leading Nazi pilot push forward on his stick to bring his guns to bear. At the same moment Brian hauled hard back on his own control stick and led us over them in a steep climbing turn to the left. In two vital seconds they lost their advantage. I saw Brian let go a burst of fire at the leading plane, saw the pilot put his machine into a half roll, and knew that he was mine. Automatically, I kicked the rudder to the left to get him at right angles, turned the gunbutton to 'Fire', and let go in a four-second burst with full deflection. He came right through my sights and I saw the tracer from all eight guns thud home. For a second he seemed to hang motionless; then a jet of red flame shot upwards and he spun out of sight.

For the next few minutes I was too busy looking after myself to think of anything, but when, after a short while, they turned and made off over the Channel, and we were ordered to our base, my mind began to work again.

It had happened.

My first emotion was one of satisfaction, satisfaction at a job adequately done, at the final logical conclusion of months of specialised training. And then I had a feeling of the essential rightness of it all. He was dead and I was alive; it could so easily have been the other way round; and that would somehow have been right too. I realised in that moment just how lucky a fighter pilot is. He has none of the personalised emotions of the soldier, handed a rifle and bayonet and told to charge. He does not even have to share the dangerous emotions of the bomber pilot who night after night must experience that childhood longing for smashing things. The fighter pilot's emotions are those of the duellist – cool, precise, impersonal. He is privileged to kill well. For if one must either kill or be killed, as now one must, it should, I feel, be done with dignity. Death should be given the setting it deserves; it should never be a pettiness; and for the fighter pilot it never can be.

From this flight Broody Benson did not return.

The engagements in which Hillary took part that week in mid-August marked an intensification of the air war and the start of the Battle of Britain, a contest for aerial superiority over the Channel without which the Germans would not mount their invasion. Although the enduring image of that summer is of Spitfire and Messerschmitt pilots duelling in the sky, the Luftwaffe's intent was in fact to break the RAF by bombing its airfields and aeroplanes on the ground.

Having been on every flight the previous day, the morning was mine to do with as I pleased. I got up slowly, gazed dispassionately at my tongue in the mirror, and wandered over to the Mess for breakfast. It must have been getting on for twelve o'clock when I came out on to the aerodrome to find the usual August heat haze forming a dull pall over everything. I started to walk across the aerodrome to the Dispersal Point on the far side. There were only two machines on the ground so I concluded that the Squadron was already up. Then I heard a shout, and our ground crew drew up in a lorry beside me. Sergeant Ross leaned out:

'Want a lift, sir? We're going round.'

'No, thanks, Sergeant. I'm going to cut across.'

This was forbidden for obvious reasons, but I felt like that.

'OK, sir. See you round there.'

The lorry trundled off down the road in a cloud of dust. I walked on across the landing ground. At that moment I heard the emotionless voice of the controller.

'Large enemy bombing formation approaching Hornchurch. All personnel not engaged in active duty take cover immediately.'

I looked up. They were still not visible. At the Dispersal Point I saw Bubble and Pip Cardell make a dash for the shelter. Three Spitfires just landed, turned about and came past me with a roar to take off down-wind. Our lorry was still trundling along the road, maybe half-way round, and seemed suddenly an awfully long way from the Dispersal Point.

I looked up again, and this time I saw them – about a dozen slugs, shining in the bright sun and coming straight on. At the rising scream of the first bomb I instinctively shrugged up my shoulders and ducked my head. Out of the corner of my eye I saw the three Spitfires. One moment they were about twenty feet up in close formation; the next catapulted apart as though on elastic. The leader went over on his back and ploughed along the runway with a rending crash of tearing fabric; No. 2 put a wing in and spun round on his airscrew, while the plane on the left was blasted wingless into the next field. I remember thinking stupidly, 'That's the shortest flight he's ever taken,' and then my feet were nearly knocked from under me, my mouth was full of dirt, and Bubble, gesticulating like a madman from the shelter entrance, was yelling, 'Run, you bloody fool, run!' I ran. Suddenly awakened to the lunacy of my behaviour, I covered the distance to that shelter as if impelled by a rocket and shot through the entrance while once again the ground rose up and hit me, and my head smashed hard against one of the pillars. I subsided on a heap of rubble and massaged it.

'Who's here?' I asked, peering through the gloom.

'Cardell and I and three of our ground crew,' said Bubble, 'and, by the Grace of God, you!'

I could see by his mouth that he was still talking, but a sudden concentration of the scream and crump of falling bombs made it impossible to hear him.

The air was thick with dust and the shelter shook and heaved at each explosion, yet somehow held firm. For about three minutes the bedlam continued, and then suddenly ceased. In the utter silence which followed nobody moved. None of us wished to be the first to look on the devastation which we felt must be outside. Then Bubble spoke. 'Praise God!' he said, 'I'm not a civilian. Of all the bloody frightening things I've ever done, sitting in that shelter was the worst. Me for the air from now on!'

It broke the tension and we scrambled out of the entrance. The runways were certainly in something of a mess. Gaping holes and great gobbets of earth were everywhere. Right in front of us a bomb had landed by my Spitfire, covering it with a shower of grit and rubble.

I turned to the aircraftsman standing beside me. 'Will you get hold of Sergeant Ross and tell him to have a crew give her an inspection.'

He jerked his head towards one corner of the aerodrome: 'I think I'd better collect the crew myself sir. Sergeant Ross won't be doing any more inspections.'

I followed his glance and saw the lorry, the roof about twenty yards away, lying grotesquely on its side.

Richard Hillary

The German ace Adolf Galland led III Gruppe of Jagdgeschwader 26. He was not afraid to speak his mind, as even Goering discovered.

A fortnight later we met the Reichsmarschall again. This time he came to visit us on the coast. The large-scale attacks of the bombers were imminent, and the air supremacy necessary for them had not been achieved to the degree expected. The British fighter force was wounded, it was true, but not beaten. And our pursuit Stuka and fighter force had naturally suffered grievous losses in material, personnel and morale. The uncertainty about the continuation of the air offensive reflected itself down to the last pilot. Goering refused to understand that his Luftwaffe, this shining and so far successful sword, threatened to turn blunt in his hand. He believed there was not enough fighting spirit and a lack of confidence in ultimate victory. By personally taking a hand, he hoped to get the best out of us.

To my mind, he went about it the wrong way. He had nothing but reproaches for the fighter force, and he expressed his dissatisfaction in the harshest terms. The theme of fighter protection was chewed over again and again. Goering clearly represented the point of view of the bombers and demanded close and rigid protection. The bomber, he said, was more important than record bag figures. I tried to point out that the Me 109 was superior in the attack and not so suitable for purely defensive purposes as the Spitfire, which, although a little slower, was much more manoeuvrable. He rejected my objection. We received many more harsh words. Finally, as his time ran short, he grew more amiable and asked what were the requirements for our squadrons. Moelders asked for a series of Me 109s with more powerful engines. The request was granted. 'And you?' Goering turned to me. I did not hesitate long. 'I should like an outfit of Spitfires for my group.' After blurting this out, I had rather a shock, for it was not really meant that way. Of course, fundamentally, I preferred our Me 109 to the Spitfire, but I was unbelievably vexed at the lack of understanding and the stubbornness with which the command gave us orders we could not execute – or only incompletely – as a result of many shortcomings for which we were not to blame. Such brazen-faced impudence made even Goering speechless. He stamped off, growling as he went.

Adolf Galland

'Shot down in flames'

Geoffrey Page Page, a Hurricane pilot, reveals the reality behind that glibly used phrase.

One moment the sky between me and thirty Dornier 215s was clear; the next it was criss-crossed with streams of white tracer from cannon shells converging on our Hurricanes.

Jumbo's machine peeled away from the attack. The distance between the German leaders and my solitary Hurricane was down to three hundred yards. Strikes from my Brownings began to flash around the port engine of one of the Dorniers.

The mass of fire from the bomber formation closed in as I fired desperately in a race to destroy before being destroyed.

The first bang came as a shock. For an instant I couldn't believe I'd been hit. Two more bangs followed in quick succession, and as if by magic a gaping hole suddenly appeared in my starboard wing.

Surprise quickly changed to fear, and as the instinct of self-preservation began to take over, the gas tank behind the engine blew up, and my cockpit became an inferno. Fear became blind terror, then agonised horror as the bare skin of my hands gripping the throttle and control column shrivelled up like burnt parchment under the intensity of the blast furnace temperature. Screaming at the top of my voice, I threw my head back to keep it away from the searing flames. Instinctively the tortured right hand groped for the release pin securing the restraining Sutton harness.

'Dear God, save me . . . save me, dear God . . .' I cried imploringly. Then, as suddenly as terror had overtaken me, it vanished with the knowledge that death was no longer to be feared. My fingers kept up their blind and bloody mechanical groping. Some large mechanical dark object disappeared between my legs and cool, relieving fresh air suddenly flowed across my burning face. I tumbled. Sky, sea, sky, over and over as a clearing brain issued instructions to outflung limbs. 'Pull the ripcord – right hand to the ripcord.' Watering eyes focused on an arm flung out in space with some strange meaty object attached at its end.

More tumbling – more sky and sea and sky, but with a blue–clad arm forming a focal point in the foreground. 'Pull the ripcord, hand,' the brain again commanded. Slowly but obediently the elbow bent and the hand came across the body to rest on the chromium ring but bounced away quickly with the agony of contact.

More tumbling but at a slower rate now. The weight of the head was beginning to tell.

Realising that pain or no pain, the ripcord had to be pulled, the brain overcame the reaction of the raw nerve endings and forced the mutilated fingers to grasp the ring and pull firmly.

It acted immediately. With a jerk the silken canopy billowed out in the clear summer sky.

Geoffrey Page Page

The author's burns were treated by Archibald MacIndoe, the New Zealand-born pioneer of plastic surgery, and he became one of the founders of MacIndoe's 'Guinea Pig Club' of patients.

‡

The war in the desert

With Hitler's progress still barred by the RAF and the English Channel, the focus of the war began to shift to North Africa after Italy's entry into the conflict. From the Mediterranean and from her possessions in East Africa and Libya she could threaten Britain's hold on Egypt and the Suez Canal, and thus her control over the Middle East and her links to India. But, as journalist Alan Moorehead realised, the desert demanded a new kind of fighting.

More and more I began to see that desert warfare resembled war at sea. Men moved by compass. No position was static. There were few if any forts to be held. Each truck or tank was as individual as a destroyer, and each squadron or tanks of guns made great sweeps across the desert as a battle-squadron at sea will vanish over the horizon. One did not occupy the desert any more than one occupied the sea. One simply took up position for a day or a week, and patrolled about it with Bren-gun carriers and light armoured vehicles. When you made contact with the enemy you manoeuvred about him for a place to strike, much as two fleets will steam into position for action. There were no trenches. There was no front line. We might patrol five hundred miles into Libya and call the country ours. The Italians might as easily have patrolled as far into the Egyptian desert without being seen. Always the essential governing principle was that desert forces must be mobile: they were seeking not the conquest of territory or position but combat with the enemy. We hunted men, not land, as a warship will hunt another warship, and care nothing for the sea on which the action is fought. And as a ship submits to the sea by the nature of its design and the way it sails, so these new mechanised soldiers were submitting to the desert. They found weaknesses in the ruthless hostility of the desert and ways to circumvent its worst moods. They used the desert. They never sought to control it. Always the desert set the pace, made the direction and planned the design. The desert offered colours in browns, yellows and greys. The army accordingly took these colours for its camouflage. There were practically no roads. The army shod its vehicles with huge balloon tyres and did without roads. Nothing except an occasional bird moved quickly in the desert. The army for ordinary purposes accepted a pace of five or six miles an hour. The desert gave water reluctantly, and often then it was brackish. The army cut its men – generals and privates – down to a gallon of water a day when they were in forward positions. There was no food in the desert. The soldier learned to exist almost entirely on tinned foods, and contrary to popular belief remained healthy on it. Mirages came that confused the gunner, and the gunner developed precision-firing to a finer art and learned new methods of establishing observation-posts close to targets. The sandstorm blew, and the tanks, profiting by it, went into action under the cover of the storm. We made no new roads. We built no houses. We did not try to make the desert livable, nor did we seek to subdue it. We found the life of the desert primitive and nomadic, and primitively and nomadically the army lived and went to war.

The Italians failed to accept these principles, and when the big fighting began in the winter it was their undoing. They wanted to be masters of the desert. They made their lives comfortable and static. They built roads and stone houses and the officers strode around in brilliant scented uniforms. They tried to subdue the desert. And in the end the desert beat them.

Alan Moorehead

Autumn 1940

The Battle of Britain still hung in the balance. On 3 September 1940, Richard Hillary was shot down.

Uncle George and the leading section took off in a cloud of dust; Brian Carbury looked across and put up his thumbs. I nodded and opened up, to take off for the last time from Hornchurch. I was flying No. 3 in Brian's section, with Stapme Stapleton on the right: the third section consisted of only two machines, so that our Squadron strength was eight. We headed south-east, climbing all out on a steady course. At about 12,000 feet we came up through the clouds: I looked down and saw them spread out below me like layers of whipped cream. The sun was brilliant and made it difficult to see even the next plane when turning. I was peering anxiously ahead, for the controller had given us warning of at least fifty enemy fighters approaching very high. When we did first sight them, nobody shouted, as I think we all saw them at the same moment. They must have been 500 to 1000 feet above us and coming straight on like a swarm of locusts. I remember cursing and going automatically into line astern: the next moment we were in among them and it was each man for himself. As soon as they saw us they spread out and dived, and the next ten minutes was a blur of twisting machines and tracer bullets. One Messerschmitt went down in a sheet of flame on my right, and a Spitfire hurtled past in a half-roll; I was weaving and turning in a desperate attempt to gain height, with the machine practically hanging on the airscrew. Then, just below me and to my left, I saw what I had been praying for – a Messerschmitt climbing and away from the sun. I closed in to 200 yards, and from slightly to one side gave him a two-second burst: fabric ripped off the wing and black smoke poured from the engine, but he did not go down. Like a fool, I did not break away, but put in another three-second burst. Red flames shot upwards and he spiralled out of sight. At that moment, I felt a terrific explosion which knocked the control stick from my hand, and the whole machine quivered like a stricken animal. In a second, the cockpit was a mass of flames: instinctively, I reached up to open the hood. It would not move. I tore off my straps and managed to force it back; but this took time, and when I dropped back into the seat and reached for the stick in an effort to turn the plane on its back, the heat was so intense that I could feel myself going. I remember a second of sharp agony, remember thinking 'So this is it!' and putting both hands to my eyes. Then I passed out.

When I regained consciousness I was free of the machine and falling rapidly. I pulled the rip-cord of my parachute and checked my descent with a jerk. Looking down, I saw that my left trouser leg was burnt off, that I was going to fall into the sea, and that the English coast was deplorably far away. About twenty feet above the water, I attempted to undo my parachute, failed, and flopped into the sea with it billowing round me. I was told later that the machine went into a spin at about 25,000 feet and that at 10,000 feet I fell out – unconscious. This may well have been so, for I discovered later a large cut on the top of my head, presumably collected while bumping round inside.

The water was not unwarm and I was pleasantly surprised to find that my life-jacket kept me afloat. I looked at my watch: it was not there. Then, for the first time, I noticed how burnt my hands were: down to the wrist, the skin was dead white and hung in shreds: I felt faintly sick from the smell of burnt flesh. By closing one eye I could see my lips, jutting out like motor tyres. The side of my parachute harness was cutting into me particularly painfully, so that I guessed my right hip was burnt. I made a further attempt to undo the harness, but owing to the pain of my hands, soon desisted.

Instead, I lay back and reviewed my position: I was a long way from land; my hands were burnt, and so, judging from the pain of the sun, was my face; it was unlikely that anyone on shore had seen me come down and even more unlikely that a ship would come by; I could float for possibly four hours in my Mae West. I began to feel that I had perhaps been premature in considering myself lucky to have escaped from the machine. After about half an hour my teeth started chattering, and to quiet them I kept up a regular tuneless chant, varying it from time to time with calls for help. There can be few more futile pastimes than yelling for help alone in the North Sea, with a solitary seagull for company, yet it gave me a certain melancholy satisfaction, for I had once written a short story in which the hero (falling from a liner) had done just this. It was rejected.

The water now seemed much colder and I noticed with surprise that the sun had gone in though my face was still burning. I looked down at my hands, and not seeing them, realised that I had gone blind. So I was going to die. It came to me like that – I was going to die, and I was not afraid. This realisation came as a surprise. The manner of my approaching death appalled and horrified me, but the actual vision of death left me unafraid: I felt only a profound curiosity and a sense of satisfaction that within a few minutes or a few hours I was to learn the great answer. I decided that it should be in a few minutes. I had no qualms about hastening my end and, reaching up, I managed to unscrew the valve of my Mae West. The air escaped in a rush and my head went under water. It is said by people who have all but died in the sea that drowning is a pleasant death. I did not find it so. I swallowed a large quantity of water before my head came up again, but derived little satisfaction from it. I tried again, to find that I could not get my face under. I was so enmeshed in my parachute that I could not move. For the next ten minutes, I tore my hands to ribbons on the spring-release catch. It was stuck fast. I lay back exhausted, and then I started to laugh.

Richard Hillary

Hillary was subsequently picked up by a rescue boat and sent to a specialist burns hospital in London.

✠

The Blitz

Unable to break the RAF, Hitler decided instead to prepare the way for the invasion by destroying first factories and then civilian morale. On 7 September more than 300 bombers headed for London. That afternoon Theodora FitzGibbon was in a pub in Chelsea with her lover Peter Rose Pulham and his friends, a little-known poet named Dylan Thomas and a young diplomat called Donald Maclean.

It was around five o'clock, the wine was all gone, and we began to think of going out for drinks at a pub. The air-raid siren had sounded a little earlier, but a warning about a week previously had amounted to very little, so we took no notice. It was, after all, still daylight. Out in the street, the sun was setting, and there was a faraway drone of aeroplanes and the sound of anti-aircraft guns. We decided to go to the King's Head and Eight Bells, a small pub on Chelsea Embankment, instead of the Six Bells. As we turned the corner there was in the sky a monstrous tower, looking like a giant puffball of smoke, away to the east. Even though it was too far off, the density of it made one's nostrils twitch with the imagined smell. We turned into the pub, normally empty at this hour, but the great menacing grey column in the east had brought many people out in search of news. The saloon bar of the pub had a long refectory table by the stairs, and several people sat there silently. It was old-fashioned in design, and over the bar, reaching almost to the counter, were panels of cut glass, with small windows on hinges which were swivelled open to give the orders. Through these foot-wide apertures the frightened eyes of the proprietors met one's own.

We decided to play a game of shove-ha'penny, a pub game of those days. It was convenient because both Peter and Sophie were left-handed, so we didn't have to keep changing sides as we spun the metal discs up the board. Men in tin hats, which we had all been issued with some time ago, came in from time to time with communiqués. When darkness came, the smoke had turned into a red bank of flames. It seemed as if they would flick out their fiery tongues and embrace the whole of London.

At about six thirty the 'all clear' sounded, and by then the sky was the colour of a blood orange, a seething, flaming mass. Donald said he would try to get home now; Dylan stayed quietly by my side. Against the now black sky, the fires shone doubly bright. After a year of the blackout it was weird to have light again, but it was an ominous brightness. It was not my night on fire-watching duty, but I thought I should report just in case. Donald walked with me to the post a few streets away. There we learned that the London docks and neighbouring boroughs had been pounded and set on fire. No, they did not want me, but would summon me if necessary. Donald brought me to the corner and went on his way.

Inside the pub, everybody was speculating as to what had happened on this sunny, Saturday, September afternoon. Jokes were made to relieve the tension; beer mugs were put down more noisily to shut out other sounds. We were glued together by dread. All our eyes were rounder, the pupils enlarged, and although we laughed, our lips twitched with alarm.

A little before nine o'clock the siren went again, and using the fires as beacons, the Luftwaffe sent wave after wave of bombers into the holocaust, until three o'clock next morning. Poplar, Bermondsey, West Ham and other places in the East End were bombed until they resembled desolate heaps of rubble, and at least a thousand people had been killed, many others trapped, wounded and made homeless. The planes flew up the Thames, which was lit up like a horrifying pantomime, past London Bridge, Victoria, Chelsea, dropping their deadly cargo indiscriminately. Nearby the flat, a gas main was hit, and a jet of white flame shot up into the darkness like a brightly lit geyser.

We did not know it then, but the winter of the bombs, or the Blitz as it was called, had begun.

Theodora FitzGibbon

Red sky at night

George Beardmore had returned to the BBC to work in the engineering section.

Following what must have been the most dangerous and was certainly the most terrifying weekend of our joint lives we have emerged unscathed and with a feeling of triumph because our nerves are still normally responsive.

It began on the Friday night when I was roof-spotting on Broadcasting House, being one of the first to do so. The sirens were sounding so many times and the alerts lasting so long that people were spending more time in their shelters than at their desks. It was therefore decided that they should go down only when warned of imminent danger by a roof-spotter. I saw the new moon sink below the horizon, a glare over the estuary which was rumoured to be an oil-tanker on fire, bunches of searchlights spring up and vanish over different quarters of the horizon, bursts of shrapnel appear in the form of sinister little smoky flashes, and finally little bunches of flares appear in the sky, dropped by an almost inaudible plane which set out over the river and toured the outskirts via (I guessed) Dalston, Highgate, Cricklewood, Bayswater, and vanished towards King-ston-on-Thames. From one of the untidiest spectacles in the world, the roof-tops of London, under the glare of the dripping flares, became one of the most majestic. At the time we thought less of the spectacle than of the danger, but nothing happened.

The bombers followed the next afternoon (Saturday) and it was this raid which so far constitutes our greatest defeat. I was at home by then and saw the sky glowing in the southeast. A group of uneasy people were watching from the Iron Bridge which, being over the railway lines heading north and south, commanded the best view. Beyond a violent flaming sky, layered by banks of cloud, nothing could be seen, however. This turned out to be the notorious Docks fire of 7 September and was far brighter than the memorable Crystal Palace fire in 1936 which we saw from the top of Shoot-up Hill, Cricklewood, taking place on the other side of London. Promiscuous bombing did not occur until Sunday night when hospitals and cinemas and shelters, the Edgware Road and Whitechapel High Street, alike suffered terribly. That Saturday night, although we were roused time and again by the dull reverberations of falling bombs and the cannonading of anti-aircraft guns, we were only frightened by three bombs, which fell among the fields of Hall's Farm, ten minutes away.

Two notes in passing, the first that when bombs fall near Jean tells the baby so that she shouldn't be frightened: 'Oh, golly, that was a big one! I bet you – I bet you we get even *bigger* ones.' But how much she is kidded I don't know. The other aside is that when Hall's milk roundsman knocked on the door next day he said: 'My ruddy 'orse's all wore out with runnin' rahnd and rahnd.'

To continue. On the Sunday night we knew that we were for it because a tremendous barrage broke out about 8.10 p.m., all the way from Uxbridge to Wembley to Northolt, dull reddish-yellow flashes stabbing the mid-air. And again (asthma was troubling me and the din woke Victoria, who would not be pacified) we heard the racket of London being bombed. One terrific crash fetched us out of bed but we never found out what happened, and it was not repeated. On my way to work by motor-bike, taking the back streets, I was compelled to go out of my way because of craters at Neasden, where also a concrete pavement was standing on end. More craters at Cricklewood, where a poor-class house had been completely demolished, and along the Edgware Road. Here I saw two refugees who might have walked straight off the front page of the *Daily Mail* – sweaty, blowsy women with disordered hair, still grinning, although possibly they had missed by inches the death that had overtaken their friends and families.

But the greatest devastation that I saw was at Chiltern Court which now looks like an East End tenement, its windows blown out, its middle ravaged by one bomb whose twin had landed plumb on Tussaud's Cinema, scattering masonry over the Euston Road, causing Tussaud's itself to collapse, turning the adjoining mews into a shambles of bricks, coping-stones, furniture, glass, and human and wax flesh. Even the large Crown Estate residences in the Outer Circle of Regent's Park, a whole arc of them, had spewed out their glass as far as the gardens. But complete, almost matter-of-fact calm in the way the police steered traffic round the debris, the firemen stood by, the Civil Defence in steel helmets stood round a WVS mobile canteen, the blue-clad heavy-mob (Heavy Rescue) were rigging up block and tackle. This was the after-the-party scene. What sort of hell it must have been a few hours earlier is anyone's guess.

Jean and I have now finally come to rest on camp-bed and couch in the drawing-room (at the back) while Victoria lies snug in her carry-cot behind the chimney breast and protected by a book-case. As a result we spent a good night last night, heedless of the planes which were ranging up and down the Thames Valley. I am to hang wire-netting over the French windows and meanwhile I push the single mattress against them, backed by another book-case, backed by an arm-chair.

We are either wise or lucky. Fletcher hasn't slept before 2 a.m. for a week, Mrs Coleman and Clarke could not reach their desks yesterday because of bombed railway-tracks, the typists are really sick with fatigue and fright. Something's got to give – these conditions can't last.

George Beardmore

13 SEPTEMBER 1940

There is a great concentration of shipping and barges in France, and it is evident that the Cabinet expect invasion at any moment. A raid starts at about 11 a.m. I go upstairs and go on with my work. At about 12.15 I meet Walter Monckton in the passage. He whispers, 'They have just dive-bombed Buckingham Palace, and hit it three times. The King's safe.' The raid continues till about 2.30. There are delayed-action bombs in St James's Park and the whole park-side of the Foreign Office has been evacuated. I cannot find any trains at all running down to Kent and I have to give up going home. Another raid begins about 3.45. Bombs are dropping close to us in Howland Street and without warning. We go down to the dug-out. I then go up to the sixth floor and look over London. There is a triumphant double-rainbow circling the City and basing itself upon St Paul's which shines in the evening sun. At 9.15 the sirens start to yell again. It is a wonderful night with a full moon. When I get back to the M. of I. [Ministry of Information], I start typing this, and as I do so, the guns boom.

Harold Nicolson

The broadcasts of the American journalist Ed Murrow made him for many people, both in the United States and in Britain, the voice of the Blitz. Here he delineates the values for which most Britons were fighting, and presciently forecasts the post-war mood of the nation.

15 SEPTEMBER 1940

During the last week you have heard much of the bombing of Buckingham Palace and probably seen pictures of the damage. You have been told by certain editors and commentators who sit in New York that the bombing of the Palace, which has one of the best air-raid shelters in England, caused a great surge of determination – a feeling of unity – to sweep this island. The bombing was called a great psychological blunder. I do not find much support for that point of view amongst Londoners with whom I've talked. They don't like the idea of their King and Queen being bombed, but, remember, this is not the last war – people's reactions are different. Minds have become hardened and callused. It didn't require a bombing of Buckingham Palace to convince these people that they are all in this thing together. There is nothing exclusive about being bombed these days. When there are houses down in your street, when friends and relatives have been killed, when you've seen that red glow in the sky night after night, when you're tired and sleepy – there just isn't enough energy left to be outraged about the bombing of a palace.

The King and Queen have earned the respect and admiration of the nation, but so have tens of thousands of humble folk who are much less well protected. If the Palace had been the only place bombed the reaction might have been different. Maybe some of those German bomb aimers are working for Goebbels instead of Goering, but if the purpose of the bombings was to strike terror to the hearts of the Britishers then the bombs have been wasted. That fire bomb on the House of Lords passed almost unnoticed. I heard a parcel of people laughing about it when one man said: 'That particular bomb wouldn't seriously have damaged the nation's war effort.'

I'm talking about those things not because the bombing of the Palace appears to have affected America more than Britain, but in order that you may understand that this war has no relation with the last one, so far as symbols and civilians are concerned. You must understand that a world is dying, that old values, the old prejudices, and the old bases of power and prestige are going.

Edward R. Murrow

Even Downing Street was not immune from the Blitz.

One evening (October 17) stands out in my mind. We were dining in the garden-room of No. 10 when the usual night raid began. My companions were Archie Sinclair, Oliver Lyttelton, and Moore-Brabazon. The steel shutters had been closed. Several loud explosions occurred around us at no great distance, and presently a bomb fell, perhaps a hundred yards away, on the Horse Guards Parade, making a great deal of noise. Suddenly I had a providential impulse. The kitchen at No. 10 Downing Street is lofty and spacious, and looks out through a large plate-glass window about twenty-five feet high. The butler and parlourmaid continued to serve the dinner with complete detachment, but I became acutely aware of this big window, behind which Mrs Landemare, the cook, and the kitchen-maid, never turning a hair, were at work. I got up abruptly, went into the kitchen, told the butler to put the dinner on the hot plate in the dining-room, and ordered the cook and the other servants into the shelter, such as it was. I had been seated again at table only about three minutes when a really very loud crash, close at hand, and a violent shock showed that the house had been struck. My detective came into the room and said much damage had been done. The kitchen, the pantry, and the offices on the Treasury side were shattered.

We went into the kitchen to view the scene. The devastation was complete. The bomb had fallen fifty yards away on the Treasury, and the blast had smitten the large, tidy kitchen, with all its bright saucepans and crockery, into a heap of black dust and rubble. The big plate-glass window had been hurled in fragments and splinters across the room, and would of course have cut its occupants, if there had been any, to pieces. But my fortunate inspiration, which I might so easily have neglected, had come in the nick of time. The underground Treasury shelter across the court had been blown to pieces by a direct hit, and the four civil servants who were doing Home Guard night-duty there were killed.

Winston Churchill

✝

After being shot down, Richard Hillary was treated for his injuries.

At this time tannic acid was the recognised treatment for burns. The theory was that in forming a hard cement it protected the skin from the air, and encouraged it to heal up underneath. As the tannic started to crack, it was to be chipped off gradually with a scalpel, but after a few months of experience, it was discovered that nearly all pilots with third-degree burns so treated developed secondary infection and septicaemia. This caused its use to be discontinued and gave us the dubious satisfaction of knowing that we were suffering in the cause of science. Both my hands were suppurating, and the fingers were already contracting under the tannic and curling down into the palms. The risk of shock was considered too great for them to do both hands. I must have been under the anaesthetic for about fifteen minutes and in that time I saw Peter Pease killed.

He was after another machine, a tall figure leaning slightly forward with a smile at the corner of his mouth. Suddenly from nowhere a Messerschmitt was on his tail about 150 yards away. For two seconds nothing happened. I had a terrible feeling of futility. Then at the top of my voice I shouted, 'Peter, for God's sake look out behind!'

I saw the Messerschmitt open up and a burst of fire hit Peter's machine. His expression did not change, and for a moment his machine hung motionless. Then it turned slowly on its back and dived to the ground. I came to, screaming his name, with two nurses and the doctor holding me down on the bed.

'All right now. Take it easy, you're not dead yet. That must have been a very bad dream.'

I said nothing. There wasn't anything to say. Two days later I had a letter from Colin. My nurse read it to me. It was very short, hoping that I was getting better and telling me that Peter was dead.

Richard Hillary

Hillary recovered sufficiently from his burns to return to flying, but was killed in a crash in 1943.

‡

Bovril – and thoughts of escape

Commander Fritz Wentzel was one of 33 survivors from the U-32, which had been sunk north-west of Ireland on 30 October. Taken by train to his POW camp, Wentzel found himself contemplating the curious British station names and entertaining the possibility that he might give his escort the slip.

The lorry drove us to the Central Station and there we got down and were taken to a train, escorted by two officers and ten soldiers. We must have looked a strange collection and people stared at us at first, but then looked away as though they were ashamed of their curiosity. No one said an unfriendly word, no one threw stones at us, no one even looked hatefully at us. In fact some of the women even looked sympathetic. One of them pressed forward as though to speak to us but she was curtly ordered to stand back by one of our escort.

A special carriage attached to an ordinary passenger train was reserved for us. There were four officers including myself, and we were kept apart from the men. As I was senior officer I was given the honour of a special compartment to myself accompanied by two British officers. The younger officer, a lieutenant, seemed to have been a teacher in civilian life and he obviously had hard and fast ideas on certain subjects and was anxious that his superior, a captain, should share them. They forgot all about me and argued away busily. My English wasn't good enough to understand what was said and I thought I would take advantage of their preoccupation to go off on a tour of inspection, but no sooner did I get up to go out into the corridor than the captain sprang up too. I indicated that I wanted to go to the lavatory, but he insisted on accompanying me. I must have shown my disappointment and he misinterpreted it.

'I expect you're feeling a bit down-hearted,' he said in a kindly voice.

By this time I had lost count of the number of enemies who had a friendly word for me.

For the rest of the journey I sat in my corner seat and looked out at the countryside. I can't remember a great deal of it, my brain was too busy, chiefly with thoughts of escape. 'You probably won't get a better opportunity,' I thought. 'And the further you go south the more favourable it will be' – we *were* going south incidentally. As far as escaping was concerned I had a certain family tradition to live up to. My uncle Günther Plüschow – my mother's brother – had been a prisoner in England during the First World War, and succeeded in escaping and getting back to Germany through Holland. I had read his book *Der Flieger von Tsingtau* perhaps a dozen times as a youngster and I knew 'how it was done'. I was to find that there was a little more to it than just knowing.

I tried to discover where we were making for from the station names. The first one was 'Bovril'. I'd never heard of it. But when the next station was 'Bovril' too, and the one after that as well, I came to the conclusion that whatever the word 'Bovril' meant it wasn't the name of a station. Later I discovered what it was and why all the station name-boards had been removed – as part of the reception arrangements for other but rather more purposeful German visitors whose arrival was expected any day now. Nowadays when I see advertisements for Bovril I always have to grin in recollection of my first train journey on British soil.

At what time we actually crossed the border I can't say, but when night fell we were obviously in England and still rolling southwards. It was pitch dark when we finally ran slowly into a big town and came to a stop. It was London. On account of air-raids there was a pretty efficient black-out and there was very little to be seen. The captain disappeared. I looked out of the window and saw him talking excitedly to one or two figures, probably officials. Something seemed to be going not quite according to plan. Then unexpectedly the lieutenant hurried off to assist the captain and I was left alone in the gloomy compartment.

It was my chance, but it came so suddenly and unexpectedly that at first I was paralysed. Then I looked out of the window on the side away from the platform. Lines of track side by side stretched away, and just visible against the skyline were dark buildings. I went cautiously through the corridor to the door and just as I pressed down the handle it was more vigorously pressed down from the outside. It opened and a dark figure climbed in with a lamp which he shone in my face. I turned back and went into my compartment to let him go on, but I was unlucky. It was the guard and he was looking with his lamp into each compartment as he went.

'This is as far as we go, sir,' he said to me when he arrived at my compartment. 'You get out here.'

'Right you are,' I said and hoped it sounded very English. After all if one of my hosts invited me to alight it would hardly be polite not to. But as I got up from my seat again something seemed to strike him and he had another look at me in the light of his lamp. Now I don't look particularly German and I think that in the ordinary way I would pass muster as an Englishman, but unfortunately I still had that damned week-old stubble which was not yet a proper beard. It must have been that because when I tried to accept his invitation he stopped me.

'Just a minute,' he said. And at that moment the penny must have dropped, for he ran to the window and started shouting for the escort.

I could have turned tail and cleared off the way he had come, running over those lines on the other side, but then the thought of the red stubble that had betrayed me robbed me of energy. Where could I go so late at night in a strange country and without a penny to bless myself with? And with that stubble? I didn't stand an earthly – certainly not in a country where everyone was clean and neat. Break in somewhere, violence? That sort of thing wasn't my strong point. So I did nothing.

Had I known that seven years as a prisoner of war lay ahead of me I might have chanced it, though whether, even if I had, it would have made any difference is another matter. In any case, the fact remains that it was the best chance of escape I ever had and I let it go. Of course, I was still quite confident in a German victory. In three months at the latest the invasion would take place and 'of course' it would be successful.

Fritz Wentzel

After a stint in a POW camp in Canada, the author finally returned home in July 1947, six years and eight months after setting foot on British soil.

‡

The Countess of Ranfurly had, with great dash and against Army regulations, managed to make her way to Cairo to be with her soldier husband, Dan.

Around six o'clock on our second evening together, when we were playing backgammon, there came a knock on our door. A short stocky officer came in. He had rather a large head shaped like an ant-hill and quick eyes under a heavy brow. 'Lady Ranfurly,' he said, 'I hope you will forgive me for intruding but I want to see you urgently.' Fear clutched my heart – obviously I had been traced.

'How do you know my name, and who told you I was here?' I began, but he interrupted: 'I know all about your recent journey and that is why I am here. I need your help.' Dan waved him to an armchair and fetched him a drink. He went on talking in a quick deft way, with his head stuck a little forward. There was something compelling about him.

'My name', he said, 'is Wingate, Orde Wingate. I am going south in five days' time. I shall raise a revolt in Abyssinia. First I shall go to Khartoum – the Emperor is there. Then I shall drop behind the lines and stay there till, with the aid of the Abyssinians and my small force, we can overthrow the Italians. Now I want you to come as my secretary – you can type, do shorthand, cope with signals?'

I nodded.

'Can you ride, and speak French?'

I nodded again.

'You might have to be dropped by parachute – you wouldn't mind that?'

'Not if I am supplied with the right kind of underwear,' I laughed.

'Lady Ranfurly, I must have an English secretary. There are none to be found in the Middle East. Will you come and help me? Can you be ready by Tuesday? You will be back in six months.'

Hermione Ranfurly

The author decided not to take up Wingate's offer. She subsequently worked in the Cairo office of SOE. Orde Wingate would later develop his ideas on irregular warfare in Burma.

Winter 1940–41

Britain Confronts Italy

In September 1940, the Tenth Italian Army had invaded Egypt and had pushed back the numerically inferior British Western Desert Force. Having been reinforced, however, by the arrival of new Matilda tanks, Sir Archibald Wavell, the Commander-in-Chief Middle East, made plans for a surprise attack on the Italians in early December at Sidi Barrani.

By far the most valuable aid in this campaign of secrecy was the misjudgement of the enemy. All the Fascists knew of the British army at this time was that it had retreated before the Germans in Belgium, Norway and France, and before the Italians in British Somaliland and the Western Desert. To the Italians in December 1940 it was inconceivable that the British could really seriously attack. They were on the defensive and had been all along. Moreover there was an interior rottenness in the Italian Intelligence, something that grew naturally out of the national weakness for exaggeration. There is, as anyone who has lived in Italy will know, nothing especially unethical in this desire to enlarge and aggrandise and embroider. Nearly every Italian I have met has a passion and a talent for bombast and display. He just can't help himself. It is a foible that has led many people into the error of believing the Italian is stupid, which he certainly is not. He proceeds with cold unsentimental logic in his inner reasoning, and makes allowances for the colourful descriptions of his friends and indeed for his own embroideries. He expects exaggerations in himself and everyone else. Nor has this in any way diminished the Italian genius for design and logic. Exaggeration never, as far as I could see, deterred the Italian from reaching decisions as well as anyone else in peace-time. But in war everything is different. Information becomes a commodity in itself. It has to be as exact as the cornerstone of a building or the barrel of a gun. And you could not overnight cure the individualistic Italian lieutenant and captain of his boastfulness.

Alan Moorehead

The Italian position at Sidi Barrani, about 250 miles from Cairo, was protected by a series of fortified camps including that at Nibeiwa, but when this was attacked by the heavily armoured Matildas, it was quickly overrun and its commander, General Maletti, was killed.

Here and there before the breaches in the walls a dead man lay spread-eagled on the ground, or collapsed grotesquely at the entrance of his dugout under a gathering cloud of flies. Some sixty or seventy mules and donkeys, recovered now from their shock at the noise of battle, nosed mournfully and hopelessly among the debris in search of fodder and water. Finding none, they would lift their heads and bray pathetically into the heavy dust-laden air. Italian light tanks were grouped at the spot on the western wall where they had huddled for a last stand and there surrendered. Others had bolted inside the fort itself and were turned this way and that, indicating how they had sought at the last moment for some formation to meet the attack. Maletti's body covered with a beribboned tunic still lay sprawled on the threshold of his tent, his beard stained with sand and sweat.

Sand was blowing now out of the immense ruts cut up by the tanks, and, walking through it, we went from one tent to another, from one dugout by subterranean passage into the next. Extraordinary things met us wherever we turned. Officers' beds laid out with clean sheets, chests of drawers filled with linen and abundance of fine clothing of every kind. Uniforms heavy with gold lace and decked with the medals and colours of the parade ground hung upon hangers in company with polished jack-boots richly spurred and pale blue sashes and belts finished with great tassels and feathered and embroidered hats and caps. An Indian came running to us through the camp with one of those silver and gilt belts – a gaudy shining thing that the Fascists sling around their shoulders on parade. We came on great blue cavalry cloaks that swathed a man to the ankles, and dressing-tables in the officers' tents were strewn with scents and silver-mounted brushes and small arms made delicately in the romantic northern arsenals of Italy.

We sat down on the open sand and ate from stores of bottled cherries and greengages; great tins of frozen hams and anchovies; bread that had been baked somehow here in the desert; and wines from Frascati and Falerno and Chianti, red and white, and Lacrimae Christi from the slopes of Vesuvius above Naples. There were wooden casks of a sweet, heady, fruity brandy, and jars of liqueurs of other kinds wrapped carefully in

envelopes of straw. For water the Italians took bottles of Recoaro minerals
– the very best in Italy – and these, like everything else, had been carted
out to them in hundreds of cases across a thousand miles of sea and desert
by ship and car and mule team.

The spaghetti was packed in long blue paper packages and stored with
great sacks of macaroni and other wheat foods as numerous as they used
to be in the shops of Italy before the war. Parmesan cheeses as big as small
cart-wheels and nearly a foot thick lay about in neat piles except where
some hungry soldier had slashed one open with his sword. Ten-pound
tins of Estratto di Pomodoro – the tomato extract vital to so many Italian
dishes – formed the bulk of the tinned stuff, which also contained many
excellent stews and delicate tinned tongue and tunny fish and small round
tins of beef. The vegetables were of every kind. Potatoes, onions, carrots,
beans, cabbages, leeks, cauliflowers, pumpkin and many other things had
been steamed down into a dry compact that readily expanded to its old
volume when soaked in warm water – a fine food for the desert. We
sampled one package that seemed at first to contain dry grass, but brewed
itself over a stove into a rich minestrone soup.

I stepped down into at least thirty dugouts, coming upon something
new and surprising in every one. The webbing and leatherwork was of
the finest; the uniforms well cut and of solid material such as the civilian
in Italy had not seen for many months. Each soldier appeared to have been
supplied with such gadgets as sewing-bags and little leather cases for his
letters and personal kit. The water containers were of new improved
design – both the aluminium tanks that strap on the shoulders and those
that one fastened to the flanks of a mule or stowed in a lorry. And over
everything, wherever I went, fell a deepening layer of sand.

Alan Moorehead

*By 11 December, more than 38,000 Italians had been taken prisoner around Sidi
Barrani for the loss of just 625 British troops. Wavell's success demonstrated that,
unlike his opponents, he had appreciated that the desert could only be fought in on
its own terms. The routed Italians were soon thrust out of both Egypt and eastern
Libya, causing Hitler to send reinforcements to his ally – the Afrika Korps.*

*The Italians' confidence had also been undermined by raids on their supply lines
and depots far behind the front. These were carried out by the Long Range Desert
Group, whose patrols went where the Italians would not. In January 1941, together*

*with Free French troops from Chad led by Lt-Col. d'Ornano, they attacked an
Italian fort at the Murzuk oasis.*

Lunch over, we set off to finish the last two miles of the journey which
had begun in Cairo eighteen days and 1500 miles before. Clayton led in
his 15-cwt, then Hewson with one troop of T patrol, and then the rest –
a quiet procession of cars, down the scarp on which we had halted, through
some broken ground, over a low ridge and into the outskirts of the
town. I wondered if the Italians had had the foresight to put even one
machine-gun post on the Sebha road. Luckily they had not, and we had
achieved the advice of their own Machiavelli:

'Those enterprises are best which can be concealed up to the moment of their
fulfilment.'

The road seemed to lead to the fort so Clayton followed it. At a well by
the roadside a group of natives gave the Fascist salute and cried 'Bon
giorno'. A little farther Clayton overtook Signor Colicchia, the postmaster,
bicycling towards the fort, and hustled the terrified official into his car as
a guide. Ahead I could now see the fort, partly hidden by trees and with
some after-lunch strollers around it. The surprise was complete.

Then things began to happen. Hewson swung off the road to the left
and opened fire on the strollers; the Guards turned to the right and started
to engage the fort. I was with Bruce Ballantyne with the other half of T
patrol who were to tackle the airfield. The hangar was now out of sight,
so from a group of natives outside a hut I seized a Sudani for a guide and
pushed him on to the truck. No doubt he thought he was going to be
murdered and he was paler than I should have thought a black man could
be. He was too scared to speak and soon fell off, but by now we could see
the hangar and were racing to beat the landing ground guards to their
machine-gun posts. Bruce with two trucks got there first and most of them
surrendered without firing, but he killed the last man, still fumbling with
his rifle, with a quick shot through the head.

Out of the corner of my eye during this confusion I had seen Clayton's
car crossing the aerodrome and wondered how he had got there. A few
minutes later he joined us with his car full of bullet holes and d'Ornano's
body in the back. Round the corner of the hangar he had run into a
machine-gun post which one of the bolder Italians had manned. Beside
him, in the front seat, Adams's Vickers gun had jammed, and before
Clayton could slam the gears into reverse d'Ornano on the back had been

killed with a bullet through the throat and also an Italian Air Force sergeant whom Clayton, having handed over the postmaster, had roped in as another guide. No doubt the Italians thought we had shot him in cold blood, but this is the truth about his death.

We got the Bofors going on to the gun post and the hangar and before long the twenty odd Italians had had enough of it and one of them appeared on the roof waving a white flag. Three dead or dying Libyans and one wounded Italian were their casualties. In the middle of it all I remember seeing, shuffling with half-bent knees across the landing ground, that so familiar African sight, a string of old women carrying firewood bundles on their heads.

Meanwhile at the fort, where Hewson had been killed and Wilson and three other men wounded, the patrols were successfully containing the garrison and a lucky mortar bomb had set the tower ablaze and burnt the flag and flagstaff. In the middle of the attack a touring car drove up to the gate. In it was the Italian commander who had probably been out to lunch and also, as some said afterwards, a woman and child. One shell from the Guards Bofors put an end to them; it was unfortunate about the woman and the child but people should arrange their lunch parties more carefully.

Bill Kennedy-Shaw

✝

Enduring the Blitz

In big cities the moon is hardly noticed amidst the tall buildings, yet we became moon-conscious. A full moon, previously welcome in the blackout, as it bathed everything in clear light, was dreaded, for it meant a raid with three to four hundred planes, and was known as a 'bomber's moon'. We learned to look at the heavens as well as the gutter, for both could be treacherous. Certain unusual sounds became immediately identifiable: the noise like iron bedsteads rattling as if thrown from a height betokened a canister of incendiary bombs, and the sound as of heavy surf breaking on shingle meant heavy lorries driving over a solid bed of broken glass. A whole new vocabulary opened up: UXBs, unexploded bombs; DAs, delayed-action bombs; canisters, not tea-caddies but containers full of incendiary bombs; an 'incident' was not a trivial thing any more, but a badly bombed building; rest centres, a euphemism for a bare room where you were given a cup of tea after being bombed; stirrup pumps; chandeliers, which were multiple flares dropped before a bomb; siren suits – one-piece garments zipped up the front, worn during raids, so that one was fully dressed; and blast, no longer a mild swear-word, but the shock-waves caused by detonation of explosives.

Despite all the horrors, the Blitz was not entirely destructive, for it produced a marked change in the attitude of British people to one another. Experiencing a common danger made for a friendliness, almost a love, amongst total strangers. People were concerned with helping their neigh-bours: there was a joke or a laugh to keep their spirits up, and a sharing of scarce commodities. The last pinch of tea, or a bottle of whisky, was offered by people one had never seen before and might never see again. Everybody was in love with life and living. In apartment houses, the owner of the basement rooms expected to share his or her bedroom with perhaps five or six people of mixed sexes. Once you have lain on a bed, even platonically, with someone for several months, it is impossible to ignore them thereafter. A painter friend of mine, Francis Butterfield, told me he would miss his oddly assorted harem when the bombing stopped. Men felt masculine for, whatever some women might say, it was with the male sex they felt safest.

Social and sexual distinctions were swept away and, when a dramatic change such as that takes place, it never goes back in quite the same way. Whatever dreariness and anxiety the middle-aged and old people felt, for the young it was undeniably exciting and stimulating. It was God's gift to naughty girls, for from the moment the sirens went, they were not expected to get home until morning when the 'all clear' sounded. In fact, they were urged to stay where they were. When it came to the pinch, where their parents were concerned, fate was far preferable to death. Certain restaurants, such as Hatchett's and the Hungaria, and all hotels provided beds for their customers. Girls went out for dinner with their night attire, toothbrushes and make-up. Young people were reluctant to contemplate death without having shared their bodies with someone else. It was sex at its sweetest: not for money or marriage, but for love of being alive and wanting to give. Many married hastily when love was kindled by flames, and many of those marriages are today still snug in their happy philo-progenitive cocoons. An interesting point is that crime and nervous dis-orders actually declined throughout this tense period.

Instinct or intuition played a singular part in one's daily life, and it was unwise to ignore it. If you felt 'safe' in a certain place, you went there regularly. During a bad raid I usually had this feeling in the Six Bells and,

when that closed, in a basement drinking club called The Gateways in
Bramerton Street. There were several of these late drinking clubs in
Chelsea (late meant until 11.30 p.m.): The Studio, next to the Town Hall,
the Pheasantry, and one in a private house in Upper Cheyne Row called,
appropriately, the Crater Club! The raids were very bad in Chelsea before
and after Christmas: the weather was beastly cold, food scarce, and what
festivity there was took place in the pubs. But this after-Christmas night I
wanted to stay home, read by the fire, and finish the remains of the meagre
Christmas food and drink.

The anti-aircraft guns rattled the windows and the clear, frosty air
intensified the whine of the bombs, which were very close. The German
bombers liked clear, frosty nights. Although not heavy smokers, when a
raid was bad we chain-smoked, and by ten o'clock were down to our last.
The pub next door was shut, for it was closing time, and the old couple
who ran it never gave a moment overtime, so there was nothing for it but
to walk up to the slot machine in the King's Road. Peter offered to go,
but on those nights I preferred to be with him. Luckily we had a shilling,
for twenty Player's cigarettes were 11½d, the halfpenny change being
enclosed in the packet. The night was bright with a full moon, searchlights
and the now customary glow of fires. Large pieces of shrapnel were clearly
visible on the pavements as we walked up Glebe Place. The King's Road
was full of activity: clanging ambulances, fire-engines and wardens racing
up towards the Town Hall. We hurried on to find a cordon around the
Six Bells, and massive chunks of heavy masonry on the ground. The front
part upstairs had been hit, and toppled into both the road and the garden
a matter of minutes before closing time. People were trapped in the back.
We helped to clear the rubble and brick; it was hard work and made us
hot, despite the cold. A small entrance was made and the stretcher bearers,
wardens and war reserve police went through. The lights still blazed, and
someone yelled, 'Turn that bloody light off!'

Several dazed but unhurt people were led out by torchlight; one had a
bottle of brandy which was passed round, and we all had a swig. Some
were 'regulars' who recognised us. The one with the purloined bottle said
jauntily:

'What happened to you tonight that you didn't cop this lot?'

There were more inside, trapped, probably dead, as they had been
sitting near the front door. Curly, the Irish barman, had gone down to the
cellar and was found, his rimless spectacles still on his snub nose, but he
was stone dead, an unbroken bottle in his hand. Almost-full pints of beer
were standing unspilt on tables in front of customers who stared at them

with unseeing eyes, for they too were dead from the blast. Similar occurrences happened every day all over London, and one learned never to persuade anyone against their will to go to a certain place.

It was towards the end of this same Christmas week that the great fire and bombing raid on the City of London took place, when the Guildhall, eight beautiful Wren churches, Guy's Hospital and hundreds of office buildings were hit, but as it was on Sunday, the latter were mercifully empty. Fire watchers saw twenty-eight incendiary bombs fall on the roof of St Paul's Cathedral, and bounce off the dome. One was blazing, and miraculously fell outwards, where it was extinguished. Indeed, amidst the wall of flame and smoke the only clear sky was around the cathedral. Londoners with a new-found love of their city watched its survival from rooftops both near and far away. With tears running down their cheeks, they said in one voice:

'The old church stood it . . .'

There was also a macabre sort of humour: a government notice told us to beware of toffee tins with a tartan design bearing the name of a well-known caterer, and also to look for a bomb with a spring which jumped out like a jack-in-the-box, and could blow off a limb. It had the delicate name of 'butterfly bomb'. One windy night, Arthur Mallett, a helper at my fire-watching station, told us of a weird, scraping, dome-like 'thing' which had chased him up Old Church Street. As he ran, so did it, faster and still faster. He turned the first corner he came to, and saw it race on about fifty yards, then stop in the middle of the street. He waited for some minutes to see if it exploded then, curiosity getting the better of him, he cautiously approached the demonic device. In the clear moonlight, he saw it was a dustbin lid.

'You can laugh at it now,' he said, 'but by Christ, I never did then.'

Theodora FitzGibbon

The American war correspondent Ernie Pyle became known for his accounts of the experiences of ordinary servicemen. In January 1941, he turned his gaze to those Londoners sheltering from the bombing in Liverpool Street underground station.

On benches on each side, as though sitting and lying on a long street-car seat, were the people, hundreds of them. And as we walked on they stretched into thousands.

In addition, there was a row of sleeping forms on the wooden floor of the tube, stretched crosswise. Their bodies took up the whole space, so we had to watch closely when we put our feet down between the sleepers.

Many of these people were old – wretched and worn old people, people who had never known many of the good things of life and who were now winding up their days on this earth in desperate discomfort.

They were the bundled-up, patched-up people with lined faces that we have seen for years sitting dumbly in waiting lines at our own relief offices at home.

There were children too, some asleep and some playing. There were youngsters in groups, laughing and talking and even singing.

There were smart-alecks and there were quiet ones. There were hard-working people of middle age who had to rise at 5 and go to work.

Some people sat knitting or playing cards or talking. But mostly they just sat. And though it was only 8 o'clock, many of the old people were already asleep.

It was the old people who seemed so tragic. Think of yourself at 70 or 80, full of pain and of the dim memories of a lifetime that has probably all been bleak. And then think of yourself now, travelling at dusk every night to a subway station, wrapping your ragged overcoat about your old shoulders and sitting on a wooden bench with your back against a curved steel wall. Sitting there all night, in nodding and fitful sleep.

Think of that as your destiny – every night, every night from now on.

Ernie Pyle

Architect Andrew Butler was given the job of inspecting damaged houses for the London borough of Chelsea.

Number 79B – that is the sort of number this house had – was uninhabited. Unlike most houses left empty, its front door was not locked because it had been split nearly in half by the adjoining explosion. It was easy therefore to put my arm in to reach the handle inside. But it was the sort of knob which turns round four or five times and then falls off. So I kicked the door and it flew half-open and stuck – due to the fact that a mat, some floorboards, and a lot of plaster had created an obstacle. I got over this rather burstingly and went into the front room. The floor and most of the furniture were entirely covered with broken glass and powdered plaster, mixed. Bits of glass were sticking in the back wall of the room. One of them jagged my sleeve. The marble surrounding the fire was lying in a heap of soot from the chimney; and the overmantel had thrown its vases under the sofa opposite. All the middle of the ceiling had come down, including the usual heavy plaster ornament and converted gas bracket. They were in a heap on the table, mixed with harmonium music and cake. The thin partition-wall next to the hall had burst open and knocked two fat stuffed birds off a shelf. The windows were voids with ragged edges and a lot of the recent rain had blown through them, soaking the armchair which had since frozen stiff. Perhaps the dreariest things of all were the torn blue blinds, hanging in shreds with dried mud from the road on them. But, as so often happens, several pictures were still hanging – one even with its glass unbroken. I put it straight.

The kitchen and other back rooms were merely squalid. A horrid mixture of glass and broken chairs, old pots, unwashed dishes and a clock lying face downwards on a bowler-hat. Plaster everywhere, in lumps and slabs and dirty powder. But the stairs were rather unusual. I suppose a tank in the roof had poured its water down them. Then, with the fierce frost of the last two days, the dying cascade had frozen and each step was a glacier. I fell over twice going up, and a long icicle from the landing hit my teeth because I failed to see it in the semi-darkness. It was not even a clean icicle but a grubby-coloured one. And the bedrooms were much the same. There was every sign of a very hurried exit. Jumbled beds with frozen sheets, clothes and shoes and handbags flung about. Half a perambulator lay by a window which had fallen in – frame and all – on top of it. The tipped-up little gas cooker had a triumphant foot through a gramophone record. And so on to the top, where the wrecking was worse. The roof was nearly uncovered. Its slates were in the beds and the cistern dangled by a feeble pipe above a squashed water-closet. Two chimney-pots had crashed against the landing banisters and pushed them over. The floors were frozen slush on slimy lino. The back wall was gone completely and the floors jutted and drooped in space. A child's doll lay on the brink, with its head off and its skirt blown up, showing its legs.

Andrew Butler

‡

The psychology of attack

In East Africa, the Italians had been pushed back to their strong defensive position near Keren, in Eritrea.

As the war went on, I grew interested in the psychology of attack and defence. However strong the defences or forlorn a hope the assault may look, the attack has the initiative and the psychological advantage, but only as long as the momentum is kept going. When it falters, the defence realises that the attack may fail, the advantage passes and the attack almost certainly will fail. There is no problem when the assault is a ram-stam affair of a single rush, but nearly every attack involves some sort of regrouping or change of line, even down to the lowly level of the platoon. With seasoned troops, this can be done without loss of momentum, even if at the moment no one is actually moving forward, but when the soldiers or their junior leaders are inexperienced and bewildered the pause to regroup can be fatal to success. This is not just due to the fact that if one goes to ground under fire, it requires a real effort of will to stand up again; it is also because in all the noise and danger of action one is inclined to think the worst. Any pause therefore can be taken by raw troops as a sign that the attack has already failed, where old sweats will sit tight until the next command reaches them.

Peter Cochrane

By the late spring of 1941 the Italians would be defeated in Eritrea and Somaliland, while Wingate's guerrilla force would enable Abyssinia's emperor, Haile Selassie, to return to the throne wrested from him by Mussolini in 1936.

‡

Greek fire

In October 1940, the Italian forces which had been occupying Albania for 18 months invaded Greece. They were repulsed, and by February 1941 had been driven back into Albania by soldiers such as Mikia Pezas.

On the seventh of February, the captain ordered our platoon to reconnoitre the ridge of the mountain to the north of the peak. It was a mild foggy day and the visibility was poor. We crossed to the other side of the forest and for nearly four hours we climbed up a narrow gorge till we reached a small plateau, half the size of a football field. It was surrounded by almost perfectly hemispherical hills, the tops of which faded in the fog. Lieutenant Floros ordered us to fix our bayonets and cross the plateau in extended order, ready for action at any moment.

'Open your eyes wide and don't walk like jaywalkers in Athens,' Panagos said to me. 'This isn't Constitution Square.'

I opened my eyes wide and walked on, looking carefully around me, but famished as I was I could not help thinking the surrounding hills looked like huge *kourambiedes* [shortbread biscuits]. I wondered how long it would take us to eat the opposite hill. But could an army feed solely on *kourambiedes*? Why not? They were very nourishing; they contained flour, walnuts, butter, eggs . . .

The sudden rattle of automatic rifles made me stop short.

'Go get them, boys! Charge uphill — there's no way back!' Floros shouted.

A tremendous cry of '*Aera!*' broke out. Everyone rushed ahead yelling. For a moment I stood open-mouthed, unable to realise what was going on.

'*Aeeraa!*' resounded all over the plateau.

I was swept forward. I ran, I yelled. For how long I could not tell. There was no time, no space; only movement and yelling. The yelling was our motive power. We scampered up the hill from all sides like wild goats. My throat hurt. I ducked my head and swallowed and stumbled, but I did not fall. Others stumbled and fell and did not get up again. In the midst I saw a parapet of rocks along the top of the hill. The barrel of an automatic rifle fired in my direction. I dropped on the snow and crawled to a rock behind which Mitso and another man had taken cover. It was big enough for three men to shoot from behind it on their knees. I shoved Mitso and he made room for me.

'What are we to do? Where's Panagos?' I asked.

'Shoot!' he replied.

I knelt behind the rock and loaded my rifle. The parapet of the Italians was at a distance of not more than thirty or forty yards, but in the prevailing mist I could see only the protruding barrels of some rifles. I aimed at them and fired. I fired again and again. I felt pleased with myself. I felt full of energy. I was doing something. I was fighting.

Someone tugged at my belt. I turned around. It was Panagos, crouching behind me.

'Go back; hand grenades,' he said, emptying the pockets of his coat. 'You two also,' he said to the others.

We crawled back and lay flat on the snow behind Panagos. He took seven grenades out of his pockets.

'Be ready to charge when the last one is thrown,' he said and picked up a hand grenade.

He knelt on his right knee and leaned back.

'This one is for Musso,' he said and the grenade flew over his head.

I saw it go up and up like a tennis ball, then it started down and I lost sight of it. The explosion filled my heart with joy. Panagos picked up another.

'This is for his sissy of a son-in-law . . .'

Again a grenade flew up. Panagos was a master. Not even Tilden could lob so well.

'. . . and this is for bottom-faced Bruno; and this for Marshal Prassa; and this for Cavallero . . .'

His voice was exultant. He turned around. His eyes shone like a madman's.

'Get ready!' he said. 'The last one is for Edda' [Mussolini's daughter].

We got on our knees, ready to rush forward. I shook all over with excitement. The explosion of Edda's grenade was the pistol shot of the race. We darted off; yet we were not the first. Some others to our left had outdistanced us. I saw them jump over the parapet. One of them was Kyriako. I saw him thrust his bayonet downwards. I vaulted over the parapet by his side. His bayonet was deep in a man's chest.

'I pierced him through, God bless me,' he said.

He stepped on the man's shoulder and pulled the bayonet out with a jerk. Scorpions were biting the wounded man's face. Blood flowed from his breast and mouth. I knelt beside him. His broad, black eyes stared at me as if I were Death. I felt cold. I felt like being kind to him.

'*Voglie qualche cosa*?' I asked.

His eyes opened wider as though he wished to speak through them. His lips moved several times but I heard no sound.

'Luisa,' he finally murmured and his eyes became glassy.

Mikia Pezas

Spring 1941

The War at Sea

Countering the U-boats

In early March 1941, the nemesis of the Royal Oak, Gunther Prien's U-47, was destroyed. Later that month two more U-boats were sunk. Here, the captain of Walker recounts how U-99 and U-100 became the first submarines to be defeated with the aid of sonar.

For half an hour later we gained contact with a certain U-boat. Our prey had not been 'killed'; he was, in fact, sneaking back towards the convoy, still bent on attack.

Recalling *Vanoc* to assist in the hunt, we set about our target with a series of carefully aimed patterns of depth-charges.

Taking it in turns to run in to the attack, pattern after pattern of depth-charges went down as we tried to get one to within the lethal range of twenty feet of our target. But he was a wily opponent and, dodging and twisting in the depths, he managed to escape destruction though heavily damaged.

Soon the waters became so disturbed by the repeated explosions, each one of which sent back an echo to the Asdic's sound beam, that we could no longer distinguish our target from the other echoes and a lull in the fight was forced upon us.

I had for some time past noticed in the distance the bobbing lights from the lifeboats of one of our sunken ships, but with an enemy to engage there was nothing for it but to harden my heart and hope that the time might come later when I could rescue the crews. This lull seemed a good opportunity and perhaps if we left the area temporarily the U-boat commander might think he had shaken us off and be tempted into some indiscretion. So, the *Vanoc* steaming round us in protection, we stopped and picked up the master and thirty-seven of the crew of the SS *J. B. White*.

This completed, the time was ripe to head quietly back to where the U-boat had last been located and perhaps catch him licking his wounds on the surface.

We had hardly got under way when I noticed that *Vanoc* was drawing ahead fast and thought perhaps she had misread the signal ordering the speed to be maintained. As I ordered a signal to be made to her, Yeoman of Signals Gerrard said, 'She's signalling to us, sir, but I can't read it as her light is flickering so badly.' I realised that *Vanoc* must be going ahead at her full speed and being, like *Walker*, an old veteran, her bridge would be shaking and rattling as her 30,000 hp drove her forward through the Atlantic swell.

Rupert Bray, on the bridge beside me, said, 'She must have sighted the U-boat.' Even as he spoke, *Vanoc* came on the air with his radio telephone, with the laconic signal: 'Have rammed and sunk U-boat.'

What a blissful moment that was for us, the successful culmination of a long and arduous fight. Something in the way of revenge for our losses in the convoy had been achieved.

There was a grim joy on board *Walker*, and not least amongst the merchant seamen from the *J. B. White*, who felt they had a personal score to settle. But for the moment our part was confined to circling *Vanoc* in protection, while she picked up the few survivors from the U-boat and examined herself for damage. We were glad of this breathing space, as, with all the depth-charges carried on the upper deck expended, the depth-charge party, led by Leading Seaman Prout, were struggling to hoist up more of these awkward heavy loads from the magazine, with the ship rolling in the Atlantic swell, and often with water swirling round their waists. They were not a moment too soon, for, as we circled *Vanoc*, I was electrified to hear the Asdic operator Able Seaman Blackhouse excitedly reporting, 'Contact, contact.' But I could hardly credit it, for not only was it unbelievable that in all the wide wastes of the Atlantic a second U-boat should turn up just where another had gone to the bottom, but I knew that there were sure to be areas of disturbed water persisting in the vicinity from our own and *Vanoc*'s wakes. The echo was not very clear and I expressed my doubts to John Langton, but Blackhouse was not to be disheartened. 'Contact, definitely submarine,' he reported, and as I listened to the ping the echo sharpened and there could be no further doubt. With a warning to the men aft to get any charges ready that they had managed to hoist into the throwers and rails, we ran into the attack. It was a great test for John Langton, for, with the maddening habit of the beautiful instruments of precision provided for us, they all elected to break down at the crucial moment. But much patient drill against just such an emergency now brought its reward. Timing his attack by the most primitive methods Langton gave the order to fire. A pattern of six depth-charges – all that could be got ready in time – went down. As they exploded, *Walker* ran on to get sea-room to turn for further attacks, but as we turned came the thrilling signal from *Vanoc* – 'U-boat surfaced astern of me.'

A searchlight beam stabbed into the night from *Vanoc*, illuminating the submarine U-99 which lay stopped. The guns' crews in both ships sprang into action and the blinding flashes from the four-inch guns and tracers from the smaller weapons made a great display, though I fear their accuracy was not remarkable. Destroyer night gunnery in such a mêlée is apt to be pretty wild and in those days, when flashless cordite was not issued to us, each salvo left one temporarily blinded. In *Walker* confusion soon reigned around the guns, for the enthusiasm of our guests from *J. B. White* knew no bounds. Joining up with the ammunition supply parties, shells came up at such a phenomenal rate that the decks were piled high with them till the guns' crews were hardly able to work their guns. But fortunately we were able very soon to cease fire as a signal lamp flashing from the U-boat, 'We are sinking,' made it clear that the action was over. Keeping end on to the U-boat in case he still had some fight left, we prepared to lower a boat in case there was a chance of a capture, but even as we did so the crew of the U-boat abandoned ship and she plunged to the bottom.

I manoeuvred *Walker* to windward of the swimming Germans and as we drifted down on to them, they were hauled on board. Some of them were in the last stages of exhaustion from the cold of those icy northern waters by the time we got them on board. Some indeed would never have made safety had not Leading Seaman Prout gone over the side fully clothed to aid them.

The last to come over the side was obviously the captain, as he swam to *Walker* still wearing his brass-bound cap. We were soon to find out that we had made indeed a notable capture, for the captain was Otto Kretschmer, leading ace of the U-boat arm, holder of the Knight's Cross with Oak Leaves and top scorer in terms of tonnage sunk.

Donald Macintyre

Kretschmer was indeed a notable prisoner since he had sunk 47 ships. He was to receive the additional award of the Swords to his Knight's Cross at the end of 1941, the decoration being smuggled into his POW camp and presented to him there.

The Battle of Cape Matapan

On 26 March, the Italian fleet entered the Aegean intending to thwart British efforts to supply Greece. Commanded by Admiral Iachino, the force consisted of one battleship – the Vittorio Veneto *– eight cruisers and thirteen destroyers. The following day the Italians attempted to engage a British supply fleet. However, a large contingent under Admiral Cunningham was approaching from Egypt and, on the 28th, aircraft from the* Formidable *torpedoed both the* Vittorio Veneto *and the cruiser* Pola. *The search continued in the dark for the wounded Italian fleet, and at about 10 o'clock the* Valiant *reported radar contact. Cunningham was on the* Warspite *when he heard the news.*

It must have been the Fleet gunnery officer, Commander Geoffrey Barnard, who gave the final order to open fire. One heard the 'ting-ting-ting' of the firing gongs. Then came the great orange flash and the violent shudder as the six big guns bearing were fired simultaneously. At the very same instant the destroyer *Greyhound*, on the screen, switched her searchlight on to one of the enemy cruisers, showing her momentarily up as a silvery-blue shape in the darkness. Our searchlights shone out with the first salvo, and provided full illumination for what was a ghastly sight. Five out of the six hit a few feet below the level of the cruiser's upper deck and burst with splashes of brilliant flame. The Italians were quite unprepared. The guns were trained fore and aft. They were helplessly shattered before they could put up any resistance. In the midst of all this there was one milder diversion. Captain Douglas Fisher, the captain of the *Warspite*, was a gunnery officer of note. When he saw the first salvo hit he was heard to say in a voice of wondering surprise: 'Good Lord! We've hit her!'

The *Valiant*, astern of us, had opened fire at the same time. She also had found her target, and when the *Warspite* shifted to the other cruiser I watched the *Valiant* pounding her ship to bits. Her rapidity of fire astonished me. Never would I have believed it possible with these heavy guns. The *Formidable* had hauled out of the line to starboard; but astern of the *Valiant* the *Barham* was also heavily engaged.

The plight of the Italian cruisers was indescribable. One saw whole turrets and masses of other heavy debris whirling through the air and splashing into the sea, and in a short time the ships themselves were nothing but glowing torches and on fire from stem to stern.

Our searchlights were still on, and just after 10.30 three Italian destroyers, which had apparently been following their cruisers, were seen coming in on our port bow. They turned, and one was seen to fire torpedoes, so the battle fleet was turned ninety degrees together to starboard to avoid them. Our destroyers were engaging, and the whole party was inextricably mixed up. The *Warspite* fired both fifteen-inch and six-inch at the enemy. To my horror I saw one of our destroyers, the *Havock*, straddled by our fire, and in my mind wrote her off as a loss. The *Formidable* also had an escape. When action was joined she hauled out to starboard at full speed, a night battle being no place for a carrier. When she was about five miles away she was caught in the beam of the *Warspite*'s searchlight sweeping on the disengaged side in case further enemy ships were present. We heard the six-inch control officer of the starboard battery get his guns on to her, and were only just in time to stop him from opening fire.

The four destroyers, *Stuart*, Captain H. M. L. Waller, Royal Australian Navy; *Greyhound*, Commander W. R. Marshall-A'Deane; *Havock*, Lieutenant G. R. G. Watkins; and *Griffin*, Lieutenant-Commander J. Lee-Barber, in company with the battle fleet were then ordered to finish off the enemy cruisers, while the battle fleet collected the *Formidable* and withdrew to the northward to keep out of their way. According to their own reports the destroyers' movements were difficult to follow; but they had a wild night and sank at least one other enemy destroyer.

At 10.45 we saw very heavy gun-fire, with star-shell and tracer, to the south-westward. Since none of our ships was on that bearing it seemed to us that either the Italians were engaging each other, or that the destroyers of our striking force might be going in to attack. Just after 11 p.m. I made a signal ordering all forces not engaged in sinking the enemy to withdraw to the north-eastward. The objects of what I now consider to have been an ill-considered signal were to give our destroyers who were mopping up a free hand to attack any sizable ship they saw, and to facilitate the assembly of the fleet next morning. The message was qualified by an order to Captain Mack and his eight destroyers of the striking force, now some twenty miles ahead, not to withdraw until he had attacked. However it had the unfortunate effect of causing Vice-Admiral Pridham-Wippell to cease his efforts to gain touch with the *Vittorio Veneto*.

Just after midnight the *Havock*, after torpedoing a destroyer and finishing her off by gun-fire, reported herself in contact with a battleship near the position where we had been in action. The battleship was Captain Mack's main objective, and the *Havock*'s report brought Mack's destroyer striking force back hot-foot from their position nearly sixty miles to the westward. An hour later, however, the *Havock* amended her report to say that it was not a battleship she had sighted but an eight-inch cruiser. Soon after 3 a.m. she sent a further message reporting herself close to the *Pola*, and, as all her torpedoes had been fired, Watkins asked whether 'to board or blow off her stern with depth-charges'.

The *Havock* had already been joined by the *Greyhound* and *Griffin*, and when Captain Mack arrived he took the *Jervis* alongside the *Pola*. That ship was in a state of indescribable confusion. Panic-stricken men were leaping over the side. On the crowded quarterdeck, littered with clothing, personal belongings and bottles, many of the sailors were drunk. There was no order or discipline of any sort, and the officers were powerless to enforce it. Having taken off the crew, Mack sank the ship with torpedoes. The *Pola*, of course, was the vessel reported by Pridham-Wippell and the *Valiant* between nine and ten the night before as lying stopped on the port side of our fleet's line of advance. She had not been under gun-fire or fired a gun, but had been torpedoed and completely crippled by one of the aircraft from the *Formidable* during the dusk attack.

Her sinking at 4.10 a.m. was the final act of the night's proceedings.

Andrew Cunningham

The Italians lost five warships and 3,000 men at Matapan. The British lost a single aircraft.

‡

Recruitment and Training

Selecting agents

The Special Operations Executive (SOE) was set up by the British to organise and carry out acts of subversion in Axis-occupied territory. Maurice Buckmaster, chief of its French section, details the qualities they looked for in potential agents.

Recruiting was, at first, rather a haphazard affair. From M.I. [Military Intelligence] we received details of officers or other ranks whose language qualifications appeared, on paper at any rate, to justify investigation. We found that the phrase 'fluent French' was not by any means always justified as an attribution. Language was, naturally, the first and vital hurdle. Schoolboy French was definitely inadequate. Among the applicants, I remember, was the son of my former school French tutor, himself a Frenchman. Here, I thought, was a likely recruit. His French should be fluent enough. I was, however, obliged to reject him on account of the British accent which five years of English public school life had grafted on to his native tongue. Many keen and courageous candidates declared themselves perfectly happy to take the risks of their tongues betraying them. But that was not the point. Any organisation of the kind we envisaged was only as strong as its weakest link, and we could not afford to jeopardise valuable agents through the inability of a colleague to speak the French of a Frenchman. It was necessary to exclude from the start all those candidates who failed to convince our examiners that they could be taken for Frenchmen by a Frenchman. This applied to appearance as well as to speech. It is true that, later in the war, we modified these strict requirements in certain cases where an officer could be sent to a *maquis* group in which he was unlikely to come into contact with either German or, worse, French officials, but at the beginning we were adamant.

Those that survived the language test were next considered from the point of view of character. Now this is a difficult thing to assess. I do not know if I can do more than say that in the type of recruit we wanted, a rugged honesty and singleness of purpose shone in his or her face. We were not concerned with physique, for we knew that training could work wonders with even the most unpromising material, but we were vitally concerned with essential guts. Now, whatever the psychiatrists, whom we rudely referred to as trick-cyclists, averred, we were more ready to back our own judgement of a face and a manner than to accept the scientific appraisal. It was probably quite wrong of us, but it worked. We may have been grossly unfair to the psychiatric gentlemen, because we were unable to tell them, for reasons of security, just what we wanted these men and women to do. We really did not mind very much if the psychiatrist diagnosed a mother fixation or a lack of leadership. It was interesting, but not conclusive, for we could probably supply a French foster-mother, and we did not always want leaders. We wanted people who would obey instructions, blindly but intelligently; people who could be inspired with confidence and passionate belief; people who would carry on, however hopeless perseverance seemed to be.

The essential difference between the successful agent and the successful junior officer seems to me to lie in the fact that the agent has to rely entirely on himself, with only a tenuous and terribly dangerous clandestine radio link with his headquarters, which might fail him at any moment.

The percentage of candidates accepted after the 'character' interview was small. We had to be absolutely certain of our envoys. It was not until they had been assessed in this manner that we introduced the subject of the job. We told them that they should not lightly undertake it, that it meant continuous strain for perhaps years on end. No holidays, no home leave, no local leave, no Sundays nor bank holidays. All the year round pitting their wits against the *Abwehr* and the French *Milice* [pro-German French Militia]. Very few took the opportunity we then afforded them for backing out. We told them that they would have to undergo an uncomfortable and arduous period of training before they would be of any use. This they accepted without demur.

We used to try to impute motives to our candidates. Did they come to us, we asked ourselves, out of boredom with their own jobs, or from motives of pecuniary gain (quite misplaced so far as our service was concerned, for we paid the pay of the rank plus a trifling extra for 'talent')? Or did they seek escape from a nagging wife or a financial embarrassment? Or were they impelled by sheer love of adventure and glamour? Or did they just drift into it? Or – and these were the interesting cases – did they come to us because they felt that only in this or similar work could they achieve their maximum contribution to the war effort?

It was sometimes difficult to tell, but it was only this last class that interested us, and it was only they who made a real success of the task. Of course, we had to guard against infiltration by enemy agents, who were quite clever enough to simulate this motive, but we had our protection against these.

We were aided in our recruiting by the advent of men and women vouched for and recommended by existing members of the service. One family contributed three brothers, another a brother and sister and cousin. It was quite a family affair, but for security reasons we seldom allowed relatives to work together. From about the beginning of 1943 we had another windfall. It was agreed that, where a Frenchman living in France had served his apprenticeship as a contact with one of our envoys, he might be sent back along the escape routes to England for training and then depart for the field again to establish a new circuit, carrying the rank of a British officer. But even so, we were, at nearly all times up to the spring of 1944, terribly short of wireless operators, essential to the building up of a circuit.

In all, during the period March 1941 to July 1944, we recruited over 460 male and forty female officers for work in the field. It has always seemed to me surprising that there were so many British or Dominion subjects, whose French was faultless, willing and anxious to undertake such supremely dangerous work. They were in no way conspicuous; the last thing we wanted in them was eccentricity. We denied them glamour, in their own interests; we made them look as homely and unremarkable as we could. In the words of one of them, they were 'just ordinary people, not particularly brave'.

Maurice Buckmaster

Of the 400 or so agents that the section sent into the field, almost 100 never returned home.

Inkerman Barracks, Woking

The right sort of training, Michael Nelson discovered, was the key to becoming a good soldier.

Our Sergeant was very keen that we should know something about the history of our Corps and take a pride in it. In fact he was anxious that we should take a pride in the whole of the British Army.

'History was made by the British Army,' he would announce as we stood rigidly to attention on the square. 'I therefore propose to give you a bit of a history lesson and by God you'd better remember every word I teaches you, or you'll never see the light of day again. Now the battle of Waterloo, that was an important date, and don't forget it, 1815. And what happened at the battle of Waterloo? The bloody frogs couldn't break the thin red line. These bloody frogs are our allies now, though a bloody lot of good they've done us. So there we are. That's the battle of Waterloo.' Here he would pause and stare along the line. 'Here you, Driver Smith. What was the date of the battle of Waterloo?'

'1815, Sergeant.'

'SIR. There's an officer on parade.'

It was a rule of the Army that if there was an officer on the parade ground, even if you couldn't see the sod because he was half a mile away, when answering the Sergeant you had to call him Sir.

'Right. Let's proceed. The next important date is 1857 because that's when the Indians mutinied, but we taught them a lesson and they've been a bloody fine army since. Got it? The next important date is the battle of Mons when the British Expeditionary Force went to the aid of the frogs and got them out of the shit the same way as it looks as if we're going to have to do this time. And what happened there? I'll tell you. A bloody great angel appeared in the sky which put the fear of God up the 'orrible Hun and inspired confidence into our boys. Right? Now we'll come a little nearer home. The Royal Army Service Corps is 147 years old this year and is descended from the Royal Waggoners, so don't let anyone tell you otherwise. Its organisation is the work of General Sir Redvers Buller and he earned the Victoria Cross, which is more than any of you fuckers will. The name of the Commandant of this barracks is Colonel Thwaite . . . spelt T–H–W–A–I–T–E. How do you spell it Driver Best?'

Driver Best was probably the dimmest man in the squad.

'Don't know, Sir.'

Our Sergeant approached Driver Best and put his face so close to him that their noses were almost touching.

'Why don't you wash your bloody ears out?' he said quietly. 'I tell you what. You're ignorant, just plain bloody ignorant. I suppose you'll tell me next that you don't know what NAAFI stands for?'

'Yes, Sir.'

'Then let me tell you. It stands for Never 'Ave Any Fags In. That's right, isn't it?'

'Yes, Sir.'

'Don't bloody well Yes me. I'll tell you what it stands for.' Here the Sergeant let himself go and roared. 'It stands for No Ambition And Fuck All Interest. Just fucking well like you, Driver Best.'

The rest of the squad tittered. Our Sergeant swung round. 'What are you lot laughing about? Take those smiles off those silly faces. Right! Let's have you! Squad, right turn! Quick March . . .'

                                                    Michael Nelson

‡

Mr Fleming's wife

London's population continued to suffer destruction and loss.

Then we talked quite freely about the raid on Wednesday night and he told me all the ghastly rituals he had been through, adding that his wife's people had offered to come to him for a bit or to take him in, but he preferred to stay where he was and be near Effie in the hospital. I admit I found the recital almost overwhelming and would have gone outside and howled or broken things and behaved like a child but for the quality of severe grandeur in the man's bearing. He had got, it seemed, beyond mere hatred of the enemy and had touched a kind of frozen detachment regarding himself; but he spoke very passionately in short staccato phrases when he said, 'This isn't a war at all. It's plain murder of ordinary folk. Why should they kill Mary? – and the girl? They didn't start the thing.

Nothing to do with it. And the parson said she died for her country. I'm sick of all that talk. What's the good of it? Where'll we be when all the people in all the countries have died for them? Doesn't get you any further. Better stop having countries. I don't believe all the Germans want to conquer the whole world. Bet there are some who think like I do – want to live quietly and do their job. It's these politicals – statesmen, they call themselves – and those business men – bloody grabbers, I call them. I know them. One came here last year. Said his name was Joshua or something. Wanted to buy up my show and me with it, just to do special frames for him. To make him richer, he meant. I told him to get out. They'll all have to get out – that lot – when this is over. We've got to try . . .'

Then he stopped and I saw he was looking at an old photograph of his wife which was hanging by the fire. He gave a short gasp and sat quite still, just staring, in the fading daylight. Only an occasional drip from the sink's tap broke the silence in the room. A room like a lot of others, I expect, all over Europe, with a plain man or woman in it enduring the maximum sorrow and wondering why.

Andrew Butler

[On Sunday 11 May] I walked out into Downing Street at 8.00 a.m. on my way to the early service at Westminster Abbey. It was really a sunny day with blue skies, but the smoke from many fires lay thick over London and obscured the sun. Burnt paper, from some demolished paper mill, was falling like leaves on a windy autumn day.

Whitehall was thronged with people, mostly sightseers but some of them Civil Defence workers with blackened faces and haggard looks. One of them, a boy of eighteen or nineteen, pointed towards the Houses of Parliament and said, 'Is that the sun?' But the great orange glow at which we were looking was the light of many fires south of the river. At Westminster Abbey there were fire-engines and the policeman at the door said to me, 'There will not be any services in the Abbey today, Sir,' exactly as if it were closed for spring cleaning. I turned towards Westminster Hall, on the roof of which I could see flames still leaping. Smoke rose from some invisible point in the pile of Parliament buildings beyond. I talked to a fireman. He showed me Big Ben, the face of which was pocked and scarred, and told me a bomb had gone right through the Tower. The one thing that had given him great pleasure during the night was that Big Ben had struck two o'clock a few minutes after being hit. It was still giving the proper time.

I stood on Westminster Bridge and thought ironically of Wordsworth and 1802. St Thomas's Hospital was ablaze, the livid colour of the sky extended from Lambeth to St Paul's, flames were visible all along the Embankment, there was smoke rising thickly as far as the eye could see. After no previous raid has London looked so wounded next day.

John Colville

✝

The Invasion of Crete

In April, the Germans came to the aid of the Italians in Yugoslavia and Greece. As they advanced, Allied troops there were withdrawn to Crete. On 20 May, the Germans stormed the island with paratroopers, the first time that they had been used en masse *in warfare. General Kurt Student deployed 23,000 airborne soldiers, among them battalion commander Baron Friedrich-August von der Heydte.*

Scarcely able to bear it any longer, I stepped once again to the open door. We were just flying over the beaches. The thin strip of surf, which looked from above like a glinting white ribbon, separated the blue waters from the yellow-green of the shore. The mountains reared up before us, and the 'planes approaching them looked like giant birds trying to reach their eyries in the rocks.

We were still flying inland as if to run against a dark mountainside. It seemed almost as though we could touch the steep slopes upon which trees and solitary buildings appeared like toys. Then our left wing dipped and we swung away from the mountain and the 'plane started to circle; but soon we straightened out again, and at that moment there came the pilot's order, 'Prepare to jump!'

Everyone rose and started to fasten his hook to the static line which ran down the centre of the body of the 'plane. And while we stood there, securing our hooks, we noticed that we were losing height, and the pressure of air became hard, almost painful, to the ear.

Next came the order, 'Ready to jump!'

In two strides I was at the door, my men pressing close behind me, and grasped the supports on either side of it. The slipstream clutched at my cheeks, and I felt as though they were fluttering like small flags in the wind.

Suddenly, a lot of little white clouds appeared from nowhere and stood poised in the air about us. They looked harmless enough, like puffs of cotton-wool, for the roar of the 'plane's engines had drowned the sound of the ack-ack shells' detonation.

Below me was the village of Alikianou. I could see people in the streets staring up at us, others running away and disappearing into doorways. The shadows of our 'planes swept like ghostly hands over the sun-drenched white houses, while behind the village there gleamed a large mirror – the reservoir – with single coloured parachutes, like autumn leaves, drifting down towards it.

Our 'plane slowed down. The moment had come.

'Go!'

I pushed with hands and feet, throwing my arms forward as if trying to clutch the black cross on the wing. And then the slipstream caught me, and I was swirling through space with the air roaring in my ears. A sudden jerk upon the webbing, a pressure on the chest which knocked the breath out of my lungs, and then – I looked upwards and saw, spread above me, the wide-open, motley hood of my parachute. In relation to this giant umbrella I felt small and insignificant. It was like descending in a lift . . . No – not a lift. Only someone who has experienced a parachute jump can know this wonderful feeling of being suspended in mid-air, this weightlessness independent of the earth. For a moment I enjoyed this silent suspension which followed the St Vitus's dance, then I looked around. To the right and left of me parachutes were hanging in the air – an infinite number of them, it seemed. And then I glanced downwards and received a shock which almost made my heart stop. It seemed that I was drifting with increasing speed towards a large reservoir which lay below me like the open mouth of a beast of prey. The waters of the reservoir loomed black and menacing, nor was there any breath of wind to urge me a little aside that I might escape drowning in the abyss. When I had marched to the front in September 1939 I had been prepared to die at some time during the war, but I had thought only of a soldier's death in battle. Could it possibly have been my destiny to be drowned in a reservoir?

The size of this reservoir grew ever larger, and I was coming nearer and nearer to it. I tried to conceive some means of escape. I tried to pray. But it was no use. I was left with only fear, fear, fear. Then suddenly there came a rough jerk. The drifting, the falling had ceased. I was down to earth again – or, at least, I was connected with the earth.

My parachute had been caught in a fig-tree growing beside the reservoir, and I was hanging by my harness over the water's edge. I unbuckled the harness, dropped, and found myself on solid ground again, all alive.

Nothing else could happen to me now, I reckoned. Anyone could come and I would fight him and show him how strong I was and how much I treasured life. I do not know if babies have any feelings when they arrive in the world from their mothers' wombs, but, if they do, theirs would be precisely the same sensation as that experienced by parachutists when they have landed after a jump . . .

Mechanically I glanced at my wrist-watch. It showed exactly 7.15 – 7.15 a.m. on May 20th, 1941. A radiant summer's morning. In an atmosphere untroubled by the smallest breeze the apparent movement of the heat-haze, which glittered and vibrated as if a myriad ghosts were dancing before my eyes, served further to increase the sensation of eeriness.

Friedrich-August von der Heydte

The author would be awarded the Knight's Cross for his leadership on Crete.
The invaders were outnumbered by the thousands of Allied soldiers on the island. Among them was an officer with the Leicestershire Regiment.

If ever there was a fillip to morale, this was it. These guns were not out of action but merely waited patiently for their target, and there it was sitting on the end of their barrel. The sound of these guns put life into us and we cheered. We had only to wait a short time before one Junkers was hit just as it was about to disgorge its load. It crashed. Perhaps the death of those parachutists was preferable to the death suffered by those who came down with their parachutes on fire, going faster and faster as they neared the earth only to be followed up by our platoons as they landed. One had the misfortune to land on top of company headquarters as we lay concealed within some standing corn. He drifted slowly to earth as I watched. When he was about ten feet from the ground seven or eight Tigers, each with a bayonet fixed, rose and approached him. That was the first time that I heard a man scream with fear.

A. W. D. Nicholls

The defenders were also attacked by the Luftwaffe:

I was still attending the patient when an enemy plane roared up and started machine-gunning the house, the bullets coming through the flimsy tile roof and badly built brick and plaster walls as if they were paper. When it had kept this up for some time, circling back again and again and finally opening up with shellfire, it became evident that the plane really was concentrating on the house for some reason or other. There was a nice deep ditch just outside, so I decided that it was best to take the patient there. I did not like moving him more than necessary for fear of starting a haemorrhage, but it seemed the lesser of two evils. So, choosing a moment when the plane had swept past and not yet returned, a Palestinian, who had remained with me, and I each grabbed one end of the blanket on which the patient was lying and carried him out. We managed to get him into the ditch and to tumble into it ourselves before the plane circled round. The latter was soon back again and kept up its machine-gunning for some time. I think it was trying to set fire to the house as many of the bullets were tracers, but, although the cottage was full of inflammable material, by some fluke it did not succeed. Finally the plane made off, and soon afterwards the stretcher arrived to remove the wounded man to the CCS.

On returning to Major Murray's HQ I learned that news had just come through that parachutists had landed just west of us and were moving in our direction.

Theodore Stephanides

Although the paratroopers were elite troops, even they found the initial resistance difficult to overcome.

In the grey light of morning we storm the vineyards on the hills at the edge of the airfield. Now our objective is before us. But they've spotted us and give us hell – and real hell at that. I see one badly injured Oberjäger holding his torn abdominal wall closed with both hands. When we stop to help him he just says: 'Get down there first, then fetch me!' Unbelievable. Oberjäger Rudi Freisch has the most enormous stroke of luck. He gets a bullet through the nose, but it goes in one side and clean out the other. (After a few days he could even blow his nose again.)

It's not good. People are getting hit all around us, and the air is full of their groans and cries of pain. We're forced to withdraw from this hill of blood and so fail to achieve our objective. Firing continues on both sides. We manage to find some cover on the rear slope, then move quickly to a white house where we can care for our wounded. The medical orderlies really have their hands full now. Then to a shallow ditch, and leap over the road into a little hollow. How many of us are there now, thirty men, forty? A heated debate follows. An Oberleutnant Hintz or Hintze from another unit wants to give the order to surrender. A Feldwebel replies curtly: 'Quite out of the question.'

Soon we hear the noise of vehicles, and orders being given in English. The only road still free is the one leading to the coast, so we move down through the bushes and the undergrowth. Everything that isn't absolutely indispensable – except weapons and ammunition – is jettisoned to make the going easier. We move along by the coast for a good hour, sometimes wading along in the sea up to our chests when that's the only way forward. Some stragglers from other units have managed to make their way to us, until finally – worn out – we reach another group of soldiers on a small hill. Under the command of Oberleutnant van Roon, a new battle group is being put together there. Oberjäger Frisch hands me my first cigarette – my God, I needed that. Tired and dispirited, we sit there with bowed heads. To top our astonishment, we discover that our East Prussian Leutnant Rikowski has turned on his heels and escaped here without his weapons and hardly any uniform. Well, we can understand most of it, but how the hell did Rikowski (who's normally so reliable) ever leave his gun behind?

New units are assembled from the remaining men and a defensive line is established. Anxious questions among us: 'How will things go?' 'How are the others doing?' 'Can we break through to Heraklion?' Despite our tiredness and despondency, hardly anyone gets any sleep . . .

Once the battle groups have been reorganised, our next objective is to make another attack on the airfield where we had suffered so many casualties. But as we advance, we suddenly see motor cycles and jeeps moving towards us. Fantastic! The mountain infantry has arrived! (The Airborne Assault Regiment, now under the command of that incredible old campaigner Oberst Ramcke, had managed to capture Maleme airfield albeit at tremendous cost. As a result, the superb mountain infantry had been able to land, and the two had joined forces to conquer the hills and drive off the enemy.)

Crete was ours. It was a heroic and bitter struggle but never forget what a tremendous toll it took in the lives of our troops. Winston Churchill was to say that, here on Crete, the spearhead of the Germany army had leapt to its death. He was right. We never recovered from it.

Martin Pöppel

Six thousand German troops, including 3,764 airborne soldiers, died during the assault on Crete. Although 17,000 Allied soldiers were taken prisoner, Hitler regarded it as a pyrrhic victory.

‡

The Bismarck

The sinking of the Hood

On 21 May, the German battleship Bismarck *left Norway under the cover of bad weather. The British made repeated attempts to locate her, and on the 23rd* Suffolk *and* Norfolk *spotted the* Bismarck *and the accompanying* Prinz Eugen *in the Denmark Strait. The next day, the* Hood *and the* Prince of Wales *engaged their rivals. Geoffrey Brooke was a gunnery officer on the* Prince of Wales.

The destroyer screen dropped astern during the night, unable to keep up the headlong rush in the pounding seas. Sporadic reports from *Norfolk* – she had contacted the *Bismarck* shortly after *Suffolk* and both cruisers were now shadowing from astern – indicated that the enemy was on much the same course, about south-west. Ours, adjusted occasionally in response, was such as to converge at a fine angle, meaning that the action would start around 06:00. It would be broad daylight in these northern waters long before this. The weather improved; the visibility was going to be good. The *Hood* was four cables (800 yards) ahead. Suddenly, 'Lookout bearing green seven-o,' and the director swung round. The time was 05:10. The light increased. It was to be a grey day with a strong north wind (Force 6) in our faces and a moderate sea. I studied the horizon again and again as the minutes passed.

'Alarm starboard! Enemy in sight. Battleship bearing green five-o. Follow director. All guns with armour-piercing *load*.' Click went the loudspeaker: 'This is your Captain speaking. The two enemy ships are in sight and we shall be opening fire any minute now. Good luck to you all.'

I could see nothing except the unbroken straight line of the horizon but, of course, the forward director was a good deal higher than ours and so could see further. The records say the time was 05:38. The loudspeaker came on the air again. 'This is the padre speaking. I am going to read a short prayer.' This he did. Though by no means irreligious, I must admit I found this distracting. But not for long. Something suddenly came up over the horizon to grow slowly but distinctly; the top of a mast. Then a little to its left something else. I shall never forget the thrill of that moment. A squat grey lump on a stalk, with bars protruding each side – the *Bismarck*'s main armament director. 'Director Target' said Mr White evenly. It grew by the second like a serpent rearing up while our rangetaker spun his wheel, trying to converge his two half-images in the face of driving spume. After widening out into a fighting top of some sort one saw that the stalk was really the top of the tower; other excrescences appeared and between these and the mast, the pointed cowl then the full width of a massive funnel. Guns began again: 'Range two seven. Inclination one-two-o left. Speed three-o.' Down below in the Transmitting Station they would be winding handwheels and pressing buttons as the details came down to them. Mesmerised, I watched the *Bismarck*'s superstructure swell as more and more of its pyramid shape – seen so often in diagrams – came into view. She was just before our beam, steaming from right to left at an angle about 30° this side of right angles.

All our Control Officers' headsets were interconnected and I heard a discussion forward about another ship. Shifting my binoculars a little I picked up a second director a good way to the left and then the performance repeated itself – stalk, lump, tower, pyramid – but on a smaller scale. Surely it must be the *Tirpitz*, only further off, i.e., on the far bow of the *Bismarck*. I swallowed hard. If it *was* the *Tirpitz* we were certainly in for something. But Guns decided it was a cruiser, reaffirming the right-hand ship as target.

We heeled to port a little, the *Bismarck* sliding a fraction to the left before the director caught up, as we altered 40° towards the enemy. It was a turn by Blue Pennant, the two ships – still only 800 yards apart – turning at the same moment so that the flagship finished up 40° on *Prince of Wales*' port bow, both steering to cut the enemy's advance at a sharper angle and so close the range much more quickly.

' "Y" turret will not bear' repeated the communication number, indicating that the turret on the quarterdeck had come up against its safety stops. I imagined Captain Aylwin, RM (the whole turret was manned by marines), fuming impotently. Though the enemy was within range, we were presumably conserving the ammunition. For some time we kept on with only the usual sounds of the sea and the voice of the Gunnery officer as he updated his calculations.

'Ready to open fire Sir!' This was to the Captain and one could not hear the reply. Surely it was yes and why weren't we firing? The whole of the *Bismarck* was now visible and I could not restrain a gasp of admiration, tinged with awe. Long and rakish with undeniably majestic lines, she was a fawnish grey, not bluish like our ships – or it may just have been the light. I noticed with a pang that all her 15-inch guns were pointing in our direction.

There was a *boom* from not far off. The *Hood* had opened fire. Seconds later 'Shoot!' said Guns. *Ting-ting* went the fire gong and I shut my eyes. BAROOM! The *Prince of Wales*' first salvo was away from 'A' and 'B' turrets. The slight concussion and the brown smoke that drifted aft (the wind dispersed it fairly quickly) brought welcome relief from inaction. My fingers moved up and down the three knobs. Suddenly a rippling yellow flash played in front of the *Bismarck*, followed by a dark cloud that, nearly blotting her out, hung for an appreciable time. She had fired. At whom? The range was 25,600 yards (nearly 13 miles) and it would take almost a minute to find out. There was a hoarse croak from a box on the bulkhead, heralding the fall of our shot, and a cluster of white columns rose to form a wall behind the *Bismarck* (and I think to the right, but that was B-C's pigeon). I pressed 'over'. BAROOM! went another salvo, following one from the *Hood*. Another flash from the *Bismarck*. More smoke. Wait. Croak. Splash. Press for another 'over'. BAROOM! Flash. On it went, Guns ordering corrections ('Left one. Down ladder shoot') in a level voice as each salvo landed, each time nearer. So far nothing seen of the enemy's shells. Presumably she was firing at the *Hood*. (The cruiser was also firing at the *Hood* but she was so far to the left that I could not see her without taking my glasses off the *Bismarck* and after the initial scrutiny I never saw her again during the action.)

BAROOM! again. Wait. Croak, splash, 'over'. BAROOM! – 'short'. We must have been firing for nearly three minutes, it was the sixth salvo, when there was the welcome sight of the great white wall partly in front and partly behind the *Bismarck*. Straddle! By all the laws we should have hit her. She did not look any different, but I did not expect her to as armour-piercing shells burst inside, normally unseen. Three more salvoes, one of which was another straddle. We were making very creditable shooting, though I had not taken in that one of our guns was not working.

Another salvo had just gone when I heard Guns warn his director layer 'Stand by to alter course to port.' This long-awaited move – presumably we were going back to the original heading so that 'Y' turret could bear for the first time – had begun to take place, in that we heeled to starboard and it became temporarily more difficult to hold the *Bismarck* steady in one's glasses, when the ship suddenly rolled upright again and then continued to heel over the opposite way; moreover, with the urgency and excessive vibration that comes only from violent rudder movement. We were going hard-a-starboard. Back towards the enemy again. What the hell was going on? There was a momentary lull. Probably the director gunner had been put off his aim, and in the comparative quiet I realised that hitherto there had been an intermittent background noise.

The ship steadied up and then began to come back to port. Dick Beckwith said 'My God! The *Hood*'s gone!'

I shot a glance up at him. He was staring horrified over his left shoulder, through his rear port. We both looked back into our glasses. Though I heard the words quite distinctly they meant nothing at that moment. It was as if that part of my brain not concerned with the long grey shape that belched flame and smoke simply was not working. I could have stood up and had a quick look (afterwards wishing I had) but it did not occur to me.

Geoffrey Brooke

The reaction on board the Bismarck *unsurprisingly was jubilant.*

Ever since the action began, I had been wondering whether I would be able to distinguish the sound of the enemy's shells hitting us from the sound of our own firing – with all the noise that was going on, that might not always be easy. Then I heard Schneider again: 'Wow, was that a misfire? That really ate into him.' Over the telephone I heard an ever louder and more excited babble of voices – it seemed as though something sensational was about to happen, if it hadn't already. Convinced that the *Suffolk* and *Norfolk* would leave us in peace for at least a few minutes, I entrusted the temporary surveillance of the horizon astern through the starboard director to one of my petty officers and went to the port director. While I was still turning it toward the *Hood*, I heard a shout, 'She's blowing up!' 'She' – that could only be the *Hood*! The sight I then saw is something I shall never forget. At first the *Hood* was nowhere to be seen; in her place was a colossal pillar of black smoke reaching into the sky. Gradually, at the foot of the pillar, I made out the bow of the battle cruiser projecting upwards at an angle, a sure sign that she had broken in two. Then I saw something I could hardly believe: a flash of orange coming from her forward guns! Although her fighting days had ended, the *Hood* was firing a last salvo. I felt great respect for those men over there.

At 05:57 one of our observers had spotted a quick-spreading fire forward of the *Hood*'s after mast: the second salvo from the *Prinz Eugen* had set fire to rocket propellant for the UP Projectors [a mortar-type weapon used in defence against aircraft]. Four minutes later, a heavy salvo from the *Bismarck* hit the *Hood* and sent a mountain of flame and a yellowish–white fireball bursting up between her masts and soaring into the sky. White stars, probably molten pieces of metal, shot out from the black smoke that followed the flame, and huge fragments, one of which looked like a main turret, whirled through the air like toys. Wreckage of every description littered the water around the *Hood*, one especially conspicuous piece remaining afire for a long time and giving off clouds of dense, black smoke.

In my director I now saw the after part of the *Hood* drift away and quickly sink. Her forward section sank slowly, and soon there was nothing to be seen where the pride of the Royal Navy, the 48,000-ton 'mighty *Hood*', had so suddenly suffered the fate Admiral Holland had in mind for the two German ships. From the time the firing began, only six minutes passed before a shell from the *Bismarck* penetrated the *Hood*'s armour protection at a point never definitely established and detonated more than 100 tons of cordite in the ammunition room of one of her after main turrets. How reminiscent of what happened to the battle cruisers *Queen Mary*, *Indefatigable*, and *Invincible* at the Battle of Jutland in 1916! The *Hood* met her end in the midst of battle. She left only three survivors in the ice-cold waters, and they were picked up by a British destroyer and landed at Reykjavik.

At their battle stations, our men were kept informed of the course of the action by the ship's watch; they heard, 'Enemy in sight' – 'Opponent has opened fire' – they waited to hear the response of our own guns. A few minutes later it came, and each salvo made the ship shudder. Salvo after salvo was leaving the *Bismarck*'s guns and her engines were running smoothly, when the men below heard, '*Hood* is burning,' and, a little later, '*Hood* is exploding.' They just stared at one another in disbelief. Then the shock passed and the jubilation knew no bounds. Overwhelmed with joy and pride in the victory, they slapped one another on the back and shook hands.

In the damage-control centre adjacent to the command centre, the First Officer's action station, Josef Statz saw a more exuberant Oels than he would have believed possible. Oels thrust the top half of his body through the pass-through between the two centres and, thrilled to the core, shouted, 'A triple *Sieg Heil* to our *Bismarck*!' The superiors had a hard time getting the men back to work and convincing them that the battle wasn't over and that every man must continue to do his duty.

Burkard von Müllenheim-Rechberg

The Swordfish attack

The Bismarck, *however, had also been damaged in the engagement, and so headed towards the French port of Brest for repairs. For two days she managed to give her pursuers the slip, but on 26 May the capital ship was located. A strike was launched*

from the carrier Ark Royal *by a flight of antiquated Swordfish torpedo bombers.*
Gerard Woods was a Fleet Air Arm Observer aboard one of them.

The minute or so which followed will be forever engraved on my memory.
There she was, a thousand yards away, big, black, cowled funnel, menacing,
with every close-range weapon stabbing flame as we steadied on our
approach, 100 knots, 100 ft, 1000 yards just as the textbook says. 'Flash'
Seager, the TAG, was sensibly crouching down in the cockpit, sitting on
a lead-covered codebook. Later he told me I was shouting my head off as
we ran in, probably true, but what it was I have no idea. All I do know is
that, as we dropped our 'tinfish', A4 'Charlie' almost leapt into the air, and
as we turned away aft tightly, we were suspended motionless for a split
second that felt like an eternity as every gun seemed to concentrate upon
us. The flak ripped through the fabric-covered fuselage like peas on a drum.
'Flash' yelled, and then Alan said, 'Christ! Just look at this lot,' as *Bismarck*
put her 15 in. guns on a flat trajectory, firing ahead of us, either intending to
blast us off the face of the earth, or as happened in fact, to make a Beechers'
Brook of water-splashes 100 ft high through which we must fly, and which
might bring us spinning down into the raging sea. 'Flash's' normally sallow
complexion looked grey, but at that time it didn't worry me, because I
had no idea what colour I was, probably even more grey than he.

As we sped aft, opening the range, and out of immediate danger, I asked
him if he was all right, and he said yes, but did not look at all happy, and
went on to say he had been hit in the buttocks, so I turned and spoke to
Alan, telling him this and giving him a course back to the ship. I saw that
Alan's flying overalls were torn in the right shoulder and asked if he was
all right. He said yes, but there was blood seeping down his back. 'How
long before we're there?' he asked. 'About 25 minutes.' 'OK, I can hold
on.' That was about the sum of our conversation. I had escaped injury but
the burst which must have wounded them both had gone clean through
my Mae West life jacket near the left shoulder, and the kapok was welling
out. At first I thought it was my tripes, but realised they weren't up there.

Gerard Woods

The Bismarck *did her best to blow the* Swordfish *out of the sky.*

Once more, the *Bismarck* became a fire-spitting mountain. The racket of
her anti-aircraft guns was joined by the roar from her main and secondary

turrets as they fired into the bubbling paths of oncoming torpedoes, creating splashes ahead of the attackers. Once more, the restricted field of my director and the dense smoke allowed me to see only a small slice of the action. The antique-looking Swordfish, fifteen of them, seemed to hang in the air, near enough to touch. The high cloud layer, which was especially thick directly over us, probably did not permit a synchronised attack from all directions, but the Swordfish came so quickly after one another that our defence did not have it any easier than it would have had against such an attack. They flew low, the spray of the heaving seas masking their landing gear. Nearer and still nearer they came, into the midst of our fire. It was as though their orders were, 'Get hits or don't come back!'

The heeling of the ship first one way and then the other told me that we were trying to evade torpedoes. The rudder indicator never came to rest and the speed indicator revealed a significant loss of speed. The men on the control platforms in the engine rooms had to keep their wits about them. 'All ahead full!' – 'All stop!' – 'All back full!' – 'Ahead!' – 'All stop!' were the ever-changing orders by which Lindemann [*Bismarck*'s captain] sought to escape the malevolent 'eels'.

As though hypnotised, I listened for the sound of an exploding torpedo mixing with the roar of our guns. It could be much worse than it was two days earlier. A hit forward of my station could be tolerated, but what about a hit aft? There was not much distance between me and our sensitive propellers and rudders, and it seemed as though these were our attackers' favourite targets. We had been under attack for perhaps fifteen minutes when I heard that sickening sound. Two torpedoes exploded in quick succession, but somewhere forward of where I was. Good fortune in misfortune, I thought. They could not have done much damage. My confidence in our armoured belt was unbounded. Let's hope that's the end of it!

Burkard von Müllenheim-Rechberg

The sinking of the Bismarck

Despite her armoured belt, the Swordfish had hit Bismarck *twice, crippling her steering gear and drastically reducing her speed. On the 27th, having been subjected to further British attacks, the Germans decided to scuttle the pride of their fleet.*

While the little group I was with was waiting to starboard, forward of turret Dora, the *Bismarck* sank still deeper by her stern and her list to port increased. The gradual emergence of more and more of her hull on the starboard side told me that the moment to jump was approaching. 'It's that time,' I said, 'inflate your life jackets, prepare to jump.' Just as earlier it was vital not to go over the side too soon, now, it was vital not to delay so long that we would be sucked down with the ship when she finally sank. 'A salute to our fallen comrades,' I called. We all snapped our hands to our caps, glanced at the flag, and jumped.

In the water we were pushed together in a bunch, as we bobbed up and down like corks. At first we swam away from the sinking ship as hard as we could to escape her suction. When I got clear by some 150 metres, I stopped and turned around for one last look and to take in everything I could about her.

What I saw was that the *Bismarck* was listing still more. She had no stability left. She was also deeper down by her stern, her bow rearing steeply out of the water. The whole starboard side of her hull, all the way to the keel, was out of the water. I scrutinised it for signs of battle damage and was surprised that I saw no trace of any. Her port side had borne the brunt of the battle, and that side of her hull may have told a different story.

When swimmers close to the bow of the ship looked back, they saw Lindemann standing on the forecastle in front of turret Anton. His messenger, a seaman, was with him. Soon, both men went forward and began climbing a steadily increasing slope. Lindemann's gestures showed that he was urging his companion to go overboard and save himself. The man refused and stayed with his commanding officer until they reached where the jackstaff had been. Then Lindemann walked out on the starboard side of the stem which, though rising even higher, was becoming more level as the ship lay over. There he stopped and raised his hand to his white cap.

Burkard von Müllenheim-Rechberg

More than 2,130 members of the Bismarck's *company were drowned. The death toll might have been lower had the British ships not called off their rescue attempts for fear of U-boat attacks.*

‡

On leave

I stayed in the same pub drinking until closing time, by which time I was more or less insensible, my main means of support being the Guardsman who kept suggesting that we should go off to the nearest YMCA and kip down together for the night, or even better, considering how posh I spoke,

I might have some rich friends in London with a nice place of their own who would be only too delighted to entertain us through the remainder of the night.

Then the black-out came down, and I could remember no more.

I awoke some eight hours later to find myself lying in a bed with a fully clothed man. On inspection he turned out to be wearing the uniform of the Royal Marines, and three pips on his shoulder indicated the rank of Captain.

I felt myself gently for any signs of damage, and finding none slid out of bed where I collapsed to the floor as an appalling stab of pain spread through my head. I managed to drag myself to the door, and having opened it, found myself in the corridor of a hotel. It wasn't until I had slipped out into the street that I realised that I was in Park Lane. The sun was shining, and even at that late or early hour, whichever way you like to look at it, the last prostitutes were still plying their trade. Not that they accosted me. I must have looked too far gone to be worth even a shilling.

There was only one thing to do, and that was to have a drink. I staggered up to Covent Garden, and made my way to one of the garden pubs where I had been welcome in the days when I had been a reporter on the *Sunday Pictorial*. There I started another day, which wasn't very much different from the day that had preceded it.

Like all leaves, this was not a satisfactory one. It did not come up to expectations, and left a nasty taste in the mouth in more senses than one. As I have said, the basis of all leaves was to have sex and drink.

Michael Nelson

‡

Rommel arrives in North Africa

By the late spring of 1941, the Axis forces stood at Halfaya Pass, near the Libyan border and the gate to Egypt. Heinz Werner Schmidt was a young officer on Rommel's staff.

Halfaya had been the scene of action before. Rommel recognised its obvious strategical importance, for it commanded the coast road from Egypt into Cyrenaica. Denied the road past Sollum and Halfaya, the enemy would be forced far south into the Desert if he aimed at an attack inside Cyrenaica. So Rommel was strengthening this sector as fast as he could, and had just sent to it the elements of the 90th Light that were still immobile through lack of transport.

Bach had just called the company commanders together for a conference. Rommel took the opportunity of giving a little talk on tactics.

'Gentlemen,' he said, 'the struggle in the desert is best compared with a battle at sea. Whoever has the weapons with the greatest range has the longest arm, exactly as at sea. Whoever has the greater mobility, through efficient motorisation and efficient lines of supply, can by swift action compel his opponent to act according to his wishes.

'Your troops here at Halfaya Pass are immobile. They are of value against motorised troops only when they are in strong and well-prepared positions. But here again the "longest arm" has the advantage. We have it – in the 88-mm. gun. It is essential for you, as immobile troops, to have the best-prepared cover, the best camouflage possible, and the best field of fire for the 88's and other pieces.'

Rommel paused and then went on, speaking with characteristic forcefulness: 'It is my intention to occupy a long defensive line stretching from the seas to Sidi Omar. The outpost positions, up to company strength, must perforce be fairly far apart; but the whole line must be planned in adequate depth towards the rear.

'Every defended point must be a complete defensive system in itself. Every weapon must be sited so that it is able to fire in every direction. I visualise the ideal arrangement of such defensive points on these lines:

'One 88-mm. "flak" gun should be sunk into the ground as deeply as the field of fire permits. From here trenches should radiate in three directions to three points – one a machine-gun position, the second a heavy mortar position, and the third a light 22-mm. anti-aircraft gun, or to a 50-mm. "pak" (anti-tank) gun. Sufficient water, ammunition, and supplies for three weeks must always be available. And every man is to sleep prepared for action.'

Rommel warmed to his subject.

'Gentlemen, a few words in regard to battle tactics. In case of an enemy attack, the fire of our arms must completely cover the gap between the defended points. Should the enemy succeed in breaking through the gaps, owing to say bad visibility, every weapon must be in position to engage towards the rear. Let it be clear that there is no such thing as a "Direction, Front," but only a "Direction, Enemy."'

He added another pronouncement: 'The final decision of any struggle if the enemy attacks will probably rest with the Panzer and motorised units behind the line. Where this decision is reached is immaterial. A battle is won when the enemy is destroyed. Remember one thing – every individual position must hold, regardless of what the general situation appears to be. Our Panzers and motorised formation will not leave you in the lurch, even if you should not see them for weeks . . . I thank you, gentlemen.'

The officers were dismissed. Bach accompanied us as we moved on to visit an Italian battery. Here, too, Rommel's concern was with ammunition supplies. Dr Hagemann translated the conversations with the Italians; but I noted that Rommel was swift to spot if the translation did not convey precisely the shade of meaning he intended. He knew more Italian than he cared to allow the Italians to perceive.

I remember that we were shelled from the east that day as we drove down 'Hellfire Pass' towards the coastal plain. The General reckoned that the fire came from self-propelled field-guns which the enemy had temporarily sent forward.

On the flat coastal plain Rommel noticed that at some defended points captured British Mark II tanks had been sunk deep in the ground with only their turrets above the surface. This intelligent employment of enemy material pleased him greatly, and we went on in high good humour.

When we reached the shore, I suggested a dip. We had no bathing trunks, but who was to worry about that in the desert front-line?

Rommel and I plunged into the cool Mediterranean. It had the lively sparkle of a blue champagne. Rommel splashed about with the gaiety of a schoolboy.

Heinz Werner Schmidt

Summer 1941

The Invasion of Russia

'May God bless our weapons!'

On 22 June 1941, Hitler began Operation Barbarossa – his war against the Soviet Union, with whom he had signed a non-aggression pact in August 1939. One hundred and fifty divisions, 2,700 aircraft, 7,000 guns and 3,300 tanks launched a surprise attack on Russian forces that were largely unprepared: only one in four of their tanks was battle-ready and little of the Soviet air force was modern. Josef Goebbels, the Nazis' propaganda minister, was closely involved in the preparations for the invasion. It was Goebbels himself who broke the news of the invasion on the radio.

22 JUNE 1941 (SUNDAY)

It is 2.30 a.m. The Führer's mood is very solemn. He intends to go to sleep for a few hours. And this is the best thing that he could do.

I go over to the ministry. It is still pitch-dark. I put my colleagues in the picture. Total amazement in all quarters. Most had guessed half, or even the whole truth. Everyone set to work immediately. Radio, press and newsreel are mobilised. Everything runs like clockwork.

I study the final telegrams again: all rubbish. Our guns will issue the last denial. I shall not say a word. Study the radio situation in Russia. We shall have our work cut out.

3.30. Now the guns will be thundering. May God bless our weapons!

Outside on the Wilhelmplatz, it is quiet and deserted. Berlin and the entire Reich are asleep. I have half an hour to spare, but I cannot sleep. I pace up and down restlessly in my room. One can hear the breath of history.

A glorious, wonderful hour has struck, when a new empire is born. Our nation is making her way up into the light.

The new fanfare sounds. Filled with power, booming and majestic. I read the Führer's proclamation to the German people over all stations. A solemn moment for me.

The burden of many weeks and months falls away.

I feel totally free.

Still a few urgent matters to settle.

Then I drive out to Schwanenwerder. The sun is already standing full and beautiful in the sky.

Outside in the garden, the birds are singing.

I tumble into bed. And sleep two hours of deep, healing sleep.

23 JUNE 1941 (MONDAY)

. . . Our air offensive had begun in grand style. With 900 Stukas and fighters. Against Russian cities, including Kiev, and against airfields. Battle has been joined along the 3000-kilometre front. The first, minor river barriers have already been crossed at all points . . .

The Russians have already suffered extremely serious aircraft losses. During one attack on Tilsit they lost twenty-two out of forty-three aircraft. Operations are proceeding according to plan . . .

I work through the afternoon at full stretch. After my reading of the Führer's proclamation, Ribbentrop added his pennyworth. The needs of vanity!

Russian movements are similar to those of the French in 1870. And her armies will suffer the same catastrophe. During the initial stages, the Russians are defending only moderately well. But their air force has suffered appalling losses at the outset: 200 planes shot down, 200 destroyed on the ground, and 200 damaged. A considerable deficit, whichever way one looks at it. We shall win. We must win, and quickly. The public mood is one of slight depression. The nation wants peace, though not at the price of defeat, but every new theatre of operations brings worry and concern.

Josef Goebbels

Barbarossa − the view on the ground

A former law student, Helmut Pabst was a signals NCO attached to an artillery unit in Army Group Centre, which was advancing towards Smolensk and, ultimately, Moscow. Pabst kept a diary in the form of letters to his family and friends in Frankfurt, notably his father who had served in the Russia campaign of 1914−17.

It's hard to believe that it started only two days ago. This time I was with the leading wave. The units moved up to their positions quietly, talking in whispers. There was a creaking of wheels − assault guns. Two nights before, we had looked over the ground; now we were waiting for the infantry. They came up in dark, ghostly columns and moved forward through the cabbage plots and cornfields. We went along with them to act as artillery liaison unit for the second battalion. In a potato field the order came 'Dig in!' No. 10 Battery was to open fire at 0305 hours.

0305. The first salvo! At the same moment everything sprang to life. Firing along the whole front – infantry guns, mortars. The Russian watch-towers vanished in a flash. Shells crashed down on all the enemy batteries, which had been located long before. In file and in line, the infantry swarmed forward. Bog, ditches; boots full of water and mud. Ahead of us the barrage crept forward from line to line. Flame-throwers advanced against the strong-points. The fire of machine-guns, and the high-pitched whip of rifle bullets. My young wireless operator, with forty pounds' load on his back, felt a bit queasy during the first half-hour. Then, at Kanopky Barracks, came the first serious resistance. The company ahead was stuck. 'Assault guns, forward!'

We were with the battalion commander on a small hill, five hundred yards from the barracks. Our first man wounded – one of the runners. We set up the wireless. Suddenly we were fired on from close quarters. A sniper. We picked up our rifles for the first time. Although we were signallers, we must have been the better shots – the sniping stopped. Our first kill.

The advance went on. We moved fast, sometimes flat on the ground, but irresistibly. Ditches, water, sand, sun. Always changing position. Thirsty. No time to eat. By ten o'clock we were already old soldiers and had seen a great deal: abandoned positions, knocked-out armoured cars, the first prisoners, the first dead Russians.

For three hours during the night we stood-to in a foxhole. Tanks were threatening our flank. At a quarter to four we went on again with the infantry. Again we were preceded by a barrage. On either side of us we could see companies fighting forward. Quite close by, flares were going up. We were right in the front line.

The first burnt-down village, with only the chimneys still standing. Here and there a shed, and the usual draw-wells. Under shell-fire for the first time. The shells make a curious singing noise: you dig in fast and make yourself flat. Constant change of position. We dump our set on the ground. Reception is good, unlike yesterday. But we have hardly taken a message before the battalion moves on. We run after it.

About three o'clock we get through the dugout line, a defile between swamps. Suddenly a halt. Someone calls: 'Anti-tank guns, forward!' The guns race through. Then there's a waste of sand, covered with clumps of broom. It extends about two kilometres to the main road and the river, by the fortress of Osowiec.

For breakfast we had a slice of bread. For lunch four of us shared an inch-thick crust. Thirst, heat, and this damned sand! We trot along wearily, taking the carrying in turns. Splashed, muddy, sand in our boots, two-day-old beards. Battalion headquarters at last, at the edge of the plain. Up by the river is our most forward post. The Russians know exactly where we are.

We dig in quickly. God knows, we're none too soon. We already know exactly when a shell's coming, and I can't help laughing when we dive headlong into our holes and crouch there like Muslims at prayer. But at last it gets too much of a good thing: the infantry pull back. We dismantle the set and make a dash whenever there's a lull in the firing. There are others running on our right and left and we all flop down in the mud at the same time. I can't stop laughing.

When we reached comparative safety, we gathered in a foxhole and waited for darkness. We shared our last cigarettes. The mosquitoes went quite mad. More signals came in. I almost went crazy decoding them, because my torch attracted more mosquitoes still. Again there were infantry coming back from the front line. We weren't quite certain what was going on.

A hill, a deep trench – we knew we must be somewhere. There was soup, and coffee – as much as we wanted. After going on two more kilometres through the dark we ended up at one of our batteries. Soon we were lying close together, pulling our jackets round our ears. The Russian shells were wishing us goodnight. When we crept out again at about four o'clock, we found ourselves a hundred yards from our headquarters.

An hour later we were marching west, then north. When night fell we were near Augustova, whose church with its two towers reminded me of Father. A bit beyond Augustova, in the direction of Grodno, we were put at readiness again. We had to be ready at half-past ten. We were woken up at half-past twelve, and eventually we started at five o'clock in the morning. The situation was changing all the time; the front was moving forward very fast. We marched towards Grodno, where we were to be used. Swamps left and right of us. A whole Russian tank brigade was supposed to be somewhere on the right, but one never gets to see such things. (Only mosquitoes – there are enough of those, and dust.)

Finally, in the evening, we got into a village by country tracks that took us through Lipsk. Everywhere pillars of dust were rising in the air and moving slowly with the columns along the roads.

The road to Kutnitza is a torrent of sand. It's all beaten down, rutted and full of craters. It pours downhill like an arid sea. Painfully we push across the slopes, sometimes winding in serpentines. Perhaps it was like that in Napoleon's campaign.

                                                                    Helmut Pabst

Barbarossa – the view from the air

Heinz Knoke was a 20-year-old Messerschmitt pilot.

22 JUNE 1941

0400 hours: general alert for all Squadrons. Every unit on the airfield is buzzing with life. All night long I hear the distant rumble of tanks and vehicles. We are only a few miles from the border.

0430 hours: all crews report to the Squadron operations room for briefing. The Commanding Officer, Captain Woitke, reads out the special order for the day to all the armed forces from the Führer.

Germany is to attack the Soviet Union!

0500 hours: the Squadron takes off and goes into action.

In our Flight four aircraft, including mine, have been equipped with a bomb-release mechanism, and I have done considerable bombing practice in recent weeks. Now there is a rack slung along the belly of my good 'Emil', carrying 100 five-pound fragmentation bombs. It will be a pleasure for me to drop them on Ivan's dirty feet.

Flying low over the broad plains, we notice endless German columns rolling eastwards. The bomber formations overhead and the dreaded Stuka dive-bombers alongside us are all heading in the same direction. We are to carry out a low-level attack on one of the Russian headquarters, situated in the woods to the west of Druskieniki.

On Russian territory, by contrast, everything appears to be asleep. We locate the headquarters and fly low over the wooden building, but there is not a Russian soldier in sight. Swooping at one of the huts, I press the bomb-release button on the control stick. I distinctly feel the aircraft lift as it gets rid of the load.

The others drop theirs at the same time. Great masses of dirt fountain up into the air, and for a time we are unable to see because of all the smoke and dust.

One of the huts is fiercely blazing. Vehicles have been stripped of their camouflage and overturned by the blast. The Ivans at last come to life.

The scene below is like an overturned ant-heap, as they scurry about in confusion. Stepsons of Stalin in their underwear flee for cover in the woods. Light flak-guns appear. I set my sights on one of them, and open up with machine-guns and both cannon. An Ivan at the gun falls to the ground, still in underwear.

And now for the next one!

Round again, and I let them have it. The Russians stand fast and begin firing back at me. 'Just wait till I take the fun out of your shooting, you bastards!'

Round yet again for another attack.

I never shot as well as this before. I come down to sixty feet, almost brushing the tree-tops in the process. Then pull up sharply in a climbing turn. My Ivans lie flat on the ground beside their gun. One of them leaps to his feet and dashes into the trees. The remainder forget to get up again.

I carry out five or six more attacks. We buzz round the camp like a swarm of hornets. Nearly all the huts are in flames. I fire at a truck. It also burns after the first burst of fire.

0556 hours: Flight landing in formation.

The Chief sees smiling faces all round when the pilots report.

At last the spell is broken. We have dreamed for a long time of doing something like this to the Bolshevists. Our feeling is not exactly one of hatred, so much as utter contempt. It is a genuine satisfaction for us to be able to trample the Bolshevists in the mud where they belong.

Heinz Knoke

The gang rape of a Russian schoolmistress

A soldier came in with some food in a pannikin. He put it down on the table, untied my hands and told me to eat. I said I did not want any food. At first he tried to persuade me, but when he saw that I meant it he wolfed up the food himself. Then I heard the sergeant's voice from a distance. The soldier seized me by the arm and said:

'Come along.' I began to tremble in every part of me, inside rather than outside. My brain was trembling. My stomach. Then I found myself in the third room, the classroom. There were a lot of German soldiers sitting round the long table. There was a smell of strange food. They were all in their shirt-sleeves. The sergeant sat at the head of the table.

'Search her!' he snapped.

This must have been a sort of signal. Two soldiers fell upon me and tore

the clothes from my body, as they had done with poor old Serge. I did
not resist. In an instant I was without any clothes on me. The Germans
broke into hurrahs and heils. I began to cry. The sergeant came up to me.
I was more terrified even than during the afternoon. I implored him to
believe me that there was no food hidden in the village. I did not know
what I was saying. The Germans guffawed like madmen. 'Food!' roared
the sergeant, 'who cares about food!' The stench of his body was awful.
Several of the others made such remarks as, 'What an innocent little thing!'
or 'She talks of food, the goose!'

The sergeant dragged me into the next room. Somebody slammed the
door behind us.

Sturman released me. There I was, face to face with that beast. Alone. I
am alone with him again now. He is here now as I write. He is here to
torture me again, so that I should go through all those horrors once
more. That is his revenge. Because I tortured him too, as he tortured me,
I killed him too. I am here with him alone and I know he is going to
torture me and kill me, just as I knew then. I am terrified and I want to
escape, but I can't. There is some compulsion, some iron will that is tying
me to this table, so that despite all the pain and suffering I am going through
I should set down what is happening to me. So that you should know and
understand. Because I know that you are the only one who will understand
me.

Everything is dissolving around me. There is no room, no walls, I am
in infinite nothingness – alone with him. I am terrified, terribly terrified,
my whole body is one huge heart, and it is thudding away everywhere, in
my temples, my throat, my chest – everywhere. Sturman is standing before
me, his face is still a human face. His grey shirt is open, I can see the thick
hair on his chest, my nostrils are assailed by his penetrating German smell.
For a moment he looks at me searchingly, then he says:

'You wanted to escape, Fräulein? what?' Now he picks up the whip
from the table and swishes it in the air. But the whip is stiff from the
coagulated blood that is on it. Serge's blood. He starts to bend the whip
and clots of dry blood fly off it in a wide arc.

'So you wanted to escape, Fräulein? You wanted to go with the officers,
what?' He kept repeating this. The room is spinning round and round. I
am beside myself. I kneel down before him and with folded hands implore
him not to hurt me. To kill me, but not to hurt me. I cry, implore, perhaps
for the first time in my life. Then with a great swish the whip crashes
down on my back. I feel a terrible stinging pain, I feel the thong of the
whip cutting into my flesh. There is something warm trickling down my

back. Blood! The idea flashes through my mind. I jump up to run away – but now the whip crashes down again. I stumble over something – or perhaps it is the blow that makes me reel – and I crash to the floor. It hurts, hurts terribly. I feel as if my flesh was being torn off me with red hot pincers. I try to scream and moan, but no sound comes from my throat, my body is shaken by soundless sobs. 'Scream, harlot!' hissed my executioner. And the whip comes crashing down a third and a fourth time.

I cannot bear it. There is a swish of the whip again. An animal howl leaves my mouth. Now he flings himself upon me.

I instinctively defend myself, I compress my hips, but he forces his knees between them. It hurts, it hurts terribly, everything hurts. I cannot resist any longer. I have no strength left.

In my torment I dig my teeth into his shoulder. There is a sticky lump in my mouth. I try to spit it out, but I can't. It chokes me, I must spit it out. Now he catches me by the hair and strikes my head against the floor. Everything is creaking, crashing within me, all around me, but there is no pain. Everything goes dark. There are big red rings dancing round my eyes then they recede more and more. I feel as if I were sinking into a bottomless pit.

'So this is death!' That is my last thought. No . . . no . . . I am still alive. God, what does this beast want of me? I implore – don't hurt me. Jimmy – our wedding. No, don't . . . it hurts. He is tearing me to pieces. My stomach . . . It hurts . . . Oh God.

A distant whining sound brings me to – it is like the yelping of a dog that is being beaten. It takes a long time before I realise that it is my own voice. I suddenly come back to reality. There is a fog before my eyes, but through it I can make him out – the sergeant is near me. His eyes are protruding, his breath is panting and wheezing into my ears. His face – his mouth is surrounded with dried blood – my blood. I try to move, but I have no strength left. There is a cruel fire burning, searing my flesh, my inside. I feel giddy. The world is spinning round with me. Then everything merges to blindness.

I come to. There is a roar of cheering, the clinking of many glasses. The sergeant is standing in the open doorway:

'The wild cat is tamed,' he is saying. 'Boys, she was a virgin. What do you say to that?'

Another burst of cheering, then he closes the door. But I am not left alone for long.

The others came in. Ten, a hundred, a thousand, one after another. They flung themselves upon me, digging into my wounds while they defiled me. I suffered terribly; I felt as if they were tearing my intestines out bit by bit. Who is this? The sergeant again? Or is it that I see his bestial face in every German? I try to move, but can't. I hurt all over, my whole body is a sea of fire, my insides . . . they have torn me to pieces. Here is another . . . another . . . another. But the grinning face is always that of the sergeant. Don't, don't, mercy.

Then everything passed. The Germans kept coming, spitting obscene words at me, guffawing as they tortured me. I saw them, but felt no pain. I was in a trance, I just guessed what was happening to me, but did not know for certain. From somewhere far away the sound of music was seeping towards me, the sound of a sentimental Schumann song. It was a long time before I realised that the sounds came from the next room, where my executioners were singing.

Then, through all the torment and horror it suddenly became light around me. The fog dispersed and I understood everything. I understood that I had been dead for a long time.

I suddenly remembered and knew – knew for certain – that I was already dead – I had died when the German beast knocked my head against the floor. That was when the beast killed my spirit.

An infinite calm swept over me when I at last understood.

These madmen do not know that they are torturing a corpse. It is still moving, it still feels, yet it is only a corpse. It hurts when they are torturing me, it hurts when they come upon me, one after the other, but I am just a corpse.

'You're laughing, harlot, you like it,' said the last German as he rolled off me and spat into my face. He did not know that he was spitting at a corpse.

Genia Demianova

The author subsequently joined the partisans, but died later during the war. It is possible that she is a fictional creation, although the event described above is typical of the treatment meted out to civilians during the war by many soldiers – of all nationalities.

✠

The War in the Air

Three kills and shot down twice – all in a day

June 21st was a sunny summer day. I remember it quite clearly, and shall never forget it. About midday the radar station reported 'Large formation of enemy aircraft approaching.' As we found out later, it was a force of Bristol Blenheim bombers with a fighter escort of about fifty Spitfires and Hurricanes. They were raiding St Omer, a favourite target of the British in those days. I gave the alarm and sent up all three wings. They soon engaged the enemy in a battle which cost both sides heavy losses.

At 12.24 I took off with the squadron detailed as the leading unit of the group, and at an altitude of 10,000 feet we sighted the British formations which had just raided the airfield of Arques, near St Omer. From a greater height I dived right through the fighter escort on to the main bomber force and attacked the right plane of the lower rear row from very close. The Blenheim caught fire immediately. Some of the crew baled out and the plane exploded on crashing near the airfield of St Omer. The time was 12.32, eight minutes after take-off. Kill no. 68.

In the meantime, my unit was wrestling with Spitfires and Hurricanes. My section companion and I were the only Germans at the moment attacking the bombers, and I immediately started my second attack. Again I managed to dive through the fighters. This time it was a Blenheim in the leading row of the formation. Flames and black smoke poured from her starboard engine, she broke away from the formation, and I saw two parachutes open. The time was 12.36. Kill no. 69.

Then Spitfires were on my tail. Tracer bullets whizzed past me. I tried to shake them off with a sharp downward bank, and got rid of my pursuer, but I had caught a packet and a layer of haze enveloped me, my right radiator was shot up, and I was leaving a long trail of smoke behind. A little later the engine seized up. Emergency landing! Luckily, I was able to make a harmless crash landing on the airfield of Calais-Marck, just below me. Half an hour later an Me 108 collected me and brought me back to my group.

After lunch the dance continued. At four o'clock there was a new alarm, 'Strong British fighter formations approaching from the Channel,' and all airworthy machines were up again and at the enemy. My faithful section companion, Rottenflieger Hegenauer, who had flown almost all the sorties against England with me during the previous year, had been shot down almost at the same time as myself, so I started alone. South-east of

Boulogne I sighted my No. 1 Wing, and decided to join them. Slightly lower and to port of them was a Spitfire formation. I immediately attacked one of the last planes of the formation – unfortunately, not *the* last, but the Spitfire I went after crashed in flames. Kill no. 70. A nice even number, I thought, as I followed her down to register the kill. I had no witness, as I was flying alone.

Hell broke loose in my crate. Now they've got you! That's what happens if you take your eye off for a couple of seconds! Something hard hit my head and arm. My aircraft was in bad shape, the wings ripped by cannon fire, and I myself was sitting half in the open. The right side of the fuselage had been shot away and fuel tank and radiator were both leaking heavily. Instinctively, I banked away to the north, noticing almost calmly as I did so that my heavily damaged plane still flew and responded tolerably well with the engine cut off. My luck has held once more, I was thinking, and I will try to glide home. My altitude was 18,000 feet.

My arm and head were bleeding, but I didn't feel any pain. No time for that. Anyhow, nothing precious was hurt. A sharp detonation tore me out of my reverie – the tank, which up to then had been gurgling away quietly, suddenly exploded and the whole fuselage was immediately aflame. Burning petrol ran into the cockpit. It was getting uncomfortably hot. Only one thought remained: Get out! Get out! Get out! The cockpit-roof release would not work – must be jammed. Shall I burn alive in here? I tore my belt open, tried to open the hinged top of the roof, but the air pressure on it was too strong. There were flames all around me. You must open it! You must not fry to death in here! Terror. Those were the most fearful seconds of my life. With a last effort I pushed my whole body against the roof. The flap opened and was torn away by the air-stream. I had already pulled her nose up but the push against the joystick did not throw me entirely clear of the burning coffin which a few minutes before was still my faithful Me 109. The parachute on which I had been sitting was caught on the fixed part of the cockpit roof. The entire plane was now in flames and was dashing down to earth with me. With my arm around the aerial mast, I tugged and pushed against anything I could find with my feet – all in vain! Should I be doomed at the last moment, although I was already half-freed? I don't know how I got free in the end, but suddenly I was falling, and turned over several times in the air. Thank God! In my excitement I nearly operated the quick harness release instead of the cord, and at the last moment noticed that I was releasing the safety catch. Another shock! The parachute and I would have arrived separately, which would have done neither of us any good. A jerk, and like a pendulum I was suspended from the open parachute. Slowly and softly I floated down to earth.

Below me a black column of smoke marked the spot where my machine had crashed. By rights I should have landed in the Forêt de Boulogne like a monkey on a tree, but the parachute only brushed a poplar and then folded up. Luckily, I landed in a soft, boggy meadow, and after the high tension of nerves and energy I had been under, collapsed immediately. I felt as wretched as a dog. Shot, and bleeding profusely from head and arm, with a painfully twisted ankle which at once started to swell, I could neither walk nor stand up. Suspicious and unfriendly French peasants came at last and carried me into a farmhouse. The first Germans I saw were men of the Todt Organisation from a nearby building site, who packed me into a car and took me back to my base at Audembert.

Everybody was already considerably worried about me, and my reception was correspondingly warm. After I had drunk an extra large cognac and smoked a cigar, essential after any kill, I felt much better. In the naval hospital at Hardinghem I was repaired by my good friend, Marine-Geschwaderarzt Dr Heim. I am especially grateful to him for allowing me to smoke on the operating table, and for not detaining me at the hospital, but letting me return to my base. I could continue to conduct operations from the ground, at least for the time being.

The news of the day's events – the Schlageter Group recorded a bag of fourteen – travelled fast, and congratulations poured in from all sides. My birthday and my seventieth kill were celebrated in a suitable manner. Osterkamp came over from Le Touquet, but what he had to tell me besides his congratulations struck me like a bolt from the blue – no one had expected anything like it, least of all myself. So far the Oak Leaves to the Knight's Cross had been the highest award for bravery, and as far as we knew there was nothing higher to win in this war. Late the same night arrived the confirmation from the Führer's Headquarters: '. . . I present you as the first officer of the German forces with the Oak Leaves with Swords to the Knight's Cross of the Iron Cross. Adolf Hitler!'

Adolf Galland

Wing Leader

By mid-1941, the RAF felt strong enough to patrol the Continent in strength, massing up to half a dozen squadrons – perhaps 60 aircraft – into wings. These offered battle to the Luftwaffe pilots who hunted the bombers that the British were often escorting (as here over Lille). Some wing leaders took their call signs from their initials: 'Dogsbody' was Douglas Bader.

'Dogsbody from Smith. 109s above. Six o'clock. About twenty-five or thirty.'

'Well done. Watch 'em and tell me when to break.'

I can see them. High in the sun, and their presence only betrayed by the reflected sparkle from highly polished windscreens and cockpit covers.

'They're coming down, Dogsbody. Break left.' And round to port we go, with Smith sliding below Bader and Cocky and me above so that we cover each other in this steep turn. We curve round and catch a glimpse of four baffled 109s climbing back to join their companions, for they can't stay with us in a turn. The keen eyes of Smith saved us from a nasty smack that time.

'Keep turning, Dogsbody. More coming down,' from Cocky.

'OK. We might get a squirt this time,' rejoins Bader. What a man, I think, what a man!

The turn tightens and in my extreme position on the starboard side I'm driving my Spitfire through a greater radius of curve than the others and falling behind. I kick on hard bottom rudder and skid down and behind the leader. More 109s hurtle down from above and a section of four angle in from the starboard flank. I look round for other Spitfires but there are none in sight. The four of us are alone over Lille.

'Keep turning. Keep turning.' (From Bader.) 'They can't stay with us.' And we keep turning, hot and frightened and a long way from home. We can't keep turning all bloody day, I think bitterly.

Cocky has not re-formed after one of our violent breaks. I take his place next to Bader and the three of us watch the Messerschmitts, time their dives and call the break into their attacks. The odds are heavily against us.

We turn across the sun and I am on the inside. The blinding light seems only two feet above Bader's cockpit and if I drop further below or he gains a little more height, I shall lose him. Already his Spitfire has lost its colour and is only a sharp, black silhouette, and now it has disappeared completely, swallowed up by the sun's fierce light. I come out of the turn and am stunned to find myself alone in the Lille sky.

The Messerschmitts come in close for the kill. At this range their camouflage looks dirty and oil-stained, and one brute has a startling black-and-white spinner. In a hot sweat of fear I keep turning and turning, and the fear is mingled with an abject humiliation that these bastards should single me out and chop me at their leisure. The radio is silent, or probably

I don't hear it in the stress of trying to stay alive. I can't turn all day. Le Touquet is seventy hostile miles away; far better to fight back and take one with me.

Four Messerschmitts roar down from six o'clock. I see them in time and curve the shuddering, protesting Spitfire to meet them, for she is on the brink of a high-speed stall. They are so certain of my destruction that they are flying badly and I fasten on to tail-end Charlie and give him a long burst of fire. He is at the maximum range, and although my shooting has no apparent effect some of my despair and fear on this fateful afternoon seems to evaporate at the faint sound of the chattering machine guns. But perhaps my attack has its just reward, for Smith's voice comes loud and clear over the radio.

'One Spit behind, Dogsbody. A thousand yards. Looks like he's in trouble.'

Then I see them. Two aircraft with the lovely curving wings that can only belong to Spitfires. I take a long breath and in a deliberately calm voice:

'It's me, Dogsbody – Johnnie.'

'OK, Johnnie. We'll orbit here for you. Drop in on my starboard. We'll get a couple of these ———'

There is no longer any question of not getting home now that I am with Bader again. He will bring us safely back to Tangmere and I know he is enjoying this, for he sounds full of confidence over the radio. A dozen Messerschmitts still shadow our small formation. They are well up-sun and waiting to strike. Smith and I fly with our necks twisted right round, like the resting mallard ducks one sees in the London parks, and all our concentration focused on the glinting shoal of 109s.

'Two coming down from five o'clock, Dogsbody. Break right,' from me. And this time mine is the smallest turn so that I am the first to meet the attack. A 109 is very close and climbing away to port. Here is a chance. Time for a quick shot and no danger of losing the other two Spitfires if I don't get involved in a long tail chase. I line up my Spitfire behind the 109, clench the spade-grip handle of the stick with both hands and send short bursts into his belly at less than a hundred yards. The 109 bursts apart and the explosion looks exactly the same as a near burst of heavy flak, a vicious flower with a poisonous glowing centre and black swirling edges.

I re-form and the Messerschmitts come in again, and this time Bader calls the break. It is well judged and the wing leader fastens on to the last 109 and I cover his Spitfire as it appears to stand on its tail with wisps of smoke plummeting from the gun ports. The enemy aircraft starts to pour white smoke from its belly and thick black smoke from the engine. They merge together and look like a long, dirty banner against the faded blue of some high cirrus cloud.

'Bloody good shooting, sir.'

'We'll get some more.'

Johnnie Johnson

In August 1941, Bader was captured after a mid-air collision above Béthune. His adversary and admirer, Adolf Galland, went to meet him.

Bader was on his guard against giving the slightest hint of any military information, and in any case we were strictly forbidden to interrogate prisoners: this was left entirely to specialists at the interrogation centres. Nevertheless, I had given instructions that nothing should be said which could even resemble a question. He did not even admit how many enemy planes he had to his credit.

'Oh, not many,' he said. He did not know how many had been recognised, and confirmations were still outstanding. 'Well, you must know approximately how many,' I urged him. 'No,' he replied, avoiding the issue defensively. 'Compared with Molders and your bag, they are so few that it's hardly worth talking about them.' Actually he had some twenty to his credit. Perhaps it really was only modesty that he did not want to talk about it with us.

Bader loosened up during the course of this free-and-easy conversation, so I proposed a little tour of our installations, which he accepted with pleasure and obvious interest. The leg which had been salvaged from the wreckage squeaked and rattled like a small armoured car. Bader asked me if we could not drop a message over England to tell his boys and his wife that he was well and to get him his spare legs, a better uniform than his battle-dress, tobacco, and a new pipe to replace the broken one he had stuck together with adhesive tape. His wife would know what to do. The spare legs were on the left in the wardrobe. I offered him some tobacco and one of my pipes, but he refused. Naturally, it was outside my province to give him a definite promise to fulfil this request, which was certainly of considerable originality, but I promised I would do my best.

The masterly way in which our airfield was camouflaged attracted his attention as an expert, and a long conversation about technical details followed, during which he praised the better points of the Messerschmitt while we praised the Spitfire. Would I allow him to sit in the cockpit of my plane? 'Why not!' Everything had to be explained to him in the smallest detail. I enjoyed the interest and understanding this great pilot showed. He would have fitted splendidly into our 'Club'.

Bader bent down to me from the cockpit of my plane, in which he was sitting, and said, 'Will you do me a great favour?' 'With pleasure, if it is in my power,' I answered. 'At least once in my life I would like to fly a Messerschmitt. Let me do just one circle over the airfield.' He said it with a smile and looked me straight in the eyes. I nearly weakened, but replied: 'If I grant your wish, I'm afraid you'll escape and I should be forced to chase after you. Now we have met, we don't want to shoot at each other again, do we?' He laughed and changed the subject. After a hearty goodbye, he went back to the hospital.

Adolf Galland

Bader had lost both legs in an accident in 1931, but had overcome his disability to return to active duty in 1939. He was, however, to spend the rest of the war as a prisoner.

☦

The Middle East

In April, a military coup brought a pro-Nazi regime to power in the former British mandate of Iraq, endangering Britain's oil supplies. An Indian division was landed at Basra, while another force set out overland from Transjordan. With the latter was the future novelist John Masters, then a career soldier with the Gurkhas.

Another relieving force arrived, having travelled across the desert from Palestine. It contained some Household Cavalry, who normally stand guard duty in Whitehall, splendid in long black boots, steel breastplates, and nodding plumes, but the majority were Yeomanry. The major-general in command was of course a regular, a cavalryman, and his first name was George. Normally this would have been a piece of information of little practical use to his subordinate officers or men, but Yeomanry were something special. At the general's final inspection before the division left England for war, he had asked one of the Yeomanry colonels whether everything was in order. The colonel replied, 'Oh, I think so, George.' The general gently pressed for details – ammunition? Vehicles? Non-coms' training? Gas-masks? The colonel scratched his head and said, 'Dash it, I don't know about any of that, George . . . but we've got forty dozen of champagne, well crated, and the pack of foxhounds is in fine fettle.'

George now took over command of all land forces from Colonel Roberts. John Strickland, of our 'A' Company, had the privilege of sitting in at one of his first conferences, and surreptitiously noted down a conversation that ran as follows:

THE GENERAL: 'Well, I think we should send a patrol up the Euphrates for fifty miles or so, to make sure no one's lying up in the desert out there.'

ONE OF HIS YEOMANRY COLONELS: 'Good idea, George.'

THE GENERAL: 'From your regiment, I thought, Harry. About a troop, with a couple of guns, eh?'

THE COLONEL: 'Oh yes, George . . . I think I'll send Charles.'

THE GENERAL (horror in his face): 'Charles? *Charles?* Do you think he'll go?'

We learned later that though 2nd Lieutenant Charles was distinctly vexed at being sent on such a piddling mission, he did finally agree to go, since George and Harry seemed to set so much store on it.

They were delightful people. My own favourite story about them concerns an early inspection, by the general, of one of the regiments. The Yeomanry colonel, going down the line introducing his officers, stopped before one captain, and said, 'This is Captain . . . Captain . . .' He shook his head, snapped his fingers and cried genially, 'Memory like a sieve! I'll be forgetting the names of me hounds next.'

                                                                    John Masters

Masters soon had to assess the mettle of a new commander, under whom he was shortly to serve in the Far East.

Slim was squarely built, with a heavy slightly undershot jaw and short greying hair. He began to speak, slowly and simply, with no affectation. He told us first that we had done a good job in the Iraqi campaign. But no one could call that a very serious business. He had already seen enough of our fighting spirit and our technical competence to know that we needed little teaching there. What he wanted to do was to prepare us, practically and above all mentally, for the heavier fighting that we must soon meet.

By now he had our whole attention. He talked a bit about matters that still needed attention – road discipline, defence against air attack, battle drills to speed up the execution of orders . . . Then he began to talk about the nature of modern war, of what it was really like when you engaged an enemy as determined, as numerous, and perhaps better armed than yourselves. Then, he said, tactics and strategy, important though they have been and still are, become less central. Situations develop which no tactical or strategical move can alter . . .

'We make the best plans we can, gentlemen, and train our wills to hold steadfastly to them in the face of adversity, and yet to be flexible to change them when events show them to be unsound, or to take advantage of an opportunity that unfolds during the battle itself. We have already trained our men to the highest possible level of skill with their weapons and in their use of minor tactics. But in the end every important battle develops to a point where there is no real control by senior commanders. Each soldier feels himself to be alone. Discipline may have got him to the place where he is, and discipline may hold him there – for a time. Co-operation with other men in the same situation can help him to move forward. Self-preservation will make him defend himself to the death, if there is no other way. But what makes him go on, alone, determined to break the will of the enemy opposite him, is morale. Pride in himself as an independent thinking man, who knows why he's there, and what he's doing. Absolute confidence that the best has been done for him, and that his fate is now in his own hands. The dominant feeling of the battlefield is loneliness, gentlemen, and morale, only morale, individual morale as a foundation under training and discipline, will bring victory.'

I went back to our camp in a thoughtful mood. Slim's sort of battle wouldn't be much of a lark, after all.

John Masters

The attractions of command

It was good fun commanding a division in the Iraq desert. It is good fun commanding a division anywhere. It is one of the four best commands in the Service – a platoon, a battalion, a division and an army. A platoon, because it is your first command, because you are young, and because, if you are any good, you know the men in it better than their mothers do and love them as much. A battalion, because it is a unit with a life of its own; whether it is good or bad depends on you alone; you have at last a real command. A division, because it is the smallest formation that is a complete orchestra of war and the largest in which every man can know you. An army, because the creation of its spirit and its leadership in battle gives you the greatest unity of emotional and intellectual experience that can befall a man.

William Slim

Syria, which was under French mandate, had sided with the Vichy regime and had been used by the Germans to provide aid to the rebellion in Iraq. In June, it was invaded by the Allies, who at first met fierce resistance.

In the earlier stages of the engagement, before heat and tiredness had worn the edge off enthusiasm, I crawled forward to an outpost to see what I could of our enemy. At dawn, when we had reached the mountain-top, we had seen a few unidentifiable figures silhouetted against the rising sun. Since then the enemy had been invisible, shooting at us through loopholes in the fort or from the neighbouring hillsides. I lay down beside a trooper. More for the fun of the thing than because he had a target, he was firing a Hotchkiss sporadically at a low built-up stone parapet about fifty yards away. Suddenly, behind the parapet, two black French soldiers (Senegalese, I believe) popped their heads up. Their two faces, under steel helmets, grinned at us, and I can still see the whiteness of their teeth and eyeballs. God knows what they thought they were doing. Probably they had never been in a battle before and, like myself, they were childishly curious to have a look at their enemy.

Or were they attempting to do something more? If men are ever to cease destroying one another, if the everlasting tit-for-tat process is ever to be halted, it will perhaps only come by an individual, a simple black man for example, standing up suddenly in the face of bullets and crying out:

'See, here I am. I don't want to kill you. Why kill me? Let us stop the battle and be friends.'

The trooper beside me was so astonished by the apparition of the two black men that he never thought of firing his Hotchkiss.

'Shoot!' I hissed at him.

He pressed the trigger and nothing happened. A cartridge had jammed. There was a simple drill for curing the stoppage, but now in his excitement, the trooper bungled it. I pushed him out of the way, grabbed the gun and ejected the cartridge.

Over the sights, I saw my burst hit the top of the parapet. The two grinning faces vanished like puppets. A little dust lingered in the air, where they had been. Thus, with the wantonness of a boy destroying some harmless bird for 'sport', I contributed my share towards the never-ending story of man's inhumanity to man. But at the time I thought I had behaved rather splendidly and the trooper was impressed too.

John Verney

By mid-July the Allies, led by Lt-Gen. Sir Maitland Wilson, were nearing Beirut and the French sought an armistice. This was signed at Acre, amid scenes of near farce.

However, at 11 p.m. all was ready for the initialling, and the journalists were ushered in. Edward Genock, the Paramount cameraman, had been concerned that the lights in the conference room would not be sufficient for his newsreel. He had obtained several reading-lamps in the barracks, and these he had joined together ready to plug into a power point in the conference room. As soon as the correspondents were admitted, Genock's assistant strode forward and took up a position with his makeshift candelabra at General Wilson's elbow. The general, a large and benign-looking man, allowed himself one astonished glance at this sudden visitation and dipped his pen for the initialling. The candelabra was plugged in, and all the lights in the room went out. Someone produced a fountain-pen torch and flashed it aimlessly among the blacked-out delegates. Others brought a staff car to the door, and turned its lights in a blinding stream upon the Frenchmen at the conference table.

It was proposed then that a motorcycle should be brought right into the room in order to shed its light upon General Wilson's papers. A dispatch rider accordingly bowled his machine up the steps and into the position lately occupied by the unfortunate holder of the candelabra. Then before the fascinated gaze of the company the soldier began to set his motorcycle in motion: a performance which would have utterly deafened everyone in that confined space. 'But I can't light the light unless I start the motor,' the soldier protested glumly. He was ordered to take his machine away and hurricane lamps were called for.

During the period of waiting it was seen that a number of unauthorised persons, hangers-on around the barracks, had crowded into the conference room to enjoy this entirely unusual spectacle. The order was given for their removal. The order, however, was not quite understood by a sergeant of police who had possibly had a training in raiding nightclubs before the war. He now flung his arms solidly across the door and announced: 'My orders are that no one who was in this room when the lights went out can leave.' At length the hurricane lamps were brought, and in an atmosphere that was beyond either laughter or tears the papers were initialled.

Alan Moorehead

‡

Life in Berlin

21 AUGUST 1941

Again the Gestapo are on the warpath. This time they hunt down anthroposophists, and leaders and members of other sects. Their fortunes are confiscated; churches, schools and meeting places are closed.

There is a story about that: 'I will let you go free,' the Gestapo man says to his victim, 'if you can tell me which of my eyes is artificial.' After long and serious consideration the anthroposophist tells him: 'The right one.'

'How did you find out?' The Gestapo man is most surprised for no one had managed to solve the riddle before.

'I noticed in your right eye, sir,' the prisoner replies, 'a vestige of human feeling.'

22 AUGUST 1941

Russia is nearing collapse. Her armies on land, sea and in the air are irrevocably destroyed.

But what a miraculous feature of this campaign: there are no German losses.

The people accept this as a matter of course. Had the Führer not promised them just that?

On the contrary, there was considerable disappointment. The victories in the West had brought home so much loot that the same was expected from the Russian front. When there was no sign of it because of the scorched earth policy of the Russians, discontent became audible.

It went even as far as free fights among women who called each other names because the husband of one was fighting unprofitably on the Russian front, while the husband of the other enjoyed life and loot peacefully as a member of the occupational army in Brussels.

Frau Krause, whom I meet in the street, draws me into a doorway and bursts into bitter tears. Her boy has been killed on the Eastern front. She must not wear mourning for him. The State denies her even this comfort.

For if all widows and orphans of the war were to go around in black clothes, the Führer's stories of negligible losses would not hold water.

23 AUGUST 1941

It looks as if today they had not advanced their customary two hundred kilometres into Russia, so Goebbels presents his deluded people with a few particularly impressive U-boat successes. If one were to take the trouble and add up the figures of the official shipping reports one would discover what imposing feats have been accomplished by the Nazi U-boats. They have sunk between ten to twenty times the entire tonnage of the world's shipping.

24 AUGUST 1941

I visited Paula today. Her husband has died.

He was an Aryan, she a Jewess.

Nevertheless, according to the law their household was Aryan and Paula enjoyed all the advantages this entailed. She was allowed to keep her jewellery, was issued with clothing coupons, had no curfew, was free to go where she pleased; in short, she was treated like a human being.

And now her Aryan husband is dead.

Even before she had time to recover from her first grief, she received an order announcing that from now on she was to regard herself as non-Aryan, all privileges were cancelled as from that day.

What a come-down!

25 AUGUST 1941

Hurray, today the British have achieved a master-stroke. My Aryan foreman lends me his midday paper. In huge headlines we are told that 'perfidious Albion' under cover of night has destroyed Berlin's most treasured cultural landmarks such as the Brandenburger Tor, the Zeughaus and all the monuments in the Siegesallee. As the greatest outrage of all they have smashed that latest symbol of Nazi glory and power, the Ehrenmal. I can hardly hide my joy at this welcome news. The foreman, who as a former socialist used to regard Nazi stories of the enemy's alleged atrocities with necessary caution, openly doubting them as the exaggerations they were, is rather impressed and upset at this news. 'No,' he ponders, 'they shouldn't have done that. It's against all the rules of straightforward warfare. Honestly, that is the last thing I would have expected the British to do. What about their famous "fair play"?'

Nevertheless, I am pleased.

I must go and see for myself.

Dead tired and as dirty as I come from the factory I take a train to the scene of these recent outrages.

Throngs of people everywhere.

I rub my eyes. This is no mirage. The Brandenburger Tor rises before me in undiminished splendour and beauty. Nothing has happened to it.

Somewhere on the ground I discover a little plaster, obviously the result of blast from an explosion nearby. Ah, and a little gold dust, shaken from the crown of the goddess of victory up there.

The museum still stands, so does the glorious Ehrenmal; nothing at all has been damaged, everything looks unchanged.

Did the little doctor put these lies into the world to keep the British from coming back a second time by convincing them that their work of destruction was done? Or did Goebbels find that a little oil was needed to stir the gradually dying flames of hatred in the hearts of the German people?

Catherine Klein

‡

The Final Solution

Rudolf Hoess, the commandant of Auschwitz, recalls the almost mundane discussions he had with two of the Reich's senior figures about the planned genocide of the Jews.

In the summer of 1941, I cannot remember the exact date, I was suddenly summoned to the Reichsführer-SS, directly by his adjutant's office. Contrary to his usual custom, Himmler received me without his adjutant being present and said in effect:

'The Führer has ordered that the Jewish question be solved once and for all and that we, the SS, are to implement that order.

'The existing extermination centres in the east are not in a position to carry out the large actions which are anticipated. I have therefore earmarked Auschwitz for this purpose, both because of its good position as regards communications and because the area can easily be isolated and camouflaged. At first I thought of calling in a senior SS officer for this job, but I changed my mind in order to avoid difficulties concerning the terms of reference. I have now decided to entrust this task to you. It is difficult and onerous and calls for complete devotion notwithstanding the difficulties that may arise. You will learn further details from Sturmbannführer

Eichmann of the Reich Security Head Office who will call on you in the immediate future.

'The departments concerned will be notified by me in due course. You will treat this order as absolutely secret, even from your superiors. After your talk with Eichmann you will immediately forward to me the plans of the projected installations.

'The Jews are the sworn enemies of the German people and must be eradicated. Every Jew that we can lay our hands on is to be destroyed now during the war, without exception. If we cannot now obliterate the biological basis of Jewry, the Jews will one day destroy the German people.'

On receiving these grave instructions, I returned forthwith to Auschwitz, without reporting to my superior at Orianenburg.

Shortly afterwards Eichmann came to Auschwitz and disclosed to me the plans for the operations as they affected the various countries concerned. I cannot remember the exact order in which they were to take place. First was to come the eastern part of Upper Silesia and the neighbouring parts of Polish territory under German rule, then, depending on the situation, simultaneously Jews from Germany and Czechoslovakia, and then finally the Jews from the West: France, Belgium and Holland. He also told me the approximate numbers of transports that might be expected, but I can no longer remember these.

We discussed the ways and means of effecting the extermination. This could only be done by gassing, since it would have been absolutely impossible to dispose by shooting of the large numbers of people that were expected, and it would have placed too heavy a burden on the SS men who had to carry it out, especially because of the women and children among the victims.

Eichmann told me about the method of killing people with exhaust gases in lorries, which had previously been used in the east. But there was no question of being able to use this for these mass transports that were due to arrive in Auschwitz. Killing with showers of carbon monoxide while bathing, as was done with mental patients in some places in the Reich, would necessitate too many buildings and it was also very doubtful whether the supply of gas for such a vast number of people would be available. We left the matter unresolved. Eichmann decided to try and find a gas which was in ready supply and which would not entail special installations for its use, and to inform me when he had done so. We inspected the area in order to choose a likely spot. We decided that a peasant farmstead situated in the north-west corner of what later became the third building sector at Birkenau would be the most suitable. It was isolated and screened by woods and hedges, and it was also not far from the railway. The bodies could be placed in long, deep pits dug in the nearby meadows. We had not at that time thought of burning the corpses. We calculated that after gas-proofing the premises then available, it would be possible to kill about 800 people simultaneously with a suitable gas. These figures were borne out later in practice.

Rudolf Hoess

Hoess was hanged by the Poles in 1947 in his own extermination camp. He was ordered to write his autobiography while he awaited trial. 'I am completely normal,' he declared, 'I led a completely normal life.'

Autumn 1941

Wartime London

Fires were started

The Luftwaffe's raids on London continued. The conflagrations that ensued were often fought by part-time volunteers. Their chronicler was William Sansom.

25 SEPTEMBER 1941
It was a blue, moonlit night and the flames blazed orange. The house stood dark and detached in its own garden of trees and shrubbery walls. It was all dark up to the top two floors and there the bright fire suddenly began. Windows sprang to life. And above, through broken rafters, the flames curled out nakedly into the night. A hail of sparks and small embers eddied round the chimneys and false turrets. The house looked like a miniature castle on fire, a pyrotechnic display piece, the kind of fire you would find drawn in a children's fairy book.

For a while we stood in the garden, playing water up from our hoses to the top windows. The lawn was dark and muddied by the water that leaked all round us. With the gunflash and the racket of shellfire and the thick mud plastering my heavy boots, I felt the scene had something of the epic Flanders. The shape of an officer hurried past. He shouted to some men, 'Take a branch up the stairs inside.' His voice echoed among the trees, a lonely voice among all this movement of fire and water. Despite the firemen, there is a deserted air about a fire. The streets to either side are empty. There is human movement only among the firemen – but they are all set upon the same object: part of the character of a real crowd is the atmosphere of a thousand different directions.

I could see fire through the staircase windows. It looked like bright sunlight behind yellow stained glass. Then, as I looked, three shadowy figures passed up the stairs silhouetted against the light. It looked as though they were walking right in the fire. Then they disappeared.

Some seconds later a cry, vague and far away, came from somewhere above that staircase. Looking at the house, seeing that the fire on the staircase was burning up, knowing that the men had passed beyond to the floor above – where the fire must have been hotter and smokier still – it seemed that they must inevitably be trapped. And that cry – how stifled and lost against the fierce open crackling of the fire.

A dark shape hurrying by. The officer again. He grabbed my arm. 'Go up and see what they want.'

Given an option, in the unhurried lights of day and peace, I would probably have found a few quick and good excuses to walk the other way. But there is something automatic in obeying an order. At a moment of that urgency, with all the deep-seated discipline laid years before at school and now incubated in the service, my heavy boots carried me straight forward. At the same time I knew, quite distinctly, that I might have hesitated to go forward voluntarily: also that I was afraid beyond the automatic reflex of the moment: also that anyway it wasn't as bad as all that because the officer could diagnose the situation more correctly than I and he would never *order* a man in where the odds were too great.

Once across the threshold I was in the smoke. A faint light came down the stairwell from the fire above. It was still dark – but here was a different texture of darkness. It was darkly opalescent. The smoke fog was thick but it held a vague, reflected light. Now and again I could just see what my boots hit. But at every step I cursed my forgotten torch. It was like blindman's buff, feeling along with arms outstretched, hoping to bang into the banisters, hoping not to drop suddenly into some obscure hole.

The smell of burning and blistered brick and wood and plaster was thicker than the smoke itself. It went so deep that I seemed to smell it with the bottom of my lungs. Water intensifies the smell. And there was plenty of water streaming down from above. I coughed and grasped along to wherever the banisters might be. The kick of the smoke was not yet strong enough to force me down to the cool air a foot or so from the floorboards.

I found the banisters by kicking along the hose track and making for the sound of the heavy water stream. Then the light got clearer and I started up the stairs. Water gushed all over the wood and the sodden carpet. I kept to the sides in case they had been weakened. I felt the wood would *melt*. The rainwater resounded constantly, in rhythm, as a hailstorm drums corrugated sheeting. I was drenched through after one flight. The water got right down into the tail of my shirt.

As I mounted so the light became clearer, I stumbled about a bit on the first landing. Through the whitish fog a broken electric lead trailed towards me. It hung from the ceiling. Within the circling smoke it seemed to weave like a submarine weed. I dodged underneath it. I had heard how a shock on your metal helmet can knock you down. This was a game the regular firemen used to play on fresh recruits in time of peace.

I was following the hose up the stairs. Then up above me I saw the first signs of fire. It came suddenly. A burning frieze a few feet away up the wall. It looked remote, undangerous. But now the heat was perceptible, the smoke thicker. It began to sting into my eyes, I called out to see how near I was to the others. I was just getting to another landing. An answering shout came from somewhere along the corridor.

The plaster was burning in one or two places. I could hear something crackling hard above my head. The sound was muffled, like the noises that come through an apartment wall. Probably the loft was well alight. As yet the ceiling screened it but at some time the ceiling would collapse. I made the landing and rounded the corner into the corridor. The first room to the left was on fire. I looked in. Nobody there. But I had forgotten the hose. This led straight along the corridor. The men would be at the end of the hose.

I went along. Some rooms were burning. These flickered with brilliant orange and deep reds. But, strangely, the next room would perhaps be quite untouched, detached in a sudden bare and negative twilight. I remember hoping the rooms on fire had burnt up most of themselves. I didn't want any flames crossing the corridor behind me.

Now I could hear the jet forcing heavily into some room ahead. I could hear the men grunting as they held the weight of the hose. It was getting hotter. I was sweating. But not with the heat so much as with running in those heavy clothes. The whole journey could not have taken more than a minute.

Then I saw them. The fireglow from the room flickered over their silver buttons and over the water on their faces and helmets and leggings. Their faces were black, like a sweep's face, with white eye-rings and pink rings round their mouths. They were all clustered round the nozzle of the hose, leaning forward against the recoil of water pressure, heads bent down to protect their faces from the singeing heat, swaying from side to side as they swept the room with a thundering broom of white water. They were up against the very end room. That was the worst part of the fire. They were all right. The floorway leading up to them was washed with water and still unburnt. When I got there, all they said was, 'For Christ's sake get back and tell them we want more pressure. Twenty bloody pounds more.' So I just went back.

William Sansom

*Charles Ritchie was a young Canadian diplomat in London, and the lover of the
novelist Elizabeth Bowen.*

In the expensive restaurants at this hour pink, well-scrubbed schoolboys
masquerading in guards' uniforms are drinking bad martinis with girlfriends in short fur capes and Fortnum and Mason shoes, who have spent
the day driving generals to the War Office or handing cups of tea and
back-chat to soldiers in canteens. Grass widows in black with diamond
clips or pearls are finding the conversation of Polish officers refreshingly
different from that of English husbands. Ugly vivacious ATS are ordering
vin rosé at the Coquille. A film actress (making the best of a patriotic part
at present) is just going through the swinging door of the Apéritif with
David Niven at her elbow. Ageing Edwardian hostesses whose big houses
are now shuttered and silent are taking little naps in their hideouts on the
third floor ('so much the safest floor, darling') at Claridge's or the Dor-
chester. Cedric (in a yachtsman's jacket) and Nigel are hipping their way
through the crowd of pansies in the Ritz bar (they all have the most madly
peculiar jobs in the Ministry of Information or the BBC). At the Travellers'
Club Harold Nicolson in his fruity voice is embellishing a story as he
settles on the leather sofa. Anne-Marie is sitting on the side of her bed at
the Ritz making eyes at herself in the mirror and trumpeting down the
telephone in Romanian French. It is a world of hotels and bars and little
pubs that have become the fashion overnight – of small drinking clubs run
by gangsters who make a nice profit out of prostitutes and the dope racket
– packed with RAF pilots, Canadian officers, blondes and slot-machines
and perhaps a baccarat table in the upstairs rooms.

And along Piccadilly from the Circus to Hyde Park Corner is an
incessant parade of prostitutes, and out of the black-out an acquisitive hand
on your arm and 'Feeling lonely, dearie?' 'Hello, my sweet' (in a Noël
Coward voice) or '*Chéri.*' In Berkeley Square the railings are down. An
old man is making a bonfire of dead leaves beside the little pavilion in the
centre of the garden.

Charles Ritchie

‡

Stuck in the mud of Odessa

German military surgeon Peter Bamm was a veteran of the First World War, but even he found the quagmire on the Russian front remarkable.

When one sees one of the roads along which reinforcements go forward to the front, the time-worn phrase 'an army worming its way along' describes the scene perfectly. Every man, every horse, every vehicle had its being twice over. Once in the control office of army command and once out here in the mud. At headquarters everything is neat and tidy; out here chaos is complete. Units become separated by many miles. No one can do anything to stop a new unit slipping from the left or right into a small gap between the marching columns. The 'road' is little more than a track – over which the light Russian peasant carts just manage to travel – hurriedly reinforced with gravel and a few broken stones. Stones are at a premium in the steppe. In a matter of hours an army's reinforcements grind a peasant track like that out of existence. This one had the added inconvenience of a ditch on either side which made it practically impossible to avoid an obstruction by cutting out into the fields.

This is the sort of thing that would happen: the back wheel of some horse-drawn vehicle in the mile-long column slips into a deep shell crater concealed by a puddle of water. The wheel breaks. The shaft rises in the air. The horses, wrenched upwards, shy and kick over the traces. One of the leads parts. The vehicle behind tries to overtake on the left but is unable to drive quite clear of the deep ruts. The right-hand back wheel of the second vehicle catches in the left-hand back wheel of the first. The horses rear and start kicking in all directions. There is no going forwards or backwards. An ammunition lorry returning empty from the front tries to pass the hopeless tangle on the narrow strip of roadway that remains. Shouts: 'We must get through!' It slowly subsides into the ditch and sticks fast. It is a private van converted to army use and is quite incapable of getting out on its own.

Now there is an impassable obstruction on the roads, on the army's supply route! Everyone becomes infected with uncontrollable fury. Everyone shouts at everyone else. Sweating, swearing, mud-spattered men start laying into sweating, shivering, mud-caked horses that are already frothing at the mouth. All at once the fury passes. Someone lights a cheroot. Someone takes the initiative. The horses are unhitched. The lorry is dragged out backwards from a ditch by horses harnessed to a swingletree attached to a rope. The vehicle with the broken wheel is emptied of its load. There is general laughter if a pale blue eiderdown or a few live geese come to light in the process. The men step into the pool of water which runs over the tops of their boots. They seize hold of the muddy wheel and shouting 'Heave! Heave!' manhandle the empty vehicle to the side. The horses are re-harnessed to the second wagon and it sets off once more. The lorry passes them, backfiring as it goes, on its way to the ammunition depot in the rear.

This scene is repeated a hundred times a day with monotonous regularity. But by each evening there has been a progression of twelve, six, occasionally only three miles. At one point a few fascines of intertwined gorse have been laid across the ditch. The whole crawling mass has meandered twenty yards on to the open field to by-pass a dud bomb which lies unexploded in the middle of the road. To left and right the fields are strewn with a weird assortment of stoves, milking stools, bedsteads, wireless-sets, munition boxes, lamps. It is like the aftermath of a flood. Every few hundred yards there is a broken-down vehicle; or a dead horse with swollen belly; or a corpse. Crows rise with a heavy flapping of wings. Tattered grey clouds chase without pause high above the living and the dead; high above beasts and men.

Peter Bamm

‡

Sidi Rezegh

On 18 November, the British commenced Operation Crusader, pushing forward into Libya. The attack, intended to forestall that expected by Rommel and to relieve the Australian garrison in the port of Tobruk, led to heavy fighting around Sidi Rezegh.

While the tanks were still locked in this bloodiest of all battles in the desert Rommel had decided upon a gamble that had the elements of genius and the wildest possible folly. He had detached a part of his tanks and armoured cars and flung them straight across the desert through the British lines of communication. A tank among unarmed lorries is like a shark among mackerel. In a spectacular night attack, the German Panzers had almost entirely overwhelmed the 5th South African Brigade and then they had plunged straight into Egypt and attempted to rejoin their infantry forces left on the frontier. British soft transports had scattered before them and confusion more deadly than shellfire spread everywhere. And now lost groups of men roamed about, passing and repassing through enemy lines. Convoys of vehicles were scattered over a hundred miles of desert, not knowing where to go. Batteries of guns and groups of tanks were left stranded in the empty desert. Men who believed they were holding the end of a continuous salient suddenly found the enemy behind them. And north of them and south of them and all round them. Then the enemy in turn would seek to carry off his booty and prisoners only to find that his own base had vanished and that he was in the midst of a strong British formation. Prisoners became gaolers. Men were captured and escaped three or four times. Half a dozen isolated engagements were going on. Field dressing stations and hospitals were taking in British and German and Italian wounded impartially, and as the battle flowed back and forth the hospitals would sometimes be under British command, sometimes under German. Both sides were using each other's captured guns, tanks and vehicles and absurd incidents were taking place. A British truck driven by a German and full of British prisoners ran up to an Italian lorry. Out jumped a platoon of New Zealanders and rescued our men. Vehicles full of Germans were joining British convoys by mistake – and escaping before they were noticed. Generals themselves were taking prisoners and corporals and brigadiers were manning machine-guns together. On the map the dispositions of the enemy and ourselves looked like an eight-decker rainbow cake, and as more and more confused information came in, Intelligence officers threw down their pencils in disgust, unable to plot the battle any further.

Alan Moorehead

Heinz Werner Schmidt, Rommel's staff officer, took part in the charge loosed at the South African positions.

'Attack!' The order was passed swiftly. The regimental commander led, standing erect in his open car. The Major's car followed with me right behind him. We headed straight for the enemy tanks. I glanced back. Behind me was a fan of our vehicles – a curious assortment of all types – spread out as far as the eye could see. There were armoured troop-carriers, cars of various kinds, caterpillars hauling mobile guns, heavy trucks with infantry, motorised anti-aircraft units. Thus we roared on towards the enemy 'barricade'.

I stared to the front fascinated. Right ahead was the erect figure of the Colonel commanding the regiment. On the left close by and slightly in rear of him was the Major's car. Tank shells were whizzing through the air. The defenders were firing from every muzzle of their 25-pounders and their little 2-pounder anti-tank guns. We raced on at a suicidal pace.

The battalion commander's car lurched and stopped suddenly – a direct hit. I had just time to notice the Colonel steadying himself. He turned sideways and dropped from the car like a felled tree. Then I had flashed past him. The Major was still ahead.

I recognised infantry positions in front of me. There was a tall, thin fellow out in the open, running backwards as if impelled by a jet from a hose. I heard bursts behind me and followed the tracer as it whipped past me into the distance ahead. How slowly tracer seems to travel! The tall fellow dropped.

We had almost reached the screen of anti-tank guns and the tanks. A cold shiver ran down my spine. I saw small round holes forming in the windscreen of my car – just as though some invisible mechanic were drilling them there. Machine-gun fire! My driver huddled lower and lower over the wheel.

The Major's car lurched and went over on its side. I was alone out in this inferno now. In front I saw nothing but belching guns.

Then suddenly there was a violent jolt, a screeching and a hiss and my car stopped dead. I saw a trench immediately ahead, leaped from the car, and plunged towards the slit. My driver leaped out even as I did. But before he could dive on his face, he suddenly stiffened up erect, spun on his axis, and then dropped limp.

I wriggled down to the comfort of Mother Earth. I was obviously in an outpost position abandoned by Sidi Rezegh defenders.

I raised my head gingerly. Where was the horde of vehicles that had been pressing on behind me?

Stopped, by God!

What was my driver doing? Was he still alive?

He lay close by – dead.

The great fan of our vehicles stood well behind me, motionless. I discovered later that they had hesitated, wavered, and pulled up when they saw their officers one by one fall ahead of them. But a junior lieutenant was still on his feet. He rallied them and called on them to advance again, an achievement for which he was awarded the Ritterkreuz.

It had been a mistake for me to lift my head. Only too obviously, I had been spotted. Missiles whanged past now, clearly aimed at me alone. With every splash of lead I hugged the earth more closely. The slit-trench was, fortunately, not too shallow. Then I heard a fluttering noise, followed by an explosion. I knew the sound only too well. It was repeated again and again. Mortars!

Now I was certain that my fate was sealed. My mouth was dry, my lips parched. I thought of home. So this, then, was the end, in a miserable hole in the dirt in Africa. But why, I reflected more philosophically, should my fate be any different from that of the Colonel or the Major, or my driver?

Then I felt a severe slap on the rump, and simultaneously an avalanche of sand almost buried my head. I knew that I had been hit. But at once I felt strangely at peace. What did death matter, after all?

And with that the firing ceased. I lay motionless for a while – I have no idea how long. Then I cautiously moved first one leg, then the other. My right leg was painful, but I could move it. Spine and pelvis, hip and thigh bones must be intact. I had suffered only the indignity of a wound in the buttock.

What now? Would the enemy advance and find me? I could not help thinking of Australian bayonets. But were these men ahead of me Australians? English? South Africans? New Zealanders?

Why on earth were our troops not continuing their advance? Where were our Panzers?

They gave me an answer. Shells began to whistle overhead from the rear. Our shelling now far outweighed the reply from the men we were facing. Light 'flak' was rattling. The squeak and roar of Panzers grew steadily louder and nearer. When the roaring was practically upon me, I staggered to my feet.

'Here is one!' roared a soldier of my own regiment, leaping at me.

In a curious mixture of fury and relief I bellowed at him: 'You idiot . . .' He hesitated, recognised me, sheered off, grinned, went on advancing. Limping, I followed.

British tanks flamed up and were knocked into silence. Others broke and raced back through the South African vehicles. Our Panzers followed them. Some received direct hits from the South African guns, but escaped damage, with the shot bursting harmlessly on the armour or bouncing off. A good number of the South African guns still seemed to be unready for action. They were not dug in, but were, some of them, still on their portees. It is, of course, possible that these were damaged or unserviceable guns, but even so they would have looked more dangerous if sited as though to meet our attack.

The South African position became one of complete chaos. Our tanks and infantry milled around among them. Soon the Brigade HQ was overrun and the Brigadier taken prisoner. The tanks fanned out and in two main columns began to mop up the infantry – the Regiment Botha men and the South African Irish. The Transvaal Scottish were farther north and were dealt with later. But before the battle was over the South Africans were attacked from every side and angle at once. They did not know where they were.

From among the wreckage ahead, among burning tanks and trucks and silent guns, enemy troops now appeared with their hands up in the air. Others were cursing over piles of spent shells, their ammunition exhausted. Their ambulance men were tending their numerous wounded.

I called for doctors and medical orderlies to assist them. Quite a number of our own people came forward. A South African officer complained that there were insufficient bandages for the wounded. I pointed silently to my own ignominious injury. The blood had flowed freely down my leg and clotted on my uniform. I looked curiously at the voluminous cape I had been wearing when I went into action. It had been rucked up above my bottom as I lay in the slit-trench. In it now were twenty-four holes – some of them neat round punctures, others jagged tears. We, too, had insufficient stocks of field-dressings or bandages for that day's work.

At dusk I had my wound dressed, and got a cup of hot tea. I slept that night on my face, in my own truck. All round lay the dead and wounded, and the prisoners. Many South Africans made off in the darkness. Others were too spent to face a desperate adventure on foot into the night and the unknown desert battlefield.

Dawn came up on the chaos of Sidi Rezegh. Wrecks still smoked. Men lay with glazed eyes staring at a sun that did not rise for them.

Heinz Werner Schmidt

The fighting at Sidi Rezegh became yet more confused. One participant was Bob Crisp, the former South African Test cricketer, who would win the DSO and MC in the desert with the Royal Tank Regiment.

I was nearly going crazy in trying to identify something and trying to determine where the enemy began and ended, and all the time asking the CO for information which he could not give me. I told Tom that I was quite sure that the infantry dug in about 2,000 yards away to the north were Jerry and that I was going to engage them with the machine gun. I had already given the gunner the order: 'Browning, traverse right. One, two thousand. Enemy infantry . . .' when I heard somebody shouting and banging on the side of the tank. I looked down at a little open tourer that had pulled up alongside and found myself staring at the three pips and crown of a tall, lean brigadier who was standing up on the front seat. I took the ear phones off to hear him ask: 'Are you in command here?'

I looked at his shoulder just to make sure, and said: 'I'm in command of this troop, sir.'

'What unit are you with?'

'Third R T R, 4th Armoured Brigade.'

'Good. There's a Jerry tank attack coming in from the west. We need you. Follow me.'

I said desperately: 'Sir, if you wait 10 minutes the whole brigade will be up.'

'If you're there in 10 minutes you'll be in time. If you're there in 15 you'll be too late,' said the long brigadier. 'Follow me.'

He sat down, said something to the fair-haired driver sitting capless beside him, and shot off down the escarpment. I told my driver to follow the car, and we bounced down. Over my shoulder I could see Tom's tank lurching down behind. On the way I explained as well as I could what had happened to my CO – that at the moment I was hurtling towards an airfield on which there were a lot of knocked-out tanks, and that if he got there in 10 minutes he'd be in time and if he got there in 15 minutes he'd be too late. I said that as near as I could judge I was just east of Point 176 on the map, and that anything he saw between him and the airfield was friendly. I could do no more, and was very relieved to hear the distant acknowledgement.

By this time we were down the slope and in amongst the infantry and gunners. They were our own all right; the grimy, weary men looked up hopefully as we passed, and I could see them yelling and giving big 'Thumbs-up' signs. We went through and beyond them in a cloud of dust. 20, 25, 30 miles an hour until the bounding tank, bucking the ridges and bushes and trenches, stretched out on the sudden smoothness of the landing ground with its crumpled planes.

30 yards ahead of me raced the little car, the blond head of the driver gleaming like the plumed helm of Navarre. Beside the driver sat the brigadier holding aloft a blue and white flag that stood straight out in the gale of their going. No wonder the dispirited troops cheered. It must have been quite a sight.

Straight across the airfield we hurtled, towards the dipping sun. I hadn't the faintest idea where we were going, nor why. I was following three pips and a crown and a stiff, blue and white flag. Now we were amongst the still-burning, depressing-looking Crusaders, and left them behind to speed through a few knocked-out Jerry tanks – a much pleasanter sight. Then we were through these on to the clean desert floor.

Suddenly the shells rained down and the flat surface was transformed into fountains of red and yellow earth and flying stones and lead through which the little car weaved and dodged and sometimes disappeared altogether in cascades of evil-smelling dirt and smoke. Miraculously it tore on and the arm that held the lofted flag never wavered.

At last, on the opposite edge of the airfield, where the scrub grew again in a straight line, the car halted and my driver pulled back on the brakes. The long brigadier stood up, looked back at me, then waved his arm widely to the westward. In the same gesture the car revved up, doubled back and like a coursing hare disappeared erratically through the shell bursts.

I looked ahead to where the brigadier had swung his arm. My stomach turned over; 1,200 yards ahead of me stretched the array of dark brown shapes, 60 or 70 monsters in solid line abreast coming steadily towards the landing ground . . . towards me. The vicious flashes at the end of their gun muzzles stood out in fearful contrast against their sombre camouflage. Behind them the sky was red with blood. I didn't need binoculars to pick out the Mark IIIs and IVs. In between moved the infantrymen, and I caught the crackle of machinegun fire.

Robert Crisp

The brigadier was Jock Campbell, whose exploits that day brought him the VC and vindicated his theory of forming mobile mixed columns of tanks, artillery and infantry.

Brewed up

'Driver, halt,' I ordered. 'Gunner, 2-pounder – traverse left – on – tank – German Mark III – eight five zero yards. Fire.' I watched Basset carefully turn the range-drum to the right range, saw him turn to his telescope and aim, noticed out of the corner of my eye that King was ready with the next round, and then the tank jolted slightly with the shock of the gun firing. Through the smoke and dust and the spurt of flame I watched intently through my binoculars the trace of the shot in flight. It curved upwards slightly and almost slowly, and then seemed to plunge swiftly towards the target. There was the unmistakable dull glow of a strike of steel on steel. 'Hit, Basset! Good shot! Fire again,' I called. Another shot and another hit, and I called, 'Good shot; but the bastard won't brew.'

As I spoke I saw the flame and smoke from the German's gun, which showed that he was at last answering. In the next instant all was chaos. There was a clang of steel on the turret front and a blast of flame and smoke from the same place, which seemed to spread into the turret, where it was followed by another dull explosion. The shock-wave which followed swept past me, still standing in the cupola, singed my hands and face and left me breathless and dazed. I looked down into the turret. It was a shambles. The shot had penetrated the front of the turret just in front of King, the loader. It had twisted the machine-gun out of its mounting. It, or a jagged piece of the torn turret, had then hit the round that King had been holding ready – had set it on fire. The explosion had wrecked the wireless, torn King's head and shoulders from the rest of his body and started a fire among the machine-gun boxes stowed on the floor. Smoke and the acrid fumes of cordite filled the turret. On the floor, licking menacingly near the main ammunition stowage bin, there were innumerable small tongues of flame. If these caught on, the charge in the rounds would explode, taking the turret and all in it with it.

I felt too dazed to move. My limbs seemed to be anchored, and I wondered vaguely how long I had been standing there and what I ought to do next. It was a miracle that the explosion had left me unharmed, though shaken. I wondered what had happened to Basset and bent into the cupola to find out. Shielded behind the gun and the recoil guard-shield, Basset, too, had escaped the main force of the explosion. The face that turned to look at me was blackened and scorched and the eyes, peering at me from the black background, seemed to be unnaturally large and startlingly terrified. For once Basset's good humour had deserted him, and the voice which I heard was shaking with emotion.

'Let's get out of 'ere, sir. Not much we can do for King, poor bastard! – 'e's 'ad it and some. An' if we 'ang around we'll catch a packet too. For Gawd's sake let's —— off quick.'

At last I awoke from my daze. 'OK, Basset. Tell Newman to bale out, and be bloody quick about it.'

As Basset bent to shout at the driver the tank was struck again, but this time on the front of the hull. When the smoke and dust cleared, Basset bent again to shout at Newman. A moment later he turned a face now sickened with horror and disgust and blurted out:

'E's 'ad it too, sir. It's took 'alf 'is chest away. For ——'s sake let's get out of 'ere.' In a frenzy of panic he tried to climb out of the narrow cupola past me, causing me to slip and delaying us both. Through my mind there flashed the thought that the German would still continue to fire until he knew that the tank was knocked out, and as yet no flames would be visible from the outside. Inside the turret there was now an inferno of fire.

Without knowing how I covered the intervening distance, I found myself lying in a small hollow some twenty yards from my stricken tank, watching the first thin tongues of flame and black smoke emerging from the turret top.

Cyril Joly

✚

The Middle East

In late August the British, having secured Iraq, moved into Persia to protect their pipelines and the overland supply route to Russia from the 3,000 German 'advisers' there. The Soviets and the British, now allies, divided the country into two zones of occupation, but eliminating received ideas about each other would prove trickier. The British troops were commanded by Bill Slim.

I was once walking with some Russian officers, one of whom did speak a little English. We passed a line of 30-cwt trucks belonging to a regiment of my allegedly armoured brigade, halted at the roadside. Suddenly the Russian touched my arm and pointed. I looked and there, seated on the running-board of a truck, sharing a bully beef lunch with a trooper, was an officer.

'Isn't that an officer?' the Russian asked.

'Yes, a major.'

'And isn't that a private soldier?' he went on.

'Yes,' I agreed, mystified.

The Russian looked bewildered.

'But', he exclaimed, 'they are feeding together.'

'Why not?' I asked. 'You can't run an officers' mess in every vehicle; on the move the crew, officers and men, must feed together.'

He shook his head.

'But British officers never eat with their men in any circumstances; they are aristocrats!'

'Not all of us,' I grinned. 'Although the one you are looking at happens to be – he's a cousin of the Queen!'

The Russian shook his head again and walked on in meditative and puzzled silence.

Slim developed his own theories about the Soviets:

I myself had served most of my military life in an Asiatic army – the Indian Army – and I came to feel more and more strongly that the Red Army was an Asiatic rather than a European one. This was not so much because many of its men were Asians, drawn from the vast areas of Asia that Russia had absorbed in her relentless, centuries-long march of conquest to the east. It went deeper than that. The Russian soldier, wherever he came from, in behaviour, living conditions, lack of outside contacts, recreations and general outlook, approximated more to the Asian than to the European. He was none the worse soldier for that; I was inclined to think he was the better. His nature inclined him to courage and patriotism, the climate of much of his homeland inured him to hardship, and his normal standard of living left him content to be without many things Western soldiers regarded as indispensable necessities – a great military advantage.

Yet the most Asiatic element in the Red Army was not its soldiers; it was the atmosphere that pervaded it from top to bottom. The severity of its discipline, the rule of fear and suspicion, the barbarity of its frequent purges, the low value it set on human life and the fanaticism it inculcated, all had a remarkable similarity to the methods of the Asiatic hordes of history – and they were formidable enough. So, with all its faults and weaknesses, was the Red Army as I saw it.

William Slim

Winter 1941–2

Pearl Harbor

On 7 December 1941, the Japanese attacked without warning the United States Pacific Fleet at its base in Hawaii, Pearl Harbor. The leader of the strike force of 353 Japanese fighters and bombers was Captain Mitsuo Fuchida of the Imperial Japanese Naval Air Service.

The selection of attack method was for my decision, to be indicated by signal pistol: one 'black dragon' for a surprise attack, two 'black dragons' if it appeared that surprise was lost. Upon either order the fighters were immediately to dash in as cover.

There was still no news from the reconnaissance planes, but I had made up my mind that we could make a surprise attack, and thereupon ordered the deployment by raising my signal pistol outside the canopy and firing one 'black dragon'. The time was 0740.

With this order dive bombers rose to 4000 metres, torpedo bombers went down almost to sea level, and level bombers came down just under the clouds. The only group that failed to deploy was the fighters. Flying above the rest of the formation, they seemed to have missed the signal because of the clouds. Realising this I fired another shot toward the fighter group. This time they noticed the signal immediately and sped toward Oahu.

This second shot, however, was taken by the commander of the dive bomber group as the second of two 'black dragons', signifying a non-surprise attack which would mean that his group should attack first, and this error served to confuse some of the pilots who had understood the original signal.

Meanwhile a reconnaissance report came in from *Chikuma*'s plane giving the locations of ten battleships, one heavy cruiser, and ten light cruisers in the harbour. It also reported a 14-metre wind from bearing 080, and clouds over the US Fleet at 1700 metres with a scale 7 density. The *Tone* plane also reported that 'the enemy fleet is not in Lahaina Anchorage'. Now I knew for sure that there were no carriers in the harbour. The sky cleared as we moved in on the target and Pearl Harbor was plainly visible from the northwest valley of the island. I studied our objective through binoculars. They were there all right, all eight of them. 'Notify all planes to launch attacks,' I ordered my radio man who immediately began tapping the key. The order went in plain code: 'To, to, to, to . . .' The time was 0749.

When Lieutenant Commander Takahashi and his dive-bombing group mistook my signal, and thought we were making a non-surprise attack, his 53 planes lost no time in dashing forward. His command was divided into two groups: one led by himself which headed for Ford Island and Hickam Field, the other, led by Lieutenant Sakamoto, headed for Wheeler Field.

The dive bombers over Hickam Field saw heavy bombers lined up on the apron. Takahashi rolled his plane sharply and went into a dive, followed immediately by the rest of his planes, and the first bombs fell at Hickam. The next places hit were Ford Island and Wheeler Field. In a very short time huge billows of black smoke were rising from these bases. The lead torpedo planes were to have started their run to the Navy Yard from over Hickam, coming from south of the bay entrance. But the sudden burst of bombs at Hickam surprised Lieutenant Commander Murata who had understood that his torpedo planes were to have attacked first. Hence he took a short cut lest the smoke from those bases cover up his targets. Thus the first torpedo was actually launched some five minutes ahead of the scheduled 0800. The time of each attack was as follows:

0755   Dive bombers at Hickam and Wheeler Field
0757   Torpedo planes at battleships
0800   Fighters strafing air bases
0805   Level bombers at battleships

After issuance of the attack order, my level bomber group kept east of Oahu going past the southern tip of the island. On our left was the Barbers Point airfield, but, as we had been informed, there were no planes. Our information indicated that a powerful anti-aircraft battery was stationed there, but we saw no evidence of it.

I continued to watch the sky over the harbour and activities on the ground. None but Japanese planes were in the air, and there were no indications of air combat. Ships in the harbour still appeared to be asleep, and the Honolulu radio broadcast continued normally. I felt that surprise was now assured, and that my men would succeed in their missions.

Knowing that Admirals Nagumo, Yamamoto, and the General Staff were anxious about the attack, I decided that they should be informed. I ordered the following message sent to the fleet: 'We have succeeded in making a surprise attack. Request you relay this report to Tokyo.' The radio man reported shortly that the message had been received by *Akagi*.

The code for a successful surprise attack was 'Tora, tora, tora . . .' Before *Akagi*'s relay of this message reached Japan, it was received by Nagato in Hiroshima Bay and the General Staff in Tokyo, directly from my plane! This was surely a long-distance record for such a low-powered transmission from an airplane, and might be attributed to the use of the word 'Tora' as our code. There is a Japanese saying, 'A tiger (tora) goes out 1000 ri (2000 miles) and returns without fail.'

I saw clouds of black smoke rising from Hickam and soon thereafter from Ford Island. This bothered me and I wondered what had happened. It was not long before I saw waterspouts rising alongside the battleships, followed by more and more waterspouts. It was time to launch our level bombing attacks so I ordered my pilot to bank sharply, which was the attack signal for the planes following us. All ten of my squadrons then formed into a single column with intervals of 200 metres. It was indeed a gorgeous formation.

The lead plane in each squadron was manned by a specially trained pilot and bombardier. The pilot and bombardier of my squadron had won numerous fleet contests and were considered the best in the Japanese Navy. I approved when Lieutenant Matsuzaki asked if the lead plane should trade positions with us, and he lifted our plane a little as a signal. The new leader came forward quickly, and I could see the smiling round face of the bombardier when he saluted. In returning the salute I entrusted the command to them for the bombing mission.

As my group made its bomb run, enemy anti-aircraft suddenly came to life. Dark grey bursts blossomed here and there until the sky was clouded with shattering near misses which made our plane tremble. Shipboard guns seemed to open fire before the shore batteries. I was startled by the rapidity of the counter-attack which came less than five minutes after the first bomb had fallen. Were it the Japanese Fleet, the reaction would not have been so quick, because although the Japanese character is suitable for offensives, it does not readily adjust to the defensive.

Suddenly the plane bounced as if struck by a huge club. 'The fuselage is holed to port,' reported the radio man behind me, 'and a steering-control wire is damaged.' I asked hurriedly if the plane was under control, and the pilot assured me that it was.

No sooner were we feeling relieved than another burst shook the plane.

My squadron was headed for *Nevada*'s mooring at the northern end of battleship row on the east side of Ford Island. We were just passing over the bay entrance and it was almost time to release our bombs. It was not easy to pass through the concentrated anti-aircraft fire. Flying at only 3000 metres, it seemed that this might well be a date with eternity.

I further saw that it was not wise to have deployed in this long single-column formation. The whole level bomber group could be destroyed like ducks in a shooting gallery. It would also have been better if we had approached the targets from the direction of Diamond Head. But here we were at our targets and there was a job to be done.

It was now a matter of utmost importance to stay on course, and the lead plane kept to its line of flight like a homing pigeon. Ignoring the barrage of shells bursting around us, I concentrated on the bomb loaded under the lead plane, pulled the safety bolt from the bomb release lever and grasped the handle. It seemed as if time was standing still.

Again we were shaken terrifically and our planes were buffeted about. When I looked out the third plane of my group was abeam of us and I saw its bomb fall! That pilot had a reputation for being careless. In training his bomb releases were poorly timed, and he had often been cautioned.

I thought, 'That damn fellow has done it again!' and shook my fist in his direction. But I soon realised that there was something wrong with his plane and he was losing gasoline. I wrote on a small blackboard, 'What happened?' and held it toward his plane. He explained, 'Underside of fuselage hit.'

Now I saw his bomb cinch lines fluttering wildly, and sorry for having scolded him, I ordered that he return to the carrier. He answered, 'Fuel tank destroyed, will follow you,' asking permission to stay with the group. Knowing the feelings of the pilot and crew, I gave the permission, although I knew it was useless to try taking that crippled and bombless plane through the enemy fire. It was nearly time for bomb release when we ran into clouds which obscured the target, and I made out the round face of the lead bombardier who was waving his hands back and forth to indicate that we had passed the release point. Banking slightly we turned right towards Honolulu, and I studied the anti-aircraft fire, knowing that we would have to run through it again. It was now concentrated on the second squadron.

While circling for another try, I looked toward the area in which the bomb from the third plane had fallen. Just outside the bay entrance I saw a large water ring close by what looked like a destroyer. The ship seemed to be standing in a floating dock, attached to both sides of the entrance like a gate boat. I was suddenly reminded of the midget submarines which were to have entered the bay for a special attack.

At the time of our sortie I was aware of these midget submarines, but knew nothing of their characteristics, operational objectives, force organisation, or the reason for their participation in the attack. In *Akagi*, Commander Shibuya, a staff officer in charge of submarine operations, had explained that they were to penetrate the harbour the night before our attack; but, no matter how good an opportunity might arise, they were not to strike until after the planes had done so.

Even now the submarines were probably concealed in the bay, awaiting the air attack. Had the entrance been left open, there would have been some opportunity for them to get out of the harbour. But in light of what I had just seen there seemed little chance of that, and, feeling now the bitterness of war, I vowed to do my best in the assigned mission.

While my group was circling over Honolulu for another bombing attempt, other groups made their runs, some making three tries before succeeding. Suddenly a colossal explosion occurred in battleship row. A huge column of dark red smoke rose to 1000 feet and a stiff shock wave reached our plane. I called the pilot's attention to the spectacle, and he observed, 'Yes, Commander, the powder magazine must have exploded. Terrible indeed!' The attack was in full swing, and smoke from fires and explosions filled most of the sky over Pearl Harbor.

My group now entered on a bombing course again. Studying battleship row through binoculars, I saw that the big explosion had been on *Arizona*. She was still flaming fiercely and her smoke was covering *Nevada*, the target of my group. Since the heavy smoke would hinder our bomber accuracy, I looked for some other ship to attack. *Tennessee*, third in the left row, was already on fire; but next in row was *Maryland*, which had not yet been attacked. I gave an order changing our target to this ship, and once again we headed into the anti-aircraft fire. Then came the 'ready' signal and I took a firm grip on the bomb release handle, holding my breath and staring at the bomb of the lead plane.

Pilots, observers, and radio men all shouted, 'Release!' on seeing the bomb drop from the lead plane, and all the others let go their bombs. I immediately lay flat on the floor to watch the fall of bombs through a peephole. Four bombs in perfect pattern plummeted like devils of doom. The target was so far away that I wondered for a moment if they would reach it. The bombs grew smaller and smaller until I was holding my breath for fear of losing them. I forgot everything in the thrill of watching them fall toward the target. They became small as poppy seeds and finally disappeared just as tiny white flashes of smoke appeared on and near the ship.

Mitsuo Fuchida

US Navy Lieutenant Clarence E. Dickinson was flying from his aircraft carrier to Pearl Harbor that morning when he was shot down by a Japanese Zero fighter. He managed to parachute out and land at Ewa Field, a few miles from Pearl Harbor. He then made his way to the target of the onslaught.

Towering before our eyes, about thirty yards or so out in the channel was the slowly moving vast grey bulk of a battleship. Beyond her, farther up the channel, I could see the *Arizona*. She lay at the far end of battleship row, her broken twisted wreckage amidships belching the blackest smoke, which kept expanding into bigger shape. One fighting top and tripod mast canted out of this incredible disorder. But on all the ships in that double two-mile lane, right to the old battleship before our eyes, guns were blasting at the planes above the harbour. Yet, all the terrific power of the biggest guns on those battleships, of turreted main and secondary batteries, of sixteen-inch and lesser guns was futile now. They were made to fight things like themselves, not gadflies in the sky. However, there on Hospital Landing the ship in front of us filled our eyes. Anywhere you looked her guns were going; eight five-inch anti-aircraft guns; lesser stuff and machine guns. Along the deck I saw wounded and men with stretchers were rushing to carry them away.

The battleship was trying to get out to sea and a lot of Jap dive bombers had been detailed to get her where she was, in the channel, where her 29,000 tons of steel hull, machinery and guns – if sunk – would choke Pearl Harbor; with the fleet inside. Where we stood, the old ship's great side seemed to loom higher than a ball park fence and her length was such (580 feet overall) you simply could not see what was happening from stem to stern with just one look. But everywhere I looked I saw organisation, men under control.

There was a tremendous ear-splitting explosion. A bomb had struck on her deck close to one of her anti-aircraft guns. Thirteen hundred men, I guess, were aboard the ship. Some were killed, more were hurt; but only one anti-aircraft gun had stopped firing. All the others were spewing lemon-coloured fire in high angles. Machine guns were rattling on the decks and on high platforms. For the first time in my life I was seeing a naval vessel in action and I was just watching in that futility in which you find yourself caught in dreams. But this was real and what was striking at the old ship was a newer weapon, my kind of weapon – dive bombers.

All the time I was watching the attack I was doing so objectively, trying to evaluate the ability of the Japanese as dive bombers. They had concentrated at least the equivalent of one of our dive bomber squadrons on the battleship. There were eighteen and possibly twenty planes detailed to this job and they went at it one by one. A dive bomber such as one of these leaves its carrier usually with no more than one big 500-pound bomb and possibly one or two smaller bombs. These planes were expecting to make a round trip of possibly 500 miles in striking at Pearl Harbor and getting back to their carriers. So they weren't raining bombs. I guess that those pilots up there would count themselves lucky to drop one bomb on a target – and get away. Every Jap bomber flying over us had his own dive to make but in that attack on the battleship they were trying to rush the job, trying desperately to sink her in the channel.

They were so eager that bombs fell first on one side of the old battleship and then on the other. Of course, each time those of us there on Hospital Landing saw that a bomb was going to fall close to us we would run. Sometimes it seemed to me as if everybody in the crowd was trying to climb up my back but those were the times when I was leading the rush. Even with those bombs landing in the water we had to throw ourselves flat before the explosion because the concussion always was terrific; if caught standing you would be knocked flat. But lying down on the concrete or on rocky earth I had a frantic impulse to claw myself into the ground. Each time as we scores of men weathered another explosion and got to our feet I was wishing for eyes at the back of my head, because while we watched the ship in front of us, at our backs the destroyer *Shaw* was being bombed.

These Japs make dives much less steep than we do. We come down at an angle of about seventy degrees. But it is standard practice for the Jap to approach his target at an angle of about fifty degrees. It is my professional hope that they continue to do this. However, one reason they make such shallow angle approaches may be so they can then use their machine guns to strafe.

For years I had been questioning statements I heard about how a man could dodge a bomb dropped from an airplane and there we were, doing it! We would see one leave a Jap plane possibly fifteen hundred feet above ground. Each time we stood fascinated. Suddenly the bomb would appear to be swelling; slanting towards us and in its fall it would actually seem to grow bigger and bigger. At some point in its fall we would have to make up our minds whether it would fall on our side of the battleship or beyond it; if beyond it we would stand and watch. Out of this experience I became wholly convinced that high altitude bombing (20,000 feet or more) is futile against ably handled ships on the open sea, unless there are such swarms of bombs falling in pattern as to make a change of course futile. Later experience was to reaffirm this conviction.

The battleship had gotten clear of the channel; she grounded on a point of land opposite the Hospital. Just at that time I had turned about to watch the bombing attack on the destroyer *Shaw*, and saw a bomb tip her bow. We could see that she was on fire after the explosion.

Immediately afterward many of us there on Hospital Landing climbed into a motor launch that had come to take us across to Ford Island. It was the kind of boat carried on battleships to take liberty parties to and from the shore. We could see that a lot of damage had been done on Ford Island. Something had been raising hell there. Three or four squadrons of PBY flying boats sometimes had been massed on the point of the island. They are big.

The PBY, a Catalina, has bunks for its crew, kitchen equipment, plumbing. It really is a flying boat. But only charred remains were left. I could distinguish the stumps of their tails. They had been burned up. There was one PBY afloat in the channel and its crew were struggling to taxi it to a cradle in which it might be pulled by tractor out of the water on to the ramp, before it could sink out there in the channel. It was full of just such big jagged holes as I had seen made in my own wing and again in that automobile on the road. This PBY had been strafed and with just one engine working the pilot and the crew were having a difficult time man-oeuvring in the wind. The dive bombing attack was in full force and our motor launch, showing a mass of heads, was the kind of target for which the strafing Japs were itching. In our situation time was passing slowly. But finally we grounded on one of the concrete ramps and stepped ashore.

Clarence E. Dickinson

Dickinson was to get his revenge at the Battle of Midway. His account of the successful dive-bombing of the Japanese aircraft carrier Kaga *can be found later.*

Seaman Second Class George Phraner was serving aboard the Arizona *as a flight of Japanese Kate bombers began to bear down on the moorings known as 'battleship row'.*

My battle station was on a forward 5-inch gun. There we were, the Japanese dropping bombs over us and we had no ammo. All the training and practising for a year and when the real thing came, we had no ammunition. As unfortunate as this was, that simple fact saved my life. Somehow the gun captain pointed at me and said 'You go aft and start bringing up the ammunition out of the magazines.' I had begun lifting shells into the hoist when a deafening roar filled the room and the entire ship shuddered. It was the forward magazine. Fifty tons of gunpowder exploding in a massive fireball disintegrating the whole forward part of the ship. Only moments before, I had stood with my gun crew just a few feet from the centre of the explosion. The lights went out and it was pitch black; a thick, acrid smoke filled the magazine locker and the metal walls began to get hot. Somehow we were able to get open the hatch and start to make our way up the ladder. I was nauseated by the smell of burning flesh, which turned out to be my own as I climbed up the hot ladder. Getting through that choking kind of smoke was a real ordeal. After a while I began to get weak and light-headed. I could feel myself losing the battle to save my own life. At that moment, I looked up and could see a small point of light through the smoke. It gave me the strength to go on. After what seemed to me like an eternity, I reached the deck gasping and choking. The warm Hawaiian air filled my lungs and cleared my head.

I glanced over the forward end of the ship to see nothing but a giant wall of flame and smoke. Behind me a marine lay dead on the deck, his body split in two. I began to realise there were dead men all around me.

George Phraner

Phraner was one of 337 men to survive the sinking of the Arizona; *1,175 others were less fortunate. The destruction of the battleship resulted in the highest loss of life ever suffered aboard one vessel by the US Navy. Five of its eight battleships were sunk and the others damaged. Crucially, however, its three aircraft carriers were elsewhere that day.*

☦

'The worst blow of the war'

Two days after the attack on Pearl Harbor, Churchill summoned his naval advisers to discuss the news from America. But the outlook was to grow blacker yet.

I convened a meeting, mostly Admiralty, in the Cabinet War Room at ten o'clock on the night of the 9th to review the naval position. We were about a dozen. We tried to measure the consequences of this fundamental change in our war position against Japan. We had lost command of every ocean except the Atlantic. Australia and New Zealand and all the vital islands in their sphere were open to attack. We had only one key weapon in our hands. The *Prince of Wales* and *Repulse* had arrived at Singapore. They had been sent to these waters to exercise that kind of vague menace which capital ships of the highest quality whose whereabouts is unknown can impose upon all hostile naval calculations. How should we use them now? Obviously they must go to sea and vanish among the innumerable islands. There was general agreement on that.

I thought myself they should go across the Pacific to join what was left of the American Fleet. It would be a proud gesture at this moment, and would knit the English-speaking world together. We had already cordially agreed to the American Navy Department withdrawing their capital ships from the Atlantic. Thus in a few months there might be a fleet in being on the west coast of America capable of fighting a decisive sea battle if need be. The existence of such a fleet and of such a fact would be the best possible shield to our brothers in Australasia. We were all much attracted by this line of thought. But as the hour was late we decided to sleep on it, and settle the next morning what to do with the *Prince of Wales* and the *Repulse*.

Within a couple of hours they were at the bottom of the sea.

I was opening my boxes on the 10th when the telephone at my bedside rang. It was the First Sea Lord. His voice sounded odd. He gave a sort of cough and gulp, and at first I could not hear quite clearly. 'Prime Minister, I have to report to you that the *Prince of Wales* and the *Repulse* have both been sunk by the Japanese – we think by aircraft. Tom Phillips [C-in-C Eastern Fleet] is drowned.' 'Are you sure it's true?' 'There is no doubt at all.' So I put the telephone down. I was thankful to be alone. In all the war I never received a more direct shock. The reader of these pages will realise how many efforts, hopes, and plans foundered with these two ships. As I turned over and twisted in bed the full horror of the news sank in upon me. There were no British or American capital ships in the Indian Ocean or the Pacific except the American survivors of Pearl Harbor, who were hastening back to California. Over all this vast expanse of waters Japan was supreme, and we everywhere were weak and naked.

Winston Churchill

Following Pearl Harbor, Hitler – who had a strategic alliance with Japan – declared war on the United States. The conflict had become truly global.

‡

Assault on the Philippines

Midday mauling

The day after the strike on Pearl Harbor, the Japanese began to mount air attacks against the Philippines (which had been an American possession since 1898). By 10 December, intelligence officer Colonel Allison Ind was already beginning to find the raids were part of his daily routine.

Somewhere in my ragged consciousness the fact registers that we are almost at the end of my watch. It's nearly noon. I've been on duty since 4.00 a.m. I am dog-weary, and my mind receives each new sensation, each new addition to the endless flow of conflicting information reports from the provinces with a dull impact – like little pellets dropping on to a limp canvas square.

Nearly noon . . .

That means it's nearly raid time. They ought to be in about 12.17 today.

What does Air Warning say?

Yes, that's more like it . . . Fifty-four heavy bombers north of Cabanatuan, proceeding southwesterly.

Fifty-four! That will be a royal slapping, if they all come at once. Gratefully I turn the smoke-filled, paper-littered office over to Lieutenant Bell. I cross the court between the legs of Headquarters building V and enter the big room with its huge horizontal map table presided over by a circle of telephonists and their spotter assistants. The map . . . No need to ask; those little composition arrows being chivvied into position by the spotter tell the story plainly enough. A formidable force of enemy bombers is converging down the mid-line of Luzon with its slower elements bearing slightly toward Manila. Already the warning has been telephoned to all headquarters and to the civil defence units. In a momentary lull in the clatter and chatter of the big room, we hear the distant wailing of the Manila and Fort McKinley sirens.

There is a shrilling of whistles.

'All unnecessary personnel, evacuate the building,' comes the shouted order, passed along the corridor.

With a resigned air, officers and men so classed – that is, those not actively required to conduct air warning and communications functions – clip into conveniently hung battle equipment and, taking gas masks and helmets, pile out of the doorway into the brilliant sunshine. Some go directly to the prepared slit trenches.

There is no confusion, no panic. Quickly we have become accustomed to this routine of meeting the unseen threat to our Headquarters and our lives. Since those first disastrous days we have learned to avoid the obvious points of shelter. No more do men run for the ditches alongside the airdrome road or those paralleling Makati Road, nor do we seek isolated clumps of trees. It's beastly hot, but the most secure camouflage against strafing is obtained by taking refuge in dried-out rice paddies, lying parallel to the little dikes, and burrowing one's way under the overhanging dry leaves left by the rice harvesters, and then lying perfectly still. I have my own particular warren about three hundred yards from the building, probably safe enough against strafing; but a near miss intended for the building – well, it could land three hundred yards away or fifty. You can outguess a bomb, but not until you see it leave the belly of the bomber – and that's difficult if you are lying well covered in an effort to identify yourself with the rest of the country.

I listened intently. Yes, there they are. That faint building up and diminishing of sound so characteristic of Japanese bomber squadrons. I burrow a little bit deeper into the paddy field; I can hear Corey and some of the other boys doing likewise.

The sun beats down like something alive, but except for this ominous drone slowly mounting in volume, there is no other thing alive in the world. The atmosphere has ceased to live. The air bears no hint of familiar movement of man or beast.

Then comes the distant clump of anti-aircraft batteries feeling their range. After each detonation the distant droning seems to cease for a tiny fraction of a second, but always it resumes. There is no slackening of its hateful purpose or song. From several quarters the guns are hammering – Cavite, Fort Mills, probably, and now the closer smash of the battery on Makati Road.

Now the small white blossoms high up in the blue, but always disappointing. Always far behind the silvery toylike formations apparently so harmlessly approaching their objectives.

F-f-fu-ut . . . f-f-fu-u-ut . . . f-f-fu-u-ut . . . f-f-fu-u-ut!

Their distant softened explosions are ridiculously tiny and ineffectual.

But not the bombs their quarries drop. Now the thudding blows shake the earth. One, two – five – ten – and more and faster until the blasts merge into one rolling thunder of destruction.

Where is it? Close – but not immediate. Sounds like Nichols Field again.

The tremendous beat of sound hurtles through the air and strikes against one like a solid thing. The thundering detonations are interrupted only, as it seems, to allow the tortured atmosphere to collect itself before the next great confusion. Again and again this gigantic drum roll.

My fingers are clutching the hot dried earth and my teeth are set. It is not fear. One soon achieves a detachment from the fact of a bombing unless he himself is part of the objective. That another objective is being smashed, even if it may be close by, leaves one with a feeling of fatalistic isolation. A miss is not only as good as a mile but as good as many miles. This, of course, is predicated upon the condition that one also be not within concussion distance. Indeed, the terrible concussion accounts for far more human damage than the actual impact of fragments against warm, soft tissue. Rather, this is the reaction of a helpless sort of anger.

But now I jerk to a new sound: the rapidly rising crescendo of a single motor in a dive.

Then there are more than big bombers in this raid! Dive bombers, or fighters, also are participating, and this one is close.

I twist violently to try to get a view through the straw. Then stop abruptly. Motion like that not only will betray my hiding place but endanger everyone concealed in this area.

'Lie still, you idiot,' I charge myself furiously, and then add in unintended facetiousness, 'or you'll die still!'

Now the whole world is filled with this bellowing thunder, punctuated sharply by the snapping of machine-gun and small-cannon fire.

Strafing . . . Ground seems to lift and suck upward toward this rushing fury.

Then my scalp contracts and I lie with paralysed rigidity. I can actually feel the cannon slugs stamping the earth like some giant riveter. They rip downward into the ground about us.

For one age-long second this stuttering line of invisible death beats toward me . . .

And passes me!

I am hot, wet, slippery with perspiration.

Now I am aware that I have been holding my breath. But I must breathe!

'Well, breathe then, you fool!' I hear myself shouting.

He must have seen us! . . . I'm going to get out of here . . . But I don't. Either he's made a quick wing over and is coming back or there is another one. I still think he can't see us, but he certainly will if anyone of us gets up and tries to make a run for it.

Besides . . . run for what . . . where?

Again that sweeping roar with lead lacing the earth. But this time the pace is more leisurely, the shooting more deliberate. And why not? There is no opposition. From far off on the Makati Road I can hear a rising storm of rifle and machine-gun fire; but there is nothing here – and why should there be? Unorganised rifle shooting has but the slightest chance of registering even a harmless hit and infinitely small possibility of establishing a really crippling impact. But it does betray the location of ground personnel, and very likely that is exactly what this attack was designed to accomplish.

But they do accomplish more.

From my earthworm shelter I can see a pillar of black smoke rising swiftly. The Headquarters building? No, it is farther north than that. Then the hangar? My curiosity becomes the greater part of imprudence and I struggle out of my cover. I am just in time to see the last act of this murderous little drama. The column of black smoke tapers down to the last resting place of the 'Royal Yacht'. A Japanese strafer, which might be either a fighter or a 97 type of fighter-bomber – it is obscured by the smoke, and its outline will not classify in my mind – is just adding the *coup de grâce* to General Claggett's flaming Douglas command plane. She was a beautiful gleaming piece of aircraft architecture. Now she makes a beautiful fire. My knees are weak, and I want to sit down. I do.

Allison Ind

‡

The Fall of Malaya and Singapore

Bicycling to victory

By managing to advance more than 600 miles in two months, the Japanese would capture the British colony of Malaya and bring off one of the great strategic triumphs of the war. Here Colonel Masanobu Tsuji, chief of operations and planning for the invasion, outlines the reasons for its success.

The main reasons for the phenomenal speed of the onslaught in the Malayan campaign were the special attention given to the equipping and training of infantry formations, and the great achievements of the Engineer Corps.

The horses of the 5th and 18th divisions, which had been fighting on the mainland of China for a number of years, had become as well trained as their masters. When it was decided to use these troops in the south, however, motor vehicles and bicycles were substituted for the horses. Each regiment of infantry was allotted roughly fifty trucks for the transport of heavy machine-guns, battalion guns, regimental guns, heavy ordnance, quick-firing guns and the like, as well as ammunition.

All officers and men who did not ride with the trucks were provided with bicycles. The divisional, army and transport units were reorganised so that their whole strength could be loaded on trucks. A division was equipped with roughly five hundred motor vehicles and six thousand bicycles. The training to accustom troops to these new conditions did not exceed a period of more than one or two months immediately before the outbreak of hostilities. It was wholly the 'Mud and Rope' model.

In Malaya, almost without exception, bridges were demolished in front of our advancing troops. When all motor transport was loaded with officers, men and equipment, it would have reduced their speed to walking pace if they had had to wait for the advance of the infantry and the repair of bridges, and it would have taken over a year to break through eleven hundred kilometres.

With the infantry on bicycles, however, there was no traffic congestion or delay. Wherever bridges were destroyed the infantry continued their advance, wading across the rivers carrying their bicycles on their shoulders, or crossing on log bridges held up on the shoulders of engineers standing in the stream. It was thus possible to maintain a hot pursuit of the enemy along the asphalt roads without giving them any time to rest or reorganise.

Mr Churchill, in his memoirs, implies that the Japanese Army before the outbreak of hostilities made secret preparations in each Malay district for comprehensive aggression – even, he says, to the storage of bicycles. With regret I have to say that these are not the facts of the case. The truth is that Japanese-manufactured bicycles, because of their cheapness, had become one of the chief exports from Japan to the whole of South-east Asia, where they were widely purchased by the inhabitants. For this reason replacements and spare parts were easily available everywhere throughout Malaya. When viewed from this angle, the incorrect observation of an Englishman, even one in Mr Churchill's position, can scarcely meet with approval.

The greatest difficulty encountered in the use of bicycles was the excessive heat, owing to which the tyres punctured easily. A bicycle repair squad of at least two men was attached to every company, and each squad repaired an average of about twenty machines a day. But such repairs were only makeshift. When the enemy were being hotly pursued, and time was pressing, punctured tyres were taken off and the bicycles ridden on the rims. Surprisingly enough they ran smoothly on the paved roads, which were in perfect condition. Numbers of bicycles, some with tyres and some without, when passing along the road, made a noise resembling that of tanks. At night when such bicycle units advanced the enemy frequently retreated hurriedly, saying, 'Here come the tanks!' 'It is the tanks, it is the tanks!'

When in trouble our troops would dive into the jungle carrying their bicycles on their shoulders. The difficulties of trying to break through jungle carrying their arms and with bicycles on their shoulders can well be imagined. When engaged in battle the troops left their bicycles in the rear with a few soldiers on guard. As soon as the enemy began to retreat our troops had to follow in close pursuit. The men guarding the bicycles would obtain the co-operation of the Malay, Indian, and Chinese residents of the locality to carry the bicycles forward to our advancing troops. Such bicycle transport units would be commanded by a Japanese soldier, not even understanding the languages of the mixture of races following him as he went forward carrying the Japanese flag at the head of his bicycle column. The men who trotted along the well-paved roads, leading hundreds of silver wheels, were surely an army in the form of a cross for the emancipation of East Asia.

Attached to the seat of each bicycle was the individual equipment of the soldier, from eight to ten *kan* [68–85 lbs] in weight. Besides this the soldier carried a light machine-gun and a small rifle over his shoulder. It was not easy work riding the bicycles for often twenty hours a day.

The British Army formations were almost completely equipped with motor cars and trucks, and whenever we were able to steal a march on them and seize bridges in front of them, or destroy their vehicles by shellfire or aeroplane bombing, their soldiers had to abandon their cars and trucks and continue their retreat on foot.

Even the long-legged Englishmen could not escape our troops on bicycles. This was the reason why they were continually driven off the road into the jungle, where, with their retreat cut off, they were forced to surrender.

Thanks to Britain's dear money spent on the excellent paved roads, and to the cheap Japanese bicycles, the assault on Malaya was easy.

Masanobu Tsuji

Malaya invaded

The Japanese had entered Thailand and Malaya at the same time as their aircraft
were attacking Pearl Harbor. Thailand surrendered within 24 hours. To the north,
Hong Kong fell on Christmas Day, and by the second week in January the Japanese
– lightly clad and, unlike their British opponents, capable of advancing at speed
through the jungle – had reached Kuala Lumpur, the second city of the Malay
peninsula. Looting soon began, watched by Ian Morrison.

The most striking sight I saw was a young Tamil coolie, naked except for
a green loincloth, who had had tremendous luck. He had found a long
cylindrical tin, three inches in diameter and a foot long, well wrapped up.
What could it contain? Obviously a tin like this could only contain some
rare and luxurious Western delicacy. He sat on the kerbstone turning the
tin round in his hands. He wished that he could read that Western language
so that he might know what the tin contained. Should he open it now or
should he wait until he got home? Curiosity got the better of him and he
decided to open the tin. Carefully he peeled off the paper and took off the
lid. Three white Slazenger tennis-balls rolled slowly out, bounced on the
pavement and then trickled into the gutter, where they soon lost their
speckless whiteness.

Ian Morrison

Ambushed by the Japanese

As they retreated towards Singapore, inexperienced and outmanoeuvred Australian
troops such as Private Russell Braddon were easy prey for the invaders.

We passed an open, mass Japanese grave which made us feel a little better.
Then, as the sun rose higher, we passed heaps of British bodies and the air
swam with humidity and the stench of death. Next we came to an
abandoned native hut. I broke in and found a tin of condensed milk
crawling with ants and half-empty. We scooped out a finger-tip full of
milk and ants each. As we started off again, two Tamils – rubber tappers –
appeared a few hundred yards ahead. They halted, startled, for a second as
they saw us, then padded swiftly off over the hill, their sarong-clad hips
swaying and their bare feet splayed wide.

We worked on a 'two-man ahead patrol' system – on the *All Clear* from
them the remaining seven moved up, whereupon the next two took over.

Thus we leap-frogged for about two hours. Hugh and I patrolled together; Harry and the first infantryman called (we now learnt) Herc; the two young sigs; and the sergeant and Sandshoes.

The latter pair were now ahead. We waited for their 'All Clear'.

'Pair of no hopers, they are,' declared Harry acidly, as he lay with his feet resting high up against a rubber tree, 'done nothing but belly-ache ever since we started.'

There was a moment's silence whilst everyone thought of the undoubted degree of the no hopers' capacity for belly-aching.

'OK,' said one of the sigs, 'she's clear up ahead.' We looked up and saw the sergeant waving us forward.

Harry got to his feet and Herc with him. Roy and Rene, the sigs, followed with the officer. Hugh and I brought up the rear. As fast as possible we walked forward to where the two belly-achers waited and then on along their patrolled beat. We had covered perhaps fifty yards of it when we cleared the first small rise in the rubber. The jungle lay cosily by our left hand. We trotted down the far side of the rise. And instantly the air was full of bullets, whilst ahead of us and to our right about fifty yards away, with automatic weapons blazing, were Japanese soldiers. We had walked straight into an ambush. The belly-achers had funked their patrol.

I didn't wait to see what happened. I was off at once, sprinting wildly, towards the jungle on the left. Beside me, I was aware without seeing him, ran Hugh. Cursing myself for every fool in the world, I thought yearningly of those four beautiful hand grenades now lying uselessly beside a canal the other side of Yong Peng.

'Stop there,' I heard the officer's clear voice directed at us, 'stop and surrender or we'll all be shot' – and my absurd army training made me falter for a second and look back. I saw Herc already bleeding from a wound in the arm; and Sandshoes and the sergeant lying on the ground; and the officer standing quite still, the sigs looking at him questioningly and Harry in outrage. Just for a second we faltered. As in any race, when one falters, it was then too late. The path to the jungle was cut by a Jap soldier with a tommy gun. We stood still, our only chance lost. Then, very slowly, very foolishly and with a sense of utter unreality, I put up my hands.

At that moment all that occurred to me was that this procedure was completely disgraceful. I have not – since then – changed my mind. I have no doubt at all that I should have continued running. One does not win battles by standing still and extending the arms upwards in the hope that one's foes have read the Hague Convention concerning the treatment of

Prisoners of War. It was unfortunate that the Army had trained me sufficiently neither to disobey instantly and without hesitation, nor to obey implicitly and without compunction. Accordingly, I had done neither: and I now stood in the recognised pose of one who optimistically seeks mercy from a conqueror whose reputation is for being wholly merciless.

The enemy patrol closed in on us. Black-whiskered men, with smutty eyes and the squat pudding faces of bullies. They snatched off our watches first of all – and then belted us with rifle butts because these did not point to the north as they swung them around under the ludicrous impression that they were compasses. They made dirty gestures at the photographs of the women-folk they took from our wallets. They threw the money in the wallets away, saying, 'Dammé, dammé, Englishu dollars': and, pointing at the King's head on the notes, they commented: 'Georgey Six number ten. Tojo number one!' And all the time two Tamils stood in the background, murmuring quietly to one another, their hips tight swathed in dirty check sarongs and their wide-splayed feet drawing restless patterns in the bare soil of the rubber plantation.

'Done a good job, haven't you, Joe?' demanded Harry savagely – but they wouldn't meet his eye. Just kept on drawing in the dirt with their toes.

Hugh picked up a $10 bill and stuffed it defiantly back in his pocket. Then they tied us up with wire, lashing it round our wrists, which were crossed behind our backs and looped to our throats. They prodded us on to the edge of a drain in the rubber. We sat with our legs in it, while they set their machine guns up facing us and about ten yards away.

'That bloody Intelligence Officer would have to be right this time of all times, wouldn't he?' demanded Harry – we all knew that he referred to the 'Japanese take no prisoners' report, and Herc, bleeding badly, nodded rather wanly.

'We must die bravely,' said the officer desperately – at which the sergeant howled for mercy. Howled and pleaded, incredibly craven. Neither he nor Sandshoes had been hit at all when I had seen them prostrate on the ground, merely frightened. The sergeant continued to bawl lustily. We sat, the nine of us, side by side, on the edge of our ready-dug grave.

The Japanese machine gunner lay down and peered along his barrel. It was my twenty-first birthday and I was not happy.

Russell Braddon

The author was to spend the rest of the war in Japanese captivity.

The fall of Singapore

Alfred Allbury, a gunner in the 18th Division, witnessed the chaos that began to envelop Britain's most formidable fortress in the Far East and which led to its capture by the Japanese within a week of their landing on Singapore Island.

My co-driver Vic Wilson and I sallied forth on nightly excursions to ammunition dumps scattered around the island – no transport could survive ten minutes on the roads by day. Once our 15 cwt was loaded, we had to deliver the shells to our guns. This called not so much for a knowledge of map reading as for the gift of clairvoyance. Jap planes and the unsuitability of the terrain for effective artillery positions kept our battery commanders roving the island in a desperate search for potential gun-sites. Those found and occupied were speedily made untenable by the sustained accuracy of the Japanese counterfire.

Vic Wilson and I had long been friends. He was an unprincipled rogue with a delightful wry sense of humour, and a healthy hatred of the war that kept him from his young wife and baby back in Charlton.

Our nightly runs soon became something of an ordeal. There was no moon and the island was plunged in Stygian gloom. In many places where trees overhung the roads I had to guide Vic forward with the glow from a cigarette; and there were rickety makeshift bridges to cross, while all around the darkened island pulsated with the animations of a thousand things that crawled, slithered and scuffled. Some of the Japanese, we had heard, had already crossed the Straits, filtered through our lines and were roaming about at will. I had a round up the barrel of my rifle, the safety catch off, and often my finger grew moist on the trigger.

By day the fifth-columnists were as ubiquitous as the palms. Certain apparently guileless gentlemen would lead their herds of cattle across our gun positions. This would be followed almost immediately by a terrific blasting from Jap shells and mortars; so we took to shooting the zealous drovers as a matter of principle. Other Japanese supporters secreted themselves in trees and further added to our discomfort by continual sniping. As Singapore was full of trees there was not much we could do about this except occasionally to loose off volleys into any tree that looked unduly suspect. I fear that many an unsuspecting and completely neutral coconut met a violent and untimely end as a result of our would-be reprisals. Certainly nothing else ever tumbled down to earth.

On February 13th we heard that the Japs had landed in force on the island, had pushed inland and that a desperate battle was raging for Bukit

Timah hill. We also heard that the Americans had landed near Penang in the Japanese rear and were pressing down behind them.

But hourly the thunder of guns drew nearer. The front line became an ever-tightening ring around the town of Singapore. It became a hazardous feat to reach the few supply-dumps still available to us, and our own guns were as elusive as the fire-flies that flitted every evening in the shadows of the wagon-lines.

On the morning of February 14th the first tentative shells landed among our supply-dumps. They quickly found the exact range and soon a searing bombardment developed that sent us scuttling into our fox-holes. The Japs were ranging on us from heights that overlooked the town. Bukit Timah was theirs after the bloodiest of struggles, the reservoir was stained crimson with the blood of those who had fought so bitterly to hold it, and the little yellow men whom we had ridiculed and despised were in swarm across the island. Already it was theirs.

Next morning Vic and I set off on a last mad jaunt taking ammunition to 'A' Troop who were dug in behind a Chinese temple to the north of Racecourse Road. Vic drove like a maniac. He had, I found, been sampling a bottle of 'John Haig'. We thundered along deserted roads, pitted and scarred with bomb-craters. Wrecked and burnt-out vehicles lay everywhere, strewn at fantastic angles. The trolley-bus cables hung across the road in desolate festoons which shivered and whined as we raced over them. A few yards from the charred remains of an ambulance were a knot of troops gathered round a cook's-wagon. From them we scrounged a mug of hot tea and found out that the guns of 'A' Troop were only a few hundred yards distant. We delivered our ammunition and an hour later rejoined Battery HQ close by the Raffles Hotel.

Here we found everyone digging like mad, preparing for a 'last stand'. In front of the hotel, filling the air with deafening cracks and the pungent fumes of cordite, were a battery of howitzers. On either side, without a scrap of cover or camouflage, stood a score of other guns. Sweating, glistening bodies loaded, slammed breeches and fired. At once came the answering crack and whine of Japanese artillery; from the high ground above the town they could judge the range to a nicety. All around us men were fixing their bayonets and automatically I did the same.

But late that afternoon came the news that we had surrendered. There was to be a cease-fire at four o'clock. We had fought and lost. And the ashes of defeat tasted bitter.

At three o'clock all but a few of the guns were silent. Ammunition had been expended. From the hills there still came the occasional bark of a

Japanese gun followed by the whine and crash of its shells. But by six o'clock, save for the spluttering of flames and the occasional explosion of ammunition, all was quiet over the island of Singapore. The carnage of the last ten days was quieted now, and in eerie silence our troops sat huddled together in puzzled but fatalistic expectancy.

Vic and I returned to our lorry, ate some tinned bacon and biscuits and stretched ourselves luxuriously for our first uninterrupted sleep for many days. We took off our boots, smoked, talked and listened to the distant caterwauling of the Japanese.

'They'll probably,' said Vic, 'be crawling round us in the night, cutting off our ears.'

But we stretched out and slept the sleep of the utterly exhausted, while around us into the tropic night rose a barbaric and discordant dirge: the victory song of the triumphant Japanese.

Alfred Allbury

General Percival surrendered Singapore to General Yamashita on 15 February 1942. More than 60,000 British, Dominion and Empire troops, including Allbury, were taken prisoner. Half would not survive their subsequent captivity.

Rice Balls

Incarcerated in Changi Prison Camp in Singapore, Russell Braddon and his fellow inmates suffered from the most debilitating afflictions.

Rice Balls is not an elegant term. It was not, however, an elegant complaint, and no picture of the life we led from 1942 to 1945 is complete without its inclusion. It was the most apparent symbol of our greatest need – vitamins – and, at the same time, of the common man's indomitable humour under even the most humiliating of afflictions. For Rice Balls, to us, meant not one of the favourite dishes of the Japanese, but the ripping raw (by the denial of even a tiny quantity of Vitamin B2) of a man's scrotum and genitals. One felt first a faint discomfort, as of chafing. Then the skin split and peeled off an area which might spread from the genitals right down the inner thighs. This entire surface then became raw and sticky and painful. As one disconsolately surveyed the damage one could not help being reminded of our red-headed sergeant major and his tinea [a fungal skin infection] that crept. By refusing us a spoonful each day of the worthless polishings taken off rice (and they could easily have given us a sackful), the

Japanese wilfully condemned their prisoners to years of living with a scrotum that was red weeping flesh. It was a constant factor in one's life that varied between acute discomfort and acute pain. But it was always there – and it thereby had its effect upon everything one thought, everything one ate, everything one stole and upon every risk one was prepared to run to alleviate the avitaminosis of which it was the most degrading symptom. It was the outward and visible sign of a physical need which was to kill thousands and send hundreds of others blind, or near blind. And because the men who suffered this affliction ironically – and aptly – applied to it the name more commonly given to a food very close to the heart of every son of Nippon, it is fitting enough, however indelicate, to use it here. We ate rice. We ate rice only. Consequently we had Rice Balls.

Russell Braddon

✛

The Russian Front

Heading east

For teenage Panzer driver Henry Metelmann, the journey through a frozen Russia was not only a taste of what was to come, but also a reminder of the nature of the regime for which he was fighting.

A long train consisting of covered wagons pulled in behind us and came to a stand. We then noticed that there were people in the wagons, most of which had small window openings about six feet above floor level, and from them we were met by staring eyes. Looking closer, we could make out that they were mainly faces of older people, with younger women amongst them – and then we also heard the voices of children. One woman opposite our window said quietly: 'Brot' (bread) and managed to push her hand out. Then two SS guards came walking along the train, each of them carrying a rifle and a pistol loose fashion over their heavy greatcoats. They looked fed–up and ill tempered, and when we asked them whether we should give the woman any bread, one said: 'To hell, you won't! They are Jews, lousy Jews, and they had their bellies filled to the brim only yesterday!' So we did nothing, just tilted our heads in a half apologetic fashion to the woman and left it at that. When the train later pulled away from us and we saw the eerie, staring eyes from every one of the passing openings, many of us felt uncomfortable, if not guilty, but none of us said anything about that encounter. All of us had heard about concentration camps, but the generally accepted understanding was that only anti-social and anti-German elements, like the Communists, homosexuals, Jews, thieves, bible punchers, gipsies and such like, were being kept in there and forced to do a decent day's work for the first time in their lives. Though we were not far from it, I am sure that none of us at that time had ever heard the name Auschwitz.

After Lemberg came the Soviet Union proper, the Ukraine. The temperature had dropped considerably and when we wanted to look out of the windows, we had first to blow little ice holes. All we could see through it was a white and endless waste, a frightening sight. So that was what was generally understood as Russia, and the thought alone of having to go out and fight in this made our hearts shudder. People in the villages were wrapped up like mummies in thick winter clothing, with little children all but disappearing in them. They were watching us all right when we steamed by, but apart from the odd small child they gave us no recognition.

Then disaster struck; all our lavatories froze up and no amount of hot water poured down could thaw them out. From then on, there was nothing left for those who could not wait for the train to stop but to get on the running board and hang on to the handles for dear life in the icy wind, and face the elements backwards. To do this effectively one had to drop one's trousers first while still in the compartment, and put on gloves. It was no pleasant sight for the other passengers, especially the wiping, which could not be done outside. To the villagers, however, watching the train go by with red and frosty German bottoms sticking out towards them, it must have been a hilarious sight, probably tinged with the revengeful thought, 'serves you right, you bastards!'

We passed a place where a battle had taken place just after Barbarossa the previous summer, somewhere near the town of Ternopol. Shot-up and burnt-out tanks, toppled over or standing forlornly rusting in the snow, gave us a horrible feeling. Our overall impression was as if they were saying to us, 'Where are you going, young lads? Don't you see what has happened to us?' Most of the tanks were Soviet, but some were German. Obviously, our interest was enormous, each one of us trying to get to the frozen window. And the sight was so awful that all that could be heard was an almost whispered 'Jesus Christ!' and when I saw one of the burnt-out Panzers exactly like mine, the thought that I could have driven that charred coffin was too much for me. A bolt of fear shot through me right to the pit of my stomach, making me the next who had to drop his trousers and put on his gloves to manure the battlefield. I was only nineteen, and did not want to die.

                                                              Henry Metelmann

The German medical corps struggled to keep up with the number of wounded requiring attention.

In Petrovka we performed operations for fifty-four hours at a stretch, from four o'clock in the morning until eleven o'clock on the next day but one. Such a thing is possible under certain conditions – good food, determination, sufficient coffee. A single gulp of brandy and one would have collapsed as if completely intoxicated. During the French campaign the other surgeon in the Main Aid Post had been wounded in the leg below the knee, with subsequent paralysis of some of the muscles, and his leg now swelled up to such an extent that his boots had to be cut open. During such an all-out effort there is an ebbing of strength, rather as in a marathon race, until after about the thirty-sixth hour one reaches almost complete exhaustion and then begins to get a second wind.

The influx of casualties had abated. I lay down, but sleep under such circumstances is impossible. I remember the bedstead: its mattress was a watering can that had been beaten flat. The advantage of a bedstead was that the rats didn't continually scamper across the sleeper. The rats were also the reason why one had to learn to sleep with one's head under the blanket.

After some indefinite time – I later discovered it had been an hour – the chief came in. 'You've got to get up. Two lung cases have come in.' With an 'I couldn't care less' movement I turned over on my side. Suddenly I heard a harsh voice. 'I am ordering you herewith to get up and continue operating.' Still half asleep I turned over again. Then a series of thoughts flashed through my fuddled brain: official orders, refusal to obey, insulting behaviour towards a superior officer, court martial! It was sufficiently frightening to arouse anybody from the deepest sleep. But I couldn't conquer my fatigue, I struggled and failed.

At first nothing happened. Suddenly the bedstead creaked. Someone sat down on the edge of my bed. A hand was laid on my arm. The harsh voice of a moment ago said: 'Be a good chap, gee up. I'm not much use at this sort of thing.' After that I got up. It was ten minutes before my bones seemed able to bear my weight.

When those fifty-four hours were over it was eleven o'clock in the morning. I crawled out of the operating den. The sun was shining. There were already a few dry patches on the village street. A soft warm wind was blowing. Between two houses stood a forlorn birch tree and the first tender green shimmered on its branches. The war had rolled on and the attack had been successful.

I pondered the episode. I was unable to recall a single patient. I only knew that I had operated on countless lung injuries. Because of favourable transport conditions we had been able to pass all abdominal cases straight on to the divisional field hospital, and in return we had dealt with all the lung cases ourselves.

As I blinked in the sunlight Sergeant Hermann, old Auntie Ju, shuffled by. He was responsible for looking after the most serious cases. As he approached I wondered how things had gone so I asked: 'Well, Hermann, how many lung cases were there?'

'Twenty-four.'

'How many are still alive?'

Sergeant Hermann paused a moment. Then he smiled and said: 'All of them.' The sun smiled. The birch tree smiled. Surgery is a wonderful thing.

I accompanied Hermann through the cottages. When we got to the one where the lung cases lay I asked if any of them wanted anything and one voice chirped up cheerfully, 'How about a fag, doctor?'

Peter Bamm

In Leningrad

The poet Vera Inber lived in Leningrad during the Baltic city's 900-day siege by the Germans. In January and February 1942 alone, 200,000 of its inhabitants died. Working in a hospital, she saw the full extent of the populace's suffering.

22 JANUARY 1942

Most of the people admitted to the hospital die in Casualty. Long trenches are dug in the cemetery, in which the bodies are laid. The cemetery guards only dig separate graves if they are bribed with bread.

There are many coffins to be seen in the streets. They are transported on sleighs. If the coffin is empty it moves easily from side to side, it skids. Once such a coffin hit my legs. A coffin with a body is usually pulled by two women. The ropes cut deeply into their shoulders, but not because the coffin is heavy; rather because the women are weak.

Recently I saw a body without a coffin. It had on the chest, under the twisted shroud, some wood shavings, apparently as a mark of dignity. One felt a professional not an amateur hand. This technical touch was more macabre than anything. It could well be that this had to be paid for by bread.

Another time, two sleighs caught by their runners. On one sleigh a spade and a crowbar were neatly tied to the lid of the coffin. The other sleigh carried logs. Truly a meeting of life and death.

Living people are frequently carried on sleighs as well. I saw two women pulling a sleigh with some difficulty. A third woman sat on it. She was holding a dead child wrapped in a small blanket. This was by the Anichkov Bridge, where Klodt's bronze horses used to be, before they were removed to a safer place.

The other day I saw an emaciated, though still young, woman having trouble with her sleigh. For on it she had put a large so-called 'modern' wardrobe from a Commission shop, and this was to be converted into a coffin.

One Sunday we walked from our gate to the Leo Tolstoy Square, and on this small stretch we met eight coffins, large and small, and a few bodies which were carried wrapped in blankets. At the same time two women were leading a third to our hospital, she being at the start of her labour. There were dark bags under her eyes – sure sign of scurvy. She was as thin as a skeleton and was hardly able to drag one foot after the other.

On another occasion I saw two women who looked like teachers or librarians pulling an old man along on a sleigh. He wore spectacles, an overcoat and a fur hat, and he lay uncomfortably on the small sleigh, leaning on his elbow, his legs dragging on the ground. 'Be careful! Do be careful!' he cried at every pothole. And those women were sweating profusely, in spite of forty degrees of frost.

Two more women were leading a man with muscular dystrophy (we have learned of the illness only here). His legs, in high felt boots, moved like artificial limbs, his eyes stared madly, as if he were possessed. The skin on his face was tightly stretched, the lips, half open, revealed teeth which seemed enlarged from hunger. His nose, sharpened as if it had melted, was covered with small sores, and the tip had bent slightly sideways. Now I know what is meant by 'gnawed by hunger'.

Faces one sees in the street are either unnaturally drawn and shiny (dropsical swellings) or green and lumpy. There is not an ounce of fat under the skin. And these desiccated skeletons are being gnawed by frost. (As I write these words I can hear a mouse, crazy with hunger, rummaging in the waste-paper basket, into which we used to throw crumbs. We call her Princess Myshkina. She hasn't even the strength to rejoice that all the cats have been eaten.)

I cannot stand the sharp, penetrating smell of pine extract. It means either that a lorry has passed carrying corpses soaked in this fluid, or that an empty lorry (usually a gas-driven one) is passing, having delivered its load. This deathly smell stays suspended in the frosty air.

This morning, when we were on our way to the icy canteen for our lunch, a man was brought to us. He was an acquaintance of Boris Yakovlevich, possibly a doctor himself. He came to beg us to admit his starving wife to hospital, and while he was begging on her behalf he fainted from hunger and it was he who was carried past us into Casualty.

And yesterday we saw a stranger in a corner by the door. He was sitting on a chair by the cupboard, where the duty nurse usually sits. His head was sunk on his chest, and his arms dropped lifelessly at his sides. All his muscles sagged, one of his galoshes had dropped by the chair.

B.Y. touched his temple, on the spot where a small muscle throbbed, and said, 'There are faint signs of life.'

After numerous telephone calls, exhausted orderlies arrived and carried the man into Casualty. Whether the man is still alive, nobody knows. He was a workman in a nearby factory. He had been given a medical certificate and was on his way to hospital. He walked through the main entrance which is now so superficially guarded, managed to reach the chair and quietly began to die, as thousands of these dystrophics are dying – sunk in an icy void.

Vera Inber

‡

Bombing strategy

After the war, Air Chief Marshal Sir Arthur Harris, who was appointed head of RAF Bomber Command in February 1942, was strongly criticised by many for his policy of area rather than precision bombing. This mode of attack – in which hundreds of aircraft saturated the target with bombs and incendiaries – was thought more likely to ensure the destruction of the objective, but inevitably caused significantly higher numbers of civilian casualties. Here Harris defends himself.

As a matter of strict calculation it was therefore obvious that the policy of destroying industrial cities, and the factories in them, was not merely the only possible one for Bomber Command at that time; it was also the best way of destroying Germany's capacity to produce war material. The morale of the enemy under bombing could be taken as an imponderable factor. Just possibly a break in morale might lead to the collapse of the enemy, and more probably bad morale would add to the loss of production resulting directly from air raid damage, but it was not necessary to take these possibilities into account; bombing, there was every reason to suppose, would cripple the enemy's war industries if it was carried out for long enough and with sufficient weight. There was no reason, of course, to confine our bombing exclusively to the large industrial cities; if this should at any time be possible it would be of great advantage to attack key-point factories outside the cities as well. And in point of fact within a month or two of my taking over the Command the force was able to seize the opportunity to bomb two key factories, one in France and the other in Germany, with a large measure of success. Moreover, now that the Americans were in the war with us, their bombers, operating by day, would be able to attack just those factories in open country or on the outskirts of towns which we could not as yet hope to attack by night in normal circumstances. The American campaign and that of our bombers would be exactly complementary, but all the facts at our disposal showed that it would not be sufficient, even if by chance it became possible, to attack only the key factories. When the Americans came to bomb Japan in force, although they had begun the war as one hundred per cent advocates of 'precision' bombing, they also discovered that it was necessary to carry out area attacks.

There is a widespread impression, which has often got into print, that I not only invented the policy of area bombing but also insisted on carrying it out in the face of the natural reluctance to kill women and children that was felt by everyone else. The facts are otherwise. Such decisions of policy are not in any case made by Commanders-in-Chief in the field but by the Ministries, by the Chiefs of Staff Committee, and by the War Cabinet. The decision to build a great force of bombers for strategic attack on industries and communications was made long before the war; the prototype of the four-engine bombers we used against Germany was designed in 1935, which gives some idea of how long it takes to organise a bomber force. The decision to attack large industrial areas instead of key factories was made before I became Commander-in-Chief.

Arthur Harris

‡

Hermann Goering

On account of his bravery in the First World War, his marriage to a Swedish aristocrat and his veneer of charm and bonhomie, Hermann Goering was often considered by foreigners to be the acceptable face of Nazism. However, it was Goering who set up the Gestapo and the first concentration camps, and he who planned the mobilisation of Germany for war in the late 1930s. He was the only Nazi ever created a Marshal of the Reich.

4 FEBRUARY 1942

Goering is leaving Rome. We had dinner at the Excelsior Hotel, and during the dinner Goering talked only about the jewels he possesses. In fact, he had some beautiful rings on his fingers. He explained that he bought them for a relatively small sum in Holland after all jewels were confiscated in Germany. I am told that he plays with his gems like a little boy with his marbles. During the trip he was nervous, so his aides brought him a small cup filled with diamonds. He placed them on the table and counted them, lined them up, mixed them together, and was happy again. One of his top officers said yesterday evening: 'He has two loves – beautiful objects and making war.' Both are expensive hobbies. He wore a great sable coat to the station, something between what automobile drivers wore in 1906 and what a high-flying prostitute wears to the opera. If any of us tried something like that we would be stoned in the streets. He, on the contrary, is not only accepted in Germany but perhaps even loved for it. That is because he has a dash of humanity.

Galeazzo Ciano

☦

In the see-saw campaign in the Western Desert, it was Rommel who had once more gained the upper hand.

There were a great many officers in the low, dark tent. They stood very stiffly, politely, their uniforms and their rugged faces stone-coloured in the lamplight. They might have been German officers carved out of rock or hardwood. Rommel came through the crowd for a moment to look at me. His face swam before my eyes, but before all these people, watching me, I was intent on being cold and dignified in spite of the dirt that covered me and Rommel asked the major if I spoke German, and the major told him, Yes, a few words.

The general looked at me for a moment or two. There was no compassion in his hard, worn face. I looked straight into his face, not caring what he thought of me. Then he spoke softly.

'He looks tired out,' he said to the others. 'Some of these Britishers have covered fantastic distances on foot in the desert.' Then he raised his voice and spoke to me slowly and distinctly.

'Do you like whisky?'

'Yes, General.'

'Bring some whisky,' he called to an orderly. The orderly brought me nearly half a glass, neat. It was Johnny Walker, I recognised it by the taste. I drank it at once, for I was suddenly afraid that there would be a toast. Rommel did not drink, but most of the others did.

'You will be well treated, Lieutenant,' Rommel told me. 'War with us is an impersonal thing. All my men have orders to treat prisoners correctly. But under an International Agreement we are obliged to hand over all prisoners, except sometimes airmen, to the Italians, our Allies.' The last word was spoken with soft, hissing emphasis, and a rustling titter swept the polite wedge of officers around us.

'War is strange indeed,' the general went on. 'Sometimes the soldier wonders that he is fighting with so-and-so against so-and-so. Well, adieu, Lieutenant. Good luck and the condolences of all officers in this tent.' The crowd in uniform, crowd of worshippers hewn from stone, closed around the great man. The major took me back to the truck, made sure the young *Aspirant* was awake to guard me, and dived back into the tent. I fell asleep while I listened to the murmur of voices and wondered what lives, German and British, depended on that eager talk.

George Millar

✚

Escape from Colditz

Oflag IVC, better known as Colditz Castle, was established as a maximum-security prison for habitual escapers; Goering even described the castle as 'escape-proof'. His boast was a vain one, because by April 1945 no fewer than 32 inmates had made 'home runs' back to Allied territory, the highest total from any POW camp in Germany. One was 24-year-old Lieutenant Airey Neave, who, accompanied by Lieutenant Toni Luteyn of the Royal Netherlands Indies Army, walked out of the castle disguised as a German officer.

On the morning of 5th January, 1942, Luteyn and I were ready to escape. We held a conference with Pat Reid and Hank Wardle and decided to try immediately after the nine o'clock *Appel* [roll-call] that evening. Our compasses, maps and a small bundle of notes were ready for hiding inside our bodies. The uniforms were now intact beneath the stage and our civilian clothes had so far escaped detection in their 'hide'. In a moment of supreme confidence, I collected the addresses of relatives of my companions. Then flushed and excited, I lay down to sleep throughout the afternoon and early evening.

A few minutes before nine I went down to the courtyard, when the snow was falling lightly. The turrets cast long shadows in the light of the moon and the steep walls enfolded me for what I believed to be the last time. There was once more the eternal sound of hundreds of men taking their meagre exercise in clogs. I stood waiting for the *Appel*, eyeing the Dutch contingent, where Luteyn was waiting ready to join me. We wore cardboard leggings painted with black polish. I wore my usual combination of battledress and sweater, and my Army boots, being brown, were also darkened with black polish. Underneath I had my 'civilian clothes' with a pair of RAF trousers. I had an overpowering sense that this was my last evening in the castle. The certainty grew with every minute, making me composed and determined.

There was a sharp order of dismissal and mingling with the dispersing prisoners, Pat Reid, 'Hank' Wardle, Luteyn and I hurried quickly into the senior officers' quarters. In the darkness of the theatre, we felt our way beneath the stage, then carefully prised up the loose floorboards. Pat Reid lifted the trap called 'Shovewood', which, on its underside, was whitewashed, disguising the hole in the ceiling of the passage below. I could see the strong, determined lines on his face as he worked in the glow of a cigarette-lighter. The trap removed, the mattress-cover rope was let down through the hole in the ceiling. Cautiously we climbed down, holding the boxes of uniforms, and landed with soft bumps on the floor of the passage.

The bright lights from the courtyard shone through the cobwebbed windows in the outer wall of the passage. Treading softly in our socks, we reached the door of the gate-bridge. Pat Reid, shining his lighter on the lock, swiftly picked it. It opened without a sound for he had oiled the hinges earlier in the week. We were in the half-light of a narrow corridor. We walked quietly across it and stopped at the door that led to the guard-house.

The German uniform overcoats were unpacked in silence and we put them over our workmen's clothes, leaving our battledress in the boxes. As we pulled on our boots there was no sound except the grating of Pat Reid's wire searching the lock. A minute passed, and suddenly came fear and exasperation. The door would not open. Beneath our feet we could hear the creaking of the gates and the voices of sentries changing guard. We stood motionless, fully dressed as German officers, and waited with pounding hearts. Pat Reid spoke in a hoarse whisper.

'I'm afraid I can't get it open!'

He continued turning the wire in the lock. I could hear the wire rasping against the rusty metal as he tried again and again to open it. Ten minutes passed in terrible suspense. Through the cobwebbed window I could see the snow falling. I folded my arms and waited. Suddenly there was a noise of old hinges creaking. A quick snap and the door swung open, showing us the dim interior of the attic.

'Good luck,' said Pat Reid, and shook hands.

We waited till the door was locked behind us and we could no longer hear his muffled steps. Then we crept carefully to the top of stone spiral stairs at an open door on the other side of the attic. A wireless in the guard-room on the ground floor was playing organ music. It was the moment to go down, for the music was loud. We walked quickly down the first flight of stairs, past the door of the officers' mess on the first floor where a light showed beneath. We waited, then stepped confidently down through darkness, into the passage beside the guard-room. The guard-room door was half-open, and I caught a glimpse of German uniforms inside, as we marched smartly into the blinding whiteness of the snow under the arc lights.

The testing time had come. I strode through the snow trying to look like a Prussian. There stood the sentry, the fallen snow covering his cap and shoulders, stamping his feet, just as I had pictured him. He saluted promptly, but he stared at us, and as our backs were turned I felt him watching. We walked on beneath the first archway and passed the second sentry without incident. Then, between the first and second archways, two under-officers talking loudly came from the Kommandantur. They began to march behind us. I felt Luteyn grow tense beside me. I clasped my hands behind my back with an air of unconcern. I might have been casually pacing an English parade ground. In a moment of excitement I had forgotten my part. 'March with your hands at your sides, you bloody fool,' came a fierce sharp whisper from my companion.

Again I saw the bicycles near the clock tower. Could they be ridden fast in this thick snow? We passed beneath the tower, saluted by the sentry, and came to the fateful wicket-gate. As Luteyn opened it I watched the under-officers, their heads bowed to the driving snow, march on across the moat bridge. Down we went into the moat, stumbling and slipping, until we reached its bed. A soldier came towards us from the married quarters. He reached us, stopped and stared deliberately. I hesitated for a moment ready to run, but Luteyn turned on him quickly and in faultless German said crossly, 'Why do you not salute?'

The soldier gaped. He saluted still looking doubtful and began to walk up the side of the moat towards the wicket-gate. We did not look back but hastened up to the path on the far side, and, passing the married quarters, came to the high oak paling which bordered the pathway above the park. We were still within the faint glare of searchlights. Every moment that we stayed on the pathway was dangerous. Lifting ourselves quickly over the paling, we landed in thick snow among the tangle of trees. My cardboard belt was torn and broken and with it into the darkness vanished the holster.

Groping among the trees we struggled through frozen leaves down the steep bank and made for the outer stone wall. It was five minutes before we were at the bottom of the slope. Helped by Luteyn, I found a foothold in the stones of the wall and sat astride the coping. The wall, descending steeply with the tree-covered slope, was shrouded in snow and ice. Each time that I tried to pull Luteyn on top, I lost my foothold and slid backwards through the steep angle of the wall. Then with numbed hands, I caught him beneath the armpits and, after great efforts, hoisted him up beside me. For a minute we sat breathless in the cold air clinging to the coping, and then jumped a distance of twelve feet. We fell heavily on the hard ground in the woods outside the castle grounds. I was bruised and shaken and frightened. I stood leaning against a tree looking at Luteyn. Another minute passed in the falling snow.

'Let's go,' I said, and we began to climb towards the east seeking the direction of Leisnig, a small town six miles away.

Airey Neave

Disguised as Dutch workmen, Neave and Luteyn crossed the Swiss frontier on 8 January, 72 hours after 'beating the castle'. At the end of 1945, Neave was to serve the war crimes indictments on the leading members of the Third Reich at Nuremberg. His account of this can be found later.

Spring 1942

Defeat in the Philippines

'I shall return'

General Douglas MacArthur's under-equipped force of 20,000 American and 110,000 Filipino troops had been holding on in the Bataan Peninsula since the Japanese attacks began in early December 1941. Although starved of supplies and reinforcements, MacArthur was reluctant to obey the order issued to him on 22 February – to leave the Philippines to the Japanese. His eventual departure proved to be extremely hazardous.

It was 7:15 on the evening of March 11th when I walked across the porch to my wife. 'Jean,' I said gently, 'it is time to go.' We drove in silence to the South Dock, where Bulkeley and PT-41 were waiting; the rest of the party was already aboard. Shelling of the waterfront had continued intermittently all day. I put Jean, Arthur, and Ah Cheu on board, and then turned slowly to look back.

On the dock I could see the men staring at me. I had lost 25 pounds living on the same diet as the soldiers, and I must have looked gaunt and ghastly standing there in my old war-stained clothes – no bemedalled commander of inspiring presence. What a change had taken place in that once beautiful spot! My eyes roamed that warped and twisted face of scorched rock. Gone was the vivid green foliage, with its trees, shrubs, and flowers. Gone were the buildings, the sheds, every growing thing. The hail of relentless bombardment had devastated, buried, and blasted. Ugly dark scars marked smouldering paths where the fire had raged from one end of the island to the other. Great gaps and forbidding crevices belched their tongues of flame. The desperate scene showed only a black mass of destruction. Through the shattered ruins, my eyes sought 'Topside,' where the deep roar of the heavy guns still growled defiance, with their red blasts tearing the growing darkness asunder. Up there, in command, was my classmate, Paul Bunker. Forty years had passed since Bunker had been twice selected by Walter Camp for the All-American team. I could shut my eyes and see again that blond head racing, tearing, plunging – 210 pounds of irresistible power. I could almost hear Quarterback Charley Daly's shrill voice barking, 'Bunker back.' He and many others up there were old, old friends, bound by ties of deepest comradeship.

Darkness had now fallen, and the waters were beginning to ripple from the faint night breeze. The enemy firing had ceased and a muttering silence had fallen. It was as though the dead were passing by the stench of destruction. The smell of filth thickened the night air. I raised my cap in farewell salute, and I could feel my face go white, feel a sudden, convulsive twitch in the muscles of my face. I heard someone ask, 'What's his chance, Sarge, of getting through?' and the gruff reply, 'Dunno. He's lucky. Maybe one in five.'

I stepped aboard PT-41. 'You may cast off, Buck,' I said, 'when you are ready.'

Although the flotilla consisted of only four battle-scarred PT boats, its size was no gauge of the uniqueness of its mission. This was the desperate attempt by a commander-in-chief and his key staff to move thousands of miles through the enemy's lines to another war theatre, to direct a new and intensified assault. Nor did the Japanese themselves underestimate the significance of such a movement.

'Tokyo Rose' had announced gleefully that, if captured, I would be publicly hanged on the Imperial Plaza in Tokyo, where the Imperial towers overlooked the traditional parade ground of the Emperor's Guard divisions. Little did I dream that bleak night that five years later, at the first parade review of Occupation troops, I would take the salute as supreme commander for the Allied Powers on the precise spot so dramatically predicted for my execution.

The tiny convoy rendezvoused at Turning Buoy just outside the mine-field at 8 p.m. Then we roared through in single file, Bulkeley leading and Admiral Rockwell in PT-34 closing the formation.

On the run to Cabra Island, many white lights were sighted – the enemy's signal that a break was being attempted through the blockade. The noise of our engines had been heard, but the sound of a PT engine is hard to differentiate from that of a bomber, and they evidently mistook it. Several boats passed. The sea rose and it began to get rough. Spiteful waves slapped and snapped at the thin skin of the little boats; visibility was becoming poorer.

As we began closing on the Japanese blockading fleet, the suspense grew tense. Suddenly, there they were, sinister outlines against the curiously peaceful formations of lazily drifting cloud. We waited, hardly breathing, for the first burst of shell that would summon us to identify ourselves. Ten seconds. Twenty. A full minute. No gun spoke; the PTs rode so low in the choppy seas that they had not spotted us.

Bulkeley changed at once to a course that brought us to the west and north of the enemy craft, and we slid by in the darkness. Again and again, this was to be repeated during the night, but our luck held.

The weather deteriorated steadily, and towering waves buffeted our tiny, war-weary, blacked-out vessels. The flying spray drove against our skin like stinging pellets of birdshot. We would fall off into a trough, then climb up the near slope of a steep water peak, only to slide down the other side. The boat would toss crazily back and forth, seeming to hang free in space as though about to breach, and then would break away and go forward with a rush. I recall describing the experience afterward as what it must be like to take a trip in a concrete mixer. The four PTs could no longer keep formation, and by 3:30 a.m. the convoy had scattered. Bulkeley tried for several hours to collect the others, but without success. Now each skipper was on his own, his rendezvous just off the uninhabited Cuyo Islands.

It was a bad night for everybody. At dawn, Lieutenant (j.g.) V. E. Schumacher, commander of PT-32, saw what he took for a Jap destroyer bearing down at 30 knots through the early morning fog. The torpedo tubes were instantly cleared for action, and the 600-gallon gasoline drums jettisoned to lighten the vessel when the time came to make a run for it. Just before the signal to fire, the onrushing 'enemy' was seen to be the PT-41 – mine.

The first boat to arrive at Tagauayan at 9:30 on the morning of March 12 was PT-34, under the command of Lieutenant R. G. Kelly. PT-32 and Bulkeley's PT-41 arrived at approximately 4 p.m. with PT-32 running out of fuel; those aboard were placed on the two other already crowded craft. A submarine which had been ordered to join us at the Cuyos did not appear. We waited as the day's stifling heat intensified, still spots on the water camouflaged as well as possible from the prying eyes of searching enemy airmen. Hours passed and at last we could wait no longer for Ensign A. B. Akers' PT-35 (it arrived two hours after we left). I gave the order to move out southward into the Mindanao Sea for Cagayan, on the northern coast. This time Rockwell's boat led and PT-41 followed. The night was clear, the sea rough and high.

Once more, huge and hostile, a Japanese warship loomed dead ahead through the dark. We were too near to run, too late to dodge. Instantly we cut engines, cleared for action – and waited. Seconds ticked into minutes, but no signal flashed from the battleship as she steamed slowly westward across our path. If we had been seen at all, we had been mistaken for part of the native fishing fleet. Our road to safety was open.

We made it into Cagayan at 7 a.m. on Friday, March 13. I called together the officers and men of both PTs. 'It was done in true naval style,' I told them. 'It gives me great pleasure and honour to award the boats' crews the Silver Star for gallantry for fortitude in the face of heavy odds.'

Brigadier General William F. Sharp, commander of the Visayan-Mindanao Force, greeted me on landing, and reported all was well with his troops. Davao was in enemy hands, but if Bataan fell, his plans for intensified guerrilla warfare were well advanced.

Four B-17s from Australia had been scheduled to meet our party. One had crashed in the waters offshore, two never reached Cagayan, and the fourth was so dangerously decrepit that General Sharp had ordered it back empty to Australia before our arrival. Of three more planes dispatched for us, two arrived around 8 p.m. on March 16. They were in bad shape, tied together, as their pilots said, 'with chewing gum and baling wire'. We took off from the Del Monte strip shortly after midnight on March 17th, the plane in which I was travelling rattling down the runway with one engine sparking and missing. We would be flying over enemy-held territory, relying on darkness to help us evade Japanese patrols. Over Timor, we were spotted and they came up after us. But we changed course from Darwin, where they figured we would land, and came in at Batchelor Field, 40 miles to the south, just as they hit the Darwin field. They discovered their mistake too late, and their dive bombers and fighters roared in at Batchelor ten minutes after I had left in another plane for Alice Springs to the south.

'It was close,' I remarked to Dick Sutherland when we landed, 'but that's the way it is in war. You win or lose, live or die – and the difference is just an eyelash.'

When we arrived at Batchelor Field, reporters pressed me for a statement. I said: 'The President of the United States ordered me to break through the Japanese lines and proceed from Corregidor to Australia for the purpose, as I understand it, of organising the American offensive against Japan, a primary object of which is the relief of the Philippines. I came through and I shall return.'

I spoke casually enough, but the phrase 'I shall return' seemed a promise of magic to the Filipinos. It lit a flame that became a symbol which focused the nation's indomitable will and at whose shrine it finally attained victory and, once again, founded freedom. It was scraped in the sands of the beaches, it was daubed on the walls of the barrios, it was stamped on the mail, it was whispered in the cloisters of the churches. It became the battle cry of a great underground swell that no Japanese bayonet could still.

Douglas MacArthur

The Bataan Death March

'Death marches' were the fate of many who became prisoners of the Japanese, who had no respect for the lives of soldiers who had surrendered. Each march had its own horrors, though that from Bataan is infamous for the brutality endured by 75,000 American and Filipino prisoners. Captains Gene Dale, John Morrett and Bert Schwarz were among them.

After the surrender, we were all taken to a concentration camp and held that night without food or water. The following afternoon we started the March of Death.

The first stage of the Death March was the steep zigzag road leading from Mariveles to Little Baguio, almost a mile straight up. We marched in single file in the deep dust, against an endless line of Jap army traffic: cavalry, tanks, artillery mounts, caissons, military trucks. We must have passed 50,000 soldiers on that march, and every Nip who felt like it would shove us or cuff us as he passed.

Kicking was nothing; they all took sideswipes at us with their hobnailed shoes until our shins were black and blue. Some of our older men would fall by the wayside in the terrific heat, and the Japs would club the stragglers to their feet. We put our arms around one another and helped ourselves along, because we knew what happened to those who dropped out. The Japs would drag them into the bushes and we would hear screams, and we would not see them again.

The Jap soldiers would snatch things from us as they passed. Bert was wearing his silver pilot wings pinned to his shirt. A little Nip made a grab for them, and instinctively Bert half-turned and gave him the hip. It was a foolish thing to do, but for some reason the soldier just turned and walked away. From then on, Bert wore the wings inside his shirt where they wouldn't be seen.

As we progressed, we began to see more and more bodies in the road, crushed by the Jap transports. Bert and Johnny were at different places along the line of march, but they both remembered one particular Filipino body along about Kilometre 160. It had been pressed as flat as a pancake by the truck tyres, and, in flattening, it had spread about twice its natural size; it was as though someone had drawn a huge caricature of a Filipino in the road. It was so flat you didn't even see what it was until you were walking on it.

Now we were half crazy with thirst. We had to get water. We would stop and drink water out of a mudhole with a dead carabao lying in the middle of it; we would scoop the water up with our cupped hands and gulp it, regardless. At one halt, Johnny crowded with some others toward a stream to fill his canteen. The men upstream shouted that several Filipino bodies were lying in the water, but the others were too thirsty to let that bother them. Johnny had some chlorine tablets and offered them around, but most of the men didn't bother. They knew they were asking for dysentery, but they were beginning to feel it wasn't going to matter.

We made about forty kilometres that day without rest, and about ten o'clock that night we were jammed into the cellar of an old Spanish stone house. It had been used as a pigsty; it would hold about fifty pigs. They shoved five hundred of us in there and locked the door and left us standing in the dark, wedged so tight we couldn't move. Several men died that night of suffocation, but the dead stood all night with the living. There was no room to fall down.

We set out again the following dawn, and we marched all that day, and all the next day, and the next. Days were beginning to run together, and events were getting blurred in our minds. We staggered on mile after mile, too dazed to know what was happening any more. Americans would die and other Americans would demand a decent burial and they would be killed for demanding burial. Now and then we would run into friends in the line. Near Little Baguio, Bert passed Captain Ed Dyess resting with his men under some trees. Bert asked him why he didn't leave on one of the planes from Bataan, and Dyess said he was sticking with his squadron. Captain Dyess was with us until he escaped from Davao a year later.

The sun beat down, the dust choked us, the smell of the dead was everywhere. We didn't even think about the dead anymore. All we thought about was water, water. We could see a glass of water in our mind, and we could almost feel it run over our tongue and down our throat, but in our mouth there was nothing but dust. It was about this time that Johnny lost his precious canteen. A Jap soldier borrowed it to take a drink, and then hung it casually on his own belt and began walking away. Johnny doubled his fist and started after him, but the others grabbed his arm and dragged him back into line.

By noon of the fifth day we could make out the stacks of the San

Fernando sugar mills in the distance, and we knew we were getting near the end of the march. A sprinkle of rain fell that afternoon; that was how we made the last few miles. We held up our mess kits to catch the rain, and we walked with our faces upturned and our parched mouths open to the sky. We were shuffling like drunken men, wandering from side to side of the road, but always keeping our eyes fixed ahead. Johnny almost passed out, and a little Air Corps pilot who was beside him put an arm around his waist and dragged him the rest of the way into town.

Gene Dale, John Morrett and Bert Schwarz

An estimated 25,000 men died during the five days of the march.

✝

The retreat from Burma

After their success in Malaya and Thailand, the Japanese pushed into Burma, threatening India itself. Rangoon fell at the start of March and the remnants of the British forces began the longest fighting retreat in the Army's history. Lt-Gen. Bill Slim had just been sent from Persia to Burma to take charge of the troops, who were supported by soldiers from China, which had been at war with Japan since its invasion in 1937.

More Japanese were coming in from the east and were reported on the river. The situation was grave. At half-past four in the afternoon, Scott reported on the radio that his men were exhausted from want of water and continuous marching and fighting. He could hold that night, he thought, but if he waited until morning his men, still without water, would be so weakened they would have little or no offensive power to renew the attack. He asked permission to destroy his guns and transport and fight his way out that night. Scott was the last man to paint an unduly dark picture. I knew his men were almost at the end of their strength and in a desperate position. I could not help wishing that he had not been so close a friend. I thought of his wife and of his boys. There were lots of other wives, too, in England, India, and Burma whose hearts would be under that black cloud a couple of miles away. Stupid to remember that now! Better get it out of my head.

I thought for a moment, sitting there with the headphones on, in the van with the operator crouching beside me, his eyes anxiously on my face.

Then I told Scott he must hang on. I had ordered a Chinese attack again with all available tanks and artillery for the next morning. If Burma Division attacked then we ought to break through, and save our precious guns and transport. I was afraid, too, that if our men came out in driblets as they would in the dark, mixed up with Japanese, the Chinese and indeed our own soldiers would fail to recognise them and their losses would be heavy. Scott took it as I knew he would. He said, 'All right, we'll hang on and we'll do our best in the morning, but, for God's sake, Bill, make those Chinese attack.'

I stepped out of the van feeling about as depressed as a man could. There, standing in a little half-circle waiting for me, were a couple of my own staff, an officer or two from the Tank Brigade, Sun, and the Chinese liaison officers. They stood there silent and looked at me. All commanders know that look. They see it in the eyes of their staffs and their men when things are really bad, when even the most confident staff officer and the toughest soldier want holding up, and they turn where they *should* turn for support – to their commander. And sometimes he does not know what to say. He feels very much alone.

'Well gentlemen,' I said, putting on what I hope was a confident, cheerful expression, 'it might be worse!'

One of the group, in a sepulchral voice, replied with a single word: 'How?'

I could cheerfully have murdered him, but instead I had to keep my temper.

'Oh,' I said, grinning, 'it might be raining!'

Two hours later, it was – hard. As I crept under a truck for shelter I thought of that fellow and wished I *had* murdered him.

William Slim

Misao Sato was a major in 215 Japanese Infantry Regiment.

Our battalion captured Schwedaung village in the early morning of 29 March 1942 after a light fight. Everybody was busy as there were about ten casualties, and positions were being set up on the south and on the north of the village where a strong enemy attack was expected. As I was standing at the three-way crossing at the south end of the village, I noticed occasional sniping fire from a certain direction. The shooting was so persistent that I sent out a section to look for the sniper, who brought back a young British soldier with his lower body stained with blood. This wounded soldier alone had bravely continued sniping from a bush.

I went to see him lying in the shade of a tree. He was young-looking, about 18 years old, a handsome British soldier. He was treated by our doctor Kikuchi. A bullet had gone through his abdomen, and the doctor told me there was no hope of survival. I asked him in my broken English, 'Where are your father and mother?' He said just a word, but clearly, 'England,' and as I asked, 'Painful?' he again said a word, 'No.' I knew that he must be suffering great pain. It is torture to be shot through the abdomen, and more painful as his intestines were ruptured.

As I looked at him closely I saw a thin stream of tears coming from his eyes. I understood that he was enduring his pain with all his might, his young, pale face contorted. Ah! his attitude was really dignified. He was doing his best to maintain the pride of the Great British Empire while his life was ending. Unconsciously I cried and held his hands. I would never forget the last minutes of that young British soldier! At that time I really discovered the origin of the strength of the British Empire.

Misao Sato

Him or me

As the main army under Slim retreated for 900 miles and two months through the Burmese jungle, some soldiers stayed behind to harry the pursuing enemy. One was Mike Calvert, who here has just emerged from a dip in the River Chindwin.

On the beach, as naked as I was, stood a Jap. A pile of clothes lay near his feet and in my first startled glance I took in the insignia of an officer on his bush shirt. It was the second time within a fortnight that I had come face to face with the enemy at a completely unexpected time and place, and for the second time we were both too startled to speak. I wondered what he was doing alone in that little cove and then I heard more splashing and shouting from the other side of the far promontory. This time the voices were Japanese.

Fantastic as it seemed I could only conclude that he was out with a patrol and had made the same decision as I had, namely to wander off on his own while his men went swimming. I watched him carefully in case he dived for his gun but he appeared to be listening for something. Then a strange gleam came into his eyes and I realised that he had heard my men.

I was baffled. If I yelled for help the Jap patrol would hear me, as well as my own. There were twelve of us but there might be twenty or thirty of them; in that case their superior numbers would give them the advantage if it came to an open fight in the confined cove.

While I was still thinking hard the Jap officer stepped into the river and came towards me. I think his mind must have been working much like mine; he could see that I was unarmed but if he used his gun it would bring both patrols running and he did not know our strength. We were behind the main retreat but for all he knew I may have collected a large band of stragglers. Anyway, he wasn't taking any chances on an open fight which would needlessly risk his men's lives. He preferred to tackle me with his bare hands.

He knew his ju-jitsu and the water on his body made him as slippery as an eel, but I was the bigger and stronger. We fought in silence except for the occasional grunt, and struggled and slipped and thrashed around until we were at times waist deep in the swirling river. It was an ungainly fight, almost in slow motion, for it is extraordinarily difficult to keep balance or move quickly and surely in two or three feet of water. Our breathing became heavier and the Jap got more vicious as he jabbed his fingers at my face in an attempt to blind me. I think it was not till then that I fully realised this would have to be a fight to the death.

I was a trained soldier, taught how to kill with a gun, or a bomb, a bayonet or even a knife in the thick of a battle. Somehow this seemed different, more personal, as the two of us, naked as we were, fought in the water. Apart from anything else I had come to admire this game little Jap. He had all the guts in the world. He could so easily have called up his men and let them fight it out but he had chosen to protect them by taking me on alone.

Now he was putting up a tremendous show and I was hard put to it to hold him. I pulled myself together. Brave or not, I had to kill him. Or he would kill me.

I was thankful for one lesson I had learned: never to take my boots off in the jungle outside camp. Other clothes can be scrambled on in a moment but boots take time, and time can cost lives. Even on this occasion I had stuck to my rule, which was just as well. I managed to grab the Jap's right wrist and force his arm behind his back. And I buried my face in his chest to stop him clawing my eyes out. Then as he lashed out with his left arm and both feet, I forced him gradually under the water. My boots gave me a firm grip and I shut my eyes and held him under the surface. His struggles grew weaker and weaker, flared again in frantic despair and then he went limp. I held on for a few seconds longer before releasing my grip. Slowly I opened my eyes and for a moment could see nothing except the eddies of water caused by his final efforts to break free. Then his body emerged on the surface a couple of yards away and floated gently off downstream.

Michael Calvert

Calvert was later to return to Burma as a senior officer with the Chindits.

'The jungle is neutral'

In one of the great feats of endurance of the war, Spencer Chapman spent more than three and a half years living in the Malayan jungle, operating with Communist guerrillas against the Japanese.

My experience is that the length of life of the British private soldier accidentally left behind in the Malayan jungle was only a few months, while the average NCO, being more intelligent, might last a year or even longer. To them the jungle seemed predominantly hostile, being full of man-eating tigers, deadly fevers, venomous snakes and scorpions, natives with poisoned darts, and a host of half-imagined nameless terrors. They were unable to adapt themselves to a new way of life and a diet of rice and vegetables; in this green hell they expected to be dead within a few weeks – and as a rule they were. The other school of thought, that the jungle teems with wild animals, fowls, and fish which are simply there for the taking, and that luscious tropical fruits – pawpaw, yams, bread-fruit and all that – drop from the trees, is equally misleading. The truth is that the jungle is neutral. It provides any amount of fresh water, and unlimited cover for friend as well as foe – an armed neutrality, if you like, but neutrality nevertheless. It is the attitude of mind that determines whether you go under or survive. 'There is nothing either good or bad, but thinking makes it so.' The jungle itself is neutral.

Spencer Chapman

✠

The attack on St Nazaire

In early 1942, the German battleship Tirpitz *was nearing completion and the British were concerned about the potential threat she would pose as a convoy raider. It was decided to destroy the only dock on the Atlantic coast large enough to*

accommodate her during repairs, that at St Nazaire. A former American destroyer,
Campbeltown, was loaded with explosives with the intention of crashing her into
the dock gates. Early on the morning of 28 March the Commando force, which also
included 16 motor launches, approached St Nazaire. It was led by Captain Robert
Ryder.

So far this was excellent. We had not only reached a position one and
three-quarter miles from our target undetected but had also, apparently,
not encountered any minefields, booms, or other unexpected obstructions,
and last, but not least, we had crossed the flats without any craft stranding.
The warning had, however, evidently been given, as at 1.22 a.m. all the
searchlights on both banks were suddenly switched on, floodlighting the
whole force. Every detail of every craft must have been clearly visible to
the enemy. In anticipation of this, however, we had taken such precautions
as we could; inadequate though they were, they helped. All the craft had
been painted a dark colour, our dirtiest and most tattered ensigns were
used, and the *Campbeltown*'s funnels had been cut on the slant, giving her
a very good resemblance to the 'Mowe'-class torpedo-boats employed by
the Germans on that coast.

Looking back at the force following us, however, it was difficult to
imagine that there could be any successful deception. Each craft, with her
silvery bow-wave, stood out clear and bright, and *Campbeltown*, rising
conspicuously over the smaller craft, could be seen by her funnel smoke
to be increasing in speed. We were challenged from the shore, first by one
of the coastal batteries and later from somewhere in the dockyard. It was
for this moment that Leading Signalman Pike, who could send and receive
German Morse, had been attached to my staff. The challenge was accompanied by sporadic flak, aimed indiscriminately at the force. It was
1.23 a.m., we were a mile and a half from our objective; ten minutes at
that speed. How long could we bluff? Although we had successfully
evaded the heavier batteries at the entrance, every minute still counted.

We did not know the correct reply to the challenge, but we instructed
them to 'Wait' and then gave the call sign of one of the German torpedo-
boats known to us. Without waiting for them to consider this, Pike
embarked on a long plain-language signal. With an 'urgent' prefix, the gist
of this was, 'Two craft, damaged by enemy action, request permission to
proceed up harbour without delay.' Firing ceased. Without finishing the
first message we made the operating signal to 'Wait' again. We had to
reply to the second station. We were about to give them a similar message
when we came under renewed fire from the north bank, heavier than the

first but still, it seemed to us, hesitant. Using our brightest Aldis lamp, we made the international signal for ships or vessels being fired on by friendly forces. The firing ceased again. Another six minutes and *Campbeltown* would be home. Our bluffing had practically achieved its object. According to our information the enemy had no heavy batteries as far up as this and he was unlikely now to sink *Campbeltown*, though a lucky hit in her steering gear or on the bridge might still make her miss her mark. Information now available confirms the valuable part played by Pike in thus delaying the enemy's fire.

By 1.27 an increasing weight of fire directed on our force left little doubt that we had been identified as hostile. We had held our fire up to the last possible moment, and now was the time to let them have it. *Campbeltown* was the first to reply. For about five minutes the sight was staggering, both sides loosing off everything they had. The air was full of tracer; not sailing majestically into the heavens as must have been a familiar sight to many during air raids, but flying horizontally, and at close range.

At the moment of opening fire, we in MGB 314 were just coming up to a guard ship anchored in the river abreast the south entrance. In the glare of the searchlights we could see her clearly and her guns. At about 200 yards three well-aimed bursts of fire from our pompom silenced her. It was indeed an unfortunate day for that vessel, as she not only received bursts of fire from each craft in turn as they passed but finally provided an excellent target for their own shore batteries, who fired on her until she scuttled herself.

After about three or four minutes of this brisk action there was a perceptible slackening in the enemy's fire. This was a triumph for the many gun-layers in the coastal craft and in the *Campbeltown*. It was, at this stage, a straight fight between the carefully sited enemy flak emplacements ashore, enjoying all the protection which concrete could afford, and the gun-layers, handling the short-range weapons on the exposed decks of their small and lively craft. Only in the *Campbeltown* had it been possible to provide a reasonable amount of steel protection, and this was largely offset by her being the most conspicuous target in our force. To our advantage, on the other hand, we were the attackers and, by evading the batteries guarding the approaches, we had arrived off our objective, with a force mounting forty or more close-range cannon. With our craft steaming past the southern entrance to the port a big percentage of our armament could concentrate on each of the enemy emplacements in turn as they passed them, and, finally, on arrival at our selected points of attack, we could reasonably expect to outnumber them locally. For all this the enemy, with their heavily protected emplacements and heavier-calibre guns (20 mm, 40 mm, and 88 mm) had the advantage.

Our triumph, therefore, although it was short-lived, was a fine feat of arms for our guncrews and for those officers and gunners' mates who in many cases stood beside the guns to assist in directing the fire. The slackening in the enemy's fire, moreover, came at the precise moment when the *Campbeltown* continued on round and in to her objective. She had increased to nineteen knots; there was a slight check as she cut the torpedo net and she hit the caisson of the lock with a crash. The exact time of impact was 1.34 a.m., four minutes after the intended time.

Robert Ryder

Ryder went ashore, where, under close and heavy fire, he supervised the evacuation of the crew from the Campbeltown. *She blew up at noon, wrecking the lock gates. Ryder was subsequently awarded the Victoria Cross.*

‡

At the end of 1941, Sir Alan Brooke, who had supervised the evacuation from Dunkirk, replaced Sir John Dill as Chief of the Imperial General Staff, Britain's senior soldier. The change was made at Churchill's insistence and the new pair were to prove a formidable combination in the steering of the war effort.

31 MARCH 1942

The last day of the first quarter of 1942, fateful year in which we have already lost a large proportion of the British Empire, and are on the high road to lose a great deal more of it!

During the last fortnight I have had for the first time since the war started a growing conviction that we are going to lose this war unless we control it very differently and fight it with more determination. But to begin with a democracy is at a great disadvantage against a dictatorship when it comes to war. Secondly a government with only one big man in it, and that one man a grave danger in many respects, is in a powerless way. Party politics, party interests, still override larger war issues. Petty jealousies colour discussions and influence destinies. Politicians still suffer from that little knowledge of military matters which gives them unwarranted confidence that they are born strategists! As a result they confuse issues, affect decisions, and convert simple problems and plans into confused tangles and hopeless muddles.

It is all desperately depressing. Furthermore it is made worse by the lack of good military commanders. Half our Corps and Divisional Commanders are totally unfit for their appointments, and yet if I were to sack them I could find no better! They lack character, imagination, drive and power of leadership. The reason for this state of affairs is to be found in the losses we sustained in the last war of all our best officers, who should now be our senior commanders. I wonder if we shall muddle through this time as we have done in the past? There are times when I wish to God I had not been placed at the helm of a ship that seems to be heading inevitably for the rocks. It is a great honour to find oneself entrusted with such a task, and the hope of saving the ship a most inspiring thought and one that does override all others. But may God help me in my task.

Alan Brooke

☦

The assassination of Heydrich

The Deputy Reich Protector for Bohemia and Moravia was one of the Third Reich's most sinister figures. A general in the SS, Reinhard Heydrich was not only head of the Reich Security Service, but also administrator of the concentration camps. It was he who chaired the Wannsee Conference in January 1942 at which the 'Final Solution' of the 'Jewish question' was put in motion. His personal rule of Czechoslovakia proved so harsh that the Czechs became determined to kill him, and in the spring of 1942 exiles in London, among them General Frantisek Moravec, the head of Czechoslovak Military Intelligence, planned an attempt on Heydrich's life.

In London a detailed tactical plan for the assassination had been worked out, and this was now explained to the men. The plan was as follows: Gabcik and Kubis would be parachuted about thirty miles south-east of Prague into a wooded hilly area which offered shelter for the descent and good approaches to Prague. After destroying all traces of their landing, as they had been taught to do, they would leave the area as quickly as possible and travel to Prague. Like all other parachutists, they would be inconspicuous, dressed and equipped in Czech-made products and carrying the necessary personal documents. (I had a special section in my department which provided all material for parachutists' use – suits, underwear, shoes, even cigarettes, matches and toothpaste, which all had to be of Czech origin. The necessary documents were also prepared with great care in London and they were forged well enough to enable the men to live legally for a time despite the thorough supervision of the Nazis.)

Prague would be their headquarters and, provided with local money, they would live during the reconnaissance period without revealing their identity or purpose to anyone.

This last point was very important. In Prague there were members of other special missions and there were members of the underground. Gabcik and Kubis, however, were to work alone. We had reports that most of the remaining underground groups were thoroughly penetrated by Gestapo provocateurs. This was why Kubis and Gabcik were instructed to contact nobody.

Heydrich's office was at Hradcany Castle, which was heavily guarded, as was his private residence in a small village named Brezany, about two miles from Prague. The most favourable place for our purpose seemed to be the road between Brezany and Prague, which Heydrich used in commuting daily between his home and Hradcany Castle.

Heydrich's car, we learned, was usually accompanied by another car or by SS guards on motorcycles, or both. This led to two important conclusions: first, Kubis and Gabcik would have to choose a spot on the road where Heydrich's car would have to slow down or even stop, such as a sharp curve or a railway crossing. For this the road from Brezany to Prague was studied in London in minute detail. Second, because of the SS guards, our soldiers would probably be unable to get near enough to Heydrich to use pistols with accuracy. A home-made bomb and machine-gun were therefore suggested as the weapons to be used.

Both men understood that an unsuccessful attempt would be a waste of energy, if not of life. We made it clear that the final details of the plan would have to be determined on the spot. Heydrich's movements would have to be observed repeatedly, his timetable and habits studied. The timing of the operation could not be fixed in London. That decision was left to Gabcik.

After completion of the mission, whether successful or not, the men were instructed to try by any available means to get to Slovakia, which was under lighter German surveillance than Bohemia and Moravia and was also Gabcik's native country, of which he had special knowledge.

I told the men to buy bicycles as soon as possible after they landed, as this would give them greater freedom of movement during the reconnaissance period and would also increase their chances of escape. We calculated these to be almost non-existent, in view of Heydrich's SS guards, but I kept thinking that if only the men managed to get out of Prague before the German police apparatus was fully brought into action, they might have a chance.

The behaviour of Kubis and Gabcik during the trying last days – the crucial period between briefing and departure – was exemplary. They understood the importance of their task and they knew that they could rely completely on each other. Like all good soldiers, they would do everything possible to save their lives, but they had no illusions. They knew that in all probability they would die with Heydrich and if there was any glory for them afterwards they would not live to enjoy it. They accepted this knowledge with heroic calm and determination. They made me think of that Roman fortitude about which I had read in the Latin classics.

In the last stages of preparations before their departure, Gabcik and Kubis were learning the topography of Prague on a huge-scale plan and I was instructing them personally. They concentrated and learned quickly. We studied the route which Heydrich customarily took and I remembered from personal experience a certain nasty corner on the outskirts of Prague where his limousine would certainly have to slow down.

The departure of Gabcik and Kubis was scheduled for the beginning of April but it had to be postponed several times because of bad weather. Finally a definite date was set for late April.

The day before they left the two men were received by President Benes. He stressed the historical importance of what they were about to do. He knew this was a do-or-die mission and I could see that – like me – he was affected by the moving simplicity with which they accepted their lot. When he said goodbye to them, there were tears in his eyes.

I had dinner with the pair before taking them to the airport. Their morale was at its highest. We ate at a little Italian restaurant round the corner from my Bayswater office. They enjoyed the food, making simple little jokes and not mentioning one word about their mission or the fact that among the equipment just issued to them were two capsules of quick-acting poison to be used on themselves in the event of unbearable torture.

At the RAF airfield the plane was waiting – a Halifax bomber, with an experienced Czech pilot, Captain Andrle. The goodbye was short and soldierly. I shook hands with Kubis and watched him climb into the plane. Then I turned to Gabcik, who had asked if he could talk to me for a few minutes in private. I wondered what he could want to ask me at this last moment after all the lengthy briefings. The idea that he might want to change his mind occurred to me, but I dismissed it. Gabcik said, 'Colonel, I'm quite embarrassed to tell you – I have a £10 debt in our restaurant. Would it be possible for you to pay it for me?'

I could only nod. Gabcik held out his hand.

'You can rely on us, Colonel. We shall fulfil our mission as ordered.'

When he returned Captain Andrle reported to me that the men had remained in high spirits during the flight and that he had dropped them in the designated area. The first phase of the operation completed successfully, there was nothing left to do but wait.

By my calculations, at least ten days must elapse before the men could make proper preparations. Two, then three weeks went by. When four weeks had elapsed and nothing happened, I began to worry. Had something gone wrong? Suddenly, on the afternoon of May 27, 1942, the news came through on the Prague radio: an official report that the Reichsprotektor Heydrich had been severely wounded in a criminal attempt to assassinate him at 10.30 that morning in the south-east suburb of Prague. A bomb had been thrown into his car and it had exploded. Two men were seen leaving the scene of the crime on bicycles. Search for them was in progress.

So that was it. Gabcik and Kubis had done it. Apparently they had fulfilled their mission according to plan and were neither killed nor captured on the spot. I liked the mention of the bicycles. Perhaps the two might after all escape from Prague before the Gestapo closed off the city.

Frantisek Moravec

Heydrich died a week later. At his funeral, Hitler called him the 'man with the iron heart'. The reprisals were predictably barbaric: 860 Czechs were executed in Prague and 395 in Brno. The village of Lidice, whose population was accused of sheltering the assassins, was obliterated. All 172 of its men were shot, its women sent to concentration camps and the children dispatched to foster homes. Gabcik and Kubis, meanwhile, were tracked down by the SS to a church in Prague. Kubis was killed by a grenade blast and Gabcik, determined not to fall into the hands of the Gestapo, shot himself.

‡

Malta besieged

Malta was of vital strategic importance to Britain, and during the first part of 1942 it came under prolonged air attack. Just enough supplies arrived by convoy to prevent the population from starving, and their spirit remained undaunted. Sybil Dobbie worked in the office of her father, General Sir William Dobbie, the island's Governor.

I remember days when raids would be almost continuous. I would get up in the morning after a more or less noisy night, and the first siren would go while I was dressing. Frequently nothing but a small reconnaissance raid would follow, and the 'Raiders Passed' would sound just as I was going down to breakfast. Towards the end of the meal the siren would go again. This would probably be something more serious; the guns would begin, and after the ADC had enquired about the plot my father would go up to the tower to watch. A rather heavy attack would follow, several waves of bombers taking part, but it would be quickly over.

By then it would be time to start for Valetta, and we would set off, stopping, perhaps, on the way to look at some fresh damage that had been done during the night or in the last raid. I would spend the morning working at Valetta Palace, and at midday, if not before, the siren would wail again and a few minutes later the red flag would go up. If the attack on one or possibly both harbours developed, Valetta, situated between the two, was too much in the forefront of the battle to be conducive to peaceful work, but we got on as best we could. The 'All Clear' would probably go while we were on our way home.

The rest of the day would be much the same. A small raid early in the afternoon would be followed by heavier ones, working up in a crescendo to the big one after tea. I remember one afternoon walking with a friend to have tea with a Maltese family who lived some distance away. We started off in one of the peaceful intervals, but a raid came on after we had gone about a mile. By the time we had reached the first village on our route planes were flying just overhead and shell splinters were pattering down all round. It seemed to be 'coming on to bomb', too (people used to talk about 'coming on to bomb' like 'coming on to rain'), and we sheltered for some time under an archway, which would at least have kept off the splinters, though very little else.

We resumed our journey as soon as it had 'cleared up', and reached our destination. The house was a beautiful one on a high ridge looking out over a cultivated plain, brilliant with crimson patches of clover, to the sea. We sat in a sun-drenched garden admiring the flowers and the view – until the enemy suddenly began to attack the next village. The open position, which I had thought so delightful, now seemed not only painfully exposed but most unpleasant, for we got only too clear a view of very heavy bombing decidedly close. It ceased and we went in to tea.

Sybil Dobbie

On 16 April 1942, Malta was awarded the George Cross for its fortitude in the face of the bombing campaign.

✝

Depth-charged

A failed torpedo attack on 26 April on an American destroyer off Cape Fear, North Carolina, had betrayed the position of U-109. A crash dive ordered by its captain, Heinrich Bleichrodt, took the submarine to the sea bed. Its hydrophone operator, Wolfgang Hirschfeld, describes the subsequent onslaught by the destroyer.

We could hear the destroyer's propellers with the naked ear. The Commander had perched himself athwart the pressure doorway so that he could maintain contact with the men in the control room and the hydrophones room.

'Give me his exact bearing, Hirschfeld.' Bleichrodt was perfectly calm despite the impending catastrophe. A depth charge attack at 240 feet on the sea bed gave little expectation of survival.

The destroyer sounded very faint in the hydrophones and it was much easier to hear him without them. Leibling shrugged. 'He was tremendously loud just now,' he assured me. In desperation I swung the indicator steering wheel around the full circle. Surely the equipment couldn't have gone out of commission before a single depth charge came down?

'He's approaching from the starboard quarter astern,' I told the Commander. 'We can't make out the exact bearing, the reception is too dispersed and weak.' Bleichrodt nodded and passed a fresh course to the helmsman in the control room.

'Boat doesn't answer the helm,' Potter called out.

'That's a good start,' said Leibling.

'Boat does not answer the depth rudders,' Berthold Seidel reported. I saw the Commander bite his lower lip. The thrashing propellers were very loud. All eyes stared upwards. The thrashing was directly overhead, then wandered quickly away to port. Just as I took a breath, there was an appalling thunderclap and the boat rolled and reeled. The hydrophones dropped from my head. A second, third, fourth thunderclap. Our head withdrew into the cradle of our arms. A giant's fist shook the boat. It sounded like the dissolution of the universe. I was choking, thinking it was the end. Here we were going to die. Slowly the main lighting failed. Around us it was now darkest night. The emergency lighting flickered on and shone with a weak glimmer. The thunder was still rolling away through the depths. The control centres reported in. No damage forward, no damage aft. This was incredible. We didn't have a single leak.

'Stop both engines and all machinery except the hydrophones

transformer,' Bleichrodt ordered. It became deathly quiet in the boat. In the sound room we could just about hear the destroyer's propellers.

'Can't you get a bearing on him?' demanded the Commander.

'We can't get a maximum accuracy, sir. He's at about 290°. Must be to do with the receivers in the bows.'

From a seat in the radio room Lt Witte said to the Commander, 'What do we do now, is he gone?' The Commander gave a grim smile. 'He's coming back, Witte. We will keep completely still. If we stir up the mud, he'll know where he has to drop.'

The destroyer was manoeuvring nearer. Lt Keller was perched on a stool near the sound room. 'Nice piece of shit we're in,' he whispered.

'Yes,' I whispered back, 'specially when I think about our oil slick.'

The thrashing noise was becoming louder. Bleichrodt looked at me enquiringly.

'Soon he'll be overhead,' I said. I glanced downhill into the bow room where the men were all curled up in naked fear. Jarschel was slowly stroking his beard. The propellers were overhead again. Leibling was rolled up on the floor like a hedgehog. We stopped breathing. I gripped the wheel of the hydrophone equipment. A crash of thunder and a huge fist shook the boat again, trying to crush the pressure hull. I tensed, expecting to hear the dread cry, 'The sea's breaking in!' The terrible thunder sawed at our nerves.

Keller had blocked his ears, but as the awful noise rolled away he grinned at me. 'They were very close that time. But their charges seem weaker than the cans the British threw us off Greenland.'

Incredibly, we had survived again without serious damage; just a few smashed instruments.

A third attack followed, in which the shock wave and thunder were even more powerful than previously; the lights went out and stayed out and we could hear the vents leaking a little water. Then the destroyer was gone.

Bleichrodt came to the radio room, picked up the microphone and said, 'Comrades, he seems to have given up. We will now free the boat and continue. Out.'

The Chief attempted to free the boat first by running the electric motors furiously in reverse while the men in the bow room stormed down the central corridor to the stern, roaring with laughter. How soon they forgot the mortal danger in which we had just found ourselves! But the boat wouldn't budge.

Witte said to me, 'The whole eastern seaboard of America has many deep holes. Scientists think that the world once had a second moon which fell to earth and exploded here.'

I crept to the control room and looked in. The Commander was leaning on the chart table, looking at the Chief Engineer's back.

'How long are you going to keep the motors running at full speed, Chief?'

Sweat stood out on Weber's forehead. He stopped the motors and swivelled round on his stool. 'We must blow the tanks, sir. Otherwise we'll never get the boat free.'

'But you'll stir the mud up. If they've got a plane up there, they'll drop a bomb on us.'

There was a long silence. We could hear the water dripping through the vents.

'We've already stirred up the mud with the propellers. We're very deep in it, and probably being slowly sucked deeper. If we are ever going to escape, we can only do it by blowing the tanks. I see no alternative.'

'Well blow them then,' said the Commander. 'It's all the same to me if we slowly suffocate down here or get blown to pieces.'

Peters opened the valves and the compressed air rattled through the piping. The motors went to full astern again. Witte gave me a sceptical glance. The boat wasn't moving. Once the air was finished, we were done for. But at last *U-109* shuddered. There was a sucking noise in the bow, then, after some heavy whirrings with the propellers, we slowly reversed out of the burrow in the mud of the sea bed, the keel bumped along the sea floor and we slithered into deeper water.

When we were well offshore the Commander surfaced the boat, and as he opened the bridge hatch he cursed loudly. The whole tower was still clogged with mud. The forward part of the boat from the peak of the bow to the Winter-garden must have worked its way deeply into a soft mud bank and this had saved us during the depth-charging.

Wolfgang Hirschfeld

With a different crew aboard, U-109 was sunk on 4 May 1943 by a British Liberator aircraft off the coast of Ireland. Bleichrodt and the author survived the war, the former winning the Knight's Cross with Oak Leaves.

‡

The enemy within

The British population was urged to be on the watch for German spies. When reports came in to the Intelligence Corps at Inverness of a flashing light seen every night at the same time on the remote Isle of Lewis, Harold Harris was sceptical that it was an agent signalling to a submarine. But, he reveals, the War Office thought it merited further investigation.

Mr Price was an amiable chap. He arrived ten days later (having taken some leave first) and without his assistant, who could not be spared for so long at the same time. They had not realised how far away it was. He asked us to lend him one of our Field Security NCOs in plain clothes, and some transport. The only transport available was an army motor-cycle, and so Mr Price, a lance-corporal in sports jacket and flannels, an army motor-cycle, and sundry equipment set sail from Kyle of Lochalsh to Stornoway and duly impressed the natives when they arrived at the scene of operations a day or two later. Mr Price visited the points from which the spy's light could be seen, set up his highly sophisticated direction-finding apparatus, and instructed our lance-corporal how to work it. Bearings were plotted on maps and the light actually pin-pointed. On the following day, with some difficulty because of the remoteness of the spot, the spy was tracked down.

Mr Price told us all about it when he returned to Inverness several days later. An ancient crofter, a man of regular habits, had no indoor sanitation in his house. Every night, before he went to bed, he walked some twenty yards across his land to a kind of cave, swinging his lantern in time with his footsteps. He put it on a ledge while he squatted down, and swung it again on his return. His story was corroborated by the evidence in the cave.

Mr Price reckoned that it was a satisfactory conclusion to a difficult case, even if it had been a long journey (about 1600 miles there and back) to discover a crofter's lavatory.

Harold Harris

So effective was MI5, Britain's counter-espionage service – and so inept the general level of agents inserted by the Germans – that during the war every single one they deployed in the United Kingdom was captured. Seventeen people in all were executed in Britain for working for the enemy.

‡

Cracks in the Axis

At the start of May, Hitler summoned Mussolini to Austria for a conference. Il
Duce *was accompanied by Ciano.*

29, 30 APRIL — 1, 2 MAY 1942

Arrival at Salzburg (the Puch station). The usual scene: Hitler, Ribbentrop,
the usual people, the usual ceremony. We are housed at the Klessheim
Castle. This is a grandiose building, once owned by the prince-bishops of
Salzburg, which has now become a guesthouse for the Führer. It is very
luxurious and well arranged: furniture, hangings, carpets, all coming from
France. They probably did not pay very much for the furnishings.

The atmosphere is extremely cordial, which makes me suspicious. The
courtesy of the Germans is always in inverse ratio to their good fortune.
Hitler looks tired; he is strong, determined, and talkative. But he is tired.
The winter months in Russia have weighed heavily upon him. I see for
the first time that he has many grey hairs.

Hitler talks with the Duce, I talk with Ribbentrop, but in two separate
rooms, and the same record is played in both. Ribbentrop, above all,
repeats his usual propaganda piece. I have recorded the conversation
elsewhere. Napoleon, the Beresina, the drama of 1812, all this is brought
to life in what he says. But the ice of Russia has been conquered by the
genius of Hitler. This is the strong dish that is served up to me. But what
about tomorrow? What does the future hold? On this issue Ribbentrop is
less explicit. An offensive against the Russians in the south with the oil
wells as a political and military objective.

When Russia will have exhausted her oil supplies she will be brought
to her knees. Then the British Conservatives, and even Churchill himself,
who, after all, is a sensible man, will bow in order to save what remains of
their battered empire. Thus spoke Ribbentrop. But what if all this doesn't
happen? What if the English, who are stubborn, decide to go on? What
course must we follow to change their minds? Airplanes and submarines,
says Ribbentrop. We go back to the 1940 formula. But that formula failed
then and was shelved in the attic. Now they pull it out once more, and,
after having dusted it thoroughly, they want to offer it to us again. I am
not convinced by it, and I say so to Ribbentrop, much to Alfieri's dismay.
Alfieri understands very little of what he hears but always says yes.

America is a big bluff. This slogan is repeated by everyone, big and small
in the conference rooms and in the antechambers. In my opinion, the

thought of what the Americans can and will do disturbs them all, and the Germans shut their eyes in order not to see. But this does not keep the more intelligent and the more honest from thinking about what America can do, and they feel shivers running down their spines.

In regard to France they feel more doubt than friendship. Laval, too, is hardly convincing. The true spirit of the French is more clearly expressed by the gesture of the typesetter who risked his life to print the newspaper with the name of Pétain changed to Putain [whore], than by all the words of the collaborationists in the pay of Vichy. In Germany they have no illusions, and are always ready to slug anybody who moves.

Hitler talks, talks, talks. Mussolini suffers, since he is in the habit of talking and, instead, practically has to keep quiet. On the second day, after lunch, when everything had been said, Hitler talked uninterruptedly for an hour and forty minutes. He omitted absolutely no argument: war and peace, religion and philosophy, art, and history. Mussolini automatically looked at his wristwatch, I had my mind on my own business, and only Cavallero, who is a phenomenon of servility, pretended he was listening in ecstasy, continually nodding his head in approval. Those, however, who dreaded the ordeal less than we did were the Germans. Poor people. They have to take it every day, and I am certain there isn't a gesture, a word, or a pause which they don't know by heart. General Jodl, after an epic struggle, finally went to sleep on the sofa. Keitel was reeling, but he succeeded in keeping his head up. He was too close to Hitler to let himself go as he would have liked to do.

One does not see any physically fit men on the streets in the cities and towns of Germany. Women, children, and old men only. Or else foreign labourers, slaves of the earth. Edda [his wife], who visited a camp of our Italian workers, found one who had been wounded on his arms by a brutal guard with a scythe. She told Hitler, who had a fit of anger and ordered all sorts of arrests and investigations. Which, however, will not change the course of things.

Losses in Russia are heavy. Ribbentrop says 270,000 dead. Our General Marras raised it to 700,000. And between amputations, frostbite, and the seriously ill who will not recover by the end of the war, the figure rises to three million.

The British air force is striking hard. Rostock and Lübeck have been literally razed to the ground. Cologne has been heavily hit. The Germans react and strike back at the English cities but with less violence. Which only partly consoles the German population, accustomed as it has always been to dish it out but never to take it.

This leads many of them, who have devastated half of Europe, to weep about the 'brutality of the English, who make many innocent Prussian families homeless'. The worst of it is that they really feel this way.

Galeazzo Ciano

✝

The Battle of the Coral Sea

With the Lexington

On 7 May, an American naval force attacked Japanese troopships making for Port Moresby, New Guinea. The Japanese aerial attempt to retaliate was initially ineffective – on one sortie 21 aircraft were lost, with some even attempting to land by mistake on the American carrier Yorktown. *The next day, however, they proved far more deadly. Journalist Stanley Johnston was on board the aircraft carrier* Lexington *during what became known as the Battle of the Coral Sea.*

'Wham!' 'Boom!' 'Tat-tat-tat-tat!!' 'Bang, bang, bang' go our anti-aircraft guns. Then a prolonged 'Whaaaaaaaaaa' of the Japanese dive-bombers coming down across our deck, all guns blasting. We can see their tracers lacing past, many of them too high to get the deck crews and too low to bother us on the bridge.

Another thought flashes through my mind: 'These fellows don't dive-bomb like our boys. They aren't coming down as steeply. They're only diving at about a 50-degree angle.' As this crosses my brain I see a black blur whip across in front of the Island about bridge high. The object clears the starboard rail by inches, hits the water and explodes. It is one of those big Jap bombs (a thousand-pounder) that would have removed all of us from the Island – the main control centre of the entire ship – had the ship's 8-inch barbettes not been removed at war's beginning, for it passed exactly through the space where the Number 2 barbette used to be.

Instinctively I duck behind the bridge rail as it flashes by. And so does everyone else who sees it come. Still squatting down behind the weather shield around the bridge, soaked by the geyser of water thrown up by the bomb blast, I reach out and measure between my thumb and forefinger, the thinness – one-eighth of an inch – of the metal plate. Ensign G. J. Hansen, the signal officer, sees this and reads my mind.

'It's not even waterproof, Mr Johnston. Won't even keep out the spray,' he grins.

11.22 a.m. – 'Whooom!' once more the *Lexington* lurches – the fourth torpedo hit.

11.22.5 a.m. – 'Baloom!!!' the fifth torpedo, all on the port side – amidships and forward.

Captain Sherman is watching the torpedoes and dive-bombers and swinging the ship – now to starboard, now to port – in a snake dance in an effort to evade the missiles. His orders to the navigating officer and helmsman continue to be in a tone of voice that might have been used in any drawing-room.

About this time I am passing in front of the wheelhouse. The skipper is standing in front of the wheel looking out and listening intently to the reports being made to him from all round. As I pass I catch his eye and brashly enough put my hand out. The Captain takes it and as we shake hands I remark: 'I think it's going to be all right, Captain.' He smiles back and squeezes my hand: 'I hope so, I hope so,' he says in his quick, quiet way.

Looking out to starboard to see how the rest of the ships are faring, I count five planes burning on the water. Japanese planes escaping after having dropped their torpedoes or bombs are being followed by our starboard guns pouring tracers into and after them. A huge waterspout leaps up near Carrier II [the *Yorktown*], my immediate reaction is 'She's hit.' (Later I discover it was a near miss by a huge bomb.)

Suddenly I see a Grumman following a Jap as he dives down toward Carrier II. They disappear into the smoke of the umbrella of bursting, heavy anti-aircraft shells and emerge into a literal hail of the machine-gun fire thrown up from her decks. The Jap releases his bomb and begins to flatten out – he bursts into flame as the bullets from our fighter rip into his petrol tanks. The Jap flames into the sea and the Grumman zooms back into the fight.

Dive-bombers are still coming down, only a second or so apart. Most of the missiles are falling towards the after-end of the ship, close, but not quite hitting. Above we see the Jap machines diving in a chain. Watching closely I see the bombs leave each plane. The aircraft follow, gradually flattening out. Their machine-guns and wing cannon wink momentarily. Each plane sweeps over the *Lexington*'s deck and then becomes a tiny shape, swiftly diminishing in size as it speeds away.

11.25 a.m. – 'Seven more torpedo planes from the port side,' the look-outs call. Our anti-aircraft fire is so hot now that the pilots in these planes are anxious to drop their fish and get away. They fail to press home their attack like the first groups. All of them are dropping their torpedoes while still in a 45-degree glide, and more than two hundred feet above the water. They then turn away instead of boring in. They never come closer than within 1,500 yards of the *Lex*.

Again we swing to avoid the torpedoes. This time it is back to starboard. All the torpedoes seem to be porpoising badly.

'Hold her steady, Captain, hold her steady,' Commander Duckworth suddenly shouts. He is out on the navigation bridge dancing up and down in his excitement, his arms spread out to each beam as if pressing the torpedoes away with his hands. 'We've got three alongside – two to port and one to starboard – they are exactly paralleling us.'

'If we veer,' Ducky yells, 'we'll collect one sure.' The skipper 'holds her' straight, and the torpedoes churn slowly on past us. We are doing 25 knots and they are doing 50, so they seem slow anyway.

11.26 a.m. – A signalman reports to Captain Sherman that one of our airmen (having been forced to bale out during the fighting) is floating on his little yellow inflated raft through the centre of the speeding fleet. He is just off our starboard bow and only a hundred yards from our track. As we sweep past him I can see him on his knees wildly cheering and waving us on. He is paying absolutely no attention to the Jap aircraft all around us and to the flying anti-aircraft stuff zipping past him from our own guns and other guns in the fleet.

Captain Sherman glances his way, instantly understanding, and over his shoulder directs a signalman to have our planeguard destroyer – the last one in the fleet – 'pick that boy up.' This is done. The destroyer draws alongside him, spins quickly, and as it slides past, engines in reverse, makes a sharp turn, drops him a line, and jerks him aboard.

11.27 a.m. – Five more Jap torpedo planes suddenly appear. In the confusion we have not seen them until they are right in the midst of the fleet. But now our anti-aircraft have opened up on them, too. These new enemies are almost at water level. They single us out, spread fanwise, and bore into our starboard side – the first attack of the day on our right.

With the entire fleet firing on them they drop their fish a long way out. The old *Lexington*, still charging ahead despite her wounds, turns once again and all these torpedoes miss her, their feathery wakes lacing the water wide off our bow.

Two more Jap planes slide in through the fleet's fire, but these turn aside from the *Lex*, pass astern of us under the barrage of our AA guns, and drop their fish at the cruiser on our port quarter. Accepting the challenge, this smartly handled ship swings quickly, avoiding both tor-pedoes. The cruiser's gun crew, meanwhile, is pouring its stuff at both the planes and someone gets a direct hit on one of them. The plane disappears in a clap of thunder and fire.

Commander Seligman is intently watching the diving Jap planes when a Marine approaches, gives a smart salute, and hands him a paper. The Commander reluctantly takes his eyes off the attackers and hastily reads the message. Crumpling the paper in his hand he disgustedly exclaims: 'This is a swell time to worry me with this – as if I didn't have enough disturbance already.'

I ask, 'What's the bother now?'

Without taking his eyes from the bombers, he replies, 'Someone wants me to worry because we have a case of *measles* aboard.'

Stanley Johnston

Despite the Lexington's *efforts, the carrier was eventually severely damaged and Captain Sherman ordered his men to abandon ship. Her loss, however, was not in vain, as the Japanese fleet heading for New Guinea was forced to turn back. It was the first check to the Japanese advance in the Pacific.*

‡

North Africa

On 27 May, Rommel outflanked the static Allied defensive line running south from Gazala to Bir Hakeim, swinging his armour out wide to assault the Eighth Army from the rear. The British mounted counter-attacks using their new, American-manufactured Grant tanks. Heinz Werner Schmidt was on the receiving end.

Shell-bursts were now erupting all round. Was I alone out here now? As I wondered this, there came a reply from behind, where Sergeant Weber was firing my third gun. He pumped out shell after shell. But there was little help in his valour.

Twelve tanks swung at us to neutralise this menace. Their guns blazed insistently at us, and they came straight on.

I dropped my glasses and rolled to the bottom of my trench, where Muller had spread a blanket. I dragged it over myself in ineffectual protection. The toes of the dead man's boots dangled six inches from my eyes.

The earth trembled. My throat was like sandpaper. This, then, was the end. I had escaped at Sidi Rezegh. But now this was it. My fiancée would be told: 'With deep regret we have to inform you that . . .' She would read that I had died a hero's death for the Fatherland. And what would it mean? That I was just a bloody mess in the sand at an unidentified spot near an unimportant point in the desert called Acroma.

A tank crunched by at the edge of my trench. I heard an English voice calling. Was it a man in the tank, or an infantryman following up with bayonet fixed?

A blanket is not much good against a bayonet. But perhaps they would not see me. Perhaps I should just lie here and go mad. Perhaps I should be killed by a shell. Perhaps another tank would crush me.

The minutes crawled by. I now heard German voices. Apparently the British were rounding up prisoners in my own sector. And here was I in the trench.

Firing had ceased. After perhaps a quarter of an hour I heard the tanks rolling off towards the south. Silence descended on the battlefield. But I still lay there like a sleeping man.

When I lifted my head the sky had dimmed from its brassy afternoon glare. Evening was coming. I saw no sign of life all round. Then I was startled by a figure that burst like a jack-in-the-box from a slit-trench some way back. It was my man Muller.

He had an anguished expression on his face. 'Are you well, *Herr Oberleutnant*?' he called to me. And he added oddly, 'I am not.'

'Get down here,' I ordered Muller. 'We shall wait until it is dark before we move.'

'*Herr Oberleutnant*,' said Muller, 'that venison was just ready when the Tommies came.'

As soon as darkness had fallen on the battlefield Muller led me back to the wadi, where the gazelle had been roasted. A haunch, still warm, lay on a sheet of iron there. Muller's flask still held coffee. We tore off hunks of the tasty but exceedingly tough meat and swallowed it.

I can still remember the feeling of the juice running down from the corners of my mouth. It was good to be alive. That sense of futility and the inevitability of death that had overwhelmed me in the slit-trench had gone. The will to live is strong in us.

Heinz Werner Schmidt

✠

The first 1,000-bomber raid

At the end of May, Air Chief Marshal Harris dispatched 1,000 bombers against a single target, gambling that success would prove that his area bombing theory was correct and would win him the resources he needed to continue the policy. He chose Cologne as the target of the raid on the night of 30 May when there was a full moon. The outcome of the mission was a turning point in the war in the air.

Over the North Sea there was, in point of fact, extremely dirty weather, but when the force reached Holland it cleared, and continued clear all the way to the target. Nearly 900 aircraft attacked out of the total of 1047, and within an hour and a half dropped 1455 tons of bombs, two-thirds of the whole load being incendiaries. The casualty rate was 3.3 per cent, with 39 aircraft missing, and, in spite of the fact that a large part of the force consisted of semi-trained crews and that many more fighters were airborne than usual, this was considerably less than the average 4.6 per cent for operations in similar weather during the previous twelve months. The medium bomber, mostly flown by crews from the OTUs, had a casualty rate of 4.5 per cent, which was remarkable, but it was still more remarkable that we lost scarcely any of the 300 heavy bombers that took part in this operation; the casualty rate for the heavies was only 1.9 per cent. These had attacked after the medium bombers, when the defences had been to some extent beaten down, and in greater concentration than was possible for the new crews in the medium bombers. The figures proved conclusively that the enemy's fighters and flak had been effectively saturated; an analysis of all reports on the attack showed that the enemy's radar location devices had been able to pick up single aircraft and follow them throughout the attack, but that the guns had been unable to engage more than a small proportion of the large concentration of aircraft.

Reconnaissance after the attack showed that 600 acres of Cologne had been devastated and this in turn conclusively proved that the passive defences of Cologne had been saturated in just the same way as its guns and searchlights had been, together with the air defence of the whole of Western Germany, by concentration of attack. The damage had increased out of all proportion to the increase of bomb tonnage; in fact, this single attack had caused very nearly as much damage in Germany – 600 acres as against 780 – as all Bomber Command's previous attacks, including the very successful attacks on Lübeck and Rostock, taken together.

I rang up Winston Churchill, who had just alighted from Washington, and told him that the operation had been successful, and that only 39 aircraft were missing, one less than my estimate of 40. I always knew from the tone and quality of Churchill's voice, quite as much as from what he actually said, whether or not he was satisfied. I knew at once that he was satisfied then. At a time when there was no other conceivable offensive weapon we could use against the Germans, and when on every front and theatre of war we were confined to purely defensive action, Churchill now knew that we had an immensely powerful weapon which would give us that initiative that only comes from taking the offensive. Churchill was all out to wage war. He certainly did not want the destruction of German cities in and for itself, or in any spirit of revenge, but he wanted above all to get on with the war and no one understood better than he the vast strategic consequences of this single operation, which proved that a serious bombing offensive against Germany itself was a real possibility. The dominating offensive weapon of the war was at last being used, nearly three years after the Germans had invaded Poland. My own opinion is that we should never have had a real bomber offensive if it had not been for the 1000-bomber attack on Cologne, an irrefutable demonstration of the power of what was to all intents and purposes a new and untried weapon.

Arthur Harris

✝

Life in the Warsaw Ghetto

In November 1940, the Jewish quarter of Warsaw was sealed off by the Nazis, effectively incarcerating its 400,000 inhabitants until they began to be transported to the extermination camp at Treblinka in 1942. One resident was teacher Abraham Lewin.

SATURDAY NIGHT, 30 MAY 1942

This day had been among the most difficult, the most nightmarish of all days that we are now living through. Firstly the round-up. Yesterday's round-up brought a rich harvest. I do not know the exact number of those seized, but by all accounts their numbers ran into the hundreds. This means that hundreds of Jewish lives are exposed to the gravest danger, the danger of destruction. This morning they were all taken away, in closed trains of course, in freight or cattle-trucks. Where they were being sent is not known for sure. I have heard from several sources that they were being sent as far away as Brobruisk to build fortifications. If this is so, it may be that their position will be even more tragic and bitter than that of those seized and sent to work-camps last year or the year before, because at that

time the Warsaw Jewish community organisation and also that of the town
nearest to the camp tried to do something for the unfortunates. Their
position was not greatly alleviated, but a certain protection and small-scale
help did reach them, and it was of some slight consolation. Today? If those
who have been rounded up are sent to the former Russian territories there
will be no one to take care of them and help them in some way. In Russia
proper there are no Jewish community organisations and the Jews have
disappeared from all those areas occupied by the Germans: either they
have retreated with the Russian army or they have been slaughtered by
the Germans. Whole Jewish towns have vanished. It is horrific, quite
horrific.

And once again we see the sad complicity of the Jewish police. With
great regret they are 'obliged' to carry out their duties and round up
people. They carry out these duties conscientiously. Thus both large
numbers of Jews are seized and the pockets of the Jewish police are filled
with ill-gotten gains. Apparently one could get released with no difficulty
for 10 zloty.

Last night we had a repetition of the Bartholomew Night action on a
smaller scale. It was another Friday night, like the infamous 18 April. The
number of those brutally murdered is said to be 11, among them a woman.
All the Jews living at 11 Mylna Street were killed, four men from one flat:
an elderly Jew, his son and his son-in-law, Rózycki, as well as his tenant.
The elder Wilner was partly paralysed. In his terror he couldn't speak and
was unable to move. The Germans put him on a chair and threw him out
of the second-floor window. The old man was killed instantly. The other
three men were taken down into the street and shot. There is also talk of
a murdered barber from 50 Nowolipie Street, and a policeman, who six
months ago had been on duty in the hospital on Stawki Street when two
Jewish reserve officers in the Polish army escaped, Gomulinski and one
other.

Also a Mrs Judt was shot. She had worked for the Germans and
had managed to obtain permits for the Jewish theatres. Altogether, as
mentioned above, 11 Jews.

The background to these murders in the night? Hard to say. One
opinion I heard was that they were all racketeers. This is, however,
not completely accurate. Thus I have heard that the Wilners owned a
brick-factory in Grodzisk; the son-in-law is supposed to have been a
teacher and a very respectable person. The barber from 50 Nowolipie
Street is said to have been a member of the Bund (the Jewish socialist
party). In short, we do not have the key to these terrible murders and none

of us has any idea what fate awaits us. All people more or less involved in the running of an organisation live each day in terror for their life.

This morning the gendarmerie drove up with Junaks on Przejazd Street and took away four Jews who were involved in smuggling. They were standing on the ruined wall at number 11, looking over to the Aryan side. I heard that Auerswald, the Nazi commissioner in charge of the ghetto, was present at the arrest and that on his orders the group was deported immediately, along with those Jews who had already been rounded up. The mother of one of those deported was sobbing pitifully outside my window.

Today a group of community officials were sitting together and for two hours a lawyer from Lwów recited to us the book of lamentations of Lwów and the whole of eastern Galicia. And what he said was so horrific and gruesome that words cannot convey what has happened. Lwów alone has lost 30,000 martyrs. The slaughter was carried out in three main stages. As soon as the Germans entered Lwów they carried out a large-scale round-up and thousands upon thousands of Jews were murdered in the prisons. The second stage took place later, when Jews had to move into the ghetto, next to the 'bridge of death' that became so tragically notorious, and the third took place in March during the great resettlement of the Lwów Jews, when up to 10,000 Jews died. In the action to dispose of people over 60 several thousand Jews were killed. The details of these events are so devastating that they are not for the pages of a diary. This must all be told in full. I hope and believe that this will one day happen, that the world's conscience will be taken by storm and that vile beast that is at the throat of the peoples of Europe and choking them to death will be bound and shackled once and for all. The lawyer from Lwów estimates that the number of dead in eastern Galicia is in excess of 100,000. All the Jewish communities along the Hungarian border have been obliterated from the face of the earth. Thus Jaremcze, which had a population of 1,000 Jews, has become *judenrein*. The same in Tatarów.

When the lawyer had finished his account of these horrors and Mr G. had thanked him, many of us had tears in our eyes.

Those two hours belong to the darkest of my life.

On my way home from this meeting I had the 'good fortune' to be stopped and made to work at loading bricks. The Germans were stopping only more respectably dressed Jews. The work lasted an hour. It wasn't so much hard work as humiliating. A soldier stood over us and yelled insults: 'Verfluchte Juden!' ['Damned Jews'] and struck one of us with the back of an iron rod. It is certainly no pleasure to taste German barbarity and Jewish servitude, even for just one hour, but I did none the less have a certain feeling of satisfaction. I have experienced at first hand, albeit in small measure, that which millions of Jews have been enduring for almost three years now. For this reason it was worthwhile.

Abraham Lewin

Lewin's diary was discovered after the war, hidden in a milk churn. It had survived; its author had not.

Summer 1942

The Battle of Midway

The tiny island of Midway was a key stepping stone in the Japanese march across the Pacific. Towards the end of May 1942, Admiral Yamamoto assembled an armada – including four aircraft carriers – he believed strong enough to annihilate any American force sent to defend the island. The Americans, however, had cracked his codes and, apprised of his intentions, lay in wait for him north-east of Midway. On the morning of 4 June, carrier-borne aircraft mounted a poorly coordinated and costly attack against the Japanese fleet, but a second wave of dive bombers, including that piloted by Clarence E. Dickinson, was more successful.

The fleet was passing under us now; we were almost at the middle of its position. Some of the craft below us were recognisable because on our ships we had collections of scale models of many Japanese ships; our own kind of voodoo. I had studied them thoroughly. Sometimes, to get a dive bomber's view I had placed a model on the deck and then, standing on a chair, looked down on it. So I was confident I could recognise at least some Japanese ships of war that I never before had seen. Certain characteristics of her silhouette made me feel sure that the most distant, that fourth carrier I had first seen coming out of the storm area, was the *Hiryu* and I guessed one of the nearer ones to be her sister ship, the *Soryu*. Now we were at an altitude between 15,000 and 16,000 feet. The next thing I heard through my headphones was the voice of Mr McCluskey.

'Earl Gallaher, you take the carrier on the left and Best, you take the carrier on the right. Earl, you follow me down.'

Lieutenant Best, assigned to the other target, was the skipper of Bombing Six. I had been unaware of it but Bombing Three, from a third carrier in our force, had been launched after we left. They had arrived at the same time and fortunately their commander had picked the one uncovered carrier in the group of three below us. I continued to be amazed by our luck. We had dreamed of catching Jap carriers but none of us had ever imagined a situation like this where we could prepare for our dive without a trace of fighter opposition; we had supposed the Jap fighters would be coming at us from all angles. I did not understand why they were not, because those bright yellow decks below were absolutely unblemished. Then I saw some of their fighters milling about, close to the water. They were finishing a job. It seems that our torpedo squadrons, one from each of the American carriers, had made an attack at noon. In considerably less than the twenty-five minutes that elapsed before we made our attack they had been destroyed except for a few who got back to the fleet. Undoubtedly the Jap fighters I saw flying close to the water had just finished the destruction of those squadrons, and probably the fighters we saw on the carriers' decks had returned aboard for refuelling. This must be the reason our bombing squadrons were able to come in unopposed.

I saw Mr McCluskey's plane and those of his two wing men, nose up and we passed under.

Right after the skipper and his division had started I kicked my rudders back and forth to cause a ducklike twitching of my tail. This was the signal for my division to attack. In my turn I pulled up my nose and in a stalled position opened my flaps. We always do this, throw the plane up and to the side on which we are going to dive, put out the flaps as brakes and then peel-off. I was the ninth man of our squadron to dive.

By the grace of God, as I put my nose down I picked up our carrier target below in front of me. I was making the best dive I had ever made. The people who came back said it was the best dive they had ever made. We were coming from all directions on the port side of the carrier, beautifully spaced.

Going down I was watching over the nose of my plane to see the first bombs land on that yellow deck. At last her fighters were taking off and that was when I felt sure I recognized her as the *Kaga*; and she was enormous. The *Kaga* and the *Akagi* were sister ships and had been converted from battleships as our *Lexington* and *Saratoga* had been converted from battle cruisers. To us *Kaga* and *Akagi* were the big names in the Japanese fleet. Very likely one, or more, of their newer carriers was better, but to us those two symbolised that which we had trained ourselves to destroy.

The carrier was racing along at thirty knots, right into the wind. She made no attempt to change course. I was coming at her a little bit astern, on the left-hand side. By the time I was at 12,000 feet I could see all the planes ahead of me in the dive. We were close together but no one plane was coming down in back of another as may easily happen.

The target was utterly satisfying. The squadron's dive was perfect. This was the absolute. After this, I felt, anything would be just anti-climax.

I saw the bombs from the group commander's section drop. They struck the water on either side of the carrier. The explosions probably grabbed at her like an ice man's tongs. Earl Gallaher was the next man to drop. I learned later that his big bomb struck the after part of the flight deck, among the parked planes, and made a tremendous explosion which fed on gasoline. I had picked as my point of aim the big red disk with its bank of white up on the bow. Near the dropping point I began to watch through my sight.

The only bombsight we use in a dive bomber is an optical tube about two feet long mounted so that the axis of the tube coincides more or less with the axis of the plane. Coming in we get what we call a position angle. The whole of the dive is really an aiming period but you do not put your eye to the sight until near the end of the dive; that is when you make minute corrections in the course of your plane, striving to keep the pipper at the middle of the optical sight just short of the target until the instant when you are going to drop. Then, allowing for the wind, you get the pipper right on the target. You are pointing the plane. As I was almost at the dropping point I saw a bomb hit just behind where I was aiming, that white circle with its blood red centre. I found out later the bomb was one dropped by Ensign Stone. I saw the deck rippling, and curling back in all directions exposing a great section of the hangar below. That bomb had a fuse set to make it explode about four feet below the deck. I knew the last plane had taken off or landed on that carrier for a long time to come. I was coming a little abaft the beam on the port side on a course that would take me diagonally across her deck to a point ahead of her island.

I dropped a few seconds after the previous bomb explosion. After the drop you must wait a fraction of a second before pulling out of the dive to make sure you do not 'throw' the bomb, spoil your aim as certainly as when you jerk, instead of squeeze, the trigger of a rifle.

I had determined during that dive that since I was dropping on a Japanese carrier I was going to see my bombs hit. After dropping I kicked my rudder to get my tail out of the way and put my plane in a stall. So I was simply standing there to watch it. I saw the 500-pound bomb hit right abreast of the island [command tower]. The two 100-pound bombs struck in the forward area of the parked planes on that yellow flight deck. Then I began thinking it was time to get myself away from there and try to get back alive.

Clarence E. Dickinson

Dickinson did make it back alive, although he ran out of fuel and had to ditch in the Pacific first.

Mitsuo Fuchida, the hero of the Japanese attack on Pearl Harbor, was on board the Akagi *when it was attacked.*

As our fighters ran out of ammunition during the fierce battle they re-turned to the carriers for replenishment, but few ran low on fuel. Service crews cheered the returning pilots, patted them on the shoulder, and shouted words of encouragement. As soon as a plane was ready again the pilot nodded, pushed forward the throttle, and roared back into the sky. This scene was repeated time and again as the desperate air struggle continued.

Preparations for a counter-strike against the enemy had continued on board our four carriers throughout the enemy torpedo attacks. One after another, planes were hoisted from the hangar and quickly arranged on the flight deck. There was no time to lose. At 10.20 Admiral Nagumo gave the order to launch when ready. On *Akagi*'s flight deck all planes were in position with engines warming up. The big ship began turning into the wind. Within five minutes all her planes would be launched.

Five minutes! Who would have dreamed that the tide of battle would shift completely in that brief interval of time?

Visibility was good. Clouds were gathering at about 3,000 metres, however, and though there were occasional breaks, they afforded good concealment for approaching enemy planes. At 10.24 the order to start launching came from the bridge by voice-tube. The Air Officer flapped a white flag, and the first Zero fighter gathered speed and whizzed off the deck. At that instant a look-out screamed: 'Hell-Divers!' I looked up to see three black enemy planes plummeting towards our ship. Some of our machine-guns managed to fire a few frantic bursts at them, but it was too late. The plump silhouettes of the American Dauntless dive-bombers quickly grew larger, and then a number of black objects suddenly floated eerily from their wings. Bombs! Down they came straight towards me! I fell intuitively to the deck and crawled behind a command post mantelet.

The terrifying scream of the dive-bombers reached me first, followed by the crashing explosion of a direct hit. There was a blinding flash and then a second explosion, much louder than the first. I was shaken by a weird blast of warm air. There was still another shock, but less severe, apparently a near-miss. Then followed a startling quiet as the barking of guns suddenly ceased. I got up and looked at the sky. The enemy planes were already gone from sight.

The attackers had got in unimpeded because our fighters, which had engaged the preceding wave of torpedo planes only a few moments earlier, had not yet had time to regain altitude. Consequently, it may be said that the American dive-bombers' success was made possible by the earlier martyrdom of their torpedo planes. Also, our carriers had no time to evade because clouds hid the enemy's approach until he dived down to the attack. We had been caught flat-footed in the most vulnerable condition possible – decks loaded with planes armed and fuelled for an attack.

Looking about, I was horrified at the destruction that had been wrought in a matter of seconds. There was a huge hole in the flight deck just behind the amidship elevator. The elevator itself, twisted like molten glass, was dropping into the hangar. Deck plates reeled upwards in grotesque configurations, planes stood tail up, belching livid flame and jet-black smoke. Reluctant tears streamed down my cheeks as I watched the fires spread, and I was terrified at the prospect of induced explosions which would surely doom the ship. I heard Masuda yelling, 'Inside! Get inside! Everybody who isn't working! Get inside!'

Unable to help, I staggered down a ladder and into the ready room. It was already jammed with badly burned victims from the hangar deck. A new explosion was followed quickly by several more, each causing the bridge structure to tremble. Smoke from the burning hangar gushed through passageways and into the bridge and ready room, forcing us to seek other refuge. Climbing back to the bridge, I could see that *Kaga* and *Soryu* had also been hit and were giving off heavy columns of black smoke. The scene was horrible to behold.

Akagi had taken two direct hits, one on the after rim of the amidship elevator, the other on the rear guard on the port side of the flight deck. Normally, neither would have been fatal to the giant carrier, but induced explosions of fuel and munitions devastated whole sections of the ship, shaking the bridge and filling the air with deadly splinters. As fire spread among the planes lined up wing to wing on the after flight deck, their torpedoes began to explode, making it impossible to bring the fires under control. The entire hangar area was a blazing inferno, and the flames moved swiftly towards the bridge.

Mitsuo Fuchida

The Japanese lost all four of their aircraft carriers, although aircraft from the Hiryu *managed to damage the* Yorktown *heavily. The news of their reverse at Midway – the gravest military defeat for the Japanese in three and a half centuries – was not revealed to their public.*

‡

Driving with the President

In mid-June, Churchill flew to Washington to discuss with Roosevelt operations for the coming year, including work on the atomic bomb. The President, who had been crippled by polio, met him at the family home in New York state, Hyde Park.

Early the next morning, the 19th, I flew to Hyde Park. The President was on the local airfield, and saw us make the roughest bump landing I have experienced. He welcomed me with great cordiality, and, driving the car himself, took me to the majestic bluffs over the Hudson River on which Hyde Park, his family home, stands. The President drove me all over the estate, showing me its splendid views. In this drive I had some thoughtful moments. Mr Roosevelt's infirmity prevented him from using his feet on the brake, clutch, or accelerator. An ingenious arrangement enabled him to do everything with his arms, which were amazingly strong and muscular. He invited me to feel his biceps, saying that a famous prize-fighter had envied them. This was reassuring; but I confess that when on several occasions the car poised and backed on the grass verges of the precipices over the Hudson I hoped the mechanical devices and brakes would show no defects. All the time we talked business, and though I was careful not to take his attention off the driving we made more progress than we might have done in formal conference.

Winston Churchill

✝

The Western Desert

The breakout from Bir Hakeim

Rommel's offensive in Libya aimed to take the port of Tobruk, protected to the west by the Gazala Line's defences. At the southern end of the line was the fortress of Bir Hakeim, held by the 1st Free French Brigade, who were commanded by Pierre Koenig. Rommel told his men it could be seized in 15 minutes, but it defied him for two weeks until the order came to withdraw on 10 June. That night, the French made a dash for it through the German lines. General Koenig was driven by his chauffeur and lover, the English-born Susan Travers, the only woman ever to serve in the Foreign Legion.

We drove on through the barren landscape. It took hours to get through all three lines of enemy armour, our route twisting this way and that to avoid the heaviest fire. We had set off shortly after midnight and four hours later we were still in the danger zone. Thankfully, a thick early morning mist descended, which shielded us. Unfortunately, it also blocked our view of what lay ahead. At one point, there was a tremendous bang on the side of the vehicle and I thought we must have been hit or driven over a mine. I spun round in my seat to check the damage, but Amilakvari, who'd seen what had happened, reassured me.

'Don't worry,' he said, 'it was just Masson's car. His driver ran into the back of you. It's wrecked and Masson's been thrown out of the roof, but he's OK. Carry on.'

I thought of the gleaming new staff car I'd driven so carefully back from Tobruk and cursed inwardly.

After driving for so long, we felt that we must surely be the other side of the enemy lines but we couldn't be sure. None of us could. We were slightly better off than the rest because we had a compass and Amilakvari was an excellent navigator. Behind us we knew that solitary soldiers and groups without compasses who had become separated from their units would be wandering around aimlessly. Some would be picked up by English patrols, some by German. We all worried that those who were lost in the desert might never be seen again.

The general ordered me to stop the car in the middle of a plateau so that Amilakvari could take a proper bearing on the compass, which wouldn't work well inside the metal car. I did as I was told, releasing my grip on the steering wheel for the first time in four hours and stretching out my cramped and boneless fingers. Every muscle in my neck and shoulders ached, every bone cried out for rest, but I knew there would be none for some time yet and I rode the pain. I refused to switch off the engine, for fear the car wouldn't start again. My head resting on the steering wheel, fighting to calm my thumping heart, I waited for my next set of instructions.

It was Amilakvari who took the initiative. He opened his door and stood on the running-board to listen and try to get a reading. He could hear nothing, no vehicles following us, no men on foot, not even the sound of distant gunfire.

The general stuck his head out of the roof and started to speak. 'We're going to have to get a move on now –' he began.

Amilakvari suddenly reached across and clamped his hand over the general's mouth. He'd heard what we could all hear now, German voices, speaking very close to us in the fog.

'*Halt! Wer ist dat?*' a German soldier barked. '*Stehen bleiben!*'

I was tempted to respond in the German I had learned in Vienna all those years ago. I wondered for a moment what they would think if they heard a woman's voice speaking in aristocratic tones in the middle of nowhere.

'Drive! *Vite!*' Amilakvari shouted, jumping back into the vehicle at the same time as the general kicked my left shoulder ferociously. I floored the accelerator once more, bumping off into the white shroud. Gunfire rang out again, and the vehicle juddered as the bullets found their mark. Looming on either side of us in the mist, we could just make out the sinister shapes of German tanks. We had inadvertently driven straight into a magnificent laager of Panzers, no doubt resting up before their planned attack on Bir Hakeim in the morning. My heart was in my mouth as I flew past the menacing silhouettes and on into the darkness, speeding as fast as I could across the desert floor. Behind us, in close pursuit, were several enemy armoured cars, headlamps full on, their beams cutting through the mist like searchlights. Somehow I managed to pull ahead some five hundred metres and take a curve down into some dead ground, up a crumbling slope the other side and behind a small cliff, finally losing our pursuers.

Once we were back out in the open, Amilakvari asked me to steer straight ahead, following the path of a single bright star we could just make out above the mist. So, with one eye on the star and the other trying to see in front of us, I bumped along. We didn't know where we were or in which direction we were heading, but we didn't dare stop. I continued driving at speed until we were several miles out in the middle of the desert.

Finally, as rosy streaks of light on the horizon heralded the dawn and the fog began to lift, we found ourselves quite alone. There was not another soul to be seen for miles and the silence of the desert was deafening. It was hard to comprehend, but by some miracle the three of us were all still alive.

Susan Travers

Bir Hakeim became a symbol of defiance for all Frenchmen who resisted the Nazis (and is commemorated by a stop on the Paris Metro). Susan Travers was awarded the Croix de Guerre for her bravery that night. She died in 2004.

The taking of Tobruk

On 20 June, Rommel began his attack on Tobruk which, held by the Australians, had frustrated him for much of the previous year. Isolated once more, it was now garrisoned largely by South Africans. Among the German troops was Heinz Werner Schmidt.

The battle was on. Away to the flank that had been jittery before, heavy machine-gun and mortar fire broke out. The Stukas dropped their noses and swooped down over our heads. They plunged at the enemy perimeter. Bombs screamed down and crashed into the minefield. Rommel had thought up a new trick in the desert. He was not bombing the defenders, but blasting a way through the minefield. One crash would be followed by another and another and a whole series: one bomb would detonate a chain of mines, like some atomic fission continuing on beyond the first explosive shock. The Stukas, their bomb-bays empty, their motors roaring, swung back low over our heads. They flew without interference, for the RAF had been driven off Gambut airfield, and the Luftwaffe had no *Huren-kähne* to harass them.

When the first bomb fell we saw a few figures ahead darting back towards shelter. Enemy outposts. But we were lying in a shallow wadi and seemed not to have been spotted. Now was the moment. We emptied our machine-gun belts in swift succession towards the ground where the enemy had disappeared, and hammered away at a barely perceptible structure that suggested the existence of a strong-point.

Our combat engineers jumped up and advanced. They carried explosives with which to destroy further wire entanglements. Then hell was let loose.

Heavy fire from the defending 11th Indian Brigade met us. From the flank one machine-gun was steadily raking us with long bursts, but the combat engineers pressed on relentlessly. They sent up Verey lights as signals to the artillery. The barrage crept farther. Then they lit their smoke candles.

This was our signal. Under cover of the smoke screen we swept forward. A few men fell. But rapid strides soon took us to the first trench. It was empty. We had cover now, and a good field of fire. Through the shell-fire from Tobruk, which was now falling behind us, our motorised infantry with anti-tank guns and Panzer support was rolling on towards the gap.

The combat engineers tackled the anti-tank ditch. It had silted up in parts. They bridged it and filled it in. The Panzers rumbled forward. Our reinforced infantry now scrambled from trench to trench. I spared a moment to look away towards our right. We had made good progress there. Our troops had swept on ahead, and were already laying flanking fire on the positions ahead of us.

Good – a great help!

We were not being heavily hammered by the Tobruk artillery, for the main weight of the enemy's shelling was being flung against the Panzers and the motorised infantry of the 15th Division. And we were almost through the stronghold line.

For a moment an unexpected minefield delayed our advance. Then the Panzers broke through, with the infantry and the anti-tank guns behind them. The Indians, particularly the 2/5 Mahrattas, hit back as best they could. But they seemed to have been stunned by the suddenness of the attack and the shock of the Stuka bombing. The 2/7 Gurkhas came racing up in Brencarriers to counter-attack. But they were swept down, swept aside, swept back by the concentrated fire of machine-guns, anti-tank guns, and mortars.

It was half-past seven or later before the Tobruk artillery really began to lay down concentrated fire on us – and then it was too late. The enemy gunners had followed the Panzers in among us. But by now we had good cover, and were glad of it.

The attack had gone according to plan, except that it had succeeded sooner than expected. We had lost a few dead and wounded, but the casualties were relatively light. Now we passed our first prisoners back, and went forward. My men linked up with some advancing troop-carriers of the 115th Rifle Regiment.

During that forenoon Rommel's Panzers, screened by a line of mobile anti-tank guns from the 1st Motorised Infantry, ploughed steadily along towards their first objective – the fork of the Tobruk–El Adem and Bardia roads, which the Tobruk defenders called King's Cross.

As early as 1941 we had known that the enemy had sited his most effective batteries in this area. We were held up by a number of batteries, at first of Royal Artillery and later, I think, of South African Artillery, but gun after gun was knocked out or overrun by our Panzers and infantry.

Other Panzers met the 4th Royal Tank Regiment near King's Cross and smashed them up. The British tanks were a scratch formation and had been hurriedly rushed forward as a counter-attack force; they seemed disorganised and were not co-ordinated with infantry support. They were no match for our Mark IIIs and Mark IVs, and by the middle of the morning only half a dozen of them were still runners. They struggled away from the scene of the action.

A few other tanks, a squadron or so, tried to attack us from where the Cameron Highlanders of the Indian Brigade were still fighting as best they could. But they, too, were smashed up by the 90th Light's anti-tank guns on the Bardia side of King's Cross. Only four of the tanks, our men said afterwards, got away from that fight.

But our Panzers were not interested in a few surviving tanks. The plan was for them to cut the fortress in two by pressing on north to the harbour.

We knew that the South Africans had not yet been engaged. They had been waiting in vain for us to attack them frontally on their sector. Now we were inside the fortress behind them. One group of our Panzers turned to the west, with portions of the 90th Light, to complete the consolidation of a west flank facing these infantry reserves of the enemy's, and to deal with the 201st Guards' Brigade.

Fourteen other Panzers, accompanied by motorised infantry from our 15th Division, raced down the road towards the harbour, despite defensive gunfire and the vain firing of infantry in trucks. Our Panzers, supported by our 115th Regiment, overran more British batteries. Soon we could see the harbour clearly. Two small ships, steaming furiously, were fleeing; we turned 88-mm. 'flak' guns on to them, but they reached the open sea.

And then we were racing past a mass of immobile trucks – the vehicles the enemy would have needed if he were ever to attempt a break-out from the fortress with his beaten garrison. We were at the harbour, according to plan, before dark. We had disorganised and disrupted Tobruk, and not even needed to exchange fire with the greater part of the garrison – Klopper's South Africans.

Rommel himself had been inside the Tobruk fortress since midday. Prisoners marched past his Mammoth at the King's Cross intersection, but few seemed to guess that the short, sturdy figure, standing with legs straddled on the roof, watching, through his field-glasses, the advance of his Panzers, was the Desert Fox himself. Rommel knew now that his ambition, his aim for fourteen months had been achieved.

General Klopper, as far as we could make out, was not far away at the time. By four o'clock in the afternoon tanks were within half a mile of him, and he seems to have shifted his headquarters then, through *force majeure*. There was little more he could do.

Thick columns of smoke mounted vertically to the heavens. Burning ammunition was exploding in dumps near the port. When the sun went down, the harbour was entirely in Rommel's hands. The Guards' Brigade – Klopper's fortress reserve – had been overrun and their headquarters destroyed. But the South Africans were still virtually intact.

During the night, Rommel planned to attack them from the rear, and drafted a special scheme for an assault, on a compass bearing between the port and Pilastrino.

Meanwhile Klopper was holding a midnight conference with his officers as to whether he should attempt a break-out – which was impossible for lack of transport – or fight to the end. He was in wireless touch with the Eighth Army. Ritchie, however, was not there, and so his only orders came from subordinates. The Eighth Army wanted to hang on for twenty-four hours. But at the same time the Eighth Army failed to get a tank force back from the Gambut region to the Tobruk perimeter to help Klopper.

The hasty plans considered by the South Africans throughout the night for a last stand were futile. In the rocky ground of the Tobruk perimeter it would have been impossible by dawn to throw up hasty new defences to face the rear of the old line. Nothing could have been improvised to stave off Rommel's attack, particularly since there was no sign of any diversion or intervention by the British armoured forces.

At a quarter to eight in the morning Klopper surrendered.

                                                    Heinz Werner Schmidt

Thirty thousand troops were taken prisoner at Tobruk. Rommel, promoted by Hitler to Field Marshal, assured him: 'I'm going on to Suez.'

Only now was the full extent of the danger realised. Churchill was in Washington when Tobruk fell, conferring with Roosevelt, and together they heard the shocking news that the whole British position in the Middle East was in danger of immediate collapse. It promised to be the greatest disaster since the fall of France. Into the Middle East for three years the British Empire had poured every man, gun and tank it could spare. Here alone the British had a front against the enemy. The loss of Egypt would precipitate a chain of misfortunes almost too disastrous to contemplate. It would force England back to the dark days of the Battle of Britain.

With Egypt would fall Malta and all British control of the Mediterranean. The Suez Canal would be lost and with it the stores and equipment worth fifty Tobruks. Suez, Port Said, Alexandria, Beyrout and Syrian Tripoli might go. Palestine and Syria could not then hope to stand and once in Jerusalem and Damascus, the Germans would be in sight of the oilwells and Turkey all but surrounded. The Red Sea would become an Axis lake and once in the Indian Ocean the Italian fleet could prey upon all the routes to Africa, India and Australia. India would be approached from both sides by the enemy. Finally, Russia's left flank would be hopelessly exposed.

All this was possible as the Germans came up to the Alamein Line on July 1st. And on that day, and the day following and the day after that the Alamein Line was in no condition to resist any sort of really determined attack whatever. It was ready to crumple. Such troops as we had left would fight – yes. But if the Germans came on the way they did at Tobruk there was no question but that the line would break. Behind Alamein the road lay fair and straight into Alexandria, a two hours' drive. There was nothing much to stop the enemy on that road. In the desert itself, beyond Alamein there was nothing much to stop their cutting the Cairo road and driving straight to Cairo.

The British fleet had left Alexandria. The demolition gangs stood ready. The town was emptied of most of its troops and those that remained were put under a curfew. Orders went out every hour for all officers to drop whatever they were doing and rejoin their units immediately.

In Cairo there was another curfew. The streets were jammed with cars that had evacuated from Alexandria and the country districts and military traffic that had come from the front. The British consulate was besieged with people seeking visas to Palestine. The east-bound Palestine trains were jammed. A thin mist of smoke hung over the British Embassy by the Nile and over the sprawling blocks of GHQ – huge quantities of secret documents were being burnt. All day a group of privates shovelled piles of maps, lists of figures, reports, estimates, codes and messages into four blazing bonfires in a vacant square of land between the GHQ buildings. Some of the RAF papers being bundled down a chute onto another fire blew over the fence and fluttered down into the crowded street outside. I went into one office and the floor was covered in ashes and the smell of burning rag hung over the whole building.

Alan Moorehead

By August, the Eighth Army was in low spirits, a mood made yet more despondent by the death shortly after his appointment of their new commander, Lt-Gen. Gott. His replacement, selected personally by Churchill, was Bernard Montgomery.

The acting Army Commander, Lt-Gen. Ramsden, met me. I knew him of old since he had commanded the Hampshire Regiment in my 8th

Division in Palestine in 1938–39; he was a very good battalion commander in those days and I had not met him since. He explained the situation to me. I cross-examined him about the Army plans for a withdrawal if Rommel attacked; certain orders had been issued about the withdrawal but they were indefinite. There was an air of uncertainty about everything in the operational line, nor was Army HQ in close touch with the HQ of the Desert Air Force.

It was clear to me that the situation was quite unreal and, in fact, dangerous. I decided at once to take action. I had been ordered not to take over command of the Eighth Army till the 15th August; it was still only the 13th. I knew it was useless to consult GHQ and that I must take full responsibility myself. I told General Ramsden he was to return at once to his corps; he seemed surprised as he had been placed in acting command of the Army, but he went. I then had lunch, with the flies and in the hot sun. During lunch I did some savage thinking. After lunch I wrote a telegram to GHQ saying that I had assumed command of Eighth Army as from 2 p.m. that day, the 13th August; this was disobedience, but there was no comeback. I then cancelled all previous orders about withdrawal.

I issued orders that in the event of enemy attack there would be *no* withdrawal; we would fight on the ground we now held and if we couldn't stay there alive we would stay there dead. I remembered an inscription I had seen in Greece when touring that country with my wife in 1933. It was carved by the Greeks at Thermopylae to commemorate those who died defending the pass over 2000 years ago, and its English version is well known:

> 'Go, tell the Spartans, thou that passeth by,
> That here, obedient to their laws, we lie.'

We would do the same, if need be.

Bernard Montgomery

Although Montgomery would gain a reputation for arrogance, his chief merit as a general was his capacity to transmit his utter confidence in his own abilities to his troops. With him at its head, the Eighth Army once more began to believe in itself.

Australians swarmed everywhere and they looked magnificent. None of us had seen such troops before. They had adopted a new uniform during the long months when they were fattening and working in the sun behind the lines. It consisted of a pair of boots, short woollen socks, a pair of khaki drill pants, a piece of string holding two identification disks round the neck, and a wide-brimmed hat turned down all the way round. Their bare backs and shoulders fascinated me. They were burnt brownish-black by the sun. Under the shining skin the muscles bulged like tennis balls.

The long siege of Tobruk had hardened and trained this 9th Division, and given them a pride in fighting. They were the Rats of Tobruk. Their long hibernation had relaxed them, filled them with good food and fresh air. They had grown tired of garrison life. They wanted to fight. They were delighted to be in the desert.

In these two years another subtler change had taken place in these Australians. To Europeans at first they had seemed boastful and quick to take offence, lax in their discipline in the field, and quarrelsome on leave. The usual thing you heard was that the Australians had an inferiority complex, and adopted a truculent, noisy manner to hide it. As an Australian living abroad, I had had many arguments about them. I had tried (quite unsuccessfully) to explain to Englishmen that the Australians' manner was the sign of their independence and the freedom of their way of life and that some of their physical vigour might not come amiss in England. To the Australians I tried (even more unsuccessfully) to point out that the Englishman's voice and reserve did not indicate animosity or contempt or weakness, and that some of the Englishman's quiet mental tenacity might not come amiss in Australia. Underneath, I knew the Australians were deeply attached to England. I believed, too, that the English had an affection for Australians that took deep root in the last war. It was usually the officers of both armies who rubbed one another up the wrong way. The men got together as soon as they began to understand one another.

Alan Moorehead

‡

The wooden wonder

To improve the effectiveness of their bombing, the RAF turned to the Australian-born Don Bennett. He gathered together crack crews into the Pathfinder Force which would drop flares to illuminate the target for the raiders, now guided by the 'Oboe' radio beam. Bennett knew which aircraft he needed for his task.

We had a few of these bomber Mosquitoes which nobody wanted, but which had been ordered in a small test order by the Ministry of Aircraft Production. They had no armament of any sort, but were indeed very fast little craft. They had a bomb bay big enough to take four of our five-hundred-pound Target Indicators, and it seemed to me that if they could achieve the ceiling we required they would be perfectly suitable. I test-flew the Mosquito by day and by night, and we got on with the 'test installation' of the Oboe equipment. At a meeting at the Air Ministry on the subject, Bomber Command and the Air Ministry both very strongly opposed the adoption of the Mosquito. They argued that it was a frail wood machine totally unsuitable for Service conditions, that it would be shot down because of its absence of gun turrets, and that in any case it was far too small to carry the equipment and an adequate Pathfinder crew. I dealt with each one of these points in turn, but finally they played their ace. They declared that the Mosquito had been tested thoroughly by the appropriate establishments and found quite unsuitable, and indeed impossible to fly at night. At this I raised an eyebrow, and said that I was very sorry to hear that it was quite impossible to fly it by night, as I had been doing so regularly during the past week and had found nothing wrong. There was a deathly silence. I got my Mosquitoes.

Don Bennett

‡

All were pressed into service in the defence of Russia, among them women trained as combat pilots. One was Tamara Pamyatnykh of the 586th Fighter Regiment.

We were to fly escort for a transport aircraft carrying Voroshilov, a member of the State Defence Committee, to the Stalingrad front. When we arrived and I got out of the cockpit to report, the officer at the airfield looked at me and asked, 'Where are the pilots?' I was a lieutenant, and when I told him we girls were the pilots, he didn't believe me. He walked around our three aircraft, saw two more girls there, and he still couldn't believe it! He asked how we were going to fly back, and I told him the same way we came here.

In August 1942, three of us were assigned a combat mission: to deliver a message to the commanding staff of the army concerning its movement. It took considerable time to fly there, and it was dark before we arrived. None of us had flown the fighters at night, we hadn't been trained in night flying at all. I could see Stalingrad burning, but I couldn't see the front line and feared we might land on an enemy airfield. At that moment the Soviet forces shot a rocket into the air to indicate the location of the airfield. We had no lights turned on, and I was afraid that one of the other two planes would land on top of mine, so I turned on my lights for just a minute, even though I had no permission to do it. Galina Burdina told me that if I hadn't done that she would have landed on top of me! We all landed safely – our first night landings.

On one combat mission with Raisa Surnachevskaya as my wingman, we were assigned to intercept and shoot down a German reconnaissance aircraft. We soon saw not one aircraft but two formations of German bombers totalling forty-two planes. We climbed until our altitude was well above them and dove down firing at the lead aircraft of the formation. Each of us shot down one bomber on our first pass through their formation. Then we turned and approached the formation again and shot down two more bombers. By that time my guns were empty, and I decided to ram one of their aircraft. I came so close to the enemy that I could see the face of the pilot. He was a huge man with a very fierce face. I was about to ram him when my plane was hit with gunfire, the wing separated from the aircraft, and I fell into a spin. It was also on fire.

I was being thrown about with so much force that my arms were flailing about, and I couldn't even get hold of the seat belt. I had already opened the canopy. My life flew in front of my eyes. I wanted to jump, but I couldn't open the belt. I didn't feel fear, but I thought I was going to die. At last I got the belt open and I didn't even jump – I was thrown out of the cockpit! I pulled the ring of my parachute, and opened. When I landed, I started touching myself to see if I had injuries because I thought I had been severely wounded. I had blood on my face, and I felt very ill. My face was hurt, and the blood was running down. When my parachute opened, I was only 150 metres from the ground.

I looked up to the sky and saw that Raisa had circled around and was making another attack on the bombers. I thought, if she makes that attack alone she will never survive. I went to the telegraph station to report to my regiment that my aircraft was down and destroyed. Then I saw Raisa walking across a field, and it was wintertime, and there was snow, and we were in our fur boots. We came together and embraced each other and had the feeling that we had both been given birth again.

But in spite of the fact we were safe and alive, I began worrying that I might be punished because my aircraft was destroyed; I wasn't afraid, but I thought something might happen because of it. Instead, we were decorated! It came over the radio that we had turned back the large formation of German bombers and shot down four of them. We were each awarded the Order of the Red Star. Then the King of England, who read of this event, sent each of us a gold watch through the Soviet Minister

of Foreign Affairs. Mine is inscribed: From the Minister of Foreign Affairs
to the brave and gallant pilot Lieutenant Tamara Pamyatnykh – from the
King of England, George VI.

Tamara Pamyatnykh

‡

Churchill meets Stalin

*In August, Churchill travelled to Moscow for his first meeting with Joseph Stalin.
The Soviet leader had strongly expressed his belief that the Western Allies could
best take the strain off him by opening a Second Front in France as soon as possible.
Churchill's task was to convince him that their forces would be better deployed first
in North Africa.*

Stalin, who had begun to look very glum, seemed unconvinced by my
argument, and asked if it was impossible to attack any part of the French
coast. I showed him a map which indicated the difficulties of making an
air umbrella anywhere except actually across the Straits. He did not seem
to understand, and asked some questions about the range of fighter planes.
Could they not, for instance, come and go all the time? I explained that
they could indeed come and go, but at this range they would have no time
to fight, and I added that an air umbrella to be of any use had to be kept
open. He then said that there was not a single German division in France of
any value, a statement which I contested. There were in France twenty-five
German divisions, nine of which were of the first line. He shook his head.
I said that I had brought the Chief of the Imperial General Staff and
General Sir Archibald Wavell with me in order that such points might be
examined in detail with the Russian General Staff. There was a point
beyond which statesmen could not carry discussions of this kind.

Stalin, whose glumness had by now much increased, said that, as he
understood it, we were unable to create a second front with any large
force and unwilling even to land six divisions. I said that this was so. We
could land six divisions, but the landing of them would be more harmful
than helpful, for it would greatly injure the big operation planned for next
year. War was war but not folly, and it would be folly to invite a disaster
which would help nobody. I said I feared the news I brought was not
good news. If by throwing in 150,000 to 200,000 men we could render
him aid by drawing away from the Russian front appreciable German

forces, we would not shrink from this course on the grounds of loss. But if it drew no men away and spoiled the prospects for 1943 it would be a great error.

Stalin, who had become restless, said that his view about war was different. A man who was not prepared to take risks could not win a war. Why were we so afraid of the Germans? He could not understand. His experience showed that troops must be blooded in battle. If you did not blood your troops you had no idea what their value was. I inquired whether he had ever asked himself why Hitler did not come to England in 1940, when he was at the height of his power and we had only 20,000 trained troops, 200 guns, and 50 tanks. He did not come. The fact was that Hitler was afraid of the operation. It was not so easy to cross the Channel. Stalin replied that this was no analogy. The landing of Hitler in England would have been resisted by the people, whereas in the case of a British landing in France the people would be on the side of the British. I pointed out that it was all the more important therefore not to expose the people of France by a withdrawal to the vengeance of Hitler and to waste them when they would be needed in the big operation in 1943.

There was an oppressive silence. Stalin at length said that if we could not make a landing in France this year he was not entitled to demand it or to insist upon it, but he was bound to say that he did not agree with my arguments.

Churchill persisted, aided by his penchant for doodles and drawings:

I then described the military advantages of freeing the Mediterranean, whence still another front could be opened. In September we must win in Egypt, and in October in North Africa, all the time holding the enemy in Northern France. If we could end the year in possession of North Africa we could threaten the belly of Hitler's Europe, and this operation should be considered in conjunction with the 1943 operation. That was what we and the Americans had decided to do.

To illustrate my point I had meanwhile drawn a picture of a crocodile, and explained to Stalin with the help of this picture how it was our intention to attack the soft belly of the crocodile as we attacked his hard snout. And Stalin, whose interest was now at a high pitch, said, 'May God prosper this undertaking.'

I emphasised that we wanted to take the strain off the Russians. If we attempted that in Northern France we should meet with a rebuff. If we tried in North Africa we had a good chance of victory, and then we could help in Europe. If we could gain North Africa Hitler would have to bring his Air Force back, or otherwise we would destroy his allies, even, for instance, Italy, and make a landing. The operation would have an important influence on Turkey and on the whole of Southern Europe, and all I was afraid of was that we might be forestalled. If North Africa were won this year we could make a deadly attack upon Hitler next year. This marked the turning-point in our conversation.

Winston Churchill

‡

Killing children

The nature of the war in the East was troubling the conscience of Panzer driver Henry Metelmann.

After having cracked the nut of Izyum and crossed the Donetz, the Great Bend of the River Don now lay invitingly open in front of us, with the Soviets unable to do anything about it. Further on to the east, we knew, stretched the Volga, Europe's mightiest river, with the city of Stalingrad along its western bank. We had been told repeatedly by our officers that reaching and conquering that city would be tantamount to the end of our thrust and that we could then look forward to a period of well-deserved rest.

We left the town of Izyum on the same day and turned south-east towards the industrial centre around Rostov on Don. When we came towards a village which stretched right across our path of advance, we let our cannons fly, just to be on the safe side, as our gunner always said. We targeted a low cottage which was partly hidden behind a high scruffy hedge and when we came closer to it, we noticed a tree with early apples on, just showing above the hedge. To replenish our supply we decided that I should pull up behind the now shattered cottage out of our officers' view and that I should fill one of our ammunition boxes with fruit while the rest of the crew stayed in position. Approaching the hedge, I heard a sobbing sound and when I stepped through the opening, I saw a girl of about twelve lying in the grass under the tree. She wore a light summer dress and I noticed pretty, puffy sleeves. Her hair was blond and tied in pigtails. Her whole left side was torn open and around her the grass was in a bloody mess. She was still moving, still in convulsion, but I could see that there was nothing anyone could do. Her mother, I presume it was her, was bending over her with her back to me. She was pleading and sobbing and calling the girl's name. Having heard me coming, she turned her head, her face wet from tears and her expression bewildered and desperate. Next to them lay a wooden plate with broken pieces of bread. The mother then slowly raised herself and when she realised who I was, a complete transformation came over her. As if with a swipe she managed to wipe away all her outward signs of grief, her face screwed up and her eyes narrowed and out of the grief showed so much hatred, so much contempt for me. The words, of which I understood only a few, screamed out of her like a torrent and hit me as seldom anything had hit me before. Though trained to be arrogant and overbearing, I knew I was guilty, and though having experienced many tight situations, there had never been anything like this. All I could manage was to mumble '*Prostite!*' (I am sorry) but I instantly realised how hopelessly wrong it was. In the agony I dropped my wooden box. '*Prostite . . . ?*' she said, 'Is that all you can say, you dare to say after what you have done? She came out to greet you, to offer you bread and salt and peace! It took some courage to do that; and you coward, you beast, what have you done to her . . . !'

I simply did not know how to react. Like a miserable coward, as she had said, I turned and ran to flee back to security amongst my mates. Falling back into my driving seat and driving off into the village where all the others had already assembled, I then told my mates what I had experienced, why I had come out without any apples, even without my box. They just looked at me quietly without saying a word, but then one of them said 'Yes, so what? One Russian girl killed by one of our shells. But why did you not bring any apples?'

We had a rest on the village green and something to eat when I saw three human bundles lying in the village street not far from us. I asked my mates how that had come about. 'Well, you know, a mother with two kids, they just ran out of the cottage at the wrong moment when we moved in, you know how it is?' Yes, I knew all right. A mother and two small children and though apparently dead, no one had gone over to have at least a look – and neither did I. Then our Captain walked across the green, and talked about our well-executed attack, about another victory, another village taken and all for Führer and Fatherland.

Henry Metelmann

✠

An extermination at Belzec

In August, SS-Lieutenant Kurt Gerstein travelled to the concentration camps in Poland, demonstrating Zyklon B as the gas to be used in the death chambers. By 18 August he had reached Belzec. There he observed the slaughter of more than 5,000 Jews in a single day.

Next day we travelled to Belzec. A small railway station had been specially built for this purpose, on a hill, due north of the Lublin–Lemberg highway, in the left corner of the demarcation line. To the south of the highway were a few houses with the inscription 'Special Command of the Waffen SS, Belzec'. The actual head of all the lethal installations, police captain Wirth, had not yet arrived, so Globocnik introduced me to SS Captain Obermeyer from Pirmasens. Obermeyer showed me only what he was obliged to. I did not see any corpses at that time, but the smell of the whole district in August heat was pestilential and there were millions of flies everywhere. Near the little two-line station was a large barrack building, the so-called 'cloakrooms', with a large valuables counter. This was followed by a room with about a hundred chairs, the barber's room. Then a narrow pathway out in the open, under birch trees, with double barbed wire on either side, and notices: To the Baths and Inhalation Rooms. Before us stood a kind of bathing hut with geraniums, then a small staircase, and then three rooms on either side, measuring five metres by five and 1 metre 90 high, with wooden doors like garages. At the far wall, difficult to see in the dark, were great wooden ramp doors. On the roof – as 'an apt little joke' – was the Star of David; and in front of the building a notice saying 'Heckenholt Foundation'. I wasn't able to see any more that afternoon.

Next morning, just before seven, I was informed that the first transport was due to arrive in ten minutes. And, in fact, in a few minutes, the first train from Lemberg arrived. The 45 carriages contained 6,700 people; 1,450 of them were already dead on arrival. Children, their faces terribly pale and fearful and the dread of death in their eyes, peered out through the barred hatches; the adults were farther up. Two hundred Ukrainians tore open the doors and whipped people out with their leather thongs. A large loudspeaker gave out instructions: 'Undress immediately, and remove your glasses, artificial limbs, dentures, etc. Surrender your valuables at the counter, no receipt given. Fasten your shoes together carefully, for collection later.' In a pile of about 25 yards high no one could possibly match them up together otherwise. Then the women and girls went to the barber, who cut off their hair in two or three snips and threw it into potato sacks. 'That's for some special purpose, for the U-boats – caulking, or something,' the SS man on duty told me.

The column started moving, a beautiful young girl in front; so they walked along the path all naked, men, women and children; without dentures, without anything. I was standing with Captain Wirth up on the ramp between the chambers. Mothers with babies at their breasts walked up hesitantly and stepped into the death chambers. A hefty SS man stood in the corner, reassuring the poor people in parsonic tones that 'Nothing at all is going to happen to you! When you get inside, just take a deep breath. This expands your lungs. It is necessary to inhale in this way to avoid illness and infection.' They asked what was to become of them and he replied: 'Of course, the men will have to work, and build houses and roads, but the women don't have to. They can help with the domestic chores or cooking, if they like.' This faint gleam of hope was enough to get some of them – poor devils – to step into the gas chambers without resistance. Most people knew better; the smell was enough for them. So they climbed up the few steps and then saw it all: mothers with tiny children, quite naked, grown-up men and women – they hesitated, but they walked into the gas chambers, pushed on by those behind them or driven by the SS with their leather whips. Without a word, most of them. A Jewess of about forty, with blazing eyes, cursed the murderers for the blood they were spilling. She received five or six strokes with a riding crop in the face from Captain Wirth personally, then she disappeared inside, too. Many people prayed. I prayed with them; I cowered in a corner and cried out loud to my God and theirs. I longed to go with them into the gas chambers; I longed to die their death with them. Then they would have found an SS man in uniform in the chambers, and the whole matter would have been treated as an unfortunate accident and consigned to oblivion. But I must not do that. First I must tell the world what I have seen here. The chambers are filling up. See that they're well packed – Captain Wirth's orders. People are standing on each other's feet. Seven to eight hundred in 25 square metres – 45 cubic metres! The SS use physical force to cram them together as tightly as possible. The doors close. Meanwhile the others wait out in the open naked. 'They do it in winter, too,' I am told. 'But that's enough to kill them,' I said. 'That's just what they're here for,' replied an SS man in his north German dialect. Then at last I understood why the whole set-up was called the Heckenholt Foundation. Heckenholt was the driver of the diesel engine, a minor technician who also built the plant. The people were to be murdered with the diesel exhaust gas; but the diesel wouldn't work. Here comes Wirth. It is embarrassing for him, one can see that; this has to happen today of all days, with me here. Yes, I see everything. I wait. My stop-watch has registered it all accurately – 50 minutes, 70 minutes; and the diesel won't start. They wait in their gas chambers. In vain. They can be heard crying and sobbing. Captain Wirth gives the Ukrainian, who is supposed to be helping Heckenholt with the diesel, thirteen strokes across the face with his riding crop. After 2 hours 49 minutes – my stop-watch registered it accurately – the diesel starts. Right up to this moment, the people in those four chambers – four times 750 people in four times 45 cubic metres – were alive. Another 25 minutes go by. Right: many of them are dead now. I can just see it, through the little window. After 28 minutes there are not many left alive. At last, after 32 minutes, they are all dead!

The men from the working party open the wooden doors from the other side. They – themselves Jews – have been promised their freedom, and a certain percentage of all valuables found, in return for their horrible duties. The dead stand upright in the chambers like columns of basalt, pressed tightly together. There would be no room to fall or even to bend over. Even in death you can recognise the families. Their hands are locked together in a death grip; it is hard to tear them apart, to make room for the next contingent. They throw out the corpses – wet with sweat and urine, and some defiled with excrement or with menstrual blood on the legs. The corpses of children fly through the air. Time is short; the Ukrainians rain their whiplashes on the working parties. Two dozen dentists clamp open the mouths, looking for gold. Gold to the left, no gold to the right. Other dentists break off the gold teeth and crowns with forceps and hammers.

Captain Wirth keeps scurrying around. He is in his element. A few workers look for gold, diamonds and valuables concealed in the anus or the genitals. Wirth calls out to me: 'Try and lift the box of gold teeth – that's only from yesterday and the day before!' And in an incredibly vulgar and ingratiating tone: 'You wouldn't believe how much gold and diamonds we find in one day – and dollars, too. Look for yourself!' Then he took me to the 'jeweller' who had to look after all these treasures, and showed me everything. Then they pointed out to me a former director of the 'Western' store in Berlin, and a violinist: 'That is a former captain in the old Austrian Imperial Army, holder of the Iron Cross Class I; he's now a camp elder and member of the Jewish working party!' The naked bodies were taken on wooden stretchers, only a few yards wide, to graves measuring 100 × 20 × 12 metres. After a few days the corpses swelled up, but caved in again shortly afterwards, so that they could throw another layer on top. Then they sprinkled about 10 centimetres of sand over the surface so that just a few solitary arms and heads protruded. I saw some Jews scrambling around on top of the corpses in one of these places, working in the graves. I was told that, through an error, those who had arrived already dead on one of the transports had not been undressed; obviously this had to be rectified to avoid their taking their clothing and valuables with them to the grave. They never took the trouble, either in Belzec or in Treblinka, to register or to count the dead. They just based their estimates on the size of the carriages . . . Captain Wirth asked me not to put forward any suggestions to Berlin for changing the set-up; but to leave everything as it was, just as if all had gone according to plan.

All my statements are literally true. I am well aware of the extraordinary implications of my allegations – and I make them before God and the whole of mankind. I swear on oath that nothing I have recorded here is an invention or an exaggeration – this is exactly what happened.

Kurt Gerstein

Gerstein was a devout Christian who had joined the SS to discover and reveal its crimes. Three days after his experience at Belzec, he encountered a Swedish diplomat on a train and told him what he knew of the genocide. The Swedes chose not to publicise the information, and at the end of the war Gerstein found himself charged as a war criminal. He hanged himself on 23 July 1945. Two days later, a letter from the diplomat arrived testifying to Gerstein's innocence.

✝

The raid on Dieppe

In order to practise landing techniques for an eventual invasion of France, the Allies decided to make a raid on the French port of Dieppe. The Germans, however, had intercepted radio transmissions dealing with its planning and on the night of 19 August were waiting for the 6,000-strong force, all but 1,000 of whom were Canadian, including war correspondent Ross Munro.

Our coxswain tried to take us in to one section of the beach and it proved the wrong spot. Before he grounded he swung the craft out again and we fumbled through the smoke to the small strip of sand which was the Puits beach. The smoke was spotty and the last thirty yards was in the clear. Geysers from artillery shells or mortar bombs shot up in our path. Miraculously we weren't hit by any of them. The din of the German ack-ack guns and machine-guns on the cliff was so deafening you could not hear the man next to you shout.

The men in our boat crouched low, their faces tense and grim. They were awed by this unexpected blast of German fire, and it was their initiation to frightful battle noises. They gripped their weapons more tightly and waited for the ramp of our craft to go down.

We bumped on the beach and down went the ramp and out poured the first infantrymen. They plunged into about two feet of water and machine-gun bullets laced into them. Bodies piled up on the ramp. Some staggered to the beach and fell. Bullets were splattering into the boat itself, wounding and killing our men.

I was near the stern and to one side. Looking out of the open bow over the bodies on the ramp, I saw the slope leading a short way up to a stone wall littered with Royal casualties. There must have been sixty or seventy of them, lying sprawled on the green grass and the brown earth. They had been cut down before they had a chance to fire a shot.

A dozen Canadians were running along the edge of the cliff towards the stone wall. They carried their weapons and some were firing as they ran. But some had no helmets, some were already wounded, their uniforms torn and bloody. One by one they were cut down and rolled down the slope to the sea.

I don't know how long we were nosed down on that beach. It may have been five minutes. It may have been twenty. On no other front have I witnessed such a carnage. It was brutal and terrible and shocked you almost to insensibility to see the piles of dead and feel the hopelessness of the attack at this point.

There was one young lad crouching six feet away from me. He had made several vain attempts to rush down the ramp to the beach but each time a hail of fire had driven him back. He had been wounded in the arm but was determined to try again. He lunged forward and a streak of red-white tracer slashed through his stomach.

I'll never forget his anguished cry as he collapsed on the blood-soaked deck: 'Christ, we gotta beat them; we gotta beat them!' He was dead in a few minutes.

The Germans were in strength on the top of the cliff and poured their fire into the gulch and on the slope which led up to the tops of the cliff crest. A high stone wall, topped with barbed wire, crossed the slope and Royals were dying by that wall.

From our battered craft lying in the centre of this wild concentration of deadly fire I could see sandbagged German positions on the top of the cliff and a large house, with rows of windows, on the left side of the cleft in the cliff. Most of the German machine-gun and rifle fire was coming from the fortified house and it wrought havoc on the tiny beach. They were firing at us at point-blank range.

There was another smaller house on the right side of the break in the cliffs and Germans were there too.

Some of the Canadians were able to return the German fire and they knocked off a number of the enemy. One German in his grey-green uniform toppled from one of the windows in the big house. Some of the less-well fortified positions were hit by fire from anti-tank rifles and Bren guns and among the Germans there were casualties.

Into the terrible German fire ran the men from our boat and I doubt if any even reached the stone wall on the slope, for mortar bombs were smashing on the slope to take the toll of those not hit by the machine-gun bullets that streaked across the whole beach almost continuously. Now the Germans on the cliff were turning their flak guns down on the beach. Our craft was the only one left.

Somehow, the Royals got the two heavy three-inch mortars in our craft down the ramp, as well as the ammunition, but they were never fired. They fell in the water as the crews were hit. The bottom of the boat was covered with soldiers who had been machine-gunned. The officer next to me, Jack Anderson of Toronto, was hit in the head and sprawled over my legs bleeding badly. A naval rating next to him had a sickening gash in his throat and was dying. A few who weren't casualties were firing back fiercely now from the boat. It was useless for them to try to make the beach. The way those men stood up and blasted back at the Germans, when they could feel even then that the attack at Puits was a lost cause, was one of the bravest things I've witnessed.

Ross Munro

The attack was a tragedy for the Canadians, almost two-thirds of whom were killed or captured. Few of their objectives were accomplished, but the disaster did teach the Allies valuable lessons in combined operations, and reinforced the Nazis' conviction that any invasion would begin with an attempt to seize a French port. Thus they began to build up their defences at harbours, rather than those on Normandy's beaches.

Autumn 1942

Guadalcanal

A night on Edson's Ridge

On 7 August 1942, the Americans landed in the Solomon Islands, north-east of Australia, an important first staging-post in their advance towards Japan itself. Once secured, the airstrip on Guadalcanal – Henderson Field – needed to be held to ensure air cover for the invading force. The key feature was a ridge to the south. This was entrusted to the 1st Marine Raider Battalion, led by Colonel Merritt Edson. The Japanese were determined to retake the island and the struggle for Guadalcanal became the most protracted of the Pacific campaign.

14 SEPTEMBER 1942

The night of the 12th–13th was mild compared to last night, when the main Jap attack hit. I had turned in early and dozed off, despite occasional bursts of firing from a distance to the south. Then I half awoke to hear the major ordering the men to the top of the ridge. He came in the tent and I asked him what was up. He said that he was moving the men up as a precaution; no details. Banta asked if he should notify the reporters in their tent. Murray said to tell them 'the situation' and they could move up if they wanted to.

I heard them all scrambling up the hill, and lay alone in the tent wondering what 'the situation' was. I called out to a sentry: 'McSwiggin, what's up?' He came over to the tent and said, in surprise, 'Didn't you get the word, Mr Merillat? Colonel Edson says quite a few Japs are filtering through his lines, and everyone has gone up to the top of the ridge.' I chose to join the others.

The fire fight to the south grew heavier and closer. But I was so tired that I dozed off for about an hour, stretched out near the D-4 tent. Then, about 2100, a terrific blast woke me up. Shells were screaming overhead. From the front, now about a quarter of a mile away, came the sound of rifles, automatic arms, machine guns, mortars, and hand grenades, and the jabbering of Japs – and maybe of marines too. (Some in the CP [command post] claimed they could hear Edson exhorting his men.)

Then I realised that the heavy stuff, the shells, were coming from our own artillery, emplaced down the hill north of us. The bombardment was terrific; it lasted all night. At times the shouting, small-arms fire, thunk-thunk of machine guns, and explosions sounded very close. After 0200 they seemed to recede, the artillery barrage following.

We were close to the batteries of 105-mm. howitzers on the one side, and close to their target, the Japanese, on the other. The shells ripped through the air right over our heads. We could hear artillery officers shout their firing orders. Two shells, falling short, hit the CP, and fragments wounded several men. The offending gun was taken out of action for the rest of the night. I sat by the D-3 tent, listening to reports on the fighting and to plans for pursuing the Japs who, in the early morning hours, seemed to be withdrawing into the jungle whence they had erupted.

But the artillery barrage grew closer again. This time, a bit wary of short bursts, I hit the deck by the message-centre shelter. Soon I was glad I had. Tracers started coming into the CP. Firing seemed to come from all sides (a common impression, I am told, on such occasions). We could make out the distinctive ping of a Jap .25-calibre rifle close by. At least one seemed to be right on the spur where the CP stood, firing at random. Now and then bullets kicked up the dirt nearby. I could have sworn the Jap was right in front of the general's house. (Later I found out he was further along the spur toward the main ridge, near the jeep park.) I slipped further down into the ravine to the north and crawled under a log that stuck up at an angle from the ground. I watched the time closely, praying for dawn.

Then, as it began to grow light, it became clear that my refuge was in full view of snipers on the west side of the ravine. Others nearby had already begun to find better cover. I dashed up the slope into the D-2 tent and hit the deck. Two others closely followed. Just as they got inside a bullet clanged against a steel plate propped near the entrance. Ducking around behind the D-2 tent I saw Colonel Buckley, also looking for cover, and asked him where everyone was (no one else was in sight). He said I could hop into one of the D-2 shelters, which I did with alacrity, to find I shared it with Martin Clemens (who didn't recognise me in the dark and was inclined to dispute my right of entry), a wounded raider, two British missionaries, and a couple of D-2 marines. By now it was about 0500. I stayed until the sky was bright.

Sniping continued all day. I got out of the CP early in the morning with the gentlemen of the press, trying to find a relatively quiet place to sleep for a while. We went down to Kukum near the Lunga. Two of the correspondents, thoroughly shaken, lit out from the CP with only their typewriters and mess gear, and took the Yippie boat to Tulagi, there to embark on a transport that was leaving the area. I decided to try to spend a quiet night outside the CP, found that Bob Barnes had an extra cot in the Quartermaster's area down in the palms near the beach, and moved in.

Herbert C. Merillat

Edson's defence of the ridge that night against a greatly superior Japanese force was recognised by the award of the Medal of Honor.

The fight for Henderson Field continued into late October, involving Marine Sergeant Mitchell Paige in vicious combat at close quarters.

About the same time as the night before we heard the Japs talking again. They were about a hundred yards from the nose. It was so damned quiet, you could hear anything. I crawled around to the men and told them to keep quiet, look forward and glue their ears to the ground. As the Japs advanced we could hear the bushes rustle. Suddenly all hell broke loose.

All of us must have seen the Japs at the same time. Grenades exploded everywhere on the ridge-nose, followed by shrieks and yells. It would have been death to fire the guns because muzzle flashes would have given away our positions and we could have been smothered and blasted by a hail of grenades. Stansbury, who was lying in the foxhole next to mine, was pulling out grenade-pins with his teeth and rolling the grenades down the side of the nose. Leipart, the smallest guy in the platoon, and my particular boy, was in his foxhole delivering grenades like a star pitcher.

Then I gave the word to fire. Machine-guns and rifles let go and the whole line seemed to light up. Pettyjohn yelled to me that his gun was out of action. In the light from the firing I could see several Japs a few feet away from Leipart. Apparently he had been hit because he was down on one knee. I knocked off two Japs with a rifle but a third drove his bayonet into Leipart. Leipart was dead; seconds later, so was the Jap. After a few minutes, I wouldn't swear to how long it was, the blitz became a hand-to-hand battle. Gaston was having trouble with a Jap officer, I remember that much. Although his leg was nearly hacked off and his rifle all cut up, Gaston finally connected his boot with the Jap's chin. The result was one slopehead with one broken neck.

Firing died down a little, so evidently the first wave was a flop. I crawled over to Pettyjohn, and while he and Faust covered me I worked to remove a ruptured cartridge and change the belt-feed pawl. Just as I was getting ready to feed in a belt of ammo, I felt something hot on my hand and a sharp vibration. Some damned slopehead with a light machine-gun had fired a full burst into the feeding mechanism and wrecked the gun.

Things got pretty bad on the second wave. The Japs penetrated our left flank, carried away all opposition and were possibly in a position to attack our ridge-nose from the rear. On the left, however, Grant, Payne and Hinson stood by. In the centre, Lock, Swanek and McNabb got it and were carried away to the rear by corpsmen [medics]. The Navy boys did a wonderful job and patched up all the casualties, but they were still bleeding like hell and you couldn't tell what was wrong with them, so I sent them back. That meant that all my men were casualties and I was on my own. It was lonely up there with nothing but dead slopeheads for company, but I couldn't tell you what I was thinking about. I guess I was really worrying about the guns, shooting as fast as I could, and getting a bead on the next and nearest Jap.

One of the guns I couldn't find because it wasn't firing. I figured the guys had been hit and had put the gun out of action before leaving. I was always very insistent that if for any reason they had to leave a gun they would put it out of action so that the Japs wouldn't be able to use it. Being without a gun myself, I dodged over to the unit on my right to get another gun and give them the word on what was going on. Kelly and Totman helped me bring the gun back towards the nose of the ridge and we zig-zagged under an enemy fire that never seemed to stop. While I was on the right flank I borrowed some riflemen to form a skirmish line. I told them to fix bayonets and follow me. Kelly and Totman fed ammo as I sprayed every inch of terrain free of Japs. Dawn was beginning to break and in the half-light I saw my own machine-gun still near the centre of the nose. It was still in working order and some Japs were crawling towards it.

We got there just in time. I left Kelly and Totman and ran over to it.

For too many moments it seemed as though the whole Japanese Army was firing at me. Nevertheless three men on the right flank thought I might be low on ammunition and volunteered to run it up to me. Stat brought one belt and he went down with a bullet in the stomach. Reilly came up with another belt. Just as he reached the gun, he was hit in the groin. His feet flew out and nearly knocked me off the gun. Then Jonjeck arrived with a belt and stopped a bullet in the shoulder. As I turned I saw a piece of flesh disappear from his neck. I told him to go back for medical aid, but he refused. He wanted to stay up there with me. There was not time to argue; so I tapped him on the chin, hard enough so that he went down. That convinced him that I wanted my order obeyed.

My ears rang when a Jap sighted in on me with his light machine-gun but luckily he went away to my left. Anyway, I decided it was too unhealthy to stay in any one place for too long, so I would fire a burst and then move. Each time I shifted, grenades fell just where I had been. Over the nose of the ridge in the tall grass, which was later burned for security, I thought I saw some movement. Right of the nose, in the grass, thirty Japs stood up. One of them was looking at me through field-glasses. I let them have it with a full burst and they peeled off like grass under a mowing machine.

After that, I guess I was so wound up that I couldn't stop. I rounded up the skirmish line, told them I was going to charge off the nose and I wanted them to be right behind me. I picked up the machine-gun, and without noticing the burning hot water jacket, cradled it in my arms. Two belts of ammo I threw round my shoulders. The total weight was about 150 pounds, but the way I felt I could have carried three more without noticing it. I fed one of the belts off my shoulders into the gun, and then started forward. A colonel dropped about four feet in front of me with his yellow belly full of good American lead. In the meantime the skirmish line came over the nose, whooping like a bunch of wild Indians. We reached the edge of the clearing where the jungle began and there was nothing left either to holler at or shoot at. The battle was over with that strange sort of quietness that always follows.

The first thing I did was to sit down. I was soaked in perspiration and steam was rising in a cloud from my gun. My hand felt funny. I looked down and saw through my tattered shirt a blister which ran from my fingertips to my forearm. Captain Ditta came running up, slapped me on the back and gave me a drink from his canteen.

For three days after the battle, we camped around the nose. They estimated that there were 110 Japs dead in front of my sector. I don't know about that, but they started to smell so horribly that we had to bury them by blasting part of the ridge over on top of them. On the third day we marched twelve miles back to the airport. I never knew what day it was, and what's more I didn't care.

Mitchell Paige

Mitchell Paige won the Medal of Honor for his actions that day.

Blueberry pie

This was my chance. Now was the time to ask these men what they were fighting for.

These men were not especial malcontents. I had heard questions like these asked by too many men to think this an outstanding group of complaints. But here they were, perhaps about to give their lives for their country, and yet exercising, until it nearly collapsed from being exercised, the right of free speech. How could men harbouring such doubts and such protests fight with enthusiasm? What was there in it for them?

And so I said: 'I wonder if I could ask you fellows one question. It's something I've been wondering about quite a bit here on this island. What would you say you were fighting for? Today, here in this valley, what are you fighting for?'

The excited flush, which had come into their faces as they asked their questions, went out again. Their faces became pale. Their eyes wandered. They looked like men bothered by a memory. They did not answer for what seemed a very long time.

Then one of them spoke, but not to me. He spoke to the others, and for a second I thought he was changing the subject or making fun of me, but of course he was not. He was answering my questions very specifically.

He whispered: 'Jesus, what I'd give for a piece of blueberry pie.'

Another whispered: 'Personally I prefer mince.'

A third whispered: 'Make mine apple with a few raisins in it and lots of cinnamon: you know, Southern style.'

Fighting for pie. Of course that is not exactly what they meant. Here, in a place where they had lived for several weeks mostly on captured Japanese rice, then finally had gone on to such delicacies as canned corned beef and Navy beans, where they were usually hungry and never given a treat – here pie was their symbol of home.

In other places there are other symbols. For some men, in places where there is plenty of good food but no liquor, it is a good bottle of scotch whisky. In other places, where there's drink but no dames, they say they'd give their left arm for a blonde. For certain men, books are the thing; for others, music; for others, movies. But for all of them, these things are just badges of home. When they say they are fighting for these things, they mean that they are fighting for home – 'to get the goddam thing over and get home'.

Perhaps this sounds selfish. It certainly sounds less dynamic than the

Axis slogans. But home seems to most Marines a pretty good thing to be fighting for. Home is where the good things are – the generosity, the good pay, the comforts, the democracy, the pie.

John Hersey

Guadalcanal was finally secured by the Americans in February 1943. One thousand six hundred Americans and 25,000 Japanese had died there.

‡

El Alamein

Though Montgomery had his weaknesses as a strategist, he was the master of the set-piece battle. By late September, with Rommel's forces low on fuel and material, and the Desert Fox himself on sick leave in Germany, he was ready to take the fight to the enemy at El Alamein, just 60 miles from Alexandria.

I was watching the training carefully and it was becoming apparent to me that the Eighth Army was very untrained. The need for training had never been stressed. Most commanders had come to the fore by skill in fighting and because no better were available; many were above their ceiling, and few were good trainers. By the end of September there were serious doubts in my mind whether the troops would be able to do what was being demanded; the plan was simple but it was too ambitious. If I was not careful, divisions and units would be given tasks which might end in failure because of the inadequate standard of training. The Eighth Army had suffered some 80,000 casualties since it was formed, and little time had been spent in training the replacements.

The moment I saw what might happen I took a quick decision. On the 6th October, just over two weeks before the battle was to begin, I changed the plan. My initial plan had been based on destroying Rommel's armour; the remainder of his army, the un-armoured portion, could then be dealt with at leisure. This was in accordance with the accepted military thinking of the day. I decided to reverse the process and thus alter the whole conception of how the battle was to be fought. My modified plan now was to hold off, or contain, the enemy armour while we carried out a methodical destruction of the infantry divisions holding the defensive system. These un-armoured divisions would be destroyed by means of a 'crumbling' process, the enemy being attacked from the flank and rear and cut off from their supplies. These operations would be carefully organised from a series of firm bases and would be within the capabilities of my troops. I did not think it likely that the enemy armour would remain inactive and watch the gradual destruction of all the unarmoured divisions; it would be launched in heavy counter-attacks. This would suit us very well, since the best way to destroy the enemy armour was to entice it to attack *our* armour in position. I aimed to get my armour beyond the area of the 'crumbling' operations. I would then turn the enemy minefields to our advantage by using them to prevent the enemy armour from interfering with our operations; this would be done by closing the approaches through the minefields with our tanks, and we would then be able to proceed relentlessly with our plans.

The success of the whole operation would depend largely on whether 30 Corps could succeed in the 'break-in' battle and establish the corridors through which the armoured divisions of 10 Corps must pass. I was certain that if we could get the leading armoured brigades through the corridors without too great delay, then we would win the battle. Could we do this? In order to make sure, I planned to launch the armoured divisions of 10 Corps into the corridors immediately behind the leading infantry divisions of 30 Corps, *and before I knew the corridors were clear.* Furthermore, I ordered that if the corridors were not completely clear on the morning of D + 1, the 24th October, the armoured divisions would fight their own way out into the open beyond the western limit of the minefields. This order was not popular with the armoured units but I was determined to see that it was carried out to the letter.

It will be seen later how infirmity of purpose on the part of certain senior commanders in carrying out this order nearly lost us the battle.

I mentioned . . . that there was a Major Williams on my intelligence staff who appeared to me to be of outstanding ability. To all who served with me in the war he was known always as Bill Williams. In a conversation one day about this time, he pointed out to me that the enemy German and Italian troops were what he called 'corseted'; that is, Rommel had so deployed his German infantry and parachute troops that they were positioned between, and in some places behind, his Italian troops all along the front, the latter being unreliable when it came to hard fighting. Bill Williams's idea was that if we could separate the two we would be very well placed, as we could smash through a purely Italian front without any great difficulty. This very brilliant analysis and idea was to be a major feature of the master plan for the 'crumbling' operations, and it paved the way to final victory at Alamein.

Bernard Montgomery

Bill Williams was in peacetime an Oxford don specialising in the cabinet government of eighteenth-century Britain. During the war he became, in the opinion of many, the best intelligence officer in either camp, and a vital part of Montgomery's armoury.

An infantry officer at Alamein

A central element of Montgomery's plan at Alamein was that the infantry would clear a path through the minefields for his armour. On the night of 23 October he began the attack with a 1,000-gun barrage along the 40 miles of the front. Moving up to the start line opposite an Italian position was H. P. Samwell, an officer with a Scottish regiment.

About 9 p.m. we moved forward and took up our positions on the start line – a taped line stretching across the open desert just in front of the forward positions. It was deathly still and a full moon lighted the bleak sand as if it were day. Suddenly the silence was broken by the crash of a single gun, and the next moment a mighty roar rent the air and the ground shook under us as salvo after salvo crashed out from hundreds of guns. Shells whined over our heads in a continuous stream, and soon we saw the enemy line lit up by bright flashes. One or two fires broke out and the ground became clearer then ever. It seemed a long time before the enemy started to reply, but finally they did so, weakly at first, then gradually growing in strength. I could imagine the German gunners having just settled in for another quiet night's sleep, tumbling out of their bivies bewildered and still half asleep. Some of them would never reach their guns, and others would arrive to find their guns blown sky high . . .

I suddenly discovered that I was still carrying my ash stick. I had meant to leave it at the rear Company HQ with the CQMS and exchange it for a rifle. I smiled to myself to think I was walking straight towards the enemy armed only with a .38 pistol and nine rounds of ammunition. Well, it was too late to do anything about it now, but I expected that someone would soon be hit and I could take his. I began to wonder, still quite impersonally, who it would be; perhaps myself! in which case I wouldn't need a rifle. Then I heard a new sound above the roar of the guns and the explosion of shells. The sharp rat-tat-tat of Breda and Spandau machine-guns – streams of tracer bullets whined diagonally across our front, not more than twenty yards ahead. We must be getting near the first enemy positions. I asked the pace-checker on my right how many paces we had done. He grinned and said he had lost count; then crump-crump-crump! a new sharper note. This was something that affected us — mortar shells were landing right among us. I heard a man on my left say, 'Oh God!' and I saw him stagger and fall. The major was shouting again. I couldn't hear what he said, but his company seemed to be already at grips with the enemy. At that moment I saw a single strand of wire ahead about breast high. I took a running jump at it and just cleared it. My sergeant, coming behind, started to climb over it and immediately there was a blinding flash and a blast of air struck me on the back of the neck. I never saw that sergeant again. I remember wondering what instinct had made me jump that wire. Strange? I hadn't been thinking of booby-traps. We had broken into a run now — why, I don't know. Nobody had given any order. A corporal on my left was firing his Bren gun from the hip. I wondered if he was really firing at anything. Then suddenly I saw a head and shoulders protruding from a hole in the ground. I had already passed it and had to turn half round. I fired my pistol three times, and then ran on to catch up the line.

The line had broken up into blobs of men all struggling together; my faithful batman was still trotting along beside me. I wondered if he had been with me while I was shooting. My runner had disappeared, though; and then I saw some men in a trench ahead of me. They were standing up with their hands above their heads screaming something that sounded like 'Mardray'. I remember thinking how dirty and ill-fitting their uniforms were, and smiled at myself for bothering about that at this time. To my left and behind me some of the NCOs were rounding up prisoners and kicking them into some sort of formation. I waved my pistol at the men in front with their hands up to sign them to join the others. In front of me a terrified Italian was running round and round with his hands above his head screaming at the top of his voice. The men I had signalled started to come out. Suddenly I heard a shout of 'Watch out!' and the next moment something hard hit the toe of my boot and bounced off. There was a blinding explosion, and I staggered back holding my arm over my eyes instinctively. Was I wounded? I looked down rather expecting to see blood pouring out, but there was nothing — a tremendous feeling of relief. I was unhurt. I looked for the sergeant who had been beside me; he had come up to take the place of the one who had fallen. At first I couldn't see him, and then I saw him lying sprawled out on his back groaning. His leg was just a tangled mess. I realised all at once what had happened: one of the enemy in the trench had thrown a grenade at me as he came out with his hands up. It had bounced off my boot as the sergeant shouted his warning, and had exploded beside him. I suddenly felt furious; an absolute uncontrollable temper surged up inside me. I swore and cursed at the enemy now crouching in the corner of the trench; then I fired at them at point-blank range – one, two, three, and then click! I had forgotten to reload. I flung my pistol away in disgust and grabbed a rifle – the sergeant's, I think – and rushed in. I believe two of the enemy were sprawled on the ground at the bottom of the square trench. I bayoneted two more and then came out again. I was quite cool now, and I started looking for my pistol, and thinking to myself there will be hell to pay with the quarter-master if I can't account for it. At the same time I wondered when I had got rid of my stick, as I couldn't remember dropping it. I felt rather sad; it had been my constant companion for two years at home. I had walked down to the pictures with my wife and had put it under the seat, and on leaving I had forgotten it, and had had to disturb a whole row of people to retrieve it. I started then to wonder what my wife was doing at that moment.

The firing had died down and groups of men were collecting round me rather vaguely; just then a man shouted and fired a single round. I afterwards learnt that one of the enemy in the trench had heaved himself up and was just going to fire into my back when my man saw him and shot him first. I didn't realise what had happened at the time.

H. P. Samwell

Shot by an Austrian soldier, whom he had subsequently wounded, Samwell later found himself sharing a trench with his adversary as shells fell about them.

Mortar shells started landing all around me. The Germans were watching our every movement, and had jumped to the conclusion that my trench was the HQ. Twice I was covered in sand, and once a red-hot piece of metal landed on my chest. The Austrian stirred uneasily and woke up. He started to raise himself by placing his hands over the edge of the trench. There was an earsplitting explosion. At first I thought our trench had been blown in. I looked carefully over the side; there was a huge crater less than five yards from the Austrian's end of the trench. Then I looked at the Austrian; he was lying half propped up against the trench looking curiously at the remains of his left hand; it had been partially blown away. I was nearly sick, but hastily tore my shirt and bound it tightly round the stump. He thanked me weakly and closed his eyes. His breathing was heavy and laboured; the poor devil was dying. I thought of his wife and children, of our talks about Austria, how damn stupid the whole thing was. First, he shoots me, then I shoot him, then we talk together as friends and share a trench where he is further wounded by his own side. Why were we fighting each other? Did it make sense? Then I thought of the massacres in Poland, France, Belgium. Yes, I suppose it was necessary. '*Wann kommt der Arzt?*' [When is the doctor coming?] he interrupted my thoughts. Mechanically I replied, '*Bald!*' [Soon] Almost petulantly he murmured, '*Bald! Bald! immer bald.*' It was no use explaining to him that we were cut off and the doctor wouldn't be coming; he would certainly be dead in a few hours, and I, too, probably if this shelling went on. My thigh was hurting infernally. I tried to read a 'News Review' my wife had sent me, but I couldn't concentrate. I had put it into my haversack at the last moment, I remember, and had purposefully left it unread for such an occasion as this, and now I didn't want to read it. I took out the photo I carried of my wife and children. How peaceful and unreal the house looked, how normal they all looked. But I didn't feel normal. I wondered if she was thinking of me at this moment; then my dream came back vividly – the bathroom – God! I was thirsty. I took another two mouthfuls of water. The Austrian stirred again and, opening his eyes, murmured, '*Wasser bitte.*' Damn him! I thought. What was the use of giving my precious water to a dying man, and an enemy at that. I was angry. Damn him, hadn't he the sense to see that he was dying, and it would be just a waste of my precious water, but I leant over and held it to his mouth. He gulped it down, and when I tried to take it from him he struggled with me, hitting out with the stump of his bandaged hand. I felt guilty, but I forced it away from him; already he had drunk a quarter of a bottle.

As I moved back to my own end of the trench a bullet whistled past my head. That damned sniper was still watching . . .

It was now early evening. The Austrian was lying peaceful, still breathing, but blood was oozing out of his mouth. I think I slept again; I was getting light-headed. I finished the second water-bottle; my thirst was more painful than the wound. I still had my batman's half-full bottle, but I couldn't use that; he would want it. Another two hours passed, and then suddenly I realised there were people round the trench. I can't remember how many, but the company commander was there and a doctor, not our own. He was wearing a forage-cap, and I thought what a risk he was taking. He was very cool and cheery. 'Hold out your arm,' he said, and he injected me with morphia. I asked him to give some to the Austrian.

He stabbed him but he scarcely stirred, and murmured, '*Der Arzt ist gekommen.*'

H. P. Samwell

The author was to be killed in the Ardennes in 1945.

The attritional 'dogfight' in the minefields that Montgomery had envisaged continued for about a week. As he had almost twice as many men and tanks as those of the combined German–Italian army, the ultimate result was not in doubt, and by 4 November he also knew (since the British had cracked the Germans' Enigma code and so could read Rommel's signals) that his adversary was on the brink of defeat.

At 2 a.m. I directed two hard punches at the 'hinges' of the final break-out area where the enemy was trying to stop us widening the gap which we had blown. That finished the battle.

The armoured car regiments went through as dawn was breaking and soon the armoured divisions got clean away into the open desert; they were now in country clear of minefields, where they could manoeuvre and operate against the enemy rear areas and retreating columns.

The armoured cars raced away to the west, being directed far afield on the enemy line of retreat.

The Italian divisions in the south, in front of 13 Corps, had nothing to do except surrender; they could not escape as the Germans had taken all their transport. I directed Horrocks to collect them in, and devoted my attention to the pursuit of Rommel's forces which were streaming westwards.

Bernard Montgomery

Retreat in the desert

Following Montgomery's successes, Rommel was forced steadily to withdraw his forces westwards. By 9 November, they were at Sidi Barrani, 200 miles from El Alamein. The tide of battle in the desert had turned for the last time.

We drove through a minor storm of enemy shells. The drivers had only one aim – to get out of range of the pursuing tanks, and their convoy discipline faltered. Contrary to orders, the trucks closed in upon each other and sometimes even raced side by side, despite the extended-order drill.

Gradually the shelling petered out. I was about to draw a sigh of relief when there was a roar and a jolt. My truck lurched to a stop: radiator and engine were smashed.

'Damn! Tanks ahead!' was the thought that flashed through my mind. 'The bastards have cut us off.'

I shouted an order to my driver, who was just slightly wounded, 'Jump to it!'

Away from here, I thought. Only speed will get us out of this jam. We leaped on the vehicle following ours.

'Forward, don't deviate!' I yelled at the driver. But there was to be no forward dash for that truck.

Again that flash, crash, and jolt. The driver and two other men in the truck were wounded. Though I was sitting in the cab too, I escaped unscathed.

As I leaped from the truck I saw to the right two brilliant flashes, and then heard two explosions.

'This is senseless,' I thought. Then I shouted: 'Dismount! Dig in!'

The command was almost unnecessary. Every vehicle had halted. Many of the men were already flat on the ground. But – extraordinary, this – there was an immediate dead calm disturbed only by a few purring engines.

Now and again a desultory shell flew overhead from our rear – a few last cracks at us from the pursuing tanks. But who the devil was firing at us from the front? Only then did the thought strike me: Are we being fired on, or have we run into a minefield?

I scarcely needed to take those few strides forward and examine the ground just behind the nearest destroyed truck. Yes, there was the tell-tale hole. Mines!

I was puzzled. My reading of the compass had been dead accurate, I was sure, despite the break-neck speed at which we had travelled. But . . . a hot prickling crept over my skin: that entrenching tool! Of course, the steel spade had caused a variation in the compass needle.

The night was fairly dark. I held the compass close to my eyes and took a bearing on its palely luminous glimmer. Then I threw the entrenching tool away and took the bearing again. As I had expected, the needle pointed considerably farther to the left.

I had been foolish. Here we now were in the middle of a minefield, with enemy tanks hard behind us. It was up to me to retrieve the situation. I wrapped my mind in calmness, made my plan, and, with the men lying prone, stepped out to look for the edge of the minefield. A soldier who had robbed a comrade, and had in consequence been dishonoured when I called him a *Schweinehund* on a battalion parade a few days before, now insisted on accompanying me. He ran about regardless of danger, examining tracks and casting an eye round for mines.

Usually, we knew, the lighter and more easily detonated anti-personnel mines were sprinkled liberally round the heavier plate mines employed against Panzers and trucks. But it seemed that here the plate mines were smaller than the usual type, and there seemed to be no anti-personnel mines.

At length I discovered a rusty strand of barbed-wire, which indicated the edge of the minefield, and I soon located the gap. We had missed it by fifty yards. Only the leading vehicles and guns were actually within the minefield. With most of the men deployed in defensive array, I had the drivers of the rear vehicles head towards the gap. Other squads were detailed for the tricky and not entirely pleasant task of man-handling the endangered vehicles and guns backward over their original tracks to the edge of the minefield. One mine exploded, but fortunately it killed no one. The Desert all round us was dead quiet. Not a shot was heard.

It took two hours to get the column safely into formation again and moving through the passage. I had lost four valuable vehicles, but none of the men were killed. At the western perimeter a squad of anxious sappers were waiting for us. No sooner had we passed than they mined the gap. Half an hour later they overtook us and sped on . . .

Just as the sun rose my battalion column was overtaken by a posse of vehicles moving at speed. Overtaking in convoy was prohibited with us, as it was with the British, whenever there was danger of intensive air attack: jammed roads caused good targets. I was about to take steps to correct the behaviour of the furious drivers passing me when there was a brief interval. I ordered the driver to slow up, slewed round, and got ready to be peremptory.

Then I recognised the approaching vehicle. It was the old familiar Mammoth. It overhauled us. On top of it, shoulders back, was an even more familiar figure. I came smartly to the salute.

Rommel waved, and gave a shout which was carried away by the wind of our passage. But his face was set and serious.

Heinz Werner Schmidt

‡

It's all set!

On 26 November, an attack by SOE operatives and andartes – *resistance fighters – destroyed the important railway bridge over the Gorgopotamos ravine in Greece, hindering the progress of German reinforcements to North Africa. The mission was SOE's most signal success to date on the European mainland, and the high point of collaboration between the two principal bands of* andartes, *the Communist ELAS and republican EDES. Among the SOE team was Denys Hamson.*

Tom said, 'It's all set', and pulled out his whistle to blow the signal. Just then the white signal cartridge was fired from the northern end of the bridge to indicate that it was clear and immediately after it the red signal from the southern post above us. We booed ironically and blew three long blasts on our whistles.

It was just after two a.m. by our watches. We lit the fuses and retired, the four of us, to our culvert fifty yards away. I was last in. The entrance faced away from the explosion and there was a good deal of water inside. The last shots had been fired a few minutes ago, and now there was an oppressive hush. The whole gorge seemed to be waiting for the explosion on which everything hung. I prayed silently. God, let there be no hitch. I dare say the other three, the sappers, Tom, Martin and Inder, were reviewing in their minds the work they had just done, to try to find a mistake. The minutes seemed to drag interminably. Tom was looking at his watch. He said, 'Two minutes up – two minutes thirty – TWO minutes FORTY-FIVE – THREE minutes.'

At three minutes fifteen seconds after we had lit our fuses, I poked my head nervously out of the culvert. I was still in the lee of the culvert, but I could see the major part of the bridge including the first masonry pier next to the steel pier we had mined. At that moment the whole scene was lit by a blinding white flash, and the crack of the explosion of two hundred-weight of high explosive so close to us hit my ears like a blow. It was so loud and sharp that for a moment I did not realise how deafening it was. The sound seemed to linger in the air for a fraction of a second and then reverberated up the Gorgopotamos ravine like thunder. The blast seemed to flow over our heads. I ducked back instinctively to let any splinters land.

Tom pushed me from behind and we scrambled out. I was first up the bank, my eyes straining towards the pier through the gloom of the moonlight. My first thought was, 'Christ, the thing is still standing', then I saw it clearer. It stood at a toppling drunken angle. It had jumped up, cut clean through on all four legs, and had come down again in a useless tangle. On the side nearest us, the spaced charges had cut out the section of eight feet on each leg, and it leant alarmingly towards us. The span between it and the first masonry pier had come clean away and lay, badly damaged, half in the river, half on the bank we stood on. The other span which it had supported to the south had also cut away and rested on the rising ground towards the shorter steel column from which it still hung by some bent girders.

I remember I roared wildly and loudly; I was too excited to put my elation into words. Tom behind me took up my roar in his hoarse tuneless voice; and then Martin and Inder joined in. Our inarticulate message carried to the waiting ears of everyone in the other parties, and sporadic cheers and shouts came from all sides of the dark gorge. I heard Chris yelling, 'Hooray, hooray.'

Denys Hamson

Winter 1942–3

Stalingrad

As Midway was to the Americans, so Stalingrad was for the Russians a turning-point in the war against their mortal foe. Both in duration and in numbers slain, the contest for the gateway to the Caucasus oilfields was a struggle on an epic scale, lasting from August 1942 until the following February and claiming the lives of 110,500 Germans and three-quarters of a million Russian troops. At least 250,000 civilians died during the siege. Much of the fighting took place in the streets of Stalingrad itself, as recounted here by a Russian officer.

21 SEPTEMBER 1942

The Germans had cut us off from our neighbours. The supply of ammunition had been cut off; every bullet was worth its weight in gold. I gave the order to economise on ammunition, to collect the cartridge-pouches of the dead and all captured weapons. In the evening the enemy again tried to break our resistance, coming up close to our positions. As our numbers grew smaller, we shortened our line of defence, we began to move back slowly towards the Volga, drawing the enemy after us, and the ground we occupied was invariably too small for the Germans to be able easily to use artillery and aircraft.

We moved back, occupying one building after another, turning them into strongholds. A soldier would crawl out of an occupied position only when the ground was on fire under him and his clothes were smouldering. During the day the Germans managed to occupy only two blocks.

At the crossroads of Krasnopiterskaya and Komsomolskaya Streets we occupied a three-storey building on the corner. This was a good position from which to fire on all corners and it became our last defence. I ordered all entrances to be barricaded, and windows and embrasures to be adapted so that we could fire through them with all our remaining weapons.

At a narrow window of the semi-basement we placed the heavy machine-gun with our emergency supply of ammunition – the last belt of cartridges. I had decided to use it at the most critical moment.

Two groups, six in each, went up to the third floor and the garret. Their job was to break down walls, and prepare lumps of stone and beams to throw at the Germans when they came up close. A place for the seriously wounded was set aside in the basement. Our garrison consisted of forty men. Difficult days began. Attack after attack broke unendingly like waves against us. After each attack was beaten off we felt it was impossible to hold off the onslaught any longer, but when the Germans launched a fresh attack, we managed to find means and strength. This lasted five days and nights.

The basement was full of wounded; only twelve men were still able to fight. There was no water. All we had left in the way of food was a few pounds of scorched grain; the Germans decided to beat us with starvation. Their attacks stopped, but they kept up the fire from their heavy-calibre machine-guns all the time.

We did not think about escape, but only about how to sell our lives most dearly – we had no other way out.

The Germans attacked again. I ran upstairs with my men and could see their thin, blackened and strained faces, the bandages on their wounds, dirty and clotted with blood, their guns held firmly in their hands. There was no fear in their eyes. Lyuba Nesterenko, a nurse, was dying, with blood flowing from a wound in her chest. She had a bandage in her hand. Before she died she wanted to help to bind someone's wound, but she failed . . .

The German attack was beaten off. In the silence that gathered around us we could hear the bitter fighting going on for Mamayev Kurgan and in the factory area of the city.

How could we help the men defending the city? How could we divert from over there a part of the enemy forces, which had stopped attacking our building?

We decided to raise a red flag over the building, so that the Nazis would not think we had given up. But we had no red material. Understanding what we wanted to do, one of the men who was severely wounded took off his bloody vest and, after wiping the blood off his wound with it, handed it over to me.

The Germans shouted through a megaphone: 'Russians! Surrender! You'll die just the same!'

At that moment a red flag rose over our building.

'Bark, you dogs! We've still got a long time to live!' shouted my orderly, Kozhushko.

We beat off the next attack with stones, firing occasionally and throwing our last grenades. Suddenly from behind a blank wall, from the rear, came the grind of a tank's caterpillar tracks. We had no anti-tank grenades. All we had left was one anti-tank rifle with three rounds. I handed this rifle to an anti-tank man, Berdyshev, and sent him out through the back to fire at the tank point-blank. But before he could get into position he was captured by German tommy-gunners. What Berdyshev told the Germans I don't know, but I can guess that he led them up the garden path, because an hour later they started to attack at precisely that point where I had put my machine-gun with its emergency belt of cartridges.

This time, reckoning that we had run out of ammunition, they came impudently out of their shelter, standing up and shouting. They came down the street in a column.

I put the last belt in the heavy machine-gun at the semi-basement window and sent the whole of the 250 bullets into the yelling, dirty-grey Nazi mob. I was wounded in the hand but did not leave go of the machine-gun. Heaps of bodies littered the ground. The Germans still alive ran for cover in panic. An hour later they led our anti-tank rifleman on to a heap of ruins and shot him in front of our eyes, for having shown them the way to my machine-gun.

There were no more attacks. An avalanche of shells fell on the building. The Germans stormed us with every possible kind of weapon. We couldn't raise our heads.

Again we heard the ominous sound of tanks. From behind a neighbouring block stocky German tanks began to crawl out. This, clearly, was the end. The guardsmen said goodbye to one another. With a dagger my orderly scratched on a brick wall: 'Rodimtsev's guardsmen fought and died for their country here.'

Anton K. Dragan

The Stalingrad Pocket

Stalingrad was not only an urban battle. A Soviet offensive on 19 November encircled the German Sixth Army to the west of the city, starving it of the supplies it needed to face the Russian winter. General Friedrich Paulus asked for permission to break out, but Hitler was determined not to lose face and told Paulus that his army of 250,000 men would be sustained by air lift. This promise was not kept. Conditions in the 'Stalingrad Pocket' became desperate, with soldiers reduced to eating the emaciated carcasses of horses, and then of their comrades, in order to survive.

When an air raid ended and circumstances permitted, we still occasionally sat together in a comradely group, and wrote to our loved ones at home, to whom our thoughts turned so fearfully and longingly in this season before Christmas. The mail service had not yet completely stopped even if letters from home arrived less and less frequently. Or a diverting discussion began. But these were mostly too self-conscious and remained tense in their obvious expediency. Occasionally, with gallows humour and in memory of a highly pleasing meal of horse stew, we sang the 'Song of the German Soldier in the East', '. . . he, who never in the pocket, ate his horse . . . !' Our feelings and thoughts could no longer get away from our cruel routine, the fatal place we were tied to for life and death, from Stalingrad and the Volga.

Life and times at Pitomnik with its desolate steppe landscape did not lack a certain uncanny romanticism. Even if air raids and dog-fights had become routine, we were often enticed out of our dug-out. Then we hunkered down amidst the snow drifts and, disregarding the danger, followed with those strange, mixed feelings of curiosity, sensation-seeking, carefreeness, enjoyment and secret horror, the breath-taking spectacle being enacted high above our heads in a combination of grace and deadly intent. The heavy thumping of the flak, the thrumming and screaming of the engines, provided an infernal accompanying music. The fighters circled among the small white clouds of exploding shells, chased and rolled over each other in vicious dog-fights until finally one went down, trailing a growing black cloud of smoke. At the beginning we still had four sleek fighters at Pitomnik, which the attacking Russians held in great respect. Occasionally a huge jet of flame erupted on the air base with an ear-splitting bang. That meant a transport, its belly crammed with fuel, had been hit after landing. Occasionally a stricken aircraft, trailing a terribly bright flame, screamed down out of the cold blue depths of the winter sky like a meteor and immediately after a huge mushrooming cloud of smoke bore witness to the end of a minute catastrophe that had devoured a man and his machine.

In the course of the weeks of December the shot-down wrecks of every conceivable type of aircraft piled up on the base at Pitomnik.

Peacefully they lay there, one next to another, from small Russian fighters to the lamed or destroyed big birds, many of which had crashed on take-off. There was even a Fieseler Storch that had frozen to the ground. But in this extensive graveyard of equipment life still pulsed feverishly even deep under the ground. The low snow walls and domes of the bunkers with their smoking chimney pipes, ineffectively camouflaged vehicles, radio stations with masts and antennas, communications trucks, occasional tents; all this gave the impression of a ghostly city where people swarmed like ants, sometimes above ground and sometimes below. And yet the place with its masses of people was lost in the never ending wilderness of snow.

It was probably the saddest and most desolate place I had laid eyes on in the east. A bare, naked, dead steppe landscape with not a bush or tree, not a village for miles around. A single trunk without branches stuck up five kilometres away in the little hamlet of Pitomnik, where a few houses were still standing, and served as a sign post. Near the hamlet were a number of *balkas*, deeply eroded, steep-banked rain gullies, that gave some protection. Occasionally an ice-grey mist from the Volga drifted over this desolate piece of ground and the wind, which cut through everything with its biting edge, blew unmercifully over the boundless snowy waste. The loneliness of the eastern expanses was depressing and this eerie feeling was increased by the early fall of darkness. We had maintained our time setting from home and this no longer fitted our sector of the front. The sun set soon after lunch and by 14.00 to 15.00 hours it was already dark, and every day this too reminded us, depressingly, here in the desolation of the snow-bound steppe, of the enormous distance that separated us from home.

Were we not all, the living and the dead, long buried in a gigantic mass grave? Thoughts like this occasionally befell me when I returned from various sectors of the front where in my role as liaison officer, I had been sent on specific assignments, or to gather urgently needed information. There, on the heights above the infamous Rossoshka valley, the men of our divisions lay in a desperate battle demanding bloody sacrifice. There in the trenches and fox-holes in the snow, the soldiers were dying of exhaustion and cold, because the steadily shrinking rations of bread and other food issued were no longer sufficient to provide the physical stamina needed to combat frost and sickness.

Only the crows swarming in the endless steppe, those horrible, greedy birds that always seemed to me to be the harbingers of doom, still found enough to eat. Yes, these croaking companions of death did very well for themselves. They rose slowly before one's feet from the frozen carcasses of the dead horses half hidden in the snow that formed a kind of trail and showed, by bloody red gashes, that hungry soldiers had cut out coveted chunks of meat with their knives or bayonets.

Whereas the air lift disappointed all expectations, the troops had to perform and suffer beyond human capacity day and night. And they did so to the extreme. The reports of losses grew more and more serious. It was as if the horsemen of the Apocalypse had ridden in, instead of the hoped for relief. The thoughts of the sufferings of our comrades, the agonies and dangers that might be ours tomorrow or the day after, never left us. If only their sacrifices were not to be in vain.

Why had we been forbidden to break out in time with the forces and energies that were now slowly and inexorably being ground down? I often recall those conversations I had overheard at the beginning of the battle, when the fatal decision to have the army dig in was taken. Had we then not looked into the future with grave concern and great anxiety? The air lift on which everything had originally depended was now clearly failing, and the fate of the army seemed to be taking its fatal course. But one great hope remained; the possibility of salvation from outside. A rapid and successful relief operation could still bring about the longed-for turning point for our desperately endangered army.

Joachim Wieder

The German retreat

Towards the end of January the Russians captured the last German-held airfield, leaving the Sixth Army without hope of succour. Like Napoleon's men before them, Joachim Wieder and his fellow soldiers began to withdraw – a difficult manoeuvre to perform when surrounded.

Nightfall soon came and saved us once again. Through the darkness we could hear the cries for help and the screams of our wounded. Here and there flames eerily rose against the sky and illuminated the gigantic, deserted snake of our vehicle column. Under the cover of darkness our decimated ranks continued their flight on foot. Death had once again passed us by.

Next day, despite great dangers, he spared us again. An hour's long march had taken us many kilometres over the snow steppe, on which, as so often before, millions of ice crystals glittered in the pitiless frost, and a penetrating east wind played its evil game from over the Volga. Russian aircraft chased through the clear, pale blue winter air in which the sun stood cold and weak. The Soviet stars on their glittering wings were clearly recognisable. Suddenly, a whole flight dived down, selecting our helpless little group of human beings as their target. Like rabbits caught in the fire from a *battue*, we scattered over the completely coverless fields of snow and then threw ourselves down with thundering hearts to burrow deeply into the snow. The hunt was repeated and once again the bullets whistled to the ground all around me.

Together with several wounded we dragged ourselves onwards until, exhausted and shattered, we finally reached the ruins and rubble of the northern Stalingrad city area. What travails did fate still hold in store for us? Death, whom I faced more often and closely in recent days than ever before, was still refusing me. But his trusted companion for many weeks, hunger, was tormenting me with tenacious power, slowly making me ripe for the end. And frost, the third murderer in the trio, had also bitten me by now, as the constant, stabbing pains in some of my limbs warned me.

Separated from our staff, our group of officers found shelter in a dark, dirty cellar while our men went to ground in a neighbouring pile of rubble. This was to be the end of our flight and our last quarters.

Joachim Wieder

Surrender

General Vasili Chuikov commanded the Russian 62nd Army, which with the 64th Army bore the brunt of the successful defence of Stalingrad. He discovered that even in defeat, his German counterparts still sang their Führer's praises.

On the evening of January 31, Gurov, Krylov and I talked in my dug-out, now spacious and light, with the captured German generals. Seeing that they were hungry and nervous and anxious about their fate, I ordered tea to be brought and invited them to have a snack. They were all dressed in parade uniform and were wearing their medals. General Otto Korfes, picking up a glass of tea and a sandwich, asked:

'What's this, propaganda?'

I answered: 'If the general thinks that the tea and the sandwiches contain propaganda, we certainly won't insist that he accept our propagandist food . . .'

My reply made the prisoners somewhat brighter, and our conversation lasted for about an hour. General Korfes spoke more than any of the others. Generals Pfeffer and Seydlitz kept silent, saying they did not understand political affairs.

In the discussion General Korfes developed the idea that the position of Germany at that time had much in common with that at the time of Frederick the Great and Bismarck. Considering Hitler's mental stature and deeds to be no less than those of Frederick and Bismarck, Korfes obviously meant that if the latter had had their setbacks and nonetheless emerged to greatness, then Hitler's defeat on the Volga did not mean the end of Hitlerism. Germany, under Hitler's leadership, would survive this defeat and would in the end be victorious. Generals Pfeffer and Seydlitz sat, from time to time uttered the words 'jawohl' or 'nein', and wept copiously.

Finally, Lieutenant-General von Seydlitz–Kurzbach asked:

'What will happen to us?'

I told him the conditions of captivity, adding that they could if they wished wear their decorations and regalia, but could not carry weapons.

'What kind of weapons?' said Pfeffer, looking interested and seeming not to understand. He glanced at Seydlitz.

'Captured generals are not allowed to carry any kind of weapons,' I repeated.

Seydlitz then took a penknife out of his pocket and handed it across to me. Of course, I returned it to him, saying that we did not consider such 'weapons' to be dangerous.

After our conversation with the captured generals, we sent them off to Front HQ, expressing the hope that they would soon get to know the real situation in the Soviet Union, so as to shake off their mistaken notions and the poison of Nazism.

Vasili Chuikov

Although Paulus surrendered, many others obeyed Hitler's order to fight to the last bullet. Of the 110,000 troops who followed Paulus into captivity, only 5,000 survived to return home after the war. The defeat at Stalingrad was met with three days of public mourning in Germany.

✠

A Jew story

Christabel Bielenberg, an Englishwoman, had married her German husband Peter in 1934 and lived in Berlin throughout the war. With Peter posted to Norway, she found herself alone with her three children and having to face the same crises of conscience as many other householders who loathed the Nazis. In early 1943, a friend, Ilse, brought round a Jewish woman seeking a place to hide.

We sat on the sofa side by side, the slight, neatly dressed woman and I. Her head was bent, the broad dark line of parting in her yellow hair showed that she would soon have to pay another visit to a safe hairdresser.

Her thin, nervous fingers never ceased twisting and turning at the wedding ring on the fourth finger of her right hand. She did not seem to realise that every side glance she gave me, every gentle answer to my questioning, was a searing accusation, indubitable proof of the rottenness of the Master Race with which my tip-tilted nose identified me. Had she children? 'No,' then softly, 'thank God.' Where was her husband now? How soon would she want to come? Her need was seemingly immediate. The priest had felt for some days that his house was being watched, and she and her husband could not allow him to risk more for them. They could not and would not go to Ilse as, being half-Jewish, she was suspect anyway. As I watched her thin nervous fingers and listened to her quiet voice, I was trying, not very successfully, to calculate just what having her in the house would entail. I would have to send the maid on holiday. The cellar? The children's bikes were kept in the cellar, and Nick was quite proud of his job at the central heating. Well, all that could be overcome, but one thing I had almost forgotten and would have to get straight. Since Peter was away, and seeing that Carl Langbehn [a lawyer and a friend of the Bielenbergs] and Hans Oster had vouched for me as being no security risk before Peter went to Norway, I would have to ask Carl first.

I found it hard to face the expression in the woman's eyes when I told her that she could stay, but that I could not give her a definite answer about her husband until late that night. The quick flash of relief, the disappointment, the shy emergent hope. 'God bless you,' she said, 'he will be in the roadway after the black-out tonight, he will wait, he knows how to hide.'

She stayed with me all that day, polishing, scrubbing, sweeping and tidying, while I hustled a rather bewildered Louisa off on an unexpected holiday. She told me her husband had been a chemist, his family and hers had been German for generations, her husband had fought in the First World War. They had not believed that Germany would cease to be their home, they had left things too late.

We played a riotous game of snakes and ladders with the boys, when I heard her laugh for the first time. She helped me cook their supper and get them to bed, and soon after she left I pushed through the gap in the hedge to the Langbehns' garden and found Carl at home, luckily alone. Knowing that he and Puppi Sarre were looking after a houseful of Jews somewhere in Potsdam, I do not think that I expected his reaction to my story. It was explosive. I had come to him for advice, well, his advice was quite definite. Under no circumstances whatsoever could I give refuge to the man, or to the woman. I did not know them, I was English, Peter was away, I had no idea what I had contemplated doing. Seeing that Nick was going to school, it could not possibly be long before I would be found out, and the punishment for giving refuge to Jews was concentration camp, plain and simple – not only for myself but for Peter. 'But –' perhaps the expression on my face showed something of a deep and very painful horror which I could feel beginning to take root somewhere behind my ribs – that twisting, turning wedding ring, the husband who knew how to move in the dark. Where were they to go? Was I to be the one to send them on their way?

Of a sudden I had rather a different Carl before me, different at least from the friend I had thought of before as a cheerful extrovert. He drew up a chair and, sitting astride it, took both of my hands in his. 'Listen, Chris,' he said gently, 'I know exactly the way you feel, do not think that I do not know. Why do you suppose I do the crazy things I do? Into the Prinz Albrechtstrasse, out of the Prinz Albrechtstrasse, pitting my wits against those SS bastards, saving the odd one here, the odd one there, but always wondering whether the next visit won't be my last, knowing all the time that single small acts of compassion are not the solution, they are stop-gaps which somehow have to be used if one wants to keep any sort of self-respect. It is little use racking our brains as to how we got into this mess. Believe me, it is the deeper issue, the elimination of the whole filthy regime which must occupy our minds day and night. Now you have come to a crossroads, a moment which most probably comes to us all. You want to show your colours, well my dear you can't, because you are not a free agent. You have your children, and while Peter is away you are my responsibility. You are British and, in spite of that fact, Hans Oster too has vouched for you, and, believe me, Oster is playing a very big game indeed. By getting yourself into trouble you – you,' he seemed to want to say more, but instead, 'would you like me to meet them outside and give them your decision?' No, I knew I could not allow him to do that if I ever wanted to look anyone easily in the face again. 'No, I'll do it,' I said, and as he took me to the door on to the terrace he told me to come back afterwards, if I felt like it. He would be there.

As soon as I pushed through the hedge again and opened our gate to the road, letting it click back shut behind me, I sensed rather than saw some movement in the darkness about me. 'What is your decision Gnädige Frau?' The voice, when it came, was quite close to me and pitched very low – it must have belonged to a small man, for I was staring out over his head. 'I can't,' I said, and I had to hold on to the railings because the pain in my side had become so intense that I could hardly breathe, 'at least –', did I hope to get rid of that pain by some sort of feeble compromise? 'at least I can't for more than a night, perhaps two.' 'Thank you,' again just the voice – the little man could not have been much taller than the railings – thanking me, in heaven's name, for two miserable days of grace. I loathed myself utterly as I went back to the house to fetch the cellar key.

The French window to the Langbehn's terrace opened immediately when I tapped on the pane. The spanking lie I had to tell Carl was still ahead, but he took one look at me and asked no questions at all. Moving quickly to the door he called his mother, who appeared in her dressing gown, radiating expertise, bustle and comfort. A colic, gall-bladder? Most likely something I had eaten, not surprising the food we got nowadays, mostly poison – substitute this, substitute that – disgusting. She had some pills though, wait now. I swallowed two obediently, and after a while the hard physical reality of pain seemed to retreat. I would have to go home, to the children; Louisa was on holiday. Carl shot a brief glance in my direction when I volunteered that bit of information, but he asked no further questions. Irmgard was obviously a straighter cup of tea than I was, or perhaps he just felt that I had had enough.

After two days the man and the woman left in the night. They left a little note. I never saw the man, but he must have been nice because the woman spoke of him with such affection. The house smelled of bees-wax, and our bits of silver shone gratefully with unaccustomed glow on the side-board in the dining room. Down in the cellar the camp bed had been folded together and the bedclothes piled neatly beside it on the stone floor. A pot of forsythia twigs had been moved and placed near the barred windows. Someone had told me that if I left them in the warm air, I would have blossom by Christmas, but I had forgotten about them, and they had flowered long since, and the branches were covered with sickly green leaves.

Christabel Bielenberg

The Bielenberg family survived the war, although Peter was for a time imprisoned in a concentration camp. Carl Langbehn was executed in October 1944.

‡

The oldest profession

The ingenuity displayed by many prisoners of war was not always directed towards attempts to escape.

Our troubles really started from the moment some of the prisoners began asking the guards if it was possible for them to be taken out for walks after working hours. The guards, banding together into a sort of guards' union, said that for five cigarettes a day they would be most pleased to take any prisoner for a walk, but naturally Lober's consent had to be obtained. Lober was only too willing to give his consent – providing that he also received five cigarettes from each man going out for a walk.

The men who went on those walks found them most pleasant, even allowing for the weather, but a little unsettling. There were so many young and attractive girls in the streets; girls who smiled provocatively and looked as if they would be very willing to grant favours if given the opportunity. With the sort of guards we had, the next step was almost inevitable.

The guards' union informed the prisoners that for cigarettes, many more cigarettes, they would be prepared to allow any prisoner to strike up an acquaintance with some girl and make a date with her for an evening meeting at some deserted spot outside the village. As Lober had already shown that he was not the sort of man to encourage private enterprise without wanting a substantial share of the profits himself, the guards omitted to inform him of the improvement they had made on the original scheme.

The scheme was so successful that it was not long before the camp was full of moon-struck men, waiting irritably until their turn came around to go out for another walk and another meeting with the newly found girl friend. As the guards had a long list of clients, they often had to wait weeks before their turn came around. None of it improved the general disposition of the camp.

But the situation did not really get out of hand until after the opening night of the *Gerfangener*'s brothel. This was an inspired idea on the part of one of the guards, who made a deal with one of the local prostitutes, and then smuggled her into the camp bath-house under the cover of darkness. After this had been safely accomplished, he came into our room and proudly announced that the brothel was now open to anyone who cared to patronise it. The bath-house was outside the compound, and twenty cigarettes was the exit fee. The guard was a little apologetic that he had to charge so much, but operational costs had been high. There had not only been the guard on the gate to fix, but also the guard on the watch-tower near the gate. The lady, now waiting expectantly in the darkness of the bath-house, would be quite content if she received either a pair of woollen socks or a bar of chocolate from each man she entertained.

Although neither Harry, Arthur, nor I were prepared to give the venture our active support, we willingly passed the news around. From the way the gates kept opening and closing for the rest of the evening, we gathered that the guard had no shortage of clients.

The camp brothel was a short-lived affair and lasted only the one night. Early next morning the guard who had organised it came storming into our room.

'The English are swine,' he shouted. 'Men without honour. They do not deserve to be treated with kindness. You do things for them and then they betray you.'

'What's the matter?' Arthur asked quietly.

The guard fumbled in his pocket and pulled out one of the thin bars of chocolate which were in all the Canadian Red Cross parcels we had been receiving lately, and also a pair of army woollen socks.

'Look at them,' the guard shouted, throwing the chocolate and socks on the table. 'Look at them, and see how the honourable English behave.'

When we examined them we found that the chocolate wrapping contained a piece of slate and that the socks were full of holes.

'Every one was the same,' the guard said bitterly. 'That poor woman didn't know she was being swindled. How could she, working in the dark, and with so many to deal with?' The thought of it all seemed to overcome him for a moment, and he lapsed into silence.

Harry chuckled softly. 'What a shower!' he said, grinning. 'They must have got together and rummaged out some of that slate that's been lying at the barracks since the huts were first built. They don't miss a trick, do they?'

'A silly thing to do, though,' Arthur said. 'Now they've spoilt it for themselves. We could have been the only prisoner-of-war camp in Germany with its own brothel.'

The guard suddenly came to life. 'The lady, of course, must be compensated.' He looked at us hopefully.

'Get out,' Arthur said evenly, 'unless you want me to tell Lober all about this – and about what happens on all those walks you take the prisoners on.'

The guard left quickly. Like the rest of the guards, he feared Lober second only to being sent to the Russian front.

Adrian Vincent

‡

North Africa

The poet Keith Douglas fought with an armoured regiment at Alamein at the age of 22 and then took part in the subsequent push through Libya towards Tripoli, during which he was forced to bail out of his burning tank.

I walked forward blindly and almost tripped over a man on the ground. He was a 'C' Squadron corporal, and his right foot was not there: the leg ended in a sort of tattered brush of bone and flesh. He said something which I could not hear, or which my mind would not grasp. After he had said it twice, I realised he was asking me not to leave him behind. To carry him seemed to my tired muscles and lungs impossible. I looked ahead and saw the sandhills stretching for an eternity, without a sign of life. 'Kneel down,' he said. 'I can get on your back.' I got on my knees and he fastened a grip on me like the old man of the sea. I tried to stand up, and at last achieved it, swaying and swearing, with the man on my back; his good leg and his stump tucked under my arms, his hands locked at my throat.

'Don't grip my throat so hard if you can help it,' I said. He relaxed his hold at once, and slid his hands down to my chest. I began to walk forward, with little idea of what I was going to do. As far as I could see I had half to three-quarters of a mile to go under the eye of the German tank commander, before I could cross a ridge and get out of his sight. No shot was fired, while I walked about fifty yards. Then an officer and two men of 'C' Squadron came out of a square pit where they were sheltering and helped me in with my burden, which we lowered carefully. Bill, the officer, had not long rejoined the regiment from a special job. He and the others began to put a shell dressing on the wounded man's leg, while I sat panting and regaining my breath. I realised I was still clutching two or three packets of Players which I had taken from my tank, so I handed them round. I told Bill about the German tank: I was still obsessed with the idea of escaping capture. I think if it had been hailing machine-gun bullets I would have stepped out into them without caring. My mind was not working properly. 'If we all stay here,' I said to Bill, 'we shall probably be captured. I think someone ought to go back and try to get a vehicle to get us out.' This was quite a sensible suggestion, but a wish was father to it. Bill agreed and said: 'You go. These are my chaps, so I'll stay. Corporal Hicks, Dumeny, Cairns, you go back.' We stood up and left the pit. A machine-gun somewhere opened up; I heard the noise of it, but did not see any sign that the shots were aimed at us. The men with me were walking along bent double as though searching the ground. I said to them: 'It's no good ducking down. If you're going to be hit you'll be hit. Run across the open ground. Run.' They began to trot reluctantly, and I ran ahead. Presently I saw two men crawling on the ground, wriggling forward very slowly in a kind of embrace.

As I came up to them I recognised one of them as Robin, the RHA Observation Officer whose aid I had been asking earlier in the day: I'd recognised first his fleece-lined suede waistcoat and polished brass shoulder titles and then his face, strained and tired with pain. His left foot was smashed to pulp, mingled with the remainder of a boot. But as I spoke to Robin saying, 'Have you got a tourniquet, Robin?' and he answered apologetically: 'I'm afraid I haven't, Keith,' I looked at the second man. Only his clothes distinguished him as a human being, and they were badly charred. His face had gone: in place of it was a huge yellow vegetable. The eyes blinked in it, eyes without lashes, and a grotesque huge mouth dribbled and moaned like a child exhausted with crying.

Robin's mangled leg was not bleeding: a paste of blood and sand, or congealed slabs of blood, covered it. I thought it would be better left as it was than bandaged, now that the air had closed it. 'I'll go on back,' I said, 'and get hold of something to pick you up, a scout car or something. Stay here.' I ran on. Before I had gone a hundred yards I was ashamed: my own mind accused me of running to escape, rather than running for help. But I hurried on, determined to silence these accusations by getting a vehicle of some kind and bringing it back, in the face of the enemy if necessary. I knew that if only I could gain the cover of the ridge and stop to think, and if I could find where the regiment had gone, I should be able to reorganise myself and go back, as I had after the first encounter with the tank.

Round a ridge of sand beside me the new lieutenant came walking. He raised a hand in salute and began to talk in a foolish flow of words about how his tank had been hit in the engine and why it had happened and how it would never have happened if only he had done such and such a thing, *und so weiter*. I walked beside him. I said: 'We must find the chaps, and get something to get the people out of those holes, and tell Piccadilly Jim how close the enemy are.' I was searching the ground ahead with my eyes, my companion looking at the ground by his feet. We almost walked past the remains of the regiment, drawn up on our left behind a ridge, because I was looking for them ahead and he was not looking at all. The nearest vehicle was Mousky's scout car, which I had had in mind, and I ran across towards it. In it sat Mousky and his driver. Another infantryman stood beside it. As we came closer I could see it was buried over its differential in sand, and would take anything up to an hour to shift. No one had yet begun to try. But beyond it was the scout car belonging to the Technical adjutant, Bert Pyeman, an ex-regular NCO, contemporary of Mac's. Bert was driving away from me. I shouted at him, but two of the Shermans fired simultaneously and my voice was drowned. Before I could shout again, my companion said: 'Look out. There's a trip wire.' I knew already; I had just tripped it. I should have thrown myself down at once, but a sort of resignation prevented me, and I walked on a few steps before the mine exploded.

I remained standing, numbed. It seemed impossible that anything could hit so hard and leave me on my feet: and as feeling came back, I shrank from movement. But the explosion of a second mine suggested to me that I ought to throw myself down, and I toppled forward and sprawled on the sand. A third mine went off, further away. I was aware of the new subaltern lying on the other side of the trip wire, which stretched between us as taut as ever. It was a bright new wire strung through wooden pegs: I realised that I had seen it and discounted it because of its newness, and because subconsciously I had come to expect such things to be cunningly hidden. People ran towards us from Mousky's scout car. I shouted to them: 'Look out for mines. Don't explode any more.' One of them said mistakenly as he came up, '*You're* all right, sir,' in a soothing sort of voice. I found I could raise one arm and waved it at Bert Pyeman whose attention the bang had attracted. He swung his little beetle of a car round and came across to us. 'Don't try to get up, Keith,' he said. I couldn't even try now: and it seemed incredible that a minute or two ago I had shouted out, for now I could only raise a whisper, in which I said: 'Can you get me out of here?' somewhat unnecessarily. 'OK old boy, we'll get you out. Can you heave yourself on to the back of the Dingo if we support you?' Bert had finished putting a very tight bandage on my right foot, which had been bleeding a lot. 'Yes, I think so,' I said.

Keith Douglas

The British entered Tripoli, which had been abandoned by the Germans, on 23 January. Douglas recovered from his wound to take part in the Normandy landings on 6 June 1944. He was killed three days later.

✢

With the Americans in Tunisia

On 8 November 1942, at the other end of North Africa, American and British troops had landed in strength in Algeria and Morocco. Operation Torch was a triumph, catching the Vichy French authorities in those countries wholly unawares. After three days they signed an armistice, prompting Hitler to occupy the area controlled by the Vichy regime on the mainland. The Allied armies then began to march east towards Tunis, intending to trap their opponents between them and the advancing Montgomery. Many of the Americans, however, were new to combat, and the going proved hard.

As dawn pierced the darkness over Monts de Tebessa to the east, we moved against the German-held positions. We ran into no opposition until we reached a point just below the first bench. It was like running up against a hornets' nest, with small arms fire filling the air with the sound of swarming bees.

A couple of sheep-herder huts made out of stone, about 10 or 12 feet square, nestled against the hillside on the far side of the sloping bench. They were defended by the stubborn German Infantry.

This was the strongest offensive action we'd experienced so far in the African campaign. When German mortars and artillery laid down barrage after barrage on our positions, the attack came to a standstill.

A machine gun on the forward edge of the bench had to be silenced before we could attack the huts. I informed my squad to prepare to move to the left, that I intended to outflank the gun, for the brush leading up to the bench afforded a fair amount of cover. We had to move with caution, for if the Germans stuck to their standard tactics, they would have men on the flanks of the MG 42 machine gun.

Gaining the protection of a large rock located to my left and a short distance up the hill became my first objective. I managed to reach the lower side of the boulder, but when I started to crawl around the right side of it, I received the shock of my life. I almost bumped into a German soldier peering around the opposite end of the large mass of rock. He wasn't more than four or five feet away. His right knee rested on the ground and his back was towards me. When he heard my combat jacket brush against the rock, he turned his head and glanced back over his left shoulder. We spotted each other at almost the same instant. As startled as we both were, the small advantage was mine, for the German was right-handed and had to swing his 'Burp Gun' around to his left before he could open fire.

For the first time in the war, I witnessed a disciplined and well-trained German soldier in action. This soldier's movements were automatic, and oh, he was fast. As he spun his body round to face me, I had the eerie feeling that I stared death in the face. The barrel of his Schmeisser moved at lightning speed, swinging in an arc towards my left side. I know my midsection must have contracted in anticipation of the bullets I knew were certain to spew from that horrible tunnel of death. I began to doubt that I'd have time to swing my Thompson the short distance to the left and pull the trigger. The advantage had been mine, but the superior training of this man from Rommel's Afrika Korps reduced the odds of me coming out of the engagement alive.

Chips of rock flew out in front of me as bullets from his 'Burp Gun' ricocheted off the boulder to my left. Hoping to throw me into a state of confusion and gain the fraction of a second advantage he needed to survive, he began to shoot, even before he'd gotten me into his line of fire.

In the heat of battle, the training I'd received instructing me to fire the Thompson in short bursts was forgotten. I did remember to keep downward pressure on the foregrip with my left hand to stop the barrel from climbing. As my finger froze on the trigger, the only thing I could think about was survival. I just knew I was going to die next to that rock, and that pock-marked boulder would stand forever as a marker next to my grave.

Not until I'd emptied my thirty-round clip of ammunition did my Thompson quit bucking, but my finger wouldn't release from the trigger. It refused to respond to my command and seemed to be in a death grip. Could I be dead on my knees and not know it? Maybe the pain would come later, for I didn't see how my life could be spared. All firing had ceased and a calm settled over the area. Even the German machine gun remained silent, its operator waiting to learn the outcome of his comrade's engagement.

In a semi-trance, I glanced down at my body. I saw no blood, except a few drops dripping from my face and hands caused by the flying chips of rock. I noticed where a couple of bullets had ripped through the left sleeve of my combat jacket. Only then did I raise my eyes and stare at the horrible sight before me. The courageous soldier was literally cut in half.

At that moment, I felt no remorse. Tense, excited and scared to death, 'Yes!' Maybe I felt as I did, because I'd been trained to kill. My mind and body were psyched up to such a high battle pitch, there was no room for compassion. That would come later.

I will never forget the astonished and determined look on that soldier's face, as he swung his 'Burp Gun' into firing position. Years later, I would awaken from a troubled sleep, wringing wet with sweat. Out of the darkness, almost life-like, that haunting face would appear, encircled in a 'Halo' of ghost-like light. The memories would be as vivid as they were the day we faced each other. I would close my tear-stained eyes and try to erase the horrible nightmare. It never left.

Fred H. Salter

Montgomery's Eighth Army continued to move towards Tunis from the east.

The morning broke unusually clear and I wandered into the village. In the main street half a dozen Tommies were washing in the horse-trough and I fell into conversation with them. They were Londoners, adolescent boys on their first campaign and enjoying a good deal of it. Their backs and chests as they washed were very white but their faces had gone scarlet through exposure. They carried on an effervescent conversation about the only three things that interest a soldier outside his regiment – the mail from home, food and women.

They were friendly and shy and very determined to do well in the war. I declined breakfast with them as my own at that moment was ready.

As I walked back to my camp the Stukas came over. They came very slowly and I suppose about eight hundred feet up, just a dozen of them with one or two fighters up above. There was ample time to run a few yards into the fields and throw oneself into the first available hollow.

It seemed for a moment they were going to sail by the village but at the last moment they altered direction, opened their flaps, and dived. The bombs tumbled out lazily, turning over and over in the morning sunshine. Then with that graceful little jump and a flick each aircraft turned upward and out of its dive and wheeled away. It all happened very slowly. They could scarcely have missed the centre of the village but they were very lucky to have hit a large truck filled with ammunition. The truck caught fire and the bullets kept blowing off in all directions, red for the tracers and white for the others. Half a dozen fires were started and the flames struggled to surge upward through the dust and smoke. One of the explosions performed the remarkable feat of killing a dove which flew through the air and struck down an officer who was in the act of talking to me. One of our men had been carrying a tin of eggs up the road and now he picked himself up ruefully from the sticky mess.

I walked over to the centre of the village keeping care to stay away from the exploding ammunition lorry. A twenty-foot steel water tank had collapsed like a fallen house of cards. The barn-like building in which we had proposed to spend the night had taken another direct hit and the coiled barbed wire had threshed about wildly in a thousand murderous tentacles. The blast had carried these fragments across to the water trough and now my six young friends were curiously huddled up and twisted over one another. It is the stillness of the dead that is so shocking. Even their boots don't seem to lie on the ground as those of a sleeping man would. They don't move at all. They seem to slump into the earth with such unnatural overwhelming tiredness; and I will never grow used to the sight of the dead.

Alan Moorehead

‡

Resistance

The Cretan runner

George Psychoundakis was one of the thousands of volunteers who constituted the rank and file of the Resistance movements across Europe. He was a messenger for the andartes, *or resistance fighters, on Crete who made full use of the cover afforded by the island's mountainous terrain.*

At that moment I heard a noise of firing and explosion in the direction of our hide-out, as if all Hell had been released. I thought at once that they had met some of our party and that they were shooting at each other. But what could we do – six men against at least two hundred Germans? The firing went on for five minutes, then stopped. I remained in the same place a long time, filled with anxiety about the fate of the others. The thick mist hid everything and I did not dare to move for fear of falling on top of the Germans, or over a precipice. I decided to go down and head for Kyriakosellia and find out what had happened. I took the downward slope in the mist, and almost reached the foothills. But there were Germans there too. Luckily I heard and saw them in time.

I climbed up again, and descended towards the village of Kampos, but on the way down I heard rifle-fire in the village and saw that the Germans were there as well.

I wondered what to do. Had those cuckolds captured everybody? I'll find somewhere to hide, I thought, and went up the mountain again. Meanwhile, dusk had begun to fall. I had had no sleep the previous night and nothing to eat for twenty-four hours. But what worried me was: what had happened to the others and how could I escape?

I headed downhill yet again, making a wide circuit. Night had fallen when I reached a foothill village between Drakona and Kampos. When I was a hundred yards from the first houses, I heard running footsteps coming my way, and, at the same second, the whole village was lit up with electric torches. I realised Germans were there also, and the footsteps were those of villagers escaping to hide. So I ran uphill again in the dark saying to myself that, to be on the safe side, I must expect everyone to be a German. I must be seen by nobody. I climbed a height half an hour above the village and went round the farther flank of the hill. Suddenly I saw the mountainside opposite ablaze with lights. I didn't know what it was at first and was very frightened, but when I reached the top of the hill I saw they were searchlights.

I climbed halfway down an overhanging precipice without realising it and almost fell down the rest. I wore myself out all night trying to get away from that accursed precipice. Climbing down, utterly exhausted, I flung myself full length at the bottom to sleep a little, betide what may. I slept a little while and was woken by rain falling on my face, so I pulled the hood of my cape farther down over my head and pressed closer into the side of the rock. Waking up again a little later, I felt a weight on top of me, but thought it was an illusion caused by my exhaustion. I opened my eyes. Day had broken, and what did I see? The whole world was white with snow, which had also completely buried me. I got up and beat it off and then headed downwards.

George Psychoundakis

Long after the war, the author was to find work as the caretaker of a German cemetery on Crete.

Heavy water

Deuterium oxide – or 'heavy water' – was vital to the German atomic weapons programme. One of the few places within Occupied Europe that could produce heavy water was the hydroelectric plant at Rjukan, Norway. Aided by SOE, a group of Norwegian agents set about destroying the installation on the night of 27–8 February 1943.

The factory buildings had seemed large from a distance. Now that we were among them, they seemed gigantic. The space between the power station and the electric-light plant was like a narrow ravine, recalling the winding alleys of Manhattan.

We waited and waited. We knew that the blowing-up party was inside to carry out its part of the task, but we did not know how things were going. Jens had a tommy-gun and a pistol. If the Germans gave the alarm, or showed any sign of realising what was going on, he would start pumping lead into the hut. I had a pistol and five or six hand-grenades. The intention was to throw them in among the Germans through the doors and windows.

'You must remember to call out *Heil Hitler* when you open the door and throw the bombs,' Jens told me.

When once we had reached our post, we both became quite calm, sensing that the operation would be successful. We knew that the Germans' lives were now completely in our hands, the only danger being that the blowing-up party might encounter unexpected difficulties inside the factory. The thin wall of the wooden hut was no protection against our automatic weapons. I was reminded of something which had happened earlier in the war. During the fighting at Tonsaasen we had surrounded a section of Germans in a wooden house. There were dead Germans hanging out of the window, and dead Germans lying inside before we had finished shooting the house to pieces.

We stood there, I dare say, for twenty minutes, but to us it seemed like a whole night – what was it like for the Chicken, Claus and Arne, who were quite alone?

At last there was an explosion, but an astonishingly small, insignificant one. Was this what we had come over a thousand miles to do? Certainly the windows were broken, and a glimmer of light spread out into the night, but it was not particularly impressive.

The Germans likewise clearly did not think that the explosion was very important: it was several minutes before they showed any signs of reacting. We had seen nothing of the blowing-up party's work, and for safety's sake Jens and I decided that we must take it calmly and wait a little longer.

A single German, unarmed, came out of the hut, went over and felt the door leading to the electric-lighting plant. It was locked, and he went in again; but a moment later he reappeared with a torch in his hand. He came over towards us and threw the light along the ground. Jens put his finger on the trigger.

'Shall I fire?'

'No. He doesn't know what has happened. Leave him as long as possible.' Our task was to blow things up, and not to shoot one German more or less.

The man directed his beam on the ground behind us, and once more Jens raised his tommy-gun. But the German turned and went in again. He probably thought the snow had exploded one of the land mines.

When we were sure that the boys were all out, we moved over towards the gate and the railway line. We discovered Claus and Arne ahead of us. We had arranged a password in advance: 'Piccadilly'. The answer was 'Leicester Square'. As Jens and I approached, we heard Arne's voice. 'Piccadilly,' he hissed. We only quickened our pace without troubling to answer. But Arne would not be put off. 'Piccadilly!' he whispered again. Jens and I grew impatient. 'Shut up, for God's sake!' we burst out simultaneously.

'What's the good of our having passwords if we don't use them?' Arne mumbled angrily when we came up to him.

Claus went on ahead, but soon returned with the news that the blowing-up party was already on the railway line.

When we had gone a little way along the line, Jens asked me if I ought not to get rid of the chloroform which we had intended for the Norwegian watchmen. I told him that I had thrown it away already. I had no desire to be chloroformed myself, and it would not take much to smash a tube to pieces. I had carefully removed fingerprints from the box before throwing it away, for the Germans had taken my fingerprints when I was arrested in 1941.

'Are you mad?' Jens cried, 'Don't you know the use of gas is forbidden in this war? And now you've started it!'

A short way down Joachim was standing by the railway line, where he had waited for us. We told him that the Germans did not know what had happened and that we had every reason to set our minds at rest.

One usually moves quickly in a retreat, and we went a good deal faster than usual as we hopped and slid down to the Maan and made our way across. The river had risen since we had first crossed it; in consequence of the thaw there was now a good deal of surface water on the ice.

When we were down in the bottom of the valley, we heard the air-raid sirens sound. This was the Germans' signal for general mobilisation in the Rjukan area. They had at last collected their wits and found out what had happened. That did not matter much to us. To capture nine desperate, well-armed men in a dark wood at night would be difficult enough for people with local knowledge; for Wehrmacht men it should be quite impossible.

On the main road things had begun to get lively. Several cars rushed past. When the last of us had crossed the road, a car came so close that we had to throw ourselves into the ditch. We saw that it was a large car with a gas generator in tow. On the other side of the valley, away on the railway line, we could see the lights of electric torches moving about. The German guards had discovered the line of our retreat.

Now we had to take to the hills. We moved as quickly as possible on the slippery ground along the line of telegraph posts. With Jens and Claus leading, on account of their local knowledge, we turned off by a sandpit just before the station for the cable railway. After walking through the wood for a couple of hundred yards we came to the Ryes road. The way to the mountains was open.

Knut Haukelid

The Germans were unable to manufacture heavy water for several months, and when they tried to ship it to Germany in 1944 the author was able to sink the transport in Lake Tinnsjo. The exploit was later filmed as The Heroes of Telemark.

‡

Churchill on de Gaulle

In London, Charles de Gaulle had become head of the French government-in-exile. Churchill's relationship with him was never an easy one, but that did not blind him to his importance to France.

In these pages various severe statements, based on events of the moment, are set down about General de Gaulle, and certainly I had continuous difficulties and many sharp antagonisms with him. There was however a dominant element in our relationship. I could not regard him as representing captive and prostrate France, nor indeed the France that had a right to decide freely the future for herself. I knew he was no friend of England. But I always recognised in him the spirit and conception which, across the pages of history, the word 'France' would ever proclaim. I understood and admired, while I resented, his arrogant demeanour. Here he was – a refugee, an exile from his country under sentence of death, in a position entirely dependent upon the goodwill of the British Government, and also now of the United States. The Germans had conquered his country. He had no real foothold anywhere. Never mind; he defied all. Always, even when he was behaving worst, he seemed to express the personality of France – a great nation, with all its pride, authority, and ambition. It was said in mockery that he thought himself the living representative of Joan of Arc, whom one of his ancestors is supposed to have served as a faithful adherent. This did not seem to me as absurd as it looked. Clemenceau, with whom it was said he also compared himself, was a far wiser and more experienced statesman. But they both gave the impression of being unconquerable Frenchmen.

Winston Churchill

Spring 1943

The Warsaw Ghetto Uprising

By April 1943, more than 300,000 Polish Jews had been taken from Warsaw and murdered at the Treblinka camp. Some 60,000 remained in the Ghetto, and when the fate of their fellows was discovered, the Jewish Fighting Organisation (ZOB) was created with the aim of putting up armed resistance to further deportations. When the SS moved into the Ghetto to begin its final liquidation, the Ghetto rose against them. One of ZOB's 600 members was Simha Rotem.

One day after the Germans began liquidating the Ghetto – on April 20 – as I stood at the observation post near the gate, I suddenly saw an SS unit approaching. With one hand I pushed the alarm button, and with the other I grabbed the fuse to the explosives. At that moment my commander, Hanoch, burst in, snatched the fuse out of my hand, and, after waiting a few seconds, exploded the mine. I was nailed to the spot, almost paralysed – a tremendous explosion! I had a fervent desire to see it with my own eyes. And I did see: crushed bodies of soldiers, limbs flying, cobblestones and fences crumbling, complete chaos. I saw and I didn't believe: German soldiers screaming in panicky flight, leaving their wounded behind. I pulled out one grenade and then another and tossed them. My comrades were also shooting and firing at them. We weren't marksmen but we did hit some. The Germans took off. But they came back later, fearful, their fingers on their triggers. They didn't walk, they ran next to the walls. We let the first group of six pass – a shame to waste ammunition on a small group. Then we burst out, with two homemade grenades, ten Molotov cocktails, and pistols in our hands. 'Shlomek – the gasoline!' I shouted to one my comrades, and hurled a grenade at the Germans. We threw the Molotov cocktails at them and they burst into flames, so we shot at the fire. A waste of the only grenade we had, and we retreated up the street, taking a position with the rest of the fighters. Quiet prevailed.

The Germans ran away, but they came back half an hour later. We welcomed them with Molotov cocktails and grenades. One of the Germans, seeing a girl at the post, called out in amazement: 'Hans, look! A woman!' and started shooting at her. But she didn't retreat. Protecting themselves with a strong fire cover, the Germans began withdrawing. One of our fighters, who had taken a position in the attic, poured shots on to the Germans near the walls, in spite of the heavy fire coming from there, and killed six of them. In the yard of a large building fronting on Swietojerska and Walowa streets, Dr Laus, one of the leaders of the Brushmakers' Area, appeared with two Germans in uniform. They were waving rifles as a sign that their intentions were peaceful. As they went from house to house, Dr Laus called on the Fighting Organisation to put down its weapons within fifteen minutes. We replied with shooting. One of the Germans was killed. Dr Laus ran away.

Some time later, the Germans returned carrying stretchers and gathered up their wounded. We took advantage of the lull to leap to another position. The enemy began using automatic weapons, machine guns and flame-throwers. They avoided coming into the Ghetto in orderly files and adopted the tactics of fighting in a populated area. Now the real siege began: the sounds of all kinds of weapons blended together – cannons, machine guns, mortars, light weapons. We all held our positions and the enemy was invisible. Despair! There was nobody to fight! The Germans took positions outside the wall and poured hellfire on to us. Suddenly, flames surrounded the building: flames and stifling smoke forced us to leave our positions. Three men covered our retreat; when we found there was nothing more we could do in the Brushmakers' Area, we decided to withdraw.

There was no advance plan for withdrawal, and not knowing what direction to turn made our situation difficult. In the chaos, I went to scout out a retreat route. I took this job because I looked Aryan, and I was wearing an SS uniform that allowed me to move around in the daytime. But there was a danger that fighters in other groups, seeing me from a distance, would think I really was an SS man and would open fire on me. As I searched, I came on a bunker at Swietojerska Street 34. When I started down, the people in the bunker saw first my boots and then my SS coat, and started screaming. I had trouble calming them down in time. We didn't think the bunker was a fit place for our group and we continued searching until we found another, well-built bunker, completely underground, whose inhabitants agreed to take us. After we gathered the whole group in that bunker, we started looking for the other two groups of the organisation, with whom we had lost contact. We wanted to turn this bunker into a gathering point for all the fighting groups in the Brushmakers' Area. Gradually, the groups began to assemble.

As commander of the mission, I had to appoint people to scout. This wasn't hard, since they volunteered. We went to search for our comrades. On the way, we came on some Germans but didn't get into battle with them. A few times we tried in vain to make contact with the other groups. As we retreated, Marek Edelman, Hanock Gutman, and I went to scout the way to the new position on Franciszkanska Street. I saw houses burning. Panicky Jews ran out, straight into the German line of fire. I tried to ignore what I saw. I clung to my mission – to find a safe and quick way to rescue my companions. Then we came on the body of Michal Klepfisz. Michal was an engineer, our 'operations man'; with the help of comrades, he had set up a small 'factory' to make Molotov cocktails. It was he who had made and planted the mine that had exploded a short while before. We didn't find his revolver on him; the Germans had certainly taken it. Before then, after the first battle, my friend Shlomo Shuster and I noticed two Jews trying to get out of the Ghetto. When we stopped them, we found documents proving that they were Gestapo agents. We took the documents from them and sent them off, figuring that the Germans would destroy them and that it would be too bad to waste our few bullets on them.

Finally, we met our two groups, who were also looking for us. We gathered all of them, eighty to a hundred members of the ZOB, in the bunker at Swietojerska 34. The people of the bunker welcomed us warmly. These 'ordinary Jews' wanted to join our ranks, but unfortunately we didn't have enough weapons. The echoes of explosions and the constant rumble of machine gun fire reached us. All night long we were busy cleaning our weapons, checking the bullets and the grenade fuses. Finally, we imposed a short rest on ourselves. In the evening, a few comrades went out to bring back Michal's body and to dig a grave for him in one of the courtyards. We dug in silence. Night fell and, between isolated shots, a momentary silence descended on the Ghetto.

Simha Rotem

For those Jews not involved in actively resisting the Germans, the next days were spent scurrying from one hiding-place to another.

It was now Tuesday, April 27, the ninth day of the uprising. Our end was very near. Early that morning violent shooting broke out in Niska Street. Dispatched to reconnoitre, Adek brought back the information that the street was full of Germans, shooting and throwing grenades into buildings. The entire length of Niska Street was one billowing sheet of smoke and flame. The fighters put up a fierce defence and our own building had joined in the shooting. We all were suffering from lack of sleep and food, but we were at high tension, gripped by a kind of ecstasy that made any effort seem within our capabilities. We knew our turn would come right after Niska Street's, but to die along with our native city seemed natural.

We heard shots in the courtyard and the baleful, '*Alles runter! Alle Juden runter!*' So it had come. Forty people held their breath and listened for every sound below. The summons was repeated several times, then silence. The noise of windowpanes being smashed. Izak peered through the peephole and whispered, white-lipped, 'They are pouring gasoline and setting fire to the staircases and apartments on the ground floor . . . Now they are coming across the courtyard.'

In perhaps half an hour the heat had become unbearable and thick billows of smoke began to fill the shelter. Our turn had come. 'Everybody follow me!' Izak called out in a terrible voice and ran for the exit. 'We're evacuating this shelter!' Below there was the sound of gunfire. Everyone rushed the narrow exit. No, not everyone. Nearly half our companions had not budged. They had chosen to take their potassium cyanide, and now they looked on with the gentle indifference of those who are no longer of this world, who can no longer be touched by such things as Nazis. '*Shma Yisroel*,' thundered the old Jew in a powerful voice none of us suspected his frail body could contain. And the voices crept through the shelter like a puff of wind: *Shma Yisroel!*

When we had made our way through the exit and found ourselves in the stairwell, the smoke and flames were just reaching the attic. Below was an inferno of fire. Our only way out was by the roof. We climbed the ladder, pushed open the trap door, and crawled over the roof to the trap door in the next building. We raised it quickly and jumped down: Izak, Adek, Bronka, Lena and I.

This building, 42 Muranowska Street, was not yet on fire. Not a soul could be seen, all the inhabitants were in the shelters and hide-outs. The house's weird silence and emptiness was like a cemetery, like ours had been an hour before. We went down to the cellar, through passages and tunnels to the rear of the building. In one of the empty apartments, on a password given by Izak, the tile oven turned on its hinges and opened the entrance to a camouflaged shelter. The shelter was cleverly built, supplied with all conveniences including running water, but nonetheless it was clear to us that it was a deathtrap. As soon as the Germans set the house on fire, the shelter's ingenious rotating oven mechanism would be heated out of shape and would not open and the occupants would be fried to death. But though we tried hard, they would not be persuaded. An awful premonition seized me and I could hardly wait until we left.

Again we sneaked through attics and staircases, tunnels and passages, and hid in cellars to which I felt instinctive revulsion.

We planned to get as far from our burning apartment house as possible and to cross to the odd-number side of the street under cover of night. The backs of the odd-side houses abutted on the backs of the Mila Street houses. Our aim was to reach a house down Mila and across Nalewki Street where there was a secret passage out of the Ghetto. By the time we reached the middle of the block, it was almost night. We were exhausted and our measly ration of biscuits and sugar lumps left us hungry.

When it got dark we set out to reconnoitre. Across the pavement was an empty plot, the remains of a building bombed out in 1939, an ideal spot for crossing the street, we thought. The problem was to find a shelter or a fighting group on the other side of the street, and we didn't have much time. German columns were moving down from both ends of the street and were bound to meet very soon. Before dawn Izak went on a scouting mission, promising to be back within three hours no matter what the outcome of his search. When he was not back at six, we could not contain our anxiety. In daylight the streets were covered by the cross fire from the German machine-gun embankments, and no one could move. We were without weapons and without a shelter.

Events overtook us . . . Again the barking machine guns downstairs and the heinous command to surrender. Broken windows, grenades, and gas bombs; smoke and flame. Already experienced in what those sounds portended, we instinctively ran up the ladder to the roof, to the trap door of the neighbouring building, and dived down. We had made it: out of the frying pan into the fire. The two German columns had met halfway and this building was already aflame, its staircase in even worse condition than the one we had just left. Smoke filled our lungs and blinded us, and we were half suffocated. Instinctively we decided to go back up to the roof, but there was no ladder. We hesitated only for the fraction of a second, then Adek climbed up on my shoulders and reached the roof. The two women pushed me up to where I could grab his outstretched hands; then we both pulled Bronka and Lena up, all but suffocated by now.

Warsaw roofs are steeply pitched, covered with tin, with a board that runs along the peak the length of the building, from trap door to trap door, from chimney to chimney. These rooftops are the exclusive domain of chimney sweeps, and figure prominently in little boys' dreams. We straddled the board and just sat there, intoxicated with the bright April sun we had not seen for ten days, greedily filling our lungs with fresh air: it was a moment of ecstatic relief. Below us the inferno raged. We could feel the whole building tremble with internal convulsions, the crash of timbers and the mounting roar of fire. The fair face of my son suddenly peered at me through the smoke, his head framed in golden curls: 'Will I ever see you again?'

'Lena,' I whispered. Never had I seen a human face change so swiftly; suddenly as I stared at it, my wife's face was drained of blood, of life. She said, 'Oh, *no!*' and turned to look at the trap door.

Catastrophe had overtaken us, indeed. In the scramble from the shelter, the little bag Lena wore around her neck had worked loose and was gone. It contained our last defence, our last refuge: cyanide. With it we remained masters of our life and death. It had been our most precious treasure, our final bulwark of hope. Its loss was the last straw: I tasted wormwood and gall.

But the fire wouldn't wait. I summed up the situation. We had two alternatives. Either we jumped from the fourth floor, or we burned alive up there. All were silent, defeated, expressionless. 'It's so hard to die!' Bronka suddenly cried out with new strength. 'Just look at this beautiful sunshine . . . At least let's try to get down. There's always time to die.' It was as if we had been waiting to hear her words. Down we went, pell-mell through smoke, flames, leaping acrobatically over collapsing stairs and dodging falling beams. Filthy, covered with soot from head to toe, we ran out of the doorway.

Vae victis!

In the courtyard a German officer in combat helmet and goggles stood with several soldiers. His left hand was raised in the air and he was studying his wrist watch intently. 'You certainly had pigs' luck,' he said when he saw us, half with approval, half with regret. 'A minute more and it would have been too late.'

Alexander Donat

The author survived being sent to both Auschwitz and Dachau, and was reunited with his wife and son after the war. The uprising was finally quelled by the Germans on 16 May. The SS commander in Warsaw, Jürgen Stroop, wrote in his report, 'Only the continuous and tireless commitment of all forces made it possible to apprehend and/or destroy 56,065 Jews. To this confirmed number must be added the Jews who lost their lives in explosions, fires, etc., whose number could not be ascertained.' Those captured in the Ghetto were sent to Treblinka and Majdenek to be gassed; in all, 2,284,000 Polish Jews were exterminated by the Nazis. Stroop was executed in Warsaw in 1951.

✝

A parachute drop goes wrong

After escaping from Norway across the North Sea, Oluf Olsen volunteered to return home to work with the underground movement. But when, on the night of 20 April, he arrived over Norway, the wind was exceptionally high and he had to decide whether to jump or not.

I was sitting on the edge of the hole again; the time was 2.07 a.m. This time the dispatcher had inherited my nervousness, and for me there was only one thing to do: to take the chance of things going right, and jump. The Halifax went lower – the contours of water, mountain and forest grew sharper – there was a terrible lot of snow – the plane swung – went straight for a few seconds – swung again – speed was reduced slightly, and the propellers set at high pitch – we went steadily lower – I was heaved to and fro – I stared at the dispatcher – green light, and 'action station' from the dispatcher, who had now raised his arm – I flung both my legs into the hole – fractions of seconds – red light . . . 'Go!' I started and – was out . . .

The wind howled in my face. I was slung round – struck my head against something, the rear wheel of the Halifax – I saw stars – many stars – a terrific jerk – more stars – a sharp pain in my back, my head – everywhere – the night was dark – I became unconscious.

The next thing I knew was that I was being jerked and flung about pretty violently; it was a little while before I really paid any attention to what was happening – and there – a few yards away, against the fearful wind, I saw the rear turret of the Halifax and the rest of the plane silhouetted against the sky. I was hanging from the plane!

If it was fear or pain which made me faint again, I cannot say, most probably both. I recovered consciousness, feeling that I was still hanging, that I was being flung up and down, to and fro at a furious pace – and I fainted again.

Before I finally recovered consciousness, a miracle must have happened: I was on my way to the ground far below. I looked up instinctively: yes, the parachute was open, but only partly. It looked to me as if some of the many silk cords which went up to the parachute had got entangled in the material and divided the whole 'umbrella' into several sections.

I looked down – far below in the darkness lay water, mountain tops and forest. I could only feel that I was falling a good deal faster than I had ever done before. But there was nothing I could do about it one way or the other. Yet there was something seriously wrong with my right foot or leg. It was hanging all wrong in relation to the left, almost at a right angle. I tried to lift my leg as I hung – but the only reaction was a stab of pain.

It was blowing hard: I was approaching a ridge just below me – dense wood – no, I was caught again by a violent gust, passed the top of the ridge and went at full speed down into the valley on the other side. I held my breath – now for it! A bunch of big fir-tops came rushing at me – the noise of branches breaking – something like a big besom hit me in the face – everything became still and strange – I had fainted again.

How long I was unconscious I do not know, but gradually and surely I came to myself again. A strange noise in my ears, a strange silence, and for a few seconds, minutes perhaps, I felt that I was dreaming – felt that I had come into quite a new world. At first I dared not move, but at last I tried. A burning pain in my back brought me back to reality, and I looked up, sideways and down.

I had landed in the top of a tree: I was hanging with my back against the trunk, and above me, a dark mass against the lighter sky, hung my pack. The fir-top itself was broken off and lay across a tree next to it and beyond, while the remains of the parachute were entangled in another. What a fantastic piece of luck! So fantastic that it could hardly be true.

It did not take me long to get hold of my commando knife and cut away the parachute straps: at the same time I twisted myself round to face the trunk, and slid down through the fir boughs as carefully as possible. I now understood what was the matter with my right leg; the knee had been dislocated and the whole lower part of my leg, with the foot, had been twisted ninety degrees out to one side. I could only hope that nothing was broken; but that a knee out of joint could be so horribly painful I should never have believed.

After numerous attempts, Olsen managed to reset his knee with the aid of a forked tree. Now limping, he needed to transport himself and his equipment across country. He was waiting for a train when another possibility presented itself.

Then a green open car came down the road at a comparatively slow speed. I must admit that I was so 'green' at that moment that I did not notice that it was a police car. In the back of it sat six Germans in full equipment with a tarpaulin over their legs. The car stopped where I sat. Involuntarily my pulse quickened.

'Got any matches?' The soldier in front leaned out and asked in a mixture of German and Norwegian. Matches, I thought – only those which are made over in England, exactly on the Norwegian pattern, but the best were good enough, no doubt. I handed him the matches without a word.

Then I had a sudden inspiration. The car was sure to be going to Drammen. Yes, quite, right, the car was going to Drammen. Could I have a lift? The commander, an *Untersturmführer* – it was he who had used the English matches with good results – demurred a little at first, but finally nodded consent. I could get in with the others on the deck behind. It was not impossible that there might be trouble on the train because I was travelling with two different tickets, so this arrangement seemed an excellent one. I man-handled my rucksack up first and climbed in myself behind it.

That was a drive I shall never forget. Beside me sat a little elderly soldier in a green uniform, who talked quite good Norwegian. What was I doing, where had I come from, what was my name, how old was I, where was I going, what were my political views, and did I know of any places where he could get some eggs in exchange for tobacco? He talked all the time with a good-natured smirk on his lips. Having satisfied his curiosity, he began to hold forth, and it was then that I first realised what kind of travelling companions I had got. For a good two days his party, along with two lorry parties from Kongsberg, had been combing the woods west of Darbu for parachutes reported to have been dropped from an English plane on the night of the 19th–20th.

I grew rigid with fear where I sat, and still more rigid when he went on to praise the style of our Norwegian rucksacks. It was the pocket in particular that was so conveniently shaped – and he demonstrated his opinion by turning and twisting the rucksack this way and that. I puffed feverishly at my pipe and tried to appear as calm as possible. (The fact was that never in my life had I been in such mortal fear as just in those minutes!) Then the conversation turned to the war, and we discussed whether the invasion of England would take place this spring or if they would wait till late in the autumn.

When we reached Mjöndal station I was not slow to take my leave and thank them for the lift. Quite remarkable how much better my knee felt during the first fifty yards away from that car!

Oluf Olsen

☦

Tunisia

On Longstop Hill

Longstop Hill barred the way to Tunis and became the scene of a bitter and prolonged struggle between the German infantry and the British First Army, which was advancing east from Algeria. It was finally taken, after four months of fighting, in late April 1943.

A profusion of things lay about all the way up the trench – empty packets of cigarettes, both British and German, water bottles and hand grenaders, half-used boxes of cartridges, German steel helmets, bits of notepaper, discarded packs and torn pieces of clothing. Through this mess the rifles and machine-guns were pointing out toward the next slope, but the men were not firing. The sun was shining strongly and they sat or leaned half in and half out of the trench. Some smoked. One man was mending a boot. Another was sewing on a button. But mostly they leaned loosely on the earth and rested. Every time an enemy gun sounded they cocked their heads mechanically and waited for the whine that would give the direction of the shot. It was only a slight movement and you did not notice them doing it at first. Sometimes the shells landed short, three or four hundred yards away, sometimes very near, perhaps only fifty yards down the slope, but anyway not on the trench. No one commented on the nearness of the shells. They had had much heavier shelling than this all night, and these spasmodic shots were only a nuisance that still had the power to hurt unless one watched.

There were several old London papers lying about. One, the *Daily Mirror*, had its last page turned upward and its thick headline read: ' "No more wars after this," says Eden.'

Seeing me looking at it, the soldier on the end of the trench said bitterly, 'They said the last war was going to end all wars. I reckon this war is supposed to start them all again.' The others in the trench laughed shortly and one or two of them made some retort. The men had greeted us with interest, but without enthusiasm. When they read the war correspondent badges on our shoulders they were full of questions and derisive comments. 'Why weren't you up here yesterday? You'd have seen something!' Then another, 'You can tell Winston Churchill we have been in the bloody line ten bloody weeks already.' Then a third, 'Are you the bastard that wrote in the paper that we're getting poached eggs for breakfast every morning?' And a fourth, 'Where's the Eighth Army? Aren't they doing

anything?' And several of them, 'How's the war going, mister? Is there
anyone doing anything besides us?'

They were hostile, bitter and contemptuous. Every second word was
an adjective I have not quoted here, and they repeated it *ad nauseam*. They
felt they were a minority that was being ordered to die (a third of them
had been killed or wounded in the night) so that a civilian majority could
sit back at home and enjoy life.

It was useless to picture these men who were winning the war for you
as immaculate and shining young heroes agog with enthusiasm for the
Cause. They had seen too much dirt and filth for that. They hated the
war. They knew it. And they were very realistic indeed about it. Instead
of sitting on an exposed hilltop in the imminent danger of death they
would have much preferred to have been on a drunk, or in bed with a
girl, or eating a steak, or going to the movies. They fought because they
were part of a system, part of a team. It was something they were obliged
to do, and now that they were in it they had a technical interest and a
pride in it. They wanted to win and get out of it – the sooner the better.
They had no high notions of glory. A great number of people at home
who referred emotionally to 'Our Boys' would have been shocked and
horrified if they had known just how the boys were thinking and behaving.
They would have regarded them as young hooligans. And this was because
the real degrading nature of war was not understood by the public at
home, and it never can be understood by anyone who has not spent
months in the trenches or in the air or at sea. More than half the army did
not know what it was because they had not been in the trenches. Only a
tiny proportion, one-fifth of the race perhaps, know what it is, and it is an
experience that sets them apart from other people. If you find the men do
not want to talk about the fighting or what they have done, it will be for
this reason only – they want to forget it.

Alan Moorehead

The fall of Tunis

*The North African campaign was marked by inspired resistance by the Germans,
despite their being hampered by a lack of supplies and by being under the control of
the Italian High Command. The Allies were handicapped by the rawness of the
American troops and by their poor liaison with one another, but when they were
finally able to unleash their armour on the plains outside Tunis, the German
defences disintegrated in a day.*

The vehicles had pulled up and at the head of the line a British officer stopped us. 'No farther,' he said. 'There are German snipers down the street. Wait until they are cleared up.' We waited in the rain, but no firing sounded and one or two of the armoured cars moved on again. In his excitement my driver tried to get ahead of the armoured cars, but I held him back, as we were already third in line and the only unarmoured vehicle on the spot except for Keating's jeep. We waited until two tanks and a Bren-gun carrier had gone ahead and then we followed.

Quite suddenly the Avenue de Bardo sprang to life. Crowds of French people rushed into the street and they were beside themselves in hysterical delight. Some rushed directly at us, flinging themselves on the running boards. A girl threw her arms round my driver's neck. An old man took a packet of cigarettes from his pocket and flung them up at us. Someone else brandished a bottle of wine. All the women had flowers that they had hastily plucked up from their gardens. A clump of roses hit me full on the mouth and there were flowers all over the bonnet of the car. Everyone was screaming and shouting and getting in the way of the vehicles, not caring whether they were run over or not. A young Frenchman, his face working with excitement, hoisted himself on to the roof of our car with a Sten gun in his hand. He screamed that he was an escaped prisoner and something else in French I did not catch, but I pushed him off, not sure whether he was friend or enemy. There were Germans walking about all over the place. They stood gaping on the pavements, standing in groups, just staring, their rifles slung over their shoulders. A Bren-gun carrier shot past us and it was full of Germans whom the Tommies had picked up, and in their excitement the crowd imagined that these Germans in the British vehicle were British and so they threw flowers at them. The Germans caught the flowers, and they sat there stiffly in the Bren-gun carrier, each man with a little posy clutched in his hand.

The double doors of a big red building on the right-hand side of the street burst open and at first I could not understand – the men who ran out, scores, hundreds of them, were British, in flat steel helmets and British battledress. Then it came to me – they were prisoners whom we had rescued. They stood in an undecided group for a moment on the sidewalk in the rain, filling their eyes with the sight of us. Then they cheered. Some of them had no heart to speak and simply looked. One man, bearded up to his eyes, cried quietly. The others yelled hoarsely. Suddenly the whole mass of men were swept with a torrent of emotional relief and wild joy. They yelled and yelled.

Handing out cigarettes, we caught their story in broken phrases. 'Four hundred of them, all officers and NCOs . . . due to sail for Italy today. Another big batch of them had sailed yesterday.'

There was an Italian lying in blood at the doorway and I asked about him. A major answered. 'He and another Italian were on guard over us. An hour ago a German armoured car went down this street and they put a burst of machine-gun bullets through the door, hoping to hit us. They didn't care about the Italian sentries and they hit this one in the head. He's dying. His friend went crazy. He rushed off down the street shooting any German he could see, and I think they killed him.'

We drove on again. On our left there was a tall and ancient stone viaduct and piles of ammunition were burning at the base of the pillars. A railway line ran beside the road. On our right there was a four-storeyed red building, a brewery. We were just level with this when the shooting started.

It started with a stream of tracer bullets, about shoulder high, skidding across the road between my vehicle and the armoured car in front. We stopped and jumped for the gutters. The crowd melted from the street, the cheering died away with a sort of strangled sigh. After the first burst there came another and another, and soon there must have been half a dozen machine-guns firing at very close range. The trouble was that one had at first no notion of where it was coming from. This was my first experience of street fighting, but I felt instinctively I wanted to get up against the wall. There were five of us in our car, Austin, Buckley, the driver and Sidney Bernstein, none of us with arms, and we groped our way along one of the side walls of the brewery.

The shooting now was continuous. Three lads suddenly jumped out of the nearest armoured car with a Bren gun. They dashed across the road, flung themselves down on the railway line, set up the gun and began firing. The Germans from the Bren-gun carrier had also jumped into the ditch beside the railway and they lay there on their backs, each man still holding his posy.

Looking up, I saw a line of bullets slapping against the brewery wall above us. As each bullet hit it sent out a little yellow flame and a spray of plaster came down on top of us. At the same moment my driver pointed up. Directly above us two German snipers were shooting out of the brewery, and we could see the barrels of their guns sticking out of a second-storey window. As yet the Germans had not seen us. Since at any moment they might look down, we crawled back to the main street. Keeping pressed against the wall, we edged our way from doorway to doorway until we reached the building where the British prisoners were kept. It was raining very heavily. There was now a second wounded man on the wooden floor. All this time the engine of our stationary car was running and the windscreen wipers were swishing to and fro. The bullets kept screaming past and above and below the car. It was in a very isolated position and directly in the path of the shooting.

After ten minutes or so the firing eased off. The tank had let fly with a couple of heavy shells and that had sobered up the snipers. We began to edge back to the brewery, hoping to get our car out before it caught fire from the tracers.

A German with blood pouring down his leg popped out of a doorway in front of me and surrendered. We waved him back toward the British prisoners. Two more Germans came out of a house with their hands up, but we were intent on getting to the car and took no notice. At the corner of the brewery two sergeants, one American and the other British, who are staff photographers, ran across the open road to their vehicle, grabbed their tommy-guns and began firing. They were enjoying the whole thing with a gusto that seemed madness at first. Yet I could understand it a little. This street fighting had a kind of Red Indian quality about it. You felt you were right up against the enemy and able to deal with him directly, your nimbleness and marksmanship against his. The American was coolly picking his targets and taking careful aim. The young Frenchman with the Sten gun turned up, and I realised now that he had been warning us about these snipers in the first place. He led the two sergeants into the brewery, kicking the door open with his foot and shooting from the hip. They sent a preliminary volley through the aperture. Presently the three of them came out with the two snipers who had been shooting above our heads. They had wounded one.

The sergeants then offered to cover us while we ran for our car. My driver was quick. He whizzed it backwards up the street, and we ran to the point a quarter of a mile back where the rest of the British column was waiting.

Clifford had been having a busy time at the crossroads. He had stopped one car with two German officers in it. They had pointed to the red crosses on their arms, but Clifford found the vehicle full of arms and he lugged them out. At the same time two snipers had run across to the house on the corner. A Tommy with a neat burst killed them as they ran. Mad things were going on. Two Italian officers marched up and demanded, in the midst of this confusion, that they should be provided with transport to return to their barracks, where they had left their waterproof coats.

Meanwhile another patrol of armoured cars had taken the right fork,

the Rue de Londres, down to the centre of the town. They took the city
entirely unawares. Hundreds of Germans were walking in the streets, some
with their girlfriends. Hundreds more were sitting drinking apéritifs in a
big pavement café. No one had warned them the British were near. The
attack had gone so quickly that here in the town there had been no
indication that the Axis line was broken. Now, suddenly, like a vision
from the sky, appeared these three British armoured cars. The Germans
rose from their seats and stared. The Tommies stared back. There was not
much they could do. Their armoured cars could not handle all these
prisoners. In the hairdressing salon next door more Germans struggled out
of the chairs and, with white sheets round their necks and lather on their
faces, stood gaping.

The three armoured cars turned back for reinforcements.

In this mad way Tunis fell that night. Here and there a German with
desperate courage emptied his gun down on the streets and hurled a
grenade or two. But for the most part these base troops in Tunis were
taken entirely off their guard and there were thousands of them. All night
there was hopeless confusion in the dark, Germans and British wandering
about together, Italians scrambling into civilian clothes and taking refuge
in the cellars, saboteurs starting new fires and igniting more dumps, men
putting out to sea in rowing boats, others grabbing bicycles and carts and
making up the roads to Cape Bon, and others again, bewildered and afraid,
simply marching along until they could find someone to whom they could
surrender. All night the fires burned, and they were still going in the
morning when the British infantry began to flood into the town in force.

Alan Moorehead

*The capture of Tunis, and the subsequent surrender of the Axis forces in North
Africa on 12 May, brought the war there to a close. Now the Allies could turn their
attention to the liberation of Europe.*

What I have seen in North Africa has altered my own feelings in one
respect. There were days when I sat in my tent alone and gloomed with
the desperate belief that it was actually possible for us to lose this war. I
don't feel that way any more. Despite our strikes and bickering and
confusion back home, America is producing and no one can deny that.
Even here at the far end of just one line the trickle has grown into an
impressive stream. We are producing at home and we are hardening

overseas. Apparently it takes a country like America about two years to become wholly at war. We had to go through that transition period of letting loose of life as it was, and then live the new war life so long that it finally became the normal life to us. It was a form of growth, and we couldn't press it. Only time can produce that change. We have survived that long passage of time, and if I am at all correct we have about changed our character and become a war nation. I can't yet see when we shall win, or over what route geographically, or by which of the many means of warfare. But no longer do I have any doubts at all that we shall win.

Ernie Pyle

‡

In mid-May, Churchill and Brooke travelled to Washington to resolve future strategy with the Americans. The British intended to pursue a Mediterranean policy, invading Italy first, then perhaps the Balkans, so as to diminish steadily Germany's strength. The Americans, suspicious of Britain's ambitions in Europe and heavily committed in the Pacific, had different priorities.

After the meeting Pound ran a small sherry party for the naval officers in charge of the ship which we were invited to attend. Now I am off to bed, and if we do not meet a submarine we should be in New York fairly early tomorrow morning. It has been a very comfortable trip, with plenty of work to fill in the time, and we should by now be ready for our conferences with the American Chiefs of Staff. I do NOT look forward to these meetings in fact I hate the thought of them. They will entail hours of argument and hard work trying to convince them that Germany must be defeated first. After much argument, they will pretend to understand, will sign many agreements and . . . will continue as at present to devote the bulk of their strength to try and defeat Japan!! In fact Casablanca will be repeated. It is all so maddening as it is not difficult in this case to see that unless our united effort is directed to defeat Germany and hold Japan the war may go on indefinitely. However it is not sufficient to see something clearly. You have got to try and convince countless people as to where the truth lies when they don't want to be acquainted with that fact. It is an exhausting process and I am very *very* tired, and shudder at the useless struggles that lie ahead.

Alan Brooke

The Americans insisted that the best way to defeat Germany was by a knockout blow through France and the outcome of the Trident conference was that, rather against British inclinations, a date was fixed for the invasion of Normandy: 1 May 1944.

‡

The Dambusters

On the night of 16 May 1943, Wing Commander Guy Gibson led 617 Squadron on what became one of the most famous raids of the war. Nineteen Lancasters, each armed with a 'bouncing bomb', took off from RAF Scampton to attack three large dams on the Ruhr, Germany's main industrial area.

The gunners had seen us coming. They could see us coming with our spotlights on over two miles away. Now they opened up and their tracers began swirling towards us; some were even bouncing off the smooth surface of the lake. This was a horrible moment: we were being dragged along at four miles a minute, almost against our will, towards the things we were going to destroy. I think at that moment the boys did not want to go. I know I did not want to go. I thought to myself, 'In another minute we shall all be dead – so what?' I thought again, 'This is terrible – this feeling of fear – if it is fear.' By now we were a few hundred yards away, and I said quickly to Pulford, under my breath, 'Better leave the throttles open now and stand by to pull me out of the seat if I get hit.' As I glanced at him I thought he looked a little glum on hearing this.

The Lancaster was really moving and I began looking through the special sight on my windscreen. Spam had his eyes glued to the bombsight in front, his hand on his button; a special mechanism on board had already begun to work so that the mine would drop (we hoped) in the right spot. Terry was still checking the height. Joe and Trev began to raise their guns. The flak could see us quite clearly now. It was not exactly inferno. I have been through far worse flak fire than that; but we were very low. There was something sinister and slightly unnerving about the whole operation. My aircraft was so small and the dam was so large; it was thick and solid, and now it was angry. My aircraft was very small. We skimmed along the surface of the lake, and as we went my gunner was firing into the defences, and the defences were firing back with vigour, their shells whistling past us. For some reason, we were not being hit.

Spam said, 'Left – little more left – steady – steady – steady – coming up.' Of the next few seconds I remember only a series of kaleidoscopic incidents.

The chatter from Joe's front guns pushing out tracers which bounced off the left-hand flak tower.

Pulford crouching beside me.

The smell of burnt cordite.

The cold sweat underneath my oxygen mask.

The tracers flashing past the windows – they all seemed the same colour now – and the inaccuracy of the gun positions near the power-station; they were firing in the wrong direction.

The closeness of the dam wall.

Spam's exultant, 'Mine gone.'

Hutch's red Verey lights to blind the flak-gunners.

The speed of the whole thing.

Someone saying over the RT, 'Good show, leader. Nice work.'

Then it was all over, and at last we were out of range, and there came over us all, I think, an immense feeling of relief and confidence.

Trevor said, 'I will get those bastards,' and he began to spray the dam with bullets until at last he, too, was out of range. As we circled round we could see a great 1,000ft column of whiteness still hanging in the air where our mine had exploded. We could see with satisfaction that Spam had been good, and it had gone off in the right position. Then, as we came closer, we could see that the explosion of the mine had caused a great disturbance upon the surface of the lake and the water had become broken and furious, as though it were being lashed by a gale. At first we thought that the dam itself had broken, because great sheets of water were slopping over the top of the wall like a gigantic basin. This caused some delay, because our mines could only be dropped in calm water, and we would have to wait until all became still again.

We waited.

We waited about ten minutes, but it seemed hours to us. It must have seemed even longer to Hoppy, who was the next to attack. Meanwhile, all the fighters had now collected over our target. They knew our game by now, but we were flying too low for them; they could not see us and there were no attacks.

At last – 'Hello, "M Mother". You may attack now. Good luck.'

'OK. Attacking.'

Hoppy, the Englishman, casual, but very efficient, keen now on only one thing, which was war. He began his attack.

He began going down over the trees where I had come from a few moments before. We could see his spotlights quite clearly, slowly closing together as he ran across the water. We saw him approach. The flak, by now, had got an idea from which direction the attack was coming, and they let him have it. When he was about 100 yards away someone said, hoarsely, over the RT: 'Hell! He has been hit.'

'M Mother' was on fire; an unlucky shot had got him in one of the inboard petrol tanks and a long jet of flame was beginning to stream out. I saw him drop his mine, but his bomb-aimer must have been wounded, because it fell straight on to the power-house on the other side of the dam. But Hoppy staggered on, trying to gain altitude so that his crew could bale out. When he had got up to about 500 ft there was a livid flash in the sky and one wing fell off; his aircraft disintegrated and fell to the ground in cascading, flaming fragments. There it began to burn quite gently and rather sinisterly in a field some 3 miles beyond the dam.

Someone said, 'Poor old Hoppy!'

Another said, 'We'll get those bastards for this.'

A furious rage surged up inside my own crew, and Trevor said, 'Let's go in and murder those gunners.' As he spoke, Hoppy's mine went up. It went up behind the power-house with a tremendous yellow explosion and left in the air a great ball of black smoke; again there was a long wait while we watched for this to clear. There was so little wind that it took a long time.

Many minutes later I told Mickey to attack; he seemed quite confident, and we ran in beside him and a little in front; as we turned, Trevor did his best to get those gunners as he had promised.

Bob Hay, Mickey's bomb-aimer, did a good job, and his mine dropped in exactly the right place. There was again a gigantic explosion as the whole surface of the lake shook, then spewed forth its cascade of white water. Mickey was all right; he got through.

But he had been hit several times and one wing-tank lost all its petrol. I could see the vicious tracer from his rear-gunner giving one gun position a hail of bullets as he swept over. Then he called up, 'OK. Attack completed.' It was then that I thought that the dam wall had moved. Of course we could not see anything, but if Jeff's theory had been correct, it should have cracked by now. If only we could go on pushing it by dropping more successful mines, it would surely move back on its axis and collapse.

Once again we watched for the water to calm down. Then in came Melvyn Young in 'D Dog'. I yelled to him, 'Be careful of the flak. It's pretty hot.'

He said, 'OK.'

I yelled again, 'Trevor's going to beat them up on the other side. He'll take most of it off you.'

Melvyn's voice again. 'OK. Thanks.' And so as 'D Dog' ran in we stayed at a fairly safe distance on the other side, firing with all guns at the defences, and the defences, like the stooges they were, firing back at us. We were both out of range of each other, but the ruse seemed to work, and we flicked on our identification lights to let them see us even more clearly. Melvyn's mine went in, again in exactly the right spot, and this time a colossal wall of water swept right over the dam and kept on going. Melvyn said, 'I think I've done it. I've broken it.' But we were in a better position to see than he, and it had not rolled down yet. We were all getting pretty excited by now, and I screamed like a schoolboy over the RT, 'Wizard show, Melvyn. I think it'll go on the next one.'

Now we had been over the Möhne for quite a long time, and all the while I had been in contact with Scampton Base. We were in close contact with the Air Officer Commanding and the Commander-in-Chief of Bomber Command, and with the scientist, observing his own greatest scientific experiment in Damology. He was sitting in the operations room, his head in his hands, listening to the reports as one after another the aircraft attacked. On the other side of the room the Commander-in-Chief paced up and down. In a way their job of waiting was worse than mine. The only difference was that they did not know that the structure was shifting as I knew, even though I could not see anything clearly.

When at last the water had all subsided I called up No. 5 – David Maltby – and told him to attack. He came in fast, and I saw his mine fall within feet of the right spot; once again the flak, the explosion and the wall of water. But this time we were on the wrong side of the wall and could not see what had happened. We watched for about five minutes, and it was rather hard to see anything, for by now the air was full of spray from these explosions, which had settled like mist on our windscreens. Time was getting short, so I called up Dave Shannon and told him to come in.

As he turned I got close to the dam wall and then saw what had happened. It had rolled over, but I could not believe my eyes. I heard someone shout, 'I think she has gone! I think she has gone!' Other voices took up the cry and quickly I said, 'Stand by until I make a recco.' I remembered that Dave was going into attack and told him to turn away and not to approach the target. We had a closer look. Now there was no doubt about it; there was a great breach 100 yards across, and the water, looking like stirred porridge in the moonlight, was gushing out and rolling into the Ruhr Valley towards the industrial centres of Germany's Third Reich.

Nearly all the flak had now stopped, and the other boys came down from the hills to have a closer look to see what had been done. There was no doubt about it at all – the Möhne Dam had been breached and the gunners on top of the dam, except for one man, had all run for their lives towards the safety of solid ground; this remaining gunner was a brave man, but one of the boys quickly extinguished his flak with a burst of well-aimed tracer. Now it was all quiet, except for the roar of the water which steamed and hissed its way from its 150 ft head. Then we began to shout and scream and act like madmen over the RT, for this was a tremendous sight, a sight which probably no man will ever see again.

Quickly I told Hutch to tap out the message, 'Nigger' [the name of his dog], to my station, and when this was handed to the Air Officer Commanding there was (I heard afterwards) great excitement in the operations room. The scientist jumped up and danced round the room.

Then I looked again at the dam and at the water, while all around me the boys were doing the same. It was the most amazing sight. The whole valley was beginning to fill with fog from the steam of the gushing water, and down in the foggy valley we saw cars speeding along the roads in front of this great wave of water, which was chasing them and going faster than they could ever hope to go. I saw their headlights burning and I saw water overtake them, wave by wave, and then the colour of the headlights underneath the water changing from light blue to green, from green to dark purple, until there was no longer anything except the water bouncing down in great waves. The floods raced on, carrying with them as they went – viaducts, railways, bridges and everything that stood in their path. Three miles beyond the dam the remains of Hoppy's aircraft were still burning gently, a dull red glow on the ground. Hoppy had been avenged.

Guy Gibson

Gibson then led the remaining five Lancasters in the attack on the Eder Dam, which was also successfully breached, flooding the surrounding area but having little lasting effect on industrial output. Their third target, the Sorpe Dam, was only partially damaged. Eight aircraft and fifty airmen failed to return. Gibson, 24, was awarded the Victoria Cross, and with it came fame and attention.

Guy Gibson, the master bomber, spent a weekend with us just after he had been awarded the Victoria Cross for blowing up the Eder and Möhne dams. He was in a rare state of excitement because Winston Churchill had invited him to dinner at 10 Downing Street on the Monday. Guy made a date with us for luncheon at one o'clock on the following day so he could report everything the great man said.

Primmie and I were at the Berkeley sharp at one – no Gibson. Two o'clock – no Gibson. We were just finishing our ersatz coffee around three o'clock when he came tottering in looking ghastly, eyes like dog's balls.

'How was it?' we asked.

'Marvellous – fabulous!' he croaked. 'God! I'm tired – that was the best yet!'

'What did he say?'

'Who?' said Gibson.

'Churchill,' I said with a touch of asperity.

Gibson looked stricken – then he clutched his head.

'Jesus Christ! – I *forgot!*'

A month later on his one hundred and twentieth bombing mission, he was shot down.

David Niven

Gibson was killed on 19 September 1944.

‡

Arrival at Auschwitz-Birkenau

Having been arrested in Germany in March 1942, a 15-year-old Polish Jewess and her mother were sent to the extermination camp at Auschwitz a year later.

It was ages before the train began to move. With no change between darkness and daylight, nothing but that electric bulb feebly on all the time, we had little sense of time and no way of working out how far we travelled.

At last guards came along and escorted women in twos and threes to the toilet. They had left it too late. By now there was mess everywhere.

I was drowsing, propped against the wire mesh, when the train slowed and finally clanked and grated to a halt. The familiar screaming and bellowing started up right away. 'Everybody out. Off the train. Get a move on!'

We scrambled down awkwardly in near-darkness. It was still night, but in the distance was a hint of dawn. There were hundreds of people stumbling about, trying to find their footing on the lumpy ground. We were dazed, unable to get our bearings. Guards moved in, screaming and shoving us into columns. We marched off along the railway line, tripping and lurching as we went. Mother and I stayed side by side.

We came to a gate with a motto above it in iron lettering, silhouetted against the sky: ARBEIT MACHT FREI – Work Brings Freedom. Men who must have been in a different part of the train were taken through the gate, along with some of the women. It was impossible to make out which women were chosen or why. The rest of us were formed into fives and went staggering on, picking our way with the help of the erratic glare from three layers of illuminated, electrified fencing. Above them stood a rank of high watch-towers.

The railway line petered out. We kept going until we were halted at another gate and a guardhouse. This was in fact the entrance to Auschwitz II, or Birkenau, though at that time we knew nothing of the names or significance of any part of this bewildering place.

A dank chill caught at us. The whole area was shrouded in a clinging grey mist. But dawn was breaking. Or was it really the dawn? A reddish glow through the mist was flickering in the weirdest way, and there was a sickly, fatty, cloying smell. Mother and I glanced at each other, baffled. Who could be roasting meat, great quantities of it, at this hour of the morning?

Whistles screeched suddenly out of the haze, and figures began to pour out of long, low huts in a wild commotion. '*Aufstehen* . . . get up.' The spaces between the huts were seething with people. '*Zahlappell. Alles aufstehen zum Zahlappell.*' Why on earth was there a roll-call at three or four in the morning?

We stumbled on our way and were driven into a long narrow building which we later heard referred to as the sauna. Women with short hair were pacing up and down, wearing striped jackets and trousers or baggy striped garments which could hardly be described as dresses. Each had a large green triangle on her left breast, identifying her as a German criminal prisoner. There was no uniformed German in sight. These hoarse-voiced prisoners were in charge of lesser prisoners, including newcomers like us; they screamed at us from force of habit, but at first none of the rasping words meant anything.

Mother stepped forward and addressed one of them politely. 'Excuse me, please, but could you tell us –'

'Haven't been here two minutes, and already you want to know so much?' The woman raised a whip. 'You'll learn soon enough.' Then she looked more closely. 'Anyway, what the hell are you doing in this camp, old woman? No room here for old people. Why weren't you sent over there?' She jerked her whip in the direction of that distant glow. 'How did you get in?'

'We've just come from prison,' said my mother. 'Thirteen of us, sentenced to hard labour.'

The woman gaped and looked almost respectful. 'Oh, you must be a political criminal. That's quite different.' It was very confusing. Having a criminal record seemed to put one immediately among the élite in this place. 'They'll be wanting you for questioning, then,' she added with some relish.

We were ordered to strip, and our clothes were thrown into large vats for decontamination. We ourselves were left under a row of cold showers for some time and then dipped in a foul-smelling, bluish-green fluid. While we were still shivering and stinging from this, the *Fryzerki*, the hairdressers, got to work. 'Arms and legs out.' We had to stretch arms and legs wide while they shaved our heads, under our armpits, and between our legs. We looked ridiculous. But even more ridiculous when we were issued with new clothing – if you could call it new. I got a pair of khaki breeches several sizes too large for me, a blouse with odd sleeves, two odd stockings and a pair of clogs. When I turned to look for my mother I couldn't make her out at first and when we did recognise each other we burst out laughing. Both of us looked so clownish. Oh, well – a black sense of humour might stand us in good stead. The uniforms, we discovered later, came from 20,000 Russian prisoners of war who had been massacred just before our arrival.

'*Anstellen, anstellen schneller, verfluchte Bande.*'

We were bullied into a long line and shuffled towards desks where a number of girl clerks sat, looking quite smart and respectable and with longer hair than those we had seen so far. They were methodically taking down particulars of all the *Zugänge*, the newcomers. I was just behind my mother, as usual, and while my documentation was being completed another woman tattooed her forearm. Mother's number was 39933. I became 39934. There was a sharp pain each time the needle dug into the skin. Not knowing anything about tattooing, I thought that when I wanted to I could easily wash the mark off. It didn't occur to me that it was permanent.

The girl tattooing my mother's arm had talked quietly to her as she did so. Had we come here straight from home? Home: the word had ceased to mean anything. Mother explained a few details, and it turned out that the girl was from our own region, not far from Bielsko. She was surprised that anyone of my mother's age had been allowed into this part of the camp instead of going 'over there'. She nodded towards the window.

'What is over there?' I asked.

'You'll find out soon enough.'

But the girl promised in an undertone that she would try to help my mother as far as possible. It might be possible to fix her up with work indoors, but not right away: nothing could be done during the six weeks of quarantine. 'I don't know if you'll last out those six weeks. The average life of a prisoner here is about three weeks.'

It was light by the time these procedures had finished. As we left the sauna, I thought I could hear music. I must be dreaming. Music, in this place, at this time of day? But in fact there was a band playing a rousing march at the gate as work parties of women streamed out.

We were told that we would be quarantined in Block 20 of *Lager A* – Camp A. As we were led off we got a full view of this section of Birkenau. Along the centre of Camp A ran a road known as the *Lagerstrasse*. On either side were the blocks: long stone-built huts with only two windows in each. To get to them we had to flounder ankle-deep through mud which clung to our wooden clogs. At the door of our block we were met by a heavily built woman, well fed and better dressed than those in the sauna but with the same gruff voice. She was boss of the hut, the *Blockälteste* or block senior, and she intended us to understand this right from the start.

'So, you're my *Zugänge*.' She put her hands on her wide hips and yelled at us. 'All right, then. Off to the meadow, the lot of you.'

The so-called meadow was a muddy patch of ground, without a blade of grass, at the back of our block. Here we had to spend the day, for no one was allowed inside the hut until night-time. It began to rain, but that made no difference: we were still forbidden to go indoors. We had had nothing to eat or drink since leaving Dresden. One of the girls timidly approached the *Blockälteste*, and was screamed at for her pains. By the time we had gone through decontamination and documentation it had been too late for breakfast here, and that was that.

Kitty Hart

Summer 1943

Yugoslavia

Following Germany's conquest of Yugoslavia in April 1941, two main sources of resistance sprang up – the royalist-leaning Chetniks of Draza Mihailovic and the Communist partisans led by Josip Broz, or 'Tito'. At first it was Mihailovic who attracted the Allies' support, but by the summer of 1943 it was becoming clear that it was Tito's forces – the most effective in Occupied Europe – who were carrying the fight to the Axis, tying down 35 divisions needed elsewhere by the Nazis and the Italians. The Germans began a ferocious sweep against Tito, which on 9 June reached his headquarters just after a British liaison mission had arrived there. Vladimir Dedijer and his wife Olga, a doctor, were both partisans.

Wednesday, June 9: Below Milinklade. – I had just closed my eyes when bombs shook me awake. Across the road from us, some fifty metres away, a scout had dropped its bombs on living targets, on one of the Fourth Brigade's battalions. A bomb fragment cut through the branches above us, but the column of Montenegrins did not stop. They just quickened their pace. And no one was wounded. Afterwards, nine Stukas came. They bombed Milinklade and the Hrcavka Valley. At eleven the Dornier bombers appeared. Bombing raids in the forest are terrible. The bombs burst among the branches and shrapnel hits everywhere. We are lying in a damp ravine; the stream laps at our legs. We are just looking toward the hour this day will end.

In the afternoon a letter arrives for Cika Janko and Vlatko. Both of them become deadly pale:

'Stari [Tito] has been wounded and one of the English killed.'

The entire Guard Battalion immediately went up above because Marko reported that they are unprotected and the Germans are approaching.

The bombs continue to fall all about us. Suddenly I hear someone calling:

'Comrade Vlado, Dedijer . . .'

Completely dishevelled, red in the face, breathless, ran a Russian nurse from Olga's surgical team.

'Comrade Vlado, Olga is calling for you. She has been seriously
wounded . . .'

Cika Janko told me I could go. The Russian calmed down.

'A bomb fell in the middle of the surgical team. It smashed Olga's
shoulder. Our doctor is wonderful. She told me, "Go, leave me; don't let
the Germans take you because of me . . ." Only, it is her fault that all the
medical equipment has been lost . . .'

We quickly climbed up Milinklade. The wounded are being brought
down in great numbers. The Russian told me that over a hundred comrades
from the Fourth Brigade were killed or wounded this morning on top of
the hill, where the airplanes spotted them on open ground.

The bombers flew overhead again. The wounded are being brought
down Milinklade in groups. The Stukas swoop down to the very tops of
the trees and drop their bombs. After them came the small reconnaissance
planes which began to bomb live targets. Seven or eight bombs were
dropped around us. The stench of gunpowder chokes us. It is completely
dark. When the smoke clears a little, I see lying next to us a comrade from
the Sixth Bosnian Brigade, a youth with wide black eyes. Both of his legs
have been blown away. His blood gushes out and, like a stream, carries off
the young beech leaves shaken down by the explosion. We could do
nothing for him. He died slowly. He waved his hand at me, whispering,
'Long live Stalin!'

I continue uphill. Beneath an oak, twenty metres above us, sat Olga. Her
entire shoulder was bandaged. Blood had penetrated through the dressing.
She looked at me with her deep black eyes and attempted to smile:

'Don't worry. It's true; the shoulder is bad.'

*At the cost of more than 100 dead, including British officer Bill Stuart, Tito's
fighters managed to break through the German net. Ten days later, however, the
pursuit was still continuing, and though her arm had been amputated Olga Dedijer's
condition was grave.*

Sunday, June 20: On the move. – I went to Medakovic. My temperature
was tormenting me. It was 39°C. Mitar called me aside at around noon. I
saw he wanted to tell me something:

'Olga's condition is very serious. We'll give you a horse. Go to her at
once.'

'I knew that yesterday. The amputation was too late. Doctor Pavletic
said that she had only a 5 percent chance of surviving . . .'

I rode for a full two hours with Gojko Mikolis on horseback. We found the Second Proletarian. They were carrying Olga on a stretcher along Romanija. She was fully conscious.

'Yesterday was horrible. I heard you were wounded. Have you had a tetanus shot?'

I did have to take a shot. Later, Stanojka Djuric came to give Olga a camphor injection, but Olga refused:

'Don't waste valuable medicine, Stanojka. Keep it for others whose lives it may save!'

The comrades put the stretcher down to rest for a while. Olga called me to her:

'Take care of Milica. Bring her up well. Don't let her become an army doctor. When you go home, tell her to remember her mother . . .'

These were her last words. We had to find new comrades to carry the stretcher. I went to the battalion commander. Olga died ten minutes later, conscious to the last.

I stood on the edge of Romanija, on the rocks, on the path which led from Stojno-Medakovic to Mokro. Night had already fallen, the wind was gusting, bending the large juniper trees. We dug Olga's grave with our bare hands and knives, because we did not have any shovels. A platoon was with me, our column's guard. All the rest had gone on ahead. We were two hours from the village where the Germans surely were. Olga lay wrapped in the white blanket. Her black hair nearly covered her entire face. The wind bent the junipers over even more, and Laza, the miner, by birth from Sekovic, a fighter in Serbia already in 1941, tore at the ground with his fists:

'Vlado, we have reached stone.'

A comrade on whom Olga had operated dug out the last bit of earth:

'She saved my life; we all loved her.'

We placed her in the shallow grave, piled up the clods of dirt and stone and made a marker, eight metres from the Romanija path, beside the very cliffs on the southeast side. Sasa Bozovic, Stanojka Djuric, three comrades from the platoon, and myself all took off our hats.

'Glory be to comrade Olga!' shouted Laza, and after him the rest of us.

We all set off into the dark forest, and reached one of the Second Proletarian's brigades in the dark, silent, walking through the dense, swampy forest. Olga had died for her people. She had died as a member of our Party. I held in my hand her watch which I had taken for Milica.

Tears began to well, first one, then two – and then an entire stream. I had much to cry for.

Vladimir Dedijer

✝

The Invasion of Sicily

On 10 July, the British and Americans landed in Sicily, the first step towards an eventual invasion of Italy and southern France. Douglas Grant was an officer in the Commandos tasked with securing the beach-head.

The landing ramp fell forward and shouting, 'Follow me!' I clambered down into the water that was disturbed into white spume by the men of the first wave struggling ashore. I lurched and stumbled forward, up to the waist in water that bellied against me, and furiously strove for the sheltering lee of the cliff to escape from the diabolic racket of machine-gun fire that whipped overhead. The smallest man in my troop fell in a pot-hole beside me and, surfacing with difficulty, unleashed an incantation of curses but still retained a firm grasp on his mortar's bipod. I made a last violent effort and found myself freed from the water and at the base of the low cliff. The cliff was not a vertical but a retreating face, up which it was easy to crawl if little weight was put on its crumbling clay jags. I climbed until it flattened out into a slope, and took cover in a sand dune as the machine-gun lashed a foot above my head along the rank of men on the skyline immediately to my front. My sergeant-major and batman joined me, and together we hurriedly ran over the rough ground along the cliff to the right, unravelling as we went the telephone cable that would be connected to the mortars on the strip of beach. Before any troop could need our fire we had to find a square house that had appeared on the aerial photographs as a solid cube, but in the darkness we could see only a foot ahead, and, when they were against the skyline, running groups of men. The wire defences were blown with a bangalore torpedo, the explosion shattering the night into a thousand fiery splinters, and we were through the reeking gap on the heels of the first troop. A track of loose stones, sheltered by a low wall and a line of rounded bushes, ran straight ahead from there along the cliff, and, slipping and cursing as the singeing cable cut our hands, we kept on until we reached the house, our objective. We fixed the telephone and, calling up the mortars, found that they were ready to fire. Lying on our bellies under cover of the house we stared ahead for the two green Verey lights to summon our fire. My heart thumped like the open palm of a hand against the ground, and my indrawn breath almost stifled me with its uncontrollable recurrence. A few shots rang out, a grenade exploded with dull percussion, and a stream of tracer fountained up into the sky, but there were otherwise few sounds of battle.

I began to get back my wind, and my senses, which had been dulled by the strenuous action, became aware again of danger. We had not examined the house in our flurry to set up the telephone, but we suddenly imagined we heard the quiet movements of someone inside. It was not the solid building which it had appeared on the aerial photograph, but a crazy hut of wattle and rushes with one door and no windows. My batman manned the telephone while the sergeant-major and I crept round to the front and flung the door open so violently that it fell off its upper hinge, at the same time covering with our revolvers the square room that our torches lit up. It was entirely empty and only the black ashes of a charcoal fire in the centre of the earth floor showed that it must have been occupied. While we were examining it, we heard the batman order the mortars into action; two green Verey lights had been sent up by the attacking troop and their signal called for supporting fire against a pre-arranged target. A dozen rounds were fired before they signalled us by a red Verey light to cease fire. The casually falling red ball thinned out and was extinguished, and immediately after its descent there were some bursts of Bren fire, the faint echo of men shouting, and then abrupt silence. We anxiously waited for any other noise by which we might guess the success of the attack, but the night had closed over the interruption as swiftly as water over a stone.

Douglas Grant

General George Patton led the US 7th Army in Sicily.

18 JULY 1943

Since the initial successful assault on the beaches before daylight on the tenth, we have continued to push along several days ahead of our assumed schedule. This has been due to the fact that having once got the enemy started, we have not let him stop, but have, so to speak, kept on his heels.

It is also due to the fact that the Italians and Germans spent tremendous effort in time, labour and money, building defensive positions. I am sure that, just as in the case of the Walls of Troy and the Roman walls across Europe, the fact that they trusted to defensive positions reduced their power to fight. Had they spent one-third as much effort in fighting as they did in building, we never could have taken the positions.

On the other hand, the Italian troops, most of whom are from Northern Italy, have fought very desperately. The German troops have not fought as well as those we destroyed in Tunisia. This is particularly true of their tanks. They have shown gallantry, but bad judgement.

The tally of prisoners, guns, etc., speaks more forcefully than words as to the success of the operation. While comparisons are odious, I believe that up to yesterday the Eighth Army had not taken over five thousand prisoners.

The enemy has been booby-trapping his dead, firing on us from the rear after we have passed through him and using dum-dum bullets. This has caused us some casualties, but has caused him a great deal more.

On the field south of Biscari Airport, where we had quite a fight, I could smell dead enemy while driving for at least six miles along the road.

The Germans have, on several occasions, put mines in behind the Italians, so that when the Italians attempt to run, they get blown up. This naturally does not make the Italians love the Germans.

There have been several very gallant instances. On the tenth, some Italian tanks entered the town of Gela, which was defended by Colonel Darby and two battalions of Rangers. Darby personally engaged one of the tanks at fifty yards with a light machine gun from his peep. When he found that these bullets would not penetrate, he hurried down to the beach, under fire of three tanks, got hold of a 37 mm. gun just unloaded, split the box of ammunition with an axe, hurried back up the hill, and went into position with his gun less than a hundred yards in front of a tank coming down on him. The first round failed to stop the tank, but the second did stop it. However, the enemy crew did not get out until Darby put a thermite grenade on top of the tank and roasted them out . . .

During the first two or three days, when we were having fighting close to the towns, the inhabitants were, to say the least, not friendly; but since we have demonstrated that we can destroy either the Germans or Italians, they have become quite Americanised and spend their time asking for cigarettes.

George Patton

A death in Sicily

The man was still semi-conscious. The chaplain knelt down beside him and two ward boys squatted alongside. The chaplain said:

'John, I'm going to say a prayer for you.'

Somehow this stark announcement hit me like a hammer. He didn't say, 'I'm going to pray for you to get well,' he just said he was going to say a prayer, and it was obvious he meant the final prayer. It was as though he had said, 'Brother, you may not know it, but your goose is cooked.'

He said a short prayer, and the weak, gasping man tried in vain to repeat the words after him. When he had finished the chaplain said, 'John, you're doing fine, you're doing fine.' Then he rose and dashed off on other business, and the ward boys went about their duties.

The dying man was left utterly alone, just lying there on his litter on the ground, lying in an aisle, because the tent was full. Of course it couldn't be otherwise, but the awful aloneness of that man as he went through the last few minutes of his life was what tormented me. I felt like going over and at least holding his hand while he died, but it would have been out of order and I didn't do it. I wish now I had.

Ernie Pyle

☦

On the Baltic coast, Leningrad was still blockaded.

24 JULY 1943. EVENING

Terrifying day! The Germans have acquired a new technique – a great number of short shellings. By this means they are inflicting a lot of casualties, as the first shell is always the most deadly, being unexpected. Besides, with this type of shelling, it is more difficult to pin-point the German batteries.

Yesterday a gas-driven lorry (not an ambulance) drove up to our casualty department, which is right opposite my window. It was full of casualties picked up on the street. The driver was a woman in army . . . (God, what a burst! I think I shall go to HQ as I'm on my own. ID isn't here, and Marietta is on duty.)

Sat in HQ for a while and came back. It's now probably about midnight. ID hasn't returned yet. He telephoned from town that he is waiting for the All Clear. He shouldn't do this. The first moments after the All Clear are just about the most dangerous. The Germans are waiting for nothing better than to start all over again.

What a lot of blood has been shed today! Another lorry-load of dead bodies has arrived. From beneath the tarpaulin legs protruded, some with the bone exposed. It's a white night and one can see all this clearly.

The lorry was about to drive up to Casualty entrance, but the doctor on duty came out, glanced under the tarpaulin and gave a thumbs-down sign. The girl driver moved on to the mortuary. None of the load needed medical help any more.

I haven't finished writing about the lorry that came during the day, yesterday. In it was a boy of 14–15 years old, an apprentice maybe, badly knocked about. His face was ashen. He was bleeding copiously. Both feet had been smashed, and hung in shreds. When he was laid on the stretcher he yelled:

'Above all . . . the waste of it . . . I'm so young, and what have they done to me! It would be better if I'd been killed! To hell with it!'

I was struck by the word 'waste'. At first I thought I'd misheard, but no. While the boy was being carried into the building, his cries still reached me: 'It's a waste!'

The boy drank a little from the mug that Efrosiniya handed to him.

The other people on the lorry were silent. The women were taken off. One was wounded in the chest, another in the legs. Her knees were burned black from gunpowder, and monstrously bloated.

All the casualties were carried out, and only some bloodstained rags were left in the lorry.

26 JULY 1943

Yesterday, again, there were many killed and wounded. The boy who had his feet torn off has died.

Important news on the radio. Mussolini has resigned.

28 JULY 1943

From yesterday's stories of surgeon B: how, during one of his operations – lancing an abscess – the blood and pus froze on his hands and covered them as tightly as a glove.

Vera Inber

Perhaps as many as 800,000 Leningraders died during the siege, which was not lifted until 27 January 1944. Vera Inber survived the war.

☦

The Downfall of Mussolini

With most of the Italian Army captive in Tunisia, and the Allied conquest of Sicily
virtually complete, on 24 July Mussolini lost a vote of confidence at a meeting of the
Fascist Grand Council. The next afternoon he went to see King Victor Emmanuel
at Villa Ada, the royal residence in Rome. At worst, he feared that the king might
withdraw from him command of the armed forces, but the Italian monarch had
belatedly realised that a more substantial change was needed.

Punctually at 5 p.m. the car entered the main gates on the Via Salaria which
had been thrown open. Everywhere within there were reinforcements of
Carabinieri, but that did not seem out of the ordinary. The King, in
Marshal's uniform, stood in the doorway of the villa. Two officers were
stationed in the hall inside. When we had entered the drawing-room, the
King, in a state of abnormal agitation, and with his features distorted, said,
clipping his words:

'My dear Duce, it's no longer any good. Italy has gone to bits. Army
morale is at rock bottom. The soldiers don't want to fight any more. The
Alpine regiments are singing a song which says they don't want to make
war on Mussolini's account any longer.' (The King repeated the verses of
the song in Piedmontese dialect.) 'The Grand Council's vote is terrific –
nineteen votes for Grandi's motion and among them four holders of the
Order of the Annunciation. You can certainly be under no illusion as to
Italy's feelings with regard to yourself. At this moment you are the most
hated man in Italy. You can no longer count on more than one friend.
You have one friend left you, I am he. That is why I tell you that you
need have no fears for your personal safety, for which I will ensure
protection. I have been thinking the man for the job now is Marshal
Badoglio. He will start by forming a government of experts for purely
administrative purposes and for the continuation of the war. In six months'
time we shall see. All Rome already knows about the Grand Council's
resolution, and they are all expecting a change.'

I replied: 'You are taking an extremely grave decision. A crisis at the
moment would mean making the people think that peace was in sight,
once the man who declared war had been dismissed. The blow to the
Army's morale would be serious. If the soldiers – Alpini or not – don't
want to make war for Mussolini any more, that doesn't matter, so long as
they are prepared to do it for you. The crisis would be considered a
triumph for the Churchill–Stalin set-up, especially for the latter, who

would see the retirement of an antagonist who has fought him for twenty years. I realise the people's hatred. I had no difficulty in recognising it last night in the midst of the Grand Council. One can't govern for such a long time and impose so many sacrifices without provoking resentments more or less temporary or permanent. In any case, I wish good luck to the man who takes the situation in hand.'

It was exactly 5.20 p.m. when the King accompanied me to the door. His face was livid and he looked smaller than ever, almost dwarfish. He shook my hand and went in again. I descended the few steps and went towards my car.

Benito Mussolini

Mussolini was arrested as he left the palace and incarcerated first at a naval base and later at a hotel in the mountains of the Gran Sasso, the highest in central Italy.

Rome hears of Mussolini's fall

Italy had never been put on a sufficiently well-organised military and industrial footing to fight a prolonged modern war, and any popularity that Mussolini had enjoyed had long since been dissipated by the deaths of numerous Italian soldiers in North Africa, the Balkans and Russia.

Midnight. The balloon has gone up! The Government has changed. Mussolini is out – Badoglio is in!

The people in the street are going mad with joy. Pandemonium is let loose! I hurry along to have a look!

26th July, 1943. To sum up this extraordinary night: about 10 p.m. Rome wireless stopped broadcasting. Then about 11.30 it gave the King's message:

'ITALIANS!

'From to-day I assume command of all the Armed Forces. In the solemn hour which falls upon the destiny of the Fatherland everyone retakes his post of duty, of faith and combat: no deviation can be tolerated, no recrimination can be allowed.

'Every Italian bows before the grave wounds which have torn the sacred soil of the Fatherland.

'Italy, by the valour of its Armed Forces, by the will of every citizen, will find the way of redemption in respect for the institutions which have always comforted the ascent.

'Italians: I am to-day more than ever united with you in unshakable faith in the immortality of the Fatherland.

'VITTORIO EMANUELE.'

This was followed by the message of Badoglio:

'ITALIANS!

'By order of His Majesty the King and Emperor, I have assumed the military government of the country with full powers.

'The war continues. Italy, seriously wounded in her invaded provinces, in her destroyed cities, will keep faith to her given word, jealous custodian of her millenary traditions.

'The ranks close in around His Majesty the King and Emperor, the living image of the country, example for all.

'The mandate received is clear and precise; it will be scrupulously executed, and anyone who imagines himself able to embarrass normal developments or attempts to disturb public order, will be inexorably punished.

'Long live Italy. Long live the King.

'PIETRO BADOGLIO.'

It was the evening of a frightfully hot day. The population was for the most part at home and undressed. Hearing the news, people rushed into the streets just as they were: in night-gowns, night-shirts, pyjamas, some in trousers and bare above the waist, some in slippers, some barefoot, all howling, yelling, screaming. Dishevelled, gaping, panting, they laughed and wept and threw themselves into each other's arms. They shouted '*Abasso Mussolini*' and '*Evviva Garibaldi*'! (Why?) They hurled down the Duce's pictures and trampled and spat on them.

An old woman who lost her husband in a Fascist prison and two sons in Abyssinia and Sicily, came running, carrying Mussolini's portrait over her head, and shrieking: 'That's all I have, that's all I have.' She then smashed it on the pavement and stamped on it, reaching in her joy the point of hysteria.

Somebody standing in the centre of a square bawled that it was no use burning black shirts. The people remembered well who had worn them. Trucks full of yelling youngsters drove along.

The 'Casa del Fascio' was raided, their furniture, books and papers were thrown into the street, where huge bonfires were made of them.

The publishing office of *Il Tevere* (a rabidly Fascist newspaper) was set on fire. People danced round clapping their hands.

The police and Carabinieri looked on, grinning. They didn't interfere at all. Only the most important points – like the Palazzo Venezia and the Palazzo Braschi where papers and documents had to be saved – were surrounded with troops.

About 2 a.m. crowds gathered in St Peter's Square, shouting, '*Evviva il Papa!*' probably under the impression that now, if ever, the Pope would be able to mediate peace.

For the hope of peace was in everybody's heart. All Italians I talked to this night were dead sure Badoglio's words: 'The war continues' had been only a face-saver. 'We shall have peace in no time,' they insisted.

I often heard anti-German shouts. A few trucks full of German soldiers, with machine-guns ready to shoot, drove through the Piazza Argentina. People screamed: 'Get after them,' but nobody moved. Many times, on seeing Germans, they shouted: 'Out with the foreigners,' and the Huns generally retreated. But I also saw them applauding a bonfire of Fascist insignia.

About 5 a.m. I was dead tired and went to bed. People continued to shout, scream and laugh. Through the mists of sleep I still heard the '*Abasso Mussolini*' and the laughter of joy.

Noon. I got up and went out again. People are still running, screaming, yelling. Everywhere the Fascist insignia are being thrown down. Firemen on huge ladders are taking them off the buildings.

The Via Nazionale and the Corso Umberto are in many places covered with pieces of broken glass and broken frames. Mussolini's pictures are still being thrown out of shops, apartments, offices. There are obviously millions of them. Buses pass full of demonstrating youths.

The population is delighted. To-day in the Mercato Generale (Great Market) everything was freely sold without rationing. People attribute it to the regained freedom. (In reality it is only due to the cowardice of the Mercato's director and his clerks, who simply didn't dare to show up.)

Spirits are as high as can be. There have been astonishingly few abuses. The gates of the Regina Coeli were broken into and the prisoners released. In the Via Volturno a couple of shops were raided, but only those belonging to notorious Fascists. A few Party men caught in the street were beaten. Passing people were stopped and asked to spit on Mussolini's busts or pictures. If they refused they were beaten too (that happened to X. from a neutral Embassy – the gang which got hold of him seemed to be one of organised Communists). Some notorious Fascist murderers, such as Pollastrini, were killed. But that was done by the families of their victims. There were a few cruelties. The Fiduciario del Partito from Trastevere was chopped to pieces in a butcher's shop. But taking it all in all one cannot imagine a quieter and smoother overthrow of a dictatorial rule after twenty-two years of its abuses.

M. DeWyss

✝

Escape or die

André Devigny was the head of the 'Gilbert' resistance network in southern France. In April 1943, he was betrayed after assassinating the police chief of Nice. He was taken to Montluc Prison, Lyons, where he was tortured by the Gestapo, headed by Klaus Barbie. Devigny was sentenced to be executed on 28 August. On the night of the 25th, with his cell-mate, he made his bid to save his life.

I knew that the moment I swung out from the roof into open space the last irrevocable decision would have been taken. By so doing I would either clinch my victory or sign my own death-warrant. While I remained on the roof it was still possible to return to my cell. Once I had begun the descent there was no way back. Despite the cool night air, my face and shirt were soaked with sweat.

'Hold on to the grappling-iron while I'm going down,' I told Gimenez. I took hold of his hands and set them in position.

Then I crouched down on the outer ledge, facing him, ready to go down the rope at the first possible moment, and waited for a train to pass. Gimenez leant over and hissed nervously in my ear: 'There's someone down below!'

'Don't worry.'

Then I looked at the sky and the stars and prayed that the rope might be strong enough, that the German sentry would not come round the corner at the wrong moment, that I would not make any accidental noise.

The waiting strained my nerves horribly. Once I began my descent there would be no more hesitation, I knew; but dear God, I thought, let that train come quickly, let me begin my descent into the abyss now, at once, before my strength fails me.

The stroke of one o'clock cut through the stillness like an axe.

Had an hour passed so quickly? The sentries' footsteps, echoing up to us with monotonous regularity, seemed to be counting out the seconds. There could not be so very many trains at this time of night.

Gimenez was showing signs of impatience. I told him to keep still. The words were hardly out of my mouth when a distant whistle broke the silence. Quickly it swelled in volume.

'This is it,' I said.

I shuffled back towards the edge of the cat-walk. Then, holding my breath, I slid myself over, gripping the rope between my knees, and holding the ledge with both hands to steady myself. At last I let go. The rope whirred upwards under my feet, the wire binding tore at my hands. I went down as fast as I could, not even using my legs.

As soon as I touched the ground I grabbed the parcel containing the second rope, and doubled across the courtyard to the low wall. I released the rope, swung the grappling iron up, hauled myself over, and dropped down on the other side, behind the doorway, leaving the rope behind for Gimenez.

The train was fading away into the distance now, towards the station. The drumming of its wheels seemed to be echoed in my heaving chest. I opened my mouth and breathed deeply to ease the pressure on my lungs. Above me I saw the dark swinging line of rope, and the sharp outline of the roof against the sky.

I stood motionless, getting my breath back and accustoming my eyes to the darkness. The sentry's footsteps rang out behind the wall, scarcely six feet away. They passed on, only to return a moment later. I pressed both hands against my beating heart. When all was quiet again I worked round to the doorway, and flattened myself against it. I felt all my human reactions being swallowed up by pure animal instinct, the instinct for self-preservation which quickens the reflexes and gives one fresh reserves of strength.

It was my life or his.

As his footsteps approached I tried to press myself into the wood against which my back was resting. Then, when I heard him change direction, I risked a quick glance out of my hiding-place to see exactly where he was.

He did exactly the same thing twice, and still I waited.

I got a good grip on the ground with my heels; I could not afford to slip. The footsteps moved in my direction, grew louder. The sentry began to turn . . .

I sprang out of my recess like a panther, and got my hands round his throat in a deadly grip. With frantic violence I began to throttle him. I was no longer a man, but a wild animal. I squeezed and squeezed, with the terrible strength of desperation. My teeth were gritting against each other, my eyes bursting out of my head. I threw back my head to exert extra pressure, and felt my fingers bite deep into his neck. Already half-strangled, the muscles of his throat torn and engorged, only held upright by my vice-like grip, the sentry still feebly raised his arms as if to defend himself; but an instant later they fell back, inert. But this did not make me let go. For perhaps three minutes longer I maintained my pressure on his throat, as if afraid that one last cry, or even the death-rattle, might give me away. Then, slowly, I loosened my blood-stained fingers, ready to close them again at the least movement; but the body remained slack and lifeless. I lowered it gently to the ground.

I stared down at the steel helmet which, fortunately perhaps, concealed the sentry's face; at the dark hunched shape of the body itself, at the sub-machine gun and the bayonet. I thought for a moment, then quickly drew the bayonet from its scabbard, gripped it by the hilt in both hands, and plunged it down with one straight, hard stroke into the sentry's back.

I raised my head, and saw that I was standing immediately below the window of cell 45. Old memories fireworked up in my mind: hunger and thirst, the beatings I had suffered, the handcuffs, the condemned man in the next cell, Fränzel spitting in my face.

My revenge had begun.

Having reached a sloping roof, Devigny needed to cross a broad track below him to reach the perimeter wall. The path was patrolled by sentries on bicycles.

Three o'clock.

Gimenez was becoming desperate. At last I decided to move. Holding the end of the rope firmly in one hand, I coiled it across my left arm like a lasso. With the other hand I grasped the grappling-iron. As soon as the sentry had pedalled past, I threw the line as hard as I could towards the opposite wall. The rope snaked up and out, and the grappling-iron fell behind the parapet. I tugged very gently on it, trying to let it find a natural anchorage. Apparently I had been successful; it held firm. A strand of barbed wire, which I had not previously noticed, rattled alarmingly as the rope jerked over it. After a little, however, it was pressed down to the level of the wall.

I gave one violent pull, but the rope did not budge. It had caught first time. I breathed again.

'Give me the other hook,' I muttered to Gimenez. I could feel him trembling.

The cyclist was coming round again now. I froze abruptly. For the first time he passed actually under the rope. When he had gone I threaded the rope through the wire loop and pulled it as tight as we could. While Gimenez held it firm to prevent it slipping, I knotted it tightly, and fixed the grappling-iron in a crevice on the near side of the parapet. In my fear of running things too fine I had actually overcalculated the amount of rope necessary; over six feet were left trailing loose on the roof. That thin line stretching across the perimeter looked hardly less fragile than the telephone-wires which followed a similar route a few yards away.

I made several further tests when the cyclist was round the other side. I unanchored the grappling-iron on our side, and then we both of us pulled on the rope as hard as we could to try out its strength.

If the truth must be told, I was horribly afraid that it would snap, and I would be left crippled in the perimeter. When I pulled on it with all my strength I could feel it stretch. One last little effort and the whole thing would be over; but I had reached the absolute end of my courage, physical endurance, and will-power alike. All the time the cyclist continued to ride round beneath us.

Four o'clock struck.

In the distance, towards the station, the red lights on the railway line still shone out. But the first glimmer of dawn was already creeping up over the horizon, and the lights showed less bright every moment. We could wait no longer.

'Over you go, Gimenez. You're lighter than I am.'

'No. You go first.'

'It's your turn.'

'I won't.'

'Go on, it's up to you.'

'No,' he said desperately, 'I can't do it.'

The cyclist turned the corner again. I shook Gimenez desperately, my fingers itching to hit him.

'Are you going, yes or no?'

'No,' he cried, 'no, *no!*'

'Shut up, for God's sake!' I said. I could not conquer his fear; I said no more. Still the German pedalled round his beat. Once he stopped almost directly beneath us, got off his machine, and urinated against the wall. It was at once a comic and terrifying sight. As time passed and the dawn approached, our chances of success grew steadily less. I knew it, yet I still hesitated. Gimenez shivered in silence.

Abruptly, as the sentry passed us yet again, I stooped forward, gripped the rope with both hands, swung out into space, and got my legs up into position. Hand over hand, my back hanging exposed above the void, I pulled myself across with desperate speed. I reached the far wall, got one arm over it, and scrambled up.

I had done it. I had escaped.

A delirious feeling of triumph swept over me. I forgot how exhausted I was; I almost forgot Gimenez, who was still waiting for the sentry to pass under him again before following me. I was oblivious to my thudding heart and hoarse breath; my knees might tremble, my face be dripping with sweat, my hands scored and bleeding, my throat choked, my head bursting, but I neither knew nor cared. All I was conscious of was the smell of life, the freedom I had won against such desperate odds. I uttered a quick and thankful prayer to God for bringing me through safely.

I moved along the top of the wall towards the courthouse buildings, where it lost height considerably. I stopped just short of a small gateway. Workmen were going past in the street outside, and I waited a few moments before jumping down. This gave Gimenez time to catch up with me.

At five o'clock we were walking down the street in our socks and shirt-sleeves – free men.

We wanted to shout out loud with joy, to run, dance, go completely mad. Never till now had I understood the full force and meaning of the word *freedom*.

André Devigny

‡

Beri beri

In Thailand, POW Russell Braddon struggled to rid himself of a degenerative nerve disease.

By this time the fluids of the wet beri beri which swamped me were flopping round in my chest, having crept up from my legs, and a most unwelcome sound it was. The Nips now abandoned their drawing of graves and crosses on the ground and instead mimed a man drowning. I had become indifferent towards many modes of death, but drowning could never be one of them. The only preventative I could think of was to consume sufficient Vitamin B tablets (they would have, of course, to be stolen from the Japs) to overcome the deficiency which caused the beri beri.

A large force of Japanese reinforcements came sloshing up the jungle trail, shoving mountain artillery along with them. Their hoarse, rhythmic shouts of 'Esau, Esau' as they pushed mountain guns along mud tracks sounded harsh and bad-tempered. They were not misleading.

Though we had just finished a particularly heavy shift we were routed out to light fires, boil water, cook food. An officer thrust his waterproof cape at me and indicated that I was to dry it. I was shivering with a malarial rigour.

Standing in front of the fire with the cape I found it impossible not to sway on my unstable legs. Soon the inevitable occurred – the cape caught alight. Before I extinguished the flame one large corner of the gentleman's garment had vanished into a tiny heap of ash and a black cloud of pungent smoke.

The gentleman himself was not slow to notice any of these things. With a hoarse 'Currah', he leapt up. He kicked, leaving a perfect impression of his toe-cap in my sodden flesh for hours afterwards: he swiped with his bayonet, cutting open the back of my head: and he then, for good measure, shoved me firmly into the fire. Bloated as I was, I was slow to move. I was surprised to notice that, though the skin bubbled and the flesh smelt singed, I felt nothing. The beri beri had at least done that for me, I reflected gratefully. On the other hand, however little it hurt, one couldn't afford to remain sprawled in a fire for long. Snowy solved the problem by ignoring the officer's bellows and dragging me out. It was all over in seconds, but it did nothing to heighten in my mind my impressions of *Bushido* or Japanese Chivalry.

Muttering to himself, as Snowy brushed me free of embers, the officer took his charred cape and placed it resentfully over his other possessions. Following his actions with a wary eye, I noticed that from the top of his haversack there protruded a large bottle of Vitamin B tablets.

When I left the guard house, so did the bottle. That night I sat up and ate solidly the small brown tablets of bran so rich in Vitamin B. They did not make easy eating, but I was a man who for a hundred days had been mocked by the Japanese as a perambulating corpse, so I continued munching. By morning the bottle was empty. I did not require my small ration of rice.

About two days later I reaped the profits of my theft. We had just gone to our bed-spaces and I was laboriously scrubbing clean (with a few drops of water in my mug and my tooth brush) the burns I had received on my hands, arms and legs as a result of being booted so unceremoniously into a fire. It suddenly became necessary to urinate. I crawled the thirty yards to our make-shift urinal and obliged, and started to crawl back to the tent. I had only gone half-way, however, when it became necessary to reverse.

Eventually, I stayed there and every ten minutes or so for two days fluid poured out of me. My chest no longer looked puffy: my stomach lost its thick pregnant look: my knees reappeared: then my ankles: then my toes. The beri beri bloated pudding was gone. In its place stood a skeleton which had never in all its life been so pleased with its physical condition than at this moment, when, according to the Japanese quartermaster's scales, it weighed eighty-one pounds.

Russell Braddon

‡

Running the gauntlet

On 17 August, the USAAF launched 376 aircraft against the ball-bearing factories at Schweinfurt and the Messerschmitt works at Regensburg, deep inside Germany. Attached to the latter mission was correspondent Beirne Lay, whose account of the dangers faced by the bomber crews ranks as one of the war's most vivid descriptions of aerial combat. The raids were made in daylight and without fighter escort, resulting in the loss of almost one in eight of the attacking force. They began to meet opposition shortly after crossing the Dutch coast.

I knew that we were in a lively fight. Every alarm bell in my brain and heart was ringing a high-pitched warning. But my nerves were steady and my brain working. The fear was unpleasant, but it was bearable. I knew that I was going to die, and so were a lot of others. What I didn't know was that the real fight, the *Anschluss* of Luftwaffe 20-mm. cannon shells, hadn't really begun. The largest and most savage fighter resistance of any war in history was rising to stop us at any cost, and our group was the most vulnerable target.

A few minutes later we absorbed the first wave of a hailstorm of individual fighter attacks that were to engulf us clear to the target in such a blizzard of bullets and shells that a chronological account is difficult. It was at 10:41, over Eupen, that I looked out the window after a minute's lull, and saw two whole squadrons, twelve Me-109s and eleven FW-190s, climbing parallel to us as though they were on a steep escalator. The first squadron had reached our level and was pulling ahead to turn into us. The second was not far behind. Several thousand feet below us were many more fighters, their noses cocked up in a maximum climb. Over the interphone came reports of an equal number of enemy aircraft deploying on the other side of the formation.

For the first time I noticed an Me-110 sitting out of range on our level out to the right. He was to stay with us all the way to the target, apparently radioing our position and weak spots to fresh *Staffeln* waiting farther down the road.

At the sight of all these fighters, I had the distinct feeling of being trapped – that the Hun had been tipped off or at least had guessed our destination and was set for us. We were already through the German fighter belt. Obviously, they had moved a lot of squadrons back in a fluid defence in depth, and they must have been saving up some outfits for the inner defence that we didn't know about. The life expectancy of our group seemed definitely limited, since it had already appeared that the fighters, instead of wasting fuel trying to overhaul the preceding groups, were glad to take a cut at us.

Swinging their yellow noses around in a wide U turn, the twelve-ship squadron of Me-109s came in from twelve to two o'clock in pairs. The main event was on. I fought an impulse to close my eyes, and overcame it.

A shining silver rectangle of metal sailed past over our right wing. I recognised it as a main-exit door. Seconds later, a black lump came hurtling through the formation, barely missing several propellers. It was a man, clasping his knees to his head, revolving like a diver in a triple somersault, shooting by us so close that I saw a piece of paper blow out of his leather jacket. He was evidently making a delayed jump, for I didn't see his parachute open.

A B-17 turned gradually out of the formation to the right, maintaining altitude. In a split second it completely vanished in a brilliant explosion, from which the only remains were four balls of fire, the fuel tanks, which were quickly consumed as they fell earthward.

I saw blue, red, yellow and aluminium-coloured fighters. Their tactics were running fairly true to form, with frontal attacks hitting the low squadron and rear attackers going for the lead and high squadrons. Some of the jerries shot at us with rockets, and an attempt at air-to-air bombing was made with little black time-fuse sticks, dropped from above, which exploded in small grey puffs off to one side of the formation. Several of the FWs did some nice deflection shooting on side attacks from 500 yards at the high group, then raked the low group on the breakaway at closer range with their noses cocked in a side slip, to keep the formation in their sights longer in the turn. External fuel tanks were visible under the bellies or wings of at least two squadrons, shedding uncomfortable light on the mystery of their ability to tail us so far from their bases.

The manner of the assaults indicated that the pilots knew where we were going and were inspired with a fanatical determination to stop us before we got there. Many pressed attacks home to 250 yards or less, or bolted right through the formation wide out, firing long twenty-second bursts, often presenting point-blank targets on the breakaway. Some committed the fatal error of pulling up instead of going down and out. More experienced pilots came in on frontal attacks with a noticeably slower rate of closure, apparently throttled back, obtaining greater accuracy. But no tactics could halt the close-knit juggernauts of our Fortresses, nor save the single-seaters from paying a terrible price.

Our airplane was endangered by various debris. Emergency hatches, exit doors, prematurely opened parachutes, bodies and assorted fragments of B-17s and Hun fighters breezed past us in the slip stream.

I watched two fighters explode not far beneath, disappear in sheets of orange flame; B-17s dropping out in every stage of distress, from engines on fire to controls shot away; friendly and enemy parachutes floating down, and, on the green carpet far below us, funeral pyres of smoke from fallen fighters, marking our trail.

On we flew through the cluttered wake of a desperate air battle, where disintegrating aircraft were commonplace and the white dots of sixty parachutes in the air at one time were hardly worth a second look. The spectacle registering on my eyes became so fantastic that my brain turned numb to the actuality of the death and destruction all around us. Had it not been for the squeezing in my stomach, which was trying to purge, I might easily have been watching an animated cartoon in a movie theatre.

The minutes dragged on into an hour. And still the fighters came. Our gunners called coolly and briefly to one another, dividing up their targets, fighting for their lives with every round of ammunition – and our lives, and the formation. The tail gunner called that he was out of ammunition. We sent another belt back to him. Here was a new hazard. We might run out of .50-calibre slugs before we reached the target.

I looked to both sides of us. Our two wing men were gone. So was the element in front of us – all three ships. We moved up into position behind the lead element of the high squadron. I looked out again on my side and saw a cripple, with one prop feathered, struggle up behind our right wing with his bad engine funnelling smoke into the slip stream. He dropped back. Now our tail gunner had a clear view. There were no more B-17s behind us. We were the last man.

I took the controls for a while. The first thing I saw when Murphy resumed flying was a B-17 turning slowly out to the right, its cockpit a mass of flames. The copilot crawled out of his window, held on with one hand, reached back for his parachute, buckled it on, let go and was whisked back into the horizontal stabiliser of the tail. I believe the impact killed him. His parachute didn't open.

I looked forward and almost ducked as I watched the tail gunner of a B-17 ahead of us take a bead right on our windshield and cut loose with a stream of tracers that missed us by a few feet as he fired on a fighter attacking us from six o'clock low. I almost ducked again when our own top-turret gunner's twin muzzles pounded away a foot above my head in the full forward position, giving a realistic imitation of cannon shells exploding in the cockpit, while I gave an even better imitation of a man jumping six inches out of his seat.

Still no let-up. The fighters queued up like a bread line and let us have it. Each second of time had a cannon shell in it. The strain of being a clay duck in the wrong end of that aerial shooting gallery became almost intolerable. Our Piccadilly Lily shook steadily with the fire of its .50s, and the air inside was wispy with smoke. I checked the engine instruments for the thousandth time. Normal. No injured crew members yet. Maybe we'd get to that target, even with our reduced fire power. Seven Fortresses from our group had already gone down and many of the rest of us were badly shot up and short-handed because of wounded crew members.

Almost disinterestedly I observed a B-17 pull out from the group preceding us and drop back to a position about 200 feet from our right wing tip. His right Tokyo tanks were on fire, and had been for a half hour. Now the smoke was thicker. Flames were licking through the blackened skin of the wing. While the pilot held her steady, I saw four crew members drop out the bomb bay and execute delayed jumps. Another bailed from the nose, opened his parachute prematurely and nearly fouled the tail. Another went out the left-waist-gun opening, delaying his opening for a safe interval. The tail gunner dropped out of his hatch, apparently pulling the ripcord before he was clear of the ship. His parachute opened instantaneously, barely missing the tail, and jerked him so hard that both his shoes came off. He hung limp in the harness, whereas the others had shown immediate signs of life shifting around in their harness. The Fortress then dropped back in a medium spiral and I did not see the pilots leave. I saw the ship, though, just before it trailed from view, belly to the sky, its wing a solid sheet of yellow flame.

Now that we had been under constant attack for more than an hour, it appeared certain that our group was faced with extinction. The sky was still mottled with rising fighters. Target time was thirty-five minutes away.

I doubt if a man in the group visualised the possibility of our getting much farther without 100 per cent loss. Gunners were becoming exhausted and nerve-tortured from the nagging strain – the strain that sends gunners and pilots to the rest home. We had been aiming point for what looked like most of the Luftwaffe. It looked as though we might find the rest of it primed for us at the target . . .

And then our weary, battered column, short twenty-four bombers, but still holding the close formation that had brought the remainder through by sheer air discipline and gunnery, turned in to the target. I knew that our bombardiers were grim as death while they synchronised their sights on the great Me-109 shops lying below us in a curve of the winding blue Danube, close to the outskirts of Regensburg. Our B-17 gave a slight lift and a red light went out on the instrument panel. Our bombs were away. We turned from the target toward the snow-capped Alps. I looked back and saw a beautiful sight – a rectangular pillar of smoke rising from the Me-109 plant. Only one burst was over and into the town. Even from this great height I could see that we had smeared the objective. The price? Cheap. 200 airmen.

Beirne Lay Jr

‡

Plan Habbakuk

One of the penalties Alan Brooke had to pay for being Chief of the Imperial General Staff was having to consider the merits of the many half-baked schemes favoured by Churchill and favourites of his such as Lord 'Dickie' Mountbatten, who was about to become Supreme Allied Commander in South-East Asia. Mountbatten had a flair for public relations and great faith in the power of technology. The two came together in the idea of aircraft carriers built cheaply from ice.

Dickie now having been let loose gave a signal, whereupon a string of attendants brought in large cubes of ice which were established at the end of the room. Dickie then proceeded to explain that the cube on the left was ordinary pure ice, whereas that on the right contained many ingredients which made it far more resilient, less liable to splinter, and consequently a far more suitable material for the construction of aircraft carriers. He then informed us that in order to prove his statements he had brought a revolver with him and intended to fire shots at the cubes to prove their properties! As he now pulled a revolver out of his pocket we all rose and discreetly moved behind him. He then warned us that he would fire at the ordinary block of ice to show how it splintered and warned us to watch the splinters. He proceeded to fire and we were subjected to a hail of ice splinters! 'There,' said Dickie, 'that is just what I told you; now I shall fire at the block on the right to show you the difference.' He fired, and there certainly was a difference; the bullet rebounded out of the block and buzzed round our legs like an angry bee!

Alan Brooke

Autumn 1943

Italy

On 8 September 1943, Marshal Pietro Badoglio, Mussolini's successor as head of government, announced that an armistice had been signed with the Allies. Though the news was met with delight by most Italians, the timing of the broadcast – before the Allied landings at Salerno the next day – allowed the Germans to start putting into action their pre-devised plan to disarm Italian troops and to occupy the country. The writer Iris Origo, who was half-American and half-English and married to an Italian, lived near Siena.

Then, as we stop at the Buonconvento barrier, we see that the soldiers are grinning from ear to ear. 'Soon you won't need these permits any more!' 'What do you mean?' – 'Haven't you heard? The Chaplain has just told us. Badoglio has spoken on the radio. There's been an armistice. *È la pace, la pace incondizionata!*' (The speaker, a small private, clearly thought this superior to any other kind of peace.) 'Thank you,' says Antonio grimly, and we drive on.

As we get nearer home and the dusk calls, we see bonfires blazing in front of the farms: the news has got here, too. And at eight-thirty p.m. we hear the official broadcast, and Badoglio's proclamation: 'The Italian Government, having recognised the impossibility of continuing an unequal struggle against overwhelming opposing forces, with the intention of saving the nation from further and graver misfortunes, has requested General Eisenhower, Commander-in-Chief of the Anglo-American Forces, for an armistice. The request has been granted. Consequently any act of hostility against the Anglo-American Forces must cease on the part of the Italian forces everywhere. They will, however, resist any attacks that may be made upon them from any quarter.'

Immediately afterwards we hear the same news from the BBC, followed by Admiral Cunningham's proclamation to the Italian Navy, telling them to sail their ships at once into Allied ports.

Outside the peasants are rejoicing, the bonfires continue, we hear sounds of laughter and merry-making. The household look at us with excited faces, in which delight is marred by a dawning uneasiness. 'What do you

think will happen next? What about the Germans?' What, indeed, about
the Germans? Presumably they will at once occupy the chief Italian towns.
Presumably, too, they will continue fighting at Naples, and later on form
another line of defence along the Apennines. But what is to be the Italian
part in all this?

Iris Origo

*On 9 September, the Americans and British began landing troops in the Bay of
Salerno, south of Naples. The invasion of mainland Italy had begun. In the first
wave was American journalist Jack Belden.*

We were still a good distance from the beach; we hadn't even reached our
line of departure; yet the German guns were on us already. As we learned
later, the Germans were so sure of where we were going to land that they
brought their defences right on to our beach. Trees, brush and all obstacles
were cut down so as to obtain a clear field of fire. Nothing was left to
chance. Machine-guns fired only in certain zones, the zones interlocked.
Almost on the water's edge, in some cases only fifty yards apart, machine-
guns threatened death to anyone coming out of the boats. Back of those
were mortars. (Only 200 yards from the beach, 88s were employed.)

This was the third landing I had made, and it was the hardest. As we
came abreast of the navy patrol vessel marking our line of departure, the
assault waves bunched up, and shells fell in among them. We needed no
order. We broke, the column went into a skirmish position and throbbed
toward shore like so many racing boats close together, side by side, with
motors roaring and spray flying.

Shells were flashing in the water, flames were yellowing the sky, and
bullets were slapping into the boat. They snapped over our heads, rattled
against the boat sides like hail and beat at the ramp door, seeming to say:
'When you open the door, I'll get you, get you, get you.' The coxswain
shouted: 'Get ready'; the boat shuddered and the ramp creaked open. A
man leaped into the void and his legs flailed the sea, which was babbling
and breaking in a white froth on the white sandy beach. I stepped down.
My legs sank down to their knees and my feet touched the sandy soil of
Italy. At last, I was on the continent of Europe.

That great and significant affair was a thing of insignificance to me then.
I was possessed by no thought of liberating a continent, but only by the
frenzied fancy that yellow tracers were flashing on the left and right,

that flares were curving in golden parabolas on to the beach, that the boats were illuminated and grey and ugly, and they were disgorging dim and menacing figures, and everything was unfriendly, miserable and wet.

I stumbled, fell on my face in the water, got up again, crawled on the beach and lay panting with a score of soldiers, went on again through sand dunes, and halted again before a line of barbed wire.

We were supposed to be the second wave, but no one seemed ahead of us. There were no wire-cutters among any of us, so we held the wire for each other and crawled through.

Flares shot up and down. They were too close and bright, so we lay down. From the indeterminate shadows around us, anxious voices were yelling as if in pain. I thought the Germans were howling but soon I distinguished the words, 'Help, help!' Momentarily, I felt horrified at what might be going on from where those voices were calling in vain for assistance.

We went on in jerks, throwing ourselves to the ground at the snap of a bullet, getting up again in anxiety when we saw how little distance we had covered and how soon the sun would come up on this denuded flat ground.

Obstacles clutched at us everywhere. We broke through the rail fences that had been interlaced with barbed wire, able to move only in single file, for we never could find enough wire-cutters. At one barricade, after we had cut our way through, we lost our balance and tumbled into a ditch filled with water and faecal matter up to our necks. When we dragged ourselves out on the other side, we had to clutch and hang on to another barrier of wire until others found the way through.

Lost, stumbling through an unfamiliar country, beset by uncertainty and slowing down from fatigue, we at last broke through our eighth barbed-wire barrier, and just before dawn emerged on a macadam highway. A few miles beyond it was a hill which we were to have seized before daylight, but which the Germans now undoubtedly held and from it looked down on us. Toward this hill the battalion commander urged his companies, which were coming by in groups of ten and twenty, having become separated from each other in the dark.

In a little while, the commander meandered off to the right down the highway.

'There's no one there but Germans,' I said, for I had seen their machine-guns firing from that direction.

'Oh, we're supposed to have somebody there,' he said; and continued walking away from the flank of our troops.

'The plans of mice and men . . .' I thought; and then I followed him.

                                                                    Jack Belden

Norman Lewis was with the British, serving with Field Security.

9 SEPTEMBER 1943

Landed on 'Red Beach', Paestum, at seven o'clock. Boatloads had been going ashore all day after a dawn shelling from the ships and a short battle for the beachhead. Now an extraordinary false serenity lay on the landward view. A great sweep of bay, thinly pencilled with sand, was backed with distant mountains gathering shadows in their innumerable folds. We saw the twinkle of white houses in orchards and groves, and distant villages clustered tightly on hilltops. Here and there, motionless columns of smoke denoted the presence of war, but the general impression was one of a splendid and tranquil evening in the late summer on one of the fabled shores of antiquity.

We hauled the motor cycles off the landing-craft, started them easily, and rode up over the wire-mesh laid across the sand, making for the cover of a wood. The corpses of those killed earlier in the day had been laid out in a row, side by side, shoulder to shoulder, with extreme precision as if about to present arms at an inspection by death. We numbered eleven: ten sergeants and a sergeant-major. Captain Cartwright, the Field Security Officer, badly smashed up in a car crash the day before we embarked, was presumably still in hospital in Oran. We had been given no briefing or orders of any kind, and so far as the Americans were concerned we might as well not have existed. This was the greatest invasion in this war so far – probably the greatest in human history – and the sea was crowded to the horizon with uncountable ships, but we were as lost and ineffective as babes in the wood. No one knew where the enemy was, but the bodies on the beach at least proved he existed. In place of the guns, tanks, armoured cars, barbed wire we had expected to see, all that had been landed in this sector of the beach were pyramids of office equipment for use by Army Headquarters. We had been issued with a Webley pistol and five rounds of ammunition apiece. Most of us had never fired a gun.

As the sun began to sink splendidly into the sea at our back we wandered at random through this wood full of chirping birds and suddenly found ourselves at the wood's edge. We looked out into an open space on a scene of unearthly enchantment. A few hundred yards away stood in a row the three perfect temples of Paestum, pink and glowing and glorious in the sun's last rays. It came as an illumination, one of the great experiences of life. But in the field between us and the temple lay two spotted cows, feet in the air. We crept back into the depths of the sheltering wood, burrowed into the undergrowth, and as soon as night fell, slept. At some time during the night I awoke in absolute darkness to the sound of movements through the bushes, then a mutter of voices in which I distinguished German words. The voices died away, and I slept again.

Norman Lewis

The Germans were caught by surprise, but gradually began to mount counter-attacks that almost drove the Allies off the beach. Two battalions of American paratroopers were dropped to provide additional support, though they met a fierce reception, as detailed in the diary of this German officer with the 16th Panzer Division later found by Alan Moorehead.

I was awakened suddenly by a violent shaking of my arm and found a guard bending over me and pointing towards the sky: 'Lieutenant! Lieutenant! Paratroops!' I was still half-asleep, but I forced my eyes open and saw the amazing sight for myself. While in the distance one heard the faint droning of the departing planes, 50–60 paratroops, still at a height of some 150 metres, swung towards the ground. As it was a bright moonlit night, one could recognise every single white fleck in the heavens. I quickly overcame the moment of terror and roused the whole Co: 'To your arms! Prepare to fire!' Like cats the gunners sprang into the turrets, and soon fourteen 20-mm guns and some 20 MGs were firing on the descending enemy. This continued until the angle of fire became too small, and our men were in danger. 'Cease fire!' Now we had to move quickly. I have mentioned before that we had camped at the foot of a thickly wooded hill. The paratroops were landing all around us, but most of them about half-way up the hill, so that they would be able, under cover of the trees, to approach close to us and place stick-grenades or similar 'toys' on our armed cars. With this in mind, I ordered all armed cars to proceed without delay to the main road and secure it from attack. When this was done, I set off towards Penta with a few men to carry out a rcn. Nothing was to be seen; we searched a few houses but could find no trace whatever of the paratroops. In this way we reached the last house in Penta, which I also intended to search. I went up to the door and found it locked. Two of my men tried to force it and finally burst it open. At the same moment, three automatic rifles opened up from the house and my men were lucky to escape injury. So that's where they were! One, two, three grenades were our prompt reply. A few bursts with our automatics and we forced our way into the house. Pitch black! I risked it and flashed my torch round the room, calling out, 'HANDS UP.' There were 8–10 paratroops, apparently wounded, in the hallway. They blinked in the light and hesitantly raised their arms. The remainder had escaped through the back door of the house, but it was too difficult to go after them then. We took the prisoners and all the material we found and started back, heavily laden.

On arrival back at the cars, the prisoners and booty were thoroughly examined. They were American paratroops from Sicily, on their first combat mission, which was to interrupt traffic on the road between Avellino and Salerno, to the rear of the German front. Among the material we found a sack with mines, two AT rifles, two light MG, two light mortars and two days' rations for 30 men. Each man was excellently equipped: one 12-mm Tommy gun, one 12-mm revolver, three hand-grenades, numerous fuses, knife, compass, maps printed on silk, a brass knuckle-duster-knife, cigarettes and excellent first-aid equipment.

During the next two days I undertook three further patrols on foot, during which I brought in another six prisoners, beating them at their own game. The patrol, which consisted of four men, armed with automatic rifles, revolvers and hand grenades, had to wrap rags round their boots – we did not have rubber soles like the Americans – and in this way could approach the enemy unnoticed. Every time we were successful.

(The diary, which covers the period September 7th to 14th ends here because the lieutenant was killed. The notebook was found on his body).

Alan Moorehead and Lieutenant Rocholl

The rescue of Mussolini

The ousted dictator was being held in a hotel atop a mountain in central Italy. An Austrian major in the SS, Otto Skorzeny, was given the task of freeing him and bringing him to Germany. Skorzeny's plan was bold: rather than attempt a conventional assault up the mountain, he decided to land his men in gliders at the top of it.

We were now much nearer the rock plateau than when we were photographing it and the conformation of the ground was more fully revealed.

It was easy to see that a landing on this 'meadow' was out of the question. My pilot, Lieutenant Meyer, must also have realised that the situation was critical, as I caught him looking all round. I was faced with a ticklish decision. If I obeyed the express orders of my General I should abandon the operation and try to glide down to the valley. If I was not prepared to do so, the forbidden crash-landing was the only alternative.

It did not take me long to decide. I called out: 'Crash landing! As near to the hotel as you can get!' The pilot, not hesitating for a second, tilted the starboard wing and down we came with a rush. I wondered for a moment whether the glider could take all the strain in the thin air, but there was little time for speculation. With the wind shrieking in our ears we approached our target. I saw Lieutenant Meyer release the parachute brake, and then followed a crash and the noise of shattering wood. I closed my eyes and stopped thinking. One last mighty heave, and we came to rest.

The bolt of the exit hatch had been wrenched away, the first man was out like a shot and I let myself fall sideways out of the glider, clutching my weapons. We were within 15 metres of the hotel! We were surrounded by jagged rocks of all sizes, which may have nearly smashed us up but had also acted as a brake so that we had taxied barely 20 metres. The parachute brake now folded up immediately behind the glider.

The first Italian sentry was standing on the edge of a slight rise at one corner of the hotel. He seemed lost in amazement. I had no time to bother about our Italian passenger, though I had noticed him falling out of the glider at my side, but rushed straight into the hotel. I was glad I had given the order that no one must fire a shot before I did. It was essential that the surprise should be complete. I could hear my men panting behind me. I knew they were the pick of the bunch and would stick to me like glue and ask no explanations.

We reached the hotel. All the surprised and shocked sentry required was a shout of '*mani in alto*' (hands up). Passing through an open door, we spotted an Italian soldier engaged in using a wireless set. A hasty kick sent his chair flying from under him and a few hearty blows from my machine-pistol wrecked his apparatus. On finding that the room had no exit into the interior of the hotel we hastily retraced our steps and went outside again.

We raced along the façade of the building and round the corner, to find ourselves faced with a terrace 2.50 to 3 metres high. Corporal Himmel offered me his back and I was up and over in a trice. The others followed in a bunch.

My eyes swept the façade and lit on a well-known face at one of the windows of the first storey. It was the Duce! Now I knew that our effort had not been in vain! I yelled at him: 'Away from the window!' and we rushed into the entrance hall, colliding with a lot of Italian soldiers pouring out. Two machine-guns were set up on the floor of the terrace. We jumped over them and put them out of action. The Carabinieri continued to stream out and it took a few far from gentle blows from my weapon to force a way through them. My men yelled out *'mani in alto'*. So far no one had fired a shot.

I was now well inside the hall. I could not look round or bother about what was happening behind me. On the right was a staircase. I leaped up it, three steps at a time, turning left along a corridor and flung open a door on the right. It was a happy choice. Mussolini and two Italian officers were standing in the middle of the room. I thrust them aside and made them stand with their backs to the door. In a moment, Untersturmführer Schwerdt appeared. He took the situation in at a glance and jostled the mightily surprised Italian officers out of the room and into the corridor. The door closed behind us.

We had succeeded in the first part of our venture. The Duce was safely in our hands. Not more than three or four minutes had passed since we had arrived!

Otto Skorzeny

Along with the pilot, the 6 ft 4 ins Skorzeny crammed himself and the bulk of Mussolini into a tiny Fieseler-Storch aircraft and flew to Rome before going on to Vienna. He was later personally decorated with the Knight's Cross by Hitler.

The 'Four Days' of Naples

At the end of September, the Neapolitans rose up against the Germans. The courage of the mostly young insurgents was witnessed by a 10-year-old girl who was to become Italy's most celebrated film star.

And then came the worst bloodbath of all – what became known as the Four Days of Naples, when ragged little boys from the slums finally rebelled against the German oppression and took matters into their own hands. What these little boys did I witnessed with my own eyes, but even so, I find it difficult to believe that what I remember actually happened. Armed with bottles filled with gasoline they had stolen from the Germans, these boys ignited rags they had stuffed into the bottles to serve as wicks, and then darted from side streets and swarmed over the huge German tanks, stuffing the bottles into the gun slits in the tanks just as the gasoline exploded. These were ragamuffin little boys, mind you, ranging from five to ten years of age, whose courage was unbelievable. They attacked tanks and trucks and installations, and no German soldier on the street was immune from their swarming attacks. Their fire bombs were exploding everywhere, and some of them had grenades and ammunition, which they had stolen from the Germans. I couldn't believe my eyes. Many of these boys were shot and killed by the Germans, their bloody little bodies dotting the streets, but nothing daunted their attacks.

I also saw them run at tanks with flaming straw held over their heads, and then somehow twist the straw into the tanks, often being killed in the process. Groups of these boys scurried around the rooftops dropping paving stones, sacks of rocks, and every manner of heavy object on troop carriers, trucks, and marchers passing below. It was a fanatical attack, waged with scissors, knives, nail-spiked boards, and virtually any potentially lethal object they could get their hands on.

For four days these incredible boys were a continual, deadly harassment. Day and night I watched them running, dodging, scurrying in and out of alleys and over walls and rooftops, ever attacking, achieving with their courage and brazen tactics what the Italian men, who were now in work camps or in hiding, had failed even to attempt.

Those boys from the slums of Naples were very much like the boys of Pozzuoli. The hard life of the slums had taken away their boyhood and required manhood of them at an early age. They ran with their flaming bottles in the face of guns firing at them, and even when wounded, persisted to their goal, if they possibly could. To my horror, I saw some of them blown up by exploding tanks when they couldn't get away in time. The most gruesome sight I saw was two German soldiers scrambling from their burning tank, themselves on fire, running after the escaping boy who had attacked their tank, firing at him with their pistols. Flames were trailing from their hair and their burning uniforms but they were intent on pursuing the little boy and trying to kill him. The three of them disappeared into an alleyway but for some time I continued to hear their pistols firing.

After four days, incredible as it may seem, the boys of Naples had brought the German army to its knees; to our amazement, the entire

German military establishment withdrew from Naples. By the end of the fifth day, there wasn't a Nazi soldier left on the streets.

							Sophia Loren

The Germans made a tactical withdrawal north from Naples, allowing the Allies to move into the city. They found it battered and starving.

9 OCTOBER 1943

This afternoon, another trip along the seafront at Santa Lucia provided a similar spectacle of the desperate hunt for food. Rocks were piled up here against the sea wall and innumerable children were at work among them. I learned that they were prising limpets off the rocks, all the winkles and sea-snails having been long since exhausted. A pint of limpets sold at the roadside fetched about two lire, and if boiled long enough could be expected to add some faint, fishy flavour to a broth produced from any edible odds and ends. Inexplicably, no boats were allowed out yet to fish. Nothing, absolutely nothing that can be tackled by the human digestive system is wasted in Naples. The butchers' shops that have opened here and there sell nothing we would consider acceptable as meat, but their displays of scraps of offal are set out with art, and handled with reverence: chickens' heads – from which the beak has been neatly trimmed – cost five lire; a little grey pile of chickens' intestines in a brightly polished saucer, five lire; a gizzard, three lire; calves' trotters two lire apiece; a large piece of windpipe, seven lire. Little queues wait to be served with these delicacies. There is a persistent rumour of a decline in the cat population of the city.

							Norman Lewis

The butterfly collector

The armistice had been the signal for thousands of Allied prisoners of war to leave the Italian camps in which they had been held before they were rounded up once more by the country's new power, the Germans. Some fetched up with partisan bands, others – including Eric Newby – began the long walk south towards the front lines.

I woke to find a German soldier standing over me. At first, with the sun behind him he was as indistinct as the peaks had become, but then he swam into focus. He was an officer and he was wearing summer battledress and a soft cap with a long narrow peak. He had a pistol but it was still in its holster on his belt and he seemed to have forgotten that he was armed because he made no effort to draw it. Across one shoulder and hanging down over one hip in a very unmilitary way he wore a large old-fashioned civilian haversack, as if he was a member of a weekend rambling club, rather than a soldier, and in one hand he held a large, professional-looking butterfly net. He was a tall, thin, pale young man of about twenty-five with mild eyes and he appeared as surprised to see me as I was to see him, but much less alarmed than I was, virtually immobilised, lying on my back without my boots and socks on.

'*Buon giorno*,' he said, courteously. His accent sounded rather like mine must, I thought. '*Che bella giornata.*'

At least up to now he seemed to have assumed that I was an Italian but as soon as I opened my mouth he would know I wasn't. Perhaps I ought to try and push him over the cliff, after all he was standing with his back to it; but I knew that I wouldn't. It seemed awful even to think of murdering someone who had simply wished me good day and remarked on what a beautiful one it was, let alone actually doing it. If ever there was going to be an appropriate time to go on stage in the part of the mute from Genoa which I had often rehearsed but never played, this was it. I didn't answer.

'*Da dove viene, lei?*' he asked.

I just continued to look at him. I suppose I should have been making strangled noises and pointing down my throat to emphasise my muteness, but just as I couldn't bring myself to assail him, I couldn't do this either. It seemed too ridiculous. But he was not to be put off. He removed his haversack, put down his butterfly net, sat down opposite me in the hollow and said:

'*Lei, non è Italiano.*'

It was not a question. It was a statement of fact which did not require an answer. I decided to abandon my absurd act.

'*Si, sono Italiano.*'

He looked at me, studying me carefully: my face, my clothes and my boots which, after my accent, were my biggest give-away, although they were very battered now.

'I think that you are English,' he said, finally, in English. 'English, or from one of your colonies. You cannot be an English deserter; you are on the wrong side of the battle front. You do not look like a parachutist or a saboteur. You must be a prisoner of war. That is so, is it not?'

I said nothing.

'Do not be afraid,' he went on. 'I will not tell anyone that I have met you, I have no intention of spoiling such a splendid day either for you or for myself. They are too rare. I have only this one day of free time and it was extremely difficult to organise the transport to get here. I am anxious to collect specimens, but specimens with wings. I give you my word that no one will ever hear from me that I have seen you or your companions if you have any.'

In the face of such courtesy it was useless to dissemble and it would have been downright uncouth to do so.

'Yes, I am English,' I said, but it was a sacrifice to admit it. I felt as if I was pledging my freedom.

He offered me his hand. He was close enough to do so without moving.

It felt strangely soft when I grasped it in my own calloused and roughened one and it looked unnaturally clean when he withdrew it.

'*Oberleutnant* Frick. Education Officer. And may I have the pleasure of your name, also?'

'Eric Newby,' I said. 'I'm a lieutenant in the infantry, or rather I was until I was put in the bag.' I could see no point in telling him that I had been in SBS, not that he was likely to have heard of it. In fact I was expressly forbidden, as all prisoners were, to give anything but my name, rank and number to the enemy.

'Excuse me? In the bag?'

'Until I was captured. It's an expression.'

He laughed slightly pedantically, but it was quite a pleasant sound. I expected him to ask me when and where I had been captured and was prepared to say Sicily, 1943, rather than 1942, which would have led to all sorts of complications; but he was more interested in the expression I had used.

'Excellent. In the bag, you say. I shall remember that. I have little opportunity now to learn colloquial English. With me it would be more appropriate to say "in the net", or, "in the bottle"; but, at least no one has put you in a prison bottle, which is what I have to do with my captives.'

Although I don't think he intended it to be, I found this rather creepy, but then I was not a butterfly hunter. His English was very good, if perhaps a little stilted. I only wished that I could speak Italian a quarter as well.

He must have noticed the look of slight distaste on my face because the next thing he said was, 'Don't worry, the poison is only crushed laurel leaves, a very old way, nothing modern from I.G. Farben.'

Now he began delving in his haversack and brought out two bottles, wrapped in brown paper which, at first, I thought must contain the laurel with which he used to knock out his butterflies when he caught them; but, in fact, they contained beer, and he offered me one of them.

'It is really excellent beer,' he said. 'Or, at least, I find it so. To my taste Italian beer is not at all good. This is from Munich. Not easy to get now unfortunately. Permit me to open it for you.'

It was cool and delicious.

Eric Newby

Following the breakout from Salerno, the Allies, including General Clark's US 5th Army, began what would prove to be a long and arduous trek up the length of Italy, a land whose hilly terrain, cut by many rivers, lends itself naturally to a defending army. Those who only had a picturesque view of Italy tended to imagine that campaigning there was an easy prospect.

It was while this fighting was in progress that I received the five Soviet Army officers who were visiting the 5th Army front. The party, including General Vasilieff and General Solodovnek, came to my van in a jovial mood, and expressed great interest in getting a close-up of the fighting.

'We want to see what the Americans are like in action against the Huns,' Vasilieff exclaimed, after discussing the valiant stand of the Red Army on the Eastern Front and the manner in which they were slaughtering the enemy. 'We would like to get right up to the front.'

I poured him another drink of vodka, which the Russians had brought, and said, 'I'll make certain that you see some fighting.'

The Russians were accompanied by three American officers, but I assigned a British officer attached to my staff, Major Renwick, who spoke Russian fluently, to see that the party got a good look at what was going on. In fact, I emphasised to Renwick that it would be unfortunate if our visitors were given any grounds for feeling that we didn't want them to see everything, because from their questions I was sure that they had been sent to our front to find out whether the Italian campaign had drawn off from the Russian front any appreciable German strength. We knew from questioning prisoners that it had, but the Russians had trouble in believing it and were inclined to regard the Italian fighting as a picnic.

Renwick proved more than able to conduct the tour. He took them up towards the rugged three-thousand-foot-high peaks of the Camino hill-mass, where enemy artillery made travel more or less hazardous on any road. He put them astride some mules, and led them up the twisting mountain-paths where American troops were struggling to overcome mines, wired booby-traps, machine-gun nests, and mortar positions concealed deep in the rocky slopes. With the help of the elements, he saw that they were rained on most of the day, and had to slither through sticky mud when they dismounted from the mules. Finally, to complete the picture, he got himself wounded by a shell-fragment.

That night, when I saw the Soviet mission at dinner-time, they were considerably less jovial than when they started out. I might even say that they were impressed by what they had seen. Later in the evening, when I questioned them about the day's trip, Vasilieff suggested that I had misunderstood his explanation of just what the mission wished to see.

'What we're most interested in,' he said, 'is logistics. We want to see how your rear elements are organised and how your supply problems are handled.'

He took another gulp from his vodka-glass. 'After all,' he added, 'we can die for Mother Russia any day in Russia. Why should we die in Italy?'

Mark Clark

Hannibal, it should be noted, chose to cross the Alps rather than fight his way up Italy.

By November 1943, American troops had pushed the Germans back to a line of fortified positions midway between Naples and Rome. With them was correspondent Richard Tregaskis.

I heard the scream of something coming, and I must have dived to the rocks instinctively. Months of conditioning on many battlefields resolved themselves in that instantaneous, life-saving reflex. Then a smothering explosion descended around me. It seemed to flood over me from above. In a fraction of a second of consciousness, I sensed that I had been hit. A curtain of fire rose, hesitated, hovered for an infinite second. In that measureless interval, an orange mist came up quickly over my horizon, like a tropical sunrise, and set again, leaving me in the dark. Then the curtain descended, gently.

I must have been unconscious for a few seconds. When a rudimentary awareness came back, I knew everything was all wrong. I realised I had been badly hit. I was still stretched on the rocks. A couple of feet from me lay my helmet which had been gashed in at least two places, one hole at the front and another ripping through the side.

Catastrophe had struck me down. My shocked perceptions groped for an understanding of what had happened. It was no use.

There was no pain. Everything seemed finished, quiet, as if time had stopped. I sat up and looked back at the path. Now I saw the motion of figures of men running up the trail at a half crouch, as a man would zigzag through shellfire. There must be danger. I was aware of that at least. I tried to shout at them, but only incoherent sounds tumbled from my mouth, and my voice rattled, as if it were coming from some place far off and beyond my control. It was like a broken, muted phonograph.

My mind formulated frantic questions. What's wrong? Why can't I talk? What am I going to do? And then I felt a slight easing of tension, a slight relaxation. I knew, then, that even though I could not utter the words, I could still think. I had lost my power of speech, not my power to understand or generate thought. It was clear to me what I wanted to say, but I couldn't say it.

By this time the men had gone, and it was evident that they were too concerned with something else to come back and pay attention to me.

A shell was coming. I knew that because I heard the sound of the approaching projectile. But the sound was just a tinny little echo of something which had once been terrifying and all-powerful. And the explosion, while it seemed to rattle my skull, was certainly not terrifying. I couldn't understand the fear written on the face of a soldier who had skidded into the ground near me as he sought to take cover from the bursting of the shell.

I tried, with my distant and almost uncontrollable voice, to talk intelligibly to the frightened soldier during the few seconds he was there. I was trying to say, 'Can you help me?' And after a number of unconnected, stumbling syllables, I finally managed two words, 'Can help?'

I heard the tinny sound of a little shell, and saw the soldier's face, hollowed by terror. He was saying, 'I can't help you, I'm too scared.' And then he was gone, running, up the trail.

Richard Tregaskis

‡

Attacking the Tirpitz

In late September 1943, the German battleship Tirpitz *was anchored in Kaafjord, Norway. Shielded by anti-torpedo nets, she believed herself immune from underwater attack. The Germans, however, had not accounted for the British X-craft, 'midget' submarines that were just 51 ft long. On the night of 21–2 September, three X-craft, each with a four-man crew, set out to sink the* Tirpitz. *The commander of X7 was Godfrey Place.*

At 0640, when X7 was close to the northward of a tanker of the *Altmark* class, the *Tirpitz* was sighted for the first time at a range of about a mile.

My intention for the attack was to go deep at a range of 500 yards, pass under the anti-torpedo nets at seventy feet and run down the length of the target from bow to stern, letting go one charge under the bridge, the other well aft and altering to port to escape under the nets on the *Tirpitz*'s starboard side.

At 0705 X7 was taken to seventy feet for the attack but stuck in the net instead of passing underneath. This time I had no intention of staying there. By similar tactics to those that extricated us before, but without breaking surface, we came out and tried again at ninety feet, this time getting more firmly stuck. On occasions when the craft is being navigated blind, it is extremely difficult to know one's position to within a hundred yards – in this case the *Tirpitz*, the nets and the shore were all within a circle of that diameter, and the gyro had again gone off the board with the excessive angles the boat had taken. Thus when X7 next came clear and started rising, the motor was stopped lest she run up the beach or on to the top of the nets and fall into enemy hands. When she broke surface I saw we were inside the close-net defences (how we got underneath I have no idea) about thirty yards from the *Tirpitz*'s port beam – 'group up, full ahead, forty feet'.

We actually hit the target's side obliquely at twenty feet and slid underneath, swinging our fore-and-aft line to the line of her keel. The first charge was let go – as I estimated, under the *Tirpitz*'s bridge – and X7 was taken about 200 feet astern to drop the other charge under the after turrets. The time was 0720. It was just as we were letting go the second charge that we heard the first signs of enemy counter-attack – but, oddly enough, we were wrong in assuming they were meant for us.

In X7 we had to guess a course that we hoped would take us back to that lucky spot where we had got under the nets on our way in; but we were not lucky. We tried in many places within a few feet of the bottom, but in vain, and rapidly lost all sense of our exact position. The gyro was still chasing its tail and the magnetic compass could not be raised for fear it would foul some wire or a portion of a net; we did use the course indicator (a form of compass that remains steady during alterations of course but does indicate true position) but the noise it made was most tiresome so we switched it off again.

The next three-quarters of an hour were very trying; exactly what track X7 made I have no idea, but we tried most places along the bottom of those nets, passing under the *Tirpitz* again more than once, and even breaking surface at times, but nowhere could we find a way out. We had to blow each time we got into the nets and the HP air was getting down to a dangerously low level – but bull-in-a-china-shop tactics were essential as our charges had been set with only an hour's delay – and those of others might go up at any time after eight o'clock. The small charges that were periodically dropped by the Germans were not likely to do us any harm and, when we were on the surface, no guns larger than light automatic weapons which caused no damage could be brought to bear – but we were sceptical about our chances against at least four tons of torpex exploding within a hundred yards. But the luck that had recently deserted us came back for a few minutes shortly after eight. We came to the surface – an original method, but we were halfway across before I realised what was happening. On the other side we dived to the bottom and at once started to get under way again to put as much distance as possible between us and the coming explosion. Sticking again in a net at sixty feet was the limit, as this confounded my estimate of our position relative to the nets. But we were not here long before the explosion came – a continuous roar that seemed to last whole minutes. The damage it caused X7 was really surprisingly small – depth gauges, trimming bubble and some lights broken; considerable but not catastrophic leaks at most hull glands; the gyro spinning with almost the speed of its rotor – but the hull was still complete. An incidental effect of the explosion was to shake us out of the net, so we sat at the bottom to review our position. We had no pumps that would work; the HP air bottles were empty, but internal venting where possible had increased the air pressure within the boat and the compressor was still working. The leaks were not immediately dangerous, but, as we had no way of pumping them out, we could not afford to delay. So we set off again, aiming at taking advantage of the confusion to get a good check on our position (I was not really certain we were even out of the nets) and then lying up and refitting on the bottom in shallow water. Nos. 1 and 3 MB tanks had to be blown to get us off bottom and with air in these open-bottom tanks, depth-keeping was impossible – we could choose only between surface and bottom. Nor was I correct in thinking we would be able to fix our position when we were on the surface (it was provoking to see the *Tirpitz* still on the surface, but that was about all that could be seen). We did another of these hops to the surface and this time the night periscope was hit; as it was probable we had only enough air for one more surface and there was no chance of getting away, we decided to abandon ship. DSEA [Davis Submarine Escape Apparatus] escape was considered, but we were not keen to risk depth-charges that were being dropped, so it was decided to try a surface surrender first. If firing did not stop at the showing of a white sweater, we could always try DSEA from the bottom after a delay to allow enemy activity to die down.

X7 was surfaced and I, gingerly, I must confess, opened the fore hatch just enough to allow the waving of a white sweater. Firing did immediately stop, so I came outside and waved the sweater more vigorously.

The Germans had put a battle-practice target some 500 yards off the starboard bow of the *Tirpitz* – probably an attempt to obscure other attacking craft's view of their target – and X7 hit this just after I came on the casing, with her extremely low buoyancy forward – one main ballast tank had presumably been hit – the curved side of this was sufficient to force the bow down so that water went into the wet-and-dry before I could shut the hatch. From Aitken's description this was probably not more than thirty gallons, but it was sufficient to send X7 to the bottom again – I was left on the battle-practice target.

Godfrey Place

Place and Aitken managed to escape from X7 and became prisoners of war, although the other two members of the craft were lost. The Tirpitz was put out of commission for six months, and the author was awarded the Victoria Cross.

‡

The Russian Front

During the autumn of 1943, the Russians began to recapture many of the towns and cities lost during Barbarossa. Helmut Pabst's mood of resignation was characteristic of that felt by many German soldiers.

Tomorrow we are to move into position. According to the Wehrmacht communiqué, the enemy has begun the expected large-scale attack west of Yelnya. The three cavalry regiments have become divisions.

I am sitting on a paliasse in the open air, waiting for the order to go forward on liaison duty. The infantry-gun shells are twittering over the heights from the East. Four tanks are breaking across the railway line in the North. The shells on No. 11 Battery creep slowly towards them, till the muzzle-flashes of their guns stand out red in the clouds of the shellbursts. They turn away clumsily.

We go forward and climb down the slopes towards the railway. Tanks and anti-tank guns are firing at individual men. We lie for a long time behind the cover of a little scarp and feel our way from bush to bush. The bushes are sparse. We are clearly silhouetted on the ridge. It's a clear, warm late-summer day. The fields of buckwheat glow rust-red in the sun. Over in the enemy's lines another village is burning. We drop into the valley of a little stream, where we find a telephone line running towards the enemy. Soon we are eating the daily bread of the infantry, high-pitched bursts of machine-gun fire, howling high-velocity shells, and slow, heavy fellows with a deep bass humming which shake the earth. The powder fumes blow across in lazy waves. At last we end up at Lieutenant Illner's. He is sitting by the stream, washing his feet: 'It's eight days since I last got out of my boots. It's a nice quiet moment . . .'

At 1730 we got the order over the wireless: 'Back at once.' At 1830 Jean Braun was waiting for us at the edge of the village. He led out the horse from the dip where he had tethered it. Half an hour later we were in the village where the gun position was. The batteries were ready to move off. Headquarters had left already. Far around us the sky was red. It was almost night. A girl was leaning from a window. She recognised me; I had been billeting for the battery. 'You not go,' she said softly. 'Oh, *panyenka*, what do you know about war!' Wren was already saddled. We rode off after the battery, overtaking dark columns. The heavy binoculars clattered and bumped on my belt. We reached the battery.

We march. It is cold. Midnight comes. The moon sails through silver clouds. The parachute-flares shine brightly like constellations. Somewhere bombs whistle. I take out my guitar: '*Weisst Du, wieviel Sternlein stehen . . . – Horch, was kommt von draussen rein! . . .*' Franz looks pale and sick, with deep lines round his mouth and eyes. He has a temperature. I feel as if my stomach had been pumped out and as if I had swallowed salt water. I have eaten one slice of bread since midday. The cart fell on its side, everything is dirty.

Let it go, it doesn't matter. It's still too cold to eat while we're marching. Let's have another song, let's smoke another cigarette, then we won't notice it so much. Slowly they fall asleep on the wagons and in the saddles. Von R has to wake up a lorry driver who lies snoring over his wheel. For kilometres behind us the column was at a standstill. At 0400 we reach our billets.

Two days later, Pabst was killed in action. His will was found on his body and sent home:

Russia, 17th April, 1942.

Dear Parents,
    I have only one anxiety: how is it possible to ease your pain? What can I do to soften the blow which no longer hurts me, but only you? I will gather all my strength to entreat you:
    My life was not completed, but it was fulfilled. It was fulfilled by your love, and it was so rich that I can only thank you again and again. Even if the other life in which I wanted to do my work as a man was hardly begun, this first life was utterly fulfilled and consummated, the one which you gave me and which you guarded, my Father, my Mother.
    I loved you very much.
    If you want to erect a small figure in my memory in the garden, let it not be with a grand gesture nor anything perpetuating sorrow. It might be a boy who smiles a little, who radiates harmony and reconciliation, or perhaps a young man who rests at peace with himself, so that my heart could become attached to it, not turned away from the world, but open to everything beautiful.
    Farewell, I loved you very much.

                                                        Helmut Pabst

The legacy of Hippocrates

Conditions in Russia were now so hellish that some German soldiers decided that self-mutilation — and the risk of a firing squad if discovered — was preferable to remaining on the front line. Their actions placed army surgeons in a quandary.

The wounded from our own division were in very low spirits; indeed, morale had sunk to zero. We had a succession of self-mutilation cases where men had shot themselves through the hand. In such cases of point-blank injury the edges of the wound are usually serrated in a characteristic manner; there are traces of blackened powder all round the wound and the fine hairs of the skin have been singed. Most experienced soldiers knew this; and from time to time, too, the Russians dropped leaflets which gave instructions on how to effect a self-mutilation that was not recognisable as such. But in practice this is virtually impossible; the expert can almost always recognise a self-inflicted wound. All such cases had to be reported and they usually ended with a court martial and a firing squad.

The first case was a young peasant lad flown out from Germany three days before after a training which had lasted only a few weeks. I examined his wound carefully: the edges were serrated and blackened. I touched it lightly with a swab; it wasn't dirt. Then I had a look at the patient – about eighteen and still quite beardless. It was clear that in desperation at having been flung so violently into hell he had suffered a mental black-out. It was clear, too, that he had no idea that what he had done might mean the end of his life. I thought for a moment. Gehrmann watched me attentively; Sergeant Fuchs, already holding mask and ether bottle in his hands, raised his enormous nose and peered over the patient's head to study the area on which I was about to operate. Both immediately recognised the sort of injury it was. I raised my eyebrows. If there should be an epidemic of self-mutilation – which under present circumstances was not impossible – we too would be lost.

I was hoist with my own petard. Since the beginning of the campaign I had deliberately set out to give all the members of the operating team some idea of the natural dignity of the science of medicine, of its ancient humanistic tradition, of the beneficial effect of this tradition on their work. I used to call the surgeon's knife the scalpel of Hippocrates and in the course of time my men had got into the way of using the phrase. And I had managed, too, to give them some idea of how great a man Hippocrates was.

Operating assistant and anaesthetist exchanged glances. Then Sergeant Fuchs, rubbing his great nose with the anaesthetic mask, said: 'Only old Hippocrates can put this right'; and then began to administer the anaesthetic. Gehrmann handed me the scalpel. I removed all traces of legal evidence by the only reliable method, cutting it away, and the wound became fairly extensive. In this manner the physician from Cos saved the life of a young German peasant in the Russian steppe; but in subsequent battles that winter it was no longer possible so to adhere to the spirit of his teachings.

Peter Bamm

‡

The Gilbert Islands

On 20 November, the Americans landed on Tarawa, a British Pacific colony north-east of the Solomons: 18,600 troops from the 2nd Marine Division stormed ashore only to encounter ferocious defence from a Japanese force less than a quarter their size, all of whom were killed. The war in the air was no less savage. On 27 November Lt-Cdr Ed 'Butch' O'Hare flew the first US night combat mission in a radar-equipped Avenger. Accompanying him against an attacking force of Japanese 'Betty' aircraft were two Hellcats, the gunner in one of which was Alvin Kernan.

We had by this time lost the Japanese planes, but a lone Betty drifted under our tail and I got off a few rounds. Phillips, true to form, began searching again. In my heart I wasn't as sure I wanted to find them as he was. The radar was our only chance, but Rand picked up no blips in any direction. He was making heavy going of it by that time and not functioning well, though trying gamely. We were now circling at some distance from the carrier, and I became increasingly disoriented. The second of the two Bettys that had crashed was burning in a long smear of gasoline on the water, and as we turned in the pitch black, I thought the ocean was the sky and the light from the burning plane another plane turning in, in a long curve for a run on us. I called out on the intercom that it was attacking and requested permission – even here this was still the battleship navy – to begin firing. Phillips, using his instruments, put me right side up again.

The ship's radar could see both us and the fighters, and the fighter director officer was trying to move us together. At this point Phillips – at O'Hare's request – turned on our running lights, and the fighters, all lighted up themselves like Christmas trees, slid suddenly in, coming down across our tail from below and aft, O'Hare on our starboard side wing one or two hundred feet away, somewhat below, Skon on the port, bright blue in the flare of their exhausts, six guns jutting out of their wings, quite scary. Canopy back, goggles up, yellow Mae West, khaki shirt, and helmet, seated aggressively forward, riding the plane hard, looking like the tough Medal of Honor recipient, American Ace he was, Butch O'Hare's face was sharply illuminated by his canopy light for one brief last moment.

This had to have been the brief moment when our group, together for the only time that night, was illuminated, and it was at that point that, attracted by our lights, one of the Bettys, as confused and blinded as we were, tried to join up on the American formation. Looking to my right, I saw a long black cigar shape climb up from below and aft of Skon and swing into formation above us on our starboard side, behind and slightly above O'Hare. Realising his fatal mistake, he [the Jap] began firing. 'Butch, this is Phil. There's a Jap on your tail. Kernan, open fire.' The intercom went dead as I began shooting back at the Betty, firing by our tail between Skon and O'Hare. The air was filled with gunfire. A long burst nearly emptied my ammunition can at the Betty to our rear, which, as the tracers arced toward him, broke away across our group to disappear in the darkness behind Skon.

Rand, in pain but staring hard out of the tunnel window, had a good view of the exchange of fire, but he missed O'Hare's plane slipping under us, just forward of Skon, and away in the dark. I thought I saw O'Hare reappear off to port, for the briefest glimpse, and then he was gone. Something whitish-grey appeared above the water, his parachute or the splash of the plane going in. Skon slid away instantly to follow O'Hare, and then returned to join up on us again when he could not find him.

Phillips took us down to drag the surface for another long half-hour before giving up and making our way about 2100 back to the *Enterprise*. Skon landed first without any trouble. But for us the evening was by no means over. We still had to make a landing on an unlighted carrier deck at night. If it had been done before, it was certainly not standard procedure, and Phillips, despite having a thousand hours as an instrument instructor, had never done it, even in practice. We homed on the white wake that marked the ship in the water, but there was no light anywhere on deck except the fluorescent wands of the landing signal officer standing on the end of the flight deck. We came in too high, and just as Phillips was about to cut the engine the landing signal officer waved us off. Full throttle, nearly stalling out, wheels, flaps, and hook down, we hung for a moment above the deck, neither rising nor falling. In the bright blue light of the exhausts I saw the huge, dark shape of the carrier's island structure just a few feet off our starboard wing, the parked planes on the deck just a few feet below, the men standing there looking up at us. We hung there for an eternity, then picked up speed all at once and flew away to go around again.

The *Enterprise* captain, Matt Gardner, must have known we would never make it with the cumbersome plane in the dark, the pilot tensed to the snapping point, so he courageously turned on the shaded lights that marked out the flight deck for the crucial moment. They could only be seen from low and aft by a plane approaching for a landing, so they didn't reveal the ship very much for very long to a submarine or the Bettys still flying about. This time it worked. We dropped heavily on the deck. The corpsmen took Rand away, Phillips disappeared to talk to the admiral, and I, still crouched on the turret seat, straightened out my legs with great pain and made my way to the head just below the flight deck, where I stood and pissed for what seemed like five minutes. Where did it all come from, on and on, emptying all the accumulated fear and tension out with the water that had built up in the longest three hours of my life, before or since.

Alvin Kernan

O'Hare's death remains a mystery. Kernan was accused of accidentally shooting him down, but the most likely explanation is that he was hit by the Betty. Phillips, Rand and Kernan were all awarded Navy Crosses. O'Hare had the posthumous honour of having Chicago's airport named for him.

☦

Madame Chiang

The Chinese, led by Chiang Kai-shek, had been fighting the Japanese since being invaded in 1937. When Japan attacked Britain's possessions in the Far East, Chiang sent soldiers to Burma, and agreed to help tie down Japanese forces in China in return for vast amounts of American aid – much of which was diverted into his own struggle against Chinese Communists. Nonetheless, in November he was invited to the Allies' Cairo Conference, together with his remarkable, American-educated wife.

This very Chinese day has remained rooted in my memory. I have never known whether Madame Chiang gatecrashed into the morning's meeting or whether she was actually invited. It makes little difference, for I feel certain she would have turned up whether she was invited or not. She was the only woman amongst a very large gathering of men, and was determined to bring into action all the charms nature had blessed her with. Although not good looking she certainly had a good figure which she knew how to display at its best. Also gifted with great charm and gracefulness, every small movement of hers arrested and pleased the eye. For instance at one critical moment her closely clinging black dress of black satin with yellow chrysanthemums displayed a slit which extended to her hip bone and exposed one of the most shapely of legs. This caused a rustle amongst those attending the conference and I even thought I heard a suppressed neigh come from a group of some of the younger members!

The trouble that lay behind all this was that we were left wondering whether we were dealing with Chiang or with Madame. Whenever he was addressed his Chinese General sitting on his right interpreted for him, but as soon as he had finished Madame said, 'Excuse me, gentlemen, I do not think that the interpreter has conveyed the full meaning to the Generalissimo!' Similarly, whenever Chiang spoke his General duly interpreted the statement, but Madame rose to say in the most perfect English, 'Excuse me, gentlemen, but the General has failed to convey to you the full meaning of the thoughts that the Generalissimo wishes to express. If you will allow me I shall put before you his real thoughts.' You were left wondering as to whom you were dealing with. I certainly felt that she was the leading spirit of the two and that I would not trust her very far.

Alan Brooke

Madame Chiang, the last survivor of the principal personalities of the war, died in 2003, aged 105.

‡

The Tehran Conference

The meeting of Churchill, Roosevelt and Chiang in Cairo resolved little, and at the end of November the first two moved on to Tehran for discussions with Stalin. It was the first time he had been involved in planning joint Allied strategy, and the former seminarian impressed all, including Alan Brooke.

This was the first occasion during the war when Stalin, Roosevelt and Winston sat round a table to discuss the war we were waging together. I found it quite enthralling looking at their faces and trying to estimate what lay behind. With Churchill of course I knew fairly well, and I was beginning to understand the workings of Roosevelt's brain, as we had had several meetings with him, but Stalin was still very much of an enigma. I had already formed a very high idea of his ability, force of character and shrewdness, but did not know yet whether he was also a strategist. I knew that Voroshilov would provide him with nothing in the shape of strategic vision. My last visit to Moscow had made that quite clear to me, when I had spent several hours with Voroshilov discussing the problem of a Second Front with him.

During this meeting and all the subsequent ones which we had with

Stalin, I rapidly grew to appreciate the fact that he had a military brain of the very highest calibre. Never once in any of his statements did he make any strategic error, nor did he ever fail to appreciate all the implications of a situation with a quick and unerring eye.

In this respect he stood out when compared with his two colleagues. Roosevelt never made any great pretence at being a strategist and left Marshall or Leahy to talk for him. Winston, on the other hand, was far more erratic, brilliant at times but far too impulsive and inclined to favour quite unsuitable plans without giving them the preliminary deep thought they required . . .

                                                                Alan Brooke

The conference revised the date of the invasion of Normandy and decided to organise a subsidiary landing in the South of France. As Brooke later realised, Stalin had rapidly appreciated that this second commitment would slow the Allies' advance from the West, enabling him to seize more territory in the East.

Roosevelt's son, Elliott, was at the conference, acting as a note-taker. He found himself in the unfortunate position of being caught between two of the larger egos of the twentieth century.

Toward the end of the meal Uncle Joe arose to propose his umpteenth toast – for a time I had been trying to keep count, but by then I was hopelessly lost – and it was on the subject of the Nazi war criminals. I cannot hope to remember his words exactly, but it ran something like this:

'I propose a salute to the swiftest possible justice for all Germany's war criminals – justice before a firing squad. I drink to our unity in dispatching them as fast as we capture them, all of them and there must be at least fifty thousand of them.'

Quick as a flash Churchill was on his feet. (By the way, the PM stuck to his favourite brandy throughout the toasting; his nightly regimen of cognac prepared him well for Russian-style conversation; but that night I suspect that even such a redoubtable tippler as he was finding his tongue thicker than usual.) His face and neck were red.

'Any such attitude', he cried, 'is wholly contrary to our British sense of justice! The British people will never stand for such mass murder. I take this opportunity to say that I feel most strongly that no one, Nazi or no, shall be summarily dealt with, before a firing squad, without proper legal trial, no matter what the known facts and proven evidence against him!'

I glanced at Stalin: he seemed hugely tickled, but his face remained serious; only his eyes twinkled as he took up the PM's challenge and drew him on, suavely pricking his arguments, seemingly careless of the fact that Churchill's temper was now hopelessly lost. At length, Stalin turned to Father and asked *his* opinion. Father, who had been hiding a smile, nevertheless felt that the moment was beginning to be too highly charged with bad feeling: it was his notion to inject a witticism.

'As usual,' he said, 'it seems to be my function to mediate this dispute. Clearly there must be some sort of compromise between your position, Mr Stalin, and that of my good friend the Prime Minister. Perhaps we could say that, instead of summarily executing fifty thousand war criminals, we should settle on a smaller number. Shall we say forty-nine thousand five hundred?'

Americans and Russians laughed. The British, taking their cue from their Prime Minister's mounting fury, sat quiet and straight-faced. Stalin, on top of the situation, pursued Father's compromise figure; he asked around the table for agreement of new estimates. The British were careful: The subject requires and deserves a great deal of study, they said. The Americans, on the other hand, were more jocular: Let's brush it off – we're still miles and miles and months and months away from Germany and conquest of the Nazis. I was hoping that Stalin would be satisfied by the early answers, and change the subject before he got to me, but if he is anything, he is persistent. The question came. Somewhat uncertainly I got to my feet.

'Well,' I said, and took a deep breath, trying to think fast through the champagne bubbles. 'Isn't the whole thing pretty academic? Look: when our armies start rolling in from the west, and your armies are still coming on from the east, we'll be solving the whole thing, won't we? Russian, American, and British soldiers will settle the issue for most of those fifty thousand, in battle, and I hope that not only those fifty thousand war criminals will be taken care of, but many hundreds of thousands more Nazis as well.' And I started to sit down again.

But Stalin was beaming with pleasure. Around the table he came, flung an arm around my shoulders. An excellent answer! A toast to my health! I flushed with pleasure, and was about to drink, for it is the Russian custom for one to drink even when it is his own health that is proposed, when all of a sudden an angry finger was being waved right at my face.

'Are you interested in damaging relations between the Allies? Do you know what you are saying? How can you dare say such a thing?' It was Churchill – and he was furious, and no fooling. Somewhat shaken to find the Prime Minister and the Marshal squabbling right over my head and feeling a little like Alice-in-Wonderland being crowded by the Hatter and the March Hare at the celebrated Tea Party, I regained my chair, sat quiet, worried stiff.

Fortunately the dinner broke up soon afterward, and I followed Father back to his apartment to apologise. After all, damaging relations between the Allies!

Father roared with laughter. 'Don't think a second about it,' he insisted. 'What you said was perfectly all right. It was fine. Winston just lost his head when everybody refused to take the subject seriously. Uncle Joe . . . the way he was needling him, he was going to take offence at what anybody said, specially if what was said pleased Uncle Joe. Don't worry, Elliott.'

'Because *you* know . . . the last thing I'd . . .'

'Forget it,' said Father, and laughed again. 'Why Winston will have forgotten all about it when he wakes up.'

But I don't think he ever did forget it. All the months I was to be stationed in England, later on, I was never again invited to spend the night at Chequers. Apparently Mr Churchill never forgets.

And after that incident I was to appreciate all the more the effectiveness of Father's ability to keep those two men thinking along constructive and broadly similar lines. It was a job such as I would never hanker for.

Elliott Roosevelt

Winter 1943–4

Crossing the lines

After his experiences in Syria, John Verney was taken prisoner while leading a raid in Sardinia. Having escaped from his POW camp in Italy with a friend, Amos, he made his way south until he stood on the banks of the River Sangro, within reach of the British positions.

I came round a bend to find myself within five yards of a German soldier. He stood in shadow and I first saw the glint of his rifle. I pressed myself flat against the rock, out of sight from him unless I moved. Very slowly I peered round to see what he was doing. There were two sudden flashes, almost in my face, and it was a few seconds before my tired mind grasped the fact that he had fired at me. I crawled backwards on my stomach and was crossing the path into the river when he fired a third time. And missed again.

I was into the river faster than a snake, and worked my way along with only my eyes and nose above water. I expected to see him at any moment on the bank above me, but I progressed safely in this way for a hundred yards, then crawled into the bushes to try and restore some warmth. I continued to crawl alternately in and out of the river for the next hour. A minefield, conveniently wired off on the south bank, suggested that I was in no-man's land, so I crossed it with infinite caution and came to a deserted and ruined village, where a black cat gave me a fright by running suddenly over the street. In early daylight I crossed the Barrea–Castel road and climbed a hill. There were shell holes everywhere in the muddy ground, but no sign of life. I opened the tin of Italian bully and scooped the meat out with my fingers. I reached the hill-top as dawn broke, but the morning mist was too thick to see anything. I longed to be challenged by a British sentry, but there were none about.

Descending the hill on the far side, I met three Italians on donkeys.

'Are there any Germans round here?' I asked them in Italian.

Suspiciously, they asked if I was German. Hearing I was English, their manner changed immediately. They embraced me and told me to keep going for half a mile when I would reach their village, Montenero, and find English soldiers everywhere.

'*Niente tedeschi, niente tedeschi!*' they laughed.

The sun broke through the morning mist as I came in sight of the village. Approaching it, I deliberately dawdled and finished the last mouthful of Italian bully.

'Well, here you are,' I said aloud. 'I suppose you'll remember the next minutes all your life.'

And I was quite right.

From a hundred yards away the much-battered buildings appeared deserted. Then I noticed a Bren-carrier behind a wall, a few trucks under camouflage netting in a yard. As I limped slowly into the main street, a solitary shell whistled overhead, exploding somewhere at the farther end. A group of British soldiers, the first I had seen, in long leather waistcoats and khaki cap-comforters, chatted unconcernedly in a doorway across the cobbles from me. I glanced shyly at them, but they took no notice. Just another bedraggled peasant haunting the ruins of his home . . .

The conventional inhibited Englishman is ill-equipped by temperament for such occasions. I would have liked to dance, to shout, to make some kind of demonstration. A Frenchman, an Australian, would have done it naturally, but somehow I could not. So I walked slowly on, holding off the pleasure of the long-awaited moment, the exclamation of surprise, the greeting from a compatriot.

English voices and laughter came from a house. I crossed the threshold and found, in what had been the peasants' kitchen but was now the usual military desolation of a billet, two half-dressed Privates cooking breakfast. One of them saw me, standing there grinning at them.

'Christ, Nobby, look what the cat's brought in,' he said.

I tried to be hearty but failed. 'I've just come through. I'm soaked. Can I warm up by your fire?' I heard my bored voice say politely.

Neither of the soldiers was much surprised by this sudden entry of what was, to all appearances, a dank and bearded Italian, who spoke fluent English with a BBC accent. Sensibly enough, they were more interested in breakfast.

'What are you? Escaped POW or something?'

'Yes.'

It didn't cause much of a sensation and they asked no more questions. They treated me, as they might have a stray dog, with a sort of cheery kindness and without fuss. In a few minutes I was sitting naked before their fire, drinking a cup of char and feeling the warmth return to my numbed body.

A Corporal and others of the section came in for their breakfast. My back view may have mildly surprised them.

'Bloke's an escaped POW,' Nobby explained.

'Lucky sod. They'll send you home,' the Corporal said, offering me a Players.

Savouring every puff of the tobacco, every sip of the tea, I wondered whether Amos was doing the same somewhere nearby. We had so often pictured just this situation in the past three months. Superstitiously, I put off asking them if they had heard of him. If they had, they would surely say so. And I didn't want to hear them say they hadn't.

Long-anticipated pleasures seldom come up to expectation. Neither the tea, the tobacco, nor even the warmth were now quite as delicious as I had imagined they would be. The scene was unreal, unbelievable. Though the soldiers' gossip around me was vivid enough.

'Ginger, go and swipe some clothes for him off the CQMS's truck,' the Corporal said to one of the men.

'Do you think the CQMS can spare me something?'

'The CQMS won't know.' Ginger winked as he left the room.

Certainly I was back with the British Army all right.

Later, in the miscellaneous garments swiped by Ginger (the CQMS would, I am sure, have supplied them voluntarily – but that, of course, would have been more trouble) I visited RHQ in another part of the village. Nothing had been heard there of Amos and the CO refused at first to credit my story that I had walked through his outposts unobserved, until I traced my route for him on the map. Evidently I had indeed walked slap through C Company's position.

'Can't think why they didn't shoot you,' the Colonel said irritably. 'Remind me to have a word with the Company Commander about that,' he added to his Adjutant.

John Verney

Amos never did cross the lines, and was presumed to have been killed in the attempt.

✠

The Burma Front

After the retreat from Burma, Slim – appointed commander of the new Fourteenth Army in late 1943 – took time to build up his men's strength, morale and skills, and to consider how best to maximise the numbers he could put in the field.

Air evacuation, in the long run, probably made the greatest difference of all to the wounded and sick. Only those who have suffered the interminable anguish of travel over rough ground or tracks by stretcher or ambulance and the long stifling railway journey for days on end, with broken limbs jolting and temperatures soaring, can realise what a difference quick, smooth, cool transport by aircraft can mean. In November 1943 we had for all transport purposes, other than the maintenance of the 81st West African Division in Arakan, only some one hundred and twenty air sorties a month, but the number was rapidly growing and with it our technique of air evacuation. Later, light aeroplanes of the Moth, Auster, or L5 type picked up the casualties on airstrips hurriedly cut out of jungle or rice-field within a mile or two of the fighting. Each little aircraft carried one lying or two sitting patients and flew them to the supply strip, anything from ten to forty miles farther back. Here the casualties were transferred to Dakotas returning empty from the supply run and flown direct to a general hospital. There were, I remember, heated arguments as to where these hospitals should be situated. Roughly, there was the choice between putting them in such hot sticky places in the plains as at Comilla or in the cool of the hills as at Shillong. I plumped for the plains, because there we could have an airstrip almost alongside the hospital; to reach the hills would have meant long and trying road journeys. So our casualties went almost direct from the battlefield to the hospital and later as convalescents by road from the plains to the hills. There was some shaking of heads among the more orthodox, but the results justified it. One such hospital took in during 1944 and 1945 over eleven thousand British casualties straight, in their filthy, blood-soaked battledress, from the front line. The total deaths in that hospital were twenty-three. Air evacuation did more in the Fourteenth Army to save lives than any other agency.

Good doctors are no use without good discipline. More than half the battle against disease is fought, not by the doctors, but by the regimental officers. It is they who see that the daily dose of mepacrine is taken, that shorts are never worn, that shirts are put on and sleeves turned down before sunset, that minor abrasions are treated before, not after, they go septic, that bodily cleanliness is enforced. When mepacrine was first introduced and turned men a jaundiced yellow, there was the usual whispering campaign among troops that greets every new remedy – the drug would render them impotent – so often the little tablet was not swallowed. An individual medical test in almost all cases will show whether it has been taken or not, but there are a few exceptions and it is difficult to prove for court-martial purposes. I, therefore, had surprise checks of whole units, every man being examined. If the overall result was less than ninety-five per cent positive I sacked the commanding officer. I only had to sack three; by then the rest had got my meaning.

Slowly, but with increasing rapidity, as all of us, commanders, doctors, regimental officers, staff officers, and NCOs, united in the drive against sickness, results began to appear. On the chart that hung on my wall the curves of admissions to hospitals and Malaria Forward Treatment Units sank lower and lower, until in 1945 the sickness rate for the whole Fourteenth Army was one per thousand per day. But at the end of 1943 that was a long way off.

He was keen to learn all he could of the enemy leaders:

We knew something of the Japanese intentions, but little of the dispositions of their reserves, and practically nothing about one of the most important factors that a general has to consider – the character of the opposing commanders. I had all the information I could obtain about Lieut.-General Kawabe, my opposite number, who, as Commander-in-Chief Burma Army Area, controlled all Japanese land and air forces in Burma, but it did not amount to much on which to build up a picture of how his mind would work. At this time, from what I had seen of his operations, I could only expect him to be, like most Japanese commanders I had met, a bold tactical planner of offensive movements, completely confident in the superiority of his troops, and prepared to use his last reserves rather than abandon a plan. Many years before, when I was working for the Staff College examination, I had studied the Russo-Japanese War, and one thing about that campaign I had always remembered. The Russians never won a battle. In almost every fight they accepted defeat while a considerable portion of their forces, in reserve, was still unused. On the other hand, the Japanese were prepared to throw in every man, and more than once tipped the scales of victory with their very last reserves. The Japanese generals we were fighting had been brought up on the lessons of that war, and all I had seen of them in this convinced me that they would run true to form and hold back nothing. This was a source of great strength to them, but also, properly taken advantage of, might, in conjunction with their overweening confidence, be a fatal weakness.

I did, however, manage to get a photograph alleged to be that of Kawabe. It showed what might have been a typical western caricature of a Japanese; the bullet head, the thick glasses, and prominent teeth were all there. To these attractions he added a long waxed moustache, extending well beyond his cheeks. I pinned this picture to the wall of my office, opposite my desk. When I needed cheering I looked at it and assured myself that, whichever of us was the cleverer general, even I was, at any rate, the better looking.

William Slim

‡

Defying the Boche

Resistance to the occupying Germans did not just take the form of sabotage. Many civilians aided airmen who had been shot down. One network of such helpers was the Comet Line, which passed escapers along a chain from Brussels to Spain. Its Belgian organisers included Anne Brusselmans. Twenty-three of her comrades were caught and executed by the Gestapo.

Before leaving with the two men for the station I had to buy a suit for Bud, and what a job it was. Why are these Americans so tall? It is so hard to find clothes to fit them. As for getting ten men like this one into a B17 it looks to me that they must have to be folded in half before entering the 'plane. Yet they say they are very comfortable inside.

The usual preparations begin as the time approaches for them to leave. First, I see that all their identity discs (or dog tags as they call them) are securely in their clothes, for if they are caught they must be able to prove they are airmen trying to escape and are not spies. Lorne has a cigarette-lighter which his mother gave him as a 21st birthday present. It has his name and address on it, so we have to find a safe place to hide this for he won't leave it behind. These men are superstitious about such things – a feeling I know well.

Afterwards, we walk down town, for the Germans are intensifying their searches and it is easier to miss a search when walking than when in a tram.

It is 3.30 p.m. We have to walk slowly, for Lorne's foot is still a little painful. He is trying his best not to limp, however, so as not to attract attention.

On our way we have to pass in front of the building where the Luftwaffe question and condemn people for helping Allied airmen. Two German soldiers are mounting guard outside, and we pass right by them. They don't even look at us, and so much the better. 'If I fly again, my first bomb will be for this place,' Lorne whispers. Then we get to the station and it is good-bye once more. A discreet V-sign, with the first two fingers of the hand, and two more gallant men are on their way.

Before the men left they helped me make a Christmas tree but we are running out of decorations for it. However, the bombers drop a lot of aluminium strips to jam the German radar screen, and we are making do with this for decorating the tree.

This is our fourth war Christmas and the children won't believe us now when we tell them it will be the last one. I have been going round the shops to see if I can find a few toys for Jacques. He is eight years old. Yvonne is twelve, and she has to understand it is impossible to give her Christmas presents. She is very reasonable about this and it makes it easier for us to tell her, but it squashes any hope she may have had. After visiting all the shops, all I could find were a few tin soldiers dressed in German uniforms, or German tanks, and German machine-guns, all marked with the German iron cross and swastika. I just will not give such toys as these to my son to play with. I would rather see him disappointed once more. But I have made up my mind that when this war is ended he and Yvonne will have all the toys they long for, even if it means I have to work until the end of my life to get them.

And so another Christmas day comes and passes in wartime. I hope it is the last one.

Anne Brusselmans

‡

The British liaison officer killed during the attack on Tito's base in June was replaced by Fitzroy Maclean. Churchill asked him to report on the effectiveness of the partisans so that he could decide whether to aid Tito or to continue supplying Mihailovic's less than whole-hearted Chetniks.

I now emphasised to Mr Churchill the other points which I had already made in my report, namely, that in my view the Partisans, whether we helped them or not, would be the decisive political factor in Jugoslavia after the war and, secondly, that Tito and the other leaders of the

Movement were openly and avowedly Communist and that the system which they would establish would inevitably be on Soviet lines and, in all probability, strongly orientated towards the Soviet Union.

The Prime Minister's reply resolved my doubts.

'Do you intend,' he asked, 'to make Jugoslavia your home after the war?'

'No, Sir,' I replied.

'Neither do I,' he said. 'And, that being so, the less you and I worry about the form of Government they set up, the better. That is for them to decide. What interests us is, which of them is doing most harm to the Germans?'

Fitzroy Maclean

‡

The destruction of the Scharnhorst

On Christmas Day 1943, the Scharnhorst *left Altenfjord in Norway to attack an Arctic convoy – JW55B – which had an escort of 14 destroyers. The battleship* Duke of York *and the light cruiser* Jamaica *were acting as 'distant cover', and on Boxing Day the former engaged the German vessel. On board* Jamaica *was Lieutenant B. B. Ramsden of the Royal Marines.*

Still the slogging match continued, flash for flash, round for round. Although the *Scharnhorst* was not firing at us directly, the shells were falling sometimes to miss the flagship and to come uncomfortably close to us. At one moment I thought the *Duke of York* was hit. Simultaneously with the burst of three eleven-inch close to her, a red glow blossomed from somewhere for'ard and lit up her entire bridge superstructure. However, it turned out to be the flash of her reply from 'A' turret, which was suffused in the billowing cordite smoke. This drifted back in arid clouds, and was most unpleasant. We turned a few points to starboard at high speed, and I could again train the director on to the *Scharnhorst*'s flickering salvos. I tried to give a running commentary over the telephone to those below, but it must have been most disjointed.

'Boxing Day, bulletin number 30.' Again the cheerful voice of the first lieutenant. 'The destroyers are now going in to attack.' I confess to having completely forgotten about them up till then, but now I blessed their presence. There was a strange lull in the gun-fire. Everyone was on tiptoe, straining to catch the first signs of their attack. The familiar flash of eleven-inch again split the darkness, and a minute or so later an incredible and terrifying noise made me momentarily crouch down again. A whole salvo had passed clean over our heads, like the tearing of a huge corrugated cardboard box – an indescribable, devilish sound. 'Come on, Adolf, no more of that,' I prayed. Again the flicker in the distance, and again we waited for it to arrive. Nothing came. Again the flash, but followed this time by star-shell illuminating the horizon. Thank God, the destroyers must be in. We remained silent and sat back more comfortably.

Then the flagship turned, slowly at first, to port, and round we went farther and farther in her faint wake until our bows were directly towards the enemy. They were getting excited below. Dead ahead were the signs of a furious engagement. Star-shell flared high, guns flashed, red beads of pompom fire ran out in livid streams, each to fade in a small white burst. Strange bursts of high-angle fire spasmodically dotted the sky, and still we ploughed on steadily and silently, and our guns pointed mutely towards the flashes ready to crash out again.

No shell came near us for almost twenty minutes. We turned to starboard, the turrets following round so that both ships presented a full broadside. I think I yelled 'Stand by again!' over the telephones, but my words were drowned by the deafening crash of gun-fire. The tracer now appeared almost horizontal, so flat was the trajectory as they rushed like fireflies to converge at a point in the darkness.

Suddenly – a bright-red glow, and in it the enemy was to be clearly seen for a brief moment. 'She's hit! My God, we've got her!' I was yelling like one possessed. We were cheering in the director. All over the ship a cheer went up, audible above the gun-fire. I had risen half standing in my seat as the wild thrill took hold of me. Again the dull glow, and in its light the sea was alive with shell-splashes from an outpouring of shells. Great columns of water stood out clearly in the brief instant of light, and I could see smoke hanging above her. I was mad with excitement until I realised that my ravings must be an incoherent babble of enthusiasm to those below as the telephones were still hanging round my head. I straightened my tin hat, sat down, and told them as calmly as I could that we could see that our shells had set her on fire, and that both the *Duke of York* and ourselves were hitting, and hitting hard.

She must have been a hell on earth. The fourteen-inch from the flagship were hitting or rocketing off from a ricochet on the sea. I had no coherent thought. The sudden knowledge that we were beating her to a standstill had gone to my head. My crew were just as bad. Nothing seemed to matter. Great flashes rent the night, and the sound of gun-fire was continuous, and yet the *Scharnhorst* replied, but only occasionally now. She was engaging the destroyers with what armament she had. We were keeping the director trained dead on her, and none of us noticed that our course had altered. The blaze and concussion of our gun-fire seemed to grow, and, as in a dream, I heard someone shout, 'The back of the director's blown in, sir.' A second later something hit me in the back, and lay there heavy and inanimate. I looked round and saw that indeed it had been blown in. The hinges had given under the blast of our turrets, and left a gaping rectangular space through which the wind and spray whistled. It occurred to me quickly that another broadside would go off any moment, and the flash come in on our unprotected backs, and so we trained on to the beam just in time. The next broadside left us dazed, but what did we care! I crawled out of my seat and crouched at the side, gripping on to a strut to steady myself for the next. 'A' and 'B' turrets were trained until the muzzle gave our director a minimum of clearance, and the shells could be passing only a few feet away from us. We clung to anything, and gazed intent on the target as the blast and flash of our broadside shook the director like a can. It was terrific.

Then faintly, but growing more loud and clear as we ceased firing, came the pipe – 'Boxing Day, bulletin number 38. Commander-in-Chief ordered *Jamaica* to go in and finish her off with torpedoes.' A moment later, divorced at last from the comfort of the flagship's heavy guns, we turned, in a sweep of spray, bows on again towards where we had last seen the *Scharnhorst*'s flash. We were alone.

How alone we felt! The tumult and the noise had died, leaving almost a hush – the hush of expectancy. All I could hear was the wind and the sea, and into the quiet came the return of foreboding and tension. Everyone was thinking – what lies ahead? When last seen the *Scharnhorst* was still firing. Had she any eleven-inch yet able to bear on us? As we closed what sudden crash of gun-fire might envelop us? God, how much nearer? A sudden large flash ahead. Wait! – no, nothing arrived near us. Still firing at the destroyers, perhaps. 'Stand by, four-inch, port side,' came the order down a voice-pipe.

I was galvanised into action. 'Train round, train round. Stop. No, a little more. There she is! Guns follow director. Enemy in sight. No deflection. You've got the range, haven't you? OK. Stand by, then.' It had come. At last we were going to open fire, and I was controlling. I was cool now, and desperately grim in concentration. I mustn't lose this chance. We were turning, turning to starboard, and again came the flicker of gun-fire right in front of us, but much more vivid and far nearer. I caught sight of a red blob, then another, which rose in front and then curved down, and it seemed to come straight for us. No, it had gone over. Again everything blurred, and was shaken as one six-inch broadside and then another was fired – straight into her. We couldn't miss at that range – 3,000 yards. I could smell the sweetish smell of burning. It must be the *Scharnhorst*. I yelled above the din for permission to open fire. We waited and waited for an answer, but none came. They probably never received it on the bridge. And then we turned away and ceased firing. My four-inch hadn't even opened up, and we were bitterly disappointed.

Star-shell from nowhere burst over our heads, bathing the whole ship in light. Surely she will open up now. We were naked, illuminated in every detail. But nothing came. No shot was fired at us, and once more everything was plunged in darkness. At 3,500 yards we turned a full half-circle, so that our starboard side was presented, and we on the port side could sit back and try to imagine what was happening. Another burst of fire and more flashes. Then we turned away and made off. There was no noise now. What had happened? Nobody seemed to know. What had become of the torpedoes? As I was trying to find out from the ADP, two distinct underwater explosions, deep and dull, made the ship quiver slightly. 'Those were our "fish" hitting!' came the cry. Still there was no noise of firing. We stood up in the director and looked around. Nothing in sight. Ten minutes passed and nothing happened. Hardly a sound could be heard above the wind and the sea. We asked the ADP if they could see anything, and they told us that there was one solitary searchlight burning on the starboard side, sweeping the sea, over which could be seen a vague pall of smoke. Minutes dragged by. What was happening? Where was everyone?

'Boxing Day, bulletin number 43,' came the pipe, and, in scarcely suppressed excitement, 'The *Scharnhorst* has been sunk. Destroyers are picking up survivors.'

B. B. Ramsden

Of the Scharnhorst's *company of 1,839, all but 36 were lost. Her sinking marked the end of the German High Seas Fleet as a threat.*

‡

Absent friends

John Comer was a flight engineer/top turret gunner with an American squadron of B-17 Flying Fortresses stationed near Cambridge at the height of the USAAF's bombing offensive against Germany. The squadron sustained heavy losses and, after completing his tour of 25 missions, he waited for news of two friends from his aircraft who still had several runs to make.

14 JANUARY 1944

I was standing in the snack bar at Chorley when I saw Lt Ferrin walk in. He was a few days behind me getting away from Ridgewell.

'When did you leave the 381st?' I asked.

'Yesterday. Got here this afternoon.'

'I read that the January eleventh mission had high losses. How did the 381st come out?'

'There was a mix-up and the planes were called back. Some of 'em didn't get the message and went on and got clobbered.'

'How many did the Group lose?'

'Quite a few. I didn't get the exact number, but it was bad!'

'You know Jim Counce and George Balmore.'

'Sure, I know 'em.'

'They were with Crozier and Cline on that mission. Did both of those ships get back OK?'

'The loss startled Col. Nazzaro because it was unexpected.'

'How about Cline and Crozier?' I sensed he was avoiding my question.

Ferrin took a deep breath and looked me in the eye. 'Crozier and Cline both went down, Comer.'

I listened in a state of shock and disbelief. For a minute I could not say anything.

'Were there any chutes – either plane?'

'Crozier's plane was seen to explode. There was hardly any chance for a survivor.' There was an icy feeling in the middle of my chest. When I recovered enough, I asked almost in a whisper, 'And the other plane?'

'Cline's ship was last seen badly damaged and engines burning – it is not known if any of the crew got out. No chutes were observed.'

At least there was a chance that Jim had time to jump, but I knew too well how fast the explosions came after engines caught fire. If anyone got out, surely Jim would be one of them, for he was close to the waist escape hatch.

'Have you seen Shutting?'

'Yes, I ran into Carl an hour ago.'

I turned away from Ferrin and stumbled blindly from the crowded bar. He followed and told me the meagre details that were known. But I had quit listening. My mind was in shock. Right then I could not talk to anyone. The night was bitterly cold and it was raining. I walked blindly in the rain without cap or raincoat for a long time because a man does not cry in front of other men; I walked until I was soaked and shaking with the cold. What Ferrin said kept coming back. 'The 533rd Squadron was almost wiped out. The mission was aborted but they did not get the message and were hit by a devastating fighter attack.' One squadron all alone so far inland was unbelievable!

There was no possible sleep for me! All night I stared into the blackness and groped for the means to accept the inevitable. At such times the mind tries to find ways to avoid the truth when it is too bitter to accept. There is some mistake! They will turn up! The word will seep back that they got out and are prisoners of war.

John Comer

Both Counce and Balmore had perished, as did one in four of all Allied bomber crews flying missions from Britain in this period of the war.

‡

The Anzio Derby

The Allied advance on Rome was held up by the Germans' dogged defence of Monte Cassino, so in late January 1944 70,000 troops were put ashore at Anzio, south of the capital, to turn the German flanks. Field Marshal Kesselring, however, reacted quickly to seal up the narrow bridgehead, where American and British soldiers were soon subject to continual air raids and heavy shelling.

In these static conditions, with nowhere safe for troops to go, there was little to do when off duty until beetle racing suddenly arrived. This caught on like wildfire, particularly amongst the Gunners and at Divisional HQ. Elaborate totes were constructed and really large money changed hands in bets. A champion beetle might fetch as much as three thousand *lire* or more, and as a thousand *lire* in those days was £2 10s., it was no mean price to pay for an insect. Runners were plentiful, for beetles seemed to be one of the chief products of the beachhead. Dig a slit trench, leave it for an hour, and the bottom would be black with beetles all trying to get out. The system of racing was simple. Various colours were painted on the beetles' backs and the runners were paraded round the ring in jam jars. Just before the 'off', or I suppose one should say when they came under starter's orders, the beetles were placed under one glass jar in the centre of the 'course'. This was a circle about six feet in diameter. At the 'off' the jar was raised and the first beetle out of the circle was the winner. A difficulty arose when, for one reason or another, it became necessary to change a beetle's colours in quick time; but at one Gunner meeting the problem was solved by attaching small flags to the beetles' backs with chewing gum.

F. C. M. Reeves

The Allies would not manage to break out of Anzio for another four months.

✠

Planning for the invasion of Normandy had reached an advanced stage.

Our intention was to assault, simultaneously, beaches on the Normandy coast immediately north of the Carentan estuary and between that area and the River Orne, with the object of securing as a base for further operations a lodgement area which was to include airfield sites and the port of Cherbourg. The left or eastern flank of the lodgement area was to include the road centre of Caen.

General Eisenhower had placed me in command of all the land forces for the assault. For this we had two armies – the Second British Army under Dempsey and the First American Army under Bradley. Later, two more armies would come into being – the First Canadian under Crerar and the Third American under Patton. It is important to understand that, once we had secured a good footing in Normandy, my plan was to *threaten* to break out on the eastern flank, that is in the Caen sector. By pursuing this threat relentlessly I intended to draw the main enemy reserves, particularly his armoured divisions, into that sector and to keep them there – using the British and Canadian forces under Dempsey for this purpose. Having got the main enemy strength committed on the *eastern* flank, my plan was to make the break-out on the *western* flank – using for this task the American forces under General Bradley. This break-out attack was to be launched southwards, and then to proceed eastwards in a wide sweep up to the Seine about Paris. I hoped that this gigantic wheel would pivot on Falaise. It aimed to cut off all the enemy forces south of the Seine, the bridges over that river below Paris having been destroyed by our air forces.

All our work was linked to this basic plot, which I explained at many conferences from February onwards.

Bernard Montgomery

✝

The Far East

With the Marines on New Guinea

In the meantime, we were constantly receiving replacements to rebuild the division. When we were back in shape, we started the well-known tough Marine Corps training. After several months of this we went to New Guinea for some advance work. We all felt it was back to the jungle for us and we were right.

This time it was a place called Cape Gloucester on the tip of New Britain Island. It was right off the eastern end of New Guinea. Once again we were going after an airfield. We boarded our LSTs [landing ships] on December 24, 1943 – a hell of a way to celebrate Christmas Eve.

These LSTs would have been all right if they'd had about one-third as many troops aboard as they did. As it was, we could hardly move. I tried to sleep up on deck on a canvas between the ribs of an F.W. Dig truck. By the time we landed, December 26th, we were all punchy from lack of sleep and seasickness. Fortunately, like the Canal, the landing was unopposed. Strangely, while the casualties on Gloucester were the lowest our division was to have in any of its campaigns, it was the first time that our battery had real eyeball-to-eyeball action with the Japanese.

It isn't the action that stands out the most to me about Cape Gloucester though, it is the awful weather. Rain, rain, rain, every day and night. Someone said the brass had picked the rainy season to go in because they felt we would surprise the enemy. Maybe so, but the area we fought in became a goddamn masterful mudslide.

The 11th picked up a unit citation here because we did such a great job slugging the guns through the mud. You'd be trying to move through the jungle when you'd find yourself up to your knees, or deeper, in a mud pit. There was a joke floating around that went like this:

This captain is looking at one of those mud pies when a helmet appears moving through the mud. Then it comes up a little higher and the captain sees a head.

'Jeez,' the captain says, 'you must be in real deep.'

'Real deep,' the Marine replies. 'Wait 'til you see the bulldozer I'm driving!'

As you can imagine, the damn diseases ran rampant. Malaria came back and so did dysentery – just think what happens to your bowels in weather like that. Even our ponchos began to disintegrate.

Then there was jungle rot. You couldn't possibly keep your socks dry, much less your boondockers. This knocked the devil out of your feet. By the time we left New Britain many of our men could hardly walk.

Another menace was those big trees. They were rotten. The shelling and the lightning were always knocking them over. Our division actually had several men killed from either lightning or falling trees.

Remember that during all this we were trying to fight a war. I did a lot of forward observing with the 7th Marines and could actually see the Japanese during some of their charges. Call them fanatical if you like, but, my God, they were brave! Our artillery and automatic weapons cut them to ribbons, but they'd come at you until they'd drop. Sometimes they'd come at you until they were close enough to toss grenades, and sometimes we'd toss them back. That Jap grenade must have had much more of a delayed action that ours did. That's the way it seemed to us anyway.

Then there was the sniper fire. I was talking to a buddy when the left side of his helmet was hit by a bullet that came out of the back side without touching the guy's head. That's about as close as you can come to the end of the ballgame. A day or two later another Marine I knew also took a slug in his helmet that came out the other end, but this time it took the poor guy's brain with it.

Well, we took our airfield, killed a lot of very brave Japanese soldiers and sometime in the early spring, they took us off New Britain.

Warner Pyne

After the war, the author became the American representative for a leading Japanese electronics firm.

The Forgotten Army

John Masters was an officer in the Gurkhas, part of Slim's Fourteenth Army.

Below the generals, below the staff . . . and above them all, were the soldiers. The theatre, and this campaign, gathered to itself, like a whirlpool, men from the ends of the earth. There were English, Irish, Welsh, and

Scots, and, in the RAF, Newfoundlanders, Australians, Canadians, New Zealanders, and South Africans. There were Chinese; there were tall, slender Negroes from East Africa, and darker, more heavily built Negroes from West Africa, with the tribal slits slashed deep into their cheeks – an infantry division of each. There were Chins, Kachins, Karens, and Burmans, mostly light brown, small-boned men in worn jungle green, doubly heroic because the Japanese held possession of their homes, often of their families, too; and, until about now, how could they be sure which side was going to win?

There were men from every state of the United States. They flew heavy bombers, they ran railroads, they drove titanic trucks at breakneck speeds through the narrow streets of primeval villages. In the back areas some behaved with a certain bombast, an air of 'We'll put this mess straight, meanwhile everything in sight belongs to us, especially your women' – which was rather galling to people who had not found it easy to get the mess straight by themselves, and had fought so long alone; but most back-area soldiers behave unpleasantly, and the Americans were merely more noticeable, with their funny accents and funny clothes – and their extra money. But, the closer you got to the front, the more you found that the Americans, whether or not they saluted with great punctilio, meant business, and the closer became the ties between them and the rest of us.

Lastly, and in by far the greatest numbers, there were the men of the Indian Army, the largest volunteer army the world has ever known. There were men from every caste and race – Sikhs, Dogras, Pathans, Madrassis, Mahrattas, Rajputs, Assamese, Kumaonis, Punjabis, Garhwalis, Naga head-hunters – and, from Nepal, the Gurkhas in all their tribes and sub-tribes, of Limbu and Rai, Thakur and Chhetri, Magar and Gurung. These men wore turbans, and steel helmets, and slouch hats, and berets, and tank helmets, and khaki shakos inherited from the eighteenth century. There were companies that averaged five feet one inch in height and companies that averaged six feet three inches. There were men as purple black as the West Africans, and men as pale and gold-wheat of skin as a lightly sun-tanned blond. They worshipped God according to the rites of the Mahayana and Hinayana, of Sunni and of Shiah, of Rome and Canterbury and Geneva, of the Vedas and the sages and the Mahabharatas, of the ten Gurus, of the secret shrines of the jungle. There were vegetarians and meat-eaters and fish-eaters, and men who ate only rice, and men who ate only wheat; and men who had four wives, men who shared one wife with four brothers, and men who openly practised sodomy. There were men who had never seen snow and men who seldom saw anything else. And Brahmins and Untouchables, both with rifle and tommy gun.

No one who saw the 14th Army in action, above all, no one who saw its dead on the field of battle, the black and the white and the brown and the yellow lying together in their indistinguishable blood on the rich soil of Burma, can ever doubt that there is a brotherhood of man; or fail to cry, What *is* Man, that he can give so much for war, so little for peace?

Lastly, there was our common, single enemy – the Japanese. They are the bravest people I have ever met. In our armies, any of them, nearly every Japanese would have had a Congressional Medal or a Victoria Cross. It is the fashion to dismiss their courage as fanaticism but this only begs the question. They believed in something, and they were willing to die for it, for any smallest detail that would help to achieve it. What else is bravery? They pressed home their attacks when no other troops in the world would have done so, when all hope of success was gone; except that it never really is, for who can know what the enemy has suffered, what is his state of mind? The Japanese simply came on, using all their skill and rage, until they were stopped, by death. In defence they held their ground with a furious tenacity that never faltered. They had to be killed, company by company, squad by squad, man by man, to the last.

By 1944 many scores of thousands of Allied soldiers had fallen unwounded into enemy hands as prisoners, because our philosophy and our history have taught us to accept the idea of surrender. By 1944 the number of Japanese captured unwounded, in all theatres of war, probably did not total one hundred. On the Burma front it was about six.

For the rest, they wrote beautiful little poems in their diaries, and practised bayonet work on their prisoners. Frugal and bestial, barbarous and brave, artistic and brutal, they were the *dushman* [enemy] and we now set about, in all seriousness, the task of killing every one of them.

John Masters

At the start of the year, Slim began to test the Japanese with a push into the Arakan, the coastal region of Burma. It was met by a savage counter-attack in February. The British, however, had now evolved a technique to deal with encircling enemy offensives, standing fast in a defensive position that could be supplied from the air. One such was known as the 'Administrative Box'. When its hospital was overrun, appalling atrocities were committed.

Wounded prisoners received no attention. Those who cried out were shot or bayoneted. Men lying helplessly in bed were killed. In one shelter were a British Lieutenant, a Major of the Gurkhas and a Signals Sergeant. They were being tended by a captain of the RAMC. Four West Yorkshires, whose defence post was overrun in the attack, joined them. When day came, they lay still so that the Japanese might not notice them. During the morning they heard a shout outside and the RAMC Captain asked:

'What do you want?'

The shout – it sounded like 'You go' – was repeated. The Captain shook his head and lay down again. 'Who is it?' asked the Lieutenant.

'It's a Jap,' said the Captain. At that moment one of the Japanese soldiers appeared and shot him through the right thigh. The Captain shouted: 'I am a doctor – Red Cross – I am a medical officer.'

The Japanese shot dead the Captain, the Gurkha Major, two British soldiers and a mess servant. The Lieutenant and the three surviving British soldiers lay still. They stayed like that all day, and when darkness came they managed to leave the hospital and find the safety of the nearest West Yorkshire post.

A British private of the RAMC – one of a party of twenty – survived to describe his experience. He was tied by his neck to another man – as they all were – kicked, cuffed and cracked over the head by rifle butts, and used as a shield on top of a trench by the Japanese when the carrier attacked. Just before dark on February 8, a Japanese officer told the twenty men: 'Come and get treatment.'

They were taken along a dried-up watercourse to a clearing with a running stream. Through the whole hot day they had been allowed only two bottles of water between them. And now they stood by the stream. But they were not allowed to drink. The Japanese opened up at them with rifles. Seventeen of them were killed. That night Lieutenant Basu and nine men who had been wounded when a mortar exploded near them lay in a watercourse, some dying, some crying for water. The Japanese shot one man and bayoneted another who cried too loudly. Just before they left, the Japanese stood in front of them, their rifles ready.

'We are Red Cross people,' said Basu – he and another doctor both had their stethoscopes slung round their necks. 'We are doctors and hospital workers. We have nothing to do with actual warfare.' Most of them wore Red Cross badges on their arms. It made no difference. The Japanese shot them all.

Lieutenant Basu was shot at twice. He was left stunned. At first he was not sure whether he was alive or dead. He felt at his ear, but there was no blood on his fingers. He could still see and his thoughts became clear once more. He realised how vulnerable he was lying there still alive. So he reached out to the body of one of his dead friends and put his hand on the wounds until it was covered with blood, and then he smeared the blood over his face and head and down his shirt front, so that the Japanese would think he, too, was mortally wounded. He slipped groaning into a trench, and there he spent the night.

Geoffrey Evans

‡

The cap

In order to survive in a Nazi concentration camp, most inmates had to abandon the moral standards to which they had previously adhered. A Jewish teenager, Roman Frister, here describes the homosexual rape to which he was subjected, and its fatal consequences.

Everyone called him Arpad Basci. He had been in more prisons than schools. He began his career as a pickpocket in the Budapest railroad station. As he grew older he took up burglary, an uncommon profession among Hungary's Jews. He was in jail so often that he became a king there. But for the German conquerors of his country he was a petty criminal – and a Jewish one at that. Long before Eichmann's deportation of Hungarian Jews, he was sent to Auschwitz. From there he was transferred to the work camp in which I met him.

Arpad Basci had a special status in the camp. An expert sculptor of chess pieces, he carved them from a rare material: bread. The camp guards who coveted his work brought him as much bread as he wished. Arpad Basci liked young boys; the young boys in the camp liked bread; and so the world went round.

He had a keen eye for spotting his new victims. The day after my arrival in the camp I was assigned to his crew of bread chewers. At night, after work, he sat five or six of us on the floor of the barracks and handed us lumps of bread. Our job was to chew them slowly, rolling them between our tongues and our palates until our saliva made them soft and malleable. From such bread alone, he explained, could he model his immortal creations. Once hardened it would withstand for ever the ravages of time, humidity, and bugs.

The bread tasted divine. Anyone swallowing a crumb would regret it. Arpad Basci was merciless. Seated opposite us, his eyes staring at each of our Adam's apples in turn, he warned that he would choke to death whoever fell into temptation. He knew how starved we were and he knew our tricks.

We spat the chewed bread onto a white linen cloth, where Arpad Basci inspected it as carefully as a jeweller grading diamonds, prodding it lightly for viscosity. Anything failing to meet his standards was scraped off the cloth and returned to the chewer. By the time I received the crust of bread that was my pay, my jaws ached.

Lights-out came at ten. At that hour we were supposed to be in our bunks with our uniforms folded and our shaven heads visible for counting. Only the kapo and Arpad Basci were allowed to move about at night. The kapo slept in a private little cubicle. Arpad Basci had his own habits.

I chewed Arpad Basci's bread for about two months before the time came for my final payment on his bread crusts. My bunkmate said nothing when Arpad Basci ordered him out of our shared bed and slipped into his place behind me. Even before he touched me I knew what was going to happen. His hand roamed my body, a shaky finger searching for the entrance. Smeared with lard, it easily found my anus and corkscrewed into it. Although I tensed my muscles to prevent him, the old man got the better of me. As soon as his finger was withdrawn his penis rammed into me with a single quick thrust. The pain was terrible. I wanted to scream. As if knowing my reaction, he covered my mouth with his hand. In it was a slice of bread. I stifled my cry and ate the bread from his hand. When I finished the first slice, a second filled my mouth. I swallowed it quickly in the hope of a third before he ejaculated. An expert rapist, he drilled into me with short, rhythmic strokes. My body felt torn apart. The sharp pain becoming a burning ache. I was bleeding.

He fell back. I swallowed the last crumbs. Only then was I overcome with humiliation and shame for having sold my honour for his bread. No, I wasn't raped. I hadn't resisted. I hadn't called for help. I hadn't even told him to stop. I had said nothing when he gave me a good-night slap on the rear and went off to sleep in his bunk.

He didn't go empty-handed. Two hours later I awoke from a draining, nightmarish dream to discover that my cap was gone. A prisoner without his standard-issue cap was as good as dead. At morning roll-call the kapo and SS officer regularly killed anyone not having one. Sometimes they played a game in which the kapo seized a cap and flung it across the parade grounds. If the owner of it stayed where he was, he was shot for being capless. If he ran to retrieve it, he was shot for 'attempting to escape'.

The son of a bitch! I cursed Arpad Basci under my breath. I had two, at most three hours left to live. Cold sweat covered my back. I felt it drop down my spine. Arpad Basci's intention was clear. He wanted to get rid of me because I knew too much. I had never paid much attention until now to the fact that his bread chewers had a way of dying or disappearing under mysterious circumstances. The last one had drowned in a tank of excrement in the camp's outhouse.

I restrained myself from going to Arpad Basci's bunk and demanding my cap back. I could identify it easily. It had bloodstains from the time I was clubbed on the head by a kapo. But what good would that do? Arpad Basci would say it wasn't mine. He would laugh or call for his friend the kapo to punish me. In the Kingdom of Evil proof or evidence meant nothing. No word was more ridiculous than 'justice'. Arpad Basci was an old and privileged prisoner while I was just a number with an arm attached. I stood no chance in an open confrontation.

I slid quietly down from my bunk. My bare feet touched the concrete floor. Its chill surface felt good and cooled my feverish brain. I looked to the left and the right. A naked bulb above the door gave the only dim light that there was. The barracks resembled a dark tunnel. I heard the breathing of the sleeping prisoners. Somebody snored. I walked down the narrow aisle between the bunks, stopping every few seconds to listen, then move on. With cat's eyes I looked for the careless prisoner who had not hidden his cap beneath his blanket. I was scared. I would be lynched if I were discovered. No one would defend me. The theft of a cap was an unpardonable crime.

My anus was burning. Someone coughed. I froze. The cougher fell silent. I took a few steps and halted, racking my mind for an alibi in case I was caught. I had once witnessed the catching of a cap thief in Auschwitz. His fellow prisoners hanged him from a rafter. They left his body hanging all day as a warning. Involuntarily, I glanced at the ceiling. That was what led me to my victim.

He was lying in a top bunk, his face covered by his blanket. The tip of his cap stuck out from the crook of his arm. I tugged it gently. He didn't awake. The cap was in my hand. I stuck it under my shirt, its rough cloth scratching my chest. I was overjoyed.

I started back to my bunk. I mustn't hurry. I listened. Silence. The pounding of my heart was the only sound I heard. I tiptoed slowly. It took me ten minutes – or was it only one? – to regain my bunk. The man on the bottom mattress turned over in his sleep. Had he seen me? I held my breath. Weary, he slept on. We all were weary. No sleeping pill was as strong as our exhaustion. I clambered up to my mattress and stuck the cap in my pocket. I couldn't sleep. I stayed awake until reveille.

Roll-call was at five. Spotlights lit up the parade grounds. A light snow was falling. The cold cut to the bone. 'Ten–tion!' shouted the kapo. We snapped to attention. The count began. I was in the second row. It was always good to be in the middle, neither too prominent nor too exposed, as far as possible from the officer's glance. In front of me, at the end of the first row, was the unassailable Arpad Basci. I recognised him by the back of his neck. It was the only one to have folds of fat on it. It belonged to a man who ate well. I recognised my cap, too, by the bloodstains.

Somewhere behind me was a man waiting to die. Only he, Arpad Basci, and I myself knew it was about to happen. Arpad Basci would be disappointed. I had no idea what the man without the cap felt. I had no qualms. I refused to think about it from his point of view. His existence didn't matter. Mine did.

The officer and the kapo walked down the lines, inspecting our uniforms, our posture, our ability to work. I counted the seconds as they counted the prisoners. I wanted it to be over. They were up to row four. The capless man didn't beg for his life. We all knew the rules of the game, the killers and the killed alike. There was no need for words. The shot rang out without warning. There was a short, dry, echoless thud. One bullet to the brain. They always shot you in the back of the skull. There was a war on. Ammunition had to be used sparingly. I didn't want to know who the man was. I was delighted to be alive.

Roman Frister

Spring 1944

Burma

The burden of command

By the start of March 1944, all was ready for the insertion by air of Orde Wingate's second Chindit expedition, which was tasked with disrupting Japanese communications behind their lines and aiding the advance of General Stilwell's Chinese troops from the north.

During the morning the gliders had been loaded with supplies, ammunition, engineer equipment, signalling stores, and men's kits. In the late afternoon the first wave, 77 Brigade Headquarters, the leading British and Gurkha infantry, and a small detachment of American airfield engineers emplaned. Each Dakota was to take two gliders. This was a heavy load, and, as far as I know, never before had these aircraft towed more than one. There had been a clash of opinion among the airmen themselves on its practicability. Cochrane, in charge of the gliders, was confident it could be done; Old, whose Combat Cargo planes would provide the tugs, maintained it was unsound. Various airmen, British and American, took sides and argument was heated. Eventually, after experiments, Wingate agreed with Cochrane, and then Baldwin and I accepted the double tow. Now as I watched the last preparations I was assailed by no doubts on that score. The Dakotas taxied into position. The tow ropes were fixed. Everyone was very quiet as the roar of engines died down and we waited for zero hour. I was standing on the airstrip with Wingate, Baldwin, and one or two more, when we saw a jeep driving furiously towards us. A couple of American airmen jumped out and confronted us with an air photograph, still wet from the developing tent. It was a picture of Piccadilly landing ground, taken two hours previously. It showed almost the whole level space, on which the gliders were to land that night, obstructed by great tree-trunks. It would be impossible to put down even one glider safely. To avoid suspicion no aircraft had reconnoitred the landing grounds for some days before the fly-in, so this photo was a complete shock to us. We looked at one another in dismay.

Wingate, though obviously feeling the mounting strain, had been quiet and controlled. Now, not unnaturally perhaps, he became very moved. His immediate reaction was to declare emphatically to me that the whole plan had been betrayed – probably by the Chinese – and that it would be dangerous to go on with it. I asked if Broadway and Chowringhee, the other proposed landing places, had been photographed at the same time. I was told they had been and that both appeared vacant and unobstructed.

Wingate was now in a very emotional state, and to avoid discussion with him before an audience, I drew him on one side. I said I did not think the Chinese had betrayed him as they certainly had no knowledge of actual landing grounds, or, as far as I knew, of the operation at all; but he reiterated that someone had betrayed the plan and that the fly-in should be cancelled. I pointed out that only one of the three landing grounds had been obstructed, and that it was the one which he had used in 1943 and of which a picture with a Dakota on it had appeared in an American magazine. We knew the Japanese were nervous of air landing and were blocking many possible landing sites in North and Central Burma; what more likely than they should include a known one we had already used, like Piccadilly. He replied that, even if Broadway and Chowringhee were not physically obstructed, it was most probable that Japanese troops were concealed in the surrounding jungle ready to destroy our gliders as they landed. With great feeling he said it would be 'murder'. I told him I doubted if these places were ambushed. Had the Japanese known of the plan I was sure they would have either ambushed or obstructed all three landing grounds. Wingate was by now calmer and much more in control of himself. After thinking for a moment, he said there would be great risk. I agreed. He paused, then looked straight at me: 'The responsibility is yours,' he said.

I knew it was. Not for the first time I felt the weight of decision crushing in on me with an almost physical pressure. The gliders, if they were to take off that night, must do so within the hour. There was no time for prolonged inquiry or discussion. On my answer would depend not only the possibility of a disaster with wide implications on the whole Burma campaign and beyond, but the lives of these splendid men, tense and waiting in and around their aircraft. At that moment I would have given a great deal if Wingate or anybody else could have relieved me of the duty of decision. But that is a burden the commander himself must bear.

I knew that if I cancelled the fly-in or even postponed it, when the men were keyed to the highest pitch, there would be a terrible reaction; we would never get their morale to the same peak again. The whole plan of campaign, too, would be thrown out.

I had promised Stilwell we would cut the communications of the enemy opposing him, and he was relying on our doing it. I had to consider also that one Chindit brigade had already marched into the area; we could hardly desert it. I was, in addition, very nervous that if we kept the aircraft crowded on the airfields as they were, the Japanese would discover them, with disastrous consequences. I knew at this time that a major Japanese offensive was about to break on the Assam front, and I calculated on Wingate's operation to confuse and hamper it. Above all, somehow I did not believe that the Japanese knew of our plan or that the obstruction of Piccadilly was evidence that they did. There was a risk, a grave risk, but not a certainty of disaster. 'The operation will go on,' I said.

William Slim

The expedition had not been betrayed – the trees at Piccadilly had been cut by chance by loggers. Slim's decision to continue with the fly-in at Broadway and Chowringhee was vindicated, and by April more than 9,000 men had been landed behind the Japanese positions.

A day in the jungle

Richard Rhodes James was the cipher officer with Lentaigne's brigade on the expedition.

At about 7.30 came that dread signal, 'Packs on,' and we shouldered our gargantuan loads, feeling again the creases and bruises of yesterday's march. That first hour was by no means the worst of the day. With the sun not properly risen and one's insides aglow with the tea of a few minutes back, we could march with ease and confidence, silent and settled, hearing only the clink of mule harness and the rattle of a badly adjusted load. The rise and fall of the equipment of the man in front had not begun to irritate and served only to emphasise the rhythm of the march. There is leisure to look around before the weight of the pack has bent the back and fixed the eyes in a weary gaze at the boots of the next man or the hooves of the mule in front. There is enchantment in this early hour more clearly defined in its contrast to the toil ahead and the troops, after they have overcome the depression of the early rise, are ready to face the day.

The enchantment is shortlived, and especially in our case with unaccustomed bodies and soft feet. The sun mounts and sheds no kindly light but a merciless glare on the column. The sweat begins to collect under the pack and flows in great salty streams from the forehead through the eyes and down the chin. All the aches and pains of yesterday appear again, to be joined by the peculiar discomforts of today. The ill-adjusted pack, the rubbing of the water-bottle or haversack, that place where the belt fails to coincide with the contours of the body, the place you long to scratch but cannot reach. And then the boots, pinching, slipping, rubbing, the socks sliding down the foot and collecting in an abrasive bundle at the heel. Having very unaccommodating feet I fared badly on that first march and suffered the extreme indignity of travelling for a whole day on a horse.

The first sign of weariness is easily recognised. It is the furtive glance at the watch, first occasionally and increasingly frequently until we glance every few minutes in a desperate hope that time has passed and the hourly halt is due. The hour seems longer and longer, as the day lengthens, and woe betide the commander who dares to trespass one minute across the boundary of that time of rest. Impressed immediately with the great monotony of the march we sought to evolve a means of keeping our minds occupied. When the hypnotist tells you to 'make your mind a blank', he is asking the impossible. And we found that our minds craved an outlet from the prison which our physical activity imposed on them. The Gurkhas, having not reached, by our standards, a very high state of mental development, did not seem to find much difficulty in sustaining interest; the noises of the jungle and the sight of game satisfied them. For the British troops the problem was more difficult and no one but the individual himself could tell how successfully he overcame it. For myself, I used the method of the marching tune, and prided myself on my ability to convert any tune into the rhythm of the march. Conscious thoughts were less easy to arrange. They varied from a pride in physical achievement, which lasted only a short time, to nostalgic memories of physical comfort. There was always a special place reserved for anticipation of the midday halt or the night's bivouac, but it was not wise to encourage these thoughts too early in the day.

The first big moment of the day has arrived and after four or five hours' marching we disperse for the midday halt. Jack Masters gives instructions: 'Signals under the big tree over there with a set one hundred yards to the right.' 'Command post under this tree.' (Selecting the choicest position.) 'Transport along the line of the trees fifty yards off the track.' 'Medical, half left by that bush.' 'Orders in twenty minutes' time.'

Each man barely reaches his allotted station before he hurls off his pack, slumps down and surveys the scene wearily. But the rest is short lived. There are mules to unload, fires to prepare, water to fetch and blistered feet to inspect. I take up my position by the wireless set and enjoy the supreme luxury of having my pack removed by Birbal. The world is acceptable again. The Brigadier is already removing his boots.

                                                         Richard Rhodes James

Aged 29, John Masters found himself in command of a brigade of Chindits, dug into a fortified position but under heavy attack by the Japanese.

The rain now fell steadily. The Deep sector looked like Passchendaele – blasted trees, feet and twisted hands sticking up out of the earth, bloody shirts, ammunition clips, holes half full of water, each containing two pale, huge-eyed men, trying to keep their rifles out of the mud, and over all the heavy, sweet stench of death, from our own bodies and entrails lying unknown in the shattered ground, from Japanese corpses on the wire, or fastened, dead and rotting, in the trees. At night the rain hissed down in total darkness, the trees ran with water and, beyond the devastation, the jungle dripped and crackled.

A Japanese light machine-gun chatters hysterically, and bullets clack and clap overhead. Two Verey lights float up, burst in brilliant whiteness. Click, click, click – boom, crash, boom, three mortar bombs burst in red-yellow flashes on the wire.

The third crisis came on May 17. On that day our Lightnings (P-38s) patrolled the valley for several hours, searching for the guns which had done us so much damage. They did not find them. Towards evening the P-38s left and I went down to the water point, as I usually did, to wash, shave, and brush up for the night's battle. While I was shaving, the enemy began to shell the block with 105s and 155s. Twelve guns or more were firing. Soap all over my face, I looked across at the ridge to the west, where the enemy had once put a mortar, and saw movement there. Mortar bombs from the ridge whistled into the block. The shelling grew more urgent and I walked quickly up to my command post – I tried never to run.

The shelling concentrated on the Deep and became a violent, continuous drumfire. My stomach felt empty and I was ready to vomit. I should have relieved the King's Own. This was more than human flesh could stand. Nothing to do now though. The attack would come in immediately after the bombardment.

The shelling increased again. For ten minutes an absolute fury fell on the Deep.

Major Heap, the second-in-command of the King's Own, tumbled in, his face streaked and bloody and working with extreme strain. 'We've had it, sir,' he said. 'They're destroying all the posts, direct hits all the time . . . all machine-guns knocked out, crews killed . . . I don't think we can hold them if . . . the men are . . .'

I didn't wait to hear what the men were. I knew. They were dead, wounded, or stunned.

I took the telephone and called Tim Brennan, commanding 26 Column of the Cameronians, and told him to bring his whole column to the ridge crest at once, with all weapons and ammunition, manhandled, ready to take over the Deep. 'Yes, sir,' he said pleasantly. I had time to call Henning and order him to spread out to occupy Brennan's positions as well as his own, before going quickly, my breath short, to the hill crest.

The shelling stopped as I reached it. Tim arrived. Johnny Boden, the mortar officer, arrived. *Now, now, the Japanese must come.* I told Boden to stand by with smoke and H.E. to cover the Cameronians; 26 Column arrived, at the double. Still no assault. Tim ran down the forward slope, his men behind him. I waited crouched on the ridge top. Ordered Boden to open up with his mortars. The enemy must have this blasted slope covered by machine-guns. I knew they had. They didn't fire. It was twilight, but down the slope in the smoke I could clearly see Cameronians jumping into the waterlogged trenches, King's Own struggling out and up towards me. The Cameronian machine-guns arrived, men bent double under the ninety-pound loads of barrel and tripod. Bombs burst, smoke rose in dense white clouds. I told the officer to move the machine-guns again, after full dark, if he could. 'Of course, sir,' he said impatiently.

The men of the King's Own passed by, very slowly, to be gathered by Heap into reserve. They staggered, many were wounded, others carried wounded men, their eyes wandered, their mouths drooped open. I wanted to cry, but dared not, could only mutter, 'Well done, well done,' as they passed.

The minutes crawled, each one a gift more precious than the first rain. I sent wire down, and ammunition, and took two machine-guns from Henning's 90 Column, and put them in trenches on the crest, ready to sweep the whole slope. Full darkness came, with rain. An hour had passed, a whole hour since the enemy bombardment ended. In our own attacks we reckoned a thirty-second delay as fatal.

With a crash of machine-guns and mortars the battle began. All night the Cameronians and the Japanese 53rd Division fought it out. Our machine-guns ripped them from the new positions. Twice the Japanese forced into the barbed wire with Bangalore torpedoes, and the blasting rain of the mortars wiped them out. At four a.m., when they launched their final assault to recover their bodies, we had defeated them.

The next morning, as the rain fell more heavily, our patrols found the enemy had gone altogether. They had left the Deep sector and the hills across the Namkwin. They had abandoned the mortar post on the westward ridge. They had all gone. The forest was full of blood and flesh, and mass graves, and bodies fallen into stream beds, and bomb craters, and thousands of cartridge cases.

I have no means of knowing how many casualties we inflicted during this first phase of the Blackpool battle, except a post-war Intelligence interrogation, when a Japanese officer said, '. . . 53 Division had little fighting against the Chindits except on one occasion only, when one regiment was annihilated near Hopin'. This was us. A guess would be eight hundred to a thousand casualties. We suffered nearly two hundred, mostly in the King's Own.

John Masters

Part of the Chindits' purpose had been to draw off Japanese troops massing for the invasion of India. The speed of Lt-Gen. Mutaguchi's strike into Assam in March, however, caught Slim by surprise. A desperate siege developed at the town of Kohima that lasted for almost two months, while Imphal, Slim's supply base, was also blockaded and had to be supplied by air during a four-month-long battle. By mid-July, however, the Japanese – weakened by the rains and short on supplies – began to withdraw, and then to retreat. Manabu Wada was a private in 138 Infantry Regiment.

Throughout our long siege of Kohima enemy fighter aircraft flew along the face of the valley in front of us and cargo planes dropped arms and water to their leading troops. Without meat, rice or rifle and machine-gun ammunition we could only watch. Occasionally our own fighters, marked with the Japanese Sun, flew in support of us against heavy anti-aircraft fire but quickly disappeared again beyond the Kohima Mountains.

It was during the battle that our Commanding Officer, Major Shibazaki, was killed by a hand grenade. That was on 18 April, a month after the commencement of the Imphal Operation. Sadly, we cut off his hands and cremated them so that his bones might one day be consecrated at the cemetery back home. One day when we were walking on a jungle road, leading men hit a piano wire between trees, causing the connected grenades to explode. Then we were fired on by machine guns and a number of our comrades were killed. I was not hit as I was in the rear.

It was not surprising that in the middle of May the British 2nd Division found it possible to recapture the hills of Kohima Ridge from us. Our losses had been dreadful. Our soldiers fought bravely, but they had no rations, no rifle or machine-gun ammunition, no artillery shells for the guns to fire. And, above all, they had no support from rear echelons. How could they have continued in such dreadful circumstances? The monsoon season had started and the Kohima region is notorious for having the heaviest rainfall in the world. In the unceasing rain there was no shelter. If one hid beneath a tree the enemy's shells would destroy not just that tree but everything around it. There was only one consolation: the rains reduced the firing but it resumed as soon as the rain stopped.

It was impossible to cook rice in the rain. Sometimes we made a fire from undergrowth and boiled vegetable matter as the only means we had of staving off our terrible hunger. When the shelling began again we entered our 'octopus traps' – holes dug in the ground to a soldier's height – but the rain flooded in so that we were chest-high in water and had to climb out. We felt we had arrived at the very limit of our endurance.

At the beginning of the Imphal Operation the regiment was 3,800 strong. When our general gave the order to withdraw to the east we were reduced to just a few hundreds still alive. Without shelter from the rains, with boots that had rotted and had to be bound with grass, we began to trudge along the deep mud paths carrying our rifles without ammunition, leaning on sticks to support our weak bodies. Our medical corps men slipped and slid as they carried the sick and wounded on stretchers or supported the 'walking wounded'. Some of the orderlies were themselves so weak that they fell to the ground again and again until their physical and moral endurance was at an end, so that when a sick man cried out in pain they simply said, 'If you complain we'll just let you go, and throw you and the stretcher down the cliff side.'

Icy rain fell mercilessly on us and we lived day and night drenched to the skin and pierced with cold. I remember how we longed for a place, any place at all, where we could take shelter and rest. Once we found a tent in the jungle; inside it were the bodies of six nurses. We had never imagined there would be female victims, especially so far over the Arakan Mountains. Why, we asked one another, had the army not taken the nurses to a place of safety? In another tent we found the bodies of three soldiers who had killed themselves. How could one ever forget such terrible, distressing sights as the dead nurses, and the soldiers who had taken their own lives? All I could do was to swear to myself that somehow, I would survive.

Our path to safety lay beyond these Arakan Mountains covered in dense jungle. In the rain, with no place to sit, we took short spells of sleep standing on our feet. The bodies of our comrades who had struggled along the track before us lay all around, rain-sodden and giving off the stench of decomposition. The bones of some bodies were exposed. Even with the support of our sticks we fell amongst the corpses again and again as we stumbled on rocks and tree roots made bare by the rain and attempted one more step, then one more step in our exhaustion.

Thousands upon thousands of maggots crept out of the bodies lying in streams and were carried away by the fast-flowing waters. Many of the dead soldiers' bodies were no more than bleached bones. I cannot forget the sight of one corpse lying in a pool of knee-high water; all its flesh and blood had been dissolved by the maggots and the water so that now it was no more than a bleached uniform.

Manabu Wada

Imphal was the turning point of the war in Burma. The Japanese suffered some 54,000 casualties as against 17,000 British – the heaviest defeat they had ever endured. From now on, the initiative lay with Slim.

‡

The Battle for Monte Cassino

With the German defenders dug into the ruins of the medieval monastery, shattered by aerial bombing, it took the Allies six months to seize Monte Cassino, the principal obstacle on the road to Rome. Here, a young Gurkha officer describes the difficulty of getting about on its slopes.

I climbed to a boulder from where it was possible to see most of the track as it snaked its way down to the base of the hill. Parts of it were obviously exposed to observers in the west end of the town although I did not know which buildings were still in German hands and which had been captured by the New Zealanders. It seemed as if I would have to cover some fifty yards or more before the track veered to the left where for a short distance

I could find protection from enemy snipers. It was impossible to see what happened after that.

I waited and waited. All was quiet. Nothing moved on the path below. Nothing moved in the town – indeed, there had been little firing down there for some time although the sound of battle behind me, around the Castle, continued as fiercely as ever. I said a prayer, the only prayer I could think of, the Lord's Prayer. Then getting quickly to my feet, charged down the track; nothing mattered but to get to A Company. It seemed as if I was going to be lucky, when something flicked off my black side-cap as I dived to the ground. I lifted my head and saw the bullet mark. As I dropped so had the bullet missed, but only just, my head. Something had prompted me into diving for cover. In a second I was covered in sweat. Cold sweat.

Everything seemed to stop; the noise of battle, the guns. Above me a lark was singing clearly and with great zest. Probably less than a minute passed but it seemed an age. A few yards away the Indians chattered on the other side of the hill, they were laughing about the young 'boy Sahib' who refused to take their advice. I longed to call out to them but knew their answer in advance.

I crawled forward and willed myself to make another dash. I prayed with great sincerity, prayed for speed, that the sniper would think that I had been hit already. Into the open zigzagging down the track at the fastest speed I had ever attempted. Once again the crack, crack, a blow on my haversack, and then the safety of another rock. Breathless, in tears and humbled to find that fear had caused my bowels to move, I lay as dead until a glance at my watch spurred me on.

Part of the lower stretch of the track was open but I covered it without any incident. What a relief it was to see the worried face of Subedar Chaturman Rai: 'Saw you come over the top and then fall. We thought you were dead, Sahib. But whatever made you come that way? The whole world could see you and you are lucky to be here.'

I agreed adding that I would explain later. I had been badly delayed already and it was important that the NCOs were briefed now so that they could carry out their tasks before darkness fell. I began giving out orders, trying to ignore shaking hands and the tell-tale wet patch down my trouser legs.

E. D. 'Birdie' Smith

The coward

Fred Salter, who had grown up in the Pennsylvania woods, regularly led night patrols out of the lines at Cassino. One evening, a newly arrived officer implied that Salter had been hiding instead of patrolling, and asked to command that night's reconnaissance mission.

For a brief moment I made a concentrated effort to relax, knowing that it is not mentally safe to venture into 'No Man's Land' with a cluttered mind. I took a moment to glance up at the Abbey that loomed above us, thinking how much it had influenced our lives. I listened to the sound of the water tinkling like a thousand bells as it flowed over the rocks in the ford. It seemed to be playing a symphony, in this orchestra pit below the Monastery. The shadows, falling up there on the stage that surrounded the jagged walls of the ancient building, danced on beams of moonlight, to the bell-like rhythm of the water. I waited.

One minute passed, then two minutes. After about five minutes elapsed, I began to wonder if something had gone wrong. Maybe the Lieutenant spotted enemy activity; if so, then the delay was understandable. After waiting another five minutes, I crawled up beside him. He remained in the same position as when I left, staring across the water towards the enemy lines. He seemed to be in a trance.

'Lieutenant,' I asked, 'have you spotted something? What's the problem?' When he didn't reply, I said, 'There's no use waiting for the moon to disappear. There's hardly a cloud in the sky. You'd better move out. We have a lot of ground to cover before we finish our patrol.'

The Lieutenant made no attempt to answer; he just sat like a statue next to that log. Realising he didn't intend to live up to his responsibilities, I decided to take charge and lead the patrol. I checked the actuator on top of my 1928 Thompson machine gun to make sure it was in firing position, then started to crawl alongside of the log in the direction of the river.

Before I'd gone a couple of feet, in a voice cracking from emotional strain, the Lieutenant whispered, 'You know, Corporal, I've been watching and listening. I haven't seen or heard any activity coming from the German lines. I believe we can wait here a little longer, then go back and report that everything is all clear. I don't believe there are any enemy troops moving around in front of our sector.'

In disgust, I looked across my shoulder at my superior officer. All the anger that I'd built up inside of me since he tried to make a good impression on the Captain came to the surface. I said, 'Lieutenant, right now, no one is more afraid to cross the river bathed in moonlight than I am. Every time I leave the safety of our lines, I get this same feeling. If you can't overcome those feelings, then you don't belong out here leading this patrol.'

I should have stopped talking and realised that the man was not responsible for his actions, but I didn't. Instead I said and did things that gnawed at my conscience for the remainder of my life. I said, 'Back at the Command Post, when the Captain gave us our orders, you spoke the truth when you told him this patrol would complete its mission. You said that he'd get the correct information when you made your report. You're supposed to be leading this patrol tonight. So help me God, you better move out right now, or you'll never leave this spot.'

I crawled back towards him. Just recently, I attached the sling of my Thompson to the front of the barrel with a swivel. The sling, draped over my shoulder, was fastened to a swivel I screwed to the top of the buttstock. This allowed my gun to remain in an upright firing position at all times. The sling modification permitted my right hand to be free so I could toss a grenade if needed.

Swinging the stock of my Thompson around with the heel of my right hand, the cutts compensator on the front of my barrel pointed directly at the Lieutenant, almost touching his belly. His mouth dropped open. As he stared down at the gun, I flipped off the safety. Later, I realised that I'd momentarily gone insane, for I took the slack off the trigger, and slowly began to apply pressure.

When he saw my trigger finger begin to move, he sucked in his stomach and hunched his shoulders but never said a word. Lifting his eyes from the gun, he looked at me in disbelief. After seeing the deranged look on my face, he must have realised he was staring at a maniac. He knew I intended to take his life.

I'll never forget the whites of his eyes that reflected in the moonlight. With my finger a breath away from applying the final pressure on the trigger, I don't know what stopped me from killing him. Thank the Good Lord, I didn't.

Fred H. Salter

The patrol completed its mission. After making its report, the Lieutenant asked to be relieved of his command and sent back to base. Salter lied about the events of that night and went unpunished.

The taking of Cassino

On 18 May 1944, after a week of continuous assaults, the Polish Carpathian Division finally raised their flag above the town, while British troops, including Fred Majdalany, swept round to the south.

At a quarter to six the earth trembled, and once again the shells started pouring overhead so thickly that at times you fancied you could see them. At the same time another lot of guns began to pound Monastery Hill in support of the Polish attack. In next to no time dust and smoke and yellow flame enveloped the Monastery itself, so that when our Dog and Baker Companies passed through Charlie Company on the stroke of six it was hidden from view. This was the kill. We were going in for the kill. The Poles were sweeping round from the right: we, two and a half miles away in the valley, were on our way to seal it off from the left. It shouldn't be long now. And once we had cut the Highway the very qualities that had made the Monastery an impregnable bastion for so long would turn it into an equally formidable death-trap. For so long the guardian and protector of its garrison, it would round on them in its death-throes and destroy them.

Compared with the previous day, we had a fairly easy advance. There were some snipers and one or two isolated machine-guns, but they didn't seem disposed to resist very strongly, and by ten Baker and Dog, assisted by fresh tanks, were nicely settled on Bluebell, another thousand yards on. We were ordered to push on as fast as possible. So Baker and Dog advanced again to the final objective line, 'Tulip', twelve hundred yards farther on. And Able, Charlie and Command Post pushed on to the area just cleared by Dog and Baker. By four o'clock in the afternoon Dog and Baker both signalled that they were established on 'Tulip' – both had OPs directly overlooking Highway Six. Both asked permission to carry on and cut the road and search beyond it. We were ordered to stay where we were, however, as the exact position of the Poles was not known and mistakes might occur if we both started milling around by the road. We dominated it from where we were. We had done what was required of us. We were to stay where we were until we had further orders. The job was nearly done.

During the night Dog and Baker were told to patrol as far as the road. Not till the following morning were we allowed to send anyone beyond it. By that time it had ceased to be a military feat. It was a formal ceremony. So John sent a special patrol of three corporals, all holders of the MM

[Military Medal]. They crossed the Highway and carried out a careful search of the gullies and ruined buildings on the far side of it, but the only Germans they could find were dead ones. Their time was not wasted, however. Each returned with a Schmeisser gun, a camera, a watch and a pair of binoculars of impeccable German manufacture. An hour later the Poles entered the Monastery. As so often happens when great events are awaited with prolonged and excessive anxiety, the announcement of the fall of Monte Cassino was rather an anticlimax. It was Thursday, 18 May. The battle had lasted a week. The job was done.

Fred Majdalany

It had taken the British XIII Corps four days, and 4,000 casualties, to advance two miles. Polish losses were, proportionately, higher still, and in all nearly 10,000 Allied soldiers were killed in the climactic battle.

✝

The Bombing of the Fatherland

An argument with Goering

Despite their heavy losses, the Allied bombers were starting to take their toll on German production capacity and civilian morale. The raiders were better protected since the introduction of fighters with long-range fuel tanks, such as the Mustang, but Goering took little account of this when berating Adolf Galland, who had become the leader of the Luftwaffe's fighter arm.

Goering began to lay increasing blame on Fighter Command and the pilots, and as I felt I had earned the right to answer him back, we were soon at loggerheads. One meeting was particularly stormy. The *Reichsmarschall* had summoned a number of squadron leaders and pilots to discuss a raid against southern Germany in which the German fighters had scored very few victories. After some general remarks, he proceeded to comment on the Fighter Command's lack of spirit. He may have been exasperated by my replies to his previous questions; at all events, he got into such a state that he hurled reproaches and accusations at us, to the effect that we had been loaded with honours and decorations, but had proved ourselves unworthy of them, that Fighter Command had been a failure as early as the Battle of Britain, and that many pilots with the highest decorations had faked their reports to get Knight's Crosses over England.

As I listened to him I got more and more furious, until finally I tore my Knight's Cross off my collar and banged it on the table. The atmosphere was tense and still. The *Reichsmarschall* had literally lost the power of speech, and I looked him firmly in the eye, ready for anything. Nothing happened, and Goering quietly finished what he had to say. For six months after that I did not wear my war decorations.

Adolf Galland

Heinz Knoke was one of the Messerschmitt pilots charged with meeting the threat posed by USAAF Fortresses.

Carefully I scan the skies. Vast layers of cloud cover the distant earth below as far as the eye can see. We are now at an altitude of 33,000 feet: it should be just right for bagging a few enemy bombers or fighters.

Vapour-trails ahead. There they are!

'I see them,' Specht reports with a crackle of his ringing voice.

'Victor, victor,' base acknowledged.

The bomber-alley lies about 6,000 feet below us – 600 to 800 of the heavy bombers are heading eastwards. Alongside and above them range the escorting fighters.

And now I am utterly absorbed in the excitement of the chase. Specht dips his left wing-tip, and we peel off for the attack. Messerschmitt after Messerschmitt follows him down.

'After them!' The radio is a babel of sound, with everybody shouting at once.

I check my guns and adjust the sights as we dive down upon the target. Then I grasp the stick with both hands, groping for the triggers with my right thumb and forefinger. I glance behind. Thunderbolts are coming down after us.

We are faster, and before they can intercept us we reach the Fortresses. Our fighters come sweeping through the bomber formation in a frontal attack. I press the triggers, and my aircraft shudders under the recoil.

'After them!'

My cannon-shells punch holes in the wing of a Fortress.

Blast! I was aiming for the control cabin.

I climb away steeply behind the formation, followed by my Flight. Then the Thunderbolts are upon us. It is a wild dog-fight. Several times I try to manoeuvre into position for firing at one of their planes. Every time

I am forced to break away, because there are two – four – five – or even ten Thunderbolts on my tail.

Everybody is milling around like mad, friend and foe alike. But the Yanks outnumber us by four or five to one. Then some Lightnings come to join in the mêlée. I get one of them in my sights. Fire!

Tracers come whizzing in a stream close past my head. I duck instinctively.

Woomf! Woomf! Good shooting!

I am forced to pull up out of it in a steep corkscrew climb, falling back on my old stand-by in such emergencies. For the moment I have a breathing space. I check the instruments and controls. All seems well. Wenneckers draws alongside and points down at four Lightnings on our left.

'After them!'

Our left wing-tips dip, and we peel off. We hurtle down towards the Lightnings as they glisten in the sun. I open fire. Too fast: I overshoot the Lightning. I wonder what to do about my excessive speed.

But now a Lightning is on my tail. In a flash, I slam the stick hard over into the left corner. The wing drops. I go down in a tight spiral dive. The engine screams. I throttle back. My aircraft shudders under the terrific strain. Rivets spring from the wing-frame. My ears pop. Slowly and very cautiously I begin to straighten out. I am thrust forward and down into the seat. My vision blacks out. I feel my chin forced down on to my chest.

A Lightning passes me, going down in flames. There is a Messerschmitt on its tail.

'Got it!'

It is Wenneckers.

A few moments later he is alongside me again. I wave to him with both hands.

'Congratulations!'

'The bastard was after your hide,' he replies.

It is the second time Wenneckers has shot a Yank from off my tail.

After we land I go up to Wenneckers to shake hands, congratulate him on his success, and – But Wenneckers interrupts before I am able to thank him: –

'No need for you to thank me, sir. I only wanted your wife not to be made a widow by that bastard. Besides, think what a nuisance to the Flight it would have been to have had to dispose of your remains!'

All the mechanics standing around greet this remark with roars of laughter. I dig the lanky lad in the ribs. We go together into the crew-room.

Meanwhile the others have also been coming in to land. This is one day we all come back.

Heinz Knoke

‡

Vengeance

Lindsay Rogers, a New Zealand surgeon, was attached to the partisans in Yugoslavia.

We opened the door of the house and entered the living room. Sitting at the table was our commandant and his commissar. Zena sat down beside them. I went to the side of the room and sat down on a three-legged stool. The Germans were brought in one by one. All their possessions were laid on the table. A faded letter, a diary, a bottle of hair oil, some rubber protectives, a postcard of a blonde girl with a message of love scratched across the corner; a photo of a group of young officers in a training camp; a picture of an old lady standing beside a farmhouse door. The commandant picked them up one by one and handed the writings to Zena, who fluently translated the German into Serbo-Croat. They were mostly simple love letters from home. The commissar started the interrogation. The official questioning took a bare five minutes. I watched Zena. A holy hate burned in her dark Jewish eyes. When it was over she asked them:

'Why do you burn down our houses and our villages?'

No answer.

'Why do you take our young women to give them disease?'

No answer.

'Why do you shoot our old women and children and torture our couriers?' No answer.

I remembered a courier patient of mine who had escaped from a German unit. He had been caught by a patrol and taken to a headquarters and asked about the movement of partisan groups. He didn't answer. They struck him on the face with their rifles and said, 'Answer you dog!' He was only seventeen. They struck him again and again until he fell. He was pulled out and locked in a room. Next day the same thing happened. No answer. Then they tied his arms with wire to a beam above his head, and from his testes they hung a brick tied with copper wire. Gradually his bladder filled, but he couldn't pass anything because of the wire. Gradually the weight strangled his genitals. The pain was terrific; not so much the blackened strangulated testes and penis, but the awful tension in his bladder. A sudden pain and the abdominal agony ended. His bladder burst and he swooned away. The next thing he recalled was a peasant lifting him down at night and carrying him into the darkness. Luckily I was near at hand and operated. But his gangrenous genitalia I couldn't replace.

'Why do you torture our partisan boys?' repeated Zena.

The German Nazi replied haughtily, 'Well, you are brigand dogs, are you not?' Fifteen minutes later they faced the firing squad and Zena and I walked slowly and silently back to our camp among the rocks.

Lindsay Rogers

✝

SOE

'The Life That I Have'

Leo Marks, the son of the owner of the famous bookshop at 84 Charing Cross Road, was SOE's chief cryptographer. He gave many agents about to be parachuted into Occupied Europe codes based on well-known poems. To Violette Szabo, he gave one he had written for a girl with whom he had been in love and who had since been killed.

I explained that some agents who were otherwise good coders often made spelling mistakes in their key-phrases, and we'd found that they weren't really happy with their poems, though they didn't always know why.

She considered the matter carefully. 'I hadn't thought of it that way.' Her expression was troubled, and she seemed to have left Orchard Court for some childhood briefing room.

She returned a few moments later to the poem-bound present. 'I shouldn't have chosen it. I couldn't spell it as a child, and I still can't . . . I'd like to change it but I suppose it's too late.'

'Do you know any others?'

'They're all nursery rhymes, and I'd feel so stupid if I used one – I know I would . . . Look, let me try another message . . .'

'How about trying another poem?'

'*Could I?*'

'Are you a quick learner?'

'I am at some things, but they're nothing to do with codes.'

The imp was back, and looked at me appealingly. 'Do you know a poem you'd like me to try?'

For the first time since Xmas Eve I thought of the words which had occurred to me on the roof of Norgeby House. I wrote them in block capitals on a sheet of squared paper, and checked the spelling before handing them over.

I then did what I could to descend from the roof.

An aircrash or two after I heard a tiny intake of breath, and turned to look at her. She was speaking the words to herself, and I felt I was intruding on her privacy.

She finally looked up at me. 'I could learn this in a few minutes. I promise you I could.'

'You're sure you want to?'

'Oh yes. Oh yes. I almost know it now.'

'Well then . . . take those few minutes, then encode two messages in it. I'll come back this time tomorrow and go through them with you.'

She promised she'd be ready.

At least I had a good reason for seeing her again.

She stood up when I entered the briefing room, waiting until I was seated opposite her, then made a simple statement of fact:

> The life that I have
> Is all that I have
> And the life that I have
> Is yours.
>
> The love that I have
> Of the life that I have
> Is yours and yours and yours.
>
> A sleep I shall have
> A rest I shall have
> Yet death will be but a pause.
>
> For the peace of my years
> In the long green grass
> Will be yours and yours and yours.

It was she who broke the silence. 'Who wrote this?'

'I'll check up, and let you know when you come back.'

I had a gut feeling that she wasn't going to, and busied myself checking the two messages she'd encoded. Each was 300 letters long, and there wasn't a single mistake in either.

Leo Marks

Violette Szabo was captured in France and executed in Ravensbruck concentration camp in 1945. She was posthumously awarded the George Cross. Leo Marks became the screenwriter of, among other films, Peeping Tom.

Kidnapping the General

In April 1944 two SOE agents, aided by resistance fighters, carried off perhaps the most audacious coup de main *of the war. Disguised as German soldiers, Bill Stanley Moss and Paddy Leigh Fermor waited at a road junction in Crete in order to flag down the car containing the island's garrison commander.*

There were five false alarms during the first hour of our watch. Two *Volkswagen*, two lorries, and one motor-cycle combination trundled past at various times, and in each of them, seated primly upright like tailors' dummies, the steel-helmeted figures of German soldiers were silhouetted against the night sky. It was a strange feeling to be crouching so close to them – almost within arm's reach of them – while they drove past with no idea that nine pairs of eyes were so fixedly watching them. It felt rather like going on patrol in action, when you find yourself very close to the enemy trenches, and can hear the sentries talking or quietly whistling, and can see them lighting cigarettes in their cupped hands.

It was already one hour past the General's routine time for making his return journey when we began to wonder if he could possibly have gone home in one of the vehicles which had already passed by. It was cold, and the canvas of our German garb did not serve to keep out the wind.

I remember Paddy asking me the time. I looked at my watch and saw that the hands were pointing close to half-past nine. And at that moment Mitso's torch blinked.

'Here we go.'

We scrambled out of the ditch on to the road. Paddy switched on his red lamp and I held up a traffic signal, and together we stood in the centre of the junction.

In a moment – far sooner than we had expected – the powerful headlamps of the General's car swept round the bend and we found ourselves floodlit. The chauffeur, on approaching the corner, slowed down.

Paddy shouted, 'Halt!'

The car stopped. We walked forward rather slowly, and as we passed the beams of the headlamps we drew our ready-cocked pistols from behind our backs and let fall the life-preservers from our wrists.

As we came level with the doors of the car Paddy asked, '*Ist dies das General's Wagen?*'

There came a muffled '*Ja, ja*' from inside.

Then everything happened very quickly. There was a rush from all sides. We tore open our respective doors, and our torches illuminated the interior of the car – the bewildered face of the General, the chauffeur's terrified eyes, the rear seats empty. With his right hand the chauffeur was reaching for his automatic, so I hit him across the head with my cosh. He fell forward, and George, who had come up behind me, heaved him out of the driving-seat and dumped him on the road. I jumped in behind the steering-wheel, and at the same moment saw Paddy and Manoli dragging the General out of the opposite door. The old man was struggling with fury, lashing out with his arms and legs. He obviously thought that he was going to be killed, and started shouting every curse under the sun at the top of his voice.

The engine of the car was still ticking over, the handbrake was on, everything was perfect. To one side, in a pool of torchlight in the centre of the road, Paddy and Manoli were trying to quieten the General, who was still cursing and struggling. On the other side George and Andoni were trying to pull the chauffeur to his feet, but the man's head was pouring with blood, and I think he must have been unconscious, because every time they lifted him up he simply collapsed to the ground again.

This was the critical moment, for if any other traffic had come along the road we should have been caught sadly unawares. But now Paddy, Manoli, Nikko, and Stratis were carrying the General towards the car and bundling him into the back seat. After him clambered George, Manoli, and Stratis – one of the three holding a knife to the General's throat to stop him shouting, the other two with their Marlin guns poking out of either window. It must have been quite a squash.

Paddy jumped into the front seat beside me.

The General kept imploring, 'Where is my hat? Where is my hat?'

The hat, of course, was on Paddy's head.

We were now ready to move. Suddenly everyone started kissing and congratulating everybody else; and Micky, having first embraced Paddy and me, started screaming at the General with all the pent-up hatred he held for the Germans. We had to push him away and tell him to shut up.

Andoni, Grigori, Nikko, and Wallace Beery were standing at the roadside, propping up the chauffeur between them, and now they waved us good-bye and turned away and started off on their long trek to the rendezvous on Mount Ida.

We started.

The car was a beauty, a brand-new Opel, and we were delighted to see that the petrol-gauge showed the tanks to be full.

We had been travelling for less than a minute when we saw a succession of lights coming along the road towards us; and a moment later we found ourselves driving past a motor convoy, and thanked our stars that it had not come this way a couple of minutes sooner. Most of the lorries were troop transports, all filled with soldiery, and this sight had the immediate effect of quietening George, Manoli, and Stratis, who had hitherto been shouting at one another and taking no notice of our attempts to keep them quiet.

When the convoy had passed Paddy told the General that the two of us were British officers and that we would treat him as an honourable prisoner of war. He seemed mightily relieved to hear this and immediately started to ask a series of questions, often not even waiting for a reply. But for some reason his chief concern still appeared to be the whereabouts of his hat – first it was the hat, then his medal. Paddy told him that he would soon be given it back, and to this the General said, '*Danke, danke.*'

It was not long before we saw a red lamp flashing in the road before us, and we realised that we were approaching the first of the traffic-control posts through which we should have to pass. We were, of course, prepared for this eventuality, and our plan had contained alternative actions which we had hoped would suit any situation, because we knew that our route led us through the centre of Heraklion, and that in the course of our journey we should probably have to pass through about twenty control posts.

Until now everything had happened so quickly that we had felt no emotion other than elation at the primary success of our venture; but as we drew nearer and nearer to the swinging red lamp we experienced our first tense moment.

A German sentry was standing in the middle of the road. As we approached him, slowing down the while, he moved to one side, presum-ably thinking that we were going to stop. However, as soon as we drew level with him – still going very slowly, so as to give him an opportunity of seeing the General's pennants on the wings of the car – I began to accelerate again, and on we went. For several seconds after we had passed the sentry we were all apprehension, fully expecting to hear a rifle-shot in our wake; but a moment later we had rounded a bend in the road and knew that the danger was temporarily past. Our chief concern now was whether or not the guard at the post behind us would telephone ahead to the next one, and it was with our fingers crossed that we approached the red lamp of the second control post a few minutes later. But we need not have had any fears, for the sentry behaved in exactly the same manner as the first had done, and we drove on feeling rather pleased with ourselves.

In point of fact, during the course of our evening's drive we passed twenty-two control posts. In most cases the above-mentioned formula sufficed to get us through, but on five occasions we came to road-blocks – raisable one-bar barriers – which brought us to a standstill. Each time, however, the General's pennants did the trick like magic, and the sentries would either give a smart salute or present arms as the gate was lifted and we passed through. Only once did we find ourselves in what might have developed into a nasty situation – but of that I shall write in a moment.

Paddy, sitting on my right and smoking a cigarette, looked quite imposing in the General's hat. The General asked him how long he would have to remain in his present undignified position, and in reply Paddy told him that if he were willing to give his parole that he would neither shout nor try to escape we should treat him, not as a prisoner, but, until we left the island, as one of ourselves. The General gave his parole immediately. We were rather surprised at this, because it seemed to us that anyone in his position might still entertain reasonable hopes of escape – a shout for help at any of the control posts might have saved him.

According to our plan, I should soon be having to spend twenty-four hours alone with Manoli and the General, so I thought it best to find out if we had any languages in common (for hitherto we had been speaking a sort of anglicised German). Paddy asked him if he spoke any English.

'*Nein*,' said the General.

'Russian?' I asked. 'Or Greek?'

'*Nein*.'

In unison: '*Parlez-vous français?*'

'*Un petit peu.*'

To which we could not resist the Cowardesque reply, 'I never think that's quite enough.'

. . . The road was clear of traffic, and it was not long before we had put several kilometres between ourselves and Heraklion. Soon we had passed the last of the control posts, and the road began to rise from the plain and wind gradually uphill. Up and up we went. We had seen the massive mountain forms in front of us as a target, but now we were among them; and high above, like a white baby curled upon a translucent canopy, we saw the crescent of the moon. Suddenly we felt quite distant from everything that had just happened – a terrific elation – and we told one another that three-quarters of the job was now over, and started discussing what sort of celebration we would have when we got back to Cairo. We sang *The Party's Over*; and then I lit a cigarette, which I thought was the best I had ever smoked in my life.

Bill Stanley Moss

The group evaded all pursuit and, after a march through the mountains, they and Kreipe were picked up by boat and taken to Cairo on 14 May.

‡

Scabies and babies

For the men of the US 82nd Airborne Division, Leicester was paradise. When unleashed from their barracks, they made it a point of honour to sample as much of the town's alcohol and as many of its women as possible.

Berkely and I seeing no particular reason to specialise on drinks or women, decided on both but with beer and gin getting top priority. In the pub we agreed to try to date the first two women we saw on the street. We were successful and both thought we had made conquests of the two most beautiful ladies in England until we began to sober up. The beverages had conferred on the damsels the same kind of beautiful perfections that Don Quixote's chivalrous idealism had on the ugly country wench he called Dulcinea del Toboso. As the alcohol loosened its grip, observation of my lady led me to discreet inquiries about her age and past history. She blushed and blurped, 'Why you blooming bloody Yank, I'm thirty-nine. I've got five children!'

Berkely took stock of his faded out, muddy-haired and foam-complexioned blonde, pondered seriously for a moment and commented, 'Mac, it is getting late, very late, and we'd better get back to camp.'

We pulled the same stunt once again and got stuck. After that we decided not to go out together, both convinced that we jinxed each other in things amorous.

We did many scabby things in England, for which I apologise to any Britisher who happens to read this narrative, but none scabbier than giving the scabies, commonly called the red itch, to the citizens of Leicester and environs. Almost every man in the 504th had caught it in Italy. Inasmuch as we would have to spend a week or two of our precious time in quarantine if the battalion and regimental surgeons learned about it, we enjoined our platoon's medics under dire threats of retribution not to mention the matter.

They agreed, having scabies themselves and wanting to go to town as badly as we did. Since the itch didn't show plainly on our hands and necks, we could hobnob undetected with the innocent British people. We gave it to the British girls, who in turn gave it to their friends and families. I confess that it was an amusing thing to watch the young chicks surreptitiously giving themselves a dig in the flanks, or slyly scratching a shapely leg, or innocently giving their bosoms a scrape with their nails, never suspecting that we understood their plight only too well and scratched ourselves discreetly and indiscreetly when the opportunity offered. It was a filthy trick to play on the chicks, but I do believe that they'd rather have had the itch than have us shut up in quarantine.

Finally after the British had already got the itch we told the medics about our plight and a great battle was launched against the bugs. They didn't quarantine us now that the British had it too. Those of us who got well of it in a hurry expertly examined our prospective dates for itch symptoms, but in spite of precautions many caught it back from their victims. We were having an itching good time in Ye Merrie Olde England.

The mayor of Leicester had welcomed the coming of the Legion, but in a few days I am certain he regretted his show of hospitality. The truth of the matter is that we conducted ourselves like uncouth barbarians. Africa, plus the campaigns in Sicily and Italy, had dissolved most of the thin veneer that civilisation spreads over the instincts. The boys simply went wild in England and didn't give two hoots in hell what they said or did. It is so easy to imagine how disconcerting it must have been for the British, who have the custom of drinking a pint or so of beer in an entire evening, meantime playing a friendly game of darts and beating their gums in a mild way, to behold the unsophisticated and inconsiderate exuberance of our boys as they poured into the pubs, took over tables, which they covered with twenty pints of beer, and invited all present to drink, particularly the girls. They frequently started arguments which ended in tipped-over tables and spilled beer. The scowling pub keeper would scurry over brandishing a mop with a martial air and scrub the floor while the jokers stood by waiting to sit down again. If he ordered them out, they laughed at him and sometimes broke glasses which they paid for, but in good-natured condescension.

Not all of our boys were so rude or got drunk every night, but enough of them were and did to give many Britishers the impression that we were a mob of cloutish rubes. I can understand why we acted as we did, but can neither condone nor justify it.

Within six weeks, pregnant women began to flock into the regimental personnel section, wanting the erring jokers to marry them or at least to make an allotment of a pound a week for sixteen years for the upbringing of the ripening love fruit. At the end of sixteen years, the youngster would presumably be large enough to forage for its own living.

The erring lovers roared and bellowed at the thought of being penalised financially over so long a time for what they regarded as a trifling matter. 'Little jokers', said the wayward expectant fathers, 'are born every day into this hard world! England needs citizens so why all the hue and cry? The nation should be grateful, not indignant!'

Ross Carter

‡

The Montgomery touch

As soldiers all across the south of England waited to embark for Normandy, Montgomery went from camp to camp addressing the troops, declaring his trust in them and breeding their confidence in him.

I suppose I have heard fifty generals addressing their soldiers, most of them with much better speeches than this. Indeed I suppose this speech in print is just about as bad as one could hope to read, outside the hearty *naïveté* of the kindergarten. Spoken by Montgomery to the soldiers who were about to run into the Atlantic Wall it had magic. No mention of God, of Divine assistance. No mention of England. Not a single eternal verity. No hate. No question of revenge. But I doubt whether the soldiers remembered the words. The words were the least of it. The whole performance succeeded because it was the expression of a wanted emotion. Without their consciously knowing it, the speech adopted an attitude which the soldiers wanted to have. At the end of it they felt they knew Montgomery as he believed he knew them. They felt that they were thinking on the same plane as he was, that they would indeed go into the assault together.

In the end Montgomery had made that speech to every British, American and Allied soldier who was to go on the landing; he must have talked to at least a million men.

Alan Moorehead

Summer 1944

D-Day

With 3 million men, 2 battleships, 23 cruisers, 105 destroyers, 1,076 other warships, 2,700 merchant ships, 2,500 landing craft, 3,500 heavy bombers, 1,700 light and medium bombers, 5,500 fighter aircraft and 2,400 transport aircraft under his command, General Dwight Eisenhower, the American given command of the Normandy invasions, had much to weigh up. The most pressing of his problems was whether the sea would be calm enough for his forces to cross the Channel. Another difficulty was working out how to prevent a certain politician from going with them.

The final conference for determining the feasibility of attacking on the tentatively selected day, June 5, was scheduled for 4 a.m. on June 4. However, some of the attacking contingents had already been ordered to sea, because if the entire force was to land on June 5, then some of the important elements stationed in northern parts of the United Kingdom could not wait for the final decision on the morning of June 4.

When the commanders assembled on the morning of June 4 the report we received was discouraging. Low clouds, high winds, and formidable wave action were predicted to make landing a most hazardous affair. The meteorologists said that air support would be impossible, naval gunfire would be inefficient, and even the handling of small boats would be rendered difficult. Admiral Ramsay thought that the mechanics of landing could be handled, but agreed with the estimate of the difficulty in adjusting gunfire. His position was mainly neutral. General Montgomery, properly concerned with the great disadvantages of delay, believed that we should go. Tedder disagreed.

Weighing all factors, I decided that the attack would have to be postponed. This decision necessitated the immediate dispatch of orders to the vessels and troops already at sea and created some doubt as to whether they could be ready twenty-four hours later in case the next day should prove favourable for the assault. Actually the manoeuvre of the ships in the Irish Sea proved most difficult by reason of the storm. That they succeeded in gaining ports, refuelling, and readying themselves to resume the movement a day later represented the utmost in seamanship and in brilliant command and staff work.

The conference on the evening of June 4 presented little, if any, added brightness to the picture of the morning, and tension mounted even higher because the inescapable consequences of postponement were almost too bitter to contemplate.

At 3.30 the next morning our little camp was shaking and shuddering under a wind of almost hurricane proportions and the accompanying rain seemed to be travelling in horizontal streaks. The mile-long trip through muddy roads to the naval headquarters was anything but a cheerful one, since it seemed impossible that in such conditions there was any reason for even discussing the situation.

When the conference started the first report given us by Group Captain Stagg and the meteorologic staff was that the bad conditions predicted the day before for the coast of France were actually prevailing there and that if we had persisted in the attempt to land on June 5 a major disaster would almost surely have resulted. This they probably told us to inspire more confidence in their next astonishing declaration, which was that by the following morning a period of relatively good weather, heretofore completely unexpected, would ensue, lasting probably thirty-six hours. The long-term prediction was not good but they did give us assurance that this short period of good weather would intervene between the exhaustion of the storm we were then experiencing and the beginning of the next spell of really bad weather.

The prospect was not bright because of the possibility that we might land the first several waves successfully and then find later build-up impracticable, and so have to leave the isolated original attacking forces easy prey to German counteraction. However, the consequences of the delay justified great risk and I quickly announced the decision to go ahead with the attack on June 6. The time was then 4.15 a.m., June 5. No one present disagreed and there was a definite brightening of faces as, without a further word, each went off to his respective post of duty to flash out his command the messages that would set the whole host in motion.

A number of people appealed to me for permission to go aboard the supporting naval ships in order to witness the attack. Every member of a staff can always develop a dozen arguments why he, in particular, should accompany an expedition rather than remain at the only post, the centre of communications, where he can be useful. Permission was denied to all except those with specific military responsibility and, of course, the allotted quotas of press and radio representatives.

Among those who were refused permission was the Prime Minster. His request was undoubtedly inspired as much by his natural instincts as a warrior as by his impatience at the prospect of sitting quietly back in London to await reports. I argued, however, that the chance of his becoming an accidental casualty was too important from the standpoint of the whole war effort and I refused his request. He replied, with complete accuracy, that while I was in sole command of the operation by virtue of authority delegated to me by both governments, such authority did not include administrative control over the British organisation. He said: 'Since this is true it is not part of your responsibility, my dear General, to determine the exact composition of any ship's company in His Majesty's Fleet. This being true,' he rather slyly continued, 'by shipping myself as a bona fide member of a ship's complement it would be beyond your authority to prevent my going.'

All of this I had ruefully to concede, but I forcefully pointed out that he was adding to my personal burdens in this thwarting of my instructions. Even, however, while I was acknowledging defeat in the matter, aid came from an unexpected source. I later heard that the King had learned of the Prime Minister's intention and, while not presuming to interfere with the decision reached by Mr Churchill, he sent word that if the Prime Minister felt it necessary to go on the expedition he, the King, felt it to be equally his duty and privilege to participate at the head of his troops. This instantly placed a different light upon the matter and I heard no more of it.

Nevertheless my sympathies were entirely with the Prime Minister. Again I had to endure the interminable wait that always intervenes between the final decision of the high command and the earliest possible determination of success or failure in such ventures. I spent the time visiting troops that would participate in the assault. A late evening visit on the 5th took me to the camp of the US 101st Airborne Division, one of the units whose participation had been so severely questioned by the air commander. I found the men in fine fettle, many of them joshingly admonishing me that I had no cause for worry, since the 101st was on the job and everything would be taken care of in fine shape. I stayed with them until the last of them were in the air, somewhere about midnight. After a two-hour trip back to my own camp, I had only a short time to wait until the first news should come in.

Dwight Eisenhower

During the night before the invasion, units were landed by glider and parachute in Normandy with the aim of disrupting the German defences and lines of communication. Major 'Rosie' Rosevere, an officer with the Royal Engineers, was given the task of destroying a bridge at Troarn.

When we were getting near, beggar me if we didn't run smack into a barbed-wire barricade across the road. By the time I saw it, it was too late. We couldn't ram it, because barbed wire is hopeless stuff and gets wrapped round everything, but by the grace of God one of our chaps had some wire-cutters with him and he cut us out. We stopped short of a crossroads at the edge of town and I sent a couple of chaps forward to look round the corner and here a really farcical situation developed. While they were looking in one direction, a German soldier appeared on a bicycle from the other direction. Well, I suppose in hindsight we should have stuck a knife in the chap, but what happened was that someone shot at him and that really set things going.

All we could do was jump aboard the jeep and make the best pace we could. I suppose we had about half a ton of explosives in the trailer and there were seven of us on the jeep, with me driving, so we couldn't make very high speed. As we came into the centre of the town, the firing started from various windows and from the ground as well; there seemed to be a Boche in every doorway firing like mad. Our chaps were firing back. One German rushed out with an MG34 and put it down in the road, but we were too quick for him and he had to whip it out of the way or we would have run him over. But he was terribly quick getting it out again and a stream of tracer went over our heads. The only thing that saved us was that there was a steep downward hill leading out of Troarn and he couldn't depress his gun far enough.

We raced down the hill, picking up speed all the time, and I nearly lost control of the darn thing. There was an appalling swerve and I think that's where we lost one of our men, our bren gunner, when he fell off the trailer.

When we got to the bridge it took us less than five minutes to set all the charges across the centre of the biggest arch and down she went.

Obviously we couldn't go back through the town, we were definitely *persona non grata* there, so we took to the fields and finally arrived back at brigade headquarters. On the way we passed a farmer milking a cow and

I told him in French that liberation was at hand. He was most unimpressed.

'Rosie' Rosevere

Although Colonel Hans von Luck had two crack Panzer Grenadier regiments at his disposal, to his immense frustration he found that he was not allowed to deploy them.

On that rainy evening [5 June], my adjutant and I were waiting for a report from No. II Battalion that the night exercise had ended. This battalion was in the area Troarn-Escoville, hence fairly near the coast, while No. I Battalion, equipped with armoured personnel carriers and armoured half-track vehicles, had taken up waiting positions further to the rear. I had given the more basic order that in the event of possible landings by Allied commando troops, the battalions and companies concerned were to attack immediately and independently; and to do so, moreover, without regard to the prohibition from the highest authority on engaging action except after clearance by High Command West. But in view of the weather report that we had been given, I had no thought of such an engagement that night.

About midnight, I heard the growing roar of aircraft, which passed over us. I wondered whether the attack was destined once again for traffic routes inland or for Germany herself. The machines appeared to be flying very low – because of the weather? I looked out of the window and was wide awake; flares were hanging in the sky. At the same moment, my adjutant was on the telephone, 'Major, paratroops are dropping. Gliders are landing in our section. I'm trying to make contact with No. II Battalion. I'll come along to you at once.'

I gave orders without hesitation, 'All units are to be put on alert immediately and the division informed. No. II Battalion is to go into action wherever necessary. Prisoners are to be taken if possible and brought to me.'

I then went to the command post with my adjutant. The 5 Company of No. II Battalion, which had gone out with blank cartridges, was not back yet from the night exercise – a dangerous situation. First reports indicated that British paratroops had dropped over Troarn. The commander of No. II Battalion had already started a counterattack with uninvolved elements and had succeeded in penetrating as far as Troarn, to which elements of the 5th Company had already withdrawn under their own steam.

We telephoned the company commander, who was in a cellar. 'Brandenburg, hold on. The battalion is already attacking and is bound to reach you in a few moments.'

'Okay,' he replied, 'I have the first prisoner here, a British medical officer of the 6th Airborne Division.'

'Send him along as soon as the position is clear.'

In the meantime, my adjutant telephoned the division. General Feuchtinger and his general-staff officer had not come back yet. We gave the orderly officer, Lieutenant Messmer, a brief situation report and asked him to obtain clearance for us for a concentrated night attack the moment the divisional commander returned.

By now, we had a slightly better idea of and grip on the situation. Prisoners who had misjudged their jumps and fallen into our hands in the course of our limited counterattack were brought in to me. Before I had them escorted away to division, in accordance with orders, we learned during our 'small talk' that the 6th Airborne Division was supposed to jump during the night in order to take the bridges over the Orne at Ranville intact and form a bridgehead east of the Orne for the landing by sea planned for the morning of 6 June.

Gradually we were becoming filled with anger. The clearance for an immediate night attack, so as to take advantage of the initial confusion among our opponents, had still not come, although our reports via division to the core and to Army Group B (Rommel) must have long since been on hand. We made a thorough calculation of our chances of successfully pushing through to the coast and preventing the formation of a bridgehead, or at least making it more difficult.

I remember the British medical officer who was brought to me as the first prisoner. In his parachute equipment he looked like any other soldier. As a good Briton, he kept his composure, but seemed deeply disappointed, and unnerved, at being taken prisoner immediately on his first mission. Since he too would only give his name and number, I began, as always with a British prisoner, to make small talk. I spoke about my last visit to London in March 1939, about Piccadilly Circus and my British friends. At that he thawed, and I learned more about British intentions and the task of the 6th Airborne Division.

The hours passed. We had set up a defensive front where we had been condemned to inactivity. The rest of the division, with the panzer regiment and Panzer Grenadier Regiment 192, was equally immobilised, though in the highest state of alert. My adjutant telephoned once more to division. Major Forster, IC and responsible for the reception of prisoners, came to the phone. He too was unable to alter the established orders. Army Group B merely informed us that it was a matter of a diversionary manoeuvre: the British had thrown out straw dummies on parachutes.

Hans von Luck

One parachutist who was no straw dummy was Private David Webster of Easy Company of the US 101st Airborne Division. Its objective was to eliminate the German infantry company at St Marie du Mont, as well as the platoon on the gun batteries at St Martin de Varreville. That, at least, was the plan.

I fell a hundred feet in three seconds, straight toward a huge flooded area shining in the moonlight. I thought I was going to fall all the way, but there was nothing I could do about it except dig my fingers into my reserve and wait to be smashed flat. I should have counted one-thousand, two-thousand, three-thousand – the general would have had me shout 'Bill Lee', but that was expecting too much – and yet all I could do was gape at the water.

Suddenly a giant snapped a whip, with me on the end, my chute popped open, and I found myself swinging wildly in the wind. Twisted in the fall, my risers were unwinding and spinning me around. They pinned my head down with my chin on the top of my rifle case and prevented me from looking up and checking my canopy. I figured that everything was all right, because at least I was floating free in the great silence that always followed the opening shock.

For several seconds, I seemed to be suspended in the sky, with no downward motion, and then all at once, the whole body of water whirled and rushed up at me.

Jesus, I thought, I'm going to drown.

I wrenched desperately at my reserve-chute's snap fasteners as the first step in preparing for a water landing. I also had to undo two leg snaps, my chest buckle, and the bellyband. The next step would have been to drop the reserve and work myself into the seat of my harness, so that I could fling my arms straight up and drop from the chute when I was ten feet above the water. I didn't even have time to begin the procedure.

We had jumped so low – about three hundred feet, instead of the scheduled seven hundred – that while I was still wrenching at the first reserve snap, I saw the whole immense sheet of water rushing up at me twenty feet below. I've had it, I thought. That goddamn Air Corps. I reached up, grasped all four risers, and yanked down hard, to fill the canopy with air and slow my descent. Just before I hit, I closed my eyes and took a deep breath of air. My feet splashed into the water.

I held my breath, expecting to sink over my head and wondering how I was going to escape from my harness underwater – and hit bottom three feet down. My chute billowed away from me in the light wind and collapsed on the surface. I went to work to free myself from my gear. Immensely relieved at the safe landing, I undid the reserve and discarded it, yanked loose the bellyband, unsnapped the leg straps and chest buckle, detached my rifle case, and let the harness sink into the swamp. I was on my own at last.

The silence ended abruptly with a long, ripping burst, burrrrrrrrp, that made me look around in fright.

That's a German machine gun, I told myself. They've seen me. The bullets cracked and popped in the air above, and as I stared openmouthed and paralysed with fright, I saw whiplike tracers darting at me from some far-off place. I dropped to my knees in the cold, black water, which tasted old and brackish, as if it had lain still for a long time, and passively waited to be killed.

Somebody wants to kill me, I thought. So this is what war is really like? I couldn't believe that somebody wanted to kill me. What had I done to them?

I wanted to go up to them and tell them that I didn't want to kill anybody, that I thought the whole war was a lot of malarkey. I don't want to hurt anybody, I would say. All I ask of the world is to be left alone.

The machine gun fired again, a longer burst that held me motionless. It was like a bad dream.

I shook my head to make sure it was true, and it was. The bullets were not in my imagination; they were real, and they were seeking me out to kill me. The gunners wouldn't even let me get close enough to talk it over with them. They wanted to kill me right here in the swamp.

The machine gun searched the area again. Far off in the night, others burped and spluttered. Enemy rifles added their popop . . . pop . . . popopop.

I waited about five minutes for someone to walk up and kill me, then my courage returned when I noticed that the shooting was all quite far away. I rose from the water, assembled my rifle, and loaded it and rammed on my bayonet. I was ready to go.

Burp ... burrrrp ... burrp ... cracklecracklecrackle ... popop ... burp ... popopop.

Lost and lonely, wrestling with the greatest fear of my life, I stood bewildered in the middle of a vast lake and looked for help.

I shivered convulsively and started to cry, then thought better of it. The hell with everything! I'm here for keeps; make the best of it. At least I can try to get out of this swamp before sunrise.

I took the little brass compass from my pocket and looked at it in the next spell of moonlight. The needle was frozen in position. I shook the compass and cursed and, holding it close, saw that it was filled with water. 'Sonofabitch,' I hissed, throwing it away. A wiseguy probably made a fortune off those compasses in the States. And now men will die because somebody gypped the government and made a fortune. Sonsofbitches.

A flare burst over the water several hundred yards away. I bowed my head and waited for the bullets to hit me like a baseball bat, but there were no bullets. The flare died out with the afterglow of a burnt match, and I looked around in the moonlight. I sought an orchard, three white lights, a crossroads village named Hébert, five hundred men from the 2nd Battalion, and all I saw was water and flares and tracers. I listened for our bugle call, and all I heard was enemy rifle and machine-gun fire.

Suddenly the whole thing struck me as ludicrous: the preparations and briefings, all the maps and sandtables. For all the good they did, the Army might as well have yanked us out of a pub and dumped us off helter-skelter to find our own way to the Germans. Instead of a regiment of over 1,500 men carefully assembled on a well-defined drop zone, D-Day was one man alone in an old swamp that the Air Corps said didn't even exist.

David K. Webster

Owing to the inexperience of many of the pilots, the men of the 101st were scattered over a wide area. By dawn, only 1,100 of the division's 6,600 troops had linked up. Nevertheless, they were still able to create much havoc behind the German positions near the beaches where the main landings were taking place.

Landing on Omaha

The American contingent came ashore in two places, stretches of coast codenamed 'Utah' and 'Omaha'. J. Robert Slaughter was a 19-year-old sergeant serving in the 116th Infantry, 29th Division.

My thinking, as we approached the beach, was that if this boat didn't hurry up and get us in I would die from seasickness. This was my first encounter with this malady. Woosiness became stomach sickness and then vomiting. At this point death is not so dreadful. I used the first thing at hand – my steel helmet. I didn't care what the Germans had to offer, I wanted to get on dry land. Nothing is worse than motion sickness, except maybe 88 mms and MG-42 machine-guns.

About 200 or 300 yards from shore we encountered the first enemy artillery fire. Near misses sent water skyward, and then it rained back on us. The British coxswain shouted to step back, he was going to lower the ramp and we were to disembark quickly. I was stationed near the front of the boat and heard Sergeant Norfleet counter, 'These men have heavy equipment and *you will take them all the way in.*' The coxswain begged, 'But we'll all be killed!' and Norfleet unholstered his .45 Colt pistol, put it to the sailor's head and ordered, 'All the way in!' The craft proceeded ashore, ploughing through the choppy water until the bow scraped the sandy bottom.

About 150 yards from shore I raised my head despite the warning from someone to 'Keep your heads down!' I could see the craft to our right taking a terrific licking from small arms. Tracer bullets were bounding and skipping off the ramp and sides as they zero'd in on the boat, which touched down a few minutes before we did. Had we not delayed a few minutes to pick up the survivors from a sunken craft, we might have taken the concentration of fire that boat took. Great plumes of water from enemy artillery and mortars kept spouting close by.

We knew then that this was not going to be a walk-in. No one thought that the enemy would give us this kind of opposition on the water's edge. We expected 'A' and 'B' Companies to have the beach secured by the time we landed. The reality was that no one else had set foot in the sector where we touched down. This turned the boys into men. Some would be very brave men, others would soon be dead men, but all of those who survived would be frightened men. Some wet their breeches, others cried unashamedly, and many just had to find it within themselves to get the job done. This is where the discipline and training took over.

As we approached the beach the ramp was lowered. Mortar and artillery shells exploded on land and in the water. Unseen snipers concealed in the cliffs were shooting down at individuals, but most havoc was from automatic weapons. The water was turning red from the blood. Explosions from artillery gunfire, the rapid-fire from nearby MG-42s, and naval gunfire firing inland was frightening.

I was stationed on the left side of the craft and about fifth from the front. Norfleet was leading the right side. The ramp was in the surf and the front of the steel craft was bucking violently up and down. As my turn came to exit, I sat on the edge of the bucking ramp, trying to time my leap on the down cycle. I sat there too long, causing a bottleneck and endangering myself as well as the men who followed. The one-inch steel ramp was going up and down in the surf, rising as much as 6 or 7 ft. I was afraid it would slam me in the head. One of our men was crushed by the door, killing him instantly. There were dead men in the water and there were live men as well. The Germans couldn't tell which was which. It was extremely hard to shed the heavy equipment, and if one were a weak swimmer, he could drown before inflating his Mae-West. I had to inflate mine to get in, even though I was a good swimmer. I remember helping Private Ernest McCanless, who was struggling to get closer in, so he wouldn't drown under all the weight. He still had one box of precious 30 cal. One of the dead, Mae-West inflated, had turned a dark colour.

There were dead men floating in the water and there were live men acting dead, letting the tide take them in. I was crouched down to chin-deep in the water when mortar shells began falling at the water's edge. Sand began to kick up from small-arms fire from the bluffs. It became apparent that it was past time to get the hell away from that killing zone and across the beach. I don't know how long we were in the water before the move was made to go. I tried to take cover behind one of the heavy timbers, and then noticed an innocent-looking mine tied to the top, so I made the decision to go for it. Getting across the beach became an obsession. The decision not to try never entered my mind.

While lying half in and half out of the water, behind one of the log poles, I noticed a GI running from right to left, trying to get across the beach. He was weighted with equipment and looked as though he was having a difficult time running. He was probably from the craft that touched down about 50 yards to our right. An enemy gunner shot him as he stumbled for cover. He screamed for a medic. One of the aid men moved quickly to help him, and he also was shot. I will never forget seeing that medic lying next to that wounded GI and both of them screaming. They died in minutes.

The tide was rushing in, and later waves of men were due, so we had to get across. I believe I was the first in my group, telling Pfc Walfred Williams, my Number One gunner, to follow. He still had his 51-pound machine-gun tripod. I had my rifle ready to fire, safety off, and had also fixed the bayonet before disembarking.

I gathered my courage and started running as fast as my long legs would carry me. I ran as low as I could to lessen the target, and since I am 6 ft 5 ins I still presented a good one. I had a long way to run – I would say a good 100 yards or more. We were loaded down with gear and all our clothes were soaking wet. Can you imagine running with shoes full of water and wet wool clothing? As I ran through a tidal pool with about six or eight inches of water, I began to stumble. I finally caught my balance and accidentally fired my rifle, barely missing my foot. I continued on to the sea wall. This is the first time I have admitted the embarrassment of inadvertently almost shooting myself!

Upon reaching the sea wall I looked back for the first time and got a glimpse of the armada out in the Channel. It was an awesome sight to behold. I also saw that Williams, Private Sal Augeri and Private Ernest McCanless were right behind. I didn't see Norfleet until later. Augeri had lost the machine-gun receiver in the water and I had got sand in my rifle. We still had one box of MG ammo but I don't believe we had a weapon that would fire. The first thing I did was take off my assault jacket and spread my raincoat so I could clean my rifle. It was then I saw bullet holes in my raincoat. I didn't realise until then that I had been targeted. I lit my first cigarette. They were wrapped in plastic, as were the matches. I had to rest and compose myself because I had become weak in the knees. It was a couple of days before I had enough appetite to eat a K-ration.

All the squad crossed the beach unscathed except Private Robert Stover and Medic Private Roland Coates, both of whom were killed. I don't know what happened to either of them. Stover was behind me in the boat and I didn't see him in the water or on the beach. (Records show Coates died of wounds on 7 June.) I didn't see Coates' fate, but knew Stover was a poor swimmer. A minor wound or accident could cause drowning in the rough surf.

J. Robert Slaughter

Almost 35,000 men landed on Omaha Beach on D-Day. More than 1,000 of them got no further, and another 3,000 were wounded.

On Sword Beach

The British destinations were 'Gold' and 'Sword'. Among those going ashore at the latter was a 26-year-old Commando officer, Major Pat Porteous VC.

We started crossing the beach. A flail tank just to my right, with its flail going looking for mines, got a direct hit by an anti-tank shell and blew up. I ordered all my chaps to throw their smoke grenades which created a big belt of smoke down our left-hand side and protected us from the pillbox. A little while later a subaltern from my unit managed to creep up to it and put a grenade into the firing slit; he won an MC.

Anyway, we got across the beach and into some sand dunes, where we organised a bit, although a lot of my chaps had been wounded. At that point I think I had lost about a quarter of my troop, either killed or wounded. Our job was to make our way to a coastal battery on the outskirts of Ouistreham, about a mile and a half away, and destroy the guns with special charges made of plastic explosive. We moved straight away and found a château with a sort of walled garden, where we cleaned our weapons and dumped our rucksacks, and then set off towards the battery.

We had to cross a big anti-tank ditch and when we got there we found someone had left a plank across it, which was just as well because one of the blokes who was carrying a specially made collapsible bridge had been killed on the beach and the bridge had been smashed to pieces.

On the way we passed a small house and a frantic Frenchman came running out and said that his wife had been wounded and asked if we had a doctor. At that very moment I heard a mortar bomb approaching and threw myself flat on the ground. The Frenchman was a little slow on the uptake, presumably he had never been mortared before, because there was an explosion and as I looked up I saw his head rolling down the road. It was very sad, kind of off-putting.

When we got to the battery, we found that the guns were dummies, just telegraph poles lashed on to wagons, and we learned afterwards from a Frenchman that the battery had been withdrawn some three or four days previously and had been re-sited a couple of miles back. In the centre of the position was a huge concrete observation tower, an enormous thing with walls about ten feet and some Germans who were at the top of it started firing at us. My signaller, who was just beside me, was shot and killed, and one of my subalterns, who had got up close to the tower, was killed when they dropped a grenade on him. He was a great friend of mine; I'd been best man at his wedding only two months before. He was trying to see if we could smoke them out, but the only access was up a single staircase in the middle and so the men inside were as safe as houses.

Patrick Porteous

Joseph Haeger was a 19-year-old German soldier with the 736th Infantry Regiment.

We held our position in the trenches for more than an hour. It was the most terrible time of my life. We were continually shelled and under fire from snipers. One of our bazookas hit a Canadian tank. We saw the flap opening and a soldier was half-way out when there was another explosion and it burst into flames with the soldier still hanging from the turret. I said to Ferdie, 'I hope we have a better death than that. I'd rather have a bullet.'

After about an hour we were ordered into a bunker, which was a command post almost entirely underground with a small observation hatch on the top. It was already full of wounded men. There were about thirty of them lying on straw blankets, absolutely terrified and crying out all the time. There was hardly any air inside and a man in the observation hole shouted that the Canadians were starting to pile earth up against the ventilators. It started to get very hot and difficult to breathe.

The company commander told us to breathe together: 'Breathe in when I say IN and out when I say OUT.' The battalion commander was firing a machine gun through a small aperture by the door. I will never forget the smell and the heat and noise inside that bunker, the cries of the wounded, the stink of exploding bullets and gases from the machine gun and the company commander yelling, 'IN, OUT, IN, OUT . . .'

Finally the company commander said to the battalion commander: 'Sir, we can't carry on. The wounded are suffocating.' The battalion commander said it was out of the question. 'We'll fight our way out of here if we have to. Count the weapons and the men preparatory to getting out.'

At that point there was almost a mutiny and some men started pulling the bolts out of their rifles in defiance. They knew that the door out of the bunker led to a trench and that on the other side of the trench the Canadians would be waiting for them.

Ferdie said to me: 'You're the only one beside the battalion commander who's got a machine gun. You'll be the first out of here, believe me.' I said: 'No, I'm not going to do it,' and I pulled out the locking pin that held the machine together. Just then the man in the observation post shouted: 'My God, they're bringing up a flame-thrower!'

We heard the 'woof' of the flame-thrower, but the flames couldn't get through the staggered sections of the ventilation shaft, although it turned red hot before our eyes. Now there was near panic. One German could speak two words of English and he kept shouting, 'Hello boys, hello boys, hello boys . . .'; the wounded were shouting their heads off and a radio operator in the corner was shouting to try and establish contact with headquarters. The battalion commander seemed oblivious to what was going on and kept firing his machine gun out of the aperture without once looking round.

People were shouting, 'We've got to do something, we've got to do something,' and eventually we took one of the dirty white sheets from one of the wounded and with the help of a broomstick pushed it out through the observation hatch. A voice from outside shouted, 'All right then, come on out.'

We dropped our weapons and made for the door, more scared of what the battalion commander would do than of the Canadians outside. Suddenly he turned round and asked the radio operator if he'd made contact. The operator shook his head. The battalion commander went very white, stepped back and then dropped his machine gun.

One of the soldiers opened the door and went out carrying the broomstick with the white sheet. Through the opening, we could see Canadian troops standing on either side of the trench. They started to shout, 'Oucha come, oucha come.'

We were made to lie down on the grass at the end of the trench, take off our equipment, boots and tunics. I said to Ferdie, 'Well, it's all over for us now.'

Joseph Haeger

Colonel von Luck had still not been ordered to attack. Hitler and the High Command believed that the Normandy landings were a bluff, and that the real invasion was still going to take place near Calais.

At daybreak, I sent my adjutant to ask divisional command post to secure us immediate clearance for a counterattack. On his arrival, Liebeskind witnessed a heated telephone conversation which Feuchtinger was evidently having with the army: 'General, I have just come back from Paris and I've seen a gigantic armada off the west coast of Cabourg, warships, supply ships, and landing craft. I want to attack at once with the entire division east of the Orne in order to push through to the coast.' But clearance was strictly denied.

Hitler, who used to work far into the night, was still asleep that early morning.

At the command post, I paced up and down and clenched my fists at the indecision of the Supreme Command in the face of the obvious facts. If Rommel had been with us instead of in Germany, he would have disregarded all orders and taken action – of that we were convinced.

We felt completely fit physically and able to cope with the situation. I concealed my anger and remained calm and matter-of-fact. My experience in previous theatres of war had taught me that the more critical a situation, or the more alarming the reports, the more calmly every experienced leader should react.

The best way to calm an excited orderly officer, or a dispatch rider coming straight from an apparently desperate situation, is to sit him down, give him a cigarette and say, 'Now tell me what has actually happened.'

So the tragedy took its course. After only a few hours, the brave fighting units in the coastal fortifications could no longer withstand the enemy pressure, or else they were smashed by the Allied naval guns; while a German panzer division, ready to engage, lay motionless behind the front and powerful Allied bomber formations, thanks to complete air superiority, covered the coastal divisions and Caen with concentrated attacks. In the early hours of the morning, from the hills east of Caen, we saw the gigantic Allied armada, the fields littered with transport gliders and the numerous observation balloons over the landing fleet, with the help of which the heavy naval guns subjected us to precision fire.

The situation forced us to regroup. Strong combat units were formed on either side of the Orne, east and west. We continued to wait for clearance for a counterattack. In view of this superiority, I thought, on seeing the landing fleet, there was no longer much chance of throwing the Allies back into the sea. Bringing up reserves was even now extremely difficult for us. The 'second front' had been established. The enemy in the east pressing with superior strength, the ceaseless bombing of our most important industrial centres and railway communications – even the bravest and most experienced troops could no longer win this war. A successful invasion, I thought, was the beginning of the end.

Hans von Luck

Raymond Paris worked for the notary public in Ste Mère-Eglise, where US Airborne troops were dropped and which was the first village to be liberated.

At this moment, however, the Germans had decided to start saturating our sector of the town with shells and in the time it took me to cross the courtyard to the trench, some ten or fifteen shells exploded in my immediate vicinity. At this point I had learned to recognise when and where shells would explode by the sound they made. If the whistling noise was thin and shrill, they would explode some distance away; if the sound was muffled and low, they would explode close by. So, when I started to cross the garden, I heard a shell coming close by and threw myself to the ground, still holding on to the bottle of milk. I was lying on the central path, close to a framework of climbing peas and it exploded in a pear tree about fifteen metres away from me, ripping it out of the ground. I continued running to the trench and I had hardly gone ten metres when a second shell exploded behind my back. I threw myself to the ground and when I looked back, I saw the pea frame had completely disintegrated. The shell had exploded more or less on the spot where I had been lying.

When I got into the trench I was overcome by a fit of violent trembling, retrospective fear, I suppose, such that I wrapped my arms around myself to try to stop it. The trembling ceased minutes later when our neighbour ran into the courtyard screaming that her husband was dead. I left the trench, accompanied her to her house and discovered that her husband had been killed in his shop by the explosion out in the street. His chest had been crushed and his right arm was missing, but worst of all his cranium had split open and his brain was lying two or three metres away from his body. I was dreadfully upset and frightened. I could hardly bear it, as one who cannot stand the sight even of an injection. I had to do something for the family. I dragged his body over on to a small couch, but I knew I had to do something about the brain which was just lying there. I took a salad bowl which happened to be handy and with some shards of glass picked up the brain, put it in the salad bowl and pushed it under the divan.

                                                                  Raymond Paris

The heavy casualties on the beaches meant that every nurse in Portsmouth would be needed, including 16-year-old Naina Beaven.

It was about two o'clock when Miss Hobbs, my nursing commandant, came into the office where I was working and said I was needed up at QA, which was Queen Alexandra's Hospital, that there were so many wounded coming back from the beaches that they desperately needed help. I ran home to tell my mother, got my uniform and then rushed up the hill to the hospital.

Another girl who I saw once a week at lectures checked in shortly after I did and we reported to Matron together. She checked our names and told us to go to this particular ward. It took us some time to get there because all the corridors were laid end to end with stretchers. Lorries were coming up from the dockyard so quickly that there wasn't room for all the wounded. The army stretcher bearers knew who was badly wounded and those who were less seriously wounded were put on the floor.

When we got to the ward we were told to start cleaning people up, giving them drinks and things. Many of them were filthy – well, they were quite young and when you're frightened you know what happens, you're all messy and dirty – so the main thing was to clean them and bed-bath them. We didn't have to treat their wounds or anything, if you took somebody's filthy battledress off and found something bad, then you would call a sister.

Mostly they were conscious but not talking much; they were mostly really, really tired and later on in the day we were told that these were the first exhaustion cases. A lot of them were so completely exhausted they didn't care one jot what happened to them. They had been on standby since the day before.

Some of them could speak, but when you are completely exhausted, not just very tired, when you are too tired to care about anything, you just want to be cleaned up and have something to drink. They weren't hungry.

As I worked with these poor exhausted soldiers, I was thinking, 'How long will it go on? If I come tomorrow and the next day, will I still be doing this?'

While I was washing and cleaning up filthy and dreadful and horrible messes and giving out water and cold milk to people who were allowed such things, two sisters came round and asked if I would be willing to work in the German prisoners' ward. They needed the same kind of help, but some nurses refused to go into their ward.

I had to go and see Matron first. I went with my friend, Win. Matron said, 'You know we have a lot of German prisoners – they were picked up very early from the beaches.' I said I didn't know, but had just been told. She said, 'Well, a lot of people won't work with them, they are either walking out or refusing to work with them. Will you do what you're doing, for them?'

Well, I was a bit meek and mild and I didn't say anything and Win looked at me and Matron said, 'Hurry up and make up your minds, because if you are not going to do it, I'll try somebody else.' Win looked at me and said, 'Oh, come on, Naina. My Eddie is out there and if somebody said they wouldn't clean him up, Mum would feel terrible.' So with that, I felt that if Win was going to do it, I'll do it. We would do it together and protect each other! I also couldn't bear the thought of my commandant saying to me, 'One of my girls wouldn't even give a prisoner a cup of water?'

Naina Beaven

By the end of 6 June, some 150,000 Allied troops had landed in France. The Second Front had been opened.

‡

Italy

A Roman triumph

On 5 June, General Mark Clark, the commander of the US 5th Army, reached Rome.

On June 5, with Gruenther and other officers, I drove along Route No. 6 into Rome. We didn't know our way round the city very well, but General Hume, who was with us, had suggested that the Town Hall on the Capitoline Hill would be a good place for me to meet my four corps commanders for a conference on our immediate plans. We wanted to push on past Rome as rapidly as possible in pursuit of the retreating enemy and towards Civitavecchia, the port of Rome, which we direly needed for unloading supplies. There were gay crowds in the streets, many of them waving flags, as our infantry marched through the capital. Flowers were stuck in the muzzles of the soldiers' rifles and of guns on the tanks. Many Romans seemed to be on the verge of hysteria in their enthusiasm for the American troops. The Americans were enthusiastic too, and kept looking for the ancient landmarks that they had read about in their history-books. It was on this day that a doughboy made the classic remark of the Italian campaign, when he took a long look at the ruins of the Colosseum, whistled softly, and said, 'Gee I didn't know our bombers had done *that* much damage in Rome!'

Our little group of jeeps wandered round the streets while we craned our necks looking at the sights, but not finding our way to the Capitoline Hill. In fact, we were lost, but we didn't like to admit it, and we didn't care very much, because we were interested in everything we saw. Eventually we found ourselves in St Peter's Square, which delighted us all and which enabled Hume to get his bearings. As we stopped to look up at the great dome of St Peter's a priest walking along the street paused by my jeep and said in English, 'Welcome to Rome. Is there any way in which I can help you?'

'Well,' I replied, 'we'd like to get to the Capitoline Hill.'

He gave us directions, and added, 'We are certainly proud of the American Fifth Army. May I introduce myself?' And he told me his name. He came from Detroit.

'My name's Clark,' I replied.

We both expressed pleasure at the meeting, and the priest started to move on. Then he stopped and took another look and said, 'What did you say your name is?' A number of Italians had gathered round by this time and were listening to our conversation. When the priest told them that I was the commander of the Fifth Army a youth on a bicycle shouted that he would lead us to the Capitoline Hill. He did, pedalling along in front of our jeep and shouting to everybody on the street to get out of the way because General Clark was trying to get to the Capitoline Hill. This, of course, merely added to the excitement that we had felt everywhere we had gone in Rome, and by the time we reached a point opposite the balcony where Mussolini used to appear for his major speeches the road was blocked by curious and cheering people.

We finally broke a path through and twisted up the hill to the Town Hall. The door was locked, and there didn't seem to be a soul about. Pounding on the big door, I reflected that it had been a curiously varied as well as a historic day. We had been lost in the ancient capital which we entered as liberators after a long and unprecedented campaign. We had been welcomed and taken in tow by a priest and a boy on a bicycle. We had almost been mobbed by excited, cheering crowds. But now we couldn't even get into the Town Hall. I pounded on the door again, not feeling much like the conqueror of Rome. Anyhow, I thought, we got to

Rome before Ike got across the Channel to Normandy. I was right about that too, but by a narrow margin. I didn't know it, but even while I stood there Ike's army was embarking. We had won the race to Rome by only two days.

Mark Clark

Although the Allies did not dally in Rome, their decision to make it an objective allowed Kesselring to regroup further north, where his forces would hold on for almost another year.

Death in the afternoon

After the Italian armistice, some former Allied POWs made common cause against the Germans with anti-Fascist groups. Stuart Hood operated with one band near Chianti.

We attacked on a hot June day. The woods were heavy with sunshine. Beetles came drifting over the bushes like bombers. There were six of us – the major, myself, four South Africans. We came to the edge of the wood and saw the bivouac tent a couple of hundred yards away across an open field of grass. There was no movement. They would be asleep in the shade or in the back of the truck. We climbed a fence and jumped down among the trailing branches of a briar. A thorn whipped back and struck a South African in the eyeball. He dropped his Sten and clapped a hand to his eye. There was a report as the jolt of the fall brought the firing pin forward on to the cartridge. At the edge of the wood a couple of figures in bathing trunks rose and peered across through the sunshine. We ran forward with a shout. They had their hands up – boys caught in a wave of fear that melted their guts and loosened their sphincters. I looked for the other two. One was by the truck in a little nest of branches he had made for shelter from the sun. He was scrabbling for a weapon. I shouted in German not to be a fool. He stood up with a grenade in his hand and tugged at the thong which would arm the fuse. When I fired he was a couple of yards away. Two shots from the Beretta. One after the other. I saw two little marks appear on his belly, just above his bathing trunks. He clapped his hands over them and fell on his back. You idiot, I said, and bent over him. His face blenched under the sunburn. He groaned a little and twisted about as if to shake off his death. Then he half sat up, looked at my face, and seized my hand, clinging to it like a frightened child. I laid him back and freed myself from his grasp. My hand was sticky with his blood. Beyond the woods the fourth of them was running through the fields, doubling and ducking. At that range there was no point in trying to catch him or to bring him down.

In the truck we found small arms ammunition – the wrong calibre – mortar bombs, and new-fangled anti-tank weapons we didn't know how to use. The wounded man lay in the shade and groaned.

We made the other two carry him and set off through the woods. In a safe spot we rested and waited for evening. He was silent now, his face a strange ashen hue. There was no haemorrhage, only a little dark blood oozing from the two holes. The flesh had closed again over the bullets. We covered him with a blanket and got water to bathe the sweat from his face. His mates sat together and watched and did not talk. After dusk a peasant cart came with a mattress and jolted him along the tracks to the nearest farmhouse. We laid him in the barn in the straw and covered him well. From time to time he would open his eyes and look at me with incredulity. A fair-haired boy with a good face lying in the mucky sweat of death.

When I went in the others were all round the table eating supper. I spoke with the boys and told them not to be afraid. Unless they did anything stupid they were safe. A doctor was coming for the one outside.

He came towards midnight, looked, felt his pulse, shrugged. There's not much to be done about it, he said. I'll give him an injection for his heart. He may last the night. Even if you got him to a hospital there's not much hope.

A South African came and stood beside us.

What does he say?

He says there's not much hope. Maybe we could leave him by the roadside tomorrow with a note. There's bound to be a convoy.

The boy stirred, opened his eyes and looked up at me in the light of the lantern.

Will I die, he asked in English, will I die?

I told him what we would do. He shut his eyes and slept.

In the morning he was worse; his breathing was laboured and irregular. Caravaggio came to report that parachutists had been dropped to us – Italian saboteurs from Bari. I took a last look at the boy and went off through the woods. I had gone about a mile when from the direction of the farmhouse I heard three bursts of fire.

Stuart Hood

‡

Kissing Botticelli's Venus

Eric Linklater made an unexpected discovery at the Tuscan castle of fellow writer and absent owner Osbert Sitwell.

Nayar and Quereshi and Vaughan Thomas had gone to explore the farther rooms, and now Vaughan Thomas, his rosy face tense with excitement, reappeared. 'The whole house is full of pictures,' he exclaimed, 'and some of the cases are labelled. They've come from the Uffizi and the Pitti Palace!'

Hastily I followed him into the next room, where a score of wooden cases stood against the walls, and then to the room beyond. There a very large picture lay upon trestles. It was spattered with little squares of semi-transparent paper, stuck for protection over imperilled areas where the paint was cracking or threatening to flake. On the near side there were cherubs, or angel-young, with delicate full lips, firm chins and candid eyes wide open over well-defined cheek-bones. Against a pale blue sky the Virgin floated in splendour. Two reverent, benign and bearded figures held a crown above her head.

We failed to recognise it. We knew now that we were in the presence of greatness, and a bewildered excitement was rising in our minds. Recognition could not yet speak plainly, but baffled by the vast improbability merely stammered. Stupidly we exclaimed, 'But that must be . . .'

'Of course, and yet . . .'

'Do you think it is?'

By this time we had gathered a few spectators. Some refugees had been sleeping in the castello – their dark bedding lay on the floor – and now, cheerfully perceiving our excitement, they were making sounds of lively approval, and a couple of men began noisily to open the shutters that darkened the last of the suite of rooms. This was a great chamber that might have served for a banquet or a ball, and as we went in the light swept superbly over a scene of battle: over the magnificent rotundities of heroic war-horses, knight tumbling knight with point of lance – and beside it, immensely tall, an austere and tragic Madonna in dark raiment upon gold.

Vaughan Thomas shouted, 'Uccello!'

I, in the same instant, cried, 'Giotto!'

For a moment we stood there, quite still, held in the double grip of amazement and delight. Giotto's Madonna and Uccello's Battle of San Romano, leaning negligently against the wall, were now like exiled royalty on the common level. They had been reduced by the circumstance of war from their own place and proper height; and they were a little dusty. We went nearer, and the refugees came round us and proudly exclaimed, 'E vero, è vero! Uccello! Giotto! Molto bello, molto antico!'

Now Vaughan Thomas is a Welshman, more volatile than I, quicker off the mark, swifter in movement, and while I remained in a pleasant stupefaction before the gaunt Virgin and the broad-bottomed cavalry, he was off in search of other treasures. A stack of pictures in the middle of the room divided it in two, and he, with Nayar and Quereshi, was on the other side when a helpful Italian took down the shutters from the far end, and let in more light. Then I heard a sudden clamour of voices, a yell of shrill delight from Nayar, and Vaughan Thomas shouting 'Botticelli!' as if he were a fox-hunter view-halloing on a hill. I ran to see what they had found, and came to a halt before the Primavera.

I do not believe that stout Cortez, when he first saw the Pacific, stood silent on a peak in Darien. I believe he shouted in wordless joy, and his men with waving arms made about him a chorus of babbling congratulation. We, before the Primavera, were certainly not mute, and the refugees – some had been sleeping side by side with Botticelli – were as loudly vocal as ourselves. They had a fine sense of occasion, and our own feeling that this was a moment in history was vigorously supported by the applause they gave to our exclamation and delight . . .

Commanding officers who have lately been engaged in battle and are roused from their entitled sleep are sometimes difficult; but fortunately for us Colonel Leeming of the Mahrattas was a good-humoured man. He listened politely, then with growing attention to what I told him. He knew there were some pictures in the house, but he had had no time to look at them, he said, and he had supposed they belonged to the family. The castello was the property of the Sitwells, who were artistic people, weren't they?

To describe the wealth of treasure that lay below him, I used all the superlatives I could put my tongue to – and still the Colonel listened, unprotesting. To the north we could hear the noise of war, and so much concern for a few yards of paint may have seemed excessive to him, whose care was men; but he was very patient. He admitted that he knew little about art, and wistfully added that if his wife were there she would be more impressed. She took a great interest in pictures, he said.

He put on his shoes and came down to look at the Primavera. He stood silent for some time, and still without comment walked slowly past the other pictures, into the adjoining rooms and back again, as though he were making his rounds of a Sunday morning after church parade. He was evidently pleased with what he saw, and now permitted himself – with a decent restraint – to be infected by our enthusiasm. He would do everything in his power to keep the pictures safe, he promised.

Several other officers had appeared, and to one of them he said: 'Have all these rooms put out of bounds, and get a guard mounted. You'll have to find somewhere else for the refugees to sleep; there's plenty of room in the place.'

We explained to the Professor [guardian of the castello] that his pictures were now under official protection – Mahratta bayonets would guard them night and day, we told him – and at once he grew boisterously happy, and danced about thanking everyone in turn . . .

In the morning we returned to Montegufoni, and found dark sentries, grave of feature and dignified in their bearing, outside the doors. Then the Professor appeared with one of the Mahrattas' English officers, and we went inside. The Colonel's orders had been strictly obeyed, and the rooms had now the untenanted peace of a museum on a fine morning. We opened the shutters, and with more leisure made further discoveries. Many pictures that we had scarcely noticed in our first excitement now appeared like distinguished guests at a party, obscured by numbers to begin with, who, when at last you meet them, are so dignified or decorative that it seems impossible they could have remained unrecognised even though their backs were turned and a multitude surrounded them. Lippo Lippis came forward smiling, a Bronzino was heartily acknowledged, Andrea del Sartos met our eyes and were more coolly received.

Beside the Giotto Madonna stood a huge equestrian portrait of Philip IV of Spain by Rubens or Velasquez? I do not know which – and peering round Philip's shoulder, absurdly coy, was the stern and antique countenance of another great Virgin. With some difficulty we moved the King and revealed a Madonna of Cimabue. In a room on the other side of the courtyard, that we had not visited before, we found Duccio's Sienese Madonna, the Rucellai Madonna. Here also were many altar-pieces, triptychs in lavish gold, and painted crucifixes of great rarity in long-darkened colours with mouths down-drawn in Byzantine pain.

Then, privily, I returned to the great room and Botticelli's Primavera. I was alone with his enchanting ladies, and standing tiptoe I was tall enough, I kissed the pregnant Venus, the Flowery Girl, and the loveliest of the Graces: her on the right. I was tempted to salute them all, but feared to be caught in vulgar promiscuity. Some day, I said, I shall see you again, aloft and remote on your proper wall in the Uffizi, and while with a decently hidden condescension I listen to the remarks of my fellow-tourists, I shall regard you with a certain intimacy with a lonely, proud and wistful memory. The officials, I thought sadly, will certainly not allow me to take a ladder into the gallery.

Eric Linklater

The legacy of war

Iris Origo returned to her farm near Siena after the fighting had washed over it.

I JULY 1944

And now we have come home. This morning Ulick sent a staff car to fetch us, and Schwester Marie and I, with the two babies and Benedetta, triumphantly drive back over the road which we had taken – so much less agreeably – ten days ago in the opposite direction. (The other children are to follow in a few days.) Plenty of shell and bomb-holes on the road and in the fields, and as we got nearer home we looked out anxiously for damages. At the Castelluccio there are some large shell-holes; the clinic, too, has been badly hit. Then, as we drive up to La Foce, chaos meets our eyes. The house is still standing, with only one shell-hole in the garden façade, another on the fattoria, and several in the roof. The latter have been caused by the explosion of a mine, the Germans' parting gift, bursting on the road to Chianciano, not thirty yards from the house. An enormous crater marks the spot, but has not blocked the road, since the Allies merely made a diversion into the field beside it.

In the garden, which has also got several shell-holes and trenches for machine-guns, they have stripped the pots off the lemons and azaleas, leaving the plants to die. The ground is strewn with my private letters and photographs, mattresses and furniture-stuffing. The inside of the house, however, is far worse. The Germans have stolen everything that took their fancy, blankets, clothes, shoes and toys, as well, of course, as anything valuable or eatable, and have deliberately destroyed much of sentimental or personal value. Every drawer of my writing-desk has been ransacked, and stained or torn-up photographs, torn out of their frames, strew the floors. In the dining-room the table is still laid, and there are traces of a drunken repast; empty wine-bottles and smashed glasses lie beside a number of my summer hats (which presumably have been tried on), together with boot-trees, toys, overturned furniture and W C paper. In the library, where the leather has been ripped off the arm-chairs and some books have been stolen, more empty bottles lie in the fireplace. The lavatory is filled to the brim with filth, and decaying meat, lying on every table, adds to the foul smell. There are innumerable flies. In our bedroom, too, it is the same, and only the nurseries, which the maids have been cleaning ever since they arrived (five hours before us) are habitable. Some of the toys have been stolen or deliberately broken, but curiously enough, the English Kate Greenaway alphabet is still upon the wall, and the children's beds are untouched. So we put the children to bed for their afternoon nap, and then go on investigating the damage. There is no water in the house, and also, of course, no light.

Antonio is away, having had to go down to Chianciano to take up his work as mayor, and cope with the spearhead AMG officials, but in the farm courtyard, in a wilderness of refuse, gravel and waste paper, a few men are standing about gloomily. They come forward to greet me – and later the fattore, too, appears, and with tears in his eyes takes both my hands in his. He and his family are all safe, but have had a very bad time. And he gives us tragic news. Gigi – our beloved gardener, with his crooked mouth and limp, with his passion for flowers, and his short temper and wry smile – Gigi has been killed by a shell in the ditch in which he had taken shelter. It was not even possible, owing to the mines that are strewn in the woods, to bring his body back to the graveyard for burial, and his son has buried him in the woods where he fell.

Iris Origo

‡

A knock at the door

In 1941, Frenchwoman Marie-Madeleine Fourcade, the 31-year-old mother of two young children, took command of what would become one of the largest intelligence-gathering networks in Occupied Europe. 'Noah's Ark' – it used animals as codenames – grew to have 3,000 members. When the Gestapo got too close to her, Fourcade was taken to England, but after D-Day she returned to France to resume her work.

I suddenly felt hungry and went into the kitchen. I absent-mindedly peeled a few tomatoes and ate them, dipping them first in fresh olive oil, a royal gift from Turtle Dove's mother. Then I went back to the drawing room to tidy up. At that moment an infernal racket broke out at the main entrance and welled up the staircase. I leapt into the hall and, seeing the bolt drawn, rushed to close it. I was too late. The door was already opening.

Exerting all my strength I pushed it, desperately trying to turn the key. If I succeeded I should gain the two minutes that were essential for escaping through the courtyard with the double exit. The banging on the door punctuated the orders that were being shouted in German, and mingled with the heavy breathing of a band of furious soldiers who were milling about on the other side.

'German police! Open!' I heard, just as my strength failed.

The wave surged in. There were two dozen of them, almost all in grey-green uniform. Among them were four civilians, one obviously a North African. 'Where's the man? Where's the man?' they screamed into my face, digging their revolvers into my chest. The soldiers carrying sub-machine guns gathered in a circle round me.

'What man?' I asked, putting on a bewildered look. 'I'm a woman and I'm on my own.'

'He went that way,' the North African said, pointing to the courtyard.

I flared up. 'There are other flats in the house. If you're looking for someone, why do you imagine he's in the first one you come to?'

'That's true,' said another civilian, who seemed to be in charge. 'We're wasting time. Let's go and see. You, watch her,' he said to a little soldier, who leaned against the mantelpiece and trained his gun on me. I heard the doors banging on the other landings and people shouting and protesting. In the half-light the grids of my messages glimmered on the table in the centre of the drawing room. It was a miracle that in their excitement they had noticed nothing. Under the watchdog's vigilant gaze, I went back to the table and quickly piled up the papers spread over it. Then pretending to blow my nose noisily I went back towards the divan in the alcove and, slipping out of my guard's line of sight for a second, I threw the whole lot as far as possible underneath.

'What are you doing?' barked the watchdog.

'I'm blowing my nose,' I said gravely, walking over to him.

'In this heat!' he commiserated. Seeing that he was ready to chat, I asked him who they were looking for. 'A man who is causing us a lot of trouble, a terrorist.'

This was my cue and I picked it up at once. 'Someone from the maquis?' I asked, pretending to be frightened.

'*Jawohl!* Someone from the maquis. He came into this house about three-quarters of an hour ago. We were sent to get him.'

'What does he look like?' I asked in a dead voice.

'Tall and fair, apparently. The Gestapo chiefs call him Grand Duke.'

At that moment the Gestapo chiefs themselves came back, still shouting.

'He's not up there; he's got away. This woman is lying to us; she wanted to gain time,' they told the North African.

'Why did you push against the door when we wanted to come in?' shouted the leader, grabbing me by the shoulders.

'Put yourself in my place. You gave me a fine old fright. I thought you were terrorists from the maquis. I stopped as soon as I heard you shout "German police".'

'That's right,' he said, withdrawing his claws. 'What are you doing here by yourself?'

I let fly. I told them I was getting away from the bombing in Toulon, as the raids were driving me mad. I hated the war and I'd come to Aix to get some peace and quiet. It was a deliberate decision. 'Can't you go about things a bit more gently?' I added, going over to the offensive. 'I've always heard the Germans were courteous. If I'd known that you were the Gestapo I'd have opened the door right away.'

Meanwhile the soldiers and civilians had been searching the flat, turning up the mattresses and easy chairs, rummaging through the cupboards, the suitcases and the fireplaces. 'What are you hoping to find?' I went on, to keep the atmosphere relaxed.

The leader described Grand Duke, going into details about his import-ance, and a big network that they had not yet been able to smash, the 'Alliance'. My blood froze. So it was *us* they were after, not me. But what then? I must go on and spin out my yarn. I blundered on, making myself seem as stupid as I possibly could.

'You see how right I was to be afraid of the man from the maquis. I heartily approve of your hunting them down. Is there any way I can help?'

The ferrets returned empty-handed. 'Nothing suspicious, chief,' said the North African.

Now completely mollified, the leader lowered his revolver: 'Here's the address of our office. If the man I've described comes back here, let me know at once.'

'Are you sure he lives here? What's his name?'

'We don't know. We only know his alias. He may have come in under the porch to throw his pursuers off the scent and then got away while these idiots were raising the alarm instead of shooting him on sight.'

Once again they split up and looked through the flat. Suddenly they pointed to the pile of cigarettes on a corner of one of the pieces of furniture. 'I see you smoke Gauloises. You've got a lot. Cigarettes are rationed.'

I began to curse my vice. Why ever had I started smoking again? 'I made a swap on the black market,' I said brazening it out. 'Some people would rather have butter.'

I offered them the Made-in-England Gauloises and lit one myself. They seemed to be in no hurry and went on standing around and smoking. Then, after a few brief orders, the soldiers picked up their weapons and moved towards the door. My heart gave a leap. I had won, they *were* going. The civilians began to say goodbye, repeating their request. I gave a silent whoop of joy. Bells rang in my ears. 'They've gone, they've gone.'

Before passing through the drawing-room door, one of them suddenly went down on all fours and looked under the divan. I saw his arm shoot underneath. Carefully he pulled out the grids, looked at them and with a triumphant gesture thrust them under his colleagues' noses.

That was that. My turn had come. I tried to think only of those who had gone before me: Navarre, Eagle, Swift, Schaerrer. The glorious band gathered round me and sustained me. It was perfectly normal; it was bound to happen to me as well. Anything else would have been unfair.

Taken to prison, she learned of a trap baited for her comrade 'Grand Duke'. If she could not escape from her cell, both of them would die.

I looked at my watch. It was midnight. Sounds came from the guardroom. Through the crack in the middle of the door I could make out the figures of soldiers going on duty and coming off and flopping down on their beds, eating, swigging great draughts of beer and swapping yarns. Moved by an uncontrollable impulse, I thumped on my door. The soldiers stopped talking and looked at one another. I went on hammering. A tall brute stood up and came and opened the door. I got him to understand that I wanted to go to the lavatory. He picked up his gun and went with me. We turned right as we went into the courtyard and he pointed the place out, keeping the door open with his foot. I studied the general layout, the vast courtyard embedded in the whole complex of the barracks. Not a hope. I quickly went back to my cell.

I must think of something else. I had five hours left in which to escape.

I lay down again on the bed. I was stupid; it was impossible; it would be better to go to sleep. I could not close my eyes. A faint gleam of light came from the window. I was suffocating. 'You must breathe, old girl, you're going mad.' I got up and went over to the window, a big, ordinary kind of opening, probably overlooking the street by which we had arrived. A thick wooden board screwed into the frame blocked four-fifths of it. It had undoubtedly been put there to prevent soldiers under punishment from communicating with the world outside while at the same time allowing the air, as well as a little light, to come in. But this meant that they must have removed the glass. There was, in fact, no proper window at all, only bars dimly outlined against the night.

I pushed the bed under the window, put the sanitary receptacle (a sort of big zinc washing-up bowl) upside down upon it, took off my shoes, climbed up and found I was level with the opening. I avidly gulped in the soft night air. I tried the bars with my forehead. They were not prison bars; simply the bars that are found on all ground floor windows the world over, strong and proud in their protective role. Without proper tools it was pointless to think of moving one from the uprights or of tearing down the wooden board. The problem was to slip somehow between the board and the bars and, once there, to push to get out.

I got down again. Behind my door the soldiers were playing cards. I reckoned that at three o'clock the guard would be changed and that those coming off duty would be only too glad to sleep. I carried on with my preparations. What a pity I hadn't brought Turtle Dove's olive oil. I would have smeared it all over my body like those Indo-Chinese burglars who, according to my father's stories, used to break into houses at night, their naked bodies covered with fat or grease so that they would slip more easily through the hands of anyone trying to catch them. They went about the job stark naked. I must go naked like them, to be as thin as possible. I took off my clothes and practised holding the little batik dress in my teeth and a few banknotes in my hand. The main thing was not to take anything that might make a noise if it dropped.

My watch showed three o'clock and, as I expected, there was a change of guard. The men coming in got into bed without a word and the light went out. Those men were really tired, as their snores immediately confirmed. I waited a few minutes, then got back into my batik dress and banged on my door. They were not the same men and so I could safely repeat the lavatory trick to test their vigilance. I banged on the door three separate times. No response but snores.

I undressed again and began my climb to freedom. Steadying myself at the top of the window opening and plunging feet first between the wooden plank and the bars was less difficult than I had feared; but I lost almost all my bank notes in the process. I immediately stopped trying to push my head between the bars that were set into the stonework on both sides of the frame; for only iron is likely to give. Methodically, I tried the rest of them. To my great surprise one gap seemed big enough to take my head provided I was prepared to push hard. I tried them all again. I was right;

only one was big enough for me to get through. I returned to it and pushed with all strength. My head went through.

At that precise moment a motor convoy swirled into the street from the left and drew up with a screech of brakes. It stopped opposite my window and I quickly withdrew my head, so sharply that I thought I had torn off my ears. The Gestapo were returning. They would find me, naked and pinned like a beetle against this board that scraped my back. What an idiot I was to have waited so long! The NCO in charge of the convoy began to shout: the raucous voice of a sentry posted a few yards to the right answered. I hadn't seen him! And I was counting on fleeing in that direction . . .

A dialogue started. The convoy had missed its way. It turned and went back. It was not the Gestapo. As it went by I saw that it was a unit that we had told London was being sent to reinforce the Normandy front. The trucks disappeared, their headlights glowing like cats' eyes, just above ground level.

Pushing my head through again was even more painful than the first time, but the pain and the fear of failure made me perspire profusely, which helped my skin to slip against the iron. After my neck I got one shoulder through, then my right leg. Squeezing my hips through was sheer agony. The pain was appalling but I knew that once the head is through the rest of the body will go, while the pain I felt would be nothing compared with what would be in store for me with the Gestapo.

I suddenly found myself down on the pavement, but the slight thud of my feet as I dropped to the ground had attracted the sentry's attention. I wrapped my dress round my neck and crouched down. '*Wer da?*' The soldier flashed his torch and its beam swept the darkness. I lay flat on the ground. I must get away quickly! Summoning up all my remaining energy I crossed the square on all fours and began to move as fast as my legs would let me, first straight ahead, then dodging from side to side, out into the vague open space that I could just make out. I ran on, stumbling into the potholes and tearing my skin on the brambles. At last, no longer hearing any sounds behind me, I put on my dress. I was free. Free!

Marie-Madeleine Fourcade

Four hundred and thirty-eight members of Fourcade's network were executed during the war. Among its achievements was the pin-pointing for British Intelligence of the Germans' rocket development site at Peenemünde.

‡

The bomb plot

On 20 July, an attempt was made on Hitler's life. The plotters, who were chiefly
aristocratic Germans and senior army officers, intended to seize power and negotiate
a peace with the Allies. It fell to Colonel Count Claus von Stauffenberg to place a
briefcase full of explosives next to Hitler at a conference. Nicolaus von Below,
Hitler's Luftwaffe adjutant, was also at the Wolfschanze HQ.

It was a warm summer's day and those of us attending the conference
assembled before the barracks hut. This circle included Puttkamer,
Bodenschatz and Graf [Count] von Stauffenberg, who since 1st July had
been Chief of Staff to Generaloberst Fromm, C-in-C Reserve Army, and
had attended at the Berghof a few days previously to present a report.
Hitler wanted to explore the idea of new panzer and infantry formations,
and today's conference was to receive information on the possibilities.
Hitler welcomed with a handshake each officer standing before the barracks
before leading the way at once into the situation room, where other senior
officers were assembled . . .

   The conference opened as usual with Heusinger's report on the Eastern
Front. I was standing a little to the side discussing the agenda for Mussolini's
visit with the three other adjutants. Heusinger made a point which interested me, and I moved to the opposite side of the table to obtain a better
view of the map. I had been there for a few minutes when the bomb
exploded. The clock said 12.40. I lost consciousness for a few seconds.
When I came to I saw around me a ruin of wood and glass. I staggered to
my feet, got out through one of the window frames, then sprinted around
the hut to the main door. My head was buzzing, I had been deafened and
I was bleeding from the head and neck. At the door a terrible scene greeted
me. Severely injured officers lay around on the floor, others were reeling
around and falling over. Hitler, sure-footed and erect, was led out by
Keitel. His uniform jacket and trousers were torn but otherwise he seemed
none the worse. He retired at once to his bunker for medical attention.
Eleven persons were found to have serious injuries and were taken to the
military hospital four kilometres distant. Everybody else had injuries in
some degree, the majority with perforated eardrums.

   I ran to the neighbouring signals barracks and passed orders to the duty
officer, Oberstleutnant Sander, to block all outgoing signals except those
from Hitler, Keitel and Jodl. Next I went to the Führerbunker, where I
found Hitler sitting in his study. As I entered I saw that he had the facial
expression of a person who has faced death and come through it almost

unscathed. He asked after my injuries and said that we had all had enormous luck. The conversation turned to the incident. Hitler dismissed any idea that Todt Organisation workers, who had been refurbishing the barracks a few days previously, might have been responsible.

By now Graf Stauffenberg had been missed and a search was made. It emerged that shortly after the beginning of the situation conference he had slipped out to the annexe on the pretence of having to make a telephone call. Without waiting for the connection to be set up, he said he had forgotten his map case and returned to a car in which Oberleutnant von Haeften, his orderly officer, was waiting. The SS FHQ-Kommandant had meanwhile raised the alarm and sentries had instructions to allow nobody to pass. Stauffenberg's car had arrived at the outer barrier but could not go through until permission had been obtained by telephone from the Kommandant's adjutant. This officer knew Stauffenberg, had taken breakfast with him that morning and assumed that Stauffenberg had to return to Berlin for service reasons. He saw no connection between Stauffenberg's hasty departure and the explosion. Thus Stauffenberg had an open road to the airfield, from where he took off for Berlin aboard an He 111 of the Army Quartermaster General.

As these details gradually became known, Stauffenberg's guilt was obvious. Himmler, now nominated C-in-C of the Reserve Army, received full powers for the criminal investigation and after a short stop at Wolfschanze flew to Berlin to be closer to events.

It was not possible to form a clear picture by phone. The flight from Rastenburg to Rangsdorf took two hours, the drive to the Reich War Ministry about another hour. Thus neither Himmler nor Stauffenberg could reach Bendlerstrasse until after 1600. This allowed us a few hours to get patched up, and I sought treatment from an Army medical officer. Goering's personal physician also took an interest in me on my return, confirmed my concussion and ordered me to bed. Goering even had an SS guard posted at my door to ensure that I did not attempt to get up. This was ridiculous, for I was the least badly hurt of the adjutants, being able to walk and fit for limited duties, for which Professor Brandt gave me permission during the course of the evening. This was necessary, for Hitler was very busy. After dinner and the evening conference we talked. He told me that Schmundt and Borgmann were very seriously hurt while Puttkamer was confined to bed with a knee injury. This meant that I needed another aide, and I asked him if I could have Oberstleutnant von Amsberg to assist me. He had been Keitel's ADC and knew the ropes at FHQ. Hitler agreed at once. What most concerned him now was who should be Chief of the Army General Staff. Zeitzler was on the sick list and Hitler did not want to see him again. He was thinking of Guderian as his successor. I advised him against this appointment and suggested other candidates. I had in mind Buhle and Krebs. But Hitler settled for Guderian.

Many more details came in that evening from Berlin. Goebbels had summoned Major Remer, commander of the Berlin Wachtbatallion, and set up a telephone conversation with Hitler in Remer's presence. Hitler told Remer to restore order by force of arms. Generaloberst Fromm, who had been replaced by Himmler as C-in-C Reserve Army and whose stance was not unequivocal, had, after some vacillation, taken the initiative in the Bendlerstrasse. He had had the ringleaders arrested and shot. These were Stauffenberg and von Haeften, General Olbricht and his Chief of Staff Ritter Mertz von Quirnheim. Generaloberst Beck was given the opportunity to take his own life. Hitler was extremely annoyed at these measures and ordered immediately that those arrested were to be brought before the People's Court.

That evening, after Mussolini's departure, Goebbels pressured Hitler into making a brief radio announcement. Goebbels said that there was great uncertainty amongst the people, which only a direct speech by Hitler could assuage. Hitler allowed himself to be persuaded and spoke that evening. He named the would-be assassins and said that 'a quite small clique of stupid officers, ambitious, unprincipled and criminal' had wanted to remove him. 'I interpret it as a confirmation of the intention of Providence', he said, 'that I shall continue to my goal as I have done previously.'

Nicolaus von Below

Princess Marie 'Missie' Vassiltchikov was a White Russian émigrée. Her noble blood and her work at the Foreign Ministry (the AA) in Berlin under Adam von Trott, another of the plotters, brought her into contact with many members of the resistance movement.

Thursday 20th July 1944 This afternoon Loremarie Schonburg and I sat chatting on the office stairs when Gottfried Bismarck burst in, bright red spots on his cheeks. I had never seen him in such a state of feverish excitement. He first drew Loremarie aside, then asked me what my plans were. I told him they were uncertain but that I would really like to get out of the AA as soon as possible. He told me I should not worry, that in a few days everything would be settled and we would all know what was going to happen to us. Then, after asking me to come to Potsdam with Loremarie as soon as possible, he jumped into his car and was gone.

I went back into my office and dialled Percy Frey at the Swiss Legation to cancel my dinner date with him, as I preferred to go out to Potsdam. While I waited, I turned to Loremarie, who was standing at the window, and asked her why Gottfried was in such a state. Could it be the *Konspiration*? (All that with the receiver in my hand!) She whispered: 'Yes! That's it! It's done. This morning!' Just then Percy replied. Still holding the receiver, I asked: 'Dead?' She answered: 'Yes, dead!' I hung up. Seized her by the shoulders and we went waltzing around the room. Then grabbing hold of some papers, I thrust them into the first drawer and shouting to the porter that we were '*dienstlich unterwegs*' ['off on official business'], we tore off to the Zoo station. On the way out to Potsdam she whispered to me the details and though the compartment was full, we did not even try to hide our excitement and joy.

Count Claus Schenck von Stauffenberg, a colonel on the General Staff, had put a bomb at Hitler's feet during a conference at Supreme HQ at Rastenburg in East Prussia. It had gone off and Adolf was dead. Stauffenberg had waited outside until the explosion and then, seeing Hitler being carried out on a stretcher covered with blood, he had run to his car, which had stood hidden somewhere, and with his ADC, Werner von Haeften, had driven to the local airfield and flown back to Berlin. In the general commotion nobody had noticed his escape.

On reaching Berlin, he had gone straight to the OKH [Army Command HQ] in the Bendlerstrasse, which had meanwhile been taken over by the plotters and where Gottfried Bismarck, Helldorf and many others were gathered . . . This evening at six an announcement would be made over the radio that Adolf was dead and that a new government had been formed. The new Reichskanzler [Chancellor of the Reich] would be Gordeler, a former mayor of Leipzig. With a socialist background, he is considered a brilliant economist. Our Count Schulenburg or Ambassador von Hassell is to be Foreign Minister. My immediate feeling was that it was perhaps a mistake to put the best brains at the head of what could only be an interim government.

By the time we had reached the Regierung in Potsdam, it was past six o'clock. I went to wash up. Loremarie hurried upstairs. Only minutes had passed when I heard dragging footsteps outside and she came in: 'A Count Stauffenberg has attempted to murder the Führer, but Providence saved him . . .'

I took her by the arm and we raced back upstairs. We found the Bismarcks in the drawing room, Melanie with a stricken expression, Gottfried pacing up and down, up and down. I was afraid to look at him. He had just got back from the Bendlerstrasse and kept repeating: 'It's just not possible! It's a trick! Stauffenberg *saw* him dead.' 'They' were staging a comedy and getting Hitler's double to go on with it. He went into his study to telephone Helldorf. Loremarie followed him and I was left alone with Melanie.

She started to moan: Loremarie had driven Gottfried to this; she had been working on him for years; if he were to die now, she, Melanie, was the one who would be left with three little children; maybe Loremarie could afford that luxury, but who would be left fatherless? Other children, not hers . . . It was really dreadful, and there was nothing I could say.

Gottfried came back into the room. He had not been able to get through to Helldorf, but he had further news: the main radio station had been lost; the insurgents had seized it but had been unable to make it work, and now it was back in SS hands. However, the officers' schools in the suburbs had taken up arms and were now marching on Berlin. And, surely enough, an hour later we heard the panzers of the Krampnotz training school rolling through Potsdam on their way to the capital. We hung out of the windows watching them go by and prayed. Nobody in the streets, which were practically empty, seemed to know what was going on. Gottfried kept insisting that he could not believe Hitler was unhurt, that 'they' were hiding something . . .

A little later the radio announced that the Führer would address the German people at midnight. We realised that only then would we know for certain whether all this was a hoax or not. And yet Gottfried refused to give up hope. According to him, even if Hitler *was* alive, his Supreme Headquarters in East Prussia was so far away that if things went well elsewhere, the regime could still be overthrown before he could regain control in Germany itself. But the rest of us were getting very uneasy.

Helldorf rang up several times. Also the Gauleiter of Brandenburg, asking the Potsdam Regierungspräsident Graf Bismarck what the devil he proposed to do, as he, the Gauleiter, understood that disorders and perhaps even a mutiny had broken out in the capital. Gottfried had the impudence to tell him that the orders from Supreme Headquarters were that the Führer wished all higher officials to stay put and await further instructions. In fact, he hoped that the insurgent troops would soon come and arrest the Gauleiter.

As night came, rumours began to circulate that the uprising was not succeeding as well as had been hoped. Somebody rang up from the airfield:

'Die Luftwaffe macht nicht mit' ['the air force isn't going along']; they wanted personal orders from Goering or from the Führer himself. Gottfried began to sound sceptical – for the first time. He said such a thing had to be done fast; every minute lost was irretrievable. It was now long past midnight and still Hitler had not spoken. It all became so discouraging that I saw no purpose in sitting up any longer and went to bed. Loremarie soon followed.

At two in the morning, Gottfried looked in and in a dead voice said: 'It was him all right!'

At dawn, we heard the tanks from Kramnitz rolling past again; they were returning to their barracks without having achieved anything.

Marie Vassiltchikov

Trott, Helldorf, Gordeler and hundreds of others were killed so that Hitler's need for revenge might be satiated. Their executions were carried out by axe, firing squad or strangulation with piano wire. Missie Vassiltchikov survived the war, and in 1946 married an American officer.

✚

Retreat in the East

On the rapidly collapsing Russian front, many German troops had become demoralised and small bands of them began to straggle homewards, living off the land and their wits. Guy Sajer was a half-French soldier in the elite Gross Deutschland division.

We were in the mountains and had just been through a town called Reghin, which at that time was known as Arlau, or Erlau. We were tramping along, grey with dust and pouring with sweat. We had miraculously escaped incorporation into several scratch formations, and our interminable, wretched column was twisting through what seemed like an infinite chain of mountains. The column was broken up into groups of varying size, in which unkempt soldiers pushed along every kind of transport to move our basic necessities.

We requisitioned the most extraordinary vehicles. Anyone who found a bicycle grabbed it, even if it had no tyres, and went on ahead of the rest to skim off anything even remotely digestible. In this district of jagged peaks and crags, we were free of enemy aircraft, but the terrain was ideal for partisans, and there were many battles to the death between them and our men, who were now fighting simply to save their skins.

In this district, one group among many others of men in a motley conglomeration of clothes was struggling to reach the mother country. Behind our glittering eyes, deeply sunk into shadowy sockets, one belief sustained us. This was that, if we managed to survive, the mother country would receive us with tenderness, and try to help us forget the unimaginable trial which was nearly over. We thought that, once we reached home, the war would be over, and that in the worst imaginable case the army would be reorganised, so that no enemy would enter Germany itself. We held to this as the one final idea which would justify our sufferings and banish the solution of suicide which others had already accepted.

Yesterday's *Landser*, members of élite units, Panzer-grenadiers who had confronted a thousand deaths to live for a chimera, clung to the idea that we had to live to be able to hope, and we had to hope passionately to be able to live as we were. We had to fight against daily ambush, and keep going no matter what, to get away from the Russians, who were hard on our heels. And we had to eat a certain minimum, which wasn't easy to do.

There were twelve in our group – many of them familiar companions: Schlesser, Frösch, Lieutenant Wollers, Lensen, Kellerman, and then Hals and me, kept together by a miracle of silent fraternity. Hals, who had grown startlingly thin, was forcing his large bony body along the narrow mountain road some four or five yards ahead of me. He often walked ahead of me, which gave me a certain sense of security, although his large body was seriously reduced. He was stripped to the waist wearing a leather belt and a band of cartridges for the Spandau across his chest. A Russian blouse, in anticipation of the cool evenings at this altitude, floated from the leather pouch that held his few possessions along with four or five grenades. His heavy steel helmet seemed to be riveted to his head, and the lice in his filthy hair must have died for lack of light.

Many men had thrown away their heavy helmets, but Hals felt his was a last link with the German Army, and that during this terrible trial we should try to remain soldiers, rather than degenerate into tramps. I kept mine too, as a sign of solidarity, dangling from my belt.

Someone up ahead shouted for us to come and see. We looked down into a leafy ravine. A camouflaged truck bearing the inscription 'WH' had crashed to the bottom. Lensen was already running down to have a closer look.

'Watch out!' someone shouted. 'It might be a trap!'

Lieutenant Wollers had joined Lensen. We drew back, certain that the partisans had arranged a booby trap, and that we would see our two companions blown to pieces any minute. However, a reassuring shout floated up from the gulf.

'A windfall! Mein Gott, it's like a whole commissary!'

Within seconds we were all running toward the miracle.

'Look at that! Chocolate, cigarettes, wurst . . .'

'Good God! And here are three bottles, too!'

'Shut up,' shouted Schlesser, 'or you'll have the whole army down here! It's a miracle no one found this before.'

'So many delicious things,' said Frösch in an almost tender voice. 'Let's all grab everything we can. We can share it out later, on the road.'

Frösch and another fellow loaded themselves heavily, and climbed back to the road to keep watch. Thousands of men were wandering very close to us; we would try to take everything. We had almost completed the job when our two look-outs shouted: 'Achtung!'

We ran into the brush and heard the distant roar of a motorcycle. The engine slowed down and seemed to stop. We ran off through the thorny growth, clutching our precious cargoes. We were used to getting out of the way in a hurry and melting into the ground when an unfriendly eye might become too interested in our existence. We could hear some noncoms shouting, and supposed that our two companions had been caught by a military patrol, perhaps even by the military police.

'Those two sods were caught with bottles under their arms,' muttered Wollers.

'Let's get out of here as fast as we can,' said Lindberg, who had just run up.

'Someone's coming down,' whispered Lensen. 'An MP – I saw his badge.'

'Hell, let's get out of here.'

Everybody ran, scattering into the bushes as if Ivan himself were at his heels. We regrouped after five or six hundred yards, hiding behind a rocky outcrop.

'I've lost enough breath because of those bastards,' said Hals. 'If they want to chase us this far, I'll take care of them.'

'You're crazy,' said Lindberg. 'Don't talk like that. What are you trying to do to us?'

'Shut up!' Hals said. 'You'll never make it home anyway. Ivan's going to get you for sure. Why don't you think for a minute of Frösch and the other fellow who've been caught?'

'We might as well eat,' said Wollers. 'I've had enough of giving orders, and sweating, and shitting in my pants like a baby when I'm scared. So let's get started. If we're going to die for it, all the more reason to fill our bellies while we can.'

Like hungry beasts, we wolfed down the contents of the tins and the other provisions, masticating loudly.

'We'd better eat it all,' Lensen said. 'If we're caught with anything in our sacks that wasn't handed out, we'll be in trouble.'

'You're right. Let's eat it all. They won't slit us open to see what's inside, although it would be just like those bastards to check our shit.'

For an hour we gorged ourselves until we were almost sick. When it grew dark, we returned to the road by a devious route. Lensen stepped out of the brush first.

'Come on, the coast is clear.'

We went on for three or four hundred yards, passing once again the hole with its unexpected windfall which had allowed us to fill our famished stomachs for a moment. There was no one in sight. We went for another two or three miles and collapsed at the side of the road.

'I can't go any further,' said Schlesser. 'We're not used to eating any more, and this is what happens.'

'Why don't we go to sleep right here?' someone said. 'That will help our digestions.'

Toward two o'clock in the morning, a large group of German soldiers came by and woke us up.

'On your feet,' shouted an old *Feldwebel*. 'Get going, or Ivan will be in Berlin before you.'

We resumed our trek. This bunch had collected several horse-drawn wagons, and for a while, we were able to ride. At daybreak, we arrived at a town built on the mountainside. Some men were splashing in an icy bathing place. Others were sleeping on the ground or on terrace walls. Further on, still others had begun their march again, toward safety, the west, the mother country, waiting to receive them, whose true condition they couldn't begin to guess.

And then there was a tree, a majestic tree, whose branches seemed to be supporting the sky. Two sacks were dangling from those branches, two empty scarecrows swinging in the wind, suspended by two short lengths of rope. We walked under them, and saw the grey, bloodless faces of hanged men, and recognised our wretched friend Frösch and his companion.

'Don't worry, Frösch,' whispered Hals. 'We ate it all.'

Lindberg hid his face in his hands and wept. I managed with difficulty to read the message scribbled on the sign tied to Frösch's broken neck.

'I am a thief and a traitor to my country.'

A short way off, some ten policemen in regulation uniform were standing beside a sidecar and a Volkswagen. As we walked by them, our eyes met theirs.

Guy Sajer

‡

The Far East

Following the death of Wingate in an air crash, the Chindits in Burma were put under the command of the American leader of the Chinese forces, Stilwell. They found themselves expected to mount conventional operations for which they were not equipped, and to remain in the jungle for months longer than anticipated. Feelings ran high.

On July 17, after a particularly bitter series of signals, my demands for a medical examination of my brigade were granted.

At nameless spots in the jungle, over the next three days, every man in the brigade was examined by medical boards consisting of two or three doctors. The strength of my four and a half battalions then totalled about 2,200 men. Those adjudged fit for any kind of action, in any theatre of operations, numbered 118, being 7 British officers, a score of British soldiers, and 90 Gurkhas. I ordered Desmond to amend the figure to 119, since he had not included me, and whatever my faults as a commander I knew one thing for sure – I was going to be the last man of my brigade out of Burma. They could say anything else, but they were never going to say I left them.

John Masters

The last Chindits were evacuated to India by air at the end of August after five months in the jungle.

Hungover on Guam

On 21 July, the Americans landed on the Pacific island of Guam. It was garrisoned by 21,000 Japanese, and to take it from them 55,000 Marines were eventually put ashore. William Manchester was one of them and, like many young men, he found hard liquor – even of the Japanese variety – too appealing to resist.

Not all Japanese liquor was stashed away on Orote, as we discovered our first day ashore on Irammiya. We were digging in for the night when little Mickey McGuire's entrenching spade hit a wooden box. 'Buried treasure,' he panted, unearthing it. 'Bullshit,' Horse said excitedly. 'That looks like schnapps!' We counted twenty-four bottles, each in its cardboard compartment. Herr von der Goltz, having advertised himself as Maine's finest epicure, was permitted to uncork the first of them and sip it. 'Rice wine,' he said, smacking his lips. 'Marvellous. Absolutely terrific.' This presented me, for the thousandth time, with the problem of leadership. I never tried to inspire the section by example. Never did an NCO run fewer risks than I did, except, perhaps, on Sugar Loaf Hill, and that came later. In the words of Walter Affitto, a Marine sergeant on Peleliu, 'I was not very military. I tried to lead the men by being a prankster, making jokes.' Obviously, turning the box in wouldn't tickle the Raggedy Ass Marines. The only sidesplitting would come at our expense, from the rear-echelon types who would dispose of it. Since any SOP order I gave would have been ignored by the Raggedy Asses, since we were already dug in, and since I was thirsty myself, I told each man that he could drink one bottle. Straws would be drawn for the five remaining bottles. What no one noticed was that the labels were not quite identical. We couldn't read the complicated kanji characters; it didn't seem to matter. Actually it mattered a great deal. Twenty-three of the bottles, bearing white labels, were wine, all right, but the label on the twenty-fourth was salmon coloured. Doubtless this had been reserved for an officer or senior NCO. It contained 110-proof sake. And I drew the straw for it.

Because my taste buds had been dulled by the wine, or my throat dried by the fear that, in combat, never lay more than a millimetre from the surface of my mind, I gulped the sake down chug-a-lug, like a beer. I remember an instant numbness, as though I had been hit by a two-by-four. Then suddenly I felt transported on to the seventh astral plane, feasting upon heaven on the half shell. I recall trying to sing a campus song:

> *Take a neck from any old bottle*
> *Take an arm from any old chair . . .*

Suddenly I was out, the first and oddest casualty of Irammiya. I lay on my back, spread out like a starfish. Night was coming swiftly; the others had their own holes to dig; there seemed to be no Japs here, so I was left in my stupor. Despite intermittent machine-gun and mortar fire throughout the night, I was quite safe. Around midnight, I later learned, the heavens opened, long shafts of rain like arrows arching down from the sky, as was customary when I arrived on a new island, but I felt nothing. One of our star shells, fired to expose any infiltrating Japs, burst overhead, illuminating me, and Colonel Krank, dug in on the safest part of the beachhead (like the Raggedy Ass Marines), saw me. He asked an NCO, 'Is Slim hit?' By now everyone else in the company knew what had happened. Krank, when told, erupted with Rabelaisian laughter – nothing is as funny to a drunk as another drunk – and dismissed the adjutant's proposal for disciplinary measures, explaining that I would be punished soon enough. Since I was comatose, I felt neither embarrassed nor threatened then. The next day, however, was another story. The colonel was right. I regained consciousness when a shaft of sunlight lanced down and blinded me through my lids. After a K-ration breakfast, in which I did not join, we saddled up and moved north with full field packs on a reconnaissance in force. I wasn't fit to stand, let alone march. My heartbeat was slower than a turtle's. The right place for me was a hospital, where I could be fed intravenously while under heavy sedation. I felt as though I had been pumped full of helium and shot through a wind tunnel. It was, without doubt, the greatest hangover of my life, possibly the worst in the history of warfare. My head had become a ganglion of screeching, spastic nerves. Every muscle twitched with pain. My legs felt rubbery. My head hung dahlialike on its stalk. I thought each step would be my last. During our hourly ten-minute breaks I simply fainted, only to waken to jeers from the colonel. I needed an emetic, or, better still, a hair of the dog. Knowing of the colonel's fondness for the grape, aware that he carried a flask which would have brought me back from this walking death, I prayed he would take pity on me. When he didn't, I prayed instead that Jap bullets would riddle his liver and leave him a weeping basket case. They didn't, but after the war I learned, with great satisfaction, that one of his platoon leaders, by then a civilian, encountered him in a bar and beat the shit out of him.

William Manchester

The Americans lost 1,300 men and nearly five times as many wounded on Guam before it fell in mid-August. Very few of its defenders were taken alive.

‡

The buzz bomb

From the middle of June, London and the South-East was menaced by a new terror, the V-1 rocket, launched from sites in France. By mid-July, 3,582 flying bombs had landed on Britain, killing 3,583 people, including 121 in the Guards' Chapel near Buckingham Palace. The rockets' speed and the random nature of their targets caused widespread fear. James Lees-Milne lived in Chelsea, close to the Thames.

FRIDAY, 28 JULY 1944

Got back in time to dine with Harold Acton and Roger Spence. I went to bed soon after 11 in our cellar. At 12.15 a bomb fell with great noise. The basement was filled with fumes, so I guessed the bomb had been pretty close. Got out of bed, put on gumboots and burberry, and walked into the road. Even in the clear light of the moon I could see a cloud of explosive steaming from the river in front of me. This fly bomb had cut out its engine, and recovered twice before finally falling. As I watched I heard people in the street shout, 'Look out, another's coming!' and they rushed down to their shelter. I was left transfixed, and knew there was no time to descend into my basement, down the rickety area steps. So I looked at the light of the bomb coming straight at me. Then the engine stopped, and I knew we were in for it. I lay flat on my face on the pavement, as close as could be to the embankment wall. I heard the bomb swish through the air. It too fell in the river, only closer than the last, and sent a spray of water over me. At dawn I met a policeman picking up a fragment of the bomb from the road. It was over a foot long. It must have hurtled over my head. I could see that all my windows and the window frames at no. 104 were out again. I saw poor Kiki Cruft at the gate of no. 97. She had been alone in the house and was rather startled. I talked to her before returning to my basement. This time I had experienced the familiar phenomenon of not registering the actual explosion of the bomb, because it was only a few yards away. I attribute it to my preparedness and the automatic instinct of tautening the whole body, including ears, to resist it. I remember hoping that my outstretched legs, which seemed so far from my cowering head, would not be cut off.

James Lees-Milne

✝

Tanks and Tank-Busting

Ken Tout was a tank gunner in 'C' squadron, the 1st Northamptonshire Yeomanry. On 7 and 8 August, he experienced 40 hours of combat in Normandy as the British sought to advance south from Caen. His tank had the call-sign '3 Baker'.

11.15 hours: I have stared at my oblong patch of landscape until I can shut my eyes and still see it detailed before me. It is a fairly simple lay-out today. It is easily demarcated by that deep gully or ravine running right across the middle of it from right to left, approximately west to east. As we have troops forward of the gully, there should not be any need to worry about the trees on this side of the dip. Over to the extreme right, between wood and orchards, I can see a patch of cornfield and the Falaise road empty beyond it. There again A Squadron stand between us and the road. They should spot any movement in that direction.

I make mental inventories of the trees and bushes. Above the point where the track finally disappears: three bushy-top trees in a solid hedgerow with light between the tree stumps; then a patch of solid woods with no light showing; an open horizon with no hedgerow; four tall trees; two large bushes; part of a gate or shed showing through a gap before two more medium bushy-top trees. If that light or gap or bush moves or disappears, it means danger, action, deeds before words, and words before thought. Fire! Report! Review! Adjust! Fire!

'Hullo, Roger 2 Baker.' (Hitler-mimic, Corporal Astley.) 'Alert! I seem to see movement half-left, a hundred yards left of roofs, but cannot yet identify. 2 Baker, over.'

'2 Baker, keep looking. Report as soon as you are sure of movement, even if you can't see what moves. Over.'

'2 Baker, OK. Off.'

I screw my eye up close to the gun sight and slowly traverse along the 2 Troop area, taking advantage of the considerable magnification to explore the intimacies of that little wilderness of trees and shadows in front of an even darker hedge. Nothing moves there . . . except green fear. The continuous sporadic traffic of shells overhead and the fitful jazz beat of explosions behind us have merged into our consciousness until we disregard them. They become like a shading of woodwind, strings and percussion, inconsequential continuing music waiting for the soloist to enter with his first clarion note.

The SLAM-CRASH of an aimed shot – direct, violent, massive –

smashes across the humdrum background of barrage. Where? What? '2 Baker. I'm bloody hit! Bale out! Hornet at . . . Gawd . . .' (. . . ? . . .) (God, that's Astley gone!)

Hornet – enemy tank or SP. Where? Where? where, where, where . . . I squeeze the grip right . . . left . . . traversing quickly, staring into the camel-shaped trees. Hornet at . . . where, where, where, the hedge, solid-topped, fairly level . . . has a gap, a gap. A gap? Why? What? 'Charlie, left of roof, hornet in hedge, over . . .' I adjust left, down, crosswires on! Stamp! Flame at muzzle. Frustrating smoke. Smoke. Smoke. Clearing to show spark of tracer leaping high into gap but another tracer from near gully flies into gap ahead of my tracer as Stan slaps my leg, loaded, down a bit, fire! Stan slaps. Stamp. Fire. Traverse. Sight. Slap. Stamp. Fire. Other flashes than mine festoon the far hedge with artificial flowers, blooming, dying, red as Flanders poppies. And as quick to wither. Normandy has poppies too.

A feather of smoke, more permanent than the transient clouds exhaled by shell bursts, wavers up to the left of the roof. I put my foot on the other pedal as solidly as on the accelerator of a car. The co-axial Browning rattles away, every fifth bullet trailing tiny tracer sparks. The first sparks dig into the roots of the hedge. I move the gun control gently up and down in a hosing motion with my left hand whilst traversing the turret slowly with my right hand. The Browning sends out fiery arrows at the hedge, perhaps half a mile away. Other tanks are brassing up the hedge in similar fashion. I keep my foot down, mentally ticking off the tens of bullets fired. A sharp click announces the end of the belt of bullets. My tiny hose of fire quenches. Beyond the hedge the single column of smoke still rises, much thicker now. Around the Robertmesnil roof a wider cloud of smoke indicates a building on fire. Whether farmhouse or barn we have no means of telling.

Keith: 'Gunner, cease fire. Operator, load AP again.'

Stan: 'Co-ax reloaded . . . 75 loaded AP.'

Me: 'I feel better for that little bit of anger.'

Bookie: 'I hope Corporal Astley feels better too.'

Me: 'What do you mean?'

Bookie: 'I mean look over to the right of the track. More smoke.'

There is indeed more smoke, over 2 Troop's position. But it is not the column of flame or pall of hideous, thick, black smoke which marks the total conflagration of a Sherman. This is a thinner, less dense spiral.

Stan: '2 Baker didn't brew up altogether. Maybe they all got out.'

Harvey: 'Astley broke off in mid-message. I reckon he's had it, poor bugger.'

Me: 'He could have snapped the plug of his mike, bailing out.'

Harvey: 'I hope nothing has happened to Astley. He's such a bloody funny bloke. Who's going to make us laugh if he's bought it? Who's going to impersonate Adolf? Who's going to shout "Ve haf goot torture for you. Ve vill pull your nails out and your balls off"'? You can't win wars without the Corporal Astleys.'

Bookie: 'We're going to have to win it without the Colonel and the B Squadron Leader and Sergeant Pearce and Corporal Astley and any other poor sod that gets in the way of a Jerry shell.'

Keith: 'Wait a mo'. We still don't know what happened. At least I think we got the Jerry gun, whatever it was, judging by the smoke.'

Stan: 'Big Chief Sioux, him read smoke signals.'

Keith: 'Yes, well, that's enough then. We're fighting a war, not running a children's party, thank you.'

We sit and watch the columns of smoke, each with its own meaning. Two narrow and faint. One wider and dense. And we wait for 2 Baker's survivors to appear over the gully, so that we can count them . . . and know the worst. For the hundredth time I mentally measure the distance from my own seat to the top of the turret. If the worst came to the worst, if we are hit, if (within seven seconds, say, if you are lucky) Stony Stratford bursts into a volcano of fire, then I may get out. A gunner's chance is about fifty-fifty. The operator's chance is less because he has to get past the gun. The driver and co-driver have a better chance in some respects because they are farther from the engine where the volcano blast will take place. Also they are not sitting on top of, and in between rows of, large shells packed with high explosives. On the other hand the driver and co-driver stand more chance of getting trapped inside the tank in an accident.

The commander has by far the quickest exit route. If he is agile, he can, with one vault, soar out of the turret top and land on the ground without touching the deck of the tank. But he risks the highest fatality rate in warfare from head injuries when, as most frequently happens, he goes into battle with his head sticking out of the turret in mid-air.

So I secretly rehearse my exit: a push of the hands on the inner turret rim, knees doubled, feet kicking against the turret wall, I spring backwards and up, arms flinging upwards, fingers hooking on to the turret hatch, touching the flat turret top to continue the vault into mid-air and out wide towards the safe ground . . . hoping to avoid the blazing hell which the back of the tank has become even whilst I am making my leap. It has happened to two of my friends who were gunners. One made his jump and hit the ground with his clothing aflame but otherwise uninjured. He said that it all happened so quickly that he did not have time to be afraid. The other gunner did not move quickly enough. He was caught inside the tank. The explosions of the ammunition, sufficient to knock out fifty tanks, served as a humane killer before the furnace began to grill him where he sat. Something in my being revolts more against the slow grilling of my flesh after death than against the sudden swift shattering of mind and body in a massive explosion.

My periscope picks up movement down the track in the gully. A black beret appears. Another. A third . . . Four! The figures trudge up the track into sight.

Stan: 'Only four. Can you see who they are, Ken?'

I swing my gun to cover the four figures. Squint through the magnifying sight. Grey, waxen faces come into focus. One with blood on his forehead. Blood on his chest. Four well-known faces. Sad but relieved. Hurt but unbowed. I count them again. Recognise them. Try to make four into five. Press the mike switch, 'Corporal Astley is not with them.'

Harvey: 'Who's going to take the piss out of bloody Hitler now then?'

The little procession heads to the Squadron Captain's tank. Halts a moment.

'Hullo, Roger Baker.' (The Squadron Captain.) '2 Baker Sunray will not be joining us for supper. Roger Baker, over.'

'Roger Baker, sorry about that. Off.'

So Corporal Astley, the orphan, will never again twiddle his moustache, shout '*Hoch, Hoch, mein Gott*' and give his impersonation of Hitler. Hitler has gained his revenge. Something evil has again entered the high summer's day. Only a thin curl of smoke now rises as a memorial to Astley where his knocked-out tank snuggles into the forest beyond our sight.

Harvey: 'Who started this rotten war, anyway?'

Ken Tout

Raymond Lallemant was a Belgian commanding the Typhoons of the RAF's 609 Squadron. They had no difficulty finding targets in the crowded pocket of land near Falaise in which the German forces were now pinioned by the Allied advance.

On August 18th I led our last attack on the Falaise enclave – my fifth sortie of the day. The bomb-line was now limited to a rectangle spanning the Trun–Falaise road for two kilometres, one kilometre deep on either side of it, and bordered to the north by the forest of Gouffern. It was thus fairly easy to identify.

Our twelve Typhoons duly took off in three sections, labelled Red, Blue and Yellow. On reaching the area, Blue and Yellow were detailed to deal with the defences, while Red attacked, but before doing so we streaked over the ground at zero feet to see what offered. Finding some tanks, I was glad to get rid of my burdensome rockets; but one or two others, who made the mistake of letting theirs off prematurely at lorries, now found themselves restricted to peppering the Tigers with their pop-gun 20-mm. cannon.

On my first swoop I was surprised by the number of tanks that still seemed to be around, but then noticed that many of them had already been put out of action. Another swoop was greeted by a burst of 88-mm. from a battery hidden in the Gouffern forest, which I promptly signalled my colleagues to avoid. Then I spotted a troop of soldiers brandishing a white flag, marching in fours towards Vimoutiers. They appeared to have had enough, but with the flak still firing at me, I decided to quench their thirst for war for good with a few bursts of cannon fire, and they went somersaulting into the ditches.

Next, my attention was attracted by a tank screened by a hedge lining the road. Two pairs of rockets, and it went up in flames that also set fire to the hedge. My dummy run however had also revealed a Tiger-Royal proceeding down the road, in the midst of its knocked-out brethren, towards a bridge next to a white inn. It stopped, but each time I tried to attack, my aim was false because it seemed to have moved while my back was turned. In this way, hedgehog fashion, it crept slowly to the cover of the inn, and I turned rapidly in order not to be cheated of my prey. Again, when I faced it, it was stationary, hoping no doubt that we could not now tell which were the derelict tanks, and which was the live one, and that we would squander our ammunition on the former. To keep it from the inn's shelter I let it think its ruse had succeeded by approaching sixty degrees off-course, and only aligning myself when already quite close to the ground. Then, as the range rapidly closed, it knew too late that I was after it. 1,000 yards . . . 900 yards . . . the inn rose up to meet me . . . 800 yards . . . my thumb stroked the firing button under the gas lever, and after a final correction to get the Tiger fully centred in the gun-sight, I let fly.

As the rockets left their rails I hardly breathed, for the slightest movement of the aircraft would upset the aim. Only when I saw the tails of the rockets converging towards the target did I pull on the stick to escape the force of the explosion. At the very moment I tilted the wing, one rocket rebounded from the road, and hitting the stone parapet of the bridge, blew it to pieces. The other was a bull's-eye. The turret flew into the air, black smoke gushed from the gaping hole, and the whole tank was engulfed in flames like a giant brazier. The Tiger-Royal had joined the cemetery of its dead brethren. Using my last rockets to attack another, I found this was extinct already.

The battery concealed in the forest of Gouffern continued to fire. The last tanks hid in the ground or dashed madly for cover. The flaming or smoking pyres of others dotted the landscape like the Last Judgment. I climbed to pass on the attack to the other sections, and presently saw four more tanks explode. But Flight-Lieutenant Carrick's plane, hit by the flak, hurtled to the ground, a flaming fire-brand on the fringe of the sector. He had been less than a week with the squadron.

As we steered for base I mused about the terrible toll of these new recruits. It was always the same. They did not all perish, but they all got hit. 'Old soldiers never die.' We veterans believed ourselves immortal, believed that danger receded in proportion to our number of missions. The greatest risk was in the first week. If a pilot lived through that, he had a chance to survive.

Ground-attack missions were the more murderous to the participants inasmuch as each one changed the order of battle. New recruits were taken along in an apprentice role, and not seldom we lost three or four at one go. Sometimes the victims would return on foot the same day, sometimes the next, but often never. As soon as one sortie was over, the squadron commander counted those who had returned, took stock of the damaged aircraft, and drew up a fresh battle-order for the next one. Our commitments demanded the use of men and aircraft to exhaustion point. Training flights for new pilots were thus a thing of the past; their very first flight took them straight into battle. There, preoccupied in locating the target and getting into position, they were caught by danger unawares, and swatted down like flies.

Raymond Lallemant

✠

The Warsaw Rising

By the end of July, Russian troops were near Warsaw. Fearing that the Soviets would become their next rulers, the Polish underground Home Army rose against the German occupiers in a bid to establish a fledgling Polish government before the Russians arrived. The battle was led by General Tadeusz Bor-Komorowski.

'Tomorrow, at seventeen hours precisely, you will start operations in Warsaw.'

The button had been pressed. Thousands of orders spread through the city that same evening.

After a good deal of deliberation, I had fixed zero hour for five o'clock. Hitherto all our activities had been timed for dawn or dusk, so this, I decided, was the best way of taking the enemy by surprise. At five o'clock the traffic in the city was at its heaviest, with people returning home from work. It would then be less difficult to conceal units moving to their appointed places in the hurrying crowd of workers coming out of offices and factories. Also, if we began then, we should have a few hours of daylight in which to take over German positions in the city before dusk, according to plan.

The next day I again met the Staff to issue final instructions and orders. This was our last meeting in hiding. On my way I walked through streets full of thousands of young men and women hurrying to their appointed posts. Many of them wore soldiers' top-boots and wind-breakers and carried rucksacks. Nearly everyone had a bag or a dispatch case; some had parcels. All this roused my anxiety and I feared for the secrecy of our zero hour. Every few paces there were German patrols, while armoured cars moved ceaselessly through the streets. Throughout the morning a fine rain fell. The insistent sound of gunfire reached us from across the Vistula. All that night and the following day the deep note of detonations was heard; it was the Germans dynamiting railway equipment near Praga.

I left Staff HQ at 2 p.m. My ADC put the pistols which we had always kept there into a portable gramophone-case, frequently used for this purpose. He took them to the Kammler Factory in the suburb of Wola, which was to be my headquarters during the rising. The factory buildings were to accommodate my immediate staff. With us were to be the Government delegate with his secretary and the Chairman of the Council of National Unity, to enable us to be in constant contact. Also on the spot was to be the radio station for transmission and reception to ensure communications with the city, the country and the world. The remainder of the Staff were to be housed in neighbouring streets. The meeting time for the staff on August 1st was fixed for between three and four o'clock.

The Home Army soldiers were still normal passers-by, mixing with the crowd of civilians and entering their assigned houses in small groups. The buildings had been chosen with care, according to a definite plan. For the most part they were corner-houses, commanding important cross-roads or facing railway stations, German barracks, stores or public works departments. Briefly, they were close to all the points which were to be attacked and taken in the first impetus. The men rang the bell of the flat indicated and handed to the occupants orders for the requisition; signed by the authorities of the rising. The inmates showed excitement but never the slightest resentment. On the contrary, they invariably did their best to help in every way and offered the soldiers their best food. The men took up their positions at windows, in attics and on chimneys. The entrances to the blocks were then closed and barricaded from within. A sentry in the courtyard forbade all inmates any access to the street for fear that the final preparations might be revealed to the enemy. Thirty minutes before zero hour, all preparations were completed. The soldiers brought out their arms and put on white-and-red arm-bands, the first open sign of a Polish army on Polish soil since the occupation. For five years they had all awaited this moment. Now the last seconds seemed an eternity. At five o'clock they would cease to be an underground resistance movement and would become once more Regular soldiers fighting in the open.

At exactly five o'clock thousands of windows flashed as they were flung open. From all sides a hail of bullets struck passing Germans, riddling their buildings and their marching formations. In the twinkling of an eye, the remaining civilians disappeared from the streets. From the entrance of houses, our men streamed out and rushed to the attack. In fifteen minutes an entire city of a million inhabitants was engulfed in the fight. Every kind of traffic ceased. As a big communications centre where roads from north, south, east and west converged, in the immediate rear of the German front, Warsaw ceased to exist. The battle for the city was on.

The Home Army found that the best means of getting around the city undetected was through its sewer system. It was, however, a hazardous and far from pleasant environment, as Bor-Komorowski himself discovered.

The entrance to the tunnel was in Krasinski Square, within 200 yards of the Germans and covered by their grenades and machine-guns. Only one by one, at varying intervals, could we get into the manhole. The party lined up against the wall of the corner house. Every few minutes a dark shadow would detach itself and dash across to the sandbags round the manhole. I went down the narrow cement wall, slipping and stumbling on the metal notches which served as steps. After a few steps I was in complete darkness and could see only a small circle of red sky high above me lit by Verey lights every few seconds. The foetid stench made me sick and brought tears to my eyes. I reached a dry ledge above the metal casing. Six feet below, the mud gurgled past. I let myself down into the sewer and found myself thigh deep in the mud. The current was so strong that I had the greatest difficulty in keeping my balance on the curved bottom. I grasped the rope held by the guide and, clutching it with all my strength, pulled myself forward a few steps to leave room for the next person. We were to start only when the whole party was lined up in the actual sewer. With the rope firmly grasped in my left hand, I kept my right on the shoulder of the man ahead of me. During the whole journey, no light of any kind was permitted and a hold on the next man was the only way of keeping together and avoiding losing the party in the darkness. Should anyone feel too bad and be unable to go on, he had to give three tugs at the rope. The guide would then stop the party.

It took an hour to assemble the whole party in the sewer. My ADC was behind the leading guide and I came after him, with the Government delegate immediately behind. Following him was my messenger girl, Basia. We moved off. After about a dozen paces, I began to get the hang of the thing and discovered how to plant my feet to move forward against the current without losing my balance, how to recognise the direction of the tunnel from the curve of its bottom, and how to use the side of the tunnel without cutting myself. Just before moving off, the guide checked the party once more and reminded everybody of their instructions for the journey: absolute necessity for complete silence – in about 300 yards we would be under the German positions; only he and his helpers who brought up the rear were allowed to use a torch; any alarm must be given by three tugs on the rope; every hour there would be a short rest. We had to go about a mile and a half. This, we hoped, would not take us longer than five hours. Ahead of the column were two soldiers with tommy-guns. We had to crouch because at that point the tunnel was no more than 5 feet high. Suddenly a woman's terrible scream rang out from behind me. Basia had fallen and the current swept her back. In the nick of time the Government delegate managed to grab her and help her to her feet again. It was only thanks to him that she was not swept away. For some minutes her scream echoed along the tunnel, and it rang in our ears even after that had died away. There was something ghastly about the echoes which resounded along these lost caves.

From time to time our route was barred by a stream of water from the roof of the tunnel where it had been damaged by the concussion of heavy shells and bombs. After a couple of these leaks I was soaked to the skin. Once I tried to do a jump through some falling water and collided with my ADC, who had stopped a moment after getting through it. I recovered my balance with difficulty, but had to step back, and found myself under the leak again. After an hour's going, we were just underneath the German positions at Krakowskie Przedmiescie. Occasionally the sewer was illuminated by light coming through an open manhole; these were the most dangerous spots, because at any moment we could be attacked by grenades. In spite of strict instructions, it was difficult for the whole column to keep silence. Everyone was exhausted and several times people lost their balance and gave the signal for a rest.

The level of the water was now lower, but the mud was thicker and progress no easier. I helped myself along by putting my hands on my knees. I had to find a new technique for advance in order not to cut my legs on the sharp scraps of rubbish lying at the bottom of the sewer. At one point the guide put his torch on for a minute or two. In its light I could see the bodies of cats lying amongst the indescribable filth and excrement. The air was becoming steadily more foetid. Only below the open manholes could we fill our lungs with comparatively fresh air. At one point we had a longer rest. We could change our positions a bit, but it was, of course, impossible to stand upright. A few moments of immobility made us all chatter with cold. Soon we went slowly on again. Leg-muscles and backs ached intolerably. The guide told us in a whisper that we had another 500 yards to go, rather less than a third of our whole journey. At last, in the distance, I made out the faint glimmer of a blue signal lamp. It looked close, but we still had another 200 yards to go. That last lap was endless. It seemed impossible to reach the flicker of blue light, which cheated us like a will-o'-the-wisp. Then the sewer narrowed and we began to crawl up a slope. Just at the end, my hand found a hanging rope. Soldiers from the manhole ahead hailed me to come up through the small aperture to the surface.

When we emerged into the street through the narrow exit of the sewer, the fresh air made us almost drunk. I personally felt as though I had suddenly been doused with icy water. It was with real difficulty that I gasped the air, while dark spots danced before my eyes. We had to lean against a wall for a time before we could recover. The entrance to the sewer was protected with sandbags and camouflaged. We were at once surrounded by the soldiers who were mounting guard at the opening. They shot questions at us, in quick succession. 'Has Bonifraterska Street been badly damaged?' 'Is such and such a house in Dluga Street still standing?' 'Have the Germans taken the whole of Muranowska?' Their families and homes were in Stare Miasto; hence the volley of questions. We were obliged to give evasive replies.

Tadeusz Bor-Komorowski

By 2 October, the Germans had crushed the Rising; 200,000 Poles were killed, and Hitler ordered any remaining buildings in the city to be demolished. Stalin had deliberately bypassed Warsaw and had let the Poles lose – he had no intention of allowing them to gain any semblance of autonomy. The Germans had done his dirty work for him, in an episode that is regarded as one of the first conflicts of the Cold War.

‡

The Liberation of Paris

Although he had been ordered to fight, the commander of the German forces in Paris, General von Choltitz, decided on 25 August to surrender the city. General Philippe Leclerc's French 4th Armoured Division entered the capital the same day. For photographer Robert Capa, returning to Paris was like a homecoming.

The road to Paris was open and every Parisian was out in the street to touch the first tank, to kiss the first man, to sing and cry. Never were there so many who were so happy so early in the morning. I felt that this entry into Paris had been made especially for me.

On a tank made by the Americans who had accepted me, riding with the Spanish Republicans with whom I had fought against fascism long years ago, I was returning to Paris – the beautiful city where I first learned to eat, drink, and love.

The thousands of faces in the finder of my camera became more and more blurred; that finder was very very wet. We drove through the *quartier* where I had lived for six years, passed my house by the Lion of Belfort. My concierge was waving a handkerchief, and I was yelling to her from the rolling tank, '*C'est moi, c'est moi!*'

Our first stop was in front of the Café de Dôme in the Montparnasse.

My favourite table was empty. Girls in light printed dresses climbed up on our tank and ersatz lipstick soon covered our faces. The best-looking of my Spaniards got more than his share, but he murmured, 'How I would prefer to be kissed by the ugliest old woman in Madrid than by the fairest girl in Paris.'

Around the Chamber of Deputies we had to fight, and some of the lipstick got washed off with blood. Late in the evening, Paris was free.

I wanted to spend my first night in the best of best hotels – the Ritz. But the hotel was already occupied. Hemingway's army had come into Paris by a different road, and after a short and happy fight had taken their main objective and liberated the Ritz from the German yokels. Red was standing guard before the entrance, happily displaying every missing front tooth. He said, in best imitation Hemingway, 'Papa took good hotel. Plenty stuff in cellar. You go up quick.'

It was all true. Papa made up with me, gave me a party, and the key to the best room in the hotel.

Robert Capa

'The Ritz is still the Ritz'

For Guards officer Peter Carrington, the chance of sampling the delights of Paris was too good to miss.

The roads were packed with huge columns of Americans. We never saw another British vehicle. Somehow we passed up the columns, mingled with them, pointed to the Union Jack on our vehicles to bamboozle our way past outraged, white-helmeted American military police. We stuck to main roads – one had no idea of the situation of the Germans, and certainly a good many small German columns were moving by minor roads in the same direction as ourselves. It was anybody's guess how far we'd get. Of fighting there was no sign. At five o'clock in the afternoon we drove into Chartres. For four years France had been beyond an impenetrable curtain of war, its enchantments recollected by those of us lucky enough to be aware of them, its people being plundered and oppressed, we supposed, by the occupying power. It was startling, on that drive, to find how normal everything and everybody appeared. Chartres, its streets filled by throngs of American soldiers, was not in the least unlike one's pictures or recollections: Normandy, with its destruction, squalor and death, was miles behind us – this didn't feel like war at all. We even found a table in a Chartres café and were able to have something to eat and drink that we hadn't cooked ourselves on a tank cooker. It was an extraordinary contrast. We drove out after half an hour, on a Paris road.

At seven o'clock we drove into Versailles. Here the great, broad avenue in front of the château was filled with milling crowds of the inhabitants, all in highly festive mood and mostly waving small tricolour flags. Our Union Jack was recognised and greeted everywhere with huge enthusiasm. Military traffic had thinned out but it was hard to believe we were near any sort of front line, and we pushed on towards Paris.

Shortly before eight o'clock we drove down the Champs Elysées. The tanks of General Leclerc's Free French Armoured Division were parked under the great avenue's trees, between the Arc de Triomphe and the Rond Point. An abandoned German Panther tank was in the Place de la Concorde, near the Jeu de Paume Gallery. Otherwise, of the enemy there was little trace.

When we had left our bivouac area that morning we had slept few nights except in a slit trench or under a tank since landing in France. We had assumed that wherever we found ourselves that night something of the same would apply – shovels were in car and jeep. We were, we imagined, moving towards the front, after all. When we reached the Place de la Concorde, however – crowds large but not overwhelming, traffic minimal – it was unclear what to do next. A slit trench and bivouac cover in the Tuileries Gardens seemed inappropriate. One of us, David Fraser, knew Paris quite well – his father had been Military Attaché until after the outbreak of war.

'I know where the Ritz is,' he said. 'Let's go there.'

We did. And – contrast of all contrasts from the battlefields we had just quitted – sitting in the Ritz were a number of well-dressed people, elegant ladies perched on bar stools chatting, sipping cocktails, looking unconcerned and somewhat indifferent to the dramatic scenes of war and peace, occupation and liberation in which we supposed we were playing a part. The impression given was that the war was a distraction, an intrusion in somewhat bad taste.

In evidence at the Ritz, however, were a good many Americans already – and a good many journalists. Another of our party was Neville Berry, a son of Lord Kemsley and himself a newspaperman in peacetime. A moment's thought convinced him that Kemsley Newspapers should open a Paris office; that the office would need a Paris bank account; and that a reasonable first charge on it would be to keep a small party of Grenadier liberators for two nights at the Ritz.

'We'd better have rooms here,' he said. 'Leave it to me.'

Half an hour and several bottles of Perrier Jouet later we sat down to a perfectly tolerable dinner, interrupted by an air-raid warning which caused disproportionate alarm, we thought. I had started to order the dinner, an order being acknowledged by the suave head waiter in perfect English. Facetiously and rather foolishly I smiled at him and said, 'Did you talk English when the Germans were here?'

He was busy writing and didn't look up as he said politely, 'No. I talked German when the Germans were here.'

It put us in our place. We gathered the last Germans had left by the back door not long before our arrival at the front. A campaign is only a campaign but the Ritz is the Ritz.

Peter Carrington

Peter Carrington was to become Britain's Foreign Secretary in 1979.

Autumn 1944

Peleliu

The assault on the Palau Islands – and in particular that on Peleliu on 15 September 1944 – was later considered by many Marines to be their most difficult assignment of the war. The Japanese commander had dispersed his troops so that their positions covered nearly every square yard of the coral island, and there was thus no single defensive line for the Marines to breach. For some, it was too much to bear.

Weary hours dragged on. We strained our eyes and ears in the dripping blackness for indications of enemy movement. We heard the usual jungle sounds caused by animals. A splash, as something fell into the water, made my heart pound and caused every muscle to tighten. Heney's inspection tours got worse. He obviously was getting more nervous with each hour.

'I wish to hell Hillbilly would grab him by the stackin' swivel and anchor him in the CP,' George mumbled.

The luminous dial of my wristwatch showed the time was after midnight. In the CP a low voice sounded, 'Oh, ah, oh' and trailed off, only to repeat the sound louder.

'What's that?' I asked George anxiously.

'Sounds like some guy havin' a nightmare,' he replied nervously. 'They sure as hell better shut him up before every Nip in this damned swamp knows our position.' We heard someone moving and thrashing around in the CP.

'Knock it off,' several men whispered near us.

'Quiet that man down!' Hillbilly ordered in a stern low voice.

'Help! help! Oh God, help me!' shouted the wild voice. The poor Marine had cracked up completely. The stress of combat had finally shattered his mind. They were trying to calm him down, but he kept thrashing around. In a firm voice filled with compassion, Hillbilly was trying to reassure the man that he was going to be all right. The effort failed. Our comrade's tragically tortured mind had slipped over the brink. He screamed more loudly. Someone pinioned the man's arms to his sides, and he screamed to the Doberman pinscher, 'Help me, dog; the Japs have got me! The Japs have got me and they're gonna throw me in the ocean.'

I heard the sickening crunch of a fist against a jaw as someone tried to knock the man unconscious. It didn't faze him. He fought like a wildcat, yelling and screaming at the top of his voice.

Our corpsman then gave him an injection of morphine in the hope of sedating him. It had no effect. More morphine; it had no effect either. Veterans though they were, the men were all getting jittery over the noise they believed would announce our exact location to any enemy in the vicinity.

'Hit him with the flat of that entrenching shovel!' a voice commanded in the CP. A horrid thud announced that the command was obeyed. The poor man finally became silent.

'Christ a'mighty, what a pity,' said a Marine in a neighboring foxhole.

'You said that right, but if the goddamn Nips don't know we're here, after all that yellin', they'll never know,' his buddy said.

A tense silence settled over the patrol. The horror of the whole affair stimulated Haney to check our positions frequently. He acted like some hyperactive demon and cautioned us endlessly to be on the alert.

When welcome dawn finally came after a seemingly endless blackness, we all had frayed nerves. I walked the few paces over to the CP to find out what I could. The man was dead. Covered with his poncho, his body lay next to the bunker. The agony and distress etched on the strong faces of Hillbilly, Hank, and the others in the CP revealed the personal horror of the night. Several of these men had received or would receive decorations for bravery in combat, but I never saw such agonised expressions on their faces as that morning in the swamp. They had done what any of us would have had to do under similar circumstances. Cruel chance had thrust the deed upon them.

Hillbilly looked at the radioman and said, 'I'm taking this patrol in. Get battalion for me.'

The radioman tuned his big pack-sized radio and got the battalion CP. Hillbilly told the battalion CO, Major Gustafson, that he wanted to bring in the patrol. We could hear the major tell Hillbilly he thought we should stay put for a couple of days until G-2 could determine the disposition of the Japanese. Hillbilly, a first lieutenant, calmly disagreed, saying we hadn't fired a shot, but because of circumstances we all had a pretty bad case of nerves. He felt strongly that we should come in. I saw several old salts raise their eyebrows and smile as Hillbilly stated his opinion. To our relief, Gus agreed with him; I have always thought it was probably because of his respect for Hillbilly's judgement.

'I'll send a relief column with a tank so you won't have any trouble coming in,' said the major's voice. We all felt comforted. The word went rapidly through the patrol that we were going in. Everyone breathed easier. In about an hour we heard a tank coming. As it forced its way through the thick growth, we saw familiar faces of Company K men with it. We placed the body on the tank, and we returned to the company's lines. I never heard an official word about the death thereafter.

Eugene Sledge

Although both MacArthur and Admiral Chester Nimitz believed that Peleliu needed to be captured to protect their flank, others believed that the weakness of the Japanese air force in the Philippines rendered it a spurious target. The battle there, which was supposed to last a few days, did not end until November, by which time almost the entire Japanese garrison of 10,000 had been killed.

‡

'A public menace'

Churchill and the unflappable Alan Brooke were a formidable team in the engine room of the British war effort, but in private Brooke became increasingly exasperated by his Prime Minister's military whims.

10 SEPTEMBER 1944

We had another meeting with Winston at 12 noon. He was again in a most unpleasant mood. Produced the most ridiculous arguments to prove that operations could be speeded up so as to leave us an option till December before having to withdraw any forces from Europe! He knows no details, has only got half the picture in his mind, talks absurdities and makes my blood boil to listen to his nonsense. I find it hard to remain civil. And the wonderful thing is that half of the population of the world imagine that Winston Churchill is one of the Strategists of History, a second Marlborough, and the other have no conception what a public menace he is and has been throughout this war! It is far better that the world should never know, and never suspect the feet of clay of that otherwise superhuman being. Without him England was lost for a certainty, with him England has been on the verge of disaster time and again.

And with it all no recognition hardly at all for those who help him except the occasional crumb intended to prevent the dog from straying too far from the table. Never have I admired and despised a man simultaneously to the same extent. Never have such opposite extremes been combined in the same human being.

Alan Brooke

✢

Arnhem

The aim of Operation Market Garden, which began on 17 September, was for Allied paratroopers to seize key bridges over the Rhine in Holland, opening up a route into Germany and shortening the war. The British 1st Airborne Division was ordered to take the bridge at Arnhem, but they encountered unexpectedly strong resistance from two SS Panzer divisions and, with reinforcements delayed, their commander, Major-General Robert 'Roy' Urquhart, found himself trapped in the attic of a house with a wounded comrade, Brigadier Lathbury.

I turned to the two officers, one of whom was Jimmy Cleminson, who had shouted the unheeded warning a few moments earlier, and the other a boyish-looking intelligence officer on Lathbury's HQ called Taylor, and said: 'We must try and get some proper medical attention for him.' At that moment I spotted a German soldier as he appeared at the window. I had an automatic in my hand and fired point-blank at a range of a few feet; the window shattered and the German dropped outside.

The Dutch couple now reappeared. They had been talking things over and, realising our plight, they now contrived to make us understand that they would take care of Lathbury and have him taken across the road into the hospital as soon as possible. In order to afford him protection from any other inquisitive German who might peer in at the window, we moved Lathbury into a space under the stairs at the top of the cellar steps, and said our farewells. Convinced that we would be taken on, we were ready for a fight when we slipped out of the back door into yet another maze of tiny, fenced gardens. We crossed these, turned right then left into another terrace house set at right angles to the one we had left. Our entry through the kitchen of 14 Zwarteweg came as a shock to Anton Derksen and family. A plump and solemn Dutchman, he pointed to the stairs just behind the door. In Dutch he tried to tell us that the Germans were already coming round the corner. I found the stairs almost too narrow for my boots, and the ceiling low for a six-footer. On the landing we paused before entering a bedroom with a single wooden bed under the window.

I glanced down into the street and saw the familiar field-grey uniforms of the Wehrmacht. Opposite was the hospital.

Cleminson took a look and then said: 'We can't get out this way. The place is crawling with 'em.'

Taylor had made a cautionary inspection at the back. 'Can we be sure of these people?' he asked, nodding in the direction of the stairs. 'There's an open attic over this room from which we might keep the entrance in view.' It was not much more than a deep shelf shaped by the slope of the roof and the bedroom ceiling. As we discussed the next move, a self-propelled gun whined to a stop almost right underneath our window. We climbed the detachable steps to the shelf, pulled them up after us, and waited. We had pistols, and we now primed our hand grenades. I had two in my blouse which I had almost forgotten about.

'Funny nobody followed us up,' Cleminson observed.

We watched the stairs.

There was no sign of any of the family we had seen on arrival. We hoped that they and their neighbours could be relied upon not to give us away, and if we had then known more about these people we would have been less troubled in mind. In those moments we expected the Germans to burst in at any time. The house remained still and silent and we could not even hear the family downstairs. I brought out a bag of sweets and a bar of chocolate Hancock had given me in exchange for my cigarettes. Outside, we could hear German voices, and occasionally from farther away, bursts of fire. We settled back, and hoped that the commotion would die down. I was suddenly struck by the size of Cleminson's moustache, one to make the RAF envious. This enormity in hirsute handlebars had earlier been lost on me but now there was little else to look at. On such a slightly built man they looked weird.

Presently, when it became obvious that the Germans did not know our whereabouts, the idiocy of the situation forced itself upon me. 'I think it's time we tried to get out,' I said. 'I don't know how you chaps feel, but we are less than useless cooped up here.' I felt that as a divisional commander I ought not to be indulging in such frolics of evasion.

'I don't think it's going to be that easy yet,' said Cleminson, 'but we can take a look.'

Taylor lowered the ladder and crossed into the bedroom to check on the street. As Cleminson and I joined him, he remarked: 'They're down there still, the SP crew.' Looking out of the window, I saw the German crew standing around only seven or eight yards away; some were smoking, others attending to spot maintenance on their vehicle.

Anything seemed better to me than to stay out of the battle in this way. There was no knowing what was happening to the division, and here was I, ineffective as a spectator and, in more senses than one, shelved. 'There's no future in this,' I suddenly announced. 'We're contributing nothing. We could lob a grenade on this thing down here and make a dash for it.' I saw that Taylor and Cleminson regarded this suggestion as more than slightly unworkable but my long absence from the centre of affairs was uppermost in my mind.

It was a big risk that seemed worth the taking.

Taylor, a brisk young officer who looked more like a schoolboy, considered that we would do better to wait. I looked at Cleminson whose magnificent spread of whiskers failed to cover up his extreme youth, and said: 'All right. We'll have a majority decision on this.' I did not feel justified in ordering them to break out with me.

'Even if we knock out the gun and its crew, which we could do quite easily,' Cleminson said, 'we would be killed or caught. I'd prefer to wait for an attack to catch up with us rather than go prowling around.' I was outvoted.

There was neither food nor water in the house – the Germans had cut off supplies of water at the mains – and the lack of indoor sanitation was a nuisance. We hated having to soil this family's living quarters, and long afterwards when I sought out the family I apologised for our unavoidable behaviour.

Outside, there was a good deal of activity around the hospital and I wondered how much of it concerned our own casualties. I was frustrated at my inability to influence the battle, and the minutes dragged through the evening and night. If I had known just how badly the battle was going elsewhere, I would certainly have attempted to reach my HQ. It is doubtful, however, if I could have succeeded.

Robert Urquhart

Urquhart and his companions were found by men of the 2nd South Staffords and the 11th Parachute Battalion the following morning. Lathbury was taken prisoner, but a week later walked out of hospital and made it back to the British lines.

Holding on at Arnhem bridge

Lt-Col. John Frost of the 2nd Parachute Battalion had taken the northern end of the bridge, but was involved in a fierce fight for it with the 9th SS Panzer Division.

Soon after first light on Wednesday morning the shelling began again. This was to be our third day of holding on under continuous enemy pressure, after three long nights of suspense and alarms. It was all the more exacting for our patience in that it followed on after that exhilarating journey from England and our successful thrust into Arnhem of the Sunday afternoon before. Now that the buildings on either side of the bridge had been destroyed and their rubble was still smouldering, the bulk of what remained of the force were concentrated round the headquarters buildings. From here we could still control the bridge. We had found a limited water supply in one of the houses, sufficient for one more day at any rate.

At last divisional headquarters came on the air and I was able to speak to the General [Urquhart]. He had been missing for two days and there had been various rumours as to his fate. It was very cheering to hear him, but he could tell me nothing more than I knew already about XXX Corps, and not anything really encouraging about the ability of the Division to get through to us. They were obviously having great difficulties themselves.

The wounded in the cellars were now lying crowded almost on top of each other, making it difficult for the doctors and orderlies to get round to attend them. I walked around the perimeter to see our defences which, though fairly secure, included some very weak places, where a determined rush by the enemy could carry them into our midst. The Luftwaffe had reappeared in considerable strength. We removed the British identification marks which we had formerly displayed all over the area as there was no sign of the RAF except for one defenceless Dakota which forlornly ran the gauntlet. We held our breath as we watched it forge its way through the puffs of black smoke.

As I was talking to Doug Crawley outside his headquarters about arranging a fighting patrol to give us more elbow-room to the north, there was a sudden savage crash beside us. I was thrown several feet and I found myself lying face downwards on the ground with pain in both legs. Doug was lying on his back not far away and he started to drag himself into the house. Stunned and bemused I did likewise and Wicks my batman came to drag me in under cover. Before long stretcher-bearers carried me to the RAP where Jimmy Logan made light of my wounds and I felt that after a rest I should be able to carry on. I sat on a box in the doorway of headquarters and vainly tried to pull myself together. I tried to swallow the whisky that remained in my flask, but this made me feel like vomiting. After a bit I got some men to carry me on to a litter in one of the cellars and tried to rest. By now the pain had localised itself to my left ankle and right shinbone.

I lay there rather dazed, hoping that the worst of the pain would lessen. Several people came to see me, but I don't remember much. The news went from bad to worse. Digby was brought in to sit beside me for a while and he told me about Jack Grayburn. Though hit several times, he refused to leave his men and died in action with them.

I told Digby that my ankle was the trouble and before long one of the MOs came in to dress it, as this had not been done before. Now I was given morphia and most of the pain went, enabling me to sleep. When I woke some bomb-happy cases were gibbering in the room. In the evening the Germans began to pound the building again. The doctors came to see me about the evacuation of the building in case of fire. I remembered discussing this with Freddie Gough on the evening before and now I sent for him. The doctors said it would take an hour to get everybody out from the cellars and so I told him to be prepared to move with all those still able to fight from new positions. The building took fire several times, and they fought the flames as best they could, but gradually the fire began to spread. One of the doctors came again to say that we would have to do something fairly quickly. I sent for Freddie once more and told him to move. I gave him my own belt with revolver and compass and we wished each other luck. Down below where I lay it was pitch black and we had to use our torches continuously.

Later I heard shouts from above of: 'Don't shoot! Only wounded are here.' George Murray suddenly appeared, wanting to know what on earth was happening. Scarcely had he gone when I heard German voices in the passage outside and sounds of the stretcher-cases being moved out. Then Wicks came in. He said he was going to stay with me till they took me out and I was very glad to see him. He went away to get a stretcher, but while he was gone a German NCO rushed in intimating that we must get out as soon as possible. With the help of one of the bomb-happy cases he dragged me up the stairs to the door. We had to move quickly outside to avoid burning debris from the house. I sat down among the stretcher-cases on the embankment leading to the bridge.

All our buildings were burning fiercely and, as I watched, the old Battalion Headquarters collapsed into a heap of smouldering rubble. The whole scene was brilliantly lit up by the flames. Both sides laboured together to bring the wounded out and I saw that the Germans were driving off in our jeeps full of bandaged men. The prisoners we had taken were standing in a group nearby, not seemingly overjoyed at their liberation. Wicks found me again and put me on a stretcher, at the same time moving me alongside Doug Crawley. As one of the orderlies was giving me an injection of morphia for the journey, I said good-bye to Wicks and thanked him for all he had done for me. He was going to get back to our people as soon as the opportunity arose.

The SS men were very polite and complimentary about the battle we had fought, but the bitterness I felt was unassuaged. No living enemy had beaten us. The battalion was unbeaten yet, but they could not have much chance with no ammunition, no rest and with no positions from which to fight. No body of men could have fought more courageously and tenaciously than the officers and men of 1st Parachute Brigade at Arnhem bridge.

John Frost

Frost and his men had held the bridge for three days and four nights. Had they not done so, it is likely that the Germans would have encircled the entire 1st Airborne Division. As it was, 6,000 were taken captive, and another 1,000 killed, but a further 2,300 managed to get away.

The Holocaust

The Countess of Ranfurly had become the secretary to General Sir 'Jumbo' Maitland Wilson, the Supreme Allied Commander in the Mediterranean.

Caserta

20 SEPTEMBER 1944

Roger Makin dined with me. After dinner I sat sewing with Coco on my shoulder and he told me the most appalling story of Lublin. He said that the Germans take Jews there by train and gas them at the rate of about two thousand a day. They burn their bodies and sell their clothes and belongings in a neighbouring shop.

Hermione Ranfurly

That the Jews deported from their homes were being systematically exterminated by the Nazis had been known to the Allied High Command, including Roosevelt, since late 1942, although the details and scale of the killings remained sketchy, and there was little that could be done since the camps were deep in German-held territory. By the middle of 1944, firm reports of the activities at Birkenau had, however, begun to reach diplomats such as Makin in London.

Disposing of the bodies at Auschwitz

A recurring theme in Holocaust memoirs is the frustration born of the inability of language to describe the horrors of the camps. One survivor of Auschwitz Vladek Spiegelman, allowed his son to depict his experiences in the form of a comic book. The result, Maus, *which depicted the Jews as mice and their guards as cats, showed that the cartoon could be just as powerful as the written word.*

Art Spiegelman

Vladek Spiegelman was reunited with his wife, Anja, after the war. Their eldest son, Richieu, died in 1943 during the liquidation of the ghetto at Zawiercie.

✝

Italy and the Balkans

The Gothic Line

The Allies reached the German fortified positions in northern Italy, the Pisa–Rimini or 'Gothic' Line, in late August 1944. Deprived of troops by the landings on the French Riviera earlier in the month, they would be held up by the Line until the early summer of the following year. Watching their initial attacks was Martha Gellhorn.

The Gothic Line, from where we stood, was a smashed village, an asphalt road and a pinkish brown hill. On this dusty mined lane leading up to the village, the road and the hill, the infantry was waiting to attack. They stood single file, spaced well apart, and did not speak. The noise of our artillery firing from the hills behind us never stopped. No one listened to it. Everyone listened to the sudden, woodpecker beats of the German machine-gun fire ahead and everyone looked to the sky on the left where the German airbursts made dark, loose, small clouds.

In front of us a bulldozer was working as bulldozers do, according to their own laws and in a world of their own. This machine was trying to fill in a portion of the deep anti-tank ditch which the Germans had dug along the entire face of the Gothic Line. The bulldozer now scraped up two mines in its wide steel shovel; the mines exploded, the bulldozer shook a little, and the driver removed his tropical helmet and cursed the situation. An infantry officer shouted something to him, and he swerved his big machine, leaving two feet cleared between the side of his shovel and the mined side of the road. Through this gap the infantry now passed. Each man seemed very alone, walking slowly and steadily toward the hills he could not see and to whatever peril those hills would offer.

The great Gothic Line, which the Germans have used as a threat ever since the Hitler Line was broken, would, under normal circumstances, be a lovely range of the Apennines. In this clear and dreaming weather that is the end of summer, the hills curve up into a water-blue sky: in the hot windless night you see the very hills only as a soft, rounded darkness under the moon. Along the Via Emilia, the road that borders the base of these hills, the Germans dynamited every village into shapeless brick rubble so that they could have a clear line of fire. In front of the flattened villages they dug their long canal to trap tanks. In front of the tank trap they cut all the trees. Among the felled trees and in the gravel bed and the low water of the Foglia River, they laid down barbed wire and they sowed their never-ending mines, the crude little wooden boxes, the small rusty tin cans, the flat metal pancakes which are the simplest and deadliest weapons in Italy.

On the range of hills that is the actual Gothic Line, the Germans built concrete machine-gun pillboxes which encircle the hills and dominate all approaches. They sank the turrets of tanks, with their long, thin snout-ended 88-mm. guns, in camouflaged pits so that nothing on wheels or tracks could pass their way. They mined some more. They turned the beautiful hills into a mountain trap four miles deep where every foot of our advance could be met with concentrated fire.

And it is awful to die when you know that the war is won anyhow. It is awful, and one would have to be a liar or a fool not to see this and not to feel it like a mystery, so that these days every man dead is a greater sorrow because the end of all this tragic dying is so near. There it was: the Gothic Line carefully planned so that every fold of the earth was used to conceal death, and the young men were walking into it, and because they have seen so much and done so much, they walked into it as if it were part of the day's work. A hellish day but still just part of the work.

Martha Gellhorn

Irregular warfare

Attached to partisans in Albania, Julian Amery found himself leading into battle some unreliable allies, soldiers from Central Asia who had been captured in the invasion of the Soviet Union and absorbed into the German Army, but who had since deserted to the guerrillas.

Back at Kurat the day passed slowly, though not without incident. This was the morning when the Tajiks murdered their NCO; a deed which convinced us that, after the excitement of mutiny, their temper urgently required the discipline of battle and the cold douche of danger. Abas Kupi came also to discuss plans; and towards midday we received the first report from the young German officer planted by us in their Corps Headquarters in Tirana. This gave us, among a mass of other information, the identifications of the post we were going to attack. It was the headquarters of the Third Battery of the 297th Artillery Regiment. With so much business, there was no time to rest before the action; and, almost as soon as we had eaten, we set out to join our forces, already concentrating behind the eastern range. We reached the assembly point at five o'clock, and climbed to the crest of the range for a further brief reconnaissance. All was quiet in the German camp; we wished each other good luck, and departed each to his allotted task.

In the morning I had agreed with a light heart to take command of the Tajiks, but, as we marched off to the attack, I was oppressed by sombre reflections. I knew nothing of their training or their ways, and spoke besides so little of their language that I could not hope to make them understand my orders in the heat of battle. This ignorance might jeopardise the whole operation; but, as I anxiously considered how to impose my will on these wild Asiatics, there suddenly came back to me a fragment from a long-forgotten conversation with a friend who had once commanded an Indian brigade:

'It doesn't matter what you say to native troops,' he had told me, 'because they won't understand you. What matters is what you do. March in front of them and they'll do whatever you do; and, if you don't run away, they'll be as good as the Guards.'

I had been in Cairo at the time, ill from jaundice, and had forgotten his words with the next glass of medicine. Now, by some strange freak of memory, the sick-bed talk was become a counsel of action; and I remembered that Ivan and Mishka at least considered the Tajiks as 'native troops'. I went, therefore, to the head of the column, though not without some apprehension; the danger from the Germans in front might be part of the day's work; but only that morning the Tajiks had murdered their NCO, and I had to steel myself not to look back too often over my shoulder.

We crossed the low ground, where a tongue of woodland stretched out from the western range, and, hurrying over the road, climbed on to the crest of the range itself. There we turned northwards, and, devoutly hoping that the Germans were off their guard, moved silently towards them through the trees. Presently we came to a low thorn fence, broken only by a stile, on the far side of which lay a clearing perhaps fifty yards wide. Beyond, the woods sloped steeply down to the enemy positions. I decided that we should cross the clearing and lie up in the fringes of the wood beyond, to wait until Maclean should begin the attack. I led the way, therefore, over the stile, and had gone perhaps ten yards when a machine-gun opened up savagely from a clump of trees some forty yards away.

I looked round to see how many of the Tajiks were already across the fence, and, as I turned my head, somehow lost my balance and fell to the ground. I thought at first that I had only slipped, and it was some time before I realised that a bullet had caught me under the chin. The wound indeed was little worse than a deep shaving cut, and caused me neither pain nor serious loss of blood. The Tajiks, however, ran back, seeing me fall; and I lay in the clearing alone. The machine-gun was silent, the gunner taking me perhaps for dead. I waited for a moment, then sprang up and ran for the fence. The German opened up at once, and his bullets hissed round me like furious insects as I vaulted the stile and made for the shelter of the trees. The Tajiks rallied when they saw me safe, and, gathering round me, opened a blind and ragged fire in the direction of the machine-gun.

I checked them as soon as I had recovered my breath and my wits, and, more by instinct than by reasoning, worked my way round the flank of the machine-gun post. When I judged we were well past it I lay down, and, while the Tajiks got into position, tried to decide what to do next. It is sometimes a weakness to see things from the other man's point of view, but, as I imagined myself among the German defenders, I knew that they were beaten. After months of inactivity they had been startled from rest, perhaps from sleep, by our approach. Their machine-gunners had seen a few Turkoman deserters, but, in the darkness of the wood, they could not tell how many were their assailants, or where the attack would come from next. Their nerves must be strained by the uncertainty; and I therefore decided not to wait for Maclean's signal but to go in to the attack.

For a few seconds I vainly racked my brains for orders which the men would understand. Then on a sudden inspiration I stood up, and, hoisting my astrakhan cap on the muzzle of my sub-machine-gun, ran forward shouting 'Hurrah'. The Tajiks did not misunderstand, and, spreading out on either side, charged through the trees, shoulders hunched and eyes glinting. The machine-gunners fled; we dropped over the crest of the ridge, and saw the huts and dug-outs of the enemy less than fifty feet below. I shouted 'Hurrah' again, and the Tajiks bounded down the hill like wolves, letting out blood-curdling yells and pouring a withering fire into the camp. As we carried the first buildings I saw a German standing twenty yards from me, stripped to the waist, with a *Schmeizer* pistol in his hand. For a moment we looked at each other without moving, then he crumpled to the ground, pressing his hands to his naked stomach. I had not heard the shot, but looked round to see Achmet grinning from ear to ear. We pressed forward, and, as I passed the dying German, I noticed that he was still a boy, with straight, fair hair and blue, staring eyes. His hands were clasped over his wound as if in prayer, and the blood was oozing quietly away through his fingers. Looking back a moment later I saw a Turkoman stripping him of his Wellington boots.

Julian Amery

Amery was the son of Leopold Amery, one of Churchill's staunchest supporters and Secretary of State for India. By contrast, Julian's brother, John, would be hanged after the war for treason.

The deal

By October, Churchill felt the need of another meeting with Stalin in Moscow. Not only were there military developments to discuss, but it was becoming clear that in the coming years the capitalist democracies would face a new threat in the form of a much-enlarged and aggressive Soviet Union. Ever the pragmatist, Churchill proposed an agreement that he hoped might prevent an imminent recurrence of war.

The moment was apt for business, so I said, 'Let us settle about our affairs in the Balkans. Your armies are in Roumania and Bulgaria. We have interests, missions, and agents there. Don't let us get at cross-purposes in small ways. So far as Britain and Russia are concerned, how would it do for you to have ninety per cent predominance in Roumania, for us to have ninety per cent of the say in Greece, and go fifty-fifty about Yugoslavia?' While this was being translated I wrote out on a half-sheet of paper:

Roumania
    Russia   90%
    The others   10%
Greece
    Great Britain   90%
        (in accord with USA)
    Russia   10%
Yugoslavia   50–50%
Hungary   50–50%
Bulgaria
    Russia   75%
    The others   25%

I pushed this across to Stalin, who had by then heard the translation. There was a slight pause. Then he took his blue pencil and made a large tick upon it, and passed it back to us. It was all settled in no more time than it takes to set down.

Of course we had long and anxiously considered our point, and were only dealing with immediate war-time arrangements. All larger questions were reserved on both sides for what we then hoped would be a peace table when the war was won.

After this there was a long silence. The pencilled paper lay in the centre of the table. At length I said, 'Might it not be thought rather cynical if it seemed we had disposed of these issues, so fateful to millions of people, in such an offhand manner? Let us burn the paper.'

'No, you keep it,' said Stalin.

Winston Churchill

Athens liberated

The Germans were being steadily pressed back on all fronts, and Allied troops landed in Greece at the start of October. On the 14th, British soldiers entered Athens. There had been terrible food shortages throughout Greece, especially in the capital, during much of the three and a half years of Nazi rule, and as many as 300,000 people had succumbed to starvation or associated illnesses. Indeed, more Greeks died during the Second World War – about 420,000 – than did Britons or Americans.

At six-thirty the war correspondents arrived and crowded into the old-fashioned room – the same room where in 1941 General Jumbo gave the order for the evacuation of the British Forces from Greece. Stiff French chairs were pushed back against the walls; the green curtains were drawn; in a glass case the swords and pistols of old General Mazaraki lay beside his blue and gold uniform. After a while someone tapped on a table and General Jumbo began to talk in a flat straightforward way. He explained how, in 1941, the Greek Government had informed him that the situation was desperate, Germans were pouring in from the north, Piraeus had been heavily bombed, the Greek Prime Minister had committed suicide. The Greeks thought it would be best for the British to leave and return later. General Jumbo said that in that dark hour the spirit of the Greek people was something he would never forget. They waved goodbye to our troops with courage and goodwill. They shouted, 'Come back again' and threw flowers at our troops as they marched away.

In this war, he continued, the Greeks had suffered greatly. They had fought hard and well against the Italians and Germans who had superior numbers and weapons. For three long years and more they had resisted the German occupation despite terrible reprisals. Their villages had been razed to the ground, their heroes shot, thousands had starved. But they held on and waited till our victories in the west and the south had pinched the Germans out of Greece. This week they had welcomed us back to Athens with the same spirit as before. General Jumbo said he hoped the great sacrifices and courage of the Greeks would not go unrewarded but unless something was done quickly to help them they would once more face starvation.

We staff gave a dinner party for the Phrances and Benski families at the Grande Bretagne Hotel. We took food because there was none to be had otherwise. Our guests were pathetically excited over our rations. They said, 'Do you mind if we eat an awful lot? We have not seen meat for so long.' They all had second helpings. Afterwards they took us to their flat. Some of their friends and a guitarist joined us and we all sat round the empty fireplace and sang their national songs. It was very gay. One of the party said to me, 'Excuse if I sing too loud. It gives me much pleasure. You see we have all had Germans billeted in our houses. One of the things we hated most was the sound of their boots along the streets and on our staircases.'

Several of the women at the party spoke English. I asked them about the German occupation. They said there had been a curfew at eight–thirty every night so the evenings had seemed endless: there was little food; radios were not allowed; nor could they visit one another. It was dangerous to talk freely lest your German lodger should overhear.

By day someone had to go out to try and find food but when they were in the streets or trams there was always the risk that the Germans would cordon off a space where they happened to be and say, 'We'll take you, and you, and you.' Then they would be taken out and shot as a reprisal for something the Greek Resistance had done, no matter whether they were connected with it or not. 'So whenever anyone went out you were not sure if you would ever see them again. It was a nightmare.' The Greeks explained to me that one of the reasons for the tremendous political dissensions in Greece today was that during the German occupation no schools or universities were allowed. The young men and boys had nothing to talk about. No news came in from outside the country. They became absorbed in politics and began to take very definite sides, either to the right or left. Fuel for revolution.

I shall never forget the gaiety and hospitality of these people. Though they had not been able to buy clothes for a long time and cosmetics are an exorbitant price, they were chic and neatly dressed. Today a Max Factor lipstick costs seven pounds sterling in Athens. I drove home in an open jeep with Colonel Zigantes and the guitarist. We made a great noise singing 'Lili Marlene'. The streets were strangely empty. People have not yet got used to going out after 8.30 p.m.

Hermione Ranfurly

The privations and terrors inflicted by the Nazis radicalised the Greek youth and laid the seeds for the forthcoming civil war between the Communists and the government restored by the British.

✝

The death of Rommel

Hitler, convinced of Rommel's complicity in the July Bomb Plot, decided that the Field Marshal should be given the choice of taking his own life or facing a public trial. Rommel's son Manfred was at home when two generals called on 14 October.

My battery, to which I had returned several weeks before, had given me leave for the 14th October. I left the gun position very early in the morning and arrived at Herrlingen at 7.00 a.m. My father was already at breakfast. A cup was quickly brought for me and we breakfasted together, afterwards taking a stroll in the garden.

'At twelve o'clock to-day two Generals are coming to see me to discuss my future employment,' my father started the conversation. 'So to-day will decide what is planned for me; whether a People's Court or a new command in the East.'

'Would you accept such a command?' I asked.

He took me by the arm, and replied: 'My dear boy, our enemy in the East is so terrible that every other consideration has to give way before it. If he succeeds in overrunning Europe, even only temporarily, it will be the end of everything which has made life appear worth living. Of course I would go.'

Shortly before twelve o'clock, my father went to his room on the first floor and changed from the brown civilian jacket which he usually wore over riding-breeches, to his Africa tunic, which was his favourite uniform on account of its open collar.

At about twelve o'clock a dark-green car with a Berlin number stopped in front of our garden gate. The only men in the house apart from my father were Captain Aldinger, a badly wounded war-veteran corporal and myself. Two generals – Burgdorf, a powerful florid man, and Maisel, small and slender – alighted from the car and entered the house. They were respectful and courteous and asked my father's permission to speak to him alone. Aldinger and I left the room. 'So they are not going to arrest him,' I thought with relief, as I went upstairs to find myself a book.

A few minutes later I heard my father come upstairs and go into my mother's room. Anxious to know what was afoot, I got up and followed him. He was standing in the middle of the room, his face pale. 'Come outside with me,' he said in a tight voice. We went into my room. 'I have just had to tell your mother,' he began slowly, 'that I shall be dead in a quarter of an hour.' He was calm as he continued: 'To die by the hand of one's own people is hard. But the house is surrounded and Hitler is charging me with high treason. "In view of my services in Africa,"' he quoted sarcastically, 'I am to have the chance of dying by poison. The two generals have brought it with them. It's fatal in three seconds. If I accept, none of the usual steps will be taken against my family, that is against you. They will also leave my staff alone.'

'Do you believe it?' I interrupted.

'Yes,' he replied. 'I believe it. It is very much in their interest to see that the affair does not come out into the open. By the way, I have been charged to put you under a promise of the strictest silence. If a single word of this comes out, they will no longer feel themselves bound by the agreement.'

I tried again. 'Can't we defend ourselves . . .' He cut me off short.

'There's no point,' he said. 'It's better for one to die than for all of us to be killed in a shooting affray. Anyway, we've practically no ammunition.' We briefly took leave of each other. 'Call Aldinger, please,' he said.

Aldinger had meanwhile been engaged in conversation by the General's escort to keep him away from my father. At my call, he came running upstairs. He, too, was struck cold when he heard what was happening. My father now spoke more quickly. He again said how useless it was to attempt to defend ourselves. 'It's all been prepared to the last detail. I'm to be given a state funeral. I have asked that it should take place in Ulm. In a quarter of an hour, you, Aldinger, will receive a telephone call from the Wagnerschule reserve hospital in Ulm to say that I've had a brain seizure on the way to a conference.' He looked at his watch. 'I must go, they've only given me ten minutes.' He quickly took leave of us again. Then we went downstairs together.

We helped my father into his leather coat. Suddenly he pulled out his wallet. 'There's still 150 marks in there,' he said. 'Shall I take the money with me?'

'That doesn't matter now, Herr Field Marshal,' said Aldinger.

My father put his wallet carefully back in his pocket. As he went into the hall, his little dachshund which he had been given as a puppy a few months before in France, jumped up at him with a whine of joy. 'Shut the dog in the study, Manfred,' he said, and waited in the hall with Aldinger while I removed the excited dog and pushed it through the study door. Then we walked out of the house together. The two generals were standing at the garden gate. We walked slowly down the path, the crunch of the gravel sounding unusually loud.

As we approached the generals they raised their right hands in salute. 'Herr Field Marshal,' Burgdorf said shortly and stood aside for my father to pass through the gate. A knot of villagers stood outside the drive. Maisel turned to me, and asked: 'What battery are you with?'

'36/7, Herr General,' I answered.

The car stood ready. The SS driver swung the door open and stood to attention. My father pushed his Marshal's baton under his left arm, and with his face calm, gave Aldinger and me his hand once more before getting in the car.

The two generals climbed quickly into their seats and the doors were slammed. My father did not turn again as the car drove quickly off up the hill and disappeared round a bend in the road. When it had gone Aldinger and I turned and walked silently back into the house. 'I'd better go up and see your mother,' Aldinger said. I went upstairs again to await the promised telephone call. An agonising depression excluded all thought.

I lit a cigarette and tried to read again, but the words no longer made sense. Twenty minutes later the telephone rang. Aldinger lifted the receiver and my father's death was duly reported. That evening we drove into Ulm to the hospital where he lay. The doctors who received us were obviously ill at ease, no doubt suspecting the true cause of my father's death. One of them opened the door of a small room. My father lay on a camp-bed in his brown Africa uniform, a look of contempt on his face.

It was not then entirely clear what had happened to him after he left us. Later we learned that the car had halted a few hundred yards up the hill from our house in an open space at the edge of the wood. Gestapo men, who had appeared in force from Berlin that morning, were watching the area with instructions to shoot my father down and storm the house if he offered resistance. Maisel and the driver got out of the car, leaving my father and Burgdorf inside. When the driver was permitted to return ten minutes or so later, he saw my father sunk forward with his cap off and the marshal's baton fallen from his hand. Then they drove off at top speed to Ulm, where the body was unloaded at the hospital; afterwards General Burgdorf drove on to Ulm Wehrmacht Headquarters where he first telephoned to Hitler to report my father's death and then to the family of one of his escort officers to compose the menu for that night's dinner. General Burgdorf, who was hated for his brutality by 99 per cent of the Officer Corps, ended his own life in Berlin in April 1945, after staggering round drunk with Bormann for several days in the Führer's bunker.

Manfred Rommel

✠

MacArthur returns to the Philippines

On 20 October, General Krueger's 6th Army landed on Leyte in the Philippines. There was little resistance from the Japanese 16th Division, and 130,000 troops were put ashore. Among them was their Supreme Commander, General Douglas MacArthur, who, after leaving the islands in 1942 when the Japanese invaded, had vowed that he would return.

The big guns on the ships opened fire at dawn. The noise, like rolling thunder, was all around us. The *Nashville*, her engines bringing to life the steel under our feet, knifed into Leyte Gulf. The ominous clouds of night still hung over the sea, fighting the sun for possession of the sky, but the blackness had given way to sombre grey, and even as we saw the black outline of the shore on the horizon, the cloak of drabness began to roll back. On every side ships were riding toward the island. The battle for Leyte had already begun.

I was on the bridge with Captain C. E. Coney. His clear, keen eyes and cool, crisp voice swung the cruiser first to port, then to starboard as he dodged floating mines. An enemy periscope suddenly spouted up, only to be blotted out as destroyers closed in with roaring depth charges. And then, just as the sun rose clear of the horizon, there was Tacloban. It had changed little since I had known it forty-one years before on my first assignment after leaving West Point. It was a full moment for me.

Shortly after this, we reached our appointed position offshore. The captain carefully hove into line and dropped anchor. Our initial vantage

point was 2 miles from the beaches, but I could clearly see the sandstrips
with the pounding surf beating down upon the shore, and in the morning
sunlight, the jungle-clad hills rising behind the town. Landings are explosive once the shooting begins, and now thousands of guns were throwing
their shells with a roar that was incessant and deafening. Rocket vapour
trails crisscrossed the sky and black, ugly, ominous pillars of smoke began
to rise. High overhead, swarms of airplanes darted into the maelstrom.
And across what would ordinarily have been a glinting, untroubled blue
sea, the black dots of the landing craft churned toward the beaches.

From my vantage point, I had a clear view of everything that took place.
Troops were going ashore at 'Red Beach', near Palo, at San Jose on 'White
Beach' and at the southern tip of Leyte on tiny Panson Island. On the
north, under Major General Franklin C. Sibert, the X Corps, made up of
the 1st Cavalry and 24th Infantry Divisions: to the south, the XXIV Corps,
under Major General John R. Hodge, consisting of the 7th and 96th
Infantry Divisions. In over-all command of ground troops was Lieutenant-
General Walter Krueger of the Sixth Army.

At 'Red Beach' our troops secured a landing and began moving inland.
I decided to go in with the third assault wave. President Osmena, accompanied by General Basilio Valdez, the Philippine Army chief of staff, and
General Carlos Romulo, my old aide, who had joined me on Bataan in
1942, had sailed with the convoy on one of the nearby transports. I took
them into my landing barge and we started for the beach. Romulo, an old
stalwart of the Quezon camp, was the resident commissioner for the
Philippines in Washington. Noted for his oratorical ability, this popular
patriot served on Bataan, and had been the radio 'Voice of Freedom' from
Corregidor.

As we slowly bucked the waves toward 'Red Beach', the sounds of war
grew louder. We could now hear the whining roar of airplane engines as
they dove over our heads to strafe and bomb enemy positions inland from
the beach. Then came the steady crump, crump of exploding naval shells.
As we came closer, we could pick up the shouts of our soldiers as they
gave and acknowledged orders. Then, unmistakably, in the near distance
came the steady rattle of small-arms fire. I could easily pick up the peculiar
fuzzy gurgle of a Japanese machine gun seemingly not more than 100 yards
from the shoreline. The smoke from the burning palm trees was in our
nostrils, and we could hear the continual snapping and crackling of flames.
The coxswain dropped the ramp about 50 yards from shore, and we waded
in. It took me only 30 or 40 long strides to reach dry land, but that was
one of the most meaningful walks I ever took. When it was done, and I

stood on the sand, I knew I was back again – against my old enemies of Bataan, for there, shining on the bodies of dead Japanese soldiers, I saw the insignia of the 16th Division, General Homma's ace unit.

Our beachhead troops were only a few yards away, stretched out behind logs and other cover, laying down fire on the area immediately inland. There were still Japanese in the undergrowth not many yards away. A mobile broadcasting unit was set up, and as I got ready to talk into the microphone, the rains came down. This is what I said:

People of the Philippines: I have returned. By the grace of Almighty God, our forces stand again on Philippine soil – soil consecrated in the blood of our two peoples. We have come dedicated and committed to the task of destroying every vestige of enemy control over your daily lives, and of restoring upon a foundation of indestructible strength, the liberties of your people.

At my side is your President, Sergio Osmena, a worthy successor of that great patriot, Manuel Quezon, with members of his cabinet. The seat of your government is now, therefore, firmly re-established on Philippine soil.

The hour of your redemption is here. Your patriots have demonstrated an unswerving and resolute devotion to the principles of freedom that challenge the best that is written on the pages of human history. I now call upon your supreme effort that the enemy may know, from the temper of an aroused people within, that he has a force there to contend with no less violent than is the force committed from without.

Rally to me. Let the indomitable spirit of Bataan and Corregidor lead on. As the lines of battle roll forward to bring you within the zone of operations, rise and strike. Strike at every favourable opportunity. For your homes and hearths, strike! For future generations of your sons and daughters, strike! In the name of your sacred dead, strike! Let no heart be faint. Let every arm be steeled. The guidance of Divine God points the way. Follow in His name to the Holy Grail of righteous victory.

President Osmena and I then walked off the beach, and picked our way into the brush behind the beach until we found a place to sit down. We had made our return and it was time to think of returning the government to constitutional authority. It was while we were finishing our discussion that the beachhead was subjected for the first time to an enemy bombing attack. It shook the log on which we sat, but that was all. As we finally got up to move, I noticed that the rain was no longer falling and that the only soldiers left near the beach were members of sniper patrols . . .

After inspecting the forward elements of our troops and the Tacloban

Airfield, I returned to the *Nashville*. That evening I ordered a co-ordinated attack by guerrillas all over the Philippines.

As I dropped off to sleep that night, the vision that danced before my tired eyes was not of bayonet, bullet, or bomb, but of an old, old man, a resident of Leyte, who stepped up to me amidst the shot and shell of the afternoon, welcoming me with outstretched arms. 'Good afternoon, Sir Field Marshal,' he said in his Visayan dialect. 'Glad to see you. It has been many years – a long, long time.'

Douglas MacArthur

The author was not able to announce the end of the campaign in the Philippines until 28 June 1945.

‡

'Girl Trouble'

Willie Mullins gets a letter

For some soldiers, the wrong kind of letter from a loved one could prove more damaging than the stress of combat. Willie Mullins and Ross Carter were serving with the US 82nd Airborne Division in Holland.

Life on the front continued its baseball rhythm of long monotonous pauses interspersed with comic and tragic incidents and moments or hours of intense anxiety and action.

The company had moved into a particularly vulnerable position on the right flank in the open fields the day Willie Mullins got a letter from his wife which did more to erode our morale than could any conceivable amount of shells, rain or hard luck. Willie loved his wife and respected her dignity enough, in spite of the biological urges which belaboured him, to stay away from the temptresses who talked love in strange tongues. He was first in line for his mail, read and reread his wife's letters and carried them with him till rain, sweat and mud made them illegible. He sent every penny he could save to her to put in the bank for the little house they planned to buy when the war was over. It had never occurred to him that the sweet young girl who sat on his knees, ran her fingers through his hair, caressed his closed eyes, and kissed him tenderly in the corners of his mouth could be a two-timer. He was fighting for her and the kind of free life he vaguely associated in his unlettered naïve thinking with the purposes of the war.

Willie had just returned from an overnight sojourn in some old houses a few yards from no man's land. It had been a strenuous night, filled with the usual tensions and noises, plus the nerve-scraping detonations of diabolically contrived new rockets we called 'screaming meemies'. This new gun rocketed six projectiles at a time, each containing thirty-five pounds of high explosives which in their trajectory shrieked with increasing sirenlike intensity, giving one the feeling of being personally pursued by a banshee from hell. They exploded in bursts of flame and sparks, sending glowing fragments for hundreds of yards in every direction. This weapon while not very accurate was hellishly terrifying. Many times during the night Willie's vision of the little house faded. His Adam's apple pistoned his dry throat and his chest tightened at the thought of dying before he held his wife on his knee again and felt the soft plush of her plump breasts pressing against him.

Berkely handed him his letter. He read it twice, his eyes bulging. First he threw it on the ground and stomped it. Next he shot at it. Then waving it he charged straight towards no man's land, cursing and storming every bound, described a wide arc and came back to our line panting and foaming.

'Having female trouble, Willie?'

'Arab, read this letter to the boys.'

The Arab read: 'Dear darling Willie, I have bad news in one way, but in another way it's good news. I am pregnant. Life was so hard without you, sweetheart. You have no idea what all I've been through. If you'd really loved me, you'd have found a way to come back from over there. I know you will understand. It will be kinda nice now, won't it, to have a little one already here when you get back. Do write, Willie boy, and tell me everything is all right. Loads of love from your loving bunny!'

The Arab finished reading the letter and handed it back to Willie with a comment that pretty well summarised our feelings.

'Willie, don't answer her! Never see her again! And in future dealings with women, Willie, don't build your life around one. Our mothers are good women so there are good women. Maybe a girl back home is okay, maybe not. As for me, a woman is a thing of beauty and a source of joy, but fragile and fleeting like a rose. "Gather in the day," *carpe diem*. That's Latin, jokers. Now, Willie, we'll get you drunk and find you a dainty damsel the next time we go on leave.'

'I can't forget her, Arab! I love her!'

'Love?' The Arab lifted his eyebrows in ironically comical disbelief. 'Love, Willie, may be a state of idiocy. You don't want to be an idiot, do you?'

'I love her, I love her, I love her!' Suddenly Willie grabbed the letter and began to run in wide circles, screaming, 'I love the bitch, I love her, I love the bitch, I love her!'

Late in the night Willie Mullins went crazy and left the front in a straitjacket.

The fear of being cuckolded was shared by the Americans' comrades-in-arms.

'It's a bloody, blooming lie, ain't it so, blokes,' said a Limey one day to Berkely, Wild Bill, the Arab and me, 'that you American blokes have been shining up to our wives back in England?'

I remembered Willie Mullins.

'Your wives wouldn't look at us, Limey!' I said.

'They're regular Penelopes, Limey!' said the Arab.

'That good or bad, Yank?'

'Good.'

'I been saying, I have, it was a bloody, blooming lie and you tell me I'm right, eh, Yanks?' he said turning to Berkely and Wild Bill.

'Every damned word of it,' they chorused.

'Let's shake hands!'

We shook hands with the reassured Limey and went our way, coddling our consciences in silent uneasiness.

Ross Carter

‡

8 NOVEMBER 1944

This evening Cyril Falls, Military Correspondent of *The Times*, came to see me. He said that he was disturbed at the system of command in France with Eisenhower commanding in two planes, namely commanding the Army, Navy and Air Forces in his capacity as Supreme Commander and at the same time pretending to command the land forces, divided into Three groups of armies directly.

He has hit the nail on the head and found the weakness of this set up which the Americans have forced on to Eisenhower. Unfortunately it becomes a political matter and the Americans, with preponderating strength of land and air forces, very naturally claim the privilege of decid-ing how the forces are to be organised and commanded. Falls had been seeing Monty and there is no doubt that Monty had been rubbing it in hard! It is however a very serious defect in our organisation and one that may have evil repercussions on the strategy of the war. I do not like the layout of the coming offensive, and doubt whether we even reach the Rhine, it is highly improbable that we should cross over before the end of the year.

Alan Brooke

Winter 1944-5

So perish all traitors

By the winter of 1944, former student Radomir Luza had become a senior figure in the Czech Resistance.

None of us was immune to informers. One day I received a report from my men near Okarec, where Hasek was active. They said a woman had turned up. She was a Czech, rather young, looking for a connection to the General Luza group. She came from some distance, where another group called Hybes was situated. Before I could respond to that information, I learned that the Soviets had taken her into their *zemljanka* [hide-out] – a serious disregard of security and an all-round idiotic move for which I angrily reproached them. We couldn't leave her there in the midst of our operation without finding out whether she was a Gestapo agent.

We had an SS uniform that Gustav Kristek had stolen from a German in Brno. I decided to stage a Gestapo raid to see what our Czech 'resister' would do when confronted by a German 'officer'. I warned the men in the *zemljanka*. 'Now, don't forget it's only a phoney raid; don't start shooting,' I told them. 'Whatever we do, there can't be any shooting.' The SS uniform was so tight, I could feel my face getting red as Lonka led us to the *zemljanka* (without a guide, I could never have found it). I made a signal to the sentry, opened the entrance to the hide-out, and shouted in my best German, 'All of you! Hands up! Don't touch your weapons. Come up slowly.' I was making German-sounding phatic noises and trying to think of other things to say when the woman emerged. She was a pretty little thing, only about twenty-two, a girl who should have been living in a college dormitory instead of a burrow. Under the coarse material of her dress one could see high, round breasts and a nice behind. I understood why the Soviets took her into their hide-out. She had cleverly told them she was carrying a child, knowing that Russians would never harass an expectant mother; but from my vast inexperience, I judged that she was not pregnant. 'Show me your identity,' I said in German.

'Wait, please,' she said, and calmly produced a piece of paper.

'Here is the telephone number. Please call this extension and ask for Gestapo Commissar Kren. He will explain my mission.'

I unbuttoned my coat just as it was about to unbutton itself, took a deep breath, and replied in Czech, 'I think I already know your mission. And as we are Czech partisans and not the SS, our mission is to root out informers like you.' Even today I am astonished that such a primitive trick worked. If I had been older, I never would have tried it. If she had been older, she never would have fallen for it. I had her walk ahead of me until we were out of earshot of the Soviets and in a relatively concealed position – about a forty-five minute walk. When she turned to face me, she was still erect, but her voice was shaking.

'You didn't shoot me on the path,' she said. I got out of her that she was working with another man, but she would not give me any further information. I wasn't even certain that she had been forced to become an informer. She did assure me that she had not sent any report since going into the *zemljanka*; therefore, if she were to be believed, the Gestapo still knew nothing of our hide-out there. According to her identity card, she had the same name as my grandmother, Marta Vecera.

She was dangerous. If she escaped, she would bring the Gestapo down on us, a big unit of machine guns swarming over the centre of our operations. We all agreed she had to be executed, but nobody was rushing to get it over with. When I returned two days later, I found her still alive and lovely, enjoying her last sunshine outside the *zemljanka* with the sentry. She raised her eyes to mine with a brave, knowing look.

'I told Yuri to take her out and give her the Hitler Kiss,' Ales explained.

'But?'

'But he crumbled like dried up horseshit. They took a little walk, chatted – and he came back with her.'

Since the Soviets had stupidly brought her into their *zemljanka*, I was determined that they would be the ones to deal with her. They finally shot her on the wayside between Bítes and Tisnov, where German troops could be seen retreating in the distance. In death, she looked thirteen. Her corpse was left in the middle of the road, a piece of paper pinned to it with the pencilled warning, 'This is the fate awaiting all Czech traitors.'

Radomir Luza

The author later learned that the informer had been forced to work for the Gestapo after she and her husband, who had been members of the Resistance, were captured. She had subsequently betrayed scores of her fellow Czechs.

‡

The Battle of the Bulge

On 16 December, 24 German divisions moved forward in a counter-offensive through the Ardennes forest on a front 80 miles long, stretching from Monschau in the north to Trier in the south. The intention was to split the Allied armies in two and drive through to Antwerp, their main supply port. For the first few days the German advance was successful, owing to bad weather which negated Allied air superiority, the confusing presence of some Germans dressed as American troops, and the sheer scale and surprise of the attack. By 19 December, the focus of the 'Battle of the Bulge' was the key road junction at Bastogne, a Belgian town held by US paratroops, including Donald Burgett.

We continued working our way forward in this manner, forcing the Germans to keep their heads down with our steady fire, until we reached their holes and began engaging them in hand-to-hand combat. Once again we were amongst them. Many of the enemy were shot as they cowered in their holes by troopers firing down on them as they ran past.

We gained overwhelming fire superiority early on, and the enemy's fire slowed to a trickle. Our machine guns and semiautomatic M1 rifles gave us a decided advantage over the Germans and their bolt-action Mausers.

Jack wasn't hitting the ground anymore. He remained standing even when the rest of us stopped and fired from the prone or on one knee. He fired his machine gun from the hip, governing the strike of his bullets by watching the tracers, like a man squirting a garden hose. All this while he was screaming at the top of his lungs. I was only a few feet from him but for the life of me I couldn't make out what he was yelling. Later someone told me that he was yelling, 'I'm a Jew! I'm a Jew! You goddamned Krauts, I'm a Jew!' And he was killing them.

One German rose up from the ground in front of Dobrich and started to run toward our left flank. Dobrich fired once and the German went down hard, bursting into flames from head to foot. He was probably carrying a Molotov cocktail on him and the bullet must have exploded it, spraying him with flaming gasoline. The snow was melting around the German's body and I heard Dobrich yell, 'Do you see that? Do you see that?'

I hit the ground hard after a short run and was searching for a target when another German, not more than three feet in front of me, raised his head up and looked me straight in the eyes. He had been lying face down on top of the snow, and I had thought he was dead. I jammed the muzzle of my rifle against his forehead and pulled the trigger. He was dead for sure now.

Bielski was lying to my left, just a few feet forward. He fired the last round from the box of ammo on his left hip and rose to his knees to reload. Taking the box of ammo from the sling on his right hip he slammed it down next to the gun, lifted the cover of the receiver, and laid the belt in place. Just as he started to close the cover, a single bullet smashed squarely into his forehead, ripped through his brain, and tore away the back of his skull. I saw steam issue from the back of his head and then he jerked back, staying upright on his knees with a shocked, wide-eyed expression on his face for a few moments, and then he fell forward over the gun. I rolled over to the gun and pulled Bielski's body off of it just as another trooper dove headfirst and slid in behind it. Bielski's body lay between me and the gun. The new trooper slammed the cover down and said he would take it from there. I felt rage boiling up with me. I shouted that it was my gun, that I would take it.

'Never mind,' he yelled back. 'I've already got it. I'll take it.' He jerked the bolt to the rear, slammed it forward, and then did it again before firing a long, sweeping burst to the left and right.

This was no time to argue. I looked up to the front, scanning the forest floor. There, just a little to the right and about two hundred feet out, I spotted two German-helmeted heads, one moving slowly to the right and the other moving to the left. Somehow I knew that one of those men had fired the shot that killed Bielski.

Taking careful aim at the helmet on the right I took the slack out of the trigger and squeezed slowly, deliberately, carefully. My rifle bucked; the head snapped back and disappeared.

'That's one,' I muttered aloud.

Carefully aligning my sights on the other helmet, which was still moving toward the left, I fired another well-placed shot. He too went down hard.

'That's two,' I said.

Second Lt Anthony 'Tony' Borrelli's 3rd Platoon, our 2nd Platoon, and men from 1st Platoon were all converging toward the ground where the main force of the enemy had dug in. The men from C Company were swinging forward on our left flank. We were amongst them. Fighting swirled around in a mad staccato of small-arms fire and paratroopers' yells. German bodies lay everywhere. We didn't look back to see who of our own we might be leaving dead in our wake. I saw an enemy head poke up out of the ground not more than fifteen feet away. I couldn't miss. I pointed my rifle like a shotgun, fired, and the head dropped straight down out of sight. Then I flopped on my belly next to a small tree, looked to see if I could spot any more Germans, and at the same time wondered if I had hit the German I'd just shot at. It dawned on me that he hadn't fallen right when I fired at him.

While I was lying there thinking about it, he suddenly popped up and, with one fluid movement, fired point-blank at me. The bullet passed between my head and the tree I was peeking around, cutting off a small, pencil-sized branch and my helmet's chinstrap. The chinstrap flipped up, striking me just under my left eye. The impact was such that I thought the bullet had passed through the left side of my head. I was stunned, more by the thought than the hit, and dropped my face into the snow, playing possum, pretending I was dead.

The German had slapped his bolt home and stood up in his foxhole, exposed from the chest up. I peeked at him though slitted eyes from under the rim of my helmet as he looked me over for a very brief moment and then took careful aim at the top of my head. My rifle was still in my right hand but lying out in front of me. I knew I could never get it up in time to shoot him. It was too late to do anything. Damn, I thought. Why did I have to go and miss? My body tensed in anticipation of the bullet strike.

At that moment something must have caught his eye, for he turned quickly to his right and fired at one of the troopers coming in from our left, one of Lieutenant Borrelli's men. Snatching my rifle up, and this time taking quick aim, I pulled the trigger as he worked his bolt. His helmet went spinning through the air and he jerked hard to one side and crumpled to the bottom of his hold. I ran over to where I could see him awkwardly folded over. I reached down and yanked him out of the hold with one hand. My bullet had entered his left cheek and taken his right ear off on its way out. I remember being amazed at my own strength. I could never have lifted a grown man out of a hole with one hand under normal conditions.

I let his body drop to the ground next to the foxhole and jumped in. I laid my rifle across his belly and used him like a sandbag while I fired. It was then that I noticed his belt buckle. It was not the square eagle stamped with the Wehrmacht's 'Gott Mit Uns' motto, but the flying eagle of the Fallschirmjäger (paratroops). Was he a German paratrooper attached to the infantry? Or was he just an infantryman wearing a piecemeal uniform? I pulled his belt from him and fastened it around my own waist to save as a souvenir of our encounter. I still have that buckle to this day.

Donald R. Burgett

The 101st Airborne Division was not relieved until Boxing Day by Patton's army, which had raced up from southern France, but it had prevented Bastogne from being taken by a force nine times its own size.

'The sonofabitch tried to make a run for it'

As Captain Charles Macdonald learned, it was not only the SS who shot prisoners.

The lead platoon advanced three hundred yards and reported that they had reached the objective. I moved again to the head of the column and saw that the two firebreaks formed an intersection. I directed the scouts to follow the clearing to the right until they should reach the north–south firebreak which should have been our left flank. We would dig in there for the night.

The column started forward and then stopped abruptly. A slow, moaning voice came from the patch of small firs growing beyond the narrow ribbon of white that was the firebreak.

'Help! Help!' the voice cried, each word slow and deliberate. 'Save me. Save me.'

Every man stopped as if each had dropped an instantaneous anchor, and rifles dropped to the ready position as if by instinct. Darkness was almost completely upon us, and the men peered in vain toward the patch of firs to determine the source of the voice.

'Help me,' the voice continued, the words heavily accented and spoken so mournfully that I could have sworn I felt the hair bristle on the back of my neck. 'I am wounded. Help me.'

'Come on out with your hands up,' someone yelled.

'I cannot come,' the voice said slowly, as if it were torture to utter each word. 'I am blind. I cannot see you.'

'Come out or we'll shoot.'

'I cannot come. Please come and get me. Do not shoot. I am blind. I cannot see.'

The same thought must have entered all our minds. This was a German trick to lure us into the open firebreak. I ran forward to the head of the column, apprehensive lest someone should decide to go out into the open toward the voice.

'Come out with your hands up or I'll shoot your nuts off, you Nazi sonofabitch!' a soldier yelled.

He fired a single shot into the underbrush.

The fir branches stirred. A dark figure emerged slowly from the brush, and I could see that it was a German soldier with his hands raised high above his head. He wore no cap or helmet, but a dirty, blood-stained bandage stretched across his forehead. Choosing each step carefully, he advanced across the firebreak.

'Do not shoot. Do not shoot.'

Two of my men grabbed him roughly and searched him for weapons.

'I have no gun,' the German said in carefully chosen English. 'My comrades have left me when I am wounded.'

'Bring him along,' I said, designating two men to walk with him. 'We'll send him back when we get where we're going.'

I noticed for the first time the bodies of two Germans near the point where we had stopped. One still breathed. An aid man examined him briefly.

'Nothing we can do,' he said. 'He's dying fast.'

I wondered how they were killed.

We continued along the edge of the trees until we crossed the north–south firebreak. I halted the column and sent a patrol from the 1st Platoon to continue to the west until they contacted the left flank of L Company. I reported our location to battalion and assigned defensive sectors to the three rifle platoons. Our main defence would face to the south, but the 3rd Platoon would defend our flank along the north–south firebreak, facing east. Numerous abandoned slit trenches filled the area, and the men began improving them for the night.

I turned my attention to the prisoner, directing the two men who were with him to take him to the A Company positions. I had lost contact with the rear CP group by radio and wanted them to contact Lieutenant Smith, who should be at the A Company positions now. The men were afraid they could not find the positions. Our circuitous route through the woods had confused them, but they said they would try.

'Would you be kind to give me cigarette?' the prisoner asked.

'Why you Nazi sonofabitch,' one of the guards answered, kicking the prisoner in the rear, 'of all the goddamned nerve. If it wasn't for you and all your —— kind, all of us could be smoking now.'

The patrol from the 1st Platoon returned. L Company's left flank was fifty yards beyond the right flank of the 1st Platoon. They were digging in for the night.

K Company reported by radio that they contacted the left flank of my 3rd Platoon and were setting up their defence along the north–south firebreak. The night was quiet except for the scrape of shovels upon frozen ground and the distant pounding of artillery.

The two men who had taken the prisoner to the rear returned. They had made a quick trip.

'Did you get him back OK?' I asked.

'Yessir,' they answered and turned quickly toward their platoons.

'Wait a minute,' I said. 'Did you find A Company? What did Lieutenant Smith say?'

The men hesitated. One spoke out suddenly.

'To tell you the truth, Cap'n, we didn't get to A Company. The sonofabitch tried to make a run for it. Know what I mean?'

'Oh, I see,' I said slowly, nodding my head. 'I see.'

Charles B. Macdonald

By the end of January, the Germans had been forced to retreat from all the initial gains they had made during the battle. It left their army severely depleted and ill-equipped for the defence of their homeland.

✝

Last days at Auschwitz

Primo Levi, a scientist and Italian Jew, had formed a guerrilla band but was arrested by the Fascists in December 1943. 'I had the good fortune to be deported to Auschwitz only in 1944,' he later wrote, 'that is, after the German Government had decided, owing to the growing scarcity of labour, to lengthen the average life-span of the prisoners destined for elimination.' At the beginning of 1945, with the Russians advancing through Poland, the Germans abandoned the camp, leaving the prisoners to fend for themselves.

22 *January*. If it is courageous to face a grave danger with a light heart, Charles and I were courageous that morning. We extended our explorations to the SS camp, immediately outside the electric wire-fence.

The camp guards must have left in a great hurry. On the tables we found plates half-full of a by-now frozen soup which we devoured with an intense pleasure, mugs full of beer; transformed into a yellowish ice, a chess board with an unfinished game. In the dormitories, piles of valuable things.

We loaded ourselves with a bottle of vodka, various medicines, newspapers and magazines and four first-rate eiderdowns, one of which is today in my house in Turin. Cheerful and irresponsible, we carried the fruits of our expedition back to the dormitory, leaving them in Arthur's care. Only that evening did we learn what happened perhaps only half an hour later.

Some SS men, perhaps dispersed, but still armed, penetrated into the abandoned camp. They found that eighteen Frenchmen had settled in the dining-hall of the SS-Waffe. They killed them all methodically, with a shot in the nape of the neck, lining up their twisted bodies in the snow on the road; then they left. The eighteen corpses remained exposed until the arrival of the Russians; nobody had the strength to bury them.

But by now there were beds in all the huts occupied by corpses as rigid as wood, whom nobody troubled to remove.

The ground was too frozen to dig graves; many bodies were piled up in a trench, but already early on the heap showed out of the hole and was shamefully visible from our window.

Only a wooden wall separated us from the ward of the dysentery patients, where many were dying and many dead. The floor was covered by a layer of frozen excrement. None of the patients had strength enough to climb out of their blankets to search for food, and those who had done it at the beginning had not returned to help their comrades. In one bed, clasping each other to resist the cold better, there were two Italians. I often heard them talking, but as I spoke only French, for a long time they were not aware of my presence. That day they heard my name by chance, pronounced with an Italian accent by Charles, and from then on they never ceased groaning and imploring.

Naturally I would have liked to have helped them, given the means and the strength, if for no other reason than to stop their crying. In the evening when all the work was finished, conquering my tiredness and disgust, I dragged myself gropingly along the dark, filthy corridor to their ward with a bowl of water and the remainder of our day's soup. The result was that from then on, through the thin wall, the whole diarrhoea ward shouted my name day and night with the accents of all the languages of Europe, accompanied by incomprehensible prayers, without my being able to do anything about it. I felt like crying, I could have cursed them.

The night held ugly surprises.

Lakmaker, in the bunk under mine, was a poor wreck of a man. He was (or had been) a Dutch Jew, seventeen years old, tall, thin and gentle. He had been in bed for three months; I have no idea how he had managed to survive the selections. He had had typhus and scarlet fever successively; at the same time a serious cardiac illness had shown itself, while he was smothered with bedsores, so much so that by now he could only lie on his stomach. Despite all this, he had a ferocious appetite. He only spoke Dutch, and none of us could understand him.

Perhaps the cause of it all was the cabbage and turnip soup, of which Lakmaker had wanted two helpings. In the middle of the night he groaned and then threw himself from his bed. He tried to reach the latrine, but was too weak and fell to the ground, crying and shouting loudly.

Charles lit the lamp (the battery showed itself providential) and we were able to ascertain the gravity of the incident. The boy's bed and the floor were filthy. The smell in the small area was rapidly becoming insupportable. We had but a minimum supply of water and neither blankets nor straw mattresses to spare. And the poor wretch, suffering from typhus, formed a terrible source of infection, while he could certainly not be left all night to groan and shiver in the cold in the middle of the filth.

Charles climbed down from his bed and dressed in silence. While I held the lamp, he cut all the dirty patches from the straw mattress and the blankets with a knife. He lifted Lakmaker from the ground with the tenderness of a mother, cleaned him as best as possible with straw taken from the mattress and lifted him into the remade bed in the only position in which the unfortunate fellow could lie. He scraped the floor with a scrap of tinplate, diluted a little chloramine and finally spread disinfectant over everything, including himself.

I judged his self-sacrifice by the tiredness which I would have had to overcome in myself to do what he had done.

Primo Levi

‡

The Yalta Conference

It was at Yalta, in the Crimea, that the post-war borders of Europe were largely determined. Stalin held many trump cards: not only was Russia's strength needed to defeat Germany, but Churchill and an ailing Roosevelt also wanted her to come into the war against Japan. The price of Stalin's help was to allow him considerable influence after the war in Eastern Europe, in particular Poland, the country whose independence had been the very cause of the war. Andrei Gromyko was a member of the Soviet negotiating team.

When Stalin spoke, which as a rule he did briefly, his opinions often grated on the ears of the Western leaders. Although his phrases in themselves were not harsh, still less crude, and he was tactful, what he said made a powerful impression.

It was striking that, while Roosevelt reacted to Stalin's remarks calmly, even with understanding, Churchill did so with barely concealed irritation. The British Prime Minister tried not to show his feelings, but his cigars gave him away. He smoked far more of them when he was tense or excited. The number of his cigar stubs was in direct proportion to the stresses of the meeting. Everyone noticed it, and mocking remarks were made about it behind his back.

It should be said in fairness that Stalin had a liking for Roosevelt – which could not be said about his attitude towards the British Prime Minister. To some extent he may have been showing sympathy for the President's infirmity, but I and other Soviet officials were convinced that a more important reason for this difference of attitude had to do with the politics of the two Western leaders.

I cannot remember a single occasion at the conference when Stalin misheard or misunderstood a major statement from either of his two partners. His memory worked like a computer and missed nothing. As never before, during the sessions in the Livadia Palace, I came to realise just what extraordinary qualities this man possessed.

Stalin made sure that every member of the Soviet delegation was fully informed about what he regarded as the most important tasks facing the conference. He ran the work of the delegation with an assurance which conveyed itself to all of us, especially those sitting at the conference table.

Despite the lack of time, Stalin still found opportunities to talk with those within the delegation who were able, because of their position, to express a judgement or maintain contact with the Americans and British. These internal meetings varied in size, depending on the circumstances. On one occasion Stalin arranged a sort of cocktail party, during which he exchanged a few words with each member of the Soviet delegation, moving about slowly and with a pensive look on his face. From time to time he came to life and even made a joke. He knew everyone by sight; in fact, it was a matter of pride to him that he knew a great many people and could remember their names and often where he had met them. It would always impress.

Stalin moved on from group to group, stopping to ask questions. It was noticeable that he himself said very little, but listened attentively to what the others were saying. I had the feeling he was working all the time, preparing himself for the next meeting of the Big Three.

Approaching me Stalin asked, 'What are the main social elements that Roosevelt can count on for support inside his country?'

I replied: 'The American President above all defends the interests of his own class, of course – the bourgeoisie. His domestic policies may encroach to some extent on the interests of the large monopolies, and right-wing extremists sometimes make the absurd accusation that he is sympathetic to socialism but it's only a propaganda ploy by people who don't want the USA to have good relations with the USSR.' After a short pause, I summed up my answer: 'At the moment, Roosevelt as President has no rival. He feels secure.'

As far as I could judge, it was to these words that Stalin attended most of all.

Stalin also organised an official dinner for Churchill and Roosevelt to which the core personnel of the three delegations were also invited. There were not too many people present and one could hear everything anyone said. Naturally, everyone was keen to hear whatever the three leaders would say. Stalin was lively and made jokes, provoking friendly laughter which helped to produce a relaxed atmosphere. Major questions were not discussed during the dinner, and mostly the three leaders threw short, pithy comments back and forth. In essence, they were agreeing that they must secure a rapid end to the destruction being wrought by Hitler's army and do their best to see that Germany never rose again as an aggressor.

I do recall one of Stalin's less formal remarks during the dinner, however: 'History has recorded many meetings of statesmen following a war. When the guns fall silent, the war seems to have made these leaders wise, and they tell each other they want to live in peace. But then, after a little while, despite all their mutual assurances, another war breaks out. Why is this? It is because some of them change their attitudes after they have achieved peace. We must try to see that doesn't happen to us in the future.'

Roosevelt said, 'I agree with you entirely. The nations can only be grateful for your words. All they want is peace.'

At that moment, Churchill was in conversation with Molotov and so did not join in.

Everyone at the Yalta conference knew that the decisions taken in the Livadia Palace had immense significance for the peaceful future of Europe. We felt we were at the focus of history and that Justice was standing by, scales in hand.

Andrei Gromyko

The author became Soviet Foreign Minister in 1957.

‡

The Eastern Front

Disobedience

As the Germans continued to retreat in the East, their discipline started to evaporate. Here, a young lieutenant – the son of an evangelical pastor – recalls how he threatened an NCO with the ultimate sanction at his disposal.

On the evening of 12 February we crept into the Mischke forester's house. It was the only house for miles around. At night it was packed full of soldiers from various units. Following Hauptmann Wild's orders I tried to get my people, insofar as they were not outside on sentry duty, together in one room alone. My attempt failed. So I had to go round trying to free up at least a few corners of rooms for us. It was important, because the forester's house was on the front line in our sector. At any moment an enemy assault unit could attack. To be able to repulse it, the unit commander had to have his people together at all times ready for combat at the shortest notice. That, however, was not guaranteed if the members of a large number of different units were lying about, mixed up in the numerous rooms.

In the very first room I met resistance from a Feldwebel. The men around him, apparently his people, made room to a certain extent willingly, but he on the other hand remained lying down. I spoke to him sharply and gave him 'as an officer the direct order' to get up immediately and to leave the room with his people. He remained unaffected. 'I will give you two minutes. If you have not obeyed my order by then I shall shoot you!' I did not wait to see the effect of my words, but went to Hauptmann Wild, to report the incident to him. Wild sat in the light of my tallow candle, not looking up, and said drily: 'Do what you want.' 'Herr Hauptmann, I just can't simply shoot the man!' I exclaimed. But Hauptmann Wild, the brave man, the fatherly comrade and the pastor, seemed to be at the end of his strength. He did not express an opinion and he took no part in what was agitating me. He shifted on to my shoulders the responsibility for deciding and acting, and once again replied tonelessly and apathetically, 'Do what you want.'

Irresolute and uncertain I turned back, fearing that the chap would still be lying in his corner. That was in fact the case. I could no longer restrain myself. Stirred up to the highest degree, I shouted at him: 'Get up immediately and leave this room, or I shall shoot you on the spot!' Inwardly I was trembling. I wondered whether the chap would obey this order.

While my trembling fingers were reaching for my holster, another Feld-webel, one of his comrades, intervened to calm and to placate me. Even his words, that the man who was refusing to obey my orders was a tried and tested and excellent soldier, I turned against him, saying that in that case he should know all the better that he had to carry out my orders like any others. But even as I was saying this, and as the Feldwebel had pointed out to me, I felt that the behaviour of the man refusing to obey my order could not have any rational cause. He was completely exhausted and at the end of his strength.

What would have happened, if I had shot the man? Nothing would have happened. As in earlier retreats and crisis situations, it had become the duty of senior officers to use weapons in cases of refusals to obey orders. They could shoot the offender immediately and without a court martial. I was therefore, formally, completely within my rights. The facts of the case clearly attested to a refusal to obey orders. Moreover, my commander had expressly given me a free hand. The order was in fact completely well founded. But what were those men doing in our sector? Were they men who had been scattered or were they deserters? To establish which it was, I was much too agitated and did not have the time. I had only time for the shot that would re-establish discipline and order.

But I did not fire it! The man was almost as exhausted as I. Probably, just like me, he had not slept during the previous days and nights. He had most likely been overwhelmed by a physical, mental, and spiritual exhaustion that left him no longer in control of his actions. It would have been the same for me, if I had not been an officer, if I had not had to be a leader and if the enormous agitation about the inconceivability of this refusal to obey orders had not then overwhelmed me. A remnant of common sense within me restored my sense of proportion. I gained enough control over myself to be able to ponder whether the insignificance of the case was worth his death. Was it right that my order should be carried out by that man? So I came to the conclusion that I should not allow myself to be guilty of his death, even if I was in every respect justified in doing so, even if it was my duty to do so.

I walked out into the dark of the February night. I was oppressed by the dichotomy of feelings of defeat that my formalistic spirit had suffered. But I was also glad of my victory over that spirit. For one trembling moment, I had held the life of that man in my hand and nearly destroyed it. Outside, the Feldwebel comrade of the mutineer joined me and said that I was 'a fine man'. He seemed suddenly to trust me, because he had recognised me as a fellow countryman. Then, in all seriousness, he proposed that I should travel to Vienna with him. He had, he said, a motorcycle and sidecar, his unit had been wiped out and he had had 'enough'. With me as an officer, he said, we would easily get through the Feldgendarmerie checkpoint and through the Heldenklaus. I was speechless. Should I now have this man arrested, taken away, and shot? I shook my head, uncomprehendingly, without saying a word. He disappeared.

Armin Scheiderbauer

The High Command organised flying courts-martial, whose dispensation of justice was brutal and haphazard. Colonel Hans von Luck, who had just been posted to the front, soon experienced their arbitrary judgement.

On Hitler's orders any incipient defeatism, desertion, failure to carry out orders or malingering were to be nipped in the bud by the imposition of death sentences as a deterrent, against which there was no appeal. On the contrary, specially selected judge advocates, who were accompanied by a firing squad, could pronounce death sentences and have them carried out immediately, without informing, let alone hearing, the man's commanding officer.

A few weeks later I too was to be confronted with one of these 'flying drumhead courts-martial'.

I had sent one of my best sergeants, the highly decorated leader of an anti-tank platoon, to our workshop in the rear, with a couple of drivers, to bring forward some armoured tractors that were being repaired. I had told him to put the screws on as we needed the vehicles urgently. He passed word to me through a messenger that he would be arriving with the vehicles the following morning. What happened then was told me the next day by one of the drivers. In tears, hardly able to control his voice, he said, 'We were sitting together in the evening, after we had made sure that the last vehicles would be finished during the night, in a little inn, eating our day's ration and talking about the future, our homes and all the other things that soldiers talk about. Suddenly the door was pushed open and in rushed a staff officer with some military policemen. "I am the Chief Judge Advocate under the direct orders of Field Marshal Schoerner. Why are you sitting about here while up at the front brave soldiers are risking their lives?"'

'My platoon leader replied: "I was ordered by my regimental commander, Colonel von Luck, to bring some armoured vehicles that are being repaired here up to the front as quickly as possible. Work will be going on through the night. We'll be able to go back to the front tomorrow morning."

'The judge advocate: "Where is your movement order?"

'Answer: "I had it from the commander by word of mouth."

'Advocate: "We know about that, that's what they all say when they want to dodge things. In the name of the Führer and by the authority of the commander in chief Army Group Centre, Field Marshal Schoerner, I sentence you to death by shooting on account of proven desertion."

' "But you can't do that," shouted our platoon leader, "I've been at the front right through the war. Here, look at my medals."

'Advocate: "But now, when it matters and everyone is needed up at the front, you soon decided you'd like to dodge things after all, didn't you? The sentence is to be carried out."

'Then the military police took our platoon leader and shot him in the garden behind the inn.'

The man could hardly go on.

'We then had to bury him under the supervision of the MPs.' Deserters were not allowed to have a cross on their graves.

'After that the advocate disappeared as fast as he had come.'

Although we were in the middle of an action, I got in touch with divisional HQ, seething with rage, and reported the unbelievable occurrence. I demanded the name of the judge advocate, so that I could prefer a charge against him.

'That will hardly be possible,' one of the officers replied. 'Our divisional commander, General Marcks, is in full and complete agreement with Schoerner's measures.'

I was appalled. So we had come to this.

'For God's sake, one of my best platoon leaders has been shot without further ado and nothing is supposed to happen? I shall make a written report and insist that the judge advocate be found.'

Military events and the bitter end made it impossible for any amends to be made for a flagrant injustice. My men of the workshop company were at least able to tend the grave properly and put up a cross with name and unit. I informed the parents that their son had unfortunately met with a soldier's death 'in the performance of his duty'.

Hans von Luck

Even the advancing Russians had to deal with problems of cowardice and lack of discipline. Here, a lieutenant describes how he tried to hold together his tank unit as it fought its way towards the German frontier.

The Germans counter-attacked after some time, but only with infantry – their tanks stayed where they were. At that time our T-34s had already driven up to us, and together with them we repelled the attack. The German infantry fell back, while the German tanks opened fire on the village, setting some houses on fire. Combat at night is generally very hard, and this engagement lasted the whole night. You cannot see a thing; you only fire at flashes or barely visible shadows. In darkness you cannot see the results of your own fire and of course it is less effective than in daytime.

As far as I remember, there were at least thirteen to fifteen Tiger tanks, but I cannot say how many infantry they had – it was too dark. Just three T-34–85 tanks supported me. The tank crews were green and it was their first battle. They rarely fired on the German tanks, being afraid that the enemy would spot their muzzle flashes, and when the houses caught fire, they tried to retreat as far as possible into the dark shadow. Although they did not retreat far, their retreat had a bad effect on the morale of my soldiers, most of whom were also green, but even the old hands were scared. They held on with their last bit of strength, but kept on firing at the enemy. However, they were all looking back at our tanks – they were afraid that the tanks would just leave us and drive to the rear. So I had to run back and forth – first to the tanks in order to stop them, if they had retreated too far, bring them back or even ask them to fire, then run to see how Guschenkov was doing, and then back to my men. The whole village was on fire, shells were exploding all around, and bullets and shell splinters flew shrieking through the air. Our DP machine-guns and submachine-guns were firing. The Germans tried to attack our flank, but Guschenkov's machine-guns cut them down almost at point-blank range and they ceased their attacks.

Nevertheless, two or three soldiers abandoned their foxholes and hid behind a hut, which was still on fire. I brought them back to their initial place – back to the trenches. If you do not nip panic in the bud, then your unit becomes uncontrollable. This is why I strictly warned the squad leaders of those two soldiers who ran away from the trenches without order. So, almost all night long I had to run back and forth from trenches to tanks and then back to trenches, all the time under enemy fire. I was steaming, I was constantly thirsty; it was good that there was a well nearby, my orderly scooped water from the well with a canteen and I gulped it down. The whole village was on fire, it was as bright as day. I had to lead almost a company in action in these conditions – two platoons and a machine-gun platoon, plus I had to force our tanks to fire, while the tanks were always trying to retreat to a safe place. This running around almost cost me my life. I could be seen for miles in the burning village, so as soon as I jumped into a foxhole, a shell exploded on its breastwork. The breastwork was smashed, while Private Ivanov and I were deafened by the explosion. The worst thing was that the trench was just a few metres from a burning house and it was too hot in that foxhole. The foxhole was clearly visible against the glare of the burning house, but the second shot never came; apparently the Germans thought we were dead. I quickly moved to another foxhole, permitting Ivanov to go to the first aid station, as he was slightly shell-shocked.

Before dawn the Germans ceased fire and then altogether disappeared from our sight. Apparently, their mission was not to destroy our battalion and the Brigade, but rather to delay our offensive for as long as possible in order to rescue their units from destruction and encirclement in another sector of the front. Despite the intensity and length of the battle, our losses were insignificant.

Evgeni Bessonov

The Russians reached the River Oder – just 50 miles from Berlin – on 31 January 1945.

☦

The Far East

Over the Irrawaddy

Following his victory at Imphal, Slim pursued the Japanese into Burma. The principal obstacle that stood between him and Rangoon was the Irrawaddy River, several miles wide at its broadest point. Slim successfully deceived the Japanese as to his intentions, and in mid-February 1945 the bulk of his army began to attempt the crossing.

To watch across the great river as dawn breaks over ancient Pagan is to hold one's breath at so much beauty. Pagan, once the capital of Burma, was in all its glory at the time of the Norman Conquest; now, silent,

ruined, and deserted, it is still noble – and very beautiful. Its twelve
hundred temples, madder red or ghostly white, rise, some like fantastic
pyramids or turreted fairy castles, others in tapering pagoda spires, from
the sage green mass of trees against the changing pastel blues, reds, and
gold of sunrise. As a foreground flows the still dark yet living sweep of
moving water. Yet as the officers of 89 Brigade gazed disconsolately
towards Pagan in the chill of early morning, they are to be forgiven if the
beauty of the scene was somewhat lost to them. They had other and less
pleasant things to think about: their attempt at crossing had definitely
failed. Then suddenly, to their surprise, they saw a small boat bearing a
white flag put off from the opposite bank. In it were two Jiffs, who, when
they came ashore, said that the Japanese had marched out of Pagan and
moved hurriedly up river, leaving only troops of the Indian National Army
to garrison the town. Their one wish, now the Japanese were gone, was
to surrender. Quickly a platoon of the Sikhs with a British officer crossed
in the only available boats. True to their word, the garrison of Pagan
marched out and with smiles laid down their arms. By evening most of
the Sikh battalion was established in the outskirts of Pagan. This incident
was, I think, the chief contribution the Indian National Army made to
either side in the Burma War.

Back at the main crossing, while all this was going on at Pagan, the
engineers were working feverishly to repair the returned boats for a new
crossing. The South Lancashire Company on the east bank reported it was
now firmly dug in and had not so far been attacked. It was, therefore,
decided to make a second effort to reinforce it. The Brigadier judged it
would take too long to reorganise the South Lancashires, so he ordered a
Punjabi battalion to make the crossing as soon as possible. The 4/15th
Punjabis, with great calmness and in excellent order, embarked on what
promised to be a most hazardous enterprise. At 9.45 a.m. their leading
company set out under the heaviest covering fire that could be provided
by artillery and air. As the boats chugged slowly across they were hardly
fired on at all; it seemed that there were still no Japanese at the actual
crossing and that even those downstream, who had taken such toll of the
South Lancashires as they drifted past, had withdrawn. Some of the boats
grounded on sandbanks but the men waded or swam ashore. The whole
company reached the beaches intact and swarmed up the cliffs. The curtain
of covering fire moved ahead of them and swept their flanks. As soon as
the boats were available the rest of the battalion began to cross, and
throughout the afternoon heavily laden craft continued to go to and fro
practically unmolested. By nightfall three battalions were over, and ferrying

had stopped as the risk of losing boats in the treacherous current in the dark became too great.

William Slim

Second Lieutenant Kazuo Imai was an officer in 215 Infantry Regiment. Although it was still below strength after its losses at Imphal, it was now ordered to attack the beaches where Slim's troops were landing.

'Enemy in the river!' someone cried. By the light of the flare bomb I saw several silhouettes of boats moving towards the beach from upstream. I could not judge whether they were boats that had drifted from the crossing or those of the enemy trying to attack us, and I called, 'Light machine gun.' The black figure lying on the ground on my left front answered, 'Machine gun, out of order.' So I cried back, 'Disassemble and clean the gun.' Then I contemplated what I should do. Mortar bombs began to fall around us and I smelled burning powder. The mortars seemed to be beyond the plateau.

A medium machine gun commanded by Lt Yokoyama was set down five metres to my right. The gun began to fire aiming at the river and over my body. It was really unbearable to lie flat so close to the front of the medium machine gun. From the shock of firing that blew up sand dust, I felt as if my internal organs would be blown out. I turned my face and tried to endure the torture. I saw the silhouette of a man fall from a boat which came close to the beach. I thought the boats were carrying enemy reinforcements. Because of the continuous shooting of the machine gun near my ear, I was deafened again.

The medium machine gun switched its aim to the plateau. I thought this an excellent time for a change and tried to raise my body but I could not stand up as my right foot was too painful. 'Platoon Leader! What are you doing?' Commander Midorikawa threw himself down, and asked, 'Are you hurt? Foot?' He sat on the sand cross-legged and watched the enemy lines which were well lit by the flare bombs, while tracer bullets flew here and there. The enemy had several firing points on the plateau just in front of us, which our machine gun was sweeping. So they were in chaos; some men ran up the slope, some slipped down to the sand, and some stood up raising both hands, probably as a sign of surrender. It was a good opportunity to charge the enemy line. Our commander cried to them twice, 'I will help you!' He said to me, 'Imai, lend me your sword.

My sword is ruined. I will rush in.' I gazed up at the coughing commander and saw something like blood coming out from his mouth, and tried to call out to him. Then a mortar bomb fell very close to me and I buried my face in the sand to cushion the explosion. When I raised my head, he was not there. Before I could ask how he was, tracer bullets came buzzing around me.

I noticed that bullets from our medium machine gun were hitting the sand in front of me. The machine gunner was dead with his head down, still pressing the trigger knob. A shadowy figure pushed aside the gunner and started to fire. A very bright flare shone on him and the enemy machine guns targeted the gun; our second gunner was shot in his face and lay prone. Undeterred, a third gunner took the position and fired, and soon the ammunition ran out. I heard the voice, 'No bullets!' and the voice of the commander, 'Machine gun, retreat!' I felt relieved to know he was well and strong. The gunner lifted and held the barrel; a very quick action. Another man who held the tripod fell down as if in a slow-motion movie.

Somebody came crawling to me. It was Lance Corporal Shimada who said, 'Platoon Leader, I got hit.' He stretched out his arm to me. His entire arm to the fingers was burning, as he said, having been hit by a flare shell. It could not be quenched even though he pushed his arm into the sand. I hesitated for a while but then told him, 'You may retreat.'

The medium machine gun had been withdrawn and we were left alone to stand fast in the sand. All light machine guns in the company, one Type 11 and two Type 99s, were jammed because of the sand. The battlefield was as bright as in daytime due to flare bombs. Unless we destroyed enemy firing points by supporting guns, it would be impossible to rush the enemy. Enemy firing became more fierce and I could hardly lift my head. By chance I remembered our Grenade-launcher Section, and called, 'Command Unit. Master Sergeant Morohashi.' This was relayed by several people and from 30 metres on my right the reply came, 'Master Sergeant Morohashi here.' As I was about to say, 'Grenade-launcher Section', several of my grenades exploded together. I was choked by the terrific explosion and lost consciousness.

When I came to myself, it was dark all around. It took me some time to understand the situation, but I realised that our troops had retreated and felt suddenly alone. I moved to my right. Though I felt several dead bodies, I could not tell who they were. Here and there cinders of flare shells were burning with blue-white flames. I saw a corpse lying face up and burning, possibly hit by a flare shell. I crawled to him and recognised him, 'Ah! Master Sergeant Morohashi.' I called out, 'Twelfth Company, Twelfth

Company!' A flare shell lit around me, and tracer bullets flew. I moved backward saying, 'Anyone wounded? We are to retreat.' Nobody reacted to my call. I could do nothing to these many dead soldiers. Suddenly I felt that I could no longer stand the fear.

I reached the beach and stepped into the river which was shallow for some distance, and lowered my body into the water. A gulp of water tasted so refreshing although it had looked dark red and turbid, and I recovered my senses. I moved along the beach downstream, half floating in the water. After a while I was almost dragged into the main stream and could hardly get to the shore. I met two soldiers limping; one was Private Iijima. A mortar shell exploded near us. I was told, 'Your sword is shining.' Indeed, I was gripping the drawn sword in my right hand.

Kazuo Imai

The attack failed, and when Slim's armour pushed on quickly to take Meiktila, their main supply base, the Japanese began to retreat eastwards.

‡

Iwo Jima

The Americans needed the island of Iwo Jima as a fighter base as well as a landing ground for bombers returning from missions over Japan itself. On 19 February, they landed on the volcanic isle, held by 21,000 troops. The invasion was expected to last eight days. However, because the Japanese had hidden themselves in a network of tunnels, the fighting lasted far longer. Here, US Marine Corps journalists describe the struggle just to take one small ridge.

Finally flame-throwers were called. They threw long jets of flaming liquid into the holes and along the curving walls of the tunnels. The roaring flames did the trick. The Marines heard the Japs howling. A few rushed out of the caves on fire. The Marines shot them or knocked them down and beat out the flames and took them prisoner. When the Marines began to hear muffled explosions inside the caves, they guessed that some of the Japs were blowing themselves up with hand grenades.

The scene became wild and terrible. More Japs rushed screaming from the caves. They tumbled over the rocks, their clothes and bodies burning fiercely. Soon the flame-throwers paused. A Marine lifted himself cautiously into view. There were no shots from the caves. A Jap with his clothes in rags hunched himself out of one hole, his arms upraised. The Marines stood up behind the rocks and waved to him to come out. The

Jap indicated that there were more who would like to surrender. The Marines motioned him to tell them to come out.

Almost forty scared and beaten men emerged from different holes. Some of them had round pudding faces. They grinned nervously and said they were Koreans. They had been forced by the Japs to stay in the caves. They said that everyone else in the caves had either been burned to death or had committed suicide.

The Marines sent them to the rear. Then they groped cautiously among the rocks from hole to hole, examining each entrance-way. Dead bodies, some hit by bullets and grenade fragments, some burned into frightful black lumps, lay in the holes. The smell was overwhelming and men turned away in disgust.

The battle of the ridge seemed over. An officer made a note to bring up demolition crews as soon as they could be spared by the front-line companies. They would seal up the holes in this troublesome ridge. The Marines gathered their casualties and drifted away. The tanks shifted into reverse and backed out. Peacefulness settled once more over the area.

But it was not for long. The sudden death, which we had come on, was to strike again from the ridge, this time bitterly close.

The same day, several hours later, Sergeant Reid Chamberlain (El Cajon, Calif.) came up to the aid station. He was on his way to a front-line company. Chamberlain was a prominent figure in the Marine Corp. He had served with General MacArthur on Bataan and Corregidor early in the war. He had escaped from Corregidor to help organise Filipino guerrilla bands. He had stayed in the Philippines a year and a half and had been commissioned a lieutenant in the US Army. Finally he had returned to America and been awarded the Distinguished Service Cross. Then he had resigned his Army commission, re-enlisted as a sergeant in the Marines, and had come overseas again. He was now a batallion runner with the 21st Regiment. He was short and handsome and wore a brown mustache.

Despite the publicity that had been given to his exploits as a guerrilla leader in the Philippines, he had stayed modest and unassuming and was one of the most popular men in the outfit.

A small group of us accompanied Chamberlain to the front-line company. We began to cross the clearing which we thought had been rid of Jap sniper fire. To escape occasional mortar shells that were dropping in the open, we clung perhaps too closely to the rocky walls of the ridge. We were picking our way among the stones and the burned Jap bodies when three shots rang out from the hillside. We scattered and tried to run behind some boulders. Chamberlain drew his pistol and looked frantically around.

There was another shot. We heard a thud. We thought the bullet had struck the curving side of the ridge.

When we reached safe spots, we paused and looked back. Our hearts beat wildly. Chamberlain was nowhere in sight. An ambulance driver and an automatic rifleman were crouched behind nearby rocks, their teeth clenched, their hands gripping their weapons. They were trying to find the hole from which the shots had come. We called Chamberlain but received no answer. Slowly we tried to edge back. Rifle shots cracked at us from serval holes, and we ducked again.

The long, rocky ridge was once more alive with enemy. Again Marines began to gather, coming up cautiously to help us. They dashed from rock to rock and slid among the boulders, trying to seek cover from the many caves that looked out at us. We told them about Chamberlain, lying somewhere among the rocks. We formed a team quickly and began crawling forward. When the Japs fired at us again, the men covering us saw where the shots were coming from. They sent a stream of automatic fire at the holes and 'buttoned up' the Japs. One burly sergeant stood straight up without a helmet on and, gritting this teeth, fired his carbine from his hip, moving directly at a hole as he fired. The jeep ambulance driver finally reached Chamberlain's body and lifted his head. A trickle of blood flowed from behind his ear. His eyes were open, but he was dead.

There is nothing you can say or do when a good friend is suddenly killed in battle. You feel stunned, angry, sad and somewhat frustrated. We could have fired point-blank the rest of the day at those holes. The Japs would only have laughed at us. In an instant they had claimed one of our best men. Chamberlain's wonderful war record had ended abruptly. After so many heroic deeds, it seemed an added tragedy that he was killed while doing nothing but walking. There was nothing anybody could do about it.

United States Marine Corps correspondents

Although it was on 23 February that the Marines famously raised the Stars and Stripes on Mount Suribachi, it was not until 26 March that all resistance ceased. Just 200 Japanese soldiers were taken prisoner.

Kamikaze

*Both on the ground and in the air, Japanese troops took pride in dying for their
cause. Tadashi Nakajima's 201st Air Group was selected by Admiral Ohnishi –
the originator of the kamikaze concept – to be the first unit to employ suicide tactics.
Nakajima's men proved willing sacrifices.*

In analysing the attitude of these men it must be remembered that they
considered kamikaze attacks merely a part of their duty. On many
occasions, I heard them express this sentiment in words such as these,
'When we became soldiers we offered our lives to the Emperor. When
we sortie, it is with the firm conviction that we will fulfil this offer to help
defeat the enemy. We would be remiss in thinking otherwise. Therefore,
"special attack" is just a name. The tactic, while unusual in form, is just
another way of performing our military obligation.'

This opinion prevailed generally and it was certainly true of the 201st
Air Group pilots in the Philippines. Their sorties were a routine matter.
There were no theatrics or hysterics. It was all in the line of duty.

In the ordinary pattern of events a kamikaze sortie would follow soon
after the sighting of an enemy task force. Let us say that a reconnaissance
detects such a target at 0800. The sighting would be radioed to headquarters
in Manila, where it would be relayed to an appropriate special attack base.
This procedure usually took about two hours. By the time the pilots were
alerted and briefed, planes readied and taking off, another two hours would
have elapsed. Thus it has to be estimated that four hours would pass
between the time the enemy task force was observed and a special attack
was on its way to strike.

In this time situation the pilots would usually be given a box luncheon
while they waited. On receipt at our base of a sighting, my own work was
completely frenzied until the planes actually took off. There was no time
for anything but essential work. When I would finally rush to brief the
pilots before their departure, some one or another of them, seeing how
busy I was, would usually offer his lunch to me.

As they awaited my briefing I would frequently hear snatches of the
pilot's conversation, such as, 'How about aiming for the funnel of a
carrier? It would probably be very effective, since a funnel is lightly
armoured.'

'Yes, but funnels are usually curved, so it is hard to hit into them.'

Such talk always seemed more like a discussion of a good fishing place
than an analysis of a rendezvous with death. Observing the pilots of the

the men of the ground crews to keep planes in the best possible condition. On occasion a pilot would come running to me at sortie time and implore, 'Commander, engine trouble! Give me another plane!'

In such a predicament it would do no good to order another plane brought up, because the rest of the flight could not wait. I would rack my brain for a satisfactory way of telling the dispirited pilot that he must abandon thoughts of making his flight that day. 'The others have already gone. It would have been impossible for you to catch them. This is sad for you but it can't be helped. Go and rest. This was an act of Divine Providence. You will have a better chance next time.'

It was always pathetic to see a pilot fail to make his sortie. He would walk away and sit alone to watch his comrades fly high into the sky. No words could console him.

Tadashi Nakajima

✠

The bombing of Dresden

On 13 and 14 February, more than 1,100 Allied bombers pulverised the historic and lightly defended German city of Dresden. Perhaps as many as 70,000 people were killed, many of them refugees from the East. Victor Klemperer and his wife Eva were among those caught up in the devastating firestorm.

We very soon heard the ever deeper and louder humming of approaching squadrons, the light went on, an explosion nearby . . . Pause in which we caught our breath, we knelt head down between the chairs, in some groups there was whimpering and weeping – approaching aircraft once again, deadly danger once again, explosion once again. I do not know how often it was repeated. Suddenly the cellar window on the back wall opposite the entrance burst open, and outside it was bright as day. Someone shouted: 'Incendiary bomb, we have to put it out!' Two people even hauled over took special care to...

mortified a pilot would feel in such a case...

trouble, the pilot's discouragement was pitiful to behold. Knowing...

likely to fail in its mission. If it returned to base because of mechanical

mechanical condition of their charges. A poorly maintained plane was

zealous in their devotion to duty, and they worried constantly about the

did his utmost to ensure its success. Plane mechanics were especially

As the special attack programme got under way, everyone concerned

all that was desirable for the task at hand.

201st Air Group, I was convinced that their spirit and morale epitomised

round with hand... called at our door 'Air-raid w...'

we have heard nothing more of either... fires were...

street was bright as day and almost empty, there was a steel-helmeted sentry

was blowing as before. As usual there was a steel-helmeted sentry...

of the wall between the two Zeughausstrasse houses (the wall of the former

synagogue with the barracks behind it). In passing I asked him whether

there was a warning. – 'Yes.' – Eva was two steps ahead of me. We came

to the entrance hall of no. 3. At that moment a big explosion nearby. I

knelt, pressing myself up against the wall, close to the courtyard door.

When I looked up, Eva had disappeared, I thought she was in our cellar. I

It was quiet, I ran across the yard to our Jews' cellar. The door was wide

open. A group of people cowered whimpering to the right of the door, I

knelt on the left, close to the window. I called out several times to Eva.

No reply. Big explosions. Again the window in the wall opposite burst

open, again it was bright as day, again water was pumped. Then an

explosion at the window close to me. Something hard and glowing hot

struck the right side of my face. I put my hand up, it was covered in blood,

I felt for my eye, it was still there. A group of Russians – where had they

come from? – pushed out of the door. I jumped over to them. I had the rucksack on my back, the grey bag with our manuscripts and Eva's jewellery in my hand, my old hat had fallen off. I stumbled and fell. A Russian lifted me up. To the side there was a vaulting, God knows of what already half-destroyed cellar. We crowded in. It was hot. The Russians ran on in some other direction, I with them. Now we stood in an open passageway, heads down, crowded together. In front of me lay a large unrecognisable open space, in the middle of it an enormous crater. Bangs, as light as day, explosions. I had no thoughts, I was not even afraid, I was simply tremendously exhausted, I think I was expecting the end. After a moment I scrambled over some vaulting or a step or a parapet into the open air, threw myself into the crater, lay flat on the ground for a while, then clambered up one side of the crater, over the edge into a telephone kiosk. Someone called out: 'This way, Herr Klemperer!' In the demolished little lavatory building close by stood Eisenmann sen. [senior], little Schor- schi in his arms. 'I don't know where my wife is.' – 'I don't know where my wife and the other children are.' – 'It's getting too hot, the wooden panelling is burning . . . over there, the hall of the Reich Bank building!' We ran into a hall, it was surrounded by flames, but looked solid. There seemed to be no more bombs exploding here, but all around everything was ablaze. I could not make out any details; I saw only flames everywhere, heard the noise of the fire and the storm, felt terribly exhausted inside. After a while Eisenmann said: 'We must get down to the Elbe, we'll get through.' He ran down the slope with the child on his shoulders; after five steps I was out of breath, I was unable to follow. A group of people were clambering up through the public gardens to the Bruhl Terrace; the route went close to fires, but it had to be cooler at the top and easier to breathe. Then I was standing at the top in the storm wind and the showers of sparks. To right and left buildings were blaze, the Belvedere and – probably – the Art Academy. Whenever the showers of sparks became too much for me on one side, I dodged to the other. Within a wider radius nothing but fires. Standing out like a torch on this side of the Elbe, the tall building at Pirnaischer Platz, glowing white; as bright as day on the other side, the roof of the Finance Ministry. Slowly thoughts came to me. Was Eva lost, had she been able to save herself, had I thought too little about her? I had wrapped the woollen blanket – *one*, I had probably lost the other with my hat – around head and shoulders, it also covered the star. In my hands I held the precious bag and – yes, also the small leather case with Eva's woollen things, how I managed to hold on to it during all the clambering about is a mystery to me. The storm again and again tore at my blanket, hurt my head. It had begun to rain, the ground was soft and wet, I did not want to put anything down, so there was serious physical strain, and that probably stupefied and distracted me. But in between there was constantly present, as dull pressure and pang of conscience, what had happened to Eva, why had I not thought enough about her? Sometimes I thought: She is more capable and courageous than I am, she will have got to safety; sometimes: If at least she didn't suffer! Then again, simply: If only the night were over!

Victor Klemperer

The author was subsequently reunited with his wife.

‡

The hazards of war

Through the dirty window-panes I was looking at Yellow Section of 274 Squadron returning from an armed reconnaissance. Only three aircraft in the circuit out of four . . . and even then one of the three seemed to have been badly damaged by flak.

Desmond called me on the phone and asked me to come at once to the Control Tower. Just as I jumped into the jeep the two first Tempests landed in formation. A cluster of red Verey lights for the guidance of the third rose from the ACP's [Aerodrome Control Pilot's] trailer. Desmond was on the balcony of the tower, microphone in hand. Without bothering about the stairs I joined him quickly by shinning up the outside ladder. 'It's Alex,' he said, handing me his field-glasses, 'give him some advice.'

Poor Alex must have caught a packet from a 37 mm., and one of the legs of his undercart was dangling pitifully, the wheel half torn off. That leg must be got up at all costs; he would never succeed in landing on his belly like this.

'Hallo Alex! Pierre here, try to get your port leg up!'

No answer. I said it again, forcing myself to speak slowly and clearly. A few seconds later, at last, Alex's voice answered in the loudspeaker, hesitant and gasping: 'Sorry, I can't.'

'Try again,' I insisted. The row of his engine at full throttle, the propeller in fine pitch, brought everybody out. I could see people climbing on the roofs of the huts and crowding at doors and windows. Hibbert and Brooker arrived, anxiously following the evolutions of the plane as it dived, climbed, waggling its wings to try and free that blasted wheel. Finally after a dive an object detached itself from the plane, but there was still the oleo-leg.

'Alex, try your CO_2 bottle!' It was his last chance. With my glasses I could see the leg begin to come slowly up in jerks, almost into the cavity in the wing.

'Hallo Pierre, I have used up my CO_2 and the leg isn't fully locked yet.'

His voice was trembling. Poor kid! How well I understood his panic, all alone up there, struggling with all that complicated machinery which had now become a death trap. I could almost see him, drenched in sweat, out of breath, desperately hammering at the undercart lever, still pushing on the CO_2 bottle lever although it was empty.

The ambulance started up and moved to the far end of the runway, keeping its engine ticking over. The fire tender followed; the crew on the running boards looking like deep-sea divers in their asbestos suits. The MO's jeep arrived. Alex called me back.

'OK Desmond, coming in for belly landing. Switching off.'

'Christ! Clostermann, tell him to bale out!' shouted Brooker. Too late, he had switched off his radio.

The Tempest began its approach. I slid down the side of the ladder and leaped into a jeep. The fire tender got into gear and moved up to the front. People started running along the perimeter track. The Tempest lost height and quickly grew bigger. The brilliant disc of the propeller suddenly broke up as Alex switched off. He levelled out perfectly. Tail and flaps down, he approached the brick runway.

I trod on the accelerator, pursued by the fire tender's bell and the siren of the ambulance.

The Tempest was about to touch down – the transparent hood flew off through the air. Now! A terrific scraping noise, the propeller buckled up and the 8 tons fell at 200 miles an hour. With a crash like thunder the plane bounced a good 30 feet into the air before our horrified eyes, turned over and crashed on to its back, tail forward, in a sheet of flame. Bricks filled the air. A muffled explosion, a blinding light and, straightaway, terrible 20-yard tongues of flame, mingled with twisting spirals of black smoke scored with vivid flashes.

I jammed on the brakes 50 yards from the furnace and jumped out, while the fire-truck literally hurled itself into the flames, spitting carbonic foam through its six high-pressure nozzles. The fire crew leapt off, armed with axes, followed by the medical orderlies.

Thirty yards away the air was so hot that it burned your throat like spirits. White sparks began to spurt from the blaze as the ammunition caught. The dry crack of the explosions and the whistling of the fragments filled the air.

One of the firemen, trying to forge into the inferno, collapsed. He was hooked out from behind, like a blackened, smoking log. He climbed out of his asbestos suit bespattered with molten aluminium, staggered, and fell on his face, vomiting. The flames roared, the smoke stung our eyes. The firemen went on pouring gallons and gallons of milky liquid which splashed, turned into steam or ran over the bricks.

The heat was getting less all the same and the shattered carcase of the Tempest began to show through the tongues of fire – the disembowelled engine showing its copper viscera besmirched with earth, the skeleton of the tail plane, the fuselage broken up into three stumps, the wings ripped by the explosion of the belts of ammunition.

The fire was now almost vanquished. A vague shifting red glow could be seen beneath the boiling foam. Wading in up to our knees, we rushed in. The horrible stench of burning rubber caught our throats and made us retch. A fine white dust of powdered aluminium fell. Then the sound of axes breaking into the remains of the cockpit.

'Easy, chaps, easy!'

The gauntleted hands tore off the tangled fragments, threw back bits of white-hot metal that fell sizzling on the grass, and then . . . I don't know what impelled me to press on, closer.

Delicately, they eased out an inchoate red and black mass, to which scraps of charred cloth still adhered. The parachute and harness straps had burnt away, but underneath the bleeding crust you could imagine the white-hot metal buckles which had gnawed their way through to the bone.

I felt the sweat congeal on my back. Completely unnerved, my legs gave way and I sat down in the slush of foam and cinders and, bent double, retched and retched.

Pierre Clostermann

Spring 1945

The Far East

The sinking of the battleship Yamato

In order to thwart the American invasion of Okinawa, the Japanese dispatched the 67,000-ton Yamato *from the Inland Sea on 6 April 1945. She was spotted by American reconnaissance flights that day, and on the 7th she was attacked by some 380 aircraft. She was sunk by five large bombs and ten torpedoes. Approximately 2,475 of her crew were lost and 269 survived. One of the survivors was Yoshida Mitsuru.*

I crawl out the look-out port and stand on the starboard bulkhead of the bridge. The survivors are lined up on the brownish belly of the ship, a distant thirty or forty metres away, all with hands raised in unison. They must just have finished three shouts of *banzai!*

In a small cluster and moving as one, they look like toy soldiers, my heart goes out to them.

The last moment of Rear Admiral Ariga Kōsaku, captain of *Yamato*:

In the anti-aircraft command post on the very top of the bridge, still wearing his helmet and flak jacket, he binds himself to the binnacle.

Having completed the final dispositions – the code-books, the command for all hands to come on deck, and so on – he shouts *banzai* three times. On finishing, he turns to look at the four surviving look-outs standing by his side.

They are too devoted to this resolute ruddy-faced captain to be able to leave him. Seeing a resolve to die together crystallising among them, he slaps each on the shoulder, encourages them to keep their spirits up, and pushes them off into the water.

The final sailor presses his last four biscuits into the captain's hands, as if to show his innermost feelings. The captain takes them with a grin. As he has the second one in his mouth, he is engulfed along with the ship.

To eat biscuits at such a time! Iron nerves without equal.

Thus the words of the chief look-out. He too was unable to leave the captain's side. In the end he was thrown into the water while standing right next to the captain; but not having lashed himself down, he floated to the surface.

Fluttering atop the main mast, the great battle ensign is about to touch the water.

As I watch, a young sailor comes forward and clambers up to the base of the mast. Would he save the battle ensign, soul of this sinking giant?

No one could have ordered him to do so.

So he has chosen this glorious duty. How proud his death!

It seems foolish to think such thoughts now, but when I drop my glances to the hull of the ship towering above the water and to its exposed undersides, it looks like a great whale.

That this vast piece of metal, 270 metres long and 40 metres wide, is about to plunge beneath the waves!

I recognise near me many shipmates. That fellow, and that one.

This one's eyebrows are very dark, that one's ears very pale. All of them have childlike expressions on their faces; better, they are all completely without expression.

For each of them, it must be a moment of absolute innocence, an instant of complete obviousness.

For all I know, I too am in the same condition.

At what do they gaze with ecstatic eyes?

The eddies, extending as far as they can see. The boiling waves, interlocking in a vast pattern.

Pure white and transparent, like ice congealing around this giant ship and propping her up.

And the sound of the waves, deafening our ears, induces still deeper rapture.

We see a sheet of white; we hear only the thundering of the turbulent waters.

'Are we sinking?' For the first time, as if on fire, I ask myself that question. The spectacle is so mysterious, so resplendent, that I am overcome with the premonition that something extraordinary is about to happen.

The water already begins to creep up on the starboard half of the ship.

Bodies flying in all directions. It is not simply a matter of being swallowed by the waves. The pressure of the water boiling up sends bodies flying like projectiles.

The bodies become mere grey dots and scatter in all directions, effortlessly, happily. Even as I watch, a whirlpool runs fifty metres in one swoop.

And spray springs up at my feet; water contorted as in a fun-house mirror, gleaming in countless angles, countless formations, glitters before my nose.

In multiple mirrors the water engulfs human figures. Some pop back up; some hang upside down in the water.

This exquisite glass design colours the uniform white of the foam, as do stripes of pure blue scattered all over this blanket of bubbles. The effect of the churning created by the many eddies?

Just as my heart delights for a moment in this beauty, this gracefulness, I am swept into a large whirlpool.

Without thinking, I draw as deep a breath as I can.

Grabbing my feet and rolling up into a ball, like a baby in the womb, I brace myself and do my utmost to avoid being injured; but the snarling whirlpool is so strong it almost wrenches off my arms and legs.

Tossed up, thrown down, beaten, torn limb from limb, I think: o world, seen with half an eye at the last moment. Even twisted and upended, how alluring your form! How exquisite your colours!

This mental image, flitting past, is welcome solace for my suffocating breast.

Not one person managed to swim far enough away in time to escape this whirlpool.

They say that with a great ship like this one, the danger zone has a radius of 300 metres.

The decision to save the men came too late and robbed us of the margin of time needed to swim that distance.

All hands dead in battle – this has become our fate.

Yoshida Mitsuru

A kamikaze attack

Geoffrey Brooke was aboard the aircraft carrier Formidable *near Leyte Gulf when it was struck.*

Suddenly, without any warning, there was the fierce 'whoosh' of an aircraft passing very fast and low overhead and I looked up in time to see a fighter plane climbing away on the starboard side, having crossed the deck from aft at 50 feet. I was thinking casually what a stupid thing to do and that he was lucky not to get shot at, with a scare on, when the starboard bow Oerlikons opened up a stream of tracer at the retreating enemy. He banked steeply, showing the Japanese red blob markings, and flew down our starboard side, the focus of a huge cone of converging yellow balls as every close-range weapon on that side began to hammer away. I thought he was certain to buy it and stood watching until he passed behind the island. I remember PO Lambe at this moment standing with his hands up as a sign to the Avenger he was directing to stop, about 30 feet from me.

Then the Jap came into view again from behind the island, banking hard to come in towards the ship from the starboard quarter, apparently unharmed and by now the target of fewer guns. His silhouette changed to a thin line with a lump in the middle, and he seemed to hang in the air as he dived for the ship.

I waited for no more but sprinted to a hatchway some 20 yards forward on the port side. Expecting to be blown to bits at each stride, I arrived at the hatch just after a tubby leading seaman of the AHP called Chambers, who had homed in from another angle. He proceeded to trip down the steel ladder step by step so I launched myself at his back and we fell in a heap to the bottom. At the same moment there was a flash and a great crash shook the ship. I gave it a second or two to subside, during which the light from the rectangle of sky above turned to deep orange, and ran back up the ladder.

It was a grim sight. At first I thought the kamikaze had hit the island and those on the bridge must be killed. Fires were blazing among several piles of wreckage on deck a little aft of the bridge, flames reached right up the side of the island, and clouds of dense black smoke billowed far above the ship. Much of the smoke came from the fires on deck but as much seemed to be issuing from the funnel and this gave the impression of damage deep below decks. The bridge windows gaped like eye sockets and most of the superstructure was burnt black. The flight deck was littered with debris, much of it on fire, and there was not a soul to be seen.

I grabbed a foam generator nozzle from its stowage nearby and ran out the hose, indicating to a rather shaken turret-safety number who was lying down between the turrets of B group, to switch on the machine. Men began to pour up from the sides of the flight deck and I pushed the foam-erupting nozzle into someone else's hands, to go round the crews of the other machines who were getting to grips with the main fire. It was very fierce with occasional machine-gun bullets 'cooking off'. Smaller fires in the tow-motor park, fire-fighter headquarters and odd bits of aircraft scattered around were attacked with hand extinguishers. The AHP were pushing unburnt aircraft clear and carrying casualties below. Some enthusiast appeared from the boat deck to cause initial confusion by playing water hoses from there on to burning oil and petrol; both float and so the fires merely spread but this was dealt with. Generally speaking the foam machines – both old and new – did good work, some blistering and almost too hot to touch. Soon there were pools and mounds of foam all over the place and the pungent smell everywhere. Large reserves of manpower materialised which did sterling work under the Commander, dragging heavy lumps of scrap iron that had been aircraft to the cranes, bringing up fresh drums of foam compound, refilling hand appliances, and generally helping to clear up. With reserves in the Fleet Train we could not tie up hangar space unprofitably and whole though badly damaged aircraft were ditched without ceremony (except for a rush for the clock!). A boat deck crane would be trained over the flight deck to collect the load on a tripping hook; the crane would be swung over the sea and the hook tripped for a fine splash . . .

The Jap pilot had started his initial dive at the ship, but finding that he was overshooting the bridge decided to pull out (luckily for most of us originally on deck) and, after firing a cannon burst, had come round again. His coolness and audacity, to say nothing of skilful handling of the machine, were indicative that high-class pilots were being used on suicide missions. Several bits of Jap pilot and aircraft were found. I collected a piece of tyre, cannon shell, and part of his bomb-release mechanism; someone found his hand with wristwatch still on it (though not going!); a yellow silk jacket was discovered for'ard and Guns was to be seen during the general clean-up poking bits of Jap off the funnel with a long pole.

Geoffrey Brooke

‡

Okinawa

The battle for the large island of Okinawa, regarded as forming part of the Japanese mainland, began on 1 April. The American landing was the biggest naval operation of the Pacific war, involving 1,200 ships and 450,000 servicemen. General Ushijima's 32nd Army – 130,000 strong – was prepared for their coming.

The ridge was about a hundred feet high, quite steep, and we were on a narrow crest. Several discarded Japanese packs, helmets, and other gear lay scattered along the crest. From the looks of the muddy soil, the place had been shelled heavily for a long time. The ridge was a putrid place. Our artillery must have killed Japanese there earlier, because the air was foul

with the odour of rotting flesh. It was just like being back at Half Moon
Hill. Off toward our front, to the south, I had only a dim view through
the gathering gloom and curtain of rain of the muddy valley below.

The men digging in on both sides of me cursed the stench and the mud.
I began moving the heavy, sticky clay mud with my entrenching shovel
to shape out the extent of the foxhole before digging deeper. Each shovelful
had to be knocked off the spade, because it stuck like glue. I was thoroughly
exhausted and thought my strength wouldn't last from one sticky shovelful
to the next.

Kneeling on the mud, I had dug the hole no more than six or eight
inches deep when the odour of rotting flesh got worse. There was nothing
to do but continue to dig, so I closed my mouth and inhaled with short,
shallow breaths. Another spadeful of soil out of the hole released a mass of
wriggling maggots that came welling up as though those beneath them
were pushing them out. I cursed, and told the NCO as he came by what
a mess I was digging into.

'You heard him, he said put the holes five yards apart.'

In disgust, I drove the spade into the soil, scooped out the insects, and
threw them down the front of the ridge. The next stroke of the spade
unearthed buttons and scraps of cloth from a Japanese army jacket buried
in the mud – and another mass of maggots. I kept on doggedly. With the
next thrust, metal hit the breastbone of a rotting Japanese corpse. I gazed
down in horror and disbelief as the metal scraped a clean track through
the mud along the dirty whitish bone and cartilage with the ribs attached.
The shovel skidded into the rotting abdomen with a squishing sound. The
odour nearly overwhelmed me as I rocked back on my heels.

I began choking and gagging as I yelled in desperation, 'I can't dig in
here! There's a dead Nip here!'

The NCO came over, looked down at my problem and at me, and
growled, 'You heard him; he said put the holes five yards apart.'

'How the hell can I dig a foxhole through a dead Nip?' I protested.

Just then the Duke came along the ridge and said, 'What's the matter,
Sledgehammer?'

I pointed to the partially exhumed corpse. Duke immediately told the
NCO to have me dig in a little to the side away from the rotting remains.
I thanked Duke and glared at the NCO. How I managed not to vomit
during that vile experience I don't know. Perhaps my senses and nerves
had been so dulled by constant foulness for so long that nothing could
evoke any other response but to cry out and move back.

I soon had a proper foxhole dug to one side of the site of my first attempt. (A few spades full of mud thrown back into that excavation did little to reduce the horrid odour.) My buddy returned, and we began to square away our gear for the coming night. There was some small-arms fire to our left, but all was quiet around us. Duke was down at the foot of the ridge behind us with a map in his hand. He called us to come down for a critique and a briefing on the next day's attack.

Glad to leave the stinking foxhole, I got up and carefully started down the slippery ridge. My buddy rose, took one step down the ridge, slipped, and fell. He slid on his belly all the way to the bottom, like a turtle sliding off a log. I reached the bottom to see him stand erect with his arms partially extended and look down at his chest and belt with a mixed expression of horror, revulsion and disbelief. He was, of course, muddy from the slide. But that was the least of it. White, fat maggots tumbled and rolled off his cartridge belt, pockets, and folds of his dungaree jacket and trousers. I picked up a stick and handed him another. Together we scraped the vile insect larvae off his reeking dungarees.

That Marine was a Gloucester veteran with whom I had shared a hole on Peleliu and Okinawa. He was as tough and as hard as any man I ever knew. But that slide was almost too much for him. I thought he was going to scream or crack up. Having to wallow in war's putrefaction was almost more than the toughest of us could bear. He shook himself like a wet dog, cursed, and threw down the stick when we got him scraped free of maggots.

Eugene Sledge

The corpses were not just those of dead soldiers. There were almost half a million civilians on Okinawa, and they too sometimes found themselves in the line of fire.

It was the fourth day when we finally reached the other side of the island. The pitch-black night was falling fast, and we hurriedly started to dig in, while we could still see our silhouettes. Suddenly, a grenade exploded in the distance, and everybody stopped and looked toward the direction we thought it had come from. We could see four dark figures moving quietly down the road. We hollered 'Toamati!' (Japanese for 'Halt!'), and they started running even faster toward us! The four of us, highly trained, scared shitless, young marines, opened fire, and watched as they fell in their tracks.

Then, a piercing scream broke the black silence. For a split second, we all froze. Someone was still alive! Then, driven into action by the sound, we ran to the fallen forms and found that they were all civilians. We had killed civilians! We had shot innocent people.

The continuous screaming was coming from a baby, still tied to its mother's back. A bullet had pierced the mother, killing her instantly, and severing the baby's arm on the way out. Shocked, my mind and body turned to ice. I was literally frozen with horror. I wanted to run, to disappear, to hide forever from the shame! God, please wake me up from this nightmare!

There was no choice. God forgive us, there was no choice! Against our will, we did the only thing we could. We ended the baby's life quickly, the cries stopping suddenly. In the silence that followed, we buried all of them. Sweat took the place of the tears we could not shed. I felt empty, lifeless, stripped of the ability to feel any emotions. The last shreds of our own innocence died that night; the sound of a baby's cry would awaken that horrible memory, for ever.

George Lince

‡

'I am remembering the first man I slew'

There was this little hut on Motobu, perched atop a low rise overlooking the East China Sea. It was a fisherman's shack, so ordinary that scarcely anyone had noticed it. I did. I noticed it because I happened to glance in that direction at a crucial moment. The hut lay between us and B Company of the First Battalion. Word had been passed that that company had been taking sniper losses. They thought the sharpshooters were in spider holes, Jap foxholes, but as I was looking that way, I saw two B Company guys drop, and from the angle of their fall I knew the firing had to come from a window on the other side of that hut. At the same time, I saw that the shack had windows on *our* side, which meant that once the rifleman had B Company pinned down, he could turn toward us. I was dug in with Barney Cobb. We had excellent defilade ahead and the Twenty-second Marines on our right flank, but we had no protection from the hut, and our hole wasn't deep enough to let us sweat it out. Every time I glanced at that shack I was looking into the empty eye socket of death.

The situation was as clear as the deduction from a Euclidean theorem, but my psychological state was extremely complicated. S.L.A. Marshall once observed that the typical fighting man is often at a disadvantage because he 'comes from a civilisation in which aggression, connected with the taking of life, is prohibited and unacceptable'. This was especially true of me, whose horror of violence had been so deep-seated that I had been unable to trade punches with other boys. But since then life had become cheaper to me. 'Two thousand pounds of education drops to a ten rupee,' wrote Kipling of the fighting on India's North-West Frontier. My plight was not unlike that described by the famous sign in the Paris zoo: 'Warning: this animal is vicious; when attacked, it defends itself.' I was responding to a basic biological principle first set down by the German zoologist Heini Hediger in his *Skizzen zu einer Tierpsychologie um und im Zirkus*. Hediger noted that beyond a certain distance, which varies from one species to another, an animal will retreat, while within it, it will attack. He called these 'flight distance' and 'critical distance'. Obviously I was within critical distance of the hut. It was time to bar the bridge, stick a finger in the dike – to do *something*. I could be quick or I could be dead.

My choices were limited. Moving inland was inconvenient; the enemy was there, too. I was on the extreme left of our perimeter, and somehow I couldn't quite see myself turning my back on the shack and fleeing through the rest of the battalion screaming, like Chicken Little, 'A Jap's after me! A Jap's after me!' Of course, I could order one of my people to take out the sniper; but I played the role of the NCO in Kipling's poem who always looks after the black sheep, and if I ducked this one, they would never let me forget it. Also, I couldn't be certain that the order would be obeyed. I was a gangling, long-boned youth, wholly lacking in what the Marine Corps called 'command presence' – charisma – and I led nineteen highly insubordinate men. I couldn't even be sure that Barney would budge. It is war, not politics, that makes strange bedfellows. The fact that I outranked Barney was in itself odd. He was a great blond buffalo of a youth, with stubby hair, a scraggly moustache, and a powerful build. Before the war he had swum breaststroke for Brown, and had left me far behind in two inter-collegiate meets. I valued his respect for me, which cowardice would have wiped out. So I asked him if he had any grenades. He didn't; nobody in the section did. The grenade shortage was chronic. That sterile exchange bought a little time, but every moment lengthened my odds against the Nip sharpshooter. Finally, sweating with the greatest fear I had known till then, I took a deep breath, told Barney, 'Cover me,' and took off for the hut at Mach 2 speed in little bounds, zigzagging and dropping every dozen steps, remembering to roll as I dropped. I was nearly there, arrowing in, when I realised that I wasn't wearing my steel helmet. The only cover on my head was my cloth Raider cap. That was a violation of orders. I was out of uniform. I remember hoping, idiotically, that nobody would report me.

Utterly terrified, I jolted to a stop on the threshold of the shack. I could feel a twitching in my jaw, coming and going like a winky light signalling some disorder. Various valves were opening and closing in my stomach. My mouth was dry, my legs quaking, and my eyes out of focus. Then my vision cleared. I unlocked the safety of my Colt, kicked the door with my right foot, and leapt inside.

My horror returned. I was in an empty room. There was another door opposite the one I had unhinged, which meant another room, which meant the sniper was in there – and had been warned by the crash of the outer door. But I had committed myself. Flight was impossible now. So I smashed into the other room and saw him as a blur to my right. I wheeled that way, crouched, gripped the pistol butt in both hands, and fired.

Not only was he the first Japanese soldier I had ever shot at; he was the only one I had seen at close quarters. He was a robin-fat, moon-faced, roly-poly little man with his thick, stubby, trunklike legs sheathed in faded khaki puttees and the rest of him squeezed into a uniform that was much too tight. Unlike me, he was wearing a tin hat, dressed to kill. But I was quite safe from him. His Arisaka rifle was strapped on in a sniper's harness, and though he had heard me, and was trying to turn toward me, the harness sling had him trapped. He couldn't disentangle himself from it. His eyes were rolling in panic. Realising that he couldn't extricate his arms and defend himself, he was backing toward a corner with a curious, crablike motion.

My first shot had missed him, embedding itself in the straw wall, but the second caught him dead-on in the femoral artery. His left thigh blossomed, swiftly turning to mush. A wave of blood gushed from the wound; then another boiled out, sheeting across his legs, pooling on the earthen floor. Mutely he looked down at it. He dipped a hand in it and listlessly smeared his cheek red. His shoulders gave a little spasmodic jerk, as though someone had whacked him on the back; then he emitted a tremendous, raspy fart, slumped down, and died. I kept firing, wasting government property.

Already I thought I detected the dark brown effluvium of the freshly slain, a sour, pervasive emanation which is different from anything else you have known. Yet seeing death at that range, like smelling it, requires no previous experience. You instantly recognise the spastic convulsion and the rattle, which in his case was not loud, but deprecating and conciliatory, like the manners of civilian Japanese. He continued to sink until he reached the earthen floor. His eyes glazed over. Almost immediately a fly landed on his left eyeball. It was joined by another. I don't know how long I stood there staring. I knew from previous combat what lay ahead for the corpse. It would swell, then bloat, bursting out of the uniform. Then the face would turn from yellow to red, to purple, to green, to black. My father's account of the Argonne had omitted certain vital facts. A feeling of disgust and self-hatred clotted darkly in my throat, gagging me.

Jerking my head to shake off the stupor, I slipped a new, fully loaded magazine into the butt of my .45. Then I began to tremble, and next to shake, all over. I sobbed, in a voice still grainy with fear: 'I'm sorry.' Then I threw up all over myself. I recognised the half-digested C-ration beans dribbling down my front, smelled the vomit above the cordite. At the same time I noticed another odour; I had urinated in my skivvies. I pondered fleetingly why our excretions become so loathsome the instant they leave the body. Then Barney burst in on me, his carbine at the ready, his face grey, as though he, not I, had just become a partner in the firm of death. He ran over to the Nip's body, grabbed its stacking swivel – its neck – and let go, satisfied that it was a cadaver. I marvelled at his courage; I couldn't have taken a step toward that corner. He approached me and then backed away, in revulsion, from my foul stench. He said: 'Slim, you stink.' I said nothing. I knew I had become a thing of tears and twitchings and dirtied pants. I remember wondering dumbly: *Is this what they mean by 'conspicuous gallantry'?*

William Manchester

The author died in 2004.

✝

Into the Reich

'It was so wonderful and so true'

With the British advancing in the north, and the Americans and the French in the centre and the south, throughout March town after town in Germany fell to the Allies. The capture of Ellershausen by the 23rd Infantry of the US 2nd Infantry Division was described by one of its company commanders as 'perfect'.

The preparatory barrage began as I turned from the tanker to return to the company. Artillery shells whistled again and again over the trees to cascade in a cloud of dust and roaring explosion upon the hapless town beyond. Heavy mortar shells plunked into 81 mm barrels and joined in the explosive tumult falling on the town. The sound of the twelve machine guns and an assortment of smaller weapons reverberated over the countryside.

I ran back to the company. The 2nd and 3rd Platoons were in position, ready for the double-time assault toward the objective.

Three sleek P-47s emerged from the clouds, the sunlight glistening against their silver wings. Down and down they dived above the town, which looked now as if it would completely disappear in the smoke and confusion of the preparatory barrage. Their machine guns and cannon began to chatter and assert themselves above the din of the battle whose privacy they had invaded. Up and up they climbed, higher into the sky; and then as if they had suddenly spotted their prey, down, down once more, their machine guns and cannon barking derisively. Then they flew away toward the east, and we could see them dive on the next town, and one of the planes dropped a bomb.

Abad tried to say something to me, but I could not hear him above the noisy demonstration before us. I made out the word 'battalion' and told him to say that we were ready.

The artillery continued to whistle and explode on the town. The mortar shells dropped unheralded upon the objective. The machine guns chattered. A freakish lull appeared in the louder noises for a second, and I heard the 'plunk' of a 60 mm mortar shell being dropped into a mortar tube somewhere behind me. The 4th Platoon artillery could not resist getting in on the action.

The lone German on the hillside was waving his white flag more frantically than ever.

I was ecstatic with an elation born of excitement. The men around me were laughing and patting one another on the back. This preparation was something for the book, and the unexpected appearance of the planes had added the finishing touch.

I looked at my watch. Four minutes to go before the barrage would lift. The men in the two assault platoons knew that the time was near and stood in half-crouches like animals waiting for the moment to spring. The smiles were gone from their faces, and in their places had come expressions of determination. It seemed impossible that any human being could survive the pasting which Ellershausen had taken and was taking, but the Germans always came out again when they were not supposed to come out.

If only they get there just as the barrage lifts!

I heard the roar of the tanks tuning up their motors. *Any minute now.* Time stood still for an instant.

Almost time now . . . almost time . . . almost . . . GO!

The machine guns stopped firing. The scouts plunged from the woods with their comrades close behind them. The artillery and mortars fired their final rounds. I saw the platoon of tanks race from the woods in single file down the highway toward the draw. To the south I could see the lead riflemen from F Company emerge from the woods. Their tanks followed. They formed an approach-march formation on the open, downward sloping hillside, and I thought of the diagrams in the Army manuals.

My own men met the tanks at the rendezvous point with split-second precision. The tankers infiltrated their steel monsters into the formation and adjusted their speed to the slower pace of the foot soldier.

The light machine gunners began to fire again, the tracers from the light guns creasing the edge of the north forest, the tracers from the heavy guns forming an umbrella of fiery steel over the heads of the advancing infantrymen. The lone German stranded on the hillside waved his white flag.

The timing, the formations were perfect. I looked at the men around me, and they looked at me and at each other. The last time we had seen an attack like this was in the training films back in the States. They didn't make attacks this way in actual battle. Something always went wrong. No, they didn't make them this way in actual battle. This was a mirage that was ridiculous because it was so wonderful and so true.

The last rounds from the artillery and mortars exploded with a roar upon the town. Orange tongues of flame licked up, up into the air from burning buildings. Black smoke billowed above the flame. The lead riflemen disappeared from sight in the first buildings of the town. The lead tank followed them. They had made it. They had crossed the open space unimpeded. The rest would be just mopping up.

Enter: the villain. A German machine gun from a haystack on the hillside to the north suddenly broke its silence and opened up on the rear elements of the assault platoons. My light gunners did not vary from their mission of neutralising the woods to the north, but the four heavy guns turned their attention to the intruder without a moment's hesitation. I saw the tracer bullets plunging into the haystack, and the hay burst into flame. *Exit: the villain.*

I cautioned the machine gunners to hold their fire until we should get past them, and I signalled my CP group forward. We moved at a half-run down the slope to the draw and the road and on toward the town. The fields on either side of us were littered with German dead. The riflemen had caught more quail on the rise than I had thought.

I entered the town with my CP group. Already at least fifty German soldiers were assembled before the second house, their hands raised high above their heads and dazed, startled expressions of incredulity on their faces. Others poured from every building as eager GIs sought them out with curses and shouts of derision. Some hurried along down the street toward the assemblage, terror written on their faces.

We moved on. I looked back and saw my support platoon move into the town and join in the mop-up operations.

The fifth house was a mass of flame. Two cows stood nearby, chewing their cuds and staring without expression at the scene of destruction. A grey-haired German farmer stood with his arm around his aged wife and stared at the burning house, tears streaming down both their faces.

'*Alles ist kaput! Alles ist kaput!*' they sobbed hysterically as we passed.

I was not impressed; instead, I was suddenly angry at them and surprised at my own anger. What right had they to stand there sobbing and blaming us for this terror? What right did they and their kind have to any emotions at all?

'Thank Adolf!' I shouted. 'Thank Hitler!' I pointed to the burning house and said, '*Der Führer!*' and laughed.

Charles B. Macdonald

A birth in the rubble

The remainder of our forces was concentrated on a small piece of territory. The Russians were using planes against us, and it was above all their air power which overwhelmed us in the end. As we stared toward the horizon, we could see that the slightest projection had been eliminated. The territory, in which, even six months ago, life must have had a certain regularity and sweetness, was now experiencing an apocalypse. It was no longer possible to move during the day. The sky was constantly filled with Russian planes, which, despite the heavy opposition of our anti-aircraft defences, always returned in constantly increasing numbers. Our defences, moreover, were continuously weakening, as the evacuation of troops began.

We were among the first to return to Gotenhafen, where certain sections of the city were already the scene of fierce combat. Within a few days, the appearance of the town had entirely changed. There were ruins everywhere, and a strong smell of gas and burning filled the air. The wide street which led down to the docks no longer had any definition. The wreckage of the buildings which had once lined it was crumbled right across the roadbed, obstructing all passage.

Along with thousands of others, we were put to work clearing away the rubble – so that trucks filled with civilians could get down to the harbour. Every five or ten minutes, planes came over, and we had to freeze where we were. The street was strafed and burned twenty or thirty times a day. Only our memories of Belgorod and Memel kept us from killing ourselves. We were no longer counting our dead and wounded: almost no one was entirely unhurt.

Heavily laden horses, which must have been spared by Supply, pulled a continuous train of sledges loaded with bodies wrapped in sacking or even paper. They had to be collected and buried with a speed which rivalled that of the Ilyushins' machine guns.

Exhausted people stood stunned and motionless on heaps of ruins, creating magnificent targets for Russian planes. As a finishing touch, the horizon to the west and southwest was reddish-black. House-to-house fighting had already begun in the outlying sections of the town, while thousands of civilians still waited down by the docks. From time to time, Russian shells reached as far as the embarkation area, and exploded there.

We were trying to snatch a short rest in a cellar, where a doctor was delivering a child. The cellar was vaulted and lit by a few hastily rigged lanterns. If the birth of a child is usually a joyful event, this particular birth only seemed to add to the general tragedy. The mother's screams no longer had any meaning in a world made of screams, and the wailing child seemed to regret the beginning of its life. Once again, there was streaming blood, like the blood in the streets, and on the earth, where we had known so much suffering, and where my appreciation of existence was continually spiralling down toward the abyss whose depths I occasionally glimpsed, defining life as a mixture of blood and suffering and groans of pain.

A short while later, after a last look at the newborn child, whose tiny cries sounded like a tinkle of delicate glass through the roar of war, we returned to the flaming street. For the child's sake, we hoped he would die before he turned twenty. Twenty is the age of ingratitude. It is too hard to be leaving life when one so much longs for it to flower.

We helped some old people, whom younger ones had left to the mercy of the Soviets. In the darkness lit up by flames, we once again performed our duty. We supported and carried the old people down to the port, where a boat was waiting for them. Planes passed over, and in spite of the blazing fires which lined the street, they once again scattered their load of death.

They killed some fifteen of our number. We had tried to pull the victims down with us on our several rapid plunges to the ground, but the old people were unable to follow us. It didn't matter though – we saved a good many of them anyhow, finally hoisting them on to a trawler, after getting them through the thickly packed crowd. The boat had to slip its lines while loading, to escape an aerial attack.

As we moved away from the shore, Wollers ran back to the stern to see if the gangplank had really been drawn in. Then he came back to us, tramping through the refugees who crowded the deck. He looked at us as if he were about to speak. Then we all turned to stare at the flames.

'Do you still have your embarkation cards?' he asked suddenly.

We all pulled out our tattered, filthy cards.

'I would have lost my head first,' muttered Grandsk.

The water slid quietly by, less than a yard below us. The boat would probably sink if the weight of its human cargo shifted. No one moved so much as a finger. Once again, we had escaped from the Russians and their fury.

Guy Sajer

Belsen

On 15 April the British liberated the concentration camp at Bergen-Belsen, near Hanover. They found 10,000 unburied corpses and 40,000 prisoners, of whom 28,000 afterwards died of illness or irreparable malnutrition.

We were now walking down the main driveway towards the first of the huts and administrative buildings. There were large crowds of civilian prisoners about, both those who strolled about in groups talking many different languages and those who sat silently on the ground. In addition there were many forms lying on the earth partly covered in rags, but it was not possible to say whether they were alive or dead or simply in the process of dying. It would be a day or two before the doctors got round to them for a diagnosis.

'There's quite a different air about the place in the last two days,' the doctor said. 'They seem much more cheerful now.'

'And the burial rate has gone down considerably,' the captain added. 'I'm handling just under three hundred a day now. It was five hundred to start with. And we are evacuating five hundred every day to the panzer training-school. It has been made into a hospital. Would you like to see the SS boys?'

We saw the women's guards first. A British sergeant threw open the cell door and some twenty women wearing dirty grey skirts and tunics were sitting and lying on the floor. 'Get up,' the sergeant roared in English.

They got up and stood to attention in a semi-circle round the room and we looked at them. Thin ones, fat ones and muscular ones; all of them ugly and one or two of them distinctly cretinous. I pointed out one, a big woman with bright golden hair and a bright pink complexion.

'She was Kramer's girl friend,' the sergeant growled. 'Nice lot, aren't they?'

There was another woman in a second room with almost delicate features, but she had the same set staring look in her eyes. The atmosphere of the reformatory school and the prison was inescapable.

Outside in the passageway there was a large blackboard ruled off in squares with white lines. Down the left-hand side of the board was a list of nationalities – 'Poles, Dutch, Russians', and so on. Spaced along the top of the board was a list of religions and political faiths – 'Communist, Jew, Atheist'. From the board one might have seen at a glance just how many prisoners were in the camp from each nation and how they were subdivided politically and religiously. However, most of the numbers appeared to have been rubbed off, and it was difficult to make out the totals exactly. Germans seemed to make up the majority of the prisoners. After them Russians and Poles. A great many were Jews. As far as one could decipher there had been half a dozen British there, one or two Americans. There had been something like fifty thousand prisoners altogether.

As we approached the cells of the SS guards the sergeant's language became ferocious.

'We have had an interrogation this morning,' the captain said. 'I'm afraid they are not a pretty sight.'

'Who does the interrogation?'

'A Frenchman. I believe he was sent up here specially from the French underground to do the job.'

The sergeant unbolted the first door and flung it back with a crack like thunder. He strode into the cell jabbing a metal spike in front of him. 'Get up,' he shouted. 'Get up; get up, you dirty bastards.'

There were half a dozen men lying or half-lying on the floor. One or two were able to pull themselves erect at once. The man nearest me, his shirt and face spattered with blood, made two attempts before he got on to his knees and then gradually on to his feet. He stood with his arms half stretched out in front of him trembling violently.

'Get up,' shouted the sergeant. They were all on their feet now, but supporting themselves against the wall. 'Get away from that wall.'

They pushed themselves out into space and stood there swaying. Unlike the women they looked not at us but vacantly in front, staring at nothing.

Same thing in the next cell and the next, where the men, who were bleeding and very dirty, were moaning something in German.

'You had better see the doctor,' the captain said. 'He's a nice specimen. He invented some of the tortures here. He had one trick of injecting creosote and petrol into the prisoners' veins. He used to go round the huts and say: "Too many people in here. Far too many." Then he used to loose off his revolver round the hut. The doctor has just finished his interrogation.'

The doctor had a cell to himself.

'Come on. Get up,' the sergeant shouted. The man was lying in his blood on the floor, a massive figure with a heavy head and a bedraggled beard. He placed his two arms on to the seat of a wooden chair, gave himself a heave and got half-upright. One more heave and be was on his feet. He flung wide his arms towards us.

'Why don't you kill me?' he whispered. 'Why don't you kill me? I can't stand any more.'

The same phrases dribbled out of his lips over and over again.

'He's been saying that all morning, the dirty bastard,' the sergeant said. We went out into the sunshine. A number of other British soldiers were standing about, all with the same hard rigid expressions on their faces, just ordinary English soldiers but changed by this expression of genuine and permanent anger.

The crowds of men and women thickened as we went farther into the camp. The litter of paper and rags and human offal grew thicker, the smell less and less bearable. At the entrance soldiers were unloading trucks filled with wooden latrines, but these had not yet been placed about the camp, so many hundreds of half-naked men and women were squatting together in the open, a scene such as you sometimes see in India – except that here it was not always possible to distinguish men from women, or indeed to determine whether they were human at all.

We drove through the filth in cars and, presently emerging on to an open space of yellow clayey soil, we came on a group of German guards flinging bodies into a pit about a hundred feet square. They brought the bodies up in hand-carts, and as they were flung into the grave a British soldier kept a tally of the numbers. When the total reached five hundred a bulldozer driven by another soldier came up and started nudging the earth into the grave. There was a curious pearly colour about the piled-up bodies, and they were small like the bodies of children. The withered skin was sagging over the bones, and all the normal features by which you know a human being had practically disappeared. Having no stomach for this sort of thing I was only able to look for a second or two, but the SS guards and even the British soldiers there appeared to have grown used to the presence of death and to be able to work in it without being sick.

'The doctors are doing a wonderful job,' the captain said. 'They are in the huts all day sorting out the living bodies from the dead, and it's not easy sometimes to tell the difference. Of course there are many who are just hopeless and they are simply left. But they are saving a lot now. We have got in all the food we want – two meals a day, at ten and six. Come on and have a look at one of the huts. We will go to the women first.'

It was a single-storey, rectangular wooden building, I suppose about a hundred feet long. Wooden bunks ran in tiers up to the ceiling, and there was a narrow passage just wide enough to allow you to pass through. Since the majority of the women there were too weak to move and had no attention whatever the stench was nauseating. Hurrying through, handkerchief to nose, one saw nothing but livid, straining faces and emaciated arms and legs under the filthy bed-clothes on either side. Many were using their last strength to moan feebly for help. These enforced animals were piled one on top of the other to the ceiling, sometimes two to a bunk.

An old hag somewhat stronger than the others was standing at the farther door. 'I'm twenty-one,' she whispered. 'No, I don't know why they put me in here. My husband is a doctor at the front. I'm a German but not Jewish. I said that I did not want to enlist in the women's organisation and they put me in here. That was eighteen months ago.'

'I've had enough of this,' I said to the captain. 'Come on,' he said. 'You've got to go through one of the men's huts yet. That's what you're here for.'

It was if anything more rancid than the one I had seen, but this time I was too sick with the stench to notice much except the sound of the voices: 'Doctor – doctor.'

As we turned towards the entrance the people round us were noticeably better in health than those at the pits and the huts. As they were able to walk some instinct drew the people away from the charnel houses and up and out towards the entrance and the ordinary sane world outside. It was all like a journey down to some Dantesque pit, unreal, leprous and frightening. And now as one emerged into the light again one's first coherent reactions were not of disgust or anger or even, I think, of pity. Something else filled the mind, a frantic desire to ask: 'Why? Why? Why?

Why had it happened?' With all one's soul one felt: 'This is not war. Nor is it anything to do with here and now, with this one place at this one moment. This is timeless and the whole world and all mankind is involved in it. This touches me and I am responsible. Why has it happened? How did we let it happen?'

We stood there in a group, a major from the commandos, a padre, three or four correspondents, having at first nothing to say, and then gradually and quietly asking one another the unspoken question.

Was it sadism? No, on the whole not. Or if it was sadism then it was sadism of a very indirect and unusual kind. Relatively little torture was carried out at this camp. The sadist presumably likes to make some direct immediate act which inflicts pain on other people. He could not obtain much satisfaction from the slow, long process of seeing people starve.

Then again the Germans were an efficient people. They needed man-power. Can one imagine anything more inefficient than letting all this valuable labour go to rot? The prisoners in Belsen were not even obliged to work. They were simply dumped in here and left to make what shift they could with a twice-daily diet of turnip stew. Incidentally this lack of work probably led to the break-up of the prisoners' morale as much as anything.

The Germans too had a normal fear of disease spreading among them-selves. And yet they let these thousands of bodies lie on the ground. It's true there was not a great deal of typhus in the camp, but it had already broken out when the German commanders approached the British and offered to cede the camp under the terms of a truce.

It was not torture which had killed the prisoners. It was neglect. The sheer indifference of the Nazis. One began to see that the most terrible thing on earth is not positive destruction nor the perverse desire to hurt and destroy. The worst thing that can happen to you is for the master to say: 'I do not care about you any more. I am indifferent.' Whether you washed or ate or laughed or died – none of this was of any consequence any more, because you as a person had no value. You were a slug on the ground, to be crushed or not to be crushed, it made no difference.

And having become attuned and accustomed to this indifference the guards were increasingly less affected by the suffering of the people around them. It was accepted that they should die. They were Russians. Russians die. Jews die. They were not even enemies. They were disease. Could you mourn or sympathise with the death throes of a germ?

Alan Moorehead

The camp's commandant, Josef Kramer, was executed in November 1945. More than 6 million Jews – a third of the people – had perished during the war.

‡

The Death of Mussolini

After his rescue by Otto Skorzeny, Mussolini became the leader of a notional Fascist government of northern Italy, the Republic of Salo, though in reality the country's rulers were now the Germans and the Allies. As the latter breached the Gothic Line and began to move on Bologna, Mussolini and his mistress, Clara Petacci, attempted to flee north in disguise, but were discovered in a lorry by partisans near Lake Como on 28 April. They were driven away and executed. One account of their end was given by an anti-Fascist named Walter Audisio, or 'Colonel Valerio'.

When we reached the spot I had previously chosen (a right-hand bend in the road and on the left the wall leading away to form a kind of square open space) I stopped the car and got out, cautioning Mussolini not to speak. I leaned up against the door of the car and whispered, 'I heard a noise . . . I'm just going to see.'

I went as far as the bend in the road then turned back and called softly: 'Quickly, get into that corner.'

Mussolini, though he obeyed promptly, did not seem very sure, as he went and stood, with Petacci on his right, with his back to the wall at the spot I had indicated. Silence.

Suddenly, pronouncing the sentence used to condemn war criminals:

'By order of the General Headquarters of the Corps of Volunteers for Liberty I am required to render justice to the Italian people.'

Mussolini appeared utterly lifeless. Petacci threw her arms round his neck and shouted: 'No, he mustn't die.'

'Go back to your place if you don't want to die too.'

The woman jumped away, back into her own place. From a distance of three yards I fired five shots into Mussolini who crumpled down on to his knees with his head leaning slightly forward. Then it was Petacci's turn.

Justice was done.

Pier Luigi Bellini delle Stelle and Urbano Lazzaro

Ignominy and revenge

Following their deaths, the bodies of Mussolini and Petacci were taken to Milan to be exhibited in a manner reminiscent of the fate of criminals centuries before. The events that followed were witnessed by the writer Philip Hamburger.

Although many Romans — and quite a few American correspondents — deplore what went on in the Piazza Loreto on the morning of Sunday, the twenty-ninth, to the Milanese these events will probably always be symbols of the north's liberation. To an outsider like myself, who happened to be on hand to see Mussolini, Clara Petacci, Pavolini, Starace, and some of the other Fascists dangling by their heels from a rusty beam in front of a gas station, the breathless, bloody scene had an air of inevitability. You had the feeling, as you have at the final curtain of a good play, that events could not have been otherwise. In many people's minds, I think, the embellishments of this upheaval — thousands of Partisans firing their machine guns into the air, Fascist bodies lying in a heap alongside the gas station, the enormous, pressing crowd — have been overemphasised and its essential dignity and purpose have been overlooked. This is best illustrated by the execution of Starace — the fanatical killer who was once secretary of the Fascist Party — who was brought into the square in an open truck at about ten-thirty in the morning. The bodies of Mussolini and the others had been hanging for several hours. I had reached the square just before the truck arrived. As it moved slowly ahead, the crowd fell back and became silent. Surrounded by armed guards, Starace stood in the middle of the truck, hands in the air, a lithe, square-jawed surly figure in a black shirt. The truck stopped for an instant close to the grotesque corpse of his old boss. Starace took one look and started to fall forward, perhaps in a faint, but was pushed back to a standing position by his guards. The truck drove ahead a few feet and stopped. Starace was taken out and placed near a white wall at the rear of the gas station. Beside him were baskets of spring flowers — pink, yellow, purple, and blue — placed there in honour of fifteen anti-Fascists who had been murdered in the same square six months before. A firing squad of Partisans shot Starace in the back, and another Partisan, perched on a beam some twenty feet above the ground, turned toward the crowd in the square and made a broad gesture of finality, much like a highly dramatic umpire calling a man out at the home plate. There were no roars or bloodcurdling yells; there was only silence, and then, suddenly, a sigh — a deep, moaning sound, seemingly expressive of release from something dark and foetid. The people in the square seemed to understand that this was a moment of both ending and beginning. Two minutes later, Starace had been strung up alongside Mussolini and the others. 'Look at them now,' an old man beside me kept saying. 'Just look at them now.'

Philip Hamburger

The author died in 2004.

‡

The Fall of Berlin

On 16 April with the Allies moving ever closer to Berlin, Stalin ordered Marshal Georgi Zhukov to make a thrust for the capital. Zhukov had 2 million men under his command, among them Lieutenant Evgeni Bessonov and his unit. The Havel Channel, 150 metres wide, was one of the last obstacles in their path.

Colonel Turkin, Majors Kozienko and Stolyarov and other officers walked up to the channel. All was silent. The battalion commander called me up and asked me where Chernyshov was. I answered that I did not know and I was the only officer in the company. Major Kozienko ordered me to find several good swimmers, volunteers, to cross the channel and bring a ferry on the other side of the channel in order to transport the rest of the company. The Germans were nowhere to be seen; no one was firing at us. Three or four brave guys volunteered, they swam across the channel; no one fired on them on the other bank and they were able to bring the ferry to our side.

Kozienko sent me across with a dozen soldiers. We did not know the capacity of the ferry, but eventually we crossed the channel safely. We went up to a mound, lay down behind it and spotted four Tiger tanks ahead of us. They were standing in a garden some 60 or 80 metres from us. The gardens were in full blossom and we could not see the tanks clearly. I sent a soldier back across the channel to report about the tanks to the battalion commander. The tanks were standing there quietly and did not show any signs of life. The entire company crossed the channel and we lay down behind this natural shelter. The battalion's battery – two 57 mm guns under the command of Lieutenants Kharmakulov and Isaev – also crossed the channel. Company commander Chernyshov also finally came running to us, he looked around and told me: 'Let's assault, not towards the tanks, but to the right, towards the city.' I objected, saying that the tanks would kill us there and squash us all with their tracks. I told him that we had to wait for our artillery to knock the tanks out first. The problem was that the tank crews of our tank regiment were really bad shooters. The Tigers, in contrast, first damaged one tank on the other side and then knocked out the second one. Lieutenants Shakulo, Mikheev and Guschenkov were away in hospitals, and Chernyshov and I were the only officers that remained in the company. Chernyshov ran to the right flank of the company and got Shakulo's platoon up to attack. Soldiers started to advance in short rushes towards Ketzin between the ugly houses and structures, closer to the road. He should not have done it, he could have lost his soldiers and have died himself, but he did not even listen to me, just cursed at me, while I could not stop him. I did not send my soldiers to attack in such a careless manner – the war was about to be over, why should I have shown such bravado? Chernyshov, however, was out of control and would often make a show.

The events that followed were even more horrible than I could imagine. I had not seen such a thing before at the front. A German APC [armoured personnel carrier] arrived and at first we did not pay attention to it, as they normally had a machine-gun mounted on them. But all of a sudden the APC started to shoot fireballs and flame and I realised that this was a flame-thrower – a horrible weapon that burnt people to ashes and could even burn a tank. The temperature of the flame was very high; if I am not mistaken, it was around 1,000 degrees Celsius. The APC threw flame several times. It was good that it was at first behind a house and the company's soldiers were out of its sight. When the APC emerged from behind the house, we were extremely lucky. Before it could throw flame at the soldiers who had not yet made to follow Chernyshov's command and at my platoon, two shots sounded from the other side of the channel, and the APC's flame liquid container exploded, killing all of its crew. The APC was knocked out by the battalion's artillery battery. They did a great job by not missing with the first shot, otherwise we would have been in big trouble. The enemy's tanks fired several rounds against the other side of the channel, turned and departed from our sight. Chernyshov again gave us the 'Forward!' order; we all stood up and entered the town. With no enemy armour in sight it was a different story. There was no enemy infantry there. As we were passing by the spot at which the flame-thrower fired, we saw the burnt bodies of our soldiers, mere ashes. It was an awful sight, although I had seen a lot of sights in the course of the war. Luckily, there were only three to five burnt soldiers, but they died because of the stupidity of one foolish commander, following an idiotic order. Later the incident was forgotten and no one recalled it. But I still recall that battle and those soldiers burnt by the flame-thrower even 60 years later . . .

At first I wanted to move forward through the gardens, not in the streets, just in case, but it did not work. Every garden with a mansion was separated from the next one by a fence, a high and strong metal mesh. We had to move forward along the street, and we did not even check the houses, which were locked – so much was Chernyshov hurrying us. It was late, but it was still light. In some places we had to fire on individual targets. Some random Fritzes were still there sometimes. I have already written that the town of Ketzin was part of our combat mission, and we were supposed to meet the troops of the first Belorussian front in the town. The town was captured by practically a single company without tanks, because they were only just starting to cross the channel on the ferries that were brought up.

Late in the evening of 24 April 1945, my platoon and company established contact with cavalry reconnaissance and the tanks of the first Belorussian front. Thus, Berlin was fully encircled by Soviet troops.

Evgeni Bessonov

'We retreated and retreated'

One of Berlin's defenders was Ulf Ollech, who helped to man an artillery battery in the suburbs.

I was only 17, but suddenly I had to shoot at human beings in order to preserve my own life. We were trained with artillery, and were stationed on one of Berlin's arterial roads, the Prenzlauer Allee, it was called. Work began at 0700 hours – practice with the artillery and training, training, training. Then we were transferred further to the north-east, to the eastern edge of Bernau. We set up positions on the road, but were then transferred at night to a place called Malchow; where we had a free field of fire on the road closer to Berlin, near the Weissensee – a free field of fire towards this road.

The Volkssturm troops were in the trenches in front of us. Behind us were residential areas with trees and houses and gardens, so that we were well camouflaged; and we expected, quite rightly, that the Red Army would come along this road straight past us. We had to be patient. During the course of one day, in terrible weather and soaking rain, walking through the trenches meant that you carried the mud and filth with you.

We spent the night there, half awake, half asleep, and the next morning, when the sun rose, we heard they were advancing along this road. Because it was an asphalt road, the Russians could see exactly whether or not someone had been laying mines there. But it was free of mines and so they advanced.

Four T-34s, two Shermans and an assault tank came along. The road had a small bend and before the first tank had reached this bend, we started firing. We had an artillery gun, which had a velocity of 1,200 metres per second, the only gun in the world from which the shell left the barrel at such a speed. That meant that the discharge and impact, especially at a distance of 200, perhaps 300 metres, was so short that you thought the discharge and the impact were the same sound. The tanks were all destroyed and the Red Army infantry at the rear of the tanks dispersed.

The wrecked tanks glowed red throughout the night and the ammunition inside exploded. We spent that night there, and the next morning the weather was dry, we discovered that the infantry units, in the shape of the Volkssturm, had gone, vanished. They were supposed to be in front of us and we had seen them the day before, but now they were nowhere to be seen.

That, of course, scared the wits out of us, because we knew that if the Red Army infantry had come at us overnight, we could never have fought them off. The next morning we ate a little and drank some tea, and then we got the order to retreat with our unit into the town proper, because the Red Army, primarily the infantry, but also the tanks, had already gone around us and broken through into the suburbs.

We retreated and retreated and we finally ended up in a flak tower – there were three of them in Berlin – and we got ourselves over to one of them. It was surprisingly comfortable. The food was good – I had the most glorious pea soup I had ever tasted in my life – and each of us had a plank bed, a cupboard, and everything was in first-class condition. We kept guard outside for four hours, then two hours inside.

The Russians started firing at the tower with their tanks. You could hear them. Their shells went 'Clack-clack' as if someone was knocking on the door. That wasn't good enough for the Russians, so they brought up some 15 cm howitzers. They managed to make tiny holes in the concrete. There were windows which were closed from the outside with heavy steel doors, I imagine that they weighed tons, and the Russians succeeded in hitting the upper hinge of one of the doors, which burst. One of them broke off, twisted off the other one and hurtled downwards. Apart from that, the flak tower wasn't badly damaged at all.

They then brought up a light artillery piece. A tank attack at night followed; they knew that we were lying in relays in the surrounding trenches. We had never experienced a tank attack at night before, and that was perhaps the most awful experience, because they attacked and we sought cover, and fought them off. Next morning we saw Russian corpses hanging over the edges of the trenches, with their machine guns dragged halfway. The Russian MGs were on wheels. You could hear when they were being pulled across a street because they rattled, 'rat-a-tat-tat'.

Then came April 30, when we learned that Hitler and his wife had committed suicide. Hitler had once said: 'I am National Socialism, if I no longer exist, there will be no more National Socialism', in other words, everything was focused upon him. We young men were very upset. We'd believed him when he'd said that. We'd grown up with it. We felt he had let us down. It was like losing an all-powerful father. What was going to happen to us now? we wondered.

It seemed hopeless for us to carry on. On May 2 we surrendered the flak tower.

Ulf Ollech

The city – and with it the Reich – fell on 2 May 1945.

The spoils of war

Because of the absence of glass any longer in most windows, all over Berlin there could be heard the screams of women being raped. Doctors later estimated that between 95,000 and 130,000 women were raped by the Red Army, of whom 10,000 subsequently died, mainly through suicide. In all, some 2 million German women are thought to have been violated in the last weeks of the war. Here a Berliner describes the rape of his wife.

The first women were fleeing from the northern parts of the city and some of them sought shelter in our cellar, sobbing that the Russians were looting all the houses, abducting the men and raping all the women and girls. I got angry, shouted I had had enough of Goebbels' silly propaganda, the time for that was past. If that was all they had to do, let them go elsewhere.

Whilst the city lay under savage artillery and rifle fire the citizens now took to looting the shops. The last soldiers withdrew farther and farther away. Somewhere in the ruins of the burning city SS-men and Hitler Youth were holding out fanatically. The crowds burst into cellars and storehouses. While bullets were whistling through the air they scrambled for a tin of fish or a pouch of tobacco.

On the morning of 1 May our flat was hit by a 21-cm. shell and almost entirely destroyed. On the same day water carriers reported that they had seen Russian soldiers. They could not be located exactly; they were engaged in house-to-house fighting which was moving very slowly. The artillery had been silent for some time when at noon on 2 May rifle fire too ceased in our district. We climbed out of our cellar.

From the street corner Russian infantry were slowly coming forward, wearing steel helmets with hand grenades in their belts and boots. The SS had vanished. The Hitler Youth had surrendered.

Bunny rushed and threw her arms round a short slit-eyed Siberian soldier who seemed more than a little surprised. I at once went off with two buckets to fetch water, but I did not get beyond the first street corner. All men were stopped there, formed into a column and marched off towards the east.

A short distance behind Alexanderplatz everything was in a state of utter turmoil and confusion. Russian nurses armed with machine-pistols were handing out loaves of bread to the German population. I took advantage of this turmoil to disappear and got back home safely. God knows where the others went.

After the first wave of combatant troops there followed reserves and supply troops who 'liberated' us in the true Russian manner. At our street corner I saw two Russian soldiers assaulting a crying elderly woman and then raping her in full view of the stunned crowd. I ran home as fast as I could. Bunny was all right so far. We had barricaded the one remaining room of our flat with rubble and charred beams in such a manner that no one outside could suspect that anyone lived there.

Every shop in the district was looted. As I hurried to the market I was met by groups of people who were laden with sacks and boxes. Vast food reserves belonging to the armed forces had been stored there. The Russians had forced the doors open and let the Germans in.

The cellars, which were completely blacked out, now became the scene of an incredible spectacle. The starving people flung themselves like beasts over one another, shouting, pushing and struggling to lay their hands on whatever they could. I caught hold of two buckets of sugar, a few boxes of preserves, sixty packages of tobacco and a small sack of coffee which I quickly took back home before returning for more.

The second raid was also successful. I found noodles, tins of butter and a large tin of sardines. But now things were getting out of hand. In order not to be trampled down themselves the Russians fired at random into the crowds with machine-pistols, killing several.

I cannot remember how I extricated myself from this screaming, shouting chaos; all I remember is that even here in this utter confusion, Russian soldiers were raping women in one of the corners.

Bunny had meanwhile made me promise not to try to interfere if anything were to happen to her. There were stories in our district of men being shot trying to protect their wives. In the afternoon two Russians entered our flat, while Bunny was sitting on the bed with the child. They looked her over for some time; evidently they were not very impressed with her. We had not washed for a fortnight, and I had expressly warned Bunny not to make herself tidy, for I thought the dirtier and more neglected she looked the safer.

But the two gentlemen did not seem to have a very high standard as far as cleanliness was concerned. With the usual words, 'Frau komm!' spoken in a menacing voice, one of them went towards her. I was about to interfere; but the other shouted 'Stoi' and jammed his machine-pistol in my chest. In my despair I shouted 'Run away, quick'; but that was, of course, impossible. I saw her quietly lay the baby aside, then she said, 'Please don't look, darling.' I turned to the wall.

When the first Russian had had enough they changed places. The second was chattering in Russian all the time. At last it was over. The man patted me on the shoulder: 'Nix Angst! Russki Soldat gut!'

Claus Fuhrmann

✟

The Death of Hitler

Albert Speer had long been part of Hitler's inner circle. Before the conflict, he was his favoured architect, but it was not until his appointment as Minister for Munitions in February 1942 that Speer began to wield real power. Towards the end of the war, his infatuation with Hitler began to pall, and he even considered killing the leader to whom he was once so devoted. On the night of 24–5 April, Speer went to Hitler's bunker in the centre of Berlin to see his Führer for the last time.

Toward midnight Eva Braun sent an SS orderly to invite me to the small room in the bunker that was both her bedroom and living room. It was pleasantly furnished; she had some of the expensive furniture which I had designed for her years ago brought from her two rooms in the upper floors of the Chancellery. Neither the proportions nor the pieces selected fitted into the gloomy surroundings. To complete the irony, one of the inlays on the doors of the chest was a four-leaf clover incorporating her initials.

We were able to talk honestly, for Hitler had withdrawn. She was the only prominent candidate for death in this bunker who displayed an admirable and superior composure. While all the others were abnormal – exaltedly heroic like Goebbels, bent on saving his skin like Bormann, exhausted like Hitler, or in total collapse like Frau Goebbels – Eva Braun radiated an almost gay serenity. 'How about a bottle of champagne for our farewell? And some sweets? I'm sure you haven't eaten in a long time.'

I was touched by her concern; she was the first person to think that I might be hungry after my many hours in the bunker. The orderly brought a bottle of Moët et Chandon, cake, and sweets. We remained alone. 'You know, it was good that you came back once more. The Führer had assumed you would be working against him. But your visit has proved the opposite to him, hasn't it?' I did not answer that question. 'Anyhow, he liked what you said to him today. He has made up his mind to stay here, and I am staying with him. And you know the rest, too, of course . . . He wanted to send me back to Munich. But I refused; I've come to end it here.'

She was also the only person in the bunker capable of humane considerations. 'Why do so many people have to be killed?' she asked. 'And it's all for nothing . . . Incidentally, you almost came too late. Yesterday the situation was so terrible it seemed the Russians would quickly occupy all of Berlin. The Führer was on the point of giving up. But Goebbels talked to him and persuaded him, and so we're still here.'

She went on talking easily and informally with me, occasionally bursting out against Bormann, who was pursuing his intrigues up to the last. But again and again she came back to the declaration that she was happy here in the bunker.

By now it was about three o'clock in the morning. Hitler was awake again. I sent word that I wanted to bid him good-bye. The day had worn me out, and I was afraid that I would not be able to control myself at our parting. Trembling, the prematurely aged man stood before me for the last time; the man to whom I had dedicated my life twelve years before. I was both moved and confused. For his part, he showed no emotion when we confronted one another. His words were as cold as his hand: 'So, you're leaving? Good. _Auf Wiedersehen_.' No regards to my family, no wishes, no thanks, no farewell. For a moment I lost my composure, said something about coming back. But he could easily see that it was a white lie, and turned his attention to something else. I was dismissed.

Ten minutes later, with hardly another word spoken to anyone, I left the Chancellor's residence. I wanted to walk once more through the neighbouring Chancellery, which I had built. Since the lights were no longer functioning, I contented myself with a few farewell minutes in the Court of Honour, whose outlines could scarcely be seen against the night sky. I sensed rather than saw the architecture. There was an almost ghostly quiet about everything, like a night in the mountains. The noise of a great city, which in earlier years had penetrated to here even during the night, had totally ceased. At rather long intervals I heard the detonations of Russian shells. Such was my last visit to the Chancellery. Years ago I had built it – full of plans, prospects, and dreams for the future. Now I was leaving the ruins of my building, and of the most significant years of my life.

Albert Speer

Speer received a 20-year term of imprisonment after the war at the Nuremberg trials. He died in London in 1981.

Götterdammerung

Traudl Junge was Hitler's secretary. Her last task for the Führer was to type his will and final testament.

I type both documents as fast as I can. My fingers work mechanically, and I am amazed to see that they make hardly any typing errors. Bormann, Goebbels and the Führer himself keep coming in to see if I've finished yet. They make me nervous and delay the work. Finally they almost tear the last sheet out of my typewriter, go back into the conference room, sign the three copies, and that very night they are sent off by courier in different directions. Colonel von Below, Heinz Lorenz and Bormann's colleague Zander take Hitler's last will and testament out of Berlin.

With that, Hitler's life is really over. Now he just wants to wait for confirmation that at least one of the documents has reached its destination. Any moment now we expect the Russians to storm our bunker, so close do the sounds of war seem to be. All our dogs are dead. The dog-walker has done his duty and shot our beloved pets before they can be torn to pieces up in the park by an enemy grenade or bomb.

Any of the guards or soldiers who have to go out in the open now are gambling with their lives. Some of our people have already been wounded. The leader of the escort commando has been shot in the leg and can't move for pain.

Almost no one stops to think of the five blonde little girls and the dark-haired boy still playing in their room, enjoying life. Their mother has now told them it's possible they may all have to be inoculated. When there are so many people living together in a small space you have to take precautions against disease. They understand that, and they're not afraid.

29 April. We're trapped here, we just sit waiting.

30 April begins like the days that went before it. The hours drag slowly by. No one knows just how to address Eva Braun now. The adjutants and orderlies stammer in embarrassment when they have to speak to the 'gnädiges Fräulein'. 'You may safely call me Frau Hitler,' she says, smiling.

She asks me into her room because she can't spend the whole time alone with her thoughts. We talk about something, anything, to distract ourselves. Suddenly she opens her wardrobe. There hangs the beautiful silver fox fur she loved so much. 'Frau Junge, I'd like to give you this coat as a goodbye present,' she says. 'I always liked to have well-dressed ladies around me – I want you to have it now and enjoy wearing it.' I thank her with all my heart, much moved. I am even glad to have it although I've no idea how, where and when I can wear it. Then we eat lunch with Hitler. The same conversation as yesterday, the day before yesterday, for many days past: a banquet of death under the mask of cheerful calm and composure. We rise from the table, Eva Braun goes to her room, and Frau Christian and I look for somewhere to smoke a cigarette in peace. I find a vacant armchair in the servants' room, next to the open door to Hitler's corridor. Hitler is probably in his room. I don't know who is with him. Then Günsche comes up to me. 'Come on, the Führer wants to say goodbye.' I rise and go out into the corridor. Linge fetches the others, Fräulein Manziarly, Frau Christian. I vaguely realise there are other people there too. But all I really see is the figure of the Führer. He comes very slowly out of his room, stooping more than ever, stands in the open doorway and shakes hands with everyone. I feel his right hand warm in mine, he looks at me but he isn't seeing me. He seems to be far away. He says something to me, but I don't hear it. I didn't take in his last words. The moment we've been waiting for has come now, and I am frozen and scarcely notice what's going on around me. Only when Eva Braun comes over to me is the spell broken a little. She smiles and embraces me. 'Please do try to get out. You may yet make your way though. And give Bavaria my love,' she says, smiling but with a sob in her voice. She is wearing the Führer's favourite dress, the black one with the roses at the neckline, and her hair is washed and beautifully done. Like that, she follows the Führer into his room – and to her death. The heavy iron door closes.

I am suddenly seized by a wild urge to get as far away from here as possible. I almost race up the stairs leading to the upper part of the bunker. But the Goebbels children are sitting halfway up, looking lost. They felt they'd been forgotten in their room. No one gave them any lunch today. Now they want to go and find their parents, and Auntie Eva and Uncle Hitler. I lead them to the round table. 'Come along, children, I'll get you something to eat. The grown-ups have so much to do today that they don't have any spare time for you,' I say as lightly and calmly as I can. I find a jar of cherries, butter some bread and feed the little ones. I talk to them to distract them. They say something about being safe in the bunker, and how it's almost fun to hear the explosions when they know the bangs can't hurt them. Suddenly there is the sound of a shot, so loud, so close that we all fall silent. It echoes on through all the rooms. 'That was a direct hit,' cries Helmut, with no idea how right he is. The Führer is dead now.

I want to be on my own. The children, satisfied, go back to their room. I stay sitting by myself on the narrow bench at the round table on the landing. There is a bottle of Steinhäger standing there, with an empty glass beside it. Automatically, I pour myself a drink and swallow the strong liquor. My watch says a few minutes after three in the afternoon. So now it's over.

Traudl Junge

Hitler shot himself through the mouth, while his wife took poison. Their bodies were taken into the courtyard by the bunker and incinerated with gasoline. Goebbels and his wife poisoned their children and then had themselves shot by an SS guard. The Russians occupied the Reichstag three hours before their deaths. The author was captured and imprisoned, but later returned to Germany to work as a secretary. She died in 2002.

Churchill hears of Hitler's death

In the middle of dinner I brought in the sensational announcement, broadcast by the Nazi wireless, that Hitler had been killed today at his post at the Reichs Chancery in Berlin and that Admiral Doenitz was taking his

place. Probably H. has in fact been dead several days, but the 1st May is a
symbolic date in the Nazi calendar and no doubt the circumstances ('fighting with his last breath against Bolshevism') were carefully invented with
an eye to the future Hitler Myth and Legend. The PM's comment over
the dinner table was: 'Well, I must say I think he was perfectly right to die
like that.' Lord B.'s [Beaverbrook] reply was that he obviously did not.

John Colville

✝

The German Surrender

*On 4 May, Montgomery received the German envoys on Lüneberg Heath, near
Lübeck.*

I had the surrender document all ready. The arrangements in the tent were
very simple – a trestle table covered with an army blanket, an inkpot, an
ordinary army pen that you could buy in a shop for twopence. There were
two BBC microphones on the table. The Germans stood up as I entered;
then we all sat down round the table. The Germans were clearly nervous
and one of them took out a cigarette; he wanted to smoke to calm his
nerves. I looked at him, and he put the cigarette away.

In that tent on Lüneberg Heath, publicly in the presence of the Press
and other spectators, I read out in English the Instrument of Surrender. I
said that unless the German delegation signed this document immediately,
and without argument on what would follow their capitulation, I would
order the fighting to continue. I then called on each member of the
German delegation by name to sign the document, which they did without
any discussion. I then signed, on behalf of General Eisenhower.

Bernard Montgomery

*Fighting was to continue elsewhere in Germany until 7 May, when the Germans
unconditionally surrendered at 2.41 p.m.*

✝

VE Day

Victory in Europe was celebrated in the Allied countries the next day. Mollie Panter-Downes was in London.

When the day finally came, it was like no other day that anyone can remember. It had a flavour of its own, an extemporaneousness which gave it something of the quality of a vast, happy village fête as people wandered about, sat, sang, and slept against a summer background of trees, grass, flowers, and water. It was not, people said, like the 1918 Armistice Day, for at no time was the reaction hysterical. It was not like the Coronation, for the crowds were larger and their gaiety, which held up all through the night, was obviously not picked up in a pub. The day also surprised the prophets who had said that only the young would be resilient enough to celebrate in a big way. Apparently the desire to assist London's celebration combusted spontaneously in the bosom of every member of every family, from the smallest babies, with their hair done up in red-white-and-blue ribbons, to beaming elderly couples who, utterly without self-consciousness, strolled up and down the streets arm in arm in red-white-and-blue paper hats. Even the dogs wore immense tricoloured bows. Rosettes sprouted from the slabs of pork in the butcher shops, which, like other food stores, were open for a couple of hours in the morning. With their customary practicality, housewives put bread before circuses. They waited in the long bakery queues, the string bags of the common round in one hand and the Union Jack of the glad occasion in the other. Even queues seemed tolerable that morning. The bells had begun to peal and, after the night's storm, London was having that perfect, hot, English summer's day which, one sometimes feels, is to be found only in the imaginations of the lyric poets.

The girls in their thin, bright dresses heightened the impression that the city had been taken over by an enormous family picnic. The number of extraordinarily pretty young girls, who presumably are hidden on working days inside the factories and government offices, was astonishing. They streamed out into the parks and streets like flocks of twittering, gaily plumaged cockney birds. In their freshly curled hair were cornflowers and poppies, and they wore red-white-and-blue ribbons around their narrow waists. Some of them even tied ribbons around their bare ankles. Strolling with their uniformed boys, arms candidly about each other, they provided a constant, gay, simple marginal decoration to the big, solemn moments of the day. The crowds milled back and forth between the Palace, Westminster, Trafalgar Square, and Piccadilly Circus, and when they got tired they simply sat down wherever they happened to be – on the grass, on doorsteps, or on the kerb – and watched the other people or spread handkerchiefs over their faces and took a nap. Everybody appeared determined to see the King and Queen and Mr Churchill at least once, and few could have been disappointed. One small boy, holding on to his father's hand, wanted to see the trench shelters in Green Park too. 'You don't want to see shelters today,' his father said. 'You'll never have to use them again, son.' 'Never?' the child asked doubtfully. 'Never!' the man cried, almost angrily. '*Never!* Understand?' In the open space before the Palace, one of the places where the Prime Minister's speech was to be relayed by loudspeaker at three o'clock, the crowds seemed a little intimidated by the nearness of that symbolic block of grey stone. The people who chose to open their lunch baskets and munch sandwiches there among the flower beds of tulips were rather subdued. Piccadilly Circus attracted the more demonstrative spirits.

By lunchtime, in the Circus, the buses had to slow to a crawl in order to get through the tightly packed, laughing people. A lad in the black beret of the Tank Corps was the first to climb the little pyramidal Angkor Vat of scaffolding and sandbags which was erected early in the war to protect the pedestal of the Eros statue after the figure had been removed to safekeeping. The boy shinnied up to the top and took a tiptoe Eros pose, aiming an imaginary bow, while the crowd roared. He was followed by a paratrooper in maroon beret, who, after getting up to the top, reached down and hauled up a blonde young woman in a very tight pair of green slacks. When she got to the top, the Tank Corps soldier promptly grabbed her in his arms and, encouraged by ecstatic cheers from the whole Circus, seemed about to enact the classic role of Eros right on the top of the monument. Nothing came of it, because a moment later a couple of GIs joined them and before long the pyramid was covered with boys and girls. They sat jammed together in an affectionate mass, swinging their legs over the sides, wearing each other's uniform caps, and calling down wisecracks to the crowd. 'My God,' someone said, 'think of a flying bomb coming down on this!' When a firecracker went off, a hawker with a tray of tin brooches of Monty's head happily yelled that comforting, sometimes fallacious phrase of the blitz nights, 'All right, mates, it's one of ours!'

All day long, the deadly past was for most people only just under the surface of the beautiful, safe present, so much so that the Government decided against sounding the sirens in a triumphant 'all clear' for fear that the noise would revive too many painful memories. For the same reason, there were no salutes of guns – only the pealing of the bells, and the whistles of tugs on the Thames sounding the doot, doot, doot, dooooot of the 'V', and the roar of the planes, which swooped back and forth over the city, dropping red and green signals toward the blur of smiling, upturned faces.

It was without any doubt Churchill's day. Thousands of King George's subjects wedged themselves in front of the Palace throughout the day, chanting ceaselessly 'We want the King' and cheering themselves hoarse when he and the Queen and their daughters appeared, but when the crowd saw Churchill there was a deep, full-throated, almost reverent roar. He was at the head of a procession of Members of Parliament, walking back to the House of Commons from the traditional St Margaret's Thanksgiving Service. Instantly, he was surrounded by people – people running, standing on tiptoe, holding up babies so that they could be told later they had seen him, and shouting affectionately the absurd little nurserymaid name, 'Winnie, Winnie!' One of two happily sozzled, very old, and incredibly dirty cockneys who had been engaged in a slow, shuffling dance, like a couple of Shakespearean clowns, bellowed, 'That's 'im, that's 'is little old lovely bald 'ead!' The crowds saw Churchill again later, when he emerged from the Commons and was driven off in the back of a small open car, rosy, smiling, and looking immensely happy. Ernest Bevin, following in another car, got a cheer too. One of the throng, an excited East Ender, in a dress with a bodice concocted of a Union Jack, shouted, 'Gawd, fancy me cheering Bevin, the chap who makes us work!' Herbert Morrison, sitting unobtrusively in a corner of a third car, was hardly recognised, and the other Cabinet Ministers did no better. The crowd had ears, eyes, and throats for no one but Churchill, and for him everyone in it seemed to have the hearing, sight, and lungs of fifty men. His slightly formal official broadcast, which was followed by buglers sounding the 'cease firing' call, did not strike the emotional note that had been expected, but he hit it perfectly in his subsequent informal speech ('My dear friends, this is your victory . . .') from a Whitehall balcony.

All day long, little extra celebrations started up. In the Mall, a model of a Gallic cock waltzed on a pole over the heads of the singing people. 'It's the Free French,' said someone. The Belgians in the crowd tagged along after a Belgian flag that marched by, its bearer invisible. A procession of students raced through Green Park, among exploding squibs, clashing dustbin lids like cymbals and waving an immense Jeyes Disinfectant poster as a banner. American sailors and laughing girls formed a conga line down the middle of Piccadilly and cockneys linked arms in the Lambeth Walk. It was a day and night of no fixed plan and no organised merriment. Each group danced its own dance, sang its own song, and went its own way as the spirit moved it. The most tolerant, self-effacing people in London on VE Day were the police, who simply stood by, smiling benignly, while soldiers swung by one arm from lamp standards and laughing groups tore down hoardings to build the evening's bonfires. Actually, the police were not unduly strained. The extraordinary thing about the crowds was that they were almost all sober. The number of drunks one saw in that whole day and night could have been counted on two hands – possibly because the pubs were sold out so early. The young service men and women who swung arm in arm down the middle of every street, singing and swarming over the few cars rash enough to come out, were simply happy with an immense holiday happiness. They were the liberated people who, like their counterparts in every celebrating capital that night, were young enough to outlive the past and to look forward to an unspoilt future. Their gaiety was very moving.

                                                            Mollie Panter-Downes

Summer 1945

On Okinawa

'The horror, the horror'

For many Japanese civilians, the battle for Okinawa was their first glimpse of the reality of a war of imperial ambitions that had hitherto been fought in distant places. Koei Kinjo was 14.

I was in this cave about 50 metres east of Maehira. It was only about two tsubo wide (72 sq. ft) inside, but it was packed with 19 people. The place was so crowded and stifling you had to get out now and then to get some fresh air.

One day, an old woman and a younger woman about 35 years old and her two children, one of them about five and the other about three, came near our place. They said they were from Nakagusuku. They'd apparently been forced out of their cave by troops and had no place to go to. They all looked awfully tired. They took refuge under a tall tree near our cave.

Perhaps they were sitting under this tree for two days or so. Then, one day when I got out of the cave, the two women were dead, perhaps killed by shell fragments. The mother had been hit by a fragment about 20 centimetres in diameter and had a big gash in her ribs. Maybe instantly killed. The old lady had been hit in her temple.

The children were safe. The baby was sucking at her mother's breast, and the older one was leaning against her body. They stayed alive like that for about three days. But when I came out again to relieve myself, I found the kids lying dead beside their mother, soaked in the rain falling all night long. I felt so bad I didn't know what to make of human lives.

Koei Kinjo

Toyo Gima was 19 and lived in Nakagusuku village.

In Makabe, there was a huge cave called Sennin Go, or One Thousand People Cave (which means it can hold 1,000 people inside). We were hiding in that cave. Only a handful of people there were civilians and the rest were soldiers.

Then Americans attacked the cave with mortar shells. The walls of the entrance were destroyed. The cave was sealed, and we couldn't get out. One of my friends was burned to death there.

So we moved deeper into the cave and lived there for about 20 days. There was enough water to drink there. Many wounded soldiers were staying near the entrance, so they were all killed when the cave was attacked, but other soldiers were safe in the inner part of the cave.

Later, we moved to another cave a little farther away from Sennin Cave. There were many civilians and soldiers in it. It was also a large cave which could house hundreds of people and there were really many people in there. I think there were more civilians than soldiers. It was in this cave that I saw this unbelievable thing.

There was a little boy about four or five years old. He was crying because he couldn't find his mother. The boy was near the entrance of the cave, where there was a hole in the ceiling.

Then, one of the soldiers said if the boy kept crying the enemy would hear him crying and they'd find us. The soldier angrily said someone should take care of the boy and asked if there were his parents in the cave. No one said anything. So they took him deeper into the cave and killed him. There was some light from this hole in the ceiling, so you could see it. They took him inside and tried to strangle him with a triangle bandage, the kind you used for dressing a wound.

I heard one of them say the cloth was too thick and they couldn't choke him to death with it. They tore the triangle cloth and made a finer string and strangled him to death with it. All the civilians who saw it were crying. I actually saw them put the string around the boy's neck, but it was so horrible I couldn't watch it to the end.

                                                                    Toyo Gima

On 21 June, General Ushijima's HQ on Hill 69 was captured. US Marines found his body inside, one of 160,000 Japanese who had died defending Okinawa. The Americans had lost 12,500 troops.

I grabbed the Tommy and followed the corpsman. He was just finishing bandaging one of the wounded Marines of the 37 mm gun crew when I got there. Other Marines were coming over to see if they could help.

Several men had been wounded by the firing when two enemy officers crept up the steep slope, threw grenades into the gun emplacement, and jumped in swinging their samurai sabres. One Marine had parried a sabre blow with his carbine. His buddy then had shot the Japanese officer who fell backwards a short distance down the slope. The sabre blow had severed a finger and sliced through the mahogany carbine forestock to the metal barrel.

The second Japanese officer lay dead on his back next to the wheel of the 37 mm gun. He was in full-dress uniform with white gloves, shiny leather leggings, Sam Browne belt, and campaign ribbons on his chest. Nothing remained of his head from the nose up – just a mass of crushed skull, brains, and bloody pulp. A grimy Marine with a dazed expression stood over the Japanese. With a foot planted firmly on the ground on each side of the enemy officer's body, the Marine held his rifle by the forestock with both hands and slowly and mechanically moved up and down like a plunger. I winced each time it came down with a sickening sound into the gory mass. Brains and blood were splattered all over the Marine's rifle, boondockers, and canvas leggings, as well as the wheel of the 37 mm gun.

The Marine was obviously in a complete state of shock. We gently took him by the arms. One of his uninjured buddies set aside the gore-smeared rifle. 'Let's get you outta here, Cobber.'

The poor guy responded like a sleepwalker as he was led off with the wounded, who were by then on stretchers. The man who had lost the finger clutched the Japanese sabre in his other hand. 'I'm gonna keep this bastard for a souvenir.'

We dragged the battered enemy officer to the edge of the gun emplacement and rolled him down the hill. Replete with violence, shock, blood, gore, and suffering, this was the type of incident that should be witnessed by anyone who has any delusions about the glory of war. It was as savage and as brutal as though the enemy and we were primitive barbarians rather than civilised men.

Eugene Sledge

‡

A General Election had been called in Britain for 5 July.

Overheard two workmen talking in the Harrow Weald teashop, a favourite rendezvous for the Council workers. Plumbers or gasfitters, I'd guess. 'Don't want him again.' A long look at the other man – so much is conveyed by looks and glances! He replied: 'Enough battles for one lifetime.' After a long pause and a sip of tea, the first man said: 'Bloody Russia,' and this time looked down at the table, interested in a drop of tea that had fallen on his donkey-jacket. The second man said: 'The old cock's just aching to wave us up and at 'em again,' to which the first man replied, having waited to see if the other was of the same mind: 'Catch me.'

They had been talking about Churchill and had thus agreed not to vote for him. Now multiply their little chat by tens of thousands and one gets the result of the Election. Those men weren't *for* Attlee, they were *against* Churchill, who in other circles is known as the Happy Warrior.

George Beardmore

Because of the need to receive votes cast abroad by servicemen, the result of the General Election would not be declared until 26 July.

‡

The Potsdam Conference

Roosevelt had died on 12 April and had been succeeded as President by Harry Truman. At the Allies' peace conference outside Berlin in July, the new American leader was studied carefully by Andrei Gromyko.

The Potsdam conference did not consist only of talks. The heads of delegation arranged various events to show their mutual respect, such as luncheons and dinners, souvenir photographs, and at all of them Stalin, Truman, Churchill and then Attlee gave the newsmen plenty of photo-opportunities.

There is a photograph of the Big Three at the conference table at Potsdam that has stuck in my mind. It has a special quality that derives, I think, from the electricity in the air. Everyone at the round table clearly feels the nervous tension. It can be seen in their faces, especially the faces of those in the front row, where the special staffs are seated. We are all in a state of extreme concentration, and this shows: nobody is smiling.

I remember another, happier occasion, when Truman had arranged a dinner. After we all got up from the table he sat down at the piano and played something he had evidently practised very carefully – he was of course well known as an able amateur pianist. When he'd finished, Stalin praised him and said laughingly: 'Ah yes, music's an excellent thing – it drives out the beast in man.'

To be truthful, it wasn't quite clear whom Stalin had in mind as the one whose beast had been driven out. Even so, Truman chose to be very pleased at his words.

Only my heightened awareness of the historic occasion can explain why I still have so many images in my mind from that conference. I particularly remember the first day.

There is Truman. He is nervous but he mobilises all his self-control so as not to show it. It looks at times as if he is about to smile, but this is a false impression. I have the feeling that the President is somehow huddled into himself. No doubt the fact that he has no experience of meetings at such a high level, and never met Stalin before, plays a part. But to give him his due he is never rude or discourteous. He is helped by the fact that all his major statements are prepared in advance, so he only has to read them. In discussion his extempore comments are usually brief, but his advisers and experts are in constant consultation with each other and from time to time pass him notes.

And Churchill. That veteran politician makes only short statements, as a rule, but he loves to stretch out individual words. The words he wants to underline are pronounced harshly. He almost never uses a prepared text. It is said that he likes to learn his speeches by heart, and my impression of him is certainly of an experienced orator who knows how to present his rhetorical stock-in-trade.

Attlee. Our delegation is right in its prediction: if Labour gets in, they'll follow essentially the same policy as the wartime Coalition. At the conference Attlee scarcely speaks. Maybe when the delegation discusses domestic policy he speaks up, but mostly he's quiet as a mouse. Maybe the experienced Labour leader is afraid of saying something that the press would pick up, and of losing Labour some support.

Stalin. He looks calm and steady. So does the Soviet delegation as a whole.

Also interesting were the dinners at which the three leaders met either to work or to relax.

One did not have to be a psychiatrist to see that each of the Big Three knew his part. Certainly two contrasting worlds – capitalist and socialist – were represented, but all three men still had to find some understanding.

Everyone listened carefully when Roosevelt spoke. We studied the twists and turns of his thinking and his sharp judgements and jokes. What he said was important for the future of the world, and we knew it.

When Churchill spoke he knew how to sparkle and make a joke, and he expressed his ideas well. One felt he was on familiar terms not only with politics but also with history: he had after all fought in the Boer War at the beginning of the century.

Then, quietly, almost casually, Stalin would begin to speak. He spoke as if only the other two were in the room. He showed neither restraint nor any desire to make an effect, yet every word sounded as if it had been specially prepared for just this occasion and just this moment.

It was noticeable that, when Stalin was speaking, even when the subject was not high policy, Roosevelt would often try to convey his attitude to what was being said, either with nods of his head or by the expression on his face.

Even at that time, it would have been hard for even the most unobservant person not to notice the authority and respect that was accorded to Stalin by the other leaders. First and foremost, this was clearly due to the unexampled feats of the Soviet people in the war. The monolithic unity of the Soviet people had made an enormous impression: the working class, the peasantry and the intelligentsia in a single upsurge had risen to defend the country against a powerful enemy.

Andrei Gromyko

At the conference, Truman revealed to Stalin the existence of the atomic bomb.

Next day, July 24, after our plenary meeting had ended and we all got up from the round table and stood about in twos and threes before dispersing, I saw the President go up to Stalin, and the two conversed alone with only their interpreters. I was perhaps five yards away, and I watched with the closest attention the momentous talk. I knew what the President was going to do. What was vital to measure was its effect on Stalin. I can see it all as if it were yesterday. He seemed to be delighted. A new bomb! Of extraordinary power! Probably decisive on the whole Japanese war! What a bit of luck! This was my impression at the moment, and I was sure he had no idea of the significance of what he was being told. Evidently in his intense toils and stresses the atomic bomb had played no part. If he had had the slightest idea of the revolution in world affairs which was in progress his reactions would have been obvious. Nothing would have been easier than for him, to say, 'Thank you so much for telling me about your new bomb. I of course have no technical knowledge. May I send my expert in these nuclear sciences to see your expert to-morrow morning?' But his face remained gay and genial and the talk between these two potentates soon came to an end. As we were waiting for our cars I found myself near Truman. 'How did it go?' I asked. 'He never asked a question,' he replied.

Winston Churchill

The following day, halfway through the conference, Churchill flew home to Britain to await the results of the General Election held three weeks before. Almost the entire world was astonished when Churchill was not returned – the British electorate now wanted social change – and Attlee took his seat at the table. On 26 July, the Potsdam Declaration called on the Japanese to surrender unconditionally. It made no mention of the atom bomb.

The new masters

For one British journalist, an encounter with some Russian soldiers at the Reich Chancellery signified the emerging political landscape of Europe.

Next morning, after trying to sleep to the whine of mosquitoes and cleaning my teeth with hock, I took the jeep and went sight-seeing. I had been told that once I could find the Tiergarten, which was equivalent to Hyde Park, I should look for the Alexanderplatz, from which I could easily make my way to the Reichstag and the Chancellery. But the Tiergarten proved to be a wildness of tree-stumps from which rose gigantic flak-towers, their concrete bulk cast in a curiously Gothic shape like Teutonic castles. Beyond, I recognised the Brandenburg Gate upon which the green, bronze group of charioteer and horses had collapsed, riddled by machine-gun fire. There stood the Reichstag, gutted and blackened by fire, red flags fluttering from walls scrawled over with Russian slogans. All around lay heaped the ruins and, where they had been cleared at a crossroads, I asked a Russian soldier in German where I could find the Alexanderplatz. He waved a square hand at the rubble around us and replied, 'Alexanderplatz'.

The Reichskanzlerei was, however, recognisable by the grandeur of its façade and neo-classical pillars and pediments around its tall windows. It, too, was in ruins, its approaches choked with rubbish, a Wehrmacht staff car lying, blown upside down, at the bottom of the steps leading to the main doors. Outside, a few Russian and American soldiers and Germans haggled over watches and cigarettes. Also outside stood Russian sentries with tommy-guns of the Chicago gangster variety and one of the Americans told me that nobody was allowed inside. Indeed, when I approached the entrance the Russians sternly waved me away.

But I had not come from London to be deterred at this moment. So, leaving the jeep, I walked down the street, turned a corner among the ruins and scrambled up into the hills of rubble. It was like climbing the steep, shale slopes of Westmorland fells but the clambering eventually led me to the side of the Chancellery and, since all its doors and windows had been blown away, entry was easy. The place had been a battlefield. The long corridors and stone stairways were littered with the aftermath of street-fighting as Aachen had been; discarded equipment, belts of ammunition, abandoned packs and mess-tins, helmets, all thick with grime. Amongst the rubbish, holes opened in the floor, blasted by bomb, or steeply plunging shell. Doors hung by a single hinge, or lay flat. Filing cabinets stood burst open by explosions, or prised open by Russian bayonets, spilling their contents: usually filed documents but, in one small room, military decorations – mostly the Iron Cross – awaiting award.

The building was empty as I picked my way through the debris, realising, partly because the design of doorway and window was becoming more imposing, and partly, I thought, by instinct, that I was approaching its heart. A series of wrecked ante-rooms opened into one another and then suddenly I knew that I was in the presence-chamber. Tall window spaces, open from floor to high ceiling, lit the great room with summer sunlight, and sparkled on the crumpled chandeliers that had crashed to the floor. A huge globe of the world lay broken into halves. In a corner by the windows, a massive desk, its top a slab of red marble, lay blown upside down. A corner of the marble had splintered and I pocketed a fragment for I knew to whom the desk had belonged. This was where Hitler had presided over Europe.

As I stood in the middle of the great room, committing its detail to memory, I heard a crunching of footsteps outside and two Russian soldiers entered, tommy-guns under arms. I smiled ingratiatingly, said '*Harasho, tovarich*' and took a packet of ten Player's cigarettes from my battledress pocket and gave it to them. While they began to open it, I waved and, still smiling, departed quickly and, scaling other dunes of rubble – one strewn with cutlery embossed with Nazi insignia – emerged from the Chancellery, wondering why the presence of the Russians made me so uneasy. That afternoon, I heard later, another trespasser was killed by treading on a mine within the Chancellery and I persuaded myself that therefore it was such risks that had led the Russians to prevent their allies from inspecting the principal prize of their shared victory.

Tom Pocock

⸸

Hiroshima

6 AUGUST 1945

Michihiko Hachiya was a director of Hiroshima Communications Hospital.

The hour was early; the morning still, warm, and beautiful. Shimmering leaves, reflecting sunlight from a cloudless sky, made a pleasant contrast with shadows in my garden as I gazed absently through wide-flung doors opening to the south.

Clad in vest and pants, I was sprawled on the living-room floor exhausted because I had just spent a sleepless night on duty as an air-raid warden in my hospital.

Suddenly, a strong flash of light startled me – and then another. So well does one recall little things that I remember vividly how a stone lantern in the garden became brilliantly lit and I debated whether this light was caused by a magnesium flare or sparks from a passing tram.

Garden shadows disappeared. The view where a moment before all had been so bright and sunny was now dark and hazy. Through swirling dust I could barely discern a wooden column that had supported one corner of my house. It was leaning crazily and the roof sagged dangerously.

Moving instinctively, I tried to escape, but rubble and fallen timbers barred the way. By picking my way cautiously I managed to reach the *roka* and stepped down into my garden. A profound weakness overcame me, so I stopped to regain my strength. To my surprise I discovered that I was completely naked. How odd! Where were my vest and pants?

What had happened?

All over the right side of my body I was cut and bleeding. A large splinter was protruding from a mangled wound in my thigh, and something warm trickled into my mouth. My cheek was torn, I discovered as I felt it gingerly, with the lower lip laid wide open. Embedded in my neck was a sizeable fragment of glass which I matter-of-factly dislodged, and with the detachment of one stunned and shocked I studied it and my blood-stained hand.

Where was my wife?

Suddenly thoroughly alarmed, I began to yell for her: 'Yaeko-san! Yaeko-san! Where are you?'

Blood began to spurt. Had my carotid artery been cut? Would I bleed to death? Frightened and irrational, I called out again: 'It's a five-hundred-ton bomb! Yaeko-san, where are you? A five-hundred-ton bomb has fallen!'

Yaeko-san, pale and frightened, her clothes torn and blood-stained, emerged from the ruins of our house holding her elbow. Seeing her, I was reassured. My own panic assuaged, I tried to reassure her.

'We'll be all right,' I explained. 'Only let's get out of here as fast as we can.'

She nodded, and I motioned for her to follow me.

The shortest path to the street lay through the house next door so through the house we went – running, stumbling, falling, and then running again until in headlong flight we tripped over something and fell sprawling into the street. Getting to my feet, I discovered that I had tripped over a man's head.

'Excuse me! Excuse me, please!' I cried hysterically. There was no answer. The man was dead. The head had belonged to a young officer whose body was crushed beneath a massive gate.

We stood in the street, uncertain and afraid, until a house across from us began to sway and then with a rending motion fell almost at our feet. Our own house began to sway, and in a minute it, too, collapsed in a cloud of dust. Other buildings caved in or toppled. Fires sprang up and whipped by a vicious wind began to spread.

It finally dawned on us that we could not stay there in the street, so we turned our steps towards the hospital. Our home was gone; we were wounded and needed treatment; and after all, it was my duty to be with my staff. This latter was an irrational thought – what good could I be to anyone, hurt as I was?

We started out, but after twenty or thirty steps I had to stop. My breath came short, my heart pounded, and my legs gave way under me. An overpowering thirst seized me and I begged Yaeko-san to find me some water. But there was no water to be found. After a little my strength somewhat returned and we were able to go on.

I was still naked, and although I did not feel the least bit of shame, I was disturbed to realise that modesty had deserted me. On rounding a corner we came upon a soldier standing idly in the street. He had a towel draped across his shoulder, and I asked if he would give it to me to cover my nakedness. The soldier surrendered the towel quite willingly but said not a word. A little later I lost the towel, and Yaeko-san took off her apron and tied it around my loins.

Our progress towards the hospital was interminably slow, until finally, my legs, stiff from drying blood, refused to carry me farther. The strength, even the will, to go on deserted me, so I told my wife, who was almost as badly hurt as I, to go on alone. This she objected to, but there was no choice. She had to go ahead and try to find someone to come back for me.

Yaeko-san looked into my face for a moment, and then, without saying a word, turned away and began running towards the hospital. Once, she looked back and waved and in a moment she was swallowed up in the gloom. It was quite dark now, and with my wife gone, a feeling of dreadful loneliness overcame me.

I must have gone out of my head lying there in the road because the next thing I recall was discovering that the clot on my thigh had been dislodged and blood was again spurting from the wound. I pressed my hand to the bleeding area and after a while the bleeding stopped and I felt better.

Could I go on?

I tried. It was all a nightmare – my wounds, the darkness, the road ahead. My movements were ever so slow; only my mind was running at top speed.

In time I came to an open space where the houses had been removed to make a fire lane. Through the dim light I could make out ahead of me the hazy outlines of the Communications Bureau's big concrete building, and beyond it the hospital. My spirits rose because I knew that now someone would find me; and if I should die, at least my body would be found.

I paused to rest. Gradually things around me came into focus. There were the shadowy forms of people, some of whom looked like walking ghosts. Others moved as though in pain, like scarecrows, their arms held out from their bodies with forearms and hands dangling. These people puzzled me until I suddenly realised that they had been burned and were holding their arms out to prevent the painful friction of raw surfaces rubbing together. A naked woman carrying a naked baby came into view. I averted my gaze. Perhaps they had been in the bath. But then I saw a naked man, and it occurred to me that, like myself, some strange thing had deprived them of their clothes. An old woman lay near me with an expression of suffering on her face; but she made no sound. Indeed, one thing was common to everyone I saw – complete silence.

Michihiko Hachiya

8 AUGUST 1945

London

After a busy morning in the office I hurried along the Strand to meet Dan and George Jellicoe for lunch at the Savoy Grill. I found them bent over the *Midday Standard* at a nice corner table. They hardly looked up when I arrived but moved the paper so I could read it too.

Across the front page, in huge letters, was one word – 'OBLITERATION'. In aghast silence we read that the Allies had dropped an Atom bomb on Hiroshima last Monday at 1.30 a.m. Four square miles, or sixty per cent of the city, were wiped out by the incredible pressure and heat. All living things were destroyed. Since then, from Guam, General Spaatz, US Air Force, has announced that reconnaissance photos, taken as soon as the seven-and-a-half-mile high mountain of dust and smoke had cleared, show the heart of the city swept as though by a bulldozer with awful thoroughness. It is rumoured that the bomb weighed only five hundred pounds.

Throughout lunch we talked of this news which eclipsed anything we had ever heard in our lives. It seemed to us that all modern inventions, even Navies, Armies and Air Forces are now out of date, dwarfed by this appalling weapon.

Walter Monckton wandered over and sat down at our table: 'This is the biggest thing which has happened since Christ came,' he said. 'The heat, the driving power of this thing, is vast. If one tenth of one per cent can completely destroy four and one tenth square miles then a full dose could destroy four thousand square miles. It means we could change the weather, melt the poles – and every aspect of trade and civilisation as we know them could be altered. This discovery is so huge that there is little one can think of that it might not change.'

On another page of the *Standard* the heading was: 'Japanese General escaped on an elephant in Burma.'

Hermione Ranfurly

On 9 August, the Americans dropped a second atomic device on the city of Nagasaki. The two bombs killed more than 200,000 people, with thousands more dying from the effects of radiation poisoning in the months and years after. Japan capitulated on 15 August.

‡

Freedom and Imprisonment

*For Australian POW Russell Braddon, the end of the war against Japan came
just in time.*

Then came a rumour that we were about to be shot the next day. And to
settle our fate – for if we were to be shot we had determined to be shot
running – the resourceful Paddy Matthews stole a wireless set and listened
in that night. That night was August 15th, 1945, and Paddy told us not to
worry, that he had just heard that the war was over. The Emperor of Japan,
overwhelmed by the power of atomic bombs and faced with the prospect
of an invasion of Nippon, had unconditionally surrendered.

Three days later even the Japanese themselves admitted that we need
no longer work. But the war had not been won: nor lost. It had simply, for
the moment, stopped. They ceased to bellow 'Currah' and instead bowed
politely when we passed. The food which they had recently declared to be
non-existent, they now produced in vast quantities so that we might eat our
fill. Likewise drugs appeared from everywhere and in profusion.

Then we all assembled, thousands upon thousands of men, until there
were 17,000 there, in Changi gaol. British paratroopers arrived and were
greeted politely by the Japanese. Then Mountbatten arrived and (though
we were ordered not to by our Administration) a few of us walked the
seventeen miles into Singapore to see him accept Itagaki's surrender. At
that brief ceremony, when Mountbatten drove fearlessly down through
hundreds of thousands of hysterical Malays and Chinese, standing upright
in an open car: when Itagaki met him on the steps of the civic hall and
handed over his sword – for that brief moment I felt that the war really
was over. But it didn't last.

I walked down to the harbour and on board the *Sussex* – where I was
fed and washed and given clean clothes by the ever-hospitable matelots of
the Royal Navy. I stayed there, smuggled away, for two days: then returned
to the gaol in a jeep with eighteen other 'sightseeing' POWs.

At the gaol I heard that the Ice-Cream Man no longer lived – which
didn't surprise me. Also that we were now in the hands of an organisation
known as RAPWI (which meant 'Rehabilitation of Allied Prisoners-of-
War and Internees' and was surely impressive enough).

When, a month later, we still languished on the Island impatiently
awaiting shipping home, RAPWI was re-christened – in the British
manner – Retain All Prisoners-of-War Indefinitely.

This seemed to sting someone into activity, for at once we were drafted into shiploads and the docks became crowded with transports.

We said all our good-byes.

Mario left, waving an excited Latin farewell, for Italy. Ron Searle and Chris departed for Britain – the one for fame, the other for medicine. Hap Kelly flew ostentatiously and swiftly back to Texas in a Skymaster, sent promptly by an ever-attentive government. David Griffin flew to Sydney and the Bar: Downer to Adelaide and the Federal Australian Parliament. Hugh went home on one ship, Piddington on another, I on a third.

The careful fabric of one's personal life, built up over four years, disintegrated at a single blow. One felt curiously alone as the ship sailed out of Singapore Harbour – except for the moment when old Harry Smith was spotted leaning, as melancholy as ever, against the rail of a ship we passed. As one man, our vessel roared: 'You'll never get off the Island,' at which Harry waved miserably and we laughed.

Then the sense of loneliness returned. All those blokes, Pommies and Australian: all those ties – gone. And then I realised, as I looked back and in the distance saw Changi's tower with its radar screen that didn't work, and above it the flagmast from which the poached egg had now vanished and the Union Jack flew, what was the trouble. This disintegration wouldn't matter if it had been caused by the *end* of the war. *That* was the trouble. For us, and for the undefeated Japanese soldiers all over South-East Asia, the war hadn't ended. It had just, momentarily, stopped. The tower slid out of view; the symbol of our captivity was gone – but now I could think only of the words of a thousand guards, of Saito himself, of Terai the intellectual who spoke English and wrote plays: 'War finish one hundred years.'

So, for those of us who had suffered under them, and for the Nipponese themselves, this was just an interlude – the Hiroshima Incident, probably, they would call it. But the war itself, of Asia against the white man, that – under one guise or another: in one place or another – still had ninety-five years to go. The trouble was, of course, that no one at home would believe it.

And with that I brightened. After all, the sea was green and clear: the sun was warm and free: there was food a'plenty and no need for anxiety as the old ship ploughed her confident way eastwards, away from Singapore. We were all going Home. That, for the moment, must be enough.

Russell Braddon

The Japanese belief that surrender was a disgrace for any soldier led them to treat their prisoners abominably. More than 12,000 Allied POWs (and 90,000 native workers) died building the Burma Railway alone. Until the last months of the war, hardly any Japanese were taken alive. Germany, incidentally, which unlike Japan had ratified the Geneva Convention, treated its Soviet captives with equal harshness; more than 90 per cent of them never returned home.

Like many Japanese, Private Yuji Aida was wary of his fate as a prisoner of the Allies.

The following day we received an issue of dried fish, sugar and soap, and at length found our way back, late at night, to the temple. It was the night of the 15th August. We suddenly became aware of a deathly stillness. It was unbelievable, but we could no longer hear the insane boom-boom of heavy artillery, nor the incessant 'da-da-da' of the heavy machine-guns. It was the very height of the monsoon season, so the noise of the rain must have been very loud and we were soaked right through to our loincloths; I have a distinct recollection of straining my ears to hear the sound of the guns as we were drying our clothes out in front of a fire. Yet the sound of the rain has vanished from my memory and all I can remember is the deathly silence of that night. Probably the noise of the rain was a symbol of safety and security for me and I simply did not hear it as a distinct sound any more. We had forgotten how peaceful night could be with no sounds of rifle-fire to be heard. So the reports were true. The war had come to an end.

And yet our hearts suddenly became heavier than they had been the day before. The significance of 'unconditional surrender' began to impress itself upon us. We had capitulated. Our arms would be given up, we would become prisoners, would be sent to a prison camp – this much was certain. But then what? Perhaps the enemy would begin reprisals against us – lynchings, even. Without doubt we would be compelled to carry out forced labour. The worn-out, emaciated figures of British prisoners of war we had seen as we were being brought to Burma crossed our minds. With bodies weakened to that extent, would we be able to endure labour forced on us at the point of the bayonet? If things went well, perhaps we would return to Japan – if there was any Japan left to return to.

I remembered the ruins of Mandalay I had seen in the spring. In that city, which reminded me of Kyoto, and in which only the walls of the royal palace remained standing, the water in the moat was a clear blue. We had cooked ourselves a meal there. But this city, which had once had a population of a hundred thousand people, had been literally annihilated. As far as the eye could see it had been transformed into acres of rubble. It had not been destroyed by incendiaries as had happened to cities in Japan – Mandalay had been bombed, and not a single brick or concrete building remained intact. I remembered seeing typewriters turned into smouldering lumps of metal lying in the rubble and there floated before my eyes a picture of the Burmese girls who passed by every day to the shops and offices on the banks of the moat. If this had happened to Japan, there wouldn't be a single trace left of our towns and cities, built as they were of wood and paper; and even if our parents were still alive, we might not know where they were, or what was happening to them. When we thought along these lines, we felt something different from the darkness of pure despair which had filled our hearts until then and a new kind of indescribable uneasiness, a great apprehension, began to come over us.

Yuji Aida

The author was held at Athlone Camp in Burma until May 1947. He was later to become professor of history at Kyoto University.

Autumn 1945 and beyond

The Japanese Surrender

The formal surrender by Japan took place on the USS Missouri on 2 September 1945. Diplomat Toshikazu Kase was a member of the Japanese delegation.

There were four destroyers with white placards hung on the mast marked A to D. We boarded the one marked B, which was the *Lansdown*, a ship which saw much meritorious service in the battle of the Pacific. As the destroyer pushed out of the harbour, we saw in the offing lines on lines of grey warships, both heavy and light, anchored in majestic array. This was the mighty pageant of the Allied navies that so lately belched forth their crashing battle, now holding in their swift thunder and floating like calm sea birds on the subjugated waters. A spirit of gay festivity pervaded the atmosphere.

After about an hour's cruise the destroyer stopped in full view of the battleship *Missouri*, which lay anchored some eighteen miles off the shore. The huge 45,000 tonner towered high above the rest of the proud squadron. High on the mast there fluttered in the wind the Stars and Stripes. It was this flag that has lighted the marching step of America's destiny on to shining victory. Today this flag of glory was raised in triumph to mark the Big Day. As we approached the battleship in a motor launch, our eyes were caught by rows of sailors massed on her broadside lining the rails, a starry multitude, in their glittering uniforms of immaculate white.

Soon the launch came alongside the battleship, and we climbed its gangway, Shigemitsu [the Japanese Foreign Minister] leading the way, heavily limping on his cane. For he walks on a wooden leg, having had his leg blown off by a bomb outrage in Shanghai some fifteen years ago. It was as if he negotiated each step with a groan and we, the rest of us, echoed it with a sigh. As we, eleven in all, climbed on to the veranda deck on the starboard side, we gathered into three short rows facing the representatives of the Allied powers across a table covered with green cloth, on which were placed the white documents of surrender. The veranda deck was animated by a motley of sparkling colours, red, gold, brown, and olive, as decorations and ribbons decked the uniforms of different cut and colour worn by the Allied representatives. There were also row upon row of American admirals and generals in sombre khaki; but what added to the festive gaiety of the occasion was the sight of the war correspondents who, monkey-like, hung on to every cliff-like point of vantage in most precarious postures. Evidently scaffolding had been specially constructed for the convenience of the cameramen, who were working frantically on their exciting job. Then there was a gallery of spectators who seemed numberless, overcrowding every bit of available space on the great ship, on the mast, on the chimneys, on the gun turrets – on everything and everywhere.

They were all thronged, packed to suffocation, representatives, journalists, spectators, an assembly of brass, braid, and brand. As we appeared on the scene we were, I felt, being subjected to the torture of the pillory. There were a million eyes beating us in the million shafts of a rattling storm of arrows barbed with fire. I felt their keenness sink into my body with a sharp physical pain. Never have I realised that the glance of glaring eyes could hurt so much.

We waited for a few minutes standing in the public gaze like penitent boys awaiting the dreaded schoolmaster. I tried to preserve with the utmost sangfroid the dignity of defeat, but it was difficult and every minute seemed to contain ages. I looked up and saw painted on the wall nearby several miniature Rising Suns, our flag, evidently in numbers corresponding to the planes and submarines shot down or sunk by the crew of the battleship. As I tried to count these markings, tears rose in my throat and quickly gathered to the eyes, flooding them. I could hardly bear the sight now. Heroes of unwritten stories, they were young boys who defied death gaily and gallantly, manning the daily thinning ranks of the suicide corps. They were just like cherry blossoms, emblems of our national character, all of a sudden blooming into riotous beauty and just as quickly going away. What do they see today, their spirit, the glorious thing, looking down on the scene of our surrender?

MacArthur walks quietly from the interior of the ship and steps to the microphones:

'We are gathered here, representatives of the major warring powers,' he said, 'to conclude a solemn agreement whereby peace may be restored. The issues, involving divergent ideals and ideologies, have been determined on the battlefields of the world and hence are not for our discussion or debate. Nor is it for us here to meet, representing as we do a majority of the people of the earth, in a spirit of distrust, malice or hatred. But rather it is for us, both victors and vanquished, to rise to that higher dignity which alone befits the sacred purposes we are about to serve, committing all our people unreservedly to faithful compliance with the obligation they are here formally to assume.

'It is my earnest hope and indeed the hope of all mankind that from this solemn occasion a better world shall emerge out of the blood and carnage of the past – a world founded upon faith and understanding – a world dedicated to the dignity of man and the fulfilment of his most cherished wish for freedom, tolerance and justice.

'The terms and conditions upon which the surrender of the Japanese Imperial Forces is here to be given and accepted are contained in the instrument of surrender now before you.

'As Supreme Commander for the Allied Powers, I announce it my firm purpose, in the tradition of the countries I represent, to proceed in the discharge of my responsibilities with justice and tolerance, while taking all necessary dispositions to insure that the terms of surrender are fully, promptly and faithfully complied with.'

In a few minutes' time the speech was over and the Supreme Commander invited the Japanese delegates to sign the instrument of surrender. Shigemitsu signed first followed by [General] Umedzu. It was eight minutes past nine when MacArthur put his signature to the documents. Other representatives of the Allied Powers followed suit in the order of the United States, China, the United Kingdom, the Soviet Union, Australia, Canada, France, the Netherlands and New Zealand.

When all the representatives had finished signing, MacArthur announced slowly: 'Let us pray that peace be now restored to the world and that God will preserve it always. These proceedings are closed.'

At that moment, the skies parted and the sun shone brightly through the layers of clouds. There was a steady drone above and now it became a deafening roar and an armada of airplanes paraded into sight, sweeping over the warships. Four hundred B-29s and 1,500 carrier planes joined in the aerial pageant in a final salute. It was over.

Toshikazu Kase

The author later became Japan's first ambassador to the United Nations. He died in 2004.

General Slim and Lord Mountbatten received the local Japanese surrender to British forces 10 days later in Singapore.

I had already, before the receipt of General MacArthur's orders, issued instructions to all my commanders as to how the Japanese surrender was to be conducted in our area. In these I had laid down that all senior Japanese officers were to surrender their swords to appropriate British commanders in front of parades of their own troops. There had been some protests at this from our Japanese experts who averred that:

(i) The Japanese officer's honour was so bound up with his Samurai sword that, rather than surrender it, he would go on fighting.
(ii) Alternatively, as the lawyers say, if he did surrender it before his men, he would never again be able to exercise command over them.
(iii) He would in fact, rather than be so publicly shamed, commit suicide.

My answers to these forebodings had been:

(i) If the Japanese liked to go on fighting, I was ready for them.
(ii) If the officers lost their soldiers' respect I could not care less as I intended to separate them from their men in any case.
(iii) If the officers committed suicide I had already prepared for this by broadcasting that any Japanese officer wishing to commit suicide would be given every facility.

I was convinced that an effective way really to impress on the Japanese that they had been beaten in the field was to insist on this ceremonial surrender of swords. No Japanese soldier who had seen his general march up and hand over his sword, would ever doubt that the Invincible Army was invincible no longer. We did not want a repetition of the German First War legend of an unconquered army. With this in mind, I was dismayed to be told that General MacArthur in his overall instruction for the surrender had decided that the 'archaic' ceremony of the surrender of swords was not to be enforced. I am afraid I disregarded his wishes. In South-East Asia all Japanese officers surrendered their swords to British officers of similar or higher rank; the enemy divisional and army commanders handed theirs in before large parades of their already disarmed troops. Field-Marshal Tarauchi's sword is in Admiral Mountbatten's hands; General Kimura's is now on my mantelpiece, where I always intended that one day it should be.

In Singapore on 12th September 1945 I sat on the left of the Supreme

Commander, Admiral Mountbatten, in the line of his Commanders-in-Chief and principal staff officers, while the formal unconditional surrender of all Japanese forces, land, sea, and air, in South-East Asia was made to him. I looked at the dull impassive masks that were the faces of the Japanese generals and admirals seated opposite. Their plight moved me not at all. For them, I had none of the sympathy of soldier for soldier, that I had felt for Germans, Turks, Italians, or Frenchmen that by the fortune of war I had seen surrender. I knew too well what these men and those under their orders had done to *their* prisoners. They sat there apart from the rest of humanity. If I had no feeling for them, they, it seemed, had no feeling of any sort, until Itagaki, who had replaced Field-Marshal Tarauchi, laid low by a stroke, leant forward to affix his seal to the surrender document. As he pressed heavily on the paper, a spasm of rage and despair twisted his face. Then it was gone and his mask was as expressionless as the rest. Outside, the same Union Jack that had been hauled down in surrender in 1942 flew again at the masthead.

The war was over.

William Slim

Forty million people had lost their lives during the Second World War.

‡

Nuremberg

In November 1945 the International Military Tribunal was established to bring the principal Nazis to account. Defendants were tried on four different charges: crimes against peace; war crimes; crimes against humanity; and conspiracy to commit crimes alleged in other courts. Twenty-one people were arraigned and the court sat until September 1946. The most senior defendant was Hermann Goering.

'This air of evil'

Airey Neave had been a prisoner of the Gestapo, and there was thus a certain justice that it should fall to him to serve the indictment on the man who had founded that organisation.

As the cell was unlocked, I braced myself to meet him. In a few seconds the door swung open. Andrus entered and Goering rose unsteadily to his feet. With his stick under his arm, Andrus stood stiffly to attention on my

right. His polished helmet glinted in the sunllight from the small barred
window. I stepped toward Goering and waited. To my left, stood the
interpreter and Mr Willey. Then came the two soldiers bearing documents.
There was no room for the other witnesses of this macabre ceremony.
They slowly assembled outside and I could hear their boots grating on the
stone floor.

The cell was crowded and I felt shut in with Goering. Once again that
urgent desire to break out came to me, as it had often done since my days
in the town gaol of Colditz. My eyes searched the cell. There was a steel
bed, a table, a chair. No piece of furniture was allowed within four feet of
the window wall. The chair was removed at night and the bed fastened to
the floor. There were signs of fresh plaster, where all bars and hooks had
been removed from the window. It was a harsh place for any prisoner. I
caught sight of the photographs of Goering's wife and small daughter on
his table. They were carefully arranged beside a pile of books.

For a time, I shunned Goering's face. It seemed an age before the rest
of the party came to a halt outside. I felt forced to take another look at the
cell. It was about thirteen feet long and nine feet wide. Opposite, was a
water closet and a washbowl with running water.

I realised at this second glance, how good the conditions were. Far
better than Plotsk in 1941. My eyes turned from the water closet back to
the photographs of the little girl, Edda Goering. It was only a month since
Sam Harris and I had studied the Dechenschule concentration camp near
Essen, where fifteen toilets were available for five hundred Krupp slaves.

The photograph of Goering's daughter, so like her father, touched me.
Then I felt suddenly angry. It was impossible to forget the Krupp guards
who caught a prisoner trying to keep a snapshot of his parents. They seized
it, tore it up, and beat him till he bled.

My apparent diffidence, which puzzled Judge Biddle and Mr Willey,
was gone. I turned and stared at Goering. It was his turn to look away
from me towards Andrus to whom he insolently referred as 'the Fire
Brigade Colonel'.

Goering was a mixture of bluff and moral cowardice. He refused to
meet my eyes but I could see that his were small and greedy. Rebecca
West, who studied him closely in the dock, likened him to those fat
women with their sleek cats seen in the late morning in doorways along
the steep streets of Marseilles. Certainly he had the look of a woman about
him and I was reminded of his passion for jewels.

It was not that Goering seemed in the least homosexual, rather the
reverse. He was, nevertheless, indefinably feminine. He appeared exquis-

itely corrupt and soft even amid the austerities of Nuremberg. My first impression was of meeting a dissolute Roman Emperor, game to the last.

Goering was now fifty-three. Since he had been in prison at Nuremberg in September, his weight had declined from twenty to fifteen stone and his grey uniform was too large. His drug intake was being reduced. His complexion was an actor's. It had a brownish tint like that of a veteran star inured to make-up and costume. Indeed, before the end of the Thousand-year Reich, Goering was seen at official parties in a toga and sandals. When he first came into the hands of Colonel Andrus, he had been a decayed and gloomy voluptuary. By October, he was once more on the stage, his health and confidence returning.

Andrus had known Goering since May when the former Reichsmarschall had been detained at Mondorf-les-Bains after his capture. He used to describe how Goering arrived with sixteen monogrammed suitcases, a red hatbox and a valet. His fingernails were varnished red. He had been indiscreetly entertained by American officers and believed he was on his way to see Eisenhower. Andrus has also written that one of the suitcases contained 20,000 paracodeine pills.

At last, Goering turned to face me. I caught the full menace of his narrow, bright eyes. His wide lips suggested nameless appetites. I was no longer afraid of him, despite this air of evil. I was struck again by his small stature and the way in which his grey Air Force uniform tunic hung loosely. He wore no badges of rank which had been stripped from him. The showmanship, the decorations, and the panoply of the Reichsmarschall of Greater Germany had vanished in the flames and dust.

This was the destined successor to Hitler; the Commander-in-Chief of the German Air Forces; the Prime Minister of Prussia and the President of the Reichstag. He now lived in a cell watched night and day by GIs. Instead of the stupendous rooms of scuttled Carinhall, with its plundered wines and looted tapestries, he lived out of a GI mess tin. No knives or forks were allowed in the cells and all food had to be eaten with a spoon. Breakfast was oatmeal and bread. Lunch: soup, fried fish, tomato sauce, beet salad, rice and coffee. Supper: bean stew, bread and tea.

I was surprised to find my voice.

'Hermann Wilhelm Goering?'

The man was still the actor. He bowed to me and smiled. I noticed that despite his age, his hair was a thick, dark brown, another hint of Hollywood. When I first entered, his mouth had twitched nervously; he seemed unsteady. Now he was in possession of the stage again. There was a trace of geniality in those cruel eyes as he gestured with one fat white hand towards the bed. It was as if to say, 'I am afraid I cannot offer you a chair.'

On my next visit to his cell, on the following day, he used those very words in a fruity voice, as I called to discuss the choice of German counsel. This day he simply said:

'*Jawohl.*'

I repeated the words agreed with Mr Willey.

'I am Major Neave, the officer appointed by the International Military Tribunal to serve upon you a copy of the indictment in which you are named as defendant.'

Goering's expression changed to a scowl, the look of a stage gangster, as the words were interpreted.

I handed him a copy of the indictment which he took in silence. He listened as I said, 'I am also asked to explain to you Article 16 of the Charter of the Tribunal.'

A copy in German was handed to him.

'If you will look at paragraph (c). You have the right to conduct your own defence before the tribunal or to have the assistance of counsel.'

My words were correct and precise. Goering looked serious and depressed as I paused.

'So it has come,' he said.

Airey Neave

The atrocity film

Gustav Gilbert was a prison psychologist employed at Nuremberg. He carefully noted the defendants' reactions to a documentary film made by the Americans about the concentration camps.

Schacht objects to being made to look at film as I ask him to move over; turns away, folds arms, gazes into gallery . . . (Film starts). Frank nods at authentication at introduction of film . . . Fritzsche (who had not seen any part of film before) already looks pale and sits aghast as it starts with scenes of prisoners burned alive in a barn . . . Keitel wipes brow, takes off headphones . . . Hess glares at screen, looking like a ghoul with sunken eyes over the footlamp . . . Keitel puts on headphone, glares at screen out of the corner of his eye . . . von Neurath has head bowed, doesn't look . . . Funk covers his eyes, looks as if he is in agony, shakes his head . . . Ribbentrop closes his eyes, looks away . . . Sauckel mops brow . . . Frank swallows hard, blinks eyes, trying to stifle tears . . . Fritzsche watches

intensely with knitted brow, cramped at the end of his seat, evidently in
agony . . . Goering keeps leaning on balustrade, not watching most of the
time, looking droopy . . . Funk mumbles something under his breath . . .
Streicher keeps watching, immobile except for an occasional squint . . .
Funk now in tears, blows nose, wipes eyes, looks down . . . Frick shakes
head at illustration of 'violent death' – Frank mutters 'Horrible!' . . .
Rosenberg fidgets, peeks at screen, bows head, looks to see how others
are reacting . . . Seyss-Inquart stoic throughout . . . Speer looks very sad,
swallows hard . . . Defence attorneys are now muttering, 'for God's sake
– terrible'. Raeder watches without budging . . . von Papen sits with hand
over brow, looking down, has not looked at screen yet . . . Hess keeps
looking bewildered . . . piles of dead are shown in a slave labour camp . . .
von Schirach watching intently, gasps, whispers to Sauckel . . . Funk crying
now . . . Goering looks sad, leaning on elbow . . . Doenitz has head
bowed, no longer watching . . . Sauckel shudders at picture of Buchenwald
crematorium oven . . . as human skin lampshade is shown, Streicher says,
'I don't believe that' . . . Goering coughing . . . Attorneys gasping . . .
Now Dachau . . . Schacht still not looking . . . Frank nods his head bitterly
and says, 'Horrible!' . . . Rosenberg still fidgeting, leans forward, looks
around, leans back, hangs head . . . Fritzsche, pale, biting lips, really seems
in agony . . . Doenitz has head buried in hands . . . Keitel now hanging
head . . . Ribbentrop looks up at screen as British officer starts to speak,
saying he has already buried 17,000 corpses . . . Frank biting his nails . . .
Frick shakes his head incredulously at speech of female doctor describing
treatment and experiments on female prisoners at Belsen . . . As Kramer is
shown, Funk says with choking voice, 'The dirty swine!' . . . Ribbentrop
sitting with pursed lips and blinking eyes, not looking at screen . . . Funk
crying bitterly, claps hand over mouth as women's naked corpses are
thrown into pit . . . Keitel and Ribbentrop look up at mention of tractor
clearing corpses, see it, then hang their heads . . . Streicher shows signs of
disturbance for first time . . . Film ends.

After showing of the film, Hess remarks, 'I don't believe it.' Goering
whispers to him to keep quiet, his own cockiness quite gone. Streicher
says something about 'perhaps in the last days'. Fritzsche retorts scornfully,
'Millions? In the last days? – No.' Otherwise there is a gloomy silence as
the prisoners file out of the courtroom.

Gustav Gilbert

Eleven of the defendants were sentenced to be hanged. Journalist Kingsbury Smith watched their executions.

Hermann Wilhelm Goering cheated the gallows of Allied justice by committing suicide in his prison cell shortly before the ten other condemned Nazi leaders were hanged in Nuremberg gaol. He swallowed cyanide he had concealed in a copper cartridge shell, while lying on a cot in his cell.

The one-time Number Two man in the Nazi hierarchy was dead two hours before he was scheduled to have been dropped through the trapdoor of a gallows erected in a small, brightly lighted gymnasium in the gaol yard, thirty-five yards from the cell block where he spent his last days of ignominy.

Joachim von Ribbentrop, foreign minister in the ill-starred regime of Adolf Hitler, took Goering's place as first to the scaffold.

Last to depart this life in a total span of just about two hours was Arthur Seyss-Inquart, former Gauleiter of Holland and Austria.

In between these two once-powerful leaders, the gallows claimed, in the order named, Field Marshal Wilhelm Keitel; Ernst Kaltenbrunner, once head of the Nazis' security police; Alfred Rosenberg, arch-priest of Nazi culture in foreign lands; Hans Frank, Gauleiter of Poland; Wilhelm Frick, Nazi minister of the interior; Fritz Sauckel, boss of slave labour, Colonel General Alfred Jodl; and Julius Streicher, who bossed the anti-Semitism drive of the Hitler Reich.

As they went to the gallows, most of the ten endeavoured to show bravery. Some were defiant and some were resigned and some begged the Almighty for mercy.

All except Rosenberg made brief, last-minute statements on the scaffold. But the only one to make any reference to Hitler or the Nazi ideology in his final moments was Julius Streicher.

Three black-painted wooden scaffolds stood inside the gymnasium, a room approximately thirty-three feet wide by eighty feet long with plaster walls in which cracks showed. The gymnasium had been used only three days before by the American security guards for a basketball game. Two gallows were used alternately. The third was a spare for use if needed. The men were hanged one at a time, but to get the executions over with quickly, the military police would bring in a man while the prisoner who preceded him still was dangling at the end of the rope.

The ten once great men in Hitler's Reich that was to have lasted for a thousand years walked up thirteen wooden steps to a platform eight feet high which also was eight feet square.

Ropes were suspended from a crossbeam supported on two posts. A new one was used for each man.

When the trap was sprung, the victim dropped from sight in the interior of the scaffolding. The bottom of it was boarded up with wood on three sides and shielded by a dark canvas curtain on the fourth, so that no one saw the death struggles of the men dangling with broken necks.

Von Ribbentrop entered the execution chamber at 1.11 a.m. Nuremberg time. He was stopped immediately inside the door by two Army sergeants who closed in on each side of him and held his arms, while another sergeant who had followed him in removed manacles from his hands and replaced them with a leather strap.

It was planned originally to permit the condemned men to walk from their cells to the execution chamber with their hands free, but all were manacled immediately following Goering's suicide.

Von Ribbentrop was able to maintain his apparent stoicism to the last. He walked steadily toward the scaffold between his two guards, but he did not answer at first when an officer standing at the foot of the gallows went through the formality of asking his name. When the query was repeated he almost shouted, 'Joachim von Ribbentrop!' and then mounted the steps without any sign of hesitation.

When he was turned around on the platform to face the witnesses, he seemed to clench his teeth and raise his head with the old arrogance. When asked whether he had any final message he said, 'God protect Germany,' in German, and then added, 'May I say something else?'

The interpreter nodded and the former diplomatic wizard of Nazidom spoke his last words in loud, firm tones: 'My last wish is that Germany realise its entity and that an understanding be reached between the East and the West. I wish peace to the world.'

As the black hood was placed in position on his head, von Ribbentrop looked straight ahead.

Then the hangman adjusted the rope, pulled the lever, and von Ribbentrop slipped away to his fate.

Field Marshal Keitel, who was immediately behind von Ribbentrop in the order of executions, was the first military leader to be executed under the new concept of international law – the principle that professional soldiers cannot escape punishment for waging aggressive wars and permitting crimes against humanity with the claim they were dutifully carrying out orders of superiors.

Keitel entered the chamber two minutes after the trap had dropped beneath von Ribbentrop, while the latter still was at the end of his rope. But von Ribbentrop's body was concealed inside the first scaffold; all that could be seen was the taut rope.

Keitel did not appear as tense as von Ribbentrop. He held his head high while his hands were being tied and walked erect toward the gallows with a military bearing. When asked his name he responded loudly and mounted the gallows as he might have mounted a reviewing stand to take a salute from German armies.

He certainly did not appear to need the help of guards who walked alongside, holding his arms. When he turned around atop the platform he looked over the crowd with the iron-jawed haughtiness of a proud Prussian officer. His last words, uttered in a full, clear voice, were translated as 'I call on God Almighty to have mercy on the German people. More than 2 million German soldiers went to their death for the fatherland before me. I follow now my sons – all for Germany.'

After his black-booted, uniformed body plunged through the trap, witnesses agreed Keitel had showed more courage on the scaffold than in the courtroom, where he had tried to shift his guilt upon the ghost of Hitler, claiming that all was the Führer's fault and that he merely carried out orders and had no responsibility.

With both von Ribbentrop and Keitel hanging at the end of their ropes there was a pause in the proceedings. The American colonel directing the executions asked the American general representing the United States on the Allied Control Commission if those present could smoke. An affirmative answer brought cigarettes into the hands of almost every one of the thirty-odd persons present. Officers and GIs walked around nervously or spoke a few words to one another in hushed voices while Allied correspondents scribbled furiously their notes on this historic though ghastly event.

In a few minutes an American Army doctor accompanied by a Russian Army doctor and both carrying stethoscopes walked to the first scaffold, lifted the curtain and disappeared within.

They emerged at 1.30 a.m. and spoke to an American colonel. The colonel swung around and facing official witnesses snapped to attention to say, 'The man is dead.'

Two GIs quickly appeared with a stretcher which was carried up and lifted into the interior of the scaffold. The hangman mounted the gallows steps, took a large commando-type knife out of a sheath strapped to his side and cut the rope.

Von Ribbentrop's limp body with the black hood still over his head was removed to the far end of the room and placed behind a black canvas curtain. This all had taken less than ten minutes.

The directing colonel turned to the witnesses and said, 'Cigarettes out, please, gentlemen.' Another colonel went out the door and over to the condemned block to fetch the next man. This was Ernst Kaltenbrunner. He entered the execution chamber at 1.36 a.m., wearing a sweater beneath his blue double-breasted coat.

With his lean haggard face furrowed by old duelling scars, this terrible successor to Reinhard Heydrich had a frightening look as he glanced around the room.

He wet his lips apparently in nervousness as he turned to mount the gallows, but he walked steadily. He answered his name in a calm, low voice. When he turned around on the gallows platform he first faced a United States Army Roman Catholic chaplain wearing a Franciscan habit. When Kaltenbrunner was invited to make a last statement, he said, 'I have loved my German people and my fatherland with a warm heart. I have done my duty by the laws of my people and I am sorry my people were led this time by men who were not soldiers and that crimes were committed of which I had no knowledge.'

This was the man, one of whose agents – a man named Rudolf Hoess – confessed at a trial that under Kaltenbrunner's orders he gassed 3 million human beings at the Auschwitz concentration camp!

As the black hood was raised over his head Kaltenbrunner, still speaking in a low voice, used a German phrase which translated means, 'Germany, good luck.'

His trap was sprung at 1.39 a.m.

Field Marshal Keitel was pronounced dead at 1.44 a.m. and three minutes later guards had removed his body. The scaffold was made ready for Alfred Rosenberg.

Rosenberg was dull and sunken-cheeked as he looked around the court. His complexion was pasty-brown, but he did not appear nervous and walked with a steady step to and up the gallows.

Apart from giving his name and replying 'no' to a question as to whether he had anything to say, he did not utter a word. Despite his avowed atheism he was accompanied by a Protestant chaplain who followed him to the gallows and stood beside him praying.

Rosenberg looked at the chaplain once, expressionless. Ninety seconds after he was swinging from the end of a hangman's rope. His was the swiftest execution of the ten.

There was a brief lull in the proceedings until Kaltenbrunner was pronounced dead at 1.52 a.m.

Hans Frank was next in the parade of death. He was the only one of the condemned to enter the chamber with a smile on his countenance.

Although nervous and swallowing frequently, this man, who was converted to Roman Catholicism after his arrest, gave the appearance of being relieved at the prospect of atoning for his evil deeds.

He answered to his name quietly and when asked for any last statement, he replied in a low voice that was almost a whisper, 'I am thankful for the kind treatment during my captivity and I ask God to accept me with mercy.'

Frank closed his eyes and swallowed as the black hood went over his head.

The sixth man to leave his prison cell and walk with handcuffed wrists to the death house was sixty-nine-year-old Wilhelm Frick. He entered the execution chamber at 2.05 a.m., six minutes after Rosenberg had been pronounced dead. He seemed the least steady of any so far and stumbled on the thirteenth step of the gallows. His only words were, 'Long live eternal Germany,' before he was hooded and dropped through the trap.

Julius Streicher made his melodramatic appearance at 2.12 a.m.

While his manacles were being removed and his hands bound, this ugly, dwarfish little man, wearing a threadbare suit and a well-worn bluish shirt buttoned to the neck but without a tie (he was notorious during his days of power for his flashy dress), glanced at the three wooden scaffolds rising up menacingly in front of him. Then he glared around the room, his eyes resting momentarily upon the small group of witnesses. By this time, his hands were tied securely behind his back. Two guards, one on each arm, directed him to Number One gallows on the left of the entrance. He walked steadily the six feet to the first wooden step but his face was twitching.

As the guards stopped him at the bottom of the steps for the identification formality he uttered his piercing scream: 'Heil Hitler!'

The shriek sent a shiver down my back.

As its echo died away an American colonel standing by the steps said sharply, 'Ask the man his name.' In response to the interpreter's query Streicher shouted, 'You know my name well.'

The interpreter repeated his request and the condemned man yelled, 'Julius Streicher.'

As he reached the platform, Streicher cried out, 'Now it goes to God.' He was pushed the last two steps to the mortal spot beneath the hangman's rope. The rope was being held back against a wooden rail by the hangman.

Streicher was swung around to face the witnesses and glared at them. Suddenly he screamed, '*Purim Fest 1946.*' (Purim is a Jewish holiday celebrated in the spring, commemorating the execution of Haman, ancient persecutor of the Jews described in the Old Testament.)

The American officer standing at the scaffold said, 'Ask the man if he has any last words.'

When the interpreter had translated, Streicher shouted, 'The Bolsheviks will hang you one day.'

When the black hood was raised over his head, Streicher said, 'I am with God.'

As it was being adjusted, Streicher's muffled voice could be heard to say, 'Adele, my dear wife.' At that instant the trap opened with a loud bang. He went down kicking. When the rope snapped taut with the body swinging wildly, groans could be heard from within the concealed interior of the scaffold. Finally, the hangman, who had descended from the gallows platform, lifted the black canvas curtain and went inside. Something happened that put a stop to the groans and brought the rope to a standstill. After it was over I was not in a mood to ask what he did, but I assume that he grabbed the swinging body and pulled down on it. We were all of the opinion that Streicher had strangled.

Then, following removal of the corpse of Frick, who had been pronounced dead at 2.20 a.m., Fritz Sauckel was brought face to face with his doom.

Wearing a sweater with no coat and looking wild-eyed, Sauckel proved to be the most defiant of any except Streicher.

Here was the man who put millions into bondage on a scale unknown since the pre-Christian era. Gazing around the room from the gallows platform he suddenly screamed, 'I am dying innocent. The sentence is wrong. God protect Germany and make Germany great again. Long live Germany! God protect my family.'

The trap was sprung at 2.26 a.m. and, as in the case of Streicher, there was a loud groan from the gallows pit as the noose snapped tightly under the weight of his body.

Ninth in the procession of death was Alfred Jodl. With the black coat-collar of his Wehrmacht uniform half turned up at the back as though hurriedly put on, Jodl entered the dismal death house with obvious signs of nervousness. He wet his lips constantly and his features were drawn and haggard as he walked, not nearly so steady as Keitel, up the gallows steps. Yet his voice was calm when he uttered his last six words on earth: 'My greetings to you, my Germany.'

At 2.34 a.m. Jodl plunged into the black hole of the scaffold. He and Sauckel hung together until the latter was pronounced dead six minutes later and removed.

The Czechoslovak-born Seyss-Inquart, whom Hitler had made ruler of Holland and Austria, was the last actor to make his appearance in this unparalleled scene. He entered the chamber at 2.38½ a.m., wearing glasses which made his face an easily remembered caricature.

He looked around with noticeable signs of unsteadiness as he limped on his left clubfoot to the gallows. He mounted the steps slowly, with guards helping him.

When he spoke his last words his voice was low but intense. He said, 'I hope that this execution is the last act of the tragedy of the Second World War and that the lesson taken from this world war will be that peace and understanding should exist between peoples. I believe in Germany.'

He dropped to death at 2.45 a.m.

With the bodies of Jodl and Seyss-Inquart still hanging, awaiting formal pronouncement of death, the gymnasium doors opened again and guards entered carrying Goering's body on a stretcher.

He had succeeded in wrecking plans of the Allied Control Council to have him lead the parade of condemned Nazi chieftains to their death. But the council's representatives were determined that Goering at least would take his place as a dead man beneath the shadow of the scaffold.

The guards carrying the stretcher set it down between the first and second gallows. Goering's big bare feet stuck out from under the bottom end of a khaki-coloured United States Army blanket. One blue-silk-clad arm was hanging over the side.

The colonel in charge of the proceedings ordered the blanket removed so that witnesses and Allied correspondents could see for themselves that Goering was definitely dead. The Army did not want any legend to develop that Goering had managed to escape.

As the blanket came off it revealed Goering clad in black silk pyjamas with a blue jacket shirt over them, and this was soaking wet, apparently the result of efforts by prison doctors to revive him.

The face of this twentieth-century freebooting political racketeer was still contorted with the pain of his last agonising moments and his final gesture of defiance.

They covered him up quickly and this Nazi warlord, who like a character out of the days of the Borgias, had wallowed in blood and beauty, passed behind a canvas curtain into the black pages of history.

Kingsbury Smith

‡

A soldier comes home

Five and a half years later I was out; my war was eventually over and after a long and uncomfortable trip from Singapore on the *Monarch of Bermuda*, filled with anticipation, relief, and a modest sense of a modest job well done, I reached my Regimental Headquarters on a dank October morning outside Guildford, where I was issued with a pork-pie hat, a cotton-tweed suit, a pair of new black shoes, a ration book and a travel warrant for Haywards Heath. Nothing could have been more prosaic, dull, or flat. Dragging a cardboard box of ill-fitting clothing to the gates on the way to the station I was accorded my last salute from a pale young Sergeant.

'Is that all there is to it?' I asked him. 'I mean, I just go?'

He smiled a weak-tea smile. 'That's all, Sir,' and then flicking a wan eye at my thin line of ribbons he added, 'thanks for the help, Sir.' He wasn't even wearing the Defence Medal. I supposed he must have been fourteen when I joined up. Help be buggered: where, I wondered, wandering down to the station, had all those years gone? A Morris Minor stopped beside me and a man asked me if I wanted a lift. I hadn't thought about a taxi – and wasn't sure of the rate of exchange even, for I had not handled English money for a long time. We drove in silence for a while. He had assumed, correctly, that I would be going to the station.

'Been away long then?' His voice was kind, not curious.

'Not long. A couple of years.'

A woman at a crossing suddenly slapped her child, shook it angrily, and then pushed her pram hurriedly over the road.

'You'll see some changes here then, after two years.'

'I expect so.'

'People are fed up really. Can't blame them, can you? A war's a war. They don't know what to do with the peace now they've got it. All at sixes and sevens.'

So, I thought, am I. What lies ahead for me now? I don't think *I'm* all that used to a peace. Two weeks left to wear the uniform which, after five years, had given me a sense of identity, then into the cotton-tweed and then what? An interview with some headmaster in December and, if I passed, a temporary job teaching at a Prep School in, of all God-forsaken places, Windlesham. Did I want to go and sit among the pines and heather of Surrey and teach scrappy Art, History and, possibly, English to a lot of stinking little boys in grey flannel suits? And supervise their cricket, I who couldn't even buckle on my pads, or tell the bails from the ball? Was this all that I was any use for now? I was, indeed, most grateful to my brother

officer who had made this temporary job even possible, for he taught, or
had taught, at the same school before the war, and had put in a good word
for me some months ago when I had written to him, in despair, saying
that I would not, after all, make the Army my career, and would be
demobilised in October without any chances of a future job, and could he
suggest something for me to do. I was not, I added, ever returning to the
theatre; I had been away too long, it would be impossible to try to start
again; and in any case I reluctantly agreed with him that he was right when
he had once said, years ago in Shrivenham where we had first met, that
acting was a pansy job. So the theatre was out . . . what could I do?
Windlesham and Cricket?

My silence in the car was impolite. I apologised.

'I know how you feel; at sixes and sevens yourself. Married, are you?'

'No . . . not married.'

'Just as well really. So many of them didn't last the first bloody leave; all
done in hysteria, really. Sad.'

At the station he pushed a packet of five cigarettes into my hand. 'Have
these, not much, might cheer you up. I can get more, don't worry. Know
a girl up at the Wheatsheaf.' He drove off before I could thank him.

'I can see you been in the sun, mate,' said a porter, shoving my box and
bits and pieces on to the rack. 'Where was you, Alamein then?'

'Calcutta . . . Java . . . Malaya.'

'Aha! The Forgotten Army, eh?'

'No . . . no! Nothing as brave as that.'

'Well, welcome home, though you won't get sunstroke where you're
going, but I expect you'll be quite glad of that. Can't stand the heat myself,
brings me out in a rash.'

Friendly, kind, solicitous; traditionally English. Like the tidy little back
gardens whipping past the window. Neat, dull, familiar. Here and there a
row of houses rubbled by a bomb, washing fluttering, children playing in
a school-yard, a red bus turning a corner. The flat October light grey; grey
as the brick houses, the autumn gardens, the pearl sky above. Through the
rumble of the wheels I heard, distinctly, the bull-frogs in the lily pool
outside my house in Bandoeng, the clatter and clack of the evening wind
in the bamboos, the soft rustle of the frangipani leaves, and the quarrelling
of the parrots, swooping low over the eaves of the house, then spiralling
upwards into the lavender sky, wheeling, diving, emerald turning to
ebony, as they splintered and scattered hurriedly into the gleaming leaves
of the great banyan tree to roost before the swift fall of night. And then
the great hush which followed; the hills across the valley gently fading

from deepest blue to blackest black, the sky vermilion and in that pure stillness the urgent, angry, reminding rat tat tat tat . . . tat tat . . . tat–a–ratter of a machine gun down on the perimeter wire.

It had been a goodish war, as far as wars go. I had survived, although I still wondered, slumped as I now was, looking out at Surrey, how the hell I had. Luck most probably. That and the very early training of my sensible parents and Lally, who had always insisted that one could do anything one wanted, if one worked for it; the working was the hardest part . . . the wanting came easier; but I had worked.

Dirk Bogarde

Acknowledgements

Minor changes to spelling and punctuation have been made to some of the extracts.

The editors and publishers wish to thank the following for permission to use copyright material:

Birlinn Ltd for material from William Manchester, *Goodbye Darkness* (2000) pp. 3–7, 288–90;

A. & C. Black Publishers Ltd for material from Anne Brusselmans, *Rendez-vous 127*, Ernest Benn (1954) pp. 103–5;

Blackwell Publishing for material from Abraham Lewin, *A Cup of Tears: Diary of a Warsaw Ghetto* (1990) pp. 106–8;

Brandt & Hochman Literary Agents, Inc. on behalf of the author for material from Charles B. MacDonald, *Company Commander*, Burford Books (1999) pp. 125–6, 186–9. Copyright © 1947, renewed 1975, by Charles B. MacDonald;

Cambridge University Press for material from D. Barlone, *A French Officer's Diary* (1942) pp. 1–5, 55–9;

Carlton Books Ltd for material from Bob Carruthers and Simon Drew, *Servants of Evil* (2001) pp. 214–16. Copyright © Edgehill Publishing Ltd, 2001;

Chambers Harrap Publishers for material from Mark Clark, *Calculated Risk*, Harrap (1951);

Chrysalis Books for material from Gerard Woods, *Wings at Sea*, Conway Maritime Press (1985) pp. 94–5;

Don Congdon Associates, Inc. on behalf of the author for material from William L. Shirer, *Berlin Diary*, Knopf (1941) pp. 77–80. Copyright © 1941, renewed 1968 by William L. Shirer;

Curtis Brown Ltd, London, on behalf of the authors or their Estates for material from Winston S. Churchill, *The Second World War* abridged version, Pimlico (2002) pp. 161–2, 217–19, 237, 243, 274, 312, 355–6, 495, 562–3, 601–2, 603, 646, 853, 945. Copyright © Winston S. Churchill, 1959; Russell Braddon, *The Naked Island*, Werner Laurie (1954) pp. 87–9, 107–11, 199–201; 260–3; and on behalf of Rosemary Lewin for material from Ronald Lewin, *The War on Land*, Hutchinson (1969) pp. 122–3. Copyright © Ronald Lewin, 1969;

Eric Dobby Publishing Ltd for material from H. W. Schmidt, *With Rommel in the Desert*, Harrap (1951) pp. 77–9, 108–11, 146–9, 182–4, 257–8;

Doubleday, a division of Random House, Inc, for material from Dwight D. Eisenhower, *Crusade in Europe*, Heinemann (1948) pp. 273–7. Copyright © 1948 by Doubleday, a division of Random House, Inc.;

Dutton, a division of Penguin Group (USA) Inc., for material from Stanley Johnston, *Queen of the Flat-Tops* (1942) pp. 140–4. Copyright © 1942 by E. P. Dutton & Company, renewed copyright © 1970 by Barbara Johnston;

Greene and Heaton Ltd on behalf of the author for material from William Sansom, *A Fireman's Journal* (1947) pp. 137–40. Copyright © William Sansom 1947;

Greenhill Books/Lionel Leventhal Ltd for material from Arthur Harris, *Bomber Offensive*, Collins (1947) pp. 108–13; Otto Skorzeny, *Skorzeny's Special Missions*, Greenhill (1997) pp. 78–80; Nicolaus von Below, *At Hitler's Side*, Greenhill (2001) pp. 208–11; Heinz Knoke, *I Flew for the Führer*, Greenhill (1997) pp. 44–8, 144–6; Evgeni Bessonov, *Tank Rider*, Greenhill (2003) pp. 155–7, 220–3; and W. Kennedy-Shaw, *Long Range Desert Group*, Collins (1945) pp. 59–60;

Grove/Atlantic, Inc, and Alexander Matthews, literary executor of the Estate of the author, for material from Martha Gellhorn, *The Face of War* (1988). Copyright © 1988 Martha Gellhorn;

Robert Hale Ltd for material from Alfred Allbury, *Bamboo and Bushido* (1955) pp. 14–17; and Ken Tout, *Tank!* (1985) pp. 103–7;

HarperCollins Publishers Ltd for material from Tom Pocock, *1945: The Dawn Came Up Like Thunder*, Collins (1983) pp. 180–2; Erwin Rommel, *The Rommel Papers*, Collins (1953) pp. 19–20, 467–8, 502–6; with Scribner, an imprint of Simon & Schuster Adult Publishing Group, for Eric Newby, *Love and War in the Appenines (When the Snow Comes, They Will Take You Away)*, Hodder & Stoughton (1951) pp. 131–3. Copyright © 1971 by Eric

Newby; and with The Free Press, a division of Simon & Schuster Adult Publishing Group, for Leo Marks, *Between Silk and Cyanide: A Codemarker's War 1941–1945* (1999) pp. 492–8. Copyright © 1998 by Leo Marks;

HarperCollins Publishers Inc. for material from Henry Berry, *Semper Fi, Mac* (1982) pp. 143–5. Copyright © 1982 by Henry Berry; Russell Miller, *Nothing Less Than Victory* (1993) pp. 208, 311–12, 379–80, 391–2, 443–4. Copyright © 1993 by Russell Miller; and John Comer, *Combat Crew*, revised edition, William Morrow (1986) pp. 264–5. Copyright © 1986, 1988 by John Comer;

A. M. Heath & Co Ltd on behalf of the authors or their Estates for material from Rikihei Inoguchi and Tadashi Nakajima, with Roger Pineau, *The Divine Wind*, Hutchinson (1959) pp. 88–90; Fred Majdalany, *The Monastery*, Bodley Head (1945); and Christabel Bielenberg, *The Past is Myself*, Corgi (1984) pp. 111–15;

Helion & Company Ltd for material from Armin Scheiderbauer, *Adventures in my Youth* (2003) pp. 148–9;

Herbig Verlagsbuchhandlung for material from Joachim Wieder, *Stalingrad und Die Verantwortung des Soldaten* [*Stalingrad – Memories and Reassessments*], ed., Heinrich Graf von Einsiedel, Cassell (2002) pp. 55–7, 98–100. Copyright © 1993 by F. A. Herbig Verlagsbuchhandlung GmbH;

David Higham Associates on behalf of the authors for material from William Slim, *Defeat into Victory*, Cassell (1956) pp. 3, 119, 179–80, 221–2, 429–30, 533–4; William Slim, *Unofficial History*, Cassell (1959) pp. 236, 326; James Lees-Milne, *Prophesying Peace*, John Murray (1977) p. 96; Kitty Hart, *Return to Auschwitz*, Sidgwick & Jackson (1981) pp. 59–63; Guy Gibson, *Enemy Coast Ahead*, Crecy (1998) pp. 244–8; Alexander Cadogan *The Cadogan Diaries*, ed., D. Dilks, Cassell/Putnam (1971) pp. 307, 433; Theodora FitzGibbon, *With Love*, Hutchinson (1982) pp. 67–8, 71–3, 79–81; and Alex Danchev, *Alan Brooke, War Diaries 1939–45*, Weidenfeld & Nicolson (2001) pp. 243–4, 401–2, 445–6, 478–9, 483, 590, 619;

Hodder and Stoughton Ltd for material from John Colville, *The Fringes of Power, Vol. I* (1985) pp. 257–8. 458; and John Colville, *The Fringes of Power, Vol. II* (1985) p. 242;

Houghton Mifflin Co. for material from General George S. Patton, *War As I Knew It* (1947) pp. 57–60. Copyright © 1947 by Beatrice Patton Walters, Ruth Patton Totten and George Smith Totten, renewed © 1975 by Major General George Patton, Ruth Patton Totten, John K. Waters and George P. Waters;

Richard Rhodes James for material from his book, *Chindit*, John Murray Publishers (1980) pp. 14–16;

Louisiana State University Press for material from David Kenyon Webster, *Parachute Infantry: An American Paratrooper's Memoir of D-Day and the Fall of the Third Reich* (1994). Copyright © 1994 by The Trustees of the Embree Family Trust; and Radomir Luza with Christina Vella, *The Hitler Kiss* (2002) pp. 189–90. Copyright © 2002 by Radomir Luza and Christina Vella;

Methuen Publishing Ltd for material from Noël Coward, *Future Indefinite*, Heinemann (1954) pp. 337–8. Copyright © 1954 The Estate of Noël Coward;

Modern Library, a division of Random House, Inc, for material from Richard Tregaskis, *Invasion Diary* (1944). Copyright © 1944 by Random House, Inc.;

John Murray Publishers for material from George Psychoundakis, *The Cretan Runner* (1955) pp. 105–6; and George Beardmore, *Civilians at War: Journals 1939–1946* (1986) pp. 42–3, 51–2, 63, 80–3;

Naval Institute Press for material from Alvin Kernan, *Crossing the Line* (1994) pp. 110–17; and with Orion Publishing Group Ltd for Matsuo Fuchida, *Midway: The Battle with Doomed Japan*, Hutchinson (1957) pp. 304–5;

William Neave on behalf of the Estate of the author for material from Airey Neave, *They Have Their Exits* (1972) pp. 89–92; and Airey Neave, *Nuremburg*, Hodder & Stoughton (1978) pp. 68–73;

Nigel Nicolson for material from Harold Nicolson, *Diaries and Letters 1939–45*, Collins (1967) pp. 34–5, 100, 112–13;

Ben Nisbet Music Ltd and Charter Film Music Ltd for Leo Marks, 'The Life That I Have', Charter Film Music Ltd (1999);

North American Heritage Press for material from Knut Haukelid, *Skis Against the Atom*, Fontana (1973) pp. 68–75.

The Orion Publishing Group Ltd for material from Victor Klemperer, *To the Bitter End*, Weidenfeld and Nicolson (1999) pp. 389–92; Roman Frister,

The Cap or The Price of a Life, Weidenfeld and Nicolson (1999) pp. 240–3; Donald Macintyre, *U-Boat Killer*, Weidenfeld and Nicolson; Traudl Junge, *Until the Final Hour*, Weidenfeld and Nicolson (2003) pp. 183–7; Robert Rhodes James, ed., *Chips: The Diaries of Sir Henry Channon*, Weidenfeld and Nicolson (1996) pp. 211–16; Rudolf Hoess, *Commandant of Auschwitz*, Weidenfeld and Nicolson (2000) pp. 183–4; Kazuo Tamayama and John Nunneley, *Tales by Japanese Soldiers*, Cassell (2000) pp. 308, 433; Guy Sajer, *The Forgotten Soldier*, Cassell (2002) pp. 465–9, 540–2; Benito Mussolini, *Memoirs*, Weidenfeld and Nicolson (1949) p. 81; with Pen and Sword Books Ltd for Geoffrey Brooks, *Hirschfeld: The Secret Diary of a U-Boat*, Cassell (2000) pp. 144–9; Paul Richey, *Fighter Pilot*, Cassell (2002) pp. 137–8; Mikia Pezas, *The Price of Liberty*, Victor Gollancz (1946) pp. 118–19; with Eric Dobby Publishing for W. Stanley Moss, *Ill Met by Moonlight*, Cassell (1999) pp. 94–102; and with Scribner, an imprint of Simon & Schuster Adult Publishing Group, for Albert Speer, *Inside the Third Reich*, trans. by Richard and Clara Wilson, Weidenfeld and Nicolson (1998) pp. 646–8. Copyright © 1969 by Verlag Ullstein GmbH, English translation copyright © 1970 by Macmillan Publishing Company;

Pan Macmillan for material from Richard Hillary, *The Last Enemy*, Macmillan (1942) pp. 2–4, 96–7, 100–102, 114–15; and Charles Ritchie, *The Siren Years*, Macmillan (1974) pp. 122, 127–8;

Pen & Sword Books for material from John Frost, *A Drop Too Many*, Cassell (1958) pp. 226–31;

Penguin Books Ltd for material from Fred Taylor, ed. and trans., *The Goebbels Diaries 1939–1941*, Hamish Hamilton (1982) pp. 424–6. Translation copyright © Fred Taylor, 1982; with Pantheon Books, a division of Random House, Inc., for Art Spiegelman, *Maus Part II: A Survivor's Tale/ And Here My Troubles Began*, Penguin Books (1992) p. 71. Copyright © Art Spiegelman, 1986, 1989, 1990, 1991; and with Curtis Brown Group Ltd on behalf of the Estate of the author for David Niven, *The Moon's a Balloon*, Hamish Hamilton (1971, 1994), pp. 227–8. Copyright © David Niven, 1971;

Peters Fraser & Dunlop Ltd on behalf of the authors for material from Arthur Koestler, *Scum of the Earth*, Eland (1991) pp. 161–3; Fitzroy Maclean, *Eastern Approaches*, Cape (1949) pp. 402–403; Eric Linklater, *Fanfare for a Tin Hat*, Macmillan (1970) pp. 433–7. Copyright © Estate of Eric Linklater, 1970; and Lord Carrington, *Reflect on Things Past* (1988) pp. 53–5. Copyright © Lord Carrington, 1988;

Phillimore & Co Ltd for material from H. R. S. Pocock, *The Memoirs of Lord Coutanche* (1975) pp. 17–20;

Pollinger Ltd on behalf of the authors or their Estates for material from Alan Moorehead, *A Year of Battle*, Hamish Hamilton (1943) pp. 242, 382–3, 393; Alan Moorehead, *Mediterranean Front*, Hamish Hamilton (1941) pp. 56–7, 62–3, 177–8; Alan Moorehead, *The End in Africa*, Hamish Hamilton (1943) pp. 517–18, 611–12, 612–15; Alan Moorehead, *Eclipse*, Hamish Hamilton (1945) pp. 43–5, 88–9; and Alan Moorehead, *African Trilogy*, Hutchinson (1943) pp. 57–8; T. Bor-Komorowski, *The Secret Army*, Gollancz (1950) pp. 214–21, 306–308; John Masters, *The Road Past Mandalay*, Michael Joseph (1961) pp. 39–40, 44–5, 161–3, 245–7, 281; and Masanobu Tsuji, *Singapore: The Japanese Version*, Constable (1962) pp. 183–5;

Random House Group Ltd for material from Vera Inber, Leningrad Diary, trans. Serge M Wolff, Hutchinson (1971) pp. 39–41, 156–7; Yuji Aida, *Prisoner of the British*, The Cresset Press (1966) pp. 7–10; Antoine de Saint Exupéry, *Flight to Arras*, William Heinemann (1942) pp. 222–3; Frantisek Moravec, *Master of Spies*, Bodley Head (1975) pp. 212–17; Pierre Clostermann, *The Big Show*, Chatto & Windus (1951) pp. 185–7; Andrei Gromyko, *Memories*, Hutchinson (1989) pp. 84–7, 112–14; with HarperCollins Publishers Inc. for A. E. Hotchner, *Sophie – Living and Loving*, Corgi (1979) pp. 41–3. Copyright © 1979 A. E. Hotchner; Russell Miller, *Nothing Less Than Victory*, Pimlico (1993) pp. 208, 311–12, 391-2, 379–80, 443–4; Dirk Bogarde, *Snakes and Ladders*, Chatto & Windus (1988) pp. 36–8; with Peters Fraser & Dunlop on behalf of the Estate of the author for Hermione, Countess of Ranfurly, *To War with Whitaker*, Heinemann (1994) pp. 67–8, 280, 293, 363–4. Copyright © Estate of Hermione Ranfurly, 1994; with Random House, Inc. for J. E. Johnson, *Wing Leader*, Ballantine Books (1957) pp. 127–8. Copyright © 1957 by Ballantine Books;

Rogers Coleridge & White Ltd on behalf of the author for material from Norman Lewis, *Naples 44*, Collins (1978) pp. 11–13, 29; Copyright © Norman Lewis 1978;

The Royal Leicestershire Regiment on behalf of the Trustees for material from an extract by Major A. W. D. Nicholls in Brigadier E. W. Underhill, *The Royal Leicestershire Regiment 17th Foot*;

Scripps Howard Foundation for material from Ernie Pyle, *Life Without*

Redemption, extracted in *Reporting World War II*, Literary Classics of America;

Simon & Schuster, Inc, for material from Clarence Dickinson and Boyden Sparkes, *The Flying Guns*, Scribner, an imprint of Simon & Schuster Adult Publishing Group (1943) pp. 31–6, 148–55. Copyright © 1942 by Charles Scribner's Sons, renewed copyright © 1970;

Spellmont Publishers for material from Martin Poppel. *Heaven and Hell* (2000) pp. 54–66;

Texas A & M University Press for material from Anne Noggle, *A Dance with Death* (1994) pp. 160–61;

Time Warner Books UK for material from Pier Luigi Bellini delle Stelle and Urbano Lazzaro, *Dongo: The Last Act (Dongo Ultima Azione)*, Macdonald London (1964) p. 182;

University of Michigan Press for material from Dedijer, *The War Diaries of Vladimir Dedijer* (1990) pp. 310–12;

The University of North Carolina Press for material from Michihiko Hachiya, *Hiroshima Diary: The Journal of a Japanese Physician, August 6–September 30, 1945*, trans. Warner Wells, MD (1955) pp. 13–16. Copyright © 1955 by the University of North Carolina Press, renewed 1995;

The University of Washington Press for material from Yoshida Mitsuru, *Requiem for Battleship Yamato* (1999) pp. 113–19;

Viking Penguin, a division of Penguin Group (USA) Inc for material from Primo Levi, *If This is a Man (Survival in Auschwitz)*, trans. Stuart Woolf (1959) pp. 165–7. Copyright © 1959 by Orion Press, Inc., © 1958 by Giulio Einaudi editore S. P. A.;

Watson Little Ltd on behalf of the Estate of the author for material from E. D. Smith, *Even the Brave Falter*, Robert Hale (1978) pp. 18–19;

A. P. Watt Ltd on behalf of the Estate of the author for material from Bernard Law Montgomery, 1st Viscount Montgomery of Alamein, *Memoirs*, Collins (1958) pp. 99–100, 119–20, 129–30, 137, 222–30, 314;

Yale University Press for material from Simha Rotem, *Memoirs of a Warsaw Ghetto Fighter: The Past With Me*, trans. Barbara Harshav (1994) pp. 34-7;

Every effort has been made to trace the copyright holders but if any have not been traced the publishers will be pleased to make the necessary arrangement at the first opportunity.

The editors would like to thank Eleo Gordon at Penguin, Tif Loehnis at Janklow & Nesbit, Hilary Frost, Katherine Massey, Harriet Walker and Julia Weston for their assistance in the preparation of *The Voice of War*.